LET'S GO

PAGES PACKED WITH ESSENTIAL INFORMATION

"Value-packed, unbeatable, accurate, and comprehensive."

—*The Los Angeles Times*

"The guides are aimed not only at young budget travelers but at the independent traveler; a sort of streetwise cookbook for traveling alone."

—*The New York Times*

"Unbeatable; good sight-seeing advice; up-to-date info on restaurants, hotels, and inns; a commitment to money-saving travel; and a wry style that brightens nearly every page."

—**The Washington Post**

THE BEST TRAVEL BARGAINS IN YOUR BUDGET

"All the dirt, dirt cheap."

—*People*

"Let's Go follows the creed that you don't have to toss your life's savings to the wind to travel—unless you want to."

—**The Salt Lake Tribune**

REAL ADVICE FOR REAL EXPERIENCES

"The writers seem to have experienced every rooster-packed bus and lunar-surfaced mattress about which they write."

—**The New York Times**

"[Let's Go's] devoted updaters really walk the walk (and thumb the ride, and trek the trail). Learn how to fish, haggle, find work—anywhere."

—*Food & Wine*

"A world-wise traveling companion—always ready with friendly advice and helpful hints, all sprinkled with a bit of wit."

—**The Philadelphia Inquirer**

A GUIDE WITH A SPIRIT AND A SOCIAL CONSCIENCE

"Lighthearted and sophisticated, informative and fun to read. [Let's Go] helps the novice traveler navigate like a knowledgeable old hand."

—*Atlanta Journal-Constitution*

"The serious mission at the book's core reveals itself in exhortations to respect the culture and the environment—and, if possible, to visit as a volunteer, a student, or a teacher rather than a tourist."

—*San Francisco Chronicle*

LET'S GO PUBLICATIONS

TRAVEL GUIDES

Australia
Austria & Switzerland
Brazil
Britain
California
Central America
Chile
China
Costa Rica
Eastern Europe
Ecuador
Egypt
Europe
France
Germany
Greece
Hawaii
India & Nepal
Ireland
Israel
Italy
Japan
Mexico
New Zealand
Peru
Puerto Rico
Southeast Asia
Spain & Portugal with Morocco
Thailand
USA
Vietnam
Western Europe

ROADTRIP GUIDE

Roadtripping USA

ADVENTURE GUIDES

Alaska
Pacific Northwest
Southwest USA

CITY GUIDES

Amsterdam
Barcelona
Boston
Buenos Aires
London
New York City
Paris
Rome
San Francisco
Washington, DC

POCKET CITY GUIDES

Amsterdam
Berlin
Boston
Chicago
London
New York City
Paris
San Francisco
Venice
Washington, DC

LET'S GO

THAILAND

Ashley R. Laporte Editor
Daniel C. Barbero Associate Editor

Researcher-Writers

Dan Gurney
Beatrice Franklin
Ross Arbes
Jeff Overall

Illiana Celia Quimbaya Map Editor
Dwight Livingstone Curtis Managing Editor

St. Martin's Press ✖ New York

HELPING LET'S GO. If you want to share your discoveries, suggestions, or corrections, please drop us a line. We appreciate every piece of correspondence, whether a postcard, a 10-page email, or a coconut. Visit Let's Go at **http://www.letsgo.com,** or send email to:

> feedback@letsgo.com
> Subject: **"Let's Go:** Thailand"

Address mail to:

> **Let's Go:** Thailand
> **67 Mount Auburn St.**
> **Cambridge, MA 02138**
> **USA**

In addition to the invaluable travel advice our readers share with us, many are kind enough to offer their services as researchers or editors. Unfortunately, our charter enables us to employ only currently enrolled Harvard students.

CONTENTS

RESEARCHER-WRITERS

Dan Gurney
Central Thailand, Northern Thailand

Last summer, Dan Gurney researched for Let's Go in Greece; this summer, he wrote to us from the many tiny cities of Northern Thailand. Whether playing foreign instruments with locals in Bo Sang or discovering hermits in the forests of Nan, Gurney never ceased to amaze us. His meticulous attention to detail and incredible work ethic made Dan a truly talented Researcher-Writer.

Jeff Overall
Central Thailand, Northeast Thailand

Outdoorsmen Jeff Overall tackled the terrain in Northeast Thailand. Neither rainstorm, nor drowned computer, nor language-barrier could keep Overall down. In fact, at one point, Jeff attended a Thai wedding. This neither surprised nor worried us (once we confirmed that he was not the one getting married). Jeff's charm, ability to connect with strangers, and love for adventure had him "sharming beers" with post office workers and kept everyone back at the office on the edge of their seats.

Ross Arbes
Central Thailand, Southern Thailand

Two summers ago, Ross Arbes toured Vietnam on a rented motorcycle, and this summer he agreed to do the same in Southern Thailand. While enjoying white-sand beaches and Ko Phangan's infamous Full Moon Party, Ross' deadpan humor and consistent honesty kept his editors impressed and his copy stellar. Ross will spend the next year traveling the world, but not researching it, and Let's Go will dearly miss him. We wish him the best of luck.

Beatrice Franklin
Central Thailand, Bangkok

Beatrice took to the streets of Bangkok and beaches of Ko Samet with unshakeable determination and an eye for everything cutting-edge. Her ability to brave ravenous ATMs and thieving monkeys alike, find a friend in every guesthouse between Lopburi and Lumphini, and convey the truth about Thailand and its wonderful people in succinct, solid prose made her invaluable to the team.

CONTRIBUTING WRITERS

Ted Osuis contributed to various *Let's Go* guides from 1980 to 1984. Since 1989, he has served the US Department of State in Manila, Philippines, as a political and administrative officer at the US Embassy to the Vatican, and as an assistant to the Permanent Representative to the UN.

Cholthira Satyawadna graduated from Chulalongkorn University, where she received degrees in Thai language and literature, and from Australian National University, where she earned a doctoral degree in anthropology. Since 1999, she has published books on Thai literature, Thai and Lao textiles, and Tai and Lawa enthnohistory.

ACKNOWLEDGMENTS

ASHLEY: Thanks to Dan for being the best side-kick one could ask for. You are brilliant and have such an amazing sense of humor. I would have been lost without you. Dwight, you kept me sane. Thanks for finding Barbero, for being so patient, and for being a true friend. Thanks to our researchers, the most badass crew ever. This book is yours; you made it all happen. Thanks Spad Thai for managing my ticket all summer. LGHQ, thank you for providing friendship, couches, food, and comfort. Thanks Jansen and Tremblay for dealing with my deadline freak-outs. Thank you Nick, Frank, and Lauren for providing an escape. Thanks to Becca for all the eyebrow raises. Thanks to my friends outside the company for allowing me to have my love affair with *Let's Go*. Finally, thanks to my family for giving me up for yet another summer. You all are my inspiration; I love you so much.

DANIEL: Ashley, for being the best, as well as a source of calm, good advice, and hilarity; thanks friend, I couldn't imagine a better summer, and sorry, I *am* sorry it's over. Thanks to Anna, Meg, Nathaniel, Dwight, Charlie, Nick, and all my comrades-in-arms at the Go; I may have spent too many hours in this office, but you folks made it worth it. Thanks to my wonderful family for their support, understanding, and *alfajores*. Thanks to my friends back home for their patience, and to Cambridge, for being a great town (whenever I did venture into it).

ILLIANA: Ashley for her sense of humor, random stories, and hard work. Dan for his dedication and tolerance of nicknames. Derek for being a champion of a leader. Mapland for its estrogen dominating awesomeness. All the RWs for their four-colored pen masterpieces. And most importantly, Nemo, for hanging out and keeping me sane.

Editor
Ashley R. Laporte
Associate Editor
Daniel C. Barbero
Managing Editor
Dwight Livingstone Curtis
Map Editor
Illiana Celia Quimbaya
Typesetter
C. Alexander Tremblay

LET'S GO

Publishing Director
Inés C. Pacheco
Editor-in-Chief
Samantha Gelfand
Production Manager
Jansen A. S. Thurmer
Cartography Manager
R. Derek Wetzel
Editorial Managers
Dwight Livingstone Curtis,
Vanessa J. Dube, Nathaniel Rakich
Financial Manager
Lauren Caruso
Publicity and Marketing Manager
Patrick McKiernan
Personnel Manager
Laura M. Gordon
Production Associate
C. Alexander Tremblay
Director of IT & E-Commerce
Lukáš Tóth
Website Manager
Ian Malott
Office Coordinators
Vinnie Chiappini, Jennifer Q. Wong
Director of Advertising Sales
Nicole J. Bass
Senior Advertising Associates
Kipyegon Kitur, Jeremy Siegfried,
John B. Ulrich
Junior Advertising Associate
Edward C. Robinson Jr.

President
Timothy J. J. Creamer
General Manager
Jim McKellar

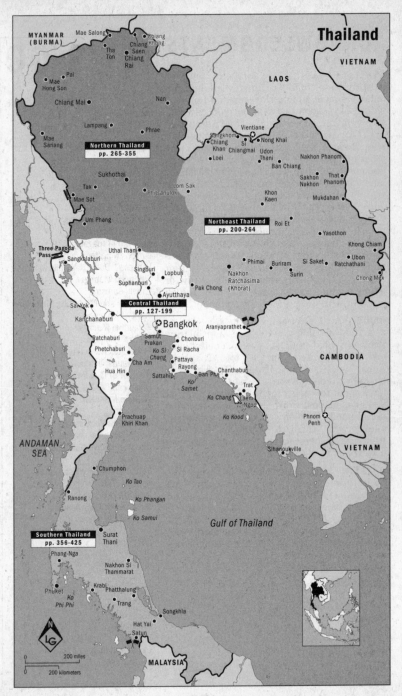

Thailand

MYANMAR (BURMA)

VIETNAM

LAOS

Northern Thailand
pp. 265-355

Mae Salong · Chiang Khong
Tha Ton · Chiang Saen · Chiang Rai
Mae Hong Son · Pai
Chiang Mai
Lampang · Phrae
Nan
Mae Sariang
Sukhothai
Tak · Phitsanulok
Mae Sot
Um Phang

Vientiane
Sangkhom · Si
Chiang Khan · Chiangmai · Nong Khai
Loei · Udon Thani
Ban Chiang
Lom Sak
Khon Kaen
Nakhon Phanom
Sakhon Nakhon · That Phanom
Mukdahan

Northeast Thailand
pp. 200-264

Roi Et
Yasothon
Khong Chiam

Three Pagoda Pass
Sangklaburi
Uthai Thani
Singburi · Lopburi
Suphanburi
Pak Chong
Nakhon Ratchasima (Khorat)
Phimai · Buriram · Si Saket · Ubon Ratchathani
Surin
Chong Mek

Central Thailand
pp. 127-199

Sai Yok
Kanchanaburi
Ayutthaya
Bangkok
Aranyaprathet

Ratchaburi
Phetchaburi
Samut Prakan · Chonburi · Si Racha
Ko Si-Chang · Pattaya · Rayong
Cha Am · Ban Pha
Hua Hin · Sattahip
Ko Samet
Chanthaburi
Trat
Ko Chang · Laem Ngop
Ko Kood

CAMBODIA

Prachuap Khiri Khan

Phnom Penh

VIETNAM

ANDAMAN SEA

Sihanoukville

Chumphon
Ko Tao
Ranong
Ko Phangan
Ko Samui

Gulf of Thailand

Southern Thailand
pp. 356-425

Surat Thani
Phang-Nga
Nakhon Si Thammarat
Krabi · Phatthalung
Phuket · Ko Phi Phi
Trang
Songkhla
Hat Yai · Satun

N
LG

0 —— 200 miles
0 —— 200 kilometers

MALAYSIA

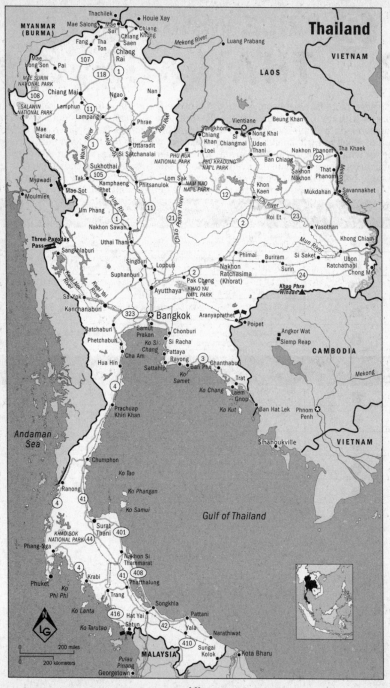

Our researchers list establishments in order of value from best to worst, honoring our favorites with the Let's Go thumbs-up (🖐). Because the best *value* is not always the cheapest *price*, we have incorporated a system of price ranges based on a rough expectation of what you will spend. For **accommodations,** we base our range on the cheapest price for which a single traveler can stay for one night. For **restaurants** and other dining establishments, we estimate the average amount one traveler will spend in one sitting. The table below tells you what you'll *typically* find in Thailand at the corresponding price range, although no system can allow for the quirks of all establishments.

ACCOMMODATIONS	RANGE	WHAT YOU'RE *LIKELY* TO FIND
①	Under US$3 Under 120฿	Single rooms, probably with fan, and occasional dorm rooms. Expect communal bathrooms and cold showers.
②	US$3-7 120-280฿	Guesthouse rooms or lower-end bungalows. You should have a fan and hot water, and may have a private bathroom.
③	US$7-12 280-480฿	A room or bungalow with private bath. Should have decent amenities, such as phone and A/C.
④	US$12-20 480-800฿	Similar to ③, but may have more amenities and will likely be in a more touristed area.
⑤	Over US$20 Over 800฿	Large hotels or upscale chains. If it's a ⑤ and it doesn't have the perks you want, you've overpaid.

FOOD	RANGE	WHAT YOU'RE *LIKELY* TO FIND
①	Under US$0.75 Under 30฿	The best way to eat in Thailand: street stalls and vendors.
②	US$0.75-2 30-80฿	Small, down-to-earth Thai restaurants. Some may not have English menus or names.
③	US$2-4 80-160฿	Slightly more upscale establishments or restaurants on islands or in touristed areas. Many will have menus in both English and Thai.
④	US$4-6 160-240฿	More touristy or foreign-themed restaurants. These may serve multiple courses.
⑤	Over US$6 Over 240฿	High-end restaurants targeting foreigners or affluent Thais. You're paying for atmosphere, not necessarily food.

DISCOVER THAILAND

A perfect blend of natural beauty, compelling culture, and some of the most welcoming citizens in the world, it's no wonder that Thailand remains one of the most accessible destinations in Southeast Asia. Though books, films, and television have tried, it's impossible to accurately describe the adventures available to travelers in Thailand; you just have to go. Explore the ancient cities of the central plains, where the ruins of great kingdoms now lie in silent majesty. Snorkel in turquise waters off the coast of a tiny southern island. Meditate among saffron-cloaked Buddhist monks in glittering golden temples. Let the mouth-watering cuisine sustain you, the surrounding beauty astonish you, and the proud people teach you as you experience their "Amazing Thailand".

FACTS AND FIGURES

OFFICIAL NAME: Kingdom of Thailand

GOVERNMENT: Constitutional monarchy

CAPITAL: Bangkok

LAND AREA: 514,000 sq. km

GEOGRAPHY: Borders Malaysia, Myanmar, Laos, and Cambodia

CLIMATE: Dry (high) season Nov.-Mar., rainy (low) season Apr.-Oct.

NATIONAL ANIMAL: *Chang Thai* (Thai elephant)

MAJOR CITIES: Bangkok, Chiang Mai

POPULATION: 65,000,000

LANGUAGE: Thai

RELIGIONS: Theravada Buddhism (95%); Islam, Christianity, Hinduism (5%)

WHEN TO GO

The low season in Thailand is marked by small crowds and reduced prices, though many beaches, islands, and trekking centers are completely closed down. Those willing to brave the crowds will find the high season more accommodating. The rainy season spans from May to September, and the dry season runs from October to May. For the most part, Thailand is hot and humid; temperatures fluctuate around 27°C (80°F) year-round everywhere except the extreme uplands of the north, where nighttime temperatures can drop dramatically (see **Average Temperatures,** p. 426).

WHAT TO DO

Thailand has enough *wats*, beaches, jungles, museums, and markets to satisfy even the most experienced traveler. No other country in the world lets you try it all—swim with sharks, shop for handicrafts, learn how to make curry, and practice your Thai. Each region brings new challenges. In Thailand, the question is not what to do, but what to do first.

BACKPACKER CENTRAL

If you're looking for a backpacker scene, Thailand is your pot of gold at the end of the rainbow. With a proliferation of charming guesthouse communities and Bangkok's position as the gateway city to Southeast Asia, Thailand a magnet for young tourists. You may run into your best friend from primary school buying spring rolls in **Bangkok** (p. 87) or that crazy guy you met two weeks ago in Vietnam getting a sun tan on **Ko Chang** (p. 151). You'll definitely meet people who have unbelieveable stories about near-death experiences with dysentery, malaria, wild tigers, Burmese border guards, or a weird guesthouse owner in **Surin** (p. 213). Most of these stories are true. **Khaosan Road** (p. 100) in Bangkok is the best place for these storytelling sessions. **Ko Samet** (p. 138), on the east coast, is the spot for low-key chilling, swimming, and snorkeling. In **Chiang Mai** (p. 265), the largest city in northern Thailand, cultural and commercial attractions abound. In the northeast, **Chiang Khan** (p. 247) is a hidden gem—a backpacking destination without the tourists. And what backpacker trip would be complete without a raging Full Moon party on **Ko Phangan** (p. 409)?

A FESTIVE OCCASION

Thailand is a country that loves its festivals, with regional and national celebrations catering to every event, object, and even fruit imaginable. The biggest bash of the year is April's **Songkran** (p. 282), or Thai New Year, a country-wide water-fight and a time to pay homage to elders, and which gets most spirited

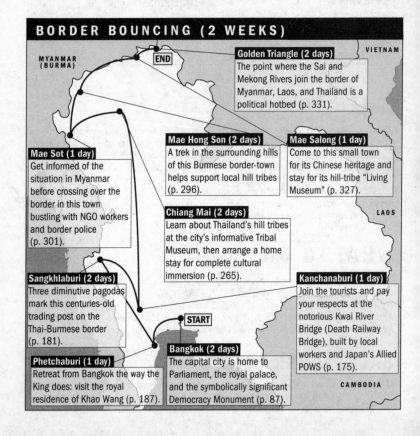

BORDER BOUNCING (2 WEEKS)

MYANMAR (BURMA)

VIETNAM

END

Golden Triangle (2 days)
The point where the Sai and Mekong Rivers join the border of Myanmar, Laos, and Thailand is a political hotbed (p. 331).

Mae Sot (1 day)
Get informed of the situation in Myanmar before crossing over the border in this town bustling with NGO workers and border police (p. 301).

Mae Hong Son (2 days)
A trek in the surrounding hills of this Burmese border-town helps support local hill tribes (p. 296).

Mae Salong (1 day)
Come to this small town for its Chinese heritage and stay for its hill-tribe "Living Museum" (p. 327).

LAOS

Chiang Mai (2 days)
Learn about Thailand's hill tribes at the city's informative Tribal Museum, then arrange a home stay for complete cultural immersion (p. 265).

Sangkhlaburi (2 days)
Three diminutive pagodas mark this centuries-old trading post on the Thai-Burmese border (p. 181).

Kanchanaburi (1 day)
Join the tourists and pay your respects at the notorious Kwai River Bridge (Death Railway Bridge), built by local workers and Japan's Allied POWS (p. 175).

START

Bangkok (2 days)
The capital city is home to Parliament, the royal palace, and the symbolically significant Democracy Monument (p. 87).

Phetchaburi (1 day)
Retreat from Bangkok the way the King does: visit the royal residence of Khao Wang (p. 187).

CAMBODIA

in Chiang Mai. The northern capital is also home to January's **Umbrella Festival** (p. 71) and February's **Flower Festival** (p. 282). All things beeswax are paraded through the streets of Ubon Ratchathani during the **Candle Festival** (p. 222) in July. Thailand's beloved fruits are feted many times in many places, from August's **Rambutan Fair** in Surat Thani (p. 395) to July's **Durian Festival** in Chanthaburi (p. 144). For a detailed listing of festivals throughout Thailand, check out **Holidays and Festivals** (p. 71). Nourish your spirit

Chiang Mai is known for its cultural heritage, and is home to more than 300 *wats*. **Wat Phra That Doi Suthep's** (p. 285), golden *chedi* attracts visitors from all over the world. **Bangkok** houses the impressive **Wat Phra Kaew** (Temple of the Emerald Buddha, p. 110), Bangkok's most-visited *wat*. **Ayutthaya's** (p. 161) collection of *wats* is among the oldest in Thailand, though many were ruined when the Burmese ransacked it in 1767. **Lopburi** (p. 167) provides similar sights with fewer crowds. **Wat Sri Chum** (p. 315) in **Sukhothai** features a 15m "talking" Buddha. Also in Sukhothai, **Wat Mahathat** (p. 315) has a beautiful lotus-shaped *chedi*, In **Khorat**, the inner sanctuary of **Wat Sala Loi** (p. 207) is shaped like a ship, symbolizing the passage of its devoted students to Nirvana. **Sala Kaew Ku** (p. 244) in **Nong Khai** was designed according to Buddhist cosmology and houses some bizarre sculptures, a few of which tower five stories high. Hidden among the millions of guesthouses and hordes of tourists in southern Thailand is **Wat Borommthat Chaiya** (p. 399). **Wat Tham Suwannakuha** (p. 365) is composed of several attached caves near **Phang-Nga**. Nearby, **Krabi's Wat Tham Sua** (p. 383) showcases Buddha's footprints, a Tiger Cave, and an inhabited monastery.

ISLAND	DESCRIPTION	BEACHES	HIGHLIGHTS
Ko Samet Central	Best beaches on the east coast.	Ao Cho (Lung Wang), ⊠ Ao Hin Khok, Ao Kiu, Ao Klang, Ao Noina, Ao Nuan, Ao Phai, ⊠ Ao Phrao, Ao Thian, Ao Tub Tim, Ao Wai, Ao Wong Duan, Hat Lung Dum, Hat Sai Kaew	Snorkeling in Ao Kiu's coral reefs, hanging out at Ao Phai, and camping under the stars on Ao Thian.
Ko Chang Central	An increasingly commercialized hot spot.	Hat Kai Bae, Hat Khlong Phrao, Hat Sai Khao	Exploring Ko Chang National Marine Park.
Ko Phi Phi South	Natural paradises beset by encroaching tourism.	Ao Lo Dalam, Maya Bay, Ao Thon Sai, Hat Hin Kohn, Hat Yao (Long Beach), Laem Him, Ma Prao	Plenty of dive sites, tours of stunning Maya Bay, and longtail boat trips.
Ko Tao South	Southeast Asia's biggest dive-training site.	Ao Chalok Ban Kao, Ao Leuk, Ao Tanote, Ao Thian, Hat Sai Ree, Laem Taa Toh, Mae Hat, Laem Nam Tok	Fantastic snorkeling and scuba diving just about anywhere on the island.
Ko Phangan South	Sun-soaked beaches by day, drunken tourists by night.	⊠ Hat Khuat (Bottle Beach), Hat Rin Nai, Hat Rin Nok, Thong Sala, Thong Nai Paan Yai, Thong Nai Paan Noi	Wild Full Moon parties, soothing Bottle Beach, and refreshing waterfalls.
Ko Samui South	An island of extremes, from McDonald's to the jungle.	Ao Bang Po, Ao Thongsai, Ao Yai Noi, Hat Bangrak (Big Buddha Beach), Hat Bo Phut, Hat Chaweng, Hat Choeng Mon, Hat Lamai, Hat Mae Nam, Laem Thongson, Na Thon	The Big Buddha, Hat Chaweng's nightlife, Ang Thong Marine National Park, and beautiful inland waterfalls.
Phuket South	Thailand's biggest and most touristed island.	Ao Bang Tao, Ao Chalong, Hat Kamala, Hat Karon, Hat Kata, Hat Nai Yang, Hat Patong, Hat Rawai, Hat Surin	Snorkeling and diving at Hat Karon and Hat Kata, gorgeous Hat Surin, and nightlife hub Hat Patong.

SNORKELERS' DELIGHT

Above water or underwater, Thailand never ceases to impress. As the largest diving-training center in Southeast Asia, **Ko Tao**, is the first stop on a Thai scuba tour. Leopard sharks and rock "swim-throughs" are just the beginning. Snorkelers will love the island's bays, **Ao Leuk** and **Ao Thian** (p. 423), or the off-beach snorkeling in Ao Tanote. A daytrip from Ko Tao to **Ko Nang Yuan** (p. 424) also yields great snorkeling. The snorkel-savy hail **Hat Karon** and **Hat Kata** on **Phuket** (p. 373) as home to some of the world's best marine life, particularly around the **Similan Islands. Ang Thong Marine National Park** (p. 406), off **Ko Samui**, is made up of 40 limestone islands that offer phenomenal snorkeling and diving, particularly at **Ko Sam Sao** (Tripod Island) and **Hat Chan Charat** (Moonlight Beach). Two of Ko Chang's outer islands, **Ko Rang** and **Ko Wai** (p. 158), are brimming with coral and sharks.

TRIBAL TALES

Northern Thailand is home to a variety of hill-tribe groups. These groups migrated to Thailand from various parts of Southeast Asia (including Myanmar and China) seeking refuge. In **Sangkhlaburi** (p. 181), a Mon village of ethnic

BEACH BABY: ISLAND HOPPING (3 WEEKS)

Ko Tao (3 days)
This small ko is one of the best diving and snorkeling sites in the world (p. 417).

Ko Samet (3 days)
Lounge on white sand beaches, swim in the clearest water on the east coast, and swig drinks by the bucket (p. 138).

CAMBODIA

Similan Islands (3 days)
This uninhabited national marine park boasts majestic rock formations, coral reefs, and amazing underwater visibility (p. 370).

START

Ko Chang (2 days)
This island has a little bit of everything: jungles, waterfalls, national parks, and beaches (p. 151).

Phuket (3 days)
Party with other internationals, splurge on a beachside bungalow, and work on that tan on this must-stop southern gateway (p. 367).

Ko Phangan (3 days)
Rest up for a Full Moon party in a secluded bungalow on the swimming sanctuary of Hat Khuat (Bottle Beach) (p. 409).

VIETNAM

END

Trang (2 days)
Hat Yong Ling's National Park is home to beautiful orchid-covered coves, bat caves, and emerald-tinged waters (p. 390).

Ko Phi Phi Ley (2 days)
After floating in this secluded island's clear waters, snorkel with colorful fish in its coral coves (p. 380).

Burmese refugees is connected to a Thai village by a wooden bridge, separating the two communities. **Mae Hong Son** (p. 292) is surrounded by Shan and Kuo Min Tang (KMT) camps and the Lisu, Hmong, and Lahu hill tribes. The Long-Necked Karen village, where residents gradually stack metal wrings around their neck, is right next door to Mae Hong Son; the Red Karen state sits just across the border. The Hmong villages in **Chiang Khong** (p. 331) remain secluded, as they are accessible only by bike during the dry season. **Chiang Mai's Tribal Museum** (p. 278) pays well-researched homage to the nine hill tribes of Thailand and the Nan National Museum in **Nan** (p. 341) also displays a thorough history of Thai hill tribes. Sample the silk products woven by Isaan women of the northeast at Village Weaver Handicrafts in **Nong Khai** (p. 241). The night market in **Chiang Rai** (p. 335) offers a plethora of hill-tribe handicrafts. For those interested in the hill-tribe lifestyle, check out the Living Museum near **Mae Salong** (p. 327).

COMMANDING CASCADES

Thailand is literally awash with waterfalls. **Mae Surin National Park** (p. 300), between **Mae Hong Son** and **Mae Sariang,** boasts the highest single-tiered waterfall in the country. One hundred and fifty meter **Haew Narok,** the tallest falls in waterfall-rich **Khao Yai National Park** (p. 202), is so precipitous that even elephants

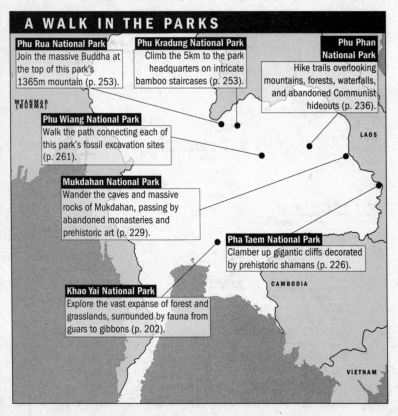

A WALK IN THE PARKS

Phu Rua National Park
Join the massive Buddha at the top of this park's 1365m mountain (p. 253).

Phu Kradung National Park
Climb the 5km to the park headquarters on intricate bamboo staircases (p. 253).

Phu Phan National Park
Hike trails overlooking mountains, forests, waterfalls, and abandoned Communist hideouts (p. 236).

MYANMAR

Phu Wiang National Park
Walk the path connecting each of this park's fossil excavation sites (p. 261).

LAOS

Mukdahan National Park
Wander the caves and massive rocks of Mukdahan, passing by abandoned monasteries and prehistoric art (p. 229).

Pha Taem National Park
Clamber up gigantic cliffs decorated by prehistoric shamans (p. 226).

CAMBODIA

Khao Yai National Park
Explore the vast expanse of forest and grasslands, surrounded by fauna from guars to gibbons (p. 202).

VIETNAM

DISCOVER

have been known to fall to their deaths. It may take three days, but the trek to **Pa La-u Falls** in **Kaeng Krachan National Park** (p. 189), with its 11 tiers of cascades, is worth it. Its nearest rival might be **Nam Tok Krathing** in **Khao Khitchakut National Park** (p. 147) near Chanthaburi, where you can swim in most of the 13 tiers of falls. After the dip, you emerge from the water into a swarm of hundreds of golden butterflies. The jungle pool at **Than Mayom Falls** (p. 157) on Ko Chang was a favorite of King Rama V and still bears his initials. The area around Tak (p. 305) provides a contrast of falls, from the deserted and soothing **Pha Peung** upper waterfalls in **Larn Sang National Park** to the stunning nine-tiered Mae Ya Pa Waterfall in **Taksin Maharat National Park.**

VENERATED BUDDHAS

Bangkok's **Wat Phra Kaew** (p. 110) houses the famous **Emerald Buddha,** Thailand's most sacred Buddha figure, while nearby **Wat Pho** (p. 111) has the largest reclining Buddha in Thailand. In **Ayutthaya, Wat Mahathat** (p. 166) holds one of the most photographed and evocative Buddha figures in the country: a tree branch-encased Buddha face. A trip to **Sukhothai** (p. 311) will bring you to **Wat Sri Chum** and King Ramkhamhaeng's famous "talking Buddha." Glass paintings and wooden Burmese dolls adorn the inside of **Wat Chong Klang** in **Mae Hong**

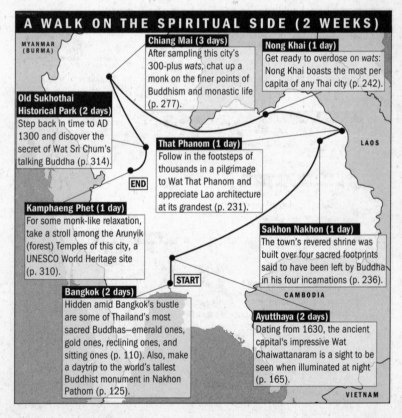

A WALK ON THE SPIRITUAL SIDE (2 WEEKS)

MYANMAR (BURMA)

LAOS

CAMBODIA

VIETNAM

Chiang Mai (3 days)
After sampling this city's 300-plus *wats*, chat up a monk on the finer points of Buddhism and monastic life (p. 277).

Nong Khai (1 day)
Get ready to overdose on *wats*: Nong Khai boasts the most per capita of any Thai city (p. 242).

Old Sukhothai Historical Park (2 days)
Step back in time to AD 1300 and discover the secret of Wat Sri Chum's talking Buddha (p. 314).

That Phanom (1 day)
Follow in the footsteps of thousands in a pilgrimage to Wat That Phanom and appreciate Lao architecture at its grandest (p. 231).

END

Kamphaeng Phet (1 day)
For some monk-like relaxation, take a stroll among the Arunyik (forest) Temples of this city, a UNESCO World Heritage site (p. 310).

Sakhon Nakhon (1 day)
The town's revered shrine was built over four sacred footprints said to have been left by Buddha in his four incarnations (p. 236).

START

Bangkok (2 days)
Hidden amid Bangkok's bustle are some of Thailand's most sacred Buddhas—emerald ones, gold ones, reclining ones, and sitting ones (p. 110). Also, make a daytrip to the world's tallest Buddhist monument in Nakhon Pathom (p. 125).

Ayutthaya (2 days)
Dating from 1630, the ancient capital's impressive Wat Chaiwattanaram is a sight to be seen when illuminated at night (p. 165).

THE BEST OF THAILAND (6 WEEKS)

MYANMAR
(BURMA)

LAOS

VIETNAM

Chiang Saen (2 days)
Come here for great views of the Golden Triangle without all of the tourists (p. 328).

Chiang Mai (5 days)
Take a cooking class, learn Thai boxing--the possibilities are endless in this city that balances tradition with modernity (p. 265).

Chiang Rai (3 days)
Glimpse authentic northern Thai culture in this slower paced yet sight-packed city (p. 335).

Mae Hong Son (2 days)
Seek sanctuary amid lush valleys and forested mountains dotted with hill-tribe villages (p. 293).

Udon Thani (2 days)
Go from this commercial center to nearby Ban Chiang, a significant archeological site (p. 237).

Old Sukhothai (2 days)
This capital of the first Thai kingdom saw a golden age of art and culture and the introduction of the Thai alphabet (p. 311).

Ayutthaya (3 days)
Celebrate Thailand's glorious past amid a concentrated collection of ancient wats (p. 161).

START

Ubon Ratchathani (2 days)
The "royal city of lotuses" is also the meditation mecca of the northeast (p. 219).

CAMBODIA

Phuket (3 days)
Tourists flock to the "Jewel of the South" for good reason: thumping nightlife, spotless sand, and top-notch resorts are hallmarks of Thailand's biggest island (p. 367).

Bangkok (6 days)
Start in this thoroughly modern metropolis, teeming with throbbing nightlife, savory international cuisine, and revered ancient wats (p. 87).

Ko Samet (3 days)
The low-key, white-sand beaches of this island are perfect for the road-weary backpacker (p. 138).

VIETNAM

Ko Tao (3 days)
Skip beach lounging and instead partake in this island's plentiful and famed aquatic activity options (p. 417).

END

Ko Phangan (3 days)
A party peninsula with or without a full moon (p. 409).

Ko Phi Phi Don (3 days)
The perfect secluded island getaway (p. 376).

MALAYSIA

Son (p. 292). The spectacular views of **Wat Tha Ton** (p. 323) form a gorgeous backdrop to the **golden dragon-headed Buddha.** In Thai history, it has been common for a bolt of lightning, a *wat*-sacking, or an accident to destroy a Buddha, only to reveal a more valuable one underneath—as happened with the **Emerald Buddha.** Most recently, in 1955, an 800-year-old stucco Buddha was dropped, cracking the stucco shell to reveal a stunning, 5-ton gold Buddha in Bangkok's **Wat Traimit** (p. 114). It is illegal to remove Buddha images from the country without the permission of the Fine Arts Department. Souvenir Buddhas, however, are not subject to these regulations.

LET'S GO PICKS: THAILAND

BEST PLACE FOR A SWIM: The multiple tiers of **Larn Sak Waterfall** in **Tak** (p. 305), or one of Thailand's many other multi-tiered marvels.

BEST HAUNTED WAT: In **Sukhothai** (p. 311), **Wat Thawet's** hellish horrors will scare even the non-Buddhist.

BEST SPA: Let the natural hot springs off the **Mae Yen River** in **Pai** (p. 288) soothe you before your traditional Thai massage.

BEST KARMA: With platforms corresponding to each level of enlighten ment, **Wat Phu Thok** in **Nong Khai** (p. 241) is not to be missed.

BEST PLACE TO ABSORB THAI FOLK CULTURE: Learn about hill-tribe costumes and the power of Thai tattoos at the **Sgt. Maj. Thawee Folk Museum** in **Phitsanulok** (p. 350).

BEST BUDDHAS: The "thousand Buddhas" tucked into caves in **Phetchaburi** (p. 184) almost beat out the **Emerald Buddha** in **Bangkok** (p. 87).

ESSENTIALS

PLANNING YOUR TRIP

BEFORE YOU GO

Passport (p. 10). Required for citizens of Australia, Ireland, New Zealand, the UK, and the US.

Visa (p. 11). Required of all travelers staying more than 30 days. Most visas take about 2 weeks to process.

Letter of Invitation (p. 11). A letter of invitation is required of those wishing to obtain a 90-day-non-immigrant visa.

Working and Studying (p. 11). Permits required for all foreigners planning to work or study in Thailand.

Required Vaccinations (p. 23).

Recommended Vaccinations (p. 23).

Vaccination/Health Certificates (p. 22). Visitors who have been in Africa or South America must have a certificate of vaccination against yellow fever. *Let's Go* lists other specifically recommended inoculations, including Japanese encephalitis.

Other Health Concerns: Malaria pills are recommended for those traveling to areas at high risk for malaria (p. 25). If your regular medical insurance policy (p. 23) does not cover travel abroad, you may wish to purchase additional coverage.

CONSULATES

THAILAND CONSULAR SERVICES ABROAD

Australia: Level 8, 131 Macquarie St., Sydney NSW 2000 (☎+61 02 9241 2542); 87 Annerley Rd., South Brisbane QLD 4102 (☎+61 07 3846 7771); Ste. 301, 566 St. Kilda Rd., Melbourne VIC 3004 (☎+61 03 9533 9100); 72 Flinders St., 1st fl., Adelaide SA 5000 (☎+61 08 8 8218 4848); 14 Victoria Avenue, Perth WA 6000 (☎+61 08 9221 3237).

Canada: 550-1040 West Geogia Street, Vancouver BC V6E 4H1 (☎+1-604 687-6400); 1501 McGill College, Bureau 2240, Montreal QC H3A 3M8 (☎+1-514-878-4466); Scotia Plaza, 40 King St. W., 41st fl., Toronto ON M5H EY4 (☎+1-416-367-6750); Suite 202, 10544, 114th St., Edmonton, Alberta T6H 3J7 (☎+1-780-439-3576); Lacey Court 344-12 Ave., SW, Calgary AB T2R OH2 (☎+1-403-266-6995).

Ireland: 18-19 Harcourt St., Dublin 2, Ireland (☎+353 1 478 6412).

UK: 9 Mount Stuart Square, Cardiff CF10 5EE (☎+44 029 2046 5777); Boodles House, 35 Lord St., Liverpool L2 9SQ (☎+44 0151 255 0504); One Victoria Square, Birmingham B1 1BD (☎+44 0121 643 9481); 4 Woodside Place, Charing Cross, Glasgow, G3 7QF (☎+44 0141 353 5090).

CONSULAR SERVICES IN THAILAND

Canada: 151 Superhighway, Tambon Tahsala, Muang, Chiang Mai 50000 (☎+66 053 242 292).

UK: 198 Bumrungraj Rd., Muang, Chiang Mai 50000 (☎+66 053 263 015). Open M-F 9-11:30am.

US: 387 Witchayanond Rd., Chiang Mai 50300 (☎+66 053 252 629). American citizen services open T and Th 8-11:30am and 1-3:30pm.

TOURIST OFFICES

Tourism Authority of Thailand (TAT): 75 Pitt St., 2nd fl., Sydney 2000 (☎+61 2 9247 7549; www.tat.or.th or www.tourismthailand.org); Brook House, 98-99 Jermyn St., 3rd fl., London SW1Y 2EE (☎+44 0870 900 2007); 61 Broadway, Ste. 2810, New York, NY 1006 (☎+011-212-432-0433); 611 North Larchmont Blvd., 1st fl., Los Angeles, CA 90004 (☎+011-323-461-9814). Website regularly updated for dates of festivals and recent news.

Ministry of Foreign Affairs: 443 Sri Ayudhaya Rd., Bangkok 10400 (☎+66 2 643 5000; www.mfa.go.th). Provides info about foreign policy updates and traveling in Thailand.

DOCUMENTS AND FORMALITIES

PASSPORTS

REQUIREMENTS

Citizens of Australia, Canada, Ireland, New Zealand, the UK, and the US need valid passports to enter Thailand and to re-enter their home countries. Thailand doesn't allow entrance if the holder's passport expires in less than six months; returning home with an expired passport is illegal and may result in a fine.

NEW PASSPORTS

Citizens of Australia, Canada, Ireland, New Zealand, the UK, and the US can apply for a passport at any passport office, selected post offices or courts of law. Citizens of these countries may also download passport applications from the official website of their country's government or passport office. Any new passport or renewal applications must be filed well in advance of the departure date, though most passport offices offer rush services for a very steep fee. Note, however, that "rushed" passports still take up to two weeks to arrive.

PASSPORT MAINTENANCE

Photocopy the page of your passport with your photo and visas, traveler's checks, serial numbers, and any other important documents. Carry one set of copies in a safe place, apart from the originals, and leave another set at home. Consulates also recommend that you carry an expired passport or an official copy of your birth certificate separate from other documents.

If you lose your passport, immediately notify the local police and your home country's nearest embassy or consulate. To expedite its replacement, you must show ID and proof of citizenship; it also helps to know all information previously recorded in the passport. In some cases, a replacement may take weeks to process, and it may be valid only for a limited time. Visas stamped in your old passport will be lost forever. In an emergency, ask for immediate temporary traveling papers that will permit you to re-enter your home country.

VISAS, INVITATIONS, AND WORK PERMITS

VISAS

Citizens of Australia, Canada, Ireland, New Zealand, the UK, and the US do not need a visa for stays up of to 30 days, but they must possess a passport, and they may be asked to show an onward or return ticket. For longer stays, travelers must apply for a 60-day tourist visa (US$35 per entry) from any Thai consulate prior to arriving in Thailand. Visas must be used within three months of issue. If you wish to sojourn in nearby countries, obtain a re-entry permit at an immigration office before departure.

Double-check entrance requirements at the nearest embassy or consulate of Thailand (see **Thai Embassies Abroad,** p. 9) for up-to-date info before departure. US citizens can consult http://travel.state.gov. US citizens can take advantage of the **Center for International Business and Travel** (☎ +1-800-925-2428), which secures visas for travel to many countries for a service charge. Travelers remaining in Thailand beyond their visa expiration date will be charged a fine upon departure payable immediately. You will also be charged a 500฿ Passenger Service Charge when departing from any of Thailand's international airports.

Entering Thailand for reasons besides tourism requires special visas. For more information, see **Beyond Tourism**, p. 76. If your reason for entering Thailand is not tourism you may need to purchase a **90-day-non-immigrant** (US$90 for single entry, US$175 for multiple entries) or transit visa (US$20) prior to your arrival. In addition to the visa application form, two passport-size pictures, and a valid passport, travelers applying for other visas may need to submit a letter from a Thai contact detailing the purpose of their visit. For more info on specific requirements please contact any Thai embassy or consulate (see p. 8) or check out the visa info at www.mfa.go.th.

If you have a 60-day tourist visa and you go to Myanmar, Cambodia, Malaysia, or Laos for a daytrip, you will lose your visa and will need to reapply. To avoid having to get a new visa when you hop across the border for a day, make photocopies of your passport (usually 5฿). Then proceed directly to Thai border control, at whichever border point you are hoping to cross, with your two photocopies of your passport. Surrender your passport to the Thai authorities, who will stamp the photocopies. Take your newly stamped photocopies and the border crossing fee to the border control authorities of the country you are entering. They will stamp your photocopies and keep one of them. All stamps are on the copies, so when you return to Thailand, you get your unmarked passport back. Foreign authorities will keep one photocopy, Thai authorities the other. Either way, when you surrender your passport photocopies, you will receive a very thin piece of paper—that piece of paper is your passport. Hold on to it if you ever want to see home again.

INVITATIONS

If applying for a 90-day-non-immigrant visa, Thailand currently requires that visitors from Australia, Canada, Ireland, New Zealand, the UK, and the US obtain an invitation from their sponsoring individual or organization.

WORK PERMITS

Admittance to a country as a traveler does not include the right to work, which is authorized only by a work permit. Those wishing to work in Thailand must apply for a 90-day-non-immigrant visa (single-entry US$65, multiple-entry US$175). For more information, **Beyond Tourism** (p. 76).

IDENTIFICATION

When traveling, always carry at least two forms of identification on your person, including a photo ID. A passport and driver's license or birth certificate will usually suffice. Never carry all of your IDs together; split them up in case of theft or loss and keep photocopies in your luggage and at home.

STUDENT, TEACHER, AND YOUTH IDENTIFICATION

The **International Student Identity Card** (ISIC), the most widely accepted form of student ID, provides discounts on some sights, accommodations, food, and transportation; access to a 24hr. emergency help line; and insurance benefits for US cardholders (see **Insurance,** p. 23). Applicants must be full-time secondary or post-secondary school students at least 12 years old. Because of the proliferation of fake ISIC cards, some services (particularly airlines) require additional proof of student identity.

The **International Teacher Identity Card** (ITIC) offers teachers the same insurance coverage as the ISIC and similar but limited discounts. To qualify for the card, teachers must be currently employed and have worked a minimum of 18hr. per week for at least one school year. For travelers who are under 26 years old but are not students, the **International Youth Travel Card** (IYTC) also offers many of the same benefits as the ISIC.

Each of these identity cards costs US$22. ISICs, ITICS, and IYTCs are valid for one year from the date of issue. To learn more about ISICs, ITICs, and IYTCs, try www.myisic.com. Many student travel agencies (p. 29) issue the cards; for a list of issuing agencies or more information, see the **International Student Travel Confederation** (ISTC) website (www.istc.org).

The **International Student Exchange Card** (ISE Card) is a similar identification card available to students, faculty, and children aged 12 to 26. The card provides discounts, medical benefits, access to a 24hr. emergency help line, and the ability to purchase student airfares. An ISE Card costs US$25; call ☎+1-800-255-8000 (in North America) or ☎+011-480-951-1177 (from all other continents) for more info or visit www.isecard.com.

CUSTOMS

Upon entering Thailand, you must declare certain items from abroad and pay a duty on the value of those articles if they exceed the allowance established by Thailand's customs service. Goods and gifts purchased at duty-free shops abroad are not exempt from duty or sales tax; "duty-free" means that you won't pay tax in the country of purchase.

Upon returning home, you must likewise declare all articles acquired abroad and pay a duty on the value of articles in excess of your home country's allowance. In order to expedite your return, make a list of any valuables brought from home and register them with customs before traveling abroad. It's a good idea to keep receipts for all goods acquired abroad. Travelers may bring one still camera with five rolls of film or one video camera with three tapes, 200 cigarettes, and one liter of alcohol. These restrictions, however, are flexible. They are meant to ensure the film equipment is for personal use only. It is illegal to remove certain species of fruit, vegetables, and plants from the country; contact the Thai government's Agricultural Regulatory Division (☎66 579 8576) for more info. The total amount of currency taken out should not exceed the amount taken in (max. 10,000฿). No authentic Buddha or Bodhisattva images, or fragments thereof, may be exported without permission from the Bangkok National Museum (☎66 02 224 1333) and the Department of Fine Arts; you must prove you are a practicing Buddhist or are using them for cultural or academic purposes. Such certification often takes three to five days to process; so make sure you leave enough time. These rules do not apply to souvenirs. For art purchased in the country, keep receipts to present to customs. For more detailed information on exportation of Buddha images or antiquities out of Thailand, see www.mfa.go.th/web/808.php.

Additionally, the Thai government has harsh penalties for drug possession and trafficking. These two offenses are often considered synonymous. The importation of firearms, weapons, and pornography is prohibited. Travelers should note that though Thailand's regulations are among the most stable in the world, customs requirements do vary.

Upon leaving Thailand, you may claim a **VAT (value added tax)** refund on goods purchased from stores advertising "VAT Refund for Tourist" (see **Taxes,** p. 16). The total amount claimed for refund cannot be less than 5000฿, including VAT. Before departure, show your goods and submit a filled-out VAT form with the original tax invoice to the Customs officers for inspection. For more information, call the VAT Refund for Tourist Office of Thailand (☎+66 02 272 9387).

MONEY

CURRENCY AND EXCHANGE

The currency chart below is based on August 2009 exchange rates between local currency and Australian dollars (AUS$), Canadian dollars (CDN$), European Union euro (EUR€), New Zealand dollars (NZ$), British pounds (UK£), and US dollars (US$). Check the currency converter on websites like www.xe.com or www.bloomberg.com for the latest exchange rates.

CURRENCY (฿)		
AUS$ = 30.53฿	20฿ = AUS$0.66	
CDN$ = 32.12฿	20฿ = CDN$0.62	
EUR€ = 51.9฿	20฿ = EUR€0.39	
NZ$ = 24.16฿	20฿ = NZ$0.83	
UK£ = 65.59฿	20฿ = UK£0.30	
US$ = 33.7฿	20฿ = US$0.59	

As a general rule, it's cheaper to convert money in Thailand than at home. While currency exchange will probably be available in your arrival airport, it's wise to bring enough foreign currency to last at least 24-72 hours.

When changing money abroad, try to go only to banks or exchange bureaus that have at most a 5% margin between their buy and sell prices. Since you lose money with every transaction, it makes sense to convert large sums at one time (unless the currency is depreciating rapidly).

If you use traveler's checks or bills, carry some in small denominations (the equivalent of US$50 or fewer) for times when you are forced to exchange money at poor rates, but bring a range of denominations since charges may be applied per check cashed. Store your money in a variety of forms; ideally, at any given time you will be carrying some cash, some traveler's checks, and an ATM and/or credit card. All travelers should also consider carrying some US dollars (about US$50 worth), which are often preferred by local tellers.

ESSENTIALS

TRAVELER'S CHECKS

Traveler's checks are one of the safest and most convenient means of carrying funds. **American Express** and Visa are the most-recognized brands. Many banks and agencies sell them for a small commission. Check issuers provide refunds if the checks are lost or stolen, and many provide additional services, such as toll-free refund hotlines abroad, emergency message services and assistance with lost and stolen credit cards or passports. Checks are accepted in most cities in Thailand, although travelers to more rural areas should carry sufficient baht to last the duration of their trip. Also, due to high incidences of fraud, Thai bank clerks tend to be suspicious of signatures, so be confident with yours. Ask about toll-free refund hotlines and the location of refund centers when purchasing checks, and always carry emergency cash.

American Express: Checks available with commission at select banks, at all AmEx offices, and online (www.americanexpress.com; US residents only). AmEx cardholders can also purchase checks by phone (☎800-528-4800). Checks available in Australian, British, Canadian, European, Japanese, and US currencies, among others. AmEx also offers the Travelers Cheque Card, a prepaid reloadable card. Cheques for Two can be signed by either of 2 people traveling together. For purchase locations or more information, contact AmEx's service centers: in Australia ☎+61 2 9271 8666, in New Zealand +64 9 367 4567, in the UK +44 1273 696 933, in the US and Canada +1-800-221-7282; elsewhere, call the US collect at +1-336-393-1111.

Travelex: Visa TravelMoney prepaid cash card and Visa traveler's checks available. For information about Thomas Cook MasterCard in Canada and the US, call ☎+1-800-223-7373, in the UK +44 0800 622 101; elsewhere, call the UK collect at +44 1733 318 950. For information about Interpayment Visa in the US and Canada, call ☎+1-800-732-1322, in the UK +44 0800 515 884; elsewhere, call the UK collect at +44 1733 318 949. For more information, visit www.travelex.com.

Visa: Checks available (generally with commission) at banks worldwide. For the location of the nearest office, call the Visa Travelers Cheque Global Refund and Assistance Center: in the UK ☎+44 0800 895 078, in the US +1-800-227-6811; elsewhere, call the UK collect at +44 2079 378 091. Checks available in British, Canadian, European, Japanese, and US currencies, among others. Visa also offers TravelMoney, a prepaid debit card that can be reloaded online or by phone. For more information on Visa travel services, see http://usa.visa.com/personal/using_visa/travel_with_visa.html.

CREDIT, DEBIT, AND ATM CARDS

Where they are accepted, credit cards often offer superior exchange rates—up to 5% better than the retail rate used by banks and other currency exchange establishments. Credit cards may also offer services such as insurance or emergency help and are sometimes required to reserve hotel rooms or rental cars. **MasterCard/Maestro/Cirrus** and **Visa/Plus** are the most frequently accepted.

American Express cards can be used at Bangkok Bank ATMs throughout Thailand. Cardholders (enrolled in the Express Cash program) can withdraw cash from their checking accounts at any of AmEx's offices and many representative offices. For more info, call ☎+1-800-227-4669 in the US (the international assistance number is ☎+1-800-732-1991) or visit www.americanexpress.com.

The use of ATM cards is widespread in Thailand. Depending on the system that your home bank uses, you can probably access your bank account from abroad. ATMs get the same wholesale exchange rate as credit cards, but there is often a limit on the amount of money you can withdraw per day (usually around US$500). There is sometimes a surcharge of US$1-5 per withdrawal.

Debit cards are as convenient as credit cards but withdraw money directly from the holder's checking account. A debit card can be used wherever its associated credit card company (usually MasterCard or Visa) is accepted. Debit cards often also function as ATM cards and can be used to withdraw cash from associated banks and ATMs in Thailand. Note, though, that ATMs are scarce in more rural areas of Thailand.

The two major international money networks are **MasterCard/Maestro/Cirrus** (for ATM locations ☎+1-800-424-7787 or www.mastercard.com) and **Visa/PLUS** (for ATM locations ☎+1-800-847-2911 or www.visa.com). Most ATMs charge a transaction fee that is paid to the bank that owns the ATM.

GETTING MONEY FROM HOME

If you run out of money while traveling, the easiest and cheapest solution is to have someone back home make a deposit to your bank account. Otherwise, consider one of the following options.

WIRING MONEY

It is possible to arrange a **bank money transfer,** which means asking a bank back home to wire money to a bank in Thailand. This is the cheapest way to transfer cash, but it's also the slowest, usually taking several days or more. Note that some banks may only release your funds in local currency, potentially sticking you with a poor exchange rate; inquire about this in advance. At Bangkok Bank you do not need to have an account in order to receive money transfers; however, you will need to present photo ID in order to claim your transfer (there is a 0.25% fee levied on every transaction; min. amount for transfer 200฿, max. 500฿). For more information on sending or receiving funds from overseas, call Bangkok Bank at ☎66 02 685 7777. Money transfer services like **Western Union** are faster and more convenient than bank transfers—but also much pricier. Western Union has many locations worldwide. To find one, visit www.westernunion.com, or call in Australia ☎+61 800 173 833, in Canada and the US +1-800-325-6000, in the UK +44 0800 833 833, or in Thailand +66 053 240 241. Several banks in Thailand, including Bank of Asia and Bank of Ayudhya, are authorized Western Union agents.

US STATE DEPARTMENT (US CITIZENS ONLY)

In serious emergencies only, the US State Department will forward money within hours to the nearest consular office, which will then disburse it according to instructions for a US$30 fee. If you wish to use this service, you must contact the Overseas Citizens Services division of the US State Department (☎+1-202-501-4444, from US ☎888-407-4747).

COSTS

The cost of your trip will vary considerably, depending on where you go, and where you stay. The most significant expense will probably be your round-trip (return) airfare to Thailand (see **Getting to Thailand,** p. 28) and a railpass or bus pass. Before you go, spend some time calculating a daily budget.

STAYING ON A BUDGET

The price difference between the cheapest options and the mid-range options in Thailand is often very small. At the moment, package tours are on the rise. Often, they offer efficient travel while still being affordable, but for many travelers, packaged deals can feel limiting. In any case, Thailand is budget friendly.

To give you a general idea, a bare-bones day in Thailand (camping or sleeping in hostels/guesthouses, buying food at supermarkets) would cost about US$10 (about 340฿) a slightly more comfortable day (sleeping in hostels/guesthouses and the occasional budget hotel, eating one meal per day at a restaurant, going out at night) would cost US$15 (500฿); and, for a luxurious day, the sky's the limit. Don't forget to factor in emergency reserve funds (at least US$200) when planning how much money you'll need.

TIPS FOR SAVING MONEY

Some simpler ways include searching out opportunities for free entertainment, splitting accommodation and food costs with trustworthy fellow travelers, and buying food in supermarkets rather than eating out. Bring a **sleepsack** (p. 18) to save on sheet charges in hostels and do your **laundry** in the sink (unless you're explicitly prohibited from doing so). Museums often have certain days once a month or once a week when admission is free; plan accordingly. If you are eligible, consider getting an ISIC or an IYTC (p. 12); many sights and museums offer reduced admission to students and youths. For getting around quickly, bikes are the most economical option. Don't forget about walking, though; you can learn a lot about a city by seeing it on foot. Drinking at bars and clubs quickly becomes expensive; it is much cheaper to buy alcohol at a supermarket and imbibe before going out. That said, do not go overboard. Though staying within your budget is important, do not do so at the expense of your health or a great travel experience.

TIPPING AND BARGAINING

Tipping in Thailand is not customary but much appreciated. The philosophy behind tipping is based on two principles: *tai boon*, the idea of merit-based tipping, and the "show-off" gesture of the giver, where the one doing the tipping is demonstrating his wealth to those with him. For Westerners, the general rule is that if an establishment includes a service charge in the bill, tipping is not necessary. In restaurants that don't levy service charges, you don't need to tip more than a 10% gratuity, but leaving the equivalent of US$2-5 is appropriate. Most people will welcome the extra baht, as the average yearly income for some regions of Thailand is as low as US$150. Foreigners should expect to pay higher entrance fees than native Thais at some places, including beaches, museums, and monuments. A *tuk-tuk* driver is not tipped unless hired as a private driver for an excursion. With metered taxis in Bangkok, however, the custom is to round up to the nearest 5฿.

Most officials are unwilling to accept bribes from foreigners, and it is unwise to initiate an under-the-table transaction. If an official demands a fee or fine that you feel may be illegal, proceed with caution. Paying the bribe might be preferable to the alternative, but keep in mind that it is also illegal. If you politely ask for a receipt, or to speak with the official's superior, you might be able to defuse the situation. As a very last resort, threatening to contact your embassy may also be effective.

TAXES

There is a 7% **VAT (value-added tax)** in Thailand levied on most items, including hotel rooms and food; it is usually already included in stated prices. Menus, tariff sheets, etc., specify if VAT is not included in the listed price. There is also a departure tax (700฿ for major international airports) that you must pay in the airport before leaving. The value of this tax varies depending on the airport from which you leave and destination to which you fly.

THE ART OF THE DEAL. In Southeast Asia, bargaining is more than a pricing system. It is an art form, and if your attitude is right, a great deal of fun. Bargaining in Thailand is a given: vendors will automatically quote you a price that is several times too high; tuk-tuks too will try to give you a run for your money. This is not a cut-throat contest, however, but a game of skill is built on a foundation of mutual respect. With the following tips and some finesse, you may be able to impress even the most hardened hawkers:

1. **Bargaining needn't be a fierce struggle laced with barbs.** Good-natured wrangling with a cheerful face may prove your best weapon.
2. **Use your poker face.** The less your face betrays your interest in the item the better. If you touch an item to inspect it, the vendor will be sure to "encourage" you to name a price or make a purchase. Coming back later to admire a trinket is a good way of ensuring that you pay a ridiculously high price. Never get too enthusiastic about the object in question.
3. **Know when to bargain.** In most cases, it's clear when it's appropriate. Most private transportation fares, like those for *tuk-tuks* and motorcycle taxis, are all fair game. Don't bargain on metered taxis or buses. Bargaining for lodging is possible, but success varies dramatically. Your chances will increase if you can state a specific reason for a better rate, like low-season discounts. It is acceptable to bargain for souvenirs at a market, but not in stores. Never bargain for produce, prepared foods on the street or in restaurants. In some stores, signs will indicate "fixed prices." When in doubt ask, "Is that your lowest price?" or whether discounts are given.
4. **Never underestimate the power of peer pressure.** Bargaining with more than one person at a time always leads to higher prices. Alternately, try having a friend discourage you from your purchase—if you seem to be reluctant, the merchant will want to drop the price to interest you again.
5. **Know when to turn away.** Refuse any vendor or driver who bargains rudely, and don't hesitate to move on to another vendor if one will not be reasonable about the final price he offers. However, to start bargaining without an intention to buy is a major faux pas. Agreeing on a price and declining it is also poor form. Turn away slowly with a smile and "thank you" upon hearing a ridiculous price—the price may plummet.
6. **Start low.** Never feel guilty offering a ridiculously low price. If it's too low the vendor simply won't sell it to you! Your starting price should be no more than one-third to one-half the asking price.

PACKING

Pack lightly. Lay out only what you absolutely need. If you plan to do a lot of hiking, also consult this book's **The Great Outdoors,** p. 41.

Luggage: If you plan to cover most of your trip on foot, a sturdy **internal frame backpack** is great. (For the basics on buying a pack.) Unless you are staying in 1 place for a large chunk of time, a suitcase will be unwieldy. A **daypack** (a small backpack or courier bag) is useful.

Clothing: It's a good idea to bring a warm jacket or wool sweater, a rain jacket (Gore-Tex® is both waterproof and breathable), sturdy shoes or hiking boots, and thick socks. Sandals are a good idea for grubby hostel showers. Extra socks too are a great addition when packing. In order to enter many temples in Thailand, dress that covers both

TOP 10 WAYS TO SAVE IN THAILAND

Any tourist can get by cheaply in Thailand, but the more savvy traveler will learn to make every baht count. Here are some tips to get you started:

1. Buy food at open-air markets instead of restaurants.
2. Visit one of Southern Thailand's famous kos in the low season, when prices and demand are substantially lower.
3. Rent a bike instead of a motorbike.
4. Get a group together for lower individual rates if you are planning to trek in the northern hills.
5. Buy your souvenirs in smaller towns to avoid inflated tourist prices.
6. Look out for flyers and coupons in weekly papers or from promoters in Bangkok that will allow you to bypass cover charges at clubs.
7. If you don't mind waiting, sharing a songthaew with other passengers before boarding will make the trip a lot cheaper.
8. Bargain! Be respectful, but don't be shy about shaving a few baht off overpriced souvenirs.
9. Learn the names of one or two Thai dishes you like, then order from the Thai menu at restaurants and skip the English one—the Thai version is often a lot cheaper.
10. If you're heading to a major resort town, try to arrive on a weekday for better room deals and availability.

the arms and the legs is required, and shoes that (at a minimum) have a strap on the heel.

Sleepsack: Some hostels require that you either provide your own linen or rent sheets from them. Making your own sleepsack: fold a full-size sheet in half the long way, then sew it closed along the long side and 1 of the short sides.

Converters and Adapters: In Thailand, electricity is 220 volts AC, enough to fry any 120V North American appliance. 220/240V electrical appliances won't work with 120V current, either. Americans and Canadians should buy an adapter (which changes the shape of the plug; US$5) and a converter (which changes the voltage; US$10-30). Don't make the mistake of using only an adapter (unless appliance instructions explicitly state otherwise). Australians and New Zealanders (who use 220V at home) won't need a converter, but will need a set of adapters to use anything electrical. For more info, check out http://kropla.com/electric.htm.

Toiletries: Condoms, deodorant, razors, tampons, and toothbrushes are often available, but it may be difficult to find your preferred brand. Contact lenses are likely to be expensive and difficult to find, so bring extra pairs and solution. Bring your glasses and a copy of your prescription in case you need emergency replacements.

First-Aid Kit: Pack bandages, a pain reliever, antibiotic cream, a thermometer, a multifunction pocketknife, tweezers, moleskin, decongestant, motion-sickness remedy, diarrhea or upset-stomach medication (Pepto Bismol or Imodium), an antihistamine, sunscreen, insect repellent, burn ointment, and a syringe for emergencies (get an explanatory letter from your doctor). If you are traveling in a malarial area of Thailand (p. 23), also bring your malaria medication.

Other Useful Items: Bring a **money belt** and a small **padlock.** Basic **outdoors equipment** (plastic water bottle, compass, waterproof matches, pocketknife, sunglasses, sunscreen, hat). Other things you're liable to forget include: an umbrella, sealable **plastic bags** (for damp clothes, soap, food, shampoo, and other spillables), an **alarm clock,** safety pins, rubber bands, a flashlight, and garbage bags. A **cell phone** can be a lifesaver on the road; see p. 37 for information on acquiring one that will work in Thailand.

Important Documents: Don't forget your passport, traveler's checks, ATM and/or credit cards, adequate ID, and photocopies of all of the aforementioned items. Check that you have any of the following: a hosteling membership card (p. 12); driver's license (p. 33); travel insurance forms (p. 23); ISIC (p. 12); and/or railpass or bus pass (p. 32).

SAFETY AND HEALTH

GENERAL ADVICE

In any type of crisis, the most important thing to do is **stay calm.** Your country's embassy abroad (p. 10) is a good resource in an emergency; registering with that embassy upon arrival in the country is a good idea. The government offices listed in the **Travel Advisories** box (p. 21) can provide information on the services they offer their citizens in case of emergencies abroad.

LOCAL LAWS AND POLICE

Thai police enforce strict drug policies and will arrest and heavily fine foreigners (and Thais) for possession and trafficking of illicit drugs. Beware of anyone offering a "free trip to Thailand" in exchange for help in transporting "luggage" or "gifts" into the country, as this method of drug trafficking has been frequently employed. It is also illegal to import more than 200 cigarettes per person into Thailand, punishable by a fine. By law, foreigners are required to carry their passports at all times (you can get arrested if caught without one).

The monarchy of Thailand is a respected institution, and it is a criminal offense to make any derisive comments about the monarchy or its members. Called *lese majeste*, offenses against the royal family can result in terms of imprisonment from three to five years. These offenses include stepping on or destroying any image of the King, such as Thai bank notes.

WHO YOU GONNA CALL? The tourist police in Bangkok can be reached by calling ☎1155 and are generally a useful resource, whether in emergency situations or in minor complications. Call this number for any issues related to tourist scams. The countrywide emergency number is ☎191. Contact the tourist police before using this number.

DRUGS AND ALCOHOL

Drugs are easily accessible in Thailand and, especially in some rural communities, drug use may seem to be common and public. Despite the glamour surrounding the Thai drug scene, which is often connected to the sex trade or the backpacker community, narcotics are illegal and travelers do get caught. Buying or selling any type of drug may lead to a stiff prison sentence. Possession of marijuana can lead to a prison sentence of up to 15 years plus a fine of 150,000฿. For more serious drug offenses, Thailand has imposed the death penalty. If you break the law, your home embassies may visit you in jail, but they cannot do anything else to help you. Often they do not even learn of arrests until a few days after they occur.

Thailand has no established minimum drinking age; however, some clubs do have a minimum age requirement (although they often do not ask for IDs from foreigners). Whenever you drink, *Let's Go* recommends that you use alcohol responsibly. Take extra safety precautions, as there have been cases of travelers being robbed after accepting drugged food or drink from strangers.

SPECIFIC CONCERNS

NATURAL DISASTERS

On December 26, 2004, a large **tsunami** hit areas of the west coast of Thailand, including Phuket, Patong, Khao Lak, and Ko Phi Phi Don. More that 5000 people were killed or missing, half of them foreign tourists. A string of hotels were also completely destroyed, though most of the hard-hit tourist areas have been rebuilt (with new safety guidelines). Travelers should educate themselves about natural dangers specific to the regions in which they are about to travel.

FLOODING. Periodically, Thailand suffers from severe flooding during the rainy season (June-Nov.). Extensive flooding in the northern provinces of Uttaradit, Phrae, Lampang, Nan, and Sukhothai occured during the week of May 22, 2006, resulted in deaths and injuries. Be careful of strong currents off Thailand's southern beaches which occasionally result in fatalities, especially when taking passenger ferries or swimming during **monsoon season** (Sept.-Oct.).

TYPHOONS. Typhoons are severe tropical storms (equivalent to hurricanes in the Atlantic) with extremely high winds. They typically occur from May to November, with the season peaking between August and October. If there is a typhoon, you should move inside, away from windows, and stay informed on the movement of the storm.

DEMONSTRATIONS AND BORDER CONFLICT

Former Prime Minister Thaksin's return to Thailand and a talk of his possible return to politics as spurred some political boycotts. There were a number of peaceful political demonstrations in Bangkok and provincial towns. As further political demonstrations may be arranged with short notice, avoid large crowds and public gatherings.

Recently, northern Thailand and its border with Myanmar have been prone to on-going conflicts between the Myanmar Army and armed opposition groups as well as clashes between Thai security forces and armed drug traffickers. In addition, bandits and drug traffickers operate in these border areas. Visitors should only travel with local guides who are familiar to the area when traveling off-road in undeveloped areas. Border closings and re-openings occur frequently. Foreigners considering traveling into Myanmar from Thailand should be aware that in the event of a border closure, they may not be able to re-enter Thailand. Check the news and your embassy for the latest information.

TERRORISM

Since January 2004, there have been almost daily attacks in the southern provinces of Naratiwat, Pattini, Yala, Satun, and Songkhla (see p. 391). Targets include civilians and government officials at hotels, bars, markets, schools; Those using transportation are targets too (see **Southern Discomfort,** p. 63). Even outside of these highly volatile areas, there is a high threat from terrorism in Thailand. Following the violence in the far south, the Thai government has taken increased security measures, but there have been isolated attacks in Bangkok, the last such attack occurring in New Year's Eve 2007. Check news and travel advisories (see **Travel Advisories,** p. 21) to get an updated list of your home country's government's advisories before departure. The box below lists offices to contact and webpages to visit to get the most updated list of your home country's government's advisories about travel.

TRAVEL ADVISORIES. The following government offices provide travel information and advisories by telephone, by fax, or via the web:

Australian Department of Foreign Affairs and Trade: ☎+61 2 6261 1111; www.dfat.gov.au.

Canadian Department of Foreign Affairs and International Trade (DFAIT): Call ☎+1-800-267-8376; www.dfait-maeci.gc.ca. Offer a free booklet, *Bon Voyage...But.*

New Zealand Ministry of Foreign Affairs: ☎+64 4 439 8000; www.mfat. govt.nz.

United Kingdom Foreign and Commonwealth Office: ☎+44 20 7008 1500; www.fco.gov.uk.

US Department of State: ☎+1-888-407-4747; http://travel.state.gov. Visit the website for the booklet, *A Safe Trip Abroad.*

ESSENTIALS

PERSONAL SAFETY

EXPLORING AND TRAVELING

To avoid unwanted attention, try to blend in as much as possible. Respecting local customs (in many cases, dressing more conservatively than you would at home) may ward off would-be hecklers. Familiarize yourself with your surroundings before setting out and carry yourself with confidence. Check maps in shops and restaurants rather than on the street. If you are traveling alone, be sure someone at home knows your itinerary and never tell anyone you meet that you're by yourself. When walking at night, stick to busy, well-lit streets and avoid dark alleyways. If you ever feel uncomfortable, leave the area as quickly and directly as you can.

There is no surefire way to avoid all the threatening situations that you might encounter while traveling, but a good **self-defense course** will give you concrete ways to react to unwanted advances. **Impact, Prepare,** and **Model Mugging** can refer you to local self-defense courses in Australia, Canada, Switzerland, and the US. Visit www.modelmugging.org for a list of nearby chapters.

If you are using a **car,** learn local driving signals and wear a seatbelt. Children under 40lb. should ride only in specially designed car seats, available for a small fee from most car-rental agencies. Study route maps before you hit the road and, if you plan on spending a lot of time driving, consider bringing spare parts. For long drives in desolate areas, invest in a cellular phone and a roadside assistance program (p. 35). Park your vehicle in a garage or well-traveled area and use a steering-wheel locking device in larger cities. Sleeping in your car is the most dangerous way to get your rest, and it's also illegal in many countries. For info on the perils of **hitchhiking,** see p. 36.

POSSESSIONS AND VALUABLES

Never leave your belongings unattended; crime can occur in even the most safe-looking hostel or hotel. Bring your own padlock for hostel lockers and don't ever store valuables in a locker. Be particularly careful on **buses** and **trains;** horror stories abound about determined thieves who wait for travelers to fall asleep. Carry your bag or purse in front of you where you can see it. When traveling with others, sleep in alternate shifts. When alone, use good judgment in selecting a train compartment: never stay in an empty one and use a lock to secure your pack to the luggage rack. Be careful if traveling at night or on overnight trains. Sleep on top bunks with your luggage stored above you (if not in bed with you) and keep important documents and valuables on your person.

There are a few steps you can take to minimize the financial risk associated with traveling. **Bring as little with you as possible.** Also, buy a few combination **padlocks** to secure your belongings either in your pack or in a hostel or train-station locker. **Carry as little cash as possible.** Keep your traveler's checks and ATM/credit cards in a **money belt**—not a "fanny pack"—along with your passport and ID cards. Lastly, **keep a small cash reserve separate from your primary stash.** This should be about US$50 (US dollars or euros are best) sewn into or stored in the depths of your pack, along with your traveler's check numbers, photocopies of your passport, birth certificate, and other important documents.

In general, Thailand has a good safety record. Nevertheless, scams abound: taxi and *tuk-tuk* drivers, guesthouse operators, and fellow travelers have all been known to attempt various con-games. In large cities, **con artists** often work in groups and may involve children. Beware of certain classics: sob stories that require money, rolls of bills "found" on the street, mustard spilled (or saliva spit) onto your shoulder to distract you while they snatch your bag. **Never let your passport and your bags out of your sight.** Hostel workers will sometimes stand at bus and train-station arrival points to recruit tired and disoriented travelers to their hostel; never believe strangers who tell you that theirs is the only hostel open. Beware of **pickpockets** in city crowds, especially on public transportation. Be alert in public telephone booths: if you must say your calling card number, do so quietly; if punching it in, make sure no one can look over your shoulder.

If you will be traveling with electronic devices, such as a laptop computer or a PDA, check whether your homeowner's insurance covers loss, theft, or damage when you travel. If not, you might consider purchasing a low-cost separate insurance policy. **Safeware** (☎+1-800-800-1492; www.safeware.com) specializes in covering computers and charges US$90 for 90-day comprehensive international travel coverage up to US$4000. However, if at all possible and if they are not absolutely necessary, leave these items at home. Using them in Thailand will make it clear that you are a tourist and will label you a target for theft.

PRE-DEPARTURE HEALTH

In your passport, write the names of any people you wish to be contacted in case of a **medical emergency** and list any allergies or medical conditions. Matching a prescription to a foreign equivalent is not always easy, safe, or possible, so, if you take **prescription drugs,** consider carrying up-to-date prescriptions or a statement from your doctor stating the medication's trade name, manufacturer, chemical name, and dosage. While traveling, be sure to keep all medication with you in your carry-on luggage. For tips on how to pack a **first-aid kit** and other health essentials, see p. 18.

In Thailand, it is helpful to know the chemical names of drugs (ie: Acetaminophen for Tylenol), as brand names you are used to may not be available.

IMMUNIZATIONS AND PRECAUTIONS

Travelers over two years old should make sure that the following vaccines are up to date: MMR (for measles, mumps, and rubella); DTaP or Td (for diphtheria, tetanus, and pertussis); IPV (for polio); Hib (for haemophilus influenza B); and HepB (for Hepatitis B). Adults traveling to the developing world on trips longer than four weeks should consider the following additional immunizations: Hepatitis A vaccine, immune globulin (IG), typhoid and cholera vaccines, particularly if traveling off the beaten paths. The Japanese encephalitis vaccine is recommended for anyone traveling in rural regions for longer than one month, particularly in the Northeastern parts of Thailand. The vaccine consists of a series of three shots, which can occasionally have severe side-effects. Additionally, the rabies vaccine and yearly influenza vaccines are recommended. While **yellow fever** is only endemic to parts of South America and sub-Saharan Africa, Thailand may deny entrance to travelers arriving from these zones without a certificate of vaccination. For recommendations on immunizations and prophylaxis, consult the Centers for Disease Control and Prevention (CDC; see **Useful Organizations and Publications,** p. 24) in the US or the equivalent in your home country, and check with a doctor for guidance.

Malaria is prevalent in most of Thailand. Strains resistant to certain prophylactics are common, so ask your doctor to recommend the best preventative drug for your region of travel. There are many schools of thought about malarial medication. It is not generally recommended for travelers staying in major cities such as Bangkok, Chiang Mai, and Pattaya. However, anyone traveling in rural areas along Thailand's borders should talk to a doctor about buying medication. Be aware certain drugs are unavailable in some parts of Thailand, so, stock up before you go. For more information, see p. 24.

INOCULATION REQUIREMENTS AND RECOMMENDATIONS. Inoculations needed for travel in Thailand vary with the length of your trip and the activities you plan to pursue. Visit your doctor at least 4-6 weeks prior to your departure to allow time for the shots to take effect. Be sure to keep your inoculation records with you as you travel: you may be required to show them to border officials.

Diphtheria and tetanus, measles, and polio: regular boosters recommended.
Typhoid: strongly recommended.
Hepatitis A or Immune Globulin (IG): recommended.
Hepatitis B: if traveling for 6 months or more, or if exposure to blood, needle-sharing, or sexual contact is likely. Important for health care workers and those who might seek medical treatment abroad.
Japanese encephalitis: only if traveling in rural areas for 4 weeks or more, or if there are outbreaks in regions you plan to visit. Elevated risk May-Oct.
Rabies: if you might be exposed to animals while you travel.
Yellow Fever: if traveling from South America, sub-Saharan Africa or other infected areas, a certificate of vaccination may be required to enter Thailand.

INSURANCE

Travel insurance covers four basic areas: medical/health problems, property loss, trip cancellation/interruption, and emergency evacuation. Though regular insurance policies may well extend to travel-related accidents, you may consider purchasing separate travel insurance if the cost of potential trip cancellation, interruption, or emergency medical evacuation is greater than you can absorb. Prices for travel insurance generally run about US$50 per week for full coverage, while trip cancellation/interruption may be purchased separately at a rate of US$3-5 per day, depending on length of stay.

Medical insurance (especially university policies) often covers costs incurred abroad; check with your provider. **Homeowners' insurance** (or your family's coverage) often covers theft during travel and loss of travel documents (passport, plane ticket, railpass, etc.) up to US$500.

ISIC and **ITIC** (see p. 12) provide basic insurance benefits to US cardholders, including US$100 per day of in-hospital sickness for up to 100 days and

US$10,000 of accident-related medical reimbursement (see www.isicus.com for details). Cardholders have access to a toll-free 24hr. helpline for medical, legal, and financial emergencies overseas. **American Express** (☎+1-800-338-1670) grants most cardholders automatic collision and theft car rental insurance on rentals made with the card.

USEFUL ORGANIZATIONS AND PUBLICATIONS

The American **Centers for Disease Control and Prevention** (CDC; ☎+1-877-FYI-TRIP; www.cdc.gov/travel) maintains an international travelers' hotline and an informative website. Consult the appropriate government agency of your home country for consular information sheets on health, entry requirements, and other issues for various countries (see the listings in the box on **Travel Advisories**, p. 21). For quick information on health and other travel warnings, call the **Overseas Citizens Services** (M-F 8am-8pm from overseas ☎+1-202-501-4444, from US +1-888-407-4747; line open M-F 8am-8pm EST), or contact a passport agency, embassy, or consulate abroad. For information on medical evacuation services and travel insurance firms, see the US government website at http://travel.state.gov/travel/abroad_health.html or the **British Foreign and Commonwealth Office** (www.fco.gov.uk). For general health information, contact the **American Red Cross** (☎+1-202-303-4498; www.redcross.org).

STAYING HEALTHY

Common sense is the simplest prescription for good health while you travel. Drink lots of fluids to prevent dehydration and constipation, and wear sturdy, broken-in shoes and clean socks. Sunscreen and heavy-duty bug spray are absolute essentials; make sure you apply regularly to stay burn- and bite-free.

ONCE IN THAILAND

ENVIRONMENTAL HAZARDS

Heat exhaustion and dehydration: Heat exhaustion leads to nausea, excessive thirst, headaches, and dizziness. Avoid it by drinking plenty of fluids, eating salty foods (e.g., crackers), abstaining from dehydrating beverages (e.g., alcohol and caffeinated beverages), and wearing sunscreen. Continuous heat stress can eventually lead to heatstroke, characterized by a rising temperature, severe headache, delirium, and cessation of sweating. Victims should be cooled off with wet towels and taken to a doctor.

Sunburn: Always wear sunscreen (SPF 30 or higher) when spending excessive amounts of time outdoors. If you are planning on spending time on the beaches of Thailand, you are at a higher risk of getting burned, even on a cloudy day. If you get sunburned, drink more fluids than usual and apply an aloe-based lotion. Severe sunburns can lead to sun poisoning, a condition that can cause fever, chills, nausea, and vomiting. Sun poisoning should always be treated by a doctor.

High Altitude: Trekkers in northern Thailand are likely to reach areas of high altitude. Allow your body a couple of days to adjust to the reduced level of oxygen before exerting yourself. Note that alcohol is more potent and UV rays are much stronger at higher elevations.

INSECT-BORNE DISEASES

Many diseases are transmitted by insects—mainly mosquitoes, fleas, ticks, and lice. Be aware of insects in wet or forested areas, especially while hiking and camping. Wear long pants and long sleeves, tuck your pants into your socks, and sleep under a mosquito net. Use insect repellents such as DEET and soak or spray your gear with permethrin (licensed in the US only for use on clothing). **Mosquitoes**—responsible for malaria, dengue fever, and Japanese encephalitis—can be particularly abundant in rice fields and in wet, swampy, or wooded areas along the border and in northern Thailand. **Ticks**—which can carry Lyme and other diseases—can be particularly dangerous in rural and forested regions. To stop the intense itch after being bitten, try calamine lotion or topical cortisone creams like Cortaid. Or, take a soothing bath with a half-cup of baking soda or oatmeal.

Malaria: Transmitted by Anopheles mosquitoes that bite at night. The incubation period varies anywhere between 10 days and 4 weeks. Early symptoms include fever, chills, aches, and fatigue, followed by high fever and sweating, sometimes with vomiting and diarrhea. See a doctor for any flu-like sickness that occurs after travel in a risk area. To reduce the risk of contracting malaria, use mosquito repellent, particularly in the evenings and when visiting forested areas. Make sure you see a doctor at least 4-6 weeks before a trip to a high-risk area to get up-to-date malaria prescriptions and recommendations. A doctor may prescribe oral prophylactics, like mefloquine or doxycycline. Be aware that mefloquine can have very serious side effects, including paranoia, psychotic behavior, and nightmares.

Japanese encephalitis: Another mosquito-borne disease, most common during the rainy season (May-Oct.) in agricultural areas near rice fields and livestock. Aside from delirium, most symptoms are flu-like: chills, headache, fever, vomiting, and muscle fatigue. Since the disease carries a high mortality rate, it is vital to go to a hospital as soon as symptoms appear. While the JE-VAX vaccine, usually given in 3 shots over a 30-day period, is effective for a year, it can cause serious side effects in some people. According to the CDC, there is little chance of being infected if you take proper precautions, such as using repellents containing DEET and sleeping under mosquito nets. The vaccine is recommended if you are planning on spending more than one month in rural Thailand or if you are going to have extensive unprotected outdoor, evening, and nighttime exposure in rural areas, such as bicycling or camping.

Yellow fever: A viral disease transmitted by mosquitoes. Derives its name from one of its most common symptoms, the jaundice caused by liver damage. While most cases are mild, the severe ones begin with fever, headache, muscle pain, nausea, and abdominal pain before progressing to jaundice, vomiting of blood, and bloody stools. While there is no specific treatment, there is an effective vaccine that offers 10 years of protection. Note that because one cannot contract this disease while in Thailand, the country does not require that travelers have this vaccine unless they have traveled to an infected area (see www.thaiembdc.org for more info).

Other insect-borne diseases: Lymphatic filariasis is a roundworm infestation transmitted by mosquitoes. Infection causes enlargement of extremities and has no vaccine. In northern Thailand, travelers who eat raw or under-cooked fish are at risk of picking up liver flukes, parasites found in the water, especially in the waters of Nong Han, the largest freshwater lake in northeast Thailand.

FOOD- AND WATER-BORNE DISEASES

Prevention is the best cure: be sure that your food is properly cooked and the water you drink is clean. Watch out for food from markets or street vendors that may have been cooked in unhygienic conditions. Other culprits are raw shellfish, unpasteurized milk, and sauces containing raw eggs. Buy bottled water or purify your own water by bringing it to a rolling boil or treating it with **iodine tablets;** note, however, that boiling is more reliable. Always wash your hands before eating or bring a quick-drying, purifying, liquid hand cleaner. It may seem like a hassle, but your bowels will thank you. Most Western

ESSENTIALS

establishments and Thai establishments that cater to tourists serve water and ice that has been purified. The menu will usually say, but it never hurts to ask.

Traveler's diarrhea: Results from drinking fecally contaminated water or eating uncooked and contaminated foods. Symptoms include nausea, bloating, and urgency. Try quick-energy, non-sugary foods with protein and carbohydrates to keep your strength up. Over-the-counter anti-diarrheals (e.g., Imodium) may counteract the problem. The most dangerous side effect is dehydration; drink 8 oz. of water with ½tsp. of sugar or honey and a pinch of salt, try uncaffeinated soft drinks, or eat salted crackers. If you develop a fever or your symptoms don't go away after 4-5 days, consult a doctor. Consult a doctor immediately for treatment of diarrhea in children.

Dysentery: Results from an intestinal infection caused by bacteria in contaminated food or water. Common symptoms include bloody diarrhea, fever, and abdominal pain and tenderness. The most common type of dysentery generally only lasts a week, but it is highly contagious. Seek medical help immediately. Dysentery can be treated with the drugs norfloxacin or ciprofloxacin (commonly known as Cipro). If you are traveling in high-risk (especially rural) regions, consider obtaining a prescription before you leave home.

Cholera: An intestinal disease caused by bacteria in contaminated food. Symptoms include diarrhea, dehydration, vomiting, and muscle cramps. See a doctor immediately; if left untreated, cholera can be lethal within hours. Antibiotics are available, but the most important treatment is rehydration. No vaccine is available in the US.

Hepatitis A: A viral infection of the liver acquired through contaminated water or shellfish from contaminated water. Symptoms include fatigue, fever, loss of appetite, nausea, dark urine, jaundice, vomiting, aches and pains, and light stools. The risk is highest in rural areas and the countryside, but it is also present in urban areas. Ask your doctor about the Hepatitis A vaccine or an injection of immune globulin.

Schistosomiasis: A parasitic disease caused when the larvae of a certain freshwater snail species penetrate unbroken skin. Symptoms include an itchy localized rash, followed in 4-6 weeks by fever, fatigue, headaches, muscle and joint aches, painful urination, diarrhea, nausea, loss of appetite, and night sweats. To avoid it, try not to swim in fresh water in areas with poor sanitation. If exposed to untreated water, rub the area vigorously with a towel and apply rubbing alcohol.

Giardiasis: Transmitted through parasites and acquired by drinking untreated water from streams or lakes. Symptoms include diarrhea, cramps, bloating, fatigue, weight loss, and nausea. If untreated, it can lead to severe dehydration. Giardiasis occurs worldwide.

Typhoid fever: Caused by the salmonella bacteria; common in villages and rural areas in Thailand. While mostly transmitted through contaminated food and water, it may also be acquired by direct contact with another person. Early symptoms include high fever, headaches, fatigue, appetite loss, constipation, and a rash on the abdomen or chest. Antibiotics can treat typhoid, but a vaccination (70-90% effective) is recommended.

OTHER INFECTIOUS DISEASES

The following diseases exist all over the world. Travelers should know how to recognize them and what to do if they suspect they have been infected.

Rabies: Transmitted through the saliva of infected animals; fatal if untreated. By the time symptoms (thirst and muscle spasms) appear, the disease is in its terminal stage. If you are bitten, wash the wound, seek immediate medical care, and try to have the animal located. A rabies vaccine, which consists of 3 shots given over a 21-day period, is available and recommended for developing world travel, but is only semi-effective.

Hepatitis B: A viral infection of the liver transmitted via blood or other bodily fluids. Symptoms, which may not surface until years after infection, include jaundice, appetite loss, fever, and joint pain. It is transmitted through unprotected sex and unclean needles. A

3-shot vaccination sequence is recommended for sexually active travelers and anyone planning to seek medical treatment abroad; it must begin 6 months before traveling.

Hepatitis C: Like Hepatitis B, but the mode of transmission differs. IV drug users, those with occupational exposure to blood, hemodialysis patients, and recipients of blood transfusions are at the highest risk, but the disease can also be spread through sexual contact or sharing items like razors and toothbrushes that may have traces of blood on them. No symptoms are usually exhibited. If untreated, Hepatitis C can lead to liver failure.

AIDS and HIV: For detailed information on Acquired Immune Deficiency Syndrome (AIDS) in Thailand, call the 24hr. National AIDS Hotline at ☎+1-800-342-2437. Note that Thailand screens incoming travelers for AIDS, primarily those planning extended visits for work or study, and denies entrance to those who test HIV-positive. Contact the consulate of Thailand for information.

Sexually transmitted infections (STIs): Gonorrhea, chlamydia, genital warts, syphilis, herpes, HPV, and other STIs are easier to catch than HIV and can be just as serious. Though condoms may protect you from some STIs, oral or even tactile contact can lead to transmission. If you think you may have contracted an STI, see a doctor immediately.

OTHER HEALTH CONCERNS

MEDICAL CARE ON THE ROAD

Hospitals in Thailand vary from region to region, but, generally, larger, centralized cities like Bangkok and Chiang Mai have high-quality facilities. Thailand's health care system is split between public and private institutions. The public system often has limited technical support and is overcrowded and bureaucratic. Private hospitals are more likely to have English-speaking doctors, language interpreters, foreign insurance claim assistance, international emergency medical evacuation access, and embassy liaison services. Private health care is so good that an epidemic of medical tourism (both cosmetic and essential) has broken out. Not only is health care in Thailand much cheaper than in most private hospitals than in the Western world, but foreigners are usually treated extremely well.

General practitioners and dentists are readily available. Most medical staff at large medical institutions speak very good English. Thai medical services are always available: walk-in services are common during the daytime and many hospitals offer 24hr. emergency room service. Unfortunately, **emergency hotlines are only useful if you speak Thai.** Watch closely at smaller rural hospitals or clincs to make sure that any instruments used during your treatment are thoroughly sanitized, and if you ever need an injection make sure the medical practitioner unwraps a brand-new syringe.

If you are concerned about obtaining medical assistance while traveling, you may wish to employ special support services. The **MedPass** from **GlobalCare, Inc.,** 6875 Shiloh Rd. East, Alpharetta, GA 30005, USA (☎+1-800-860-1111; www.global-care.net), provides 24hr. international medical assistance, support, and medical evacuation resources. The **International Association for Medical Assistance to Travelers** (**IAMAT;** US ☎+1-716-754-4883, Canada +1519-836-0102; www.iamat.org) has free membership, lists English-speaking doctors worldwide, and offers detailed info on immunization requirements and sanitation. If your regular insurance policy does not cover travel abroad, you may wish to purchase additional coverage (p. 23).

Those with medical conditions (such as diabetes, allergies to antibiotics, epilepsy, or heart conditions) may want to obtain a **MedicAlert** membership (US$40 per year), which includes among other things a stainless-steel ID tag and a 24hr. collect-call number. Contact the MedicAlert Foundation International, 2323 Colorado Ave., Turlock, CA 95382, USA (☎+1-888-633-4298, outside US 209-668-3333; www.medicalert.org).

WOMEN'S HEALTH

Women traveling in unsanitary conditions are vulnerable to **urinary tract** (including **bladder** and **kidney**) infections. Thailand's hot and humid climate also makes women especially susceptible to **vaginal yeast infections.** Wearing loose trousers or a skirt and cotton underwear will help, as will over-the-counter remedies like Monistat or Gyne-Lotrimin. Bring supplies from home if you are prone to infection, as they may be difficult to find on the road. In a pinch, some travelers use natural alternatives such as a plain yogurt and lemon juice douche.

Tampons, pads, and **contraceptive devices** are widely available. Most toiletries can be found in Western establishments like UK's Boots on Khaosan Rd. and malls on Silom Rd. in Bangkok. Women using birth control pills should bring enough to allow for possible loss or extended stays. Also bring a prescription, since forms of the pill vary considerably. If you need contraceptive services, contact the Planned Parenthood Association of Thailand in Bangkok, 8 Soi Vibhavadi-Rangsit 44, Vibhavadi-Rangsit Road Ladyao, Chatuchak, Bangkok 10900 (☎+66 02 941 2320; www.ppat.or.th). English is the primary language spoken at the branch. **Abortion** is legal in Thailand, but only in cases where the woman's health is in danger or she has been raped.

TOILETS

Toilets in Thailand are truly unique. While many establishments have Western toilets, some don't, especially the farther away you get from big cities. If you do encounter a **squat toilet,** don't panic; using one may take some practice, but it is very manageable. Most squat toilets are porcelain bowls set in the ground with raised foot grooves on either side. You are expected to put a foot on either side of the bowl and then squat down. The toilet there will be a container of water and a small bucket, which is used both to wash yourself and flush the toilet (scoop water in the bucket, pour the water in the toilet, and the water will disappear). You may want to carry toilet paper with you, but putting this in the toilet is not a good idea. Instead, many establishments provide a wastepaper basket for their disposal. Also a bottle of hand sanitizer may come in handy.

GETTING TO THAILAND

BY PLANE

When it comes to airfare, a little effort can save you a bundle. Courier fares are the cheapest for those whose plans are flexible enough to deal with the restrictions. Tickets sold by consolidators and standby seating are also good deals, but last-minute specials, airfare wars, and charter flights often beat these fares. The key is to hunt around, be flexible, and ask about discounts. Students, seniors, and those under 26 should never pay full price for a ticket.

AIRFARES

Airfares to Thailand peak between November and December and again between July and August. The cheapest times to travel are also during the rainy season. Mid-week (M-Th morning) round-trip flights run US$40-50 cheaper than weekend flights, but they are generally more crowded and less likely to permit frequent-flier upgrades. Not fixing a return date ("open return") or arriving in and departing from different cities ("open-jaw") can be pricier than round-trip flights. Patching one-way flights together is the most expensive way to travel. Flights between Thailand's capitals or regional hubs—Bangkok, Chiang Mai, Ko Samui—tend to be cheaper, and domestic flights can usually be purchased just hours in advance.

Round-the-world (RTW) tickets usually include at least five stops and are valid for about a year; prices range US$1200-5000. Try **Star Alliance,** a consortium of 16 airlines including United Airlines (www.staralliance.com).

BUDGET AND STUDENT TRAVEL AGENCIES

While knowledgeable agents specializing in flights to (your country/region) can make your life easy, they may not spend the time to find you the lowest possible fare—they get paid on commission. Travelers holding ISIC and IYTC (p. 12) qualify for big discounts from student travel agencies. Most flights from budget agencies are on major airlines, but in peak season some may sell seats on less reliable chartered aircraft.

STA Travel, 5900 Wilshire Blvd., Ste. 900, Los Angeles, CA 90036, USA (24hr. reservations and info ☎+1-800-781-4040; www.statravel.com). A student and youth travel organization with over 150 offices worldwide (check their website for a listing of all their offices), including US offices in Boston, Chicago, Los Angeles, New York City, Seattle, San Francisco, and Washington, DC. Ticket booking, travel insurance, railpasses, and more. Walk-in offices are located throughout Australia (☎+61 3 9207 5900), New Zealand (☎+64 9 309 9723), and the UK (☎+44 8701 630 026).

Travel CUTS (Canadian Universities Travel Services Limited), 187 College St., Toronto, ON M5T 1P7, Canada (☎+1-888-592-2887; www.travelcuts.com). Offices across Canada and the US including Los Angeles, New York City, Seattle, and San Francisco.

USIT, 19-21 Aston Quay, Dublin 2, Ireland (☎+353 1 602 1904; www.usit.ie). Ireland's leading student/budget travel agency has 20 offices throughout Northern Ireland and the Republic of Ireland. Offers programs to work, study, and volunteer worldwide.

COMMERCIAL AIRLINES

The commercial airlines' lowest regular offer is the **APEX (Advance Purchase Excursion)** fare, which provides confirmed reservations and allows "open-jaw" tickets. Generally, reservations must be made seven to 21 days ahead of departure, with seven- to 14-day minimum-stay and up to 90-day maximum-stay restrictions. These fares carry hefty cancellation and change penalties (fees rise in summer). Book peak-season APEX fares early. Use **Expedia** (www.expedia.com) or **Travelocity** (www.travelocity.com) to get an idea of the lowest published fares, then use the resources outlined here to try to beat those fares. Low-season fares should be appreciably cheaper than the high-season (Nov.-Feb.) ones listed here.

TRAVELING FROM NORTH AMERICA

Basic round-trip fares to Thailand are expensive: at their cheapest they are still US$800-4000 to Bangkok; US$2000-6000 to Chiang Mai; and US$1500-4000 to Phuket. Standard commercial carriers like **United** (☎800-538-2929; www.ual.com) will probably offer the most convenient flights, but they may not be the cheapest, unless you manage to grab a special promotion or airfare-war ticket. Check **Thai Airways** (US ☎800-426-5204, Thailand ☎66 02 265 5555; www.thai-airways.com) and **Bangkok Airways** (US ☎866-226-4565, Thailand ☎02 265 5555; www.bangkokair.com) for discounts.

Basic round-trip fares to Thailand range from roughly UK£450-1500. Check British Airways (☎+1-800-247-9297; www.britishairways.com). Asian-based airlines like **China Airlines** (US ☎+1-800 227 5118; www.china-airlines.com),

Korean Air (Thailand ☎+66 2635 0465-9; www.koreanair.com), **Singapore Airlines** (Thailand ☎+66 2353 6000; www.singaporeair.com), or Hong Kong-based **Cathay Pacific Airways** (Thailand ☎+66 2263 0606; www.cathaypacific.com) may also have cheaper flights, depending on when you book.

TRAVELING FROM AUSTRALIA AND NEW ZEALAND

Basic round-trip fares to Thailand roughly cost AUS$850-3000 from Australia; from New Zealand NZ$950-2500. Check **Qantas** (☎+61 29 691 3636; www.qantas.com.au) for low fares.

BY BUS

Travelers often reach Thailand by bus from Cambodia, Laos, Malaysia, or Myanmar. A/C buses are usually comfortable and reliable. Other, non-A/C buses offer sparse leg room and bumpy rides. Inquire about purchasing tickets, as some buses require reservations in advance, whereas others sell tickets upon departure and don't leave the station until full. Check visa availability before taking a bus ride; visas may not always be available at the border and in most cases must be acquired in advance in other towns. Most tourist cafes can help you with info and reservations.

BY LAND

Overland border-crossing points represent legal points of transit between Southeast Asian countries. Check local news agencies and embassies to confirm which border-crossing points are open. Though Thailand's border-crossing regulations remain stable, those of its neighboring countries do not. The result is unpredictable closings of crossing points, particularly with Malaysia.

BORDER CROSSINGS
Cambodia: Aranyaprathet to **Poipet** (see p. 159), from **Chong Jiam** (p. 216), or via a **Trat-Sihanoukville** boat (p. 151).
Laos: Chiang Khong to **Houie Xay** (p. 332), **Nong Khai** to **Vientiane** (see p. 245), **Nakhon Phanom** to **Tha Kaek** (p. 234), **Mukdahan to Savannakhet** (p. 229), **Chong Mek** to **Vang Tao** (p. 223).
Myanmar: Mae Sot (p. 303), or the **Three Pagoda Pass** (p. 183). Border crossing points close frequently and unexpectedly, so check at the local embassy first.

GETTING AROUND THAILAND

From buses to *tuk-tuks*, you'll find detailed info on transportation options in the Local Transportation section of each city.

LOCAL TRANSPORTATION	
Motorcycle taxi	A death-defying ride on the back of a speeding motorcycle. One passenger only.
Samlor	A 3-wheeled vehicle, more primitive than the tuk-tuk (below). Can be man-powered (pedaled) or motorized.
Songthaew	Four-wheeled pickup with two parallel rows of seats running along the bed. More room but less spunk than a tuk-tuk (below).
Tuk-tuk	A noisy three-wheeled truck that spatters and sputters on every road in Thailand.

BY PLANE

It's possible to travel by plane within Thailand, but be aware of possible safety risks. **Thai Airways** (p. 29) offers extensive domestic connections. **Bangkok Airways'** (p. 29) a popular choices if going to Ko Samui and Phuket. **Air Asia** (www.airasia.com) and **PBAir** (www.pbair.com) also offer flights to major cities.

BY BUS OR TRAIN

Public buses are the cheapest and easiest way to travel short distances, but take blue A/C buses for longer transits. These buses generally cost twice as much, but make fewer stops, and are mostly used by tourists.

The **State Railway of Thailand** (☎+66 02 621 8701; www.thailandrailway.com) operates an efficient, cheap rail system with three main train routes starting in Bangkok: north to Chiang Mai, south to Malaysia and Singapore, and northeast to Nong Khai and Ubon Ratchathani. Minor routes connect Bangkok to Kanchanaburi and cities north of the eastern seaboard such as Si Racha and Aranyaprathet. For long rides (over 3hr.), **third-class** travel is not ideal. Train fares given in this book are usually for third-class travel on regular trains; depending on the type of train and class of travel, your fare may vary. **Second-class** sleeping berths carry an additional charge of 350-430ß above standard second-class rates (depending on the type of train, fan or A/C, and upper or lower bunk) and often sell out. **Rapid** (140-190ß extra), **Express** (160-210ß extra), and **Special Express** (80ß extra) trains come next in price and are speedier than ordinary trains.

AIRCRAFT SAFETY. The airlines of developing world nations do not always meet safety standards. The Official Airline Guide (www.oag.com) and many travel agencies can tell you the type and age of aircraft on a particular route. This can be especially useful in Southeast Asia, where less reliable equipment is often used for internal or short flights. The International Airline Passengers Association (US ☎+1-800-821-4272, UK +44 20 8681 6555) provides region-specific safety info. The Federal Aviation Administration (www.faa.gov) reviews the airline authorities for countries whose airlines enter the US. US State Department travel advisories (☎+011-202-647-5225) sometimes involve foreign carriers, especially when terrorist bombings or hijackings may be a threat.

BY CAR

Travel by car is largely unnecessary because of the wide range of public transportation options available to travelers. It's also something best avoided for the sake of safety, especially in Bangkok, where city traffic and a lack of adherence to driving regulations are notorious. Other good rental options, such as bicycles and motorbikes, are also plentiful. A great resource for information on international automobile travel is the Association for Safe International Road Travel (www.asirt.org).

RENTING

Car rental is not only uncommon but also unreliable. All the same, cars can be rented in major cities. For information on renting a car in Bangkok, see p. 97.

RENTAL AGENCIES

You can generally make reservations before you leave by calling major international offices in your home country. However, occasionally the price and other information that they give doesn't jive with what the local offices in your country will tell you. Try checking with both offices to make sure you get the best price and the most accurate information. Local desk numbers are included in town listings; for home-country numbers, call your toll-free directory.

To rent a car from most establishments in Thailand, you need to be at least 21 years old. Some agencies require renters to be 25, and most charge those 21-25 an additional insurance fee (around 200฿ per day). Policies and prices vary from agency to agency. Small local operations occasionally rent to people under 21, but be sure to ask about the insurance coverage and deductible, and always check the fine print. Rental agencies in Thailand include:

AVIS (www.avis.com), on the 1st fl. of Meeting Hall at the Bangkok International Airport. Open daily 24hr. Other locations: 2/12 Wireless Rd., Bangkok 10330 (☎+66 02 255 5300), open daily 8am-6pm; Royal Princess Chiang Mai Hotel, 122 Chang Klan Rd., Chiang Mai (☎+66 053 281 0336), open daily 8am-8pm; 60/27 Chiang Mai Airport, Chiang Mai 50200, open daily 7am-9pm.

Budget Rental, (international reservations US and Canada ☎800-472-3325; www.budget.com) has 2 main locations in Bangkok: 335/16 Don Muang Railway Station, Viphavadee Rungsit Rd., Bangkok 10320 (☎+66 2 566 5067), open daily 24hr.; 19/23 Royal City Ave., New Petchburi Rd., Bangkok 10320 (☎+66 2 203 0250), open daily 7:30am-7:30pm. One location in Chiang Mai: Tambon Haiya 201/2 Mahidol Rd., Tumbon Suthep Muang, Chiang Mai 50100 (☎+66 53 202 8712), open daily 8am-7pm.

COSTS AND INSURANCE

Rental car prices start at around 2200฿ per day for a subcompact car. Expect to pay more for larger cars and for 4WD. Cars with automatic transmission can cost much more per day than cars with manual transmission (stick shift), and in some places, automatic transmission is hard to find in the first place. It is virtually impossible, no matter where you are, to find an automatic 4WD.

Remember that if you are driving a conventional rental vehicle on an unpaved road in a rental car, you are almost never covered by insurance; ask about this before leaving the rental agency. Be aware that cars rented on an **American Express** or **Visa/MasterCard Gold** or **Platinum** credit card in Thailand might *not* carry the automatic insurance that they would in some other countries; check with your credit-card company. Insurance plans from rental companies almost always come with an **excess** of around 5000฿ for conventional vehicles. This means that the insurance bought from the rental company only applies to damages over the excess; damages up to that amount must be covered by your existing insurance plan. Many rental companies in Thailand require you to buy a **Collision Damage Waiver (CDW),** which will waive the excess in the case of a collision. **Loss Damage Waivers (LDWs)** do the same in the case of theft or vandalism.

National chains often allow one-way rentals (picking up in one city and dropping off in another). There is usually a minimum hire period and sometimes an extra drop-off charge of several hundred US dollars.

DRIVING PERMITS AND CAR INSURANCE

INTERNATIONAL DRIVING PERMIT (IDP)

If you plan to drive a car while in Thailand, you must be over 21 and have an International Driving Permit (IDP).

Your IDP, valid for one year, must be issued in your own country before you depart. An application for an IDP usually requires one or two photos, a current local license, an additional form of identification, and a fee. To apply, contact your home country's automobile association. Be vigilant when purchasing an IDP online or anywhere other than your home automobile association. Many vendors sell permits of questionable legitimacy for higher prices.

CAR INSURANCE

Most credit cards cover standard insurance. If you rent, lease, or borrow a car, you will need a **green card,** or **International Insurance Certificate,** to certify that you have liability insurance and that it applies abroad. Green cards can be obtained at car rental agencies, car dealers (for those leasing cars), some travel agents, and some border crossings. Rental agencies may require you to purchase theft insurance in countries that they consider to have a high risk of auto theft.

ON THE ROAD

Driving in Thailand can be confusing at best, and downright dangerous at worst. Avoid driving in Bangkok at any cost. In the rest of Thailand, drivers tend to ignore international driving rules, and cars travel on both sides of the road without discrimination. While road signs are constantly being updated, many are still only in Thai script. Asking for directions can be difficult if locals do not speak English. If you decide to drive, get a good road map, such as the **Thailand Atlas,** by **Roadway,** or the **Thailand Atlas,** by **Lotus Image.** Local tourist offices or guesthouses may also have maps.

A better option may be chauffeured vans, which can be rented out to small groups. The driver, who often serves as an impromptu tour guide, can take you wherever you wish. The vans are comparably priced to rental cars, and arrangements can be made by most upscale hotels.

The price of gas is just about the only thing you won't need to worry about if driving in Thailand; in Bangkok, a gallon of gasoline is about US$1.60.

DANGERS

Thailand's roads vary from the wide, vehicle-crammed streets of Bangkok to the unpaved, mountainous roads of its *kos* and more rural areas. If you choose to drive, be aware of these varying road conditions and exercise caution. Speeding is one of the major dangers on Thai roadways. It's also essential to be wary of other drivers who may be under the influence of alcohol and drugs. The number of alcohol-related road fatalities increases during the holidays.

CAR ASSISTANCE
International SOS Services (Thailand) Limited, (www.internationalsos.com), 11th fl. Diethelm Tower B, 931 Wireless Rd., Lumpini, Pathumwan, Bangkok 10330, Thailand. Provides roadside assistance and other emergency services to members.

MOTORBIKE BY-LAWS. Riding a motorbike will probably be the most dangerous thing you do in Thailand. Many shops will rent motorbikes to anyone, regardless of his or her ability to drive. Each year, too many tourists are injured or die in motorbike-related accidents. *Let's Go* recommends alternate methods of transportation. But, when there is no other choice, keeping a few things in mind will make your trip much safer. Before you leave the rental shop, be sure you know how to ride your bike and that it is in good condition. Document any dents before you leave to avoid a hassle later. Whenever possible, protect your eyes by wearing goggle-style sunglasses; designer knockoffs are sold all over Thailand. Stick to the shoulder of the road. It's easy to get turned around, especially if you're used to driving on the right side of the road; force of habit often kicks in on roundabouts and U-turns. On highways, motorbikes are expected only to occupy the far left shoulder so as to leave room for other traffic. Wear lots of clothing—at least jeans and closed-toed shoes. When skin hits asphalt at high rates of speed, the asphalt always wins. Always be aware of traffic, which often jumps across to the other side of the road. Wear your helmet. They're required by law in Thailand, although most people ignore that fact. Given the mountains of evidence that prove time and again that they save lives, you'd have to be pretty hard-headed not to wear one.

BY BOAT, BICYCLE, MOPED, ETC.

Almost every kind of personal vehicle short of a pogo stick can be rented in Thailand. Motorbikes and bicycles are the most common and often quite convenient. Always rent a helmet. If possible, ask other travelers in the area what their experience has been with local rental agencies before renting. Also be sure to test-drive the vehicle or bike before you agree to pay for it.

Walking around in Thai cities can be a bit confusing. The street numbering system (see below) and street signs are indecipherable to the uninitiated. As there is no official transliteration system, Thai street names are often spelled in multiple ways, even in the same city. Minor roads that split off of a main thoroughfare are called *soi* (alleys), although they can often be sizable roads.

BY THUMB

LET'S NOT GO. *Let's Go* never recommends hitchhiking as a safe means of transportation, and none of the information presented here is intended to do so.

Let's Go strongly urges you to consider the risks before you choose to hitchhike. Hitching means entrusting your life to a stranger and risking assault, sexual harassment, theft, and unsafe driving. For women traveling alone (or even in pairs), hitching is just too dangerous. A man and a woman are a less dangerous combination; two men will have a harder time getting a lift, while three men will go nowhere. Hitching is legal in Thailand, albeit not extremely common. Though the Thai people are kind and generous, it is never a safe option. Pay the extra baht, and take something official.

KEEPING IN TOUCH

BY EMAIL AND INTERNET

Thailand is an Internet savvy country. Internet cafes crowd Bangkok and Chiang Mai, and there's a good chance that all but the most remote small towns and villages have at least one cyber cafe. Online rates are also often cheap, though rates can run anything from 0.5-3฿ per min. Many guesthouses and hotels also offer Internet and Wi-fi service—sometimes even free of charge.

BY TELEPHONE

PLACING INTERNATIONAL CALLS. To call Thailand from home or to call home from Thailand, dial:
1. The **international dialing prefix.** To call from **Australia,** dial 0011; **Canada** or the **US,** 011; **Ireland, New Zealand,** or the **UK,** 00; **Thailand,** 66.
2. The **country code** of the country you want to call. To call **Australia,** dial 61; **Canada** or the **US,** 1; **Ireland,** 353; **New Zealand,** 64; the **UK,** 44; **Thailand,** 66.
3. The **city/area code.** *Let's Go* lists the city/area codes for cities and towns in Thailand opposite the city or town name, next to a ☎, as well as in every phone number. If the first digit is a zero (e.g., 020 for London), omit the zero when calling from abroad (e.g., dial 20 from **Canada** to reach **London**).
4. The **local number.**

CALLING HOME FROM THAILAND

Prepaid phone cards are a common and relatively inexpensive means of calling abroad. Each one comes with a Personal Identification Number (PIN) and a toll-free access number. You call the access number and then follow the directions for dialing your PIN. To purchase prepaid phone cards, check online for the best rates; www.callingcards.com is a good place to start. Online providers generally send your access number and PIN via email, with no actual "card" involved. You can also call home with prepaid phone cards purchased in Thailand.

CALLING WITHIN THAILAND

The simplest way to call within the country is to use a coin-operated phone. **Prepaid phone cards** (available at many restaurants, shops, and guest houses), usually save time and money in the long run. Phone rates typically tend to be highest in the morning, lower in the evening, and lowest on Sunday and late at night.

Computerized phones will tell you how much time, in units, you have left on your card. Another kind of prepaid telephone card comes with a PIN and a toll-free access number. Instead of inserting the card into the phone, you call the access number and follow the directions on the card. These cards can be used to make international as well as domestic calls.

CELLULAR PHONES

Cellular phones, from the normal garden-variety flip phone to the more exotic (and entertaining, one can guess) karaoke phone, are extremely popular in Thailand. They are also extremely useful, as cell phone coverage includes all urban and most rural areas of the country. They can be found in cell phone or electronic stores in most large towns and cities, and many are readily available at airports.

The international standard for cell phones is **Global System for Mobile Communication** (GSM). To make and receive calls in Thailand you will need a GSM-compatible phone and a **SIM (Subscriber Identity Module) card,** a country-specific, thumbnail-sized chip that gives you a local phone number and plugs you into the local network. Many SIM cards are prepaid, and incoming calls are frequently free. You can buy additional cards or vouchers (usually available at convenience stores) to "top up" your phone. For more information on GSM phones, check out www.telestial.com, www.orange.co.uk, www.roadpost.com, or www.planetomni.com. Companies like **Cellular Abroad** (www.cellularabroad.com) rent cell phones that work in a variety of destinations around the world.

GSM PHONES. Just having a GSM phone doesn't mean you're necessarily good to go when you travel abroad. The majority of GSM phones sold in the United States operate on a different **frequency** (1900) than international phones (900/1800) and will not work abroad. Tri-band phones work on all three frequencies (900/1800/1900) and will operate through most of the world. Additionally, some GSM phones are **SIM-locked** and will only accept SIM cards from a single carrier. You'll need a **SIM-unlocked** phone to use a SIM card from a local carrier when you travel.

TIME DIFFERENCES

Thailand is seven hours ahead of **Greenwich Mean Time (GMT).** It is 14hr. ahead of Vancouver and San Francisco, 11hr. ahead of New York, 6hr. ahead of London, 3hr. behind Sydney, and 5hr. behind Auckland, although the actual time differences depend on **Daylight Saving Time (DST),** which Thailand does not observe (see below). A useful resource is the World Time Server (www.worldtimeserver.com), which lists the current time in numerous locations worldwide, as well as whether the location is operating on Standard Time or DST. Take note that

ESSENTIALS

from early April to late October **Bangkok** will be 1hr. further behind the other countries in the chart below.

BY MAIL

SENDING MAIL HOME FROM THAILAND

Airmail is the best way to send mail home from Thailand. **Aerogrammes,** printed sheets that fold into envelopes and travel via airmail, are available at post offices. Write "airmail," on the front. Most post offices will charge exorbitant fees or simply refuse to send aerogrammes with enclosures. Surface mail is by far the cheapest and slowest way to send mail. It takes one to two months to cross the Atlantic and one to three to cross the Pacific—good for heavy items you won't need for a while, such as souvenirs that you've acquired along the way.

SENDING MAIL TO THAILAND

To ensure timely delivery, mark envelopes "airmail". In addition to the standard postage system whose rates are listed below, **Federal Express** (Australia ☎+61 13 26 10, Canada and the US +1-800-463-3339, Ireland +353 800 535 800, New Zealand +64 800 733 339, the UK +44 8456 070 809; www.fedex.com) handles express mail services from most countries to Thailand. Sending a postcard within Thailand costs 2฿, while sending letters (up to 20g) domestically requires 3฿.

There are several ways to arrange pick up of letters sent to you while you are abroad. Mail can be sent via **Poste Restante** (General Delivery) to almost any city or town in Thailand with a post office, and is generally reliable. Address **Poste Restante** letters like so:

Geoff CURFMAN

Poste Restante

Bangkok, Thailand

The mail will go to a special desk in the central post office, unless you specify a post office by street address or postal code. It's best to use the largest post office, since mail may be sent there regardless. It is usually safer and quicker, though more expensive, to send mail express or registered. Bring your passport (or other photo ID) for pickup; there may be a small fee. If the clerks insist that there is nothing for you, ask them to check under your first name as well. *Let's Go* lists post offices under the **Practical Information** section.

ACCOMMODATIONS

HOSTELS

Many hostels are laid out dorm-style, often with large single-sex rooms and bunk beds, although private rooms that sleep two to four are becoming more common. They sometimes have kitchens and utensils for your use, bike or moped rentals, storage areas, transportation to airports, breakfast and other meals, laundry facilities, and Internet. However, there can be drawbacks: some hostels close during certain daytime "lockout" hours, have a curfew, don't accept reservations, impose a maximum stay, or, less frequently, require that you do chores. In Thailand, a dorm bed in a hostel will average around 80-120฿ and a private room around 100-300฿. There are certain standard features that we do not include in our hostel listings. Unless we state otherwise, you can expect that every hostel has no lockout, no curfew, some system of secure luggage storage, and no key deposit.

HOSTELLING INTERNATIONAL

Joining the youth hostel association in your own country (listed below) automatically grants you membership privileges in **Hostelling International (HI)**, a federation of national hosteling associations. Non-HI members may be allowed to stay in some hostels, but will have to pay extra to do so. HI hostels are scattered throughout Thailand (most are in Bangkok and Chiang Mai) and are sometimes less expensive than private hostels. HI's umbrella organization's website (www.hihostels.com), which lists the web addresses and phone numbers of all national associations, can be a great place to begin researching hostels in a specific region. Other comprehensive hosteling websites include www.hostels.com and www.hostelplanet.com.

Most HI hostels in Thailand also honor **guest memberships**—you'll get a blank card with space for six validation stamps. Each night you'll pay a nonmember supplement (one-sixth the membership fee) and earn one guest stamp; six stamps makes you a member. A new membership benefit is the FreeNites program, which allows hostelers to gain points toward free rooms. Most student travel agencies (p. 29) sell HI cards, as do all of the national hosteling organizations listed below. All prices listed below are valid for one-year memberships unless otherwise noted.

Australian Youth Hostels Association (AYHA), 422 Kent St., Sydney, NSW 200 (☎+61 2 9261 1111; www.yha.com.au). AUS$52, under 18 AUS$19.

Hostelling International-Canada (HI-C), 205 Catherine St., Ste. 400, Ottawa, ON K2P 1C3 (☎+1-613-237-7884; www.hihostels.ca). CDN$35, under 18 free.

Hostelling International Northern Ireland (HINI), 22-32 Donegall Rd., Belfast BT12 5JN (☎+44 2890 32 47 33; www.hini.org.uk). UK£15, under 25 UK£10.

Youth Hostels Association of New Zealand Inc. (YHANZ), Level 1, 166 Moorhouse Ave., P.O. Box 436, Christchurch (☎+64 3 379 9970, in NZ 0800 278 299; www.yha.org.nz). NZ$40, under 18 free.

Youth Hostels Association (England and Wales), Trevelyan House, Dimple Rd., Matlock, Derbyshire DE4 3YH (☎+44 8707 708 868; www.yha.org.uk). UK£16, under 26 UK£10.

Hostelling International-USA, 8401 Colesville Rd., Ste. 600, Silver Spring, MD 20910 (☎+1-301-495-1240; www.hiayh.org). US$28, under 18 free.

Thai Youth Hostels Association, 25/14 Phitsanulok Road, Si Sao Thewet, Dusit (☎02 628 7413; www.tyha.org). Non-Thai residents can only purchase guest stamp membership here.

OTHER TYPES OF ACCOMMODATIONS

HOTELS, GUESTHOUSES, AND PENSIONS

Hotel singles in Thailand cost about US$ 7-15 (280-600฿) per night, doubles US$ 10-20 (400-800฿). You'll typically share a hall bathroom; a private bathroom will cost extra. Smaller guesthouses also tend to be less expensive (singles about US$5-10, 200-400฿). If you make **reservations** in writing, indicate your night of arrival and the number of nights you plan to stay. The hotel will send you a confirmation and may request payment for the first night.

UNIVERSITY DORMS

Many **colleges** and **universities** open their residence halls to travelers when school is not in session; some do so even during term time. Getting a room may take a couple of phone calls and require advanced planning, but rates tend to be low and many offer free local calls and Internet access.

HOME EXCHANGES AND HOSPITALITY CLUBS

Home exchange offers the traveler various types of homes (houses, apartments, condominiums, villas, even castles in some cases), plus the opportunity to live like a native and to cut down on accommodation fees. For more information, contact **HomeExchange.com Inc.,** P.O. Box 787, Hermosa Beach, CA 90254, USA (☎+1-310 798 3864 or toll-free 800-877-8723; www.homeexchange.com) or **Intervac International Home Exchange** (☎+33 61 618 2022; www.intervac.com).

Hospitality clubs link their members with individuals or families abroad who are willing to host travelers for free or for a small fee to promote cultural exchange and general good karma. In exchange, members usually must be willing to host travelers in their own homes; a small fee may also be required. **The Hospitality Club** (www.hospitalityclub.org) is a good place to start. **Servas** (www.servas.org) is an established, more formal, peace-based organization, and requires a fee and an interview to join. Other hospitality organizations include **GlobalFreeloaders** (www.globalfreeloaders.com) and **CouchSurfing International** (www.couchsurfing.com). An Internet search will find many other organizations, some of which cater to special interests (e.g., women, GLBT travelers, or members of certain professions). As always, use common sense when planning to stay with or host someone you do not know.

LONG-TERM ACCOMMODATIONS

Travelers planning to stay in Thailand for extended periods of time may find it most cost-effective to rent an apartment. A basic one-bedroom (or studio) apartment in Bangkok will range 5000-25,000฿ per month, depending on quality and location. Besides the rent itself, prospective tenants are usually also required to front a security deposit (often one month's rent) and the last month's rent. Serviced apartments may be easier to procure but are also more expensive: expect to pay 18,000฿ or more per month.

The purchase of Thai real estate by foreigners is both increasingly common and encouraged by the government. There are a number of websites catering to foreigners; many Thai real estate companies, such as **Acute Realty** (www. thaiapartment.com), advertise online. A good overview of housing options can be found at www.thailandguru.com/home-housing.html.

Another option for those staying for a significant amount of time are **YMCAs/ YWCAs.** Though not overly common, Thailand plays host to several YMCA and YWCA hostels. Listings of hostels, and contact information for the National Council of YMCAs, is available through the World Alliance of YMCAs (www.ymca.int).

CAMPING

It's possible to camp in many parks and beaches, although the practice isn't very widespread. Nearly all national parks have designated camping areas, though they almost certainly will require registration or a fee in order to camp, so be sure to check with park headquarters before pitching your tent. As always, exercise caution and don't camp alone—women especially should be careful. For more information on outdoor activities in Thailand, see **The Great Outdoors** (below).

THE GREAT OUTDOORS

The **Great Outdoor Recreation Page** (www.gorp.com) provides excellent general information for travelers planning on camping or spending time in the outdoors.

 LEAVE NO TRACE. Let's Go encourages travelers to embrace the "Leave No Trace" ethic, which, when followed, minimizes human impact on natural environments. Trekkers and wilderness enthusiasts should set up camp on durable surfaces, use cookstoves instead of campfires, bury human waste away from water supplies, bag trash and carry it out with them, and respect wildlife and the physical environment. For more detailed info, contact the **Leave No Trace Center for Outdoor Ethics**, P.O. Box 997, Boulder, CO 80306, USA (☎+1-800-332-4100 or 303-442-8222; www.lnt.org).

ESSENTIALS

NATIONAL PARKS

Thailand's national parks are among its best kept secrets. From deep jungle to sparkling beaches, thousands of acres of land in more than 100 parks, wildlife sanctuaries, and nature reserves across the country are protected by Thailand's **Royal Forest Department** (www.forest.go.th/default_e.asp). These magnificent places provide refuge for endangered species of plants and wildlife, and for *farang* who need a break from each other.

Thailand's web of national parks includes such giants as Kaeng Krachan National Park and Doi Inthanon National Park. Although most parks are open to tourists, they are rarely open to public transportation; the easiest way to access them is by renting (or the more expensive option of chartering) a car. Many of Thailand's parks are listed as daytrips in this guide due to their proximity to other cities or towns, but renting a car is often the only feasible way of seeing them in a day. Many parks will charge a modest entrance fee, and some offer accommodations such as bungalows; check at the central ranger station upon arrival.

WILDERNESS SAFETY

Staying warm, dry, and **well hydrated** is key to a happy wilderness experience. For any hike, prepare yourself for an emergency by packing a first-aid kit, a reflector, a whistle, high-energy food, extra water, rain gear, a hat, mittens, and extra socks. For warmth, wear wool or insulating synthetic materials designed for the outdoors. Cotton is a bad choice since it takes so long to dry.

Check **weather forecasts** often, and pay attention to the skies when hiking, as weather patterns can change suddenly. Always let someone—a friend, your hostel, a park ranger, or a local hiking organization—know when and where you are going. Know your physical limits and do not attempt a hike beyond your ability. See **Safety and Health** (p. 19) for information on outdoor medical concerns.

ORGANIZED ADVENTURE TRIPS

Organized adventure tours offer another way of exploring the wild. Activities include hiking, biking, skiing, canoeing, kayaking, rafting, climbing, photo safaris, and archaeological digs. Tourism bureaus often can suggest parks, trails, and outfitters. Organizations that specialize in camping and outdoor equipment such as EMS and REI (see above) are also good sources for info. Below is one such example; a more comprehensive listing of adventure opportunities can be found in the **Beyond Tourism** section of this guide (p. 76).

Specialty Travel Index, P.O. Box 458, San Anselmo, CA 94979, USA (US ☎+1-888-624-4030, elsewhere +1-415-455-1643; www.specialtytravel.com).

ESSENTIALS

HILL TRIBES AND TREKKING

The safest bet when searching for tour guides is to use companies that meet **TAT** regulations (p. 279). Reputable operations should make reports from former customers available. Trekking companies, guides, and customers are required by TAT regulations to be registered with the tourist police. TAT publishes a list of trekking agencies, indicating those that use licensed guides who have studied at the Tribal Research Institute in Chiang Mai. Most companies provide insurance, food, accommodations, transportation, and some extra supplies. Go in a group of eight or fewer people, as smaller groups are less disruptive. The best way to learn about hill tribe culture is to hire a personal guide. Make sure your guide speaks both English and the languages of the villages on your itinerary.

HEALTH AND SECURITY

Bring a first-aid kit, sunscreen, a hat, mosquito repellent, a water bottle, and long pants. Some regions contain malarial mosquitoes; be sure to get the proper medications before you go (see **Insect-Borne Diseases,** p. 24). Before embarking on a trek, try to find a safe place to leave valuables in your absence. TAT recommends that trekkers utilize a bank safety deposit box, as there have been numerous reports of credit cards being lifted from guesthouse "security" boxes. Bandits have been known to raid trekking groups. Should this occur, hand over your belongings to the bandits to avoid physical harm. TAT discourages independent trekking.

TREKKING ETIQUETTE

Hill-tribe societies are being rapidly integrated into Thai society. Their unique, centuries-old cultures are ever changing, and there is no question that tourism speeds up the process. **Always ask permission from the specific people you want to photograph before doing so.** Some individuals or even whole villages may object even if your guide says it is okay. Respect the people, their culture, and their way of life. Be particularly respectful of hill-tribe beliefs, and be mindful about what you touch. For example, the gate at the entrance to an Akha village marks the point past which spirits may not enter: do not touch this. Use the old hiking maxim: see it as it is, leave it as it was.

WHEN TO GO

Of northern Thailand's three distinct seasons, the cool season (Oct.-Feb.) is the best time for trekking. The vegetation is most lush and temperatures are usually in the mid-20s °C by day, falling to near freezing at night. In the rainy season (July-Sept.), paths are muddy and raging rivers make rafting fun but dangerous. In the hot season (Mar.-May), the land is parched and the air is dry.

WATER SPORTS

Most scuba agencies require that you have a **Professional Association of Diving Instructors (PADI)** certification in order to dive with them. The **Open Water Diving** course is the beginner course; its "performance-based" progress means that it will last as long as it takes for you to pass. Most diving courses consist of a educational section, a skill-training section, and four training dives. There is a 183m nonstop swimming requirement or 300m nonstop snorkel and a 10min. water treading or floating session. **Ko Tao** is the largest diving training center in Southeast Asia. In addition to having some of the best snorkeling and diving in the world, the island also has a plethora of scuba agencies, which are the island's primary source of income. (For specific listings, see **Ko Tao,** p. 417.) All of Ko Tao's scuba agencies are PADI certified, which means that there can be no more than eight students with an instructor at any time. To get your certification before your trip, see the listings of PADI certification sites in Australia, Canada, the US, and Europe at www.padi.com. It also has listings of dive sites worldwide.

SNORKELING

Unlike scuba diving, snorkeling requires no training—anyone can grab a mask and jump right in. Since most snorkeling takes place in water only 1m deep, popping your head above water is always an option. The breathing technique takes adjustment, however; practice by the shore before heading for deeper waters. Travelers can also take classes at scuba centers. Nearly all cater to both snorkeling and scuba diving.

HEALTH RESTRICTIONS

While PADI only mandates average health for certification, a prudent traveler will check with his or her doctor before signing up for a scuba course. Travelers with respiratory and heart ailments should be particularly careful with both diving and snorkeling. Contact lens wearers should not have a problem using them with a scuba or snorkeling mask, but prescription masks are also available.

SAFETY

Before you head out, check with local agencies and fellow backpackers about water conditions, currents, geological features of the area, and weather conditions. A strong current or an unexpected boulder can be extremely dangerous. Always check your equipment in shallow water before using it and swim with a buddy.

When buying or renting gear, make sure that the retailer is both reliable and reputable. There are many discount stores offering top quality merchandise, but keep in mind that the oxygen meter needs to be precise when you are 20m under the sea.

CORAL PRESERVATION

Before any trip, it is always a good idea to learn about the marine life in the waters you hope to explore. This will not only improve the quality and enjoyment of the excursion but will give you an idea of which species are particularly delicate and prone to destruction. Never stand or kneel near coral—simply touching it can kill it. And try not to disturb the environment; passive observation provides better sights anyway.

SPECIFIC CONCERNS

SUSTAINABLE TRAVEL

As the number of travelers on the road rises, the detrimental effect they can have on natural environments is an increasing concern. With this in mind, *Let's Go* promotes the philosophy of sustainable travel. Through a sensitivity to issues of ecology and sustainability, today's travelers can be a powerful force in preserving and restoring the places they visit.

Ecotourism, a rising trend in sustainable travel, focuses on the conservation of natural habitats—mainly, on how to use them to build up the economy without exploitation or overdevelopment. Travelers can make a difference by doing advance research, by supporting organizations and establishments that pay attention to their carbon "footprint," and by patronizing establishments that strive to be environmentally friendly.

Travelers in Thailand are especially likely to enter ecologically sensitive areas. Avoid buying natural souvenirs such as **teeth, hides, coral, butterflies,** or **turtle shells.** Products made of animals often come at the expense of endangered species. Women should consider buying hygiene products with minimal packaging. Choose glass bottles over less-recyclable plastic equivalents and reuse plastic bags. Bucket showers and squat toilets are more water-efficient than their Western counterparts. **Carry a water bottle or canteen;** where tap water is unsafe, purifying tablets, iodine drops, or a small water purifier to save buying countless plastic water bottles!

ECOTOURISM RESOURCES. For more information on environmentally responsible tourism, contact one of the organizations below:

Conservation International, 2011 Crystal Dr., Ste. 500, Arlington, VA 22202, USA (☎+1-800-406-2306 or 703-341-2400; www.conservation.org).

Green Globe 21, Green Globe vof, Verbenalaan 1, 2111 ZL Aerdenhout, the Netherlands (☎+31 23 544 0306; www.greenglobe.com).

International Ecotourism Society, 1333 H St. NW, Ste. 300E, Washington, DC 20005, USA (☎+1-202-347-9203; www.ecotourism.org).

United Nations Environment Program (UNEP), 39-43 Quai André Citroën, 75739 Paris Cedex 15, France (☎+33 1 44 37 14 50; www.uneptie.org/pc/tourism).

RESPONSIBLE TRAVEL

Your tourist dollars can make a big impact on the destinations you visit. The choices you make during your trip can have powerful effects on local communities—for better or for worse. Travelers who care about the destinations and environments they explore should make themselves aware of the social and cultural implications of their choices. Simple decisions such as buying local products, paying fair prices for products or services, and attempting to speak the local language can have a strong, positive effect on the community.

Community-based tourism aims to channel tourist dollars into the local economy by emphasizing tours and cultural programs that are run by members of the host community. This type of tourism also benefits the tourists themselves, as it often takes them beyond the traditional tours of the region. Thailand is a prime location for this kind of tourism, from visiting environmental conservation projects to learning Thai cooking in northern towns (see **Beyond Tourism,** (p. 76)). The Ethical Travel Guide (UK£13), a project of Tourism Concern (☎+44 20 7133 3330; www.tourismconcern.org.uk), is an excellent resource for information on community-based travel, with a directory of 300 establishments in 60 countries.

Social and environmental problems are often tied up with tourism in Thailand. While popular, visits to the hill tribe villages of the north often degrade local villages and can disrupt native culture (see **Life and Times,** (p. 49)). **People for the Ethical Treatment of Animals (PETA)** has called attention to the alleged mistreatment of elephants in Thailand's elephant camps. Some of these camps may employ inhumane training techniques. Keep this in mind when planning itineraries including elephant treks or elephant camps.

TRAVELING ALONE

Traveling alone can be extremely beneficial, providing a sense of independence and a greater opportunity to connect with locals. On the other hand, solo travelers are more vulnerable targets of harassment and street theft. If you are traveling alone, look confident, try not to stand out as a tourist, and be especially careful in deserted or very crowded areas. Stay away from areas that are not well lit. If questioned, never admit that you are traveling alone. Maintain regular contact with someone at home who knows your itinerary, and always research your destination before traveling. For more tips, pick up *Traveling Solo* by Eleanor Berman (Globe Pequot Press; US$18), visit www.travelaloneandloveit.com, or subscribe to **Connecting: Solo Travel Network,** 689 Park Rd., Unit 6, Gibsons, BC V0N 1V7, Canada (☎+1-604-886-9099; www.cstn.org; membership US$30-48).

WOMEN TRAVELERS

Women exploring on their own inevitably face some additional safety concerns. Consider staying in hostels which offer single rooms that lock from the inside or in religious organizations with single-sex rooms. It's a good idea to stick to centrally located accommodations and to avoid solitary late-night treks or metro rides.

Always carry extra cash for a phone call, bus, or taxi. **Hitchhiking** is never safe for lone women, or even for two women traveling together. Look as if you know where you're going and approach older women or couples for directions if you're lost or feeling uncomfortable in your surroundings. Generally, the less you look like a tourist, the better off you'll be. **Dress conservatively,** especially in rural areas. Wearing a conspicuous **wedding band** sometimes helps to prevent unwanted advances.

Your best answer to verbal harassment is no answer at all; feigning deafness, sitting motionless, and staring straight ahead at nothing in particular will usually do the trick. The extremely persistent can sometimes be dissuaded by a firm, loud, and very public "Go away!" in the appropriate language. Don't hesitate to seek out a police officer or a passerby if you are being harassed. Memorize the emergency numbers in places you visit, and consider carrying a whistle on your keychain. A self-defense course will both prepare you for a potential attack and raise your level of awareness of your surroundings (see **Personal Safety,** p. 21). Also, it might be a good idea to talk with your doctor about the health concerns that women face when traveling (p. 28).

ESSENTIALS

TOP TEN MARKETS

Finding a market in Thailand isn't hard, but finding an exciting one is. Here are our picks:

1. **Chatuchak Market:** With over 9000 individual stalls, Bangkok's weekend market is not only the biggest in the world, but it also has great bargains on regional crafts (p. 119).

2. **Punchard:** Browse for Isaan silk, axe pillows, and bronze in Ubon Ratchathani (p. 223).

3. **Lanyai Market:** Buy a festive flower necklace at this fragrant Chiang Mai market (see p. 282).

4. **Sangkhlaburi's Handicrafts Market:** This border-town market has traditional Burmese fabrics for sale (p. 184).

5. **Bo Sang:** This colorful village specializes in paper-umbrella-making, but find similar umbrellas for less at nearby Chiang Mai's Night Market (p. 282).

6. **Dan Kwian Village:** Everything from pottery to jewelry is available at this clay-specializing village (p. 208).

7. **Mae Sai:** Buy pots of white tanakha makeup, an all-purpose Burmese skin treatment, in markets all over town. (see p. 324).

8. **Suan Lum Night Bazaar:** Bangkok's bazaar offers fun and an unlimited gift options (p. 120).

9. **Chiang Rai's Night Market:** Find an endless supply of hill-tribe products (p. 339).

10. **Floating Markets:** Buy bananas and Thai handicrafts from floating vendors throughout Thailand (p. 125).

GLBT TRAVELERS

The spirit of Buddhist tolerance and non-confrontation make Thailand accepting, if not actively supportive, of same-sex relationships. Most Thais are horrified at the idea of discriminating against a person because of his sexual orientation. There are no legal restrictions against homosexuality between consenting adults, and little social stigma is attached to it. Yet, given Thai society's strong emphasis on continuing the family lineage, many lesbians and gays feel pressure to stay closeted.

The absence of blatant discrimination based on sexual orientation in Thai society, however, takes away any impetus for the gay community to mobilize itself. It comes as no surprise, then, that informal social networks predominate over political organizations. Globalization has posed a unique set of challenges regarding homosexuality. On the one hand, many educated, upper-class Thais have absorbed homophobic prejudices from Westerners. On the other hand, Thais who have had contact with Western gay movements have returned to Thailand to spearhead domestic awareness campaigns. Thai health officials are beginning to recognize the issues of homosexuality in their crusade against HIV/AIDS, so more attention is likely to be focused on the GLBT community in the future.

Gender norms as a whole are different in Thailand, and foreign ideas and preconceptions will serve for little. Camaraderie between members of the same sex, particularly between men, is much more common than travelers may be used to. For example, hand-holding between men has entirely different implications than it has in Western culture. In any case, most Thais believe that sexuality is a private matter and should be treated with discretion, regardless of one's sexual orientation. Public displays of affection are frowned upon under any circumstance.

Regardless, a booming gay nightlife—much of it divorced from the sex industry—remains quite accessible to foreigners and makes Thailand an extremely popular destination for gay travelers. As a result, Thai tourism officials have seen the economic benefits of gay bars and establishments. Conversely, lesbian communities, often inaccessible to outsiders, remain largely underground, and their nightlife comparatively subdued.

To avoid hassles at airports and border crossings, transgendered travelers should make sure that all of their travel documents consistently report the same gender. Many countries (including the US, the UK, Canada, Ireland, Australia, and New Zealand) will amend the passports of post-operative transsexuals to reflect their physical gender, although governments are generally less willing to amend documents for pre-operative transsexuals and other transgendered individuals.

Listed below are contact organizations, mail-order catalogs, and publishers that offer materials addressing some specific concerns. **Out and About** (www.planetout.com) offers a weekly newsletter addressing travel concerns and a comprehensive site addressing gay travel concerns. The online newspaper **365gay.com** also has a travel section (www.365gay.com/travel/travelchannel.htm).

Gay's the Word, 66 Marchmont St., London WC1N 1AB, UK (☎+44 20 7278 7654; http://freespace.virgin.net/gays.theword). The largest gay and lesbian bookshop in the UK, with both fiction and non-fiction titles. Mail-order service available.

Giovanni's Room, 345 S. 12th St., Philadelphia, PA 19107, USA (☎+1-215-923-2960; www.queerbooks.com). An international lesbian and gay bookstore with mail-order service (carries many of the publications listed below).

International Lesbian and Gay Association (ILGA), Avenue des Villas 34, 1060 Brussels, Belgium (☎+32 2 502 2471; www.ilga.org). Provides political information, such as homosexuality laws of individual countries.

> **ADDITIONAL RESOURCES: GLBT**
>
> *Spartacus 2005-2006: International Gay Guide.* Bruno Gmunder Verlag (US$33).
> *Damron Men's Travel Guide, Damron Road Atlas, Damron Accommodations Guide, Damron City Guide,* and *Damron Women's Traveller.* Damron Travel Guides (US$18-24). For info, call ☎+1-800-462-6654 or visit www.damron.com.
> *The Gay Vacation Guide: The Best Trips and How to Plan Them,* by Mark Chesnut. Kensington Books (US$15). *Gayellow Pages USA/Canada,* by Frances Green. Gayellow Pages (US$20). They also publish regional editions. Visit Gayellow pages online at http://gayellowpages.com.

TRAVELERS WITH DISABILITIES

Thailand is ill-equipped to accommodate disabled travelers and has a poor record of accepting people with disabilities. Many Thais believe people with physical disabilities were immoral in past lives and are bearers of bad luck. Furthermore, it is also a cultural belief that a person's physical disabilities are emblematic of other mental and emotional disabilities. Though these attitudes still persist in Thailand, they are slowly changing. The 1997 Constitution and 1998 Declaration on the Rights of Thai People with Disabilities have reflected the government's attempts to give the issue national attention, as well as to facilitate the participation of people with disabilities in society. In 2001, Thailand received the Franklin D. Roosevelt International Disability Award for its progress toward fulfilling the goals set out by the United Nations World Programme of Action Concerning Disabled Persons. Bold disabled travelers will find many people eager to aid them.

However, hard limitations remain. Hospitals cannot be relied upon to replace broken braces or prostheses. Orthopedic materials, even in Bangkok, are often faulty at best. Most public transportation is completely inaccessible. Rural areas have no sidewalks, and larger cities are packed with curbs and steps.

Those with disabilities should inform airlines and hotels of their disabilities when making reservations; some time may be needed to prepare special accommodations. Call ahead to restaurants, museums, and other facilities to find out if they are wheelchair-accessible. Guide-dog owners should inquire as to the quarantine policies beforehand.

USEFUL ORGANIZATIONS

Accessible Journeys, 35 W. Sellers Ave., Ridley Park, PA 19078, USA (☎+1-800-846-4537; www.disabilitytravel.com). Designs tours for wheelchair users and slow walkers. The site has tips and forums for all travelers.

Flying Wheels Travel, 143 W. Bridge St., Owatonna, MN 55060, USA (☎+1-507-451-5005; www.flyingwheelstravel.com). Specializes in escorted trips to Europe for people with physical disabilities; plans custom trips worldwide.

Mobility International USA (MIUSA), P.O. Box 10767, Eugene, OR 97440, USA (☎+1-541-343-1284; www.miusa.org). Provides a variety of books and other publications containing information for travelers with disabilities.

Society for Accessible Travel and Hospitality (SATH), 347 5th Ave., Ste. 610, New York, NY 10016, USA (☎+1-212-447-7284; www.sath.org). An advocacy group that publishes free online travel information. Annual membership US$49, students and seniors US$29.

MINORITY TRAVELERS

People in Thailand are largely accepting of minority travelers. However, travelers of African descent have reported stray incidents of harassment and discrimination. It is widely reported that they find it difficult to find teaching jobs in Thailand. These travelers are advised not to travel alone in rural areas.

DIETARY CONCERNS

Vegetarian dishes abound in Thailand. The travel section of the **The Vegetarian Resource Group's** website, at www.vrg.org/travel, has a comprehensive list of organizations and websites that are geared toward helping vegetarians and vegans traveling abroad. Vegetarians will find numerous resources on the web; try www.vegdining.com, www.happycow.net, and www.vegetariansabroad.com, for starters.

Travelers who keep kosher should contact synagogues in larger cities for information on kosher restaurants. The website www.shamash.org/kosher provides a small list of kosher restaurants in Bangkok; contact synagogues in larger cities for more information. If you are strict in your observance, you may have to prepare your own food on the road.

The Muslim presence in Thailand makes halal food an integral part of the national cuisine (especially in the Yawi-speaking regions of the south). Consult www.zabihah.com for more info.

LET'S GO ONLINE. Plan your next trip on our newly redesigned website, **www.letsgo.com.** It features the latest travel info on your favorite destinations, as well as tons of interactive features: make your own itinerary, read blogs from our trusty researcher-writers, browse our photo library, watch exclusive videos, check out our newsletter, find travel deals, and buy new guides. We're always updating and adding new features, so check back often!

LIFE AND TIMES

The only country in Southeast Asia never to have been colonized, Thailand has a proud history that continues to influence the spirit of Thai society. The country's love for its King, flag, and national anthem is felt in each bustling street and quiet countryside, despite current political unrest. Tourism is Thailand's lifeblood; fifteen years ago one million people descended on the "Land of Smiles" each year. Today, that number has risen to an estimated 10 million. There are sights to satiate every traveler's desires: beachgoers head to the picturesque islands off the eastern and southern coasts, while more adventurous travelers trek through hill-tribe homelands in the mountainous north. Others explore the ancient cities of Central Thailand, where the ruins of great kingdoms now lie in silent majesty, a testament to a glorious past. For travelers new to Southeast Asia, there is no better place to start than "Amazing Thailand."

◪HIGHLIGHTS OF THAILAND

BEACHES. Ko Samet (p. 138) and **Ko Chang** (p. 151), off the east coast, are easy on the wallet and easy going. Down south, **Ko Samui** (p. 401), **Ko Phangan** (p. 409), and **Ko Tao** (p. 417) offer a more raucous brand of sun and fun with a broader slate of aquatic activities. **Krabi's** (p. 381) seaside cliffs offer world-class climbing.

HIKING AND TREKKING. Northern Thailand (p. 265) offers an impressive range of affordable treks. Less-touristed **Mae Hong Son** (p. 292) and **Sangkhlaburi** (p. 181) have activities ranging from elephant excursions to river rafting.

HANGING OUT. Towns along the Mekong, including **Chiang Khan** (p. 247) and **Nakhon Phanom** (p. 232), are unparalleled spots to unwind and take in stunning natural settings. **Kanchanaburi** (p. 171) is the place to go for top-notch accommodations and tasty cuisine. Tiny **Pai** (p. 288), nestled in the northern highlands, has a host of bubbling natural hot springs.

CULTURAL HERITAGE. The temples and palaces of **Bangkok** (p. xx), the ancient capitals of **Sukhothai** (p. 311) and **Ayutthaya** (p. 161), and the Khmer ruins of **Phimai** (p. 208) are enthralling and accessible. **Chiang Mai** (p. 265) is not to be missed for its stunning architectural legacy and religious significance.

NIGHTLIFE. Bangkok (p. 87), **Chiang Mai** (p. 265), **Ko Phangan** (p. 409), **Ko Samui** (p. 401), and **Khon Kaen** (p. 256) hit the dance floor when the rest of the kingdom hits the hay.

LAND

The diverse beauty of Thailand's physical expanse is a geographer's dream and a cartographer's headache. Despite the country's small size, it contains a plethora of topological features. It is perhaps best known for its southern *kos* (islands), whose white beaches, coral reefs, gushing waterfalls, and shimmering turquoise waters have drawn paradise seekers the world over. Still, the mainland holds gems of its own. From the river-rich and peak-encrusted north crowned by Doi Inthanon (Thailand's highest point), to the fertile "rice bowl" that is the central plains, to the semi-arid plateau that blankets the northeast and meets the mighty Mekong River, every corner is a visual feast.

PEOPLE

DEMOGRAPHICS

Use of the word "Thai" began in the 20th century when the country shed the name "Siam" for "Thailand". "Thai" is a political and geographical designation referring to all citizens of the country. "Tai" refers to the ethnic Tai-Kadai people, who speak Tai-based languages, live mostly in China, Laos, and Myanmar (where they are known as the Shan), and account for 75% of the population of Thailand. Historically, starvation and poverty at home have contributed to a high Chinese immigration rate, and the Chinese are now Thailand's largest minority at about 12% of the population. Malay-speaking Muslims constitute another 2.3% of the population and are concentrated in the south, while hill-tribe groups including the Karen, Hmong, Yao, Lahu, Akha, and Lisu form a small but distinctive minority in the north.

LANGUAGE

Like the people themselves, the Thai language has absorbed influences over time from languages including English, Chinese, and Sanskrit while still retaining its distinctive characteristics. Thai is a **tonal** language and consists of five tones—mid, low, high, rising, and falling—which define a word just as much as its script does. The first Thai **alphabet** was created by King Ramkhamhaeng of Sukhothai in 1283 and was based on Mon and Khmer script, and it has survived almost entirely intact to this day. Thai **grammar** is delightfully simple: there are no suffixes, genders, articles, declensions, or plurals in spoken Thai. Like English, it is written from left to right, but it lacks capital letters and punctuation. Thanks to its grammatical simplicity, Thai vocabulary readily lends itself to adaptation, especially in the creation of compound words to describe objects. For example, the word "ice" in Thai, *nam khaeng*, literally translates to "solid water." Western concepts and scientific and technological terms are somewhat more difficult to create by combining existing Thai words. To remedy the situation, the **Royal Institute** convenes a committee of linguists to concoct new vocabulary words by delving into Pali and Sanskrit. The national language has four major dialects that have developed in northern, northeastern, southern, and central Thailand. Central Thai (also known as Bangkok Thai) is the standard dialect and is taught in schools (see **Appendix**, p. 426 for specific phrases). In addition to regional dialects, Thai also has four different categories of vocabulary and syntax whose use depends on the social status of the speaker relative to his audience. The most distinctive of these is the royal language, **rachasap**, used mainly for state or official occasions. Following *rachasap* are the dialect used to address religious figures, the **polite vernacular**, used on a daily basis, and the **slang** of casual conversation.

RELIGION

Theravada Buddhism may be the state religion in all but name—the Thai Constitution requires that the reigning monarch be Buddhist, and any speech that insults Buddhism is strictly prohibited—but it is not officially designated as such in order to guarantee complete freedom of religion for all citizens. The government does sanction certain religious groups. Since 1984, though, the government has not recognized any new faiths, including the Church of Jesus Christ of Latter Day Saints. However, foreign missionaries may work and followers of other religions can worship in the country freely whether they're registered with the government or not. Government-issued National Identity Cards began to include a religious designation in 1999 in the interest of providing an easier means of identifying individuals requiring a Muslim burial. This designation, however, is optional; card-holders can choose whether or not they would like to declare their faith.

THERAVADA BUDDHISM. As the religion of about 95% of the Thai people, Theravada ("the way of the elders") Buddhism informs both faith and lifestyle. Buddhist spirituality is founded upon the **Four Noble Truths:** there is suffering; the source of suffering is desire; the absence of desire enables a cessation of suffering; and that cessation is achieved through an adherence to the **Eightfold Path,** which is a path of virtue, mental cultivation, and wisdom. Anti-materialism, forgiveness, and a vigorous spirit that has mastered tranquility are all characteristics of this highly scriptural religion. The **Spirit of Free Enquiry** is central to Buddhism: Buddha encouraged his followers to investigate his teaching for themselves instead of adhering to it blindly. This teaching inspires a high degree of tolerance for difference—racial, religious, or ethnic—and teaches kindness and compassion in the hope that individuals can live in harmony with the people, creatures, and the natural environment around them. In Thailand, Buddhist *wats*, or places of worship, play a central role in religious life, and the monks that inhabit them command great respect. Monks, too, are a common sight; their saffron robes, shaved heads, and gentle manner serve as a reminder of the search for inner peace that is the mainstay of Theravada Buddhism. It is an accepted **male rite of passage** to serve temporarily (usually about three months) in the monkhood. The goal of this religious service is increased maturity and spirituality in everyday life. In Thailand (unlike in Myanmar and Sri Lanka), the female Thervada **Bhikkhuni** (nun) lineage was never established and thus most Thais believe women have no place in monastic life. Still, there are the occasional exceptions, like the nuns of Dhammajarinee Wittaya in Chiang Mai.

MAHAYANA BUDDHISM. In the first century, a group of Buddhists viewed Theravada as too restrictive and ascetic. This group began to develop into its own school: Mahayana ("larger vehicle"). Mahayana teaches that it is impossible for individuals to achieve their own Nirvana. They believe that while removal from life experience is the ultimate object of enlightenment, they can only approach it. According to Mahayana Buddhism, **Nirvana** will only come when all of humankind is ready for salvation, and consequently prizes the relief of universal suffering. Although it is more popular today in other parts of Southeast Asia, Mahayana Buddhism is still practiced in Thailand, mainly by ethnic Chinese and Vietnamese immigrants. There is a particularly large ethnic Chinese community in Phuket that practices a combination of Mahayana Buddhism and Taoism.

ISLAM. Muslims constitute Thailand's largest religious minority and account for 4.6% of the population. The vast majority are Sunni; only 1 or 2% of Thai Muslims are Shi'a. Most are concentrated close to the Malaysian border in southern Thailand—the south actually contains more mosques than *wats*—and many are originally of **Malay** descent. Though a minority, Muslims in Thailand are able to practice their religion freely. In the south, employers observe Muslim holidays and holy days, and all employees are given one month's paid leave to travel to Mecca. In the wake of violent incidents in southern Thailand, the government has become more wary of possible separatist movements in that region (see **Southern Discomfort,** p. 63).

ON THE ROAD TO GENDER EQUALITY

Over three decades ago, Thailand began its journey toward freedom when people sacrificed their lives to oppose a dictatorship and demand democracy. However, there are still larger problems facing Thailand. Under Thai law, men and women are regarded on equal terms—Article 80 of the Thai Constitution commits the state to promoting gender equality, while Article 90 mandates that one-third of the Extraordinary House Committee has to be constituted by women's organizations when women's issues are on the agenda—but women are still strikingly underrepresented on all political levels. Their representation in the Lower House amounts to a mere 4.8 percent.

Women's labor employment rates are only slightly lower than men's (95.4% versus 96.7%). Despite general improvement since the Asian Economic Crisis of 1997, the economic situation of women is still more difficult than that of men. They constitute the majority of the jobless, and many women are still forced to work in the informal sector without any kind of benefits. Where membership in the labor unions is composed of both women and men, men still outnumber women in terms of participation; in 1993, men accounted for 60% of the total numbers in 839 labor unions. In 2003, there were only 138 women out of 1066 executive officers of state enterprises' unions (12%), while in private sector unions, women constituted 4,143 of 12,215 executive officers (33.39%).

Women's access to educational institutions is comparatively good. Still, there are still wide gaps between young men and women concerning graduate education; male enrollment is considerably higher than female enrollment (17.3% versus 12.8%). Women also have a higher illiteracy rate (11.5%) than men (7.3%).

The period from 1995-2006 saw women's political participation increase at both local and national levels. There has been an increase in the number of women candidates for the Lower House as well as in the National Parliament, but women's chances of having their names submitted as national candidates is quite small. Chance of election is even smaller. Among 37 parties taking part in the most recent election in 2005, 147 women's names (18.15%) were placed on the party list, but only eight of them went on to become members of Parliament in the 'party list' category. The first two women senators were appointed in 1949; within this year, the first woman was coincidently elected to the Parliament. The last appointment of senators was made in 2006, but women's representation in the Senate is still very small, peaking at only 10% as of 2006.

The first official policy statement of the Thai government to address issues of women in power and decision-making was made in 1995, marking an increasing awareness of gender issues. In 1997, the Chuan Leekpai government resolved "to promote gender equality by amending laws, regulations and rules to provide the opportunity for women and men to engage in a career or to have an administration and decision-making role both in the public and private sectors on equal terms in line with the Constitution." In 2001, the Thaksin government further affirmed an "aim to promote women's rights, role and status, develop women's capability to enable them to fully participate in community development ... in terms of economic, social and political rights, ... including the promotion of gender equality in governmental service sectors."

NGOs have insisted that the cabinet consider the equitable appointment of women in national committees where major decisions are made. A few high-profile national committees now have some seats for women, particularly the National Human Rights Commission (NHRC), where the gender balance is roughly equal (six men to five women), but it is still chaired by a senior male member.

Although the number of women in leading positions remains low, Thailand is fueled by a strong and diverse women's liberation movement. Women leaders in academic structures promote democratic development by encouraging women's political participation and fighting to reduce the gender gap in parliament and political bodies. However, the transition to gender equality will only be ongoing in the years to come.

-Cholthira Satyawadhna

CHRISTIANITY. Christianity first emerged in Thailand in the 16th and 17th centuries, brought by missionaries of various Christian sects. Today, however, Thailand's Christian population remains proportionally the smallest of any Asian nation at 0.05%, with almost half of that group resides in and around Chiang Mai. Roman Catholic enclaves can be found among the Vietnamese and Lao populations, while missionaries have focused their energies on several of the northern hill tribes.

HINDUISM. Despite the fact that it constitutes such a small religious minority in Thailand, Hinduism plays a large role in Thai society. Pre-Buddhist Thailand adopted many religious, artistic, and political influences from the firmly Hindu Khmer Empire, and as a result, much of the ceremony surrounding the Thai king became infused with Hindu ritual. Far less than 1% of modern Thai are Hindu, most of whom are immigrants from India living in Bangkok, which has four major Hindu temples. Since mandatory religious instruction in schools is solely focused on Buddhism and Islam, the Hindu community keeps traditional subjects like Hindi and Sanskrit alive in its own school in Bangkok.

ANIMISM. Animism is an ancient form of worship predating both Hinduism and Buddhism. Followers of Animism believe that natural objects and phenomena, such as mountains and storms, possess living spirits that are appeased only by offerings. **Spirit houses,** small shelters provided as a residence for local spirits, are ubiquitous in and around Thai homes (p. 65). Although Animism is a very distinct practice from Thai Buddhism, its beliefs have been incorporated by the latter in the form of astrology and fortune-telling, the practice of which is extremely popular in Thai society. Today, most Animists are found among the northern hill tribes and the Chao Lay of the Andaman Sea.

FLORA AND FAUNA

Thailand's diverse topology yields a wealth of plant and animal species. Intrepid visitors to the country encounter come of the world's best scuba diving, birdwatching, and trekking. Even the world's best veterinarians travel to Thailand to care for endangered wildlife in its many sanctuaries and nature preserves.

PLANTS

PLENTY OF PETALS. Thailand has more than 27,000 flowering species, ranging from bamboo to fruit trees to the **Ratchaphruek,** the country's national flower. Although many **orchid** species are endangered, Thailand is home to 1000 different types, and boasts a major orchid industry. The white or pink **lotus,** seen floating on ponds or depicted in Buddhist art, is a sacred symbol of wisdom, purity, peace, and compassion. Legend has it that it became sacred when one blossom grew from each of the young Buddha's first seven footsteps. The scarlet (poisonous) **poinsettia,** a flower associated with Christian winters in the West, is popular in Thailand, especially in the Chiang Mai province. During the winter months, its bright, cheerful blooms compensate for the fewer hours of daylight. Flowers are a part of daily Thai life: they can be cooked or boiled as food, used as decoration, or included in traditional Thai ceremonies, and Thai remedies employ common roots and berries for medicinal purposes.

RICE AND EVERYTHING NICE. Not only is rice Thailand's most important crop and a staple of national cuisine, but it also has religious significance: rice is celebrated as an example of nature's powers of sustenance. Early each morning (mainly in smaller villages), residents leave an offering of rice for the Buddhist monks who collect donations of food and basic daily necessities in a practice known as *Binderbaht*. These offerings are particularly significant during harvest festivals (timing varies by region), when it is customary to celebrate all of earth's living things and the human labor that brings them into the home.

RELIGIOSI-TREE. It is believed that Buddha attained enlightenment in the shade of the **Bodhi tree.** Those grown from a cutting of the original tree in India are the most precious, but all Bodhi trees command respect. Long branches, an irregularly shaped trunk, and heart-shaped leaves are its most noticeable traits. Buddha is also said to have sat in the shade of the Rose Apple tree, meditating on man's sufferings. The tree's enormous branches (13m) protected Buddha thousands of years ago; they now do the same for Thais. The Chomphu Phukha tree in Nan's **Doi Phuka National Park** (p. 345) is extremely rare, though it isn't the only one in the world, as locals claim. When it blooms in February, it becomes a regional attraction.

WILDLIFE

ENDANGERED ANIMALS. As a primarily Buddhist people, Thais tend to regard animals in the same way they would regard other human beings. This attitude is even reflected in Thai media: almost daily, special interest articles appear in the well-respected *Bangkok Post* about various animals whose names, personalities, and salient characteristics are well known. Recently, however, animals have been making the news for serious reasons: Thailand is home to a number of endangered species. The **elephant,** used for centuries as both the primary means of transportation in Thailand and as a battle animal, is today drugged into docility, overworked, and underfed by illegal loggers. Therefore, despite being considered sacred, elephant numbers have diminished by almost 40% in the past ten years. The **Asiatic Black Bear** and the **Malaysian Sun Bear,** the world's smallest bear, are both native to Thailand and also on the endangered species list, thanks to poaching. A popular pet in Southeast Asia, the Sun Bear's skin is so loose that when it is grabbed by an attacker, it is able to turn around completely and defend itself. Though the practice is illegal, both species are poached for their skins, and older bears are killed for medicinal purposes—the recipes for many traditional remedies for inflammation, fevers, and liver disease include the gallbladder and bile of these bears. Herbal alternatives to these recipes exist, but the products containing actual animal parts are far more popular. Discovered in Thailand in 1974 and found nowhere else in the world, **Kitti's Hog-Nosed Bat,** which, at the size of a bumblebee, may be the world's smallest mammal, is also endangered. So too is the **Giant Mekong Catfish,** which weighs in at up to 300kg.

SAVE THE TREES. In 1961, 54% of Thailand was covered in some type of forest; by 1988, extensive logging and urban development reduced this number to 28%. In response, the Thai government set in place conservation measures, most notably the 1992 Environmental Protection Act, a law that was heralded as the dawn of environmental awareness in the country. Thailand is now home to a number of national parks, wildlife sanctuaries, and forest reserves, whose total area covers an impressive 13% of Thailand. However, pollution, illegal logging (and subsequent damage due to flooding), and population growth have all continued to plague the country's wildlife. Additionally, the growth of Thailand's two major cities, Bangkok and Chiang Mai, has caused its own environmental concerns: high air- and water-pollution rates. Moreover, according to Thailand's Department of Mineral Resources, Bangkok is sinking about 5cm per year. Developed atop a vast swamp with numerous canals, the "Venice of the East" is beset by the problems of industrialization, a set of issues the country has yet to address.

HISTORY

ENTER THE TAI

Human habitation in what is now Thailand was present but faint until the coming of agriculture and bronze in the second millennium BC. Remains discovered at **Ban Chiang** (p. 241) in the Khorat Plateau suggest that farmers settled there around 2500 BC. During the following milennia, various Tai-Kadai tribes moved south into northern Myanmar, Thailand, and Laos, merging with Mon and Khmer peoples and establishing small principalities, or "*muang.*" Scholars disagree about the origins of the Thai people. Some argue that their ancestors came from Mongolia or northern China, while others trace the sources to northeast Thailand. Buddhism was introduced to the region that is now Thailand at the time of the Dvaravati kingdom, which began to flourish in northern Thailand in the seventh century AD.

THE SUKHOTHAI PERIOD (AD 1238-1350)

In the early part of the 13th century, none of the minor city-states that populated modern-day Thailand were strong enough to individually challenge the powerful Khmer empire to the north, but in 1238, two Thai chieftans, **Khun Bang Klang Thao** and **Khun Pha Muang**, rebelled and moved north. They established the kingdom of Sukhothai, considered to be the first independent Thai polity. **King Si Sri Inthrathit** was its first ruler. Sukhothai, meaning "Dawn of Happiness," reached its zenith in power and size (incorporating portions of present-day Laos, Thailand, Singapore, Malaysia, and much of Myanmar) in 1275, when **King Ramkhamhaeng the Great** ascended the throne.

Modern Thai ideals of the benevolent monarch and his place in society originate in the Sukhothai period. Ramkhamhaeng's rule marked the first unification of Thais under a single monarch, and he worked tirelessly to better the condition of his people by abolishing slavery and codifying Sukhothai's first formal laws. Ramkhamhaeng also invited Ceylonese monks to come to Sukhothai to "purify" the kingdom's Khmer-influenced syncretic Buddhism; as a result, the Ceylonese school of Theravada Buddhism was established, and it remains the main religion in Thailand to this day. A famous inscription believed to be from this period reads, "In the water there are fish, in the fields there is rice. Whoever wants to trade in elephants, so trades....Whoever wants to trade in silver and gold, so trades. The faces of the citizens are happy." It is no wonder everyone was smiling: King Ramkhamhaeng abolished taxes and built a bell in front of his palace so that his subjects could ring it at any time, confident that he would arbitrate justly. In 1283, the King achieved his

2500 BC
Farmers settle at Ban Chiang.

AD 651
First kingdom of Thai tribes forms. 7-12th Centuries Dvaravati era.

1238
Kingdom of Sukhothai founded by King Si Sri Inthrathit.

1275
King Ramkhamhaeng ascends the throne.

1283
Thai alphabet established by King Ramkhamhaeng.

1350
Kingdom of Ayutthaya founded.

14th-16th Centuries
Ayutthaya grows in stature and number of temples.

1511
Portuguese establish contact with Ayutthaya.

1605-1662
Spanish, Dutch, English, Danish, and French arrive.

1688
French expelled from the kingdom.

most longstanding reform by introducing the Thai **alphabet,** which not only became a symbol of the nation's cultural and political independence but also effectively unified Thailand's myriad city-states under one common identity. Other Thai states such as **Lanna** (established by King Mengrai in Chiang Mai) and **Phayao** (located in the northern part of modern Thailand) also flourished contemporaneously, with the former becoming a center of Buddhist scholarship and evangelism.

GOLDEN AGE OF AYUTTHAYA (1351-1767)

After Ramkhamhaeng's death in 1317, the Sukhothai kingdom began to decline, and in 1350, King **U Thong** (later called King Ramathibodi I) established a rival kingdom centered on the magnificent island-city of **Ayutthaya.** It would serve as the capital of Siam for the next four centuries, a period which is now considered to be the "golden age" of Thai history. The most significant development of the kingdom was its incorporation of the Khmer concept of the absolute monarch into Thai royal custom; the king was no longer the paternal figure of the Sukhothai period, but a divine and transcendent man physically removed from his subjects. In this imperial climate, the kingdom of Ayutthaya conquered Sukhothai and continued to expand. Ayutthaya's location in the central plains region made it safe from external invasions during the rainy season, which was marked by massive flooding. Thus the kingdom was able to turn inward and develop the complex system of administration that was the prototype of modern Thai bureaucracy. To complement this administrative structure, Thai society began to develop complex internal hierarchies. The lowest rung on the social ladder was **phrai,** commoners and slaves; above them were **khunnang,** or nobles. At the top were **chao,** the princes. **Monks** remained the one social group that could bridge these divisions.

The rise of Ayutthaya also coincided with the arrival of European imperialists. A dispute over the Malacca territory brought the **Portuguese** into the picture in 1511. The Portuguese were followed by a veritable stampede of curious foreign visitors, beginning with the **Spanish,** followed by the **Dutch, English,** and **Danish,** and concluding with the **French** in 1662. This did not hinder Ayutthaya's rise; under **King Narai,** who ruled from 1656 to 1688, Ayutthaya reached its peak of power and influence, boasting a population nearly double that of 17th-century London. In 1688, however, while the king was seriously ill, his chief minister (a Greek named **Constantine Phaulkon**) was accused of conspiring to replace Narai with a puppet-king loyal to France. Phaulkon had successfully kept the Dutch and English at bay, but permitted the French to station over 500 troops throughout Ayutthaya. Once he recovered, King Narai cut off relations with the French and executed Phaulkon for his French connections. Ayutthaya had limited contact with foreigners after the debacle with France.

TROUBLED TIMES (1767-82)

The influx of European forces during Ayutthaya's period of expansion may have been a major source of distraction for the Siamese, but the true threat to their kingdom did not come from the Europeans. Disaster swept in from the northwest in 1763, in the form of a Burmese army bent on revenging an almost 200-year-old military defeat. In 1767, after a 15-month siege, they stormed Ayutthaya, burning it to the ground and destroying culturally and religiously significant manuscripts, paintings, and sculptures. Only a few thousand out of over one million original inhabitants escaped the slaughter, including **General Phraya Taksin** and a few hundred of his followers. After regrouping on the east coast, Taksin led an army of several thousand men to expel the Burmese; within 15 years, the Thais had successfully recaptured Chiang Mai, Cambodia, and parts of Laos. Taksin ruled from his new capital at **Thonburi,** just across the river from Bangkok. Soon after winning the war, however, he began to suffer from the unfortunate misconception that he was a reincarnation of the Buddha, most likely due to some form of mental illness. Needless to say, Taksin's declaration was poorly received in court. He was executed in royal fashion: he was thrown into a velvet sack (so as not to spill any royal blood) and then beaten to death with a sandalwood club. Commander-in-chief **Thong Duang** was recalled from his campaign in Cambodia and crowned **King Rama I** in 1782, marking the beginning of the **Chakri** dynasty.

1767
Burmese annex, sack, and burn Ayutthaya.

1767-83
General Taksin reclaims Thai kingdom.

RISE OF THE CHAKRI (1782-1868)

When it became apparent that Thonburi was vulnerable to the Burmese and unable to accommodate major expansion, Rama I moved the capital across the Chao Phraya River to **Bangkok.** There he built his most lasting legacy, the Grand Palace and Royal Chapel, now the Temple of the Emerald Buddha (p. 110), and unified the kingdom's many fiefdoms. Rama I also translated the Indian epic *Ramayana* into Thai, and edited and codified Thai law into the innovative Kotmai Tra Samdung (Three Seals Code), which addressed the interrelationship between economic, political, and military power. During his reign, Laos, Cambodia, and what is now northern Thailand were added to the kingdom.

Siam's illustriousness only increased with the ascension of King Mongkut, or **King Rama IV,** to the throne in 1851; his rule was one of the most significant transitional periods in Thai history. Unfairly portrayed as a flippant and frivolous monarch in Margaret Landon's *Anna and the King of Siam*, Mongkut was actually a serious man, having spent the reign of his half-brother, **King Rama III,** in the monkhood, traveling extensively throughout the kingdom and mastering subjects such as English, Latin, and Western history. In order to strengthen Siam and silence his Western critics, Rama IV negotiated a trade treaty with the British in 1855, carrying Siam out of 150 years of virtual isolation.

1782
King Rama I comes to power.

1785
Bangkok becomes capital; King Rama I builds Grand Palace.

1851
King Rama IV ascends the throne.

1855
King signs treaty with British, imports Western technology.

LIFE AND TIMES

COLONIALISM AVERTED (1868-1932)

1868-1910
The reign of King Rama V.

When malaria cut Mongkut's rule short, the government fell into the able hands of his teenage son, **Prince Chulalongkorn**, who was crowned **King Rama V.** Chulalongkorn's 42 years of rule were marked by the abolition of slavery, reforms to the Thai justice, education, and public welfare systems, and courageous foreign policy in an era of aggressive European colonialism. In 1893, after prolonged tension between France and Siam in the northeast, two French gunboats shelled Siamese defenses at the mouth of the Chao Phraya River and moved into Bangkok. Thanks to the swift diplomatic action of Foreign Minister **Prince Devawongse**, war between the two countries was averted. A subsequent treaty in 1896 with the French established Siam as a regional **buffer state,** guaranteeing its independence. In the treaty, Siam ceded much of the territory that is modern Laos and Cambodia to the French and what is now peninsular Malaysia to the British.

1893
Franco-Siamese Crisis: French ships enter Bangkok.

1897
Rama V is the first Thai monarch to travel to Europe.

1908
First statue of a Thai king (Rama V) erected.

1909
Siam gives up claims to peninsular Malaysia.

By the time of his death in 1910, Rama V had become esconced as the most revered Thai monarch in modern history; October 23 (the anniversary of his death) is now a national holiday, Chulalongkorn Day. In 1910, upon his death, his son **King Vajiravudh** took the throne. The Oxford-educated Vajiravudh oversaw the founding of Chulalongkorn University (p. 115), now Thailand's most prestigious university, in honor of his father, and solidified the country's Western relations by declaring war against Germany in 1917 and sending a small number of troops to fight with the Allies in **WWI.** After the war's end, Thailand became a member of the **League of Nations** in 1920. In a less internationally-acclaimed move, Vajiravudh wrote a book about overseas Chinese in Siam entitled *The Jews of the Orient*, a work whose intense focus on nationalism was only heightened through Vajiravudh's adoption of the concept of surnames (which had not previously existed in Thailand), coining hundreds of them himself. Under this system, Siam's ethnic Chinese were forced either to assimilate or be branded as foreigners.

MILITARY, MONARCHY, DEMOCRACY (1932-1942)

1932
Absolute monarchy abolished; People's Party comes to power in a bloodless coup.

The Great Depression of the 1930s hit Siam just as hard as the rest of the world, and **King Rama VII** had to cut wages and raise taxes. Prominent, discontented academics and intellectuals blamed the royal government for Siam's financial woes and demanded a civil constitution. In June 1932, civil officials and the military launched a bloodless coup which effectively transformed Thailand from an absolute monarchy into a **constitutional one.** Proclaiming themselves the **People's Party,** the revolutionaries, led by **Major Luang Phibun Songkhram** (commonly known as Phibun) and **Dr. Pridi Phanomyong,** moved quickly to occupy high government posts. Phanomyong outlined a socialist economic plan that would nationalize land

1933
Dr. Pridi Banomyong advocates socialist economic plan.

and labor, but conservative leaders were horrified by his proposal and forced him into exile. Unable to manage the crisis, King Rama VII abdicated in 1935 and went into a voluntary exile in England, where he died six years later. Rama VII was replaced by his nephew, 10-year-old **Ananda Mahidol** (later **King Rama VIII**), whose age and education in Switzerland prevented him from governing, so a regent council was established to rule in his place. As the country experimented with **constitutions** granting varying degrees of democracy, the pendulum of Thai political power swung back and forth between the increasingly powerful military and the civilian bureaucratic elite. Thailand received its current name in 1939, when Phibun, by then firmly in charge, officially renamed the country. In 1940, Phibun requested that France return the territories that it had taken just a few decades earlier. The French were reluctant, to say the least, and subsequent military skirmishes only ended when the occupying Japanese intervened to arbitrate. The 1941 **Tokyo Convention** returned much of French Indochina to Thai control. Later, under Japanese pressure, Thailand would join **World War II** on the Axis side.

WORLD WAR, COLD WAR (1942-1971)

On December 8, 1941, the day after the bombing of Pearl Harbor, Japan invaded Thailand. Under pressure from Japanese occupiers, the Thai Ambassador to the United States reluctantly went to American Secretary of State Cordell Hull, saying he was obligated to deliver a declaration that he did not want to deliver. Hull suggested that he not deliver it. The ambassador concurred, but Thai troops invaded Burma alongside the Japanese. At the same time, a 'Free Thai' movement was working against the Japanese and the Phibun regime. As the war turned against the Axis, Field Marshal Phibun Songkhram faced mounting opposition and ultimately resigned as prime minister, to be replaced by opposition leader **Pridi Phanomyong**. But the anti-royalist Phanomyong was also forced to resign when the newly returned Rama VIII died mysteriously in 1946. After the ascension of **Pumipohn Adunyadayt (King Rama IX)** to the throne, and a brief civilian interlude, the civilian government fell to a second coup led by Phibun. After his second fall in 1957, the military staged a coup d'état during the general elections, under the leadership of Field Marshal **Sarit Thanarat**. The new government nullified the Consititution and re-established full military control while cracking down on the drug trade and suppressing Communist propaganda. By the time of Thanarat's death in 1963, Thailand had become a staunch US ally in Southeast Asia. Under his successor, **Thanom Kittikachorn**, US forces were permitted to build air bases in Thailand for the war in Vietnam. Thailand became more actively involved in international affairs, joining the **United Nations** in 1946 and even sending troops on a UN mission to Korea in 1950.

1935
King Rama VII goes into voluntary exile in England.

1941
Tokyo Convention: France returns Indochinese territory to Thailand.

1941
Pacific war engulfs Southeast Asia.

1942
Thai Field Marshal declares war on Allies; ambassador refuses to honor declaration.

1946
Thailand joins the United Nations.

1957
Military coup d'état during general elections; Field Marshal Sarit Thanarat takes over.

1964
First US military personnel stationed in Thailand.

1967
Association of Southeast Asian Nations (ASEAN) founded.

LIFE AND TIMES

REPRESSION AND REVOLUTION (1971-1980)

1973
Students and workers hold pro-democracy demonstrations.

1974
Interim government establishes new constitution.

1976
Government quells demonstrations, resulting in the October Massacre.

By 1973, Thailand had been under full military rule for over a decade. But, while the government was static, the nation had undergone rapid economic growth, and its patience with military juntas was wearing thin. In June of 1973, students and workers held demonstrations in the streets, calling for a democratic government. By October 13, tens of thousands had gathered in front of the **Democracy Monument** in Bangkok (built to commemorate the the end of absolute monarchial rule) in the largest protest in Thai history. The military attacked the crowd, killing hundreds. In the bloody aftermath, King Bhumibol called for the resignation of Field Marshal Thanom (who fled the country) and appointed **Professor Sanya Dharmasakti** as interim prime minister. A new constitution sparked an era of democratic rule cut short by increased political polarization. Protests began to break out across Bangkok, and military troops responding to a sit-in at **Thammasat University** in October of 1976 shot, clubbed to death, and hanged more than 300 protestors in what came to be called the October Massacre. Newly appointed prime minister Thanin Kraivichien oversaw an even more repressive regime. The following years saw instability and military infighting.

PREMOCRACY (1980-1992)

1988
First elected, non-military Prime Minister since 1977.

In 1980, with the election of the new prime minister General **Prem Tinsulanonda**, Thailand gained much needed and long awaited political stability. Immediately after his appointment, Prem departed from his predecessors in a surprising move: he retired from the military in a symbolic act of separation from decades of military and political entanglement. There was a revival of democratic politics under Tinsulanonda's "Premocracy," but corruption increased under his successor, Chatichai Choonhavan. Early in 1991, the army launched a successful bloodless coup under General **Suchinda Kraprayoon,** who suspended the constitution, dissolved the legislature, and curtailed general freedoms. Accusations that the army influenced the framing of a new constitution in order to institutionalize its own rule spurred hundreds of thousands of pro-democracy protesters to hold a demonstration in May 1992. The military injured and killed hundreds of people, many of whom were strategically located in front of the Democracy Monument and Western TV cameras. A horrified King Bhumibol forced Suchinda out of office and appointed **Anand Panyarachun** as interim prime minister.

1991
Army launches bloodless coup, dissolves legislature, abolishes constitution.

1992
Troops kill hudnreds of protestors on Suchinda's orders.

1992-96
Economic prosperity slows down.

1996
Stock market crashes.

MONEY PROBLEMS (1992-1998)

When Panyarachun fired the top four military officers in August 1992, it marked a renewed effort in Thai politics to separate the government from the military. Subsequent regimes, however, faced charges of corruption and mismanagement, and the resulting political instability damaged

Thailand's previously spectacular 8-10% annual growth rates. By 1996, Thailand had its highest inflation rate in five years, 0% export growth, and a 30% drop in stock market prices, and tougher times were still to come. Then-Prime Minister **Banharn Silpa-archa** was harshly criticized for meddling in economic affairs and was held responsible for the nation's dire economic situation. In July 1997, heavy external debts and financial deregulation culminated in the collapse of the Thai baht during what is now known as the **Asian Financial Crisis.** Economists discovered the hard way that the corruption- and debt-ridden national economic infrastructure was too weak to absorb the shock and rebound from it. Waves of **currency devaluations,** accompanied by economic and political havoc, spread across Southeast Asia. The **International Monetary Fund (IMF)** initiated a US$17.2 billion emergency international rescue package for Thailand in August of that year, but the crisis continued; the baht's value fell 40%, more than 350 factories shut down, and Thailand's stock market hit a nine-year low. From 1985 to 1995, Thailand had maintained the highest growth rate in the world, but by January of 1998, its currency hit the lowest point in history: 56฿ to the US$.

1997
Asian Financial Crisis.

2000
"Amazing Thailand" launched by TAT.

2001
PM Thaksin Shinawatra elected in landslide victory.

2004
Violence erupts in the south of Thailand.

LIFE AND TIMES

THAILAND TODAY

With positive growth rates since 1999, Thailand seems to be well on its way to economic recovery. The **Tourism Authority of Thailand (TAT)** inaugurated the ambitious **"Amazing Thailand"** campaign to boost the economy, and in February 2000, officials declared the worst of the economic crisis to be over. Today, Thailand's economy is one of the fastest-growing in Southeast Asia, largely due to the efforts of charismatic Prime Minister **Thaksin Shinawatra.** Allegations of rampant corruption, however, plagued Thaksin's administration, and reached a crisis point in March 2006, when massive protests called for his resignation. He resorted to running a highly controversial snap election marred by boycotts and suspicious results. Another election was scheduled, but the military lost patience and seized power in September 2006. Facing little opposition, the military suspended democratic rule and liberties, eventually drawing up a new constitution. Parliamentary elections were held in December 2007, but the military remains in the background, and political tensions have remained unresolved. Thailand faces other problems as well: violence broke out in the predominantly Muslim south (p. 63) in January 2004 in the form of a series of bombings and attacks on the government, and violence continues in that region, with 2,700 dead.

KING BHUMIBOL ADULYADEJ (RAMA IX)

King Rama IX was born in December 1927 in Cambridge, Massachusetts, while his parents were studying medical-related fields at Harvard University and Simmons College. The young king ascended to the throne at the age of 18, so his actual coronation was postponed by four years so that he could finish his education. The longest-reigning monarch in the world, Bhumibol is also one of the most beloved; he is revered for his dedication to the underprivileged, his role in resolving government conflicts, and his commitment to the peace and unity of his country. As a constitutional monarch, he exercises little visible power, but his word commands tremendous loyalty and respect. His official titles are

Head of State, Head of the Armed Forces, and Upholder of All Religions. The three "rights" that accompany these positions are to encourage, to warn, and to be consulted. Since 1974, he has become particularly active in **reforestation projects** in order to preserve Thailand's flora and fauna. King Bhumibol has also been heavily influenced by his parents' medical careers and places a great deal of emphasis on **health care.** The King also devotes himself to a variety of hobbies: he is a world-class yachtsman, as well as a famous composer, with 43 jazz and blues compositions to his name.

HOOKED ON THAILAND

According to the United States Central Intelligence Agency, Thailand is considered to be a **drug money-laundering center.** Whether it be in the form of **opium, cocaine,** or other substances, narcotics and their sale have a strong presence in Thailand. Some argue that this trend arose with the increase in tourism, while others blame it on the drugs' addictive qualities. Either way, widespread violence and the **AIDS/HIV** epidemic (both linked to the drug trade) have resulted in a nation-wide crackdown.

On January 28th 2003, former Prime Minister Thaksin signed an order that promised a "concerted effort of the nation to overcome drugs." The year-long effort to rid the country of its drug problem resulted in more than 2,700 deaths and tens of thousands of arrests. While this campaign has helped to crack down on the drug trade, some fear that its violence may only make it harder to identify and treat intravenous drug users afflicted with HIV/AIDS. Still, the effort is felt in certain areas of Thailand. Full moon parties, once saturated with ectasy, opium, and acid, are now subject to the watchful gaze of the Thai police who frequently set-up roadblocks and checkpoints in an attempt to rid their country of these harmful drugs (see **Sex, Drugs, and Lunar Cycles, p. 415**).

THE SEX INDUSTRY AND AIDS

While traditional gender roles in Thailand are more equally balanced than in many other countries, Thailand has garnered an international reputation for its **sex industry.** Many young girls and boys enter prostitution as an escape from rural poverty; estimates of the number of sex workers in the country vary but range anywhere from 200,000 to nearly 2 million, with the majority of them female. While prostitution has been illegal since 1960, it is tacitly accepted and tolerated, making Thailand a destination for Western and Japanese "sex tours." This industry accounts for an estimated 3 percent of Thailand's economy, or about US $4.3 billion a year, and has numerous links to government corruption and organized crime.

Thailand's sex trade was made all the more controversial due to the growth of the **Acquired Immune Deficiency Syndrome (AIDS)** to epidemic status in parts of Thailand during the late 1990s. By the end of 1999, the combination of thriving sex and intravenous drug industries resulted in 66,000 HIV/AIDS deaths in Thailand, the first country in Southeast Asia to experience the epidemic. Medical researchers warned that the country's AIDS-related deaths would total approximately 286,000 by the beginning of the new millennium, and many feared that the disease was spreading to new sectors of Thai society. Today, these trends are slowly reversing. The effects of safe-sex practices such as condom use, first advocated in the early 1990s by **Senator Mechai Viravaidya** (justly dubbed **"Mr. Condom"**) and his "100 Percent Condom" plan, are now becoming apparent in HIV/AIDS statistics. The use of condoms in commercial sex is up from 14% to over 90%, and protective measures have resulted in a 90% decrease in the rate of sexually transmitted diseases (STDs). The government has thus taken a more pragmatic approach towards its sex industry and HIV/AIDS, creating cooperative partnerships between health workers, police, and sex workers themselves. However, complacency after previous success in the crusade for safer sex spurred a resurgence in infections, and in 2005 Viravaidya announced a new campaign that aims to counter it.

SOUTHERN DISCOMFORT

Although Thais pride themselves on their religious tolerance, their government does not always follow the same path. The southernmost provinces of Thailand—Narathiwat, Pattani, Songhkla, and Yala, once the independent Sultanate of Pattani—only came under Thai rule in 1902 and have been restless ever since. The local population is overwhelmingly Muslim and speaks Yawi, a Malay dialect. Local separatists, angered by heavy-handed nationalist policies under the dictatorship of Phibun Songkhram in the 30s and feeling estranged from the Buddhist Thai government, began a violent insurgency in the 70s. The government under Prem Tinsulanonda in the 80s changed course, emphasizing negotiation, cultural rights, increased funding, and political representation. Violence died down throughout the 90s, but following the disbanding of joint task forces, local governments, and declaration of martial law under Prime Minister Thaksin, there was a resurgence of violence. In January 2004, armed men burned schools, looted weapons, and killed four Thai soldiers in the South. Scattered bombings and shootings plagued the area until the conflict came to a head in April of 2004, with militant raids on police stations and government buildings. The police fought back, killing an estimated 112 poorly-armed fighters. The Prime Minister assumed even more sweeping powers, including the detention of suspects for seven days, censorship of newspapers, and broad wiretapping authority.

The military government following Thaksin took a more conciliatory approach, but violence has continued, fueled by the conflict of previous years, and combined nationalism and religious sentiment. The tendency of insurgents to make no claims on violent attacks and operate under a high level of secrecy compounds the difficulty of negotiation or effective quelling of the violence. The current military regime's refusal to discuss autonomy for the south or begin trials for human rights abuses committed by officials may play a role in the continued conflict. In the meantime, violence is likely to continue, and it is not clear how many more will be added to the current death toll of over 3000.

YOU SAY BURMA, I SAY MYANMAR. In 1989, the Burmese government changed the official name of the country from Burma to Myanmar. The name change has been adopted by most members of the international press, and the country's official UN designation is Myanmar. However, many governments don't recognize the name in a show of non-recognition of the government and refer to it by its traditional name of Burma. For the sake of clarity, *Let's Go: Thailand* uses "Myanmar" when referring to the modern government and territory, and "Burmese" when referring to people, language, or culture.

BORDER RELATIONS

Thailand is bordered by Cambodia, Laos, Malaysia, and Myanmar and has had shaky relationships with each of these countries. From historical battles to present-day policy skirmishes, a variety of events have contributed to the tension often felt around Thailand's 8000km perimeter. Sporadic border disputes with neighbors are sometimes compounded by cultural clashes, like the 2003 riots in Cambodia over a Thai soap opera star's claim that Angkor Wat belonged to Thailand. At the present, however, peace prevails through cooperation on

LIFE AND TIMES

issues such as drug trafficking, membership in the Association of Southeast Asian Nations (ASEAN), and continued good relations abroad with the US.

THAI-BURMESE RELATIONS. Since the Burmese sacked the Thai capital of Ayutthaya in 1767 (p. 161), Thai-Burmese relations have been off-and-on at best. Issues such as illicit drugs and border tensions contribute to the Thai-Burmese bout, as both Thai and Burmese drug lords have long been producing methamphetamine and smuggling it into one another's countries as well as into China and India. The Burmese border area is littered with **landmines,** used by the military regime and the numerous rebel groups fighting against it. Make sure to check with the local tourist authority for information specific to the area you are planning to visit. The border between Thailand and Myanmar has also been crossed by hundreds of thousands of Burmese refugees. These immigrants are a constant presence in the border provinces of Thailand. The devastation wrought by **Cyclone Nargis** in 2008, is likely to complicate this issue even further.

CULTURE

NATIONAL SYMBOLS

ROYALS

In 2001, a Scottish national made the nearly-fatal mistake of urinating on a picture of the king, an action that under Thai law, carries the death penalty. He got lucky and was only deported after substantial jail time, but his ordeal nevertheless stands testament to the fact that Thais hold their royal family—especially the king—in high reverence and view the monarchy as the embodiment of Thai values. Do not speak disparagingly of the Monarchy, and avoid dropping, defacing, or stepping on currency or stamps, which carry the king's portrait. When near a portrait of King Bhumibol or any past Thai king, never raise your head above the head in the portrait. Be especially careful in restaurants and public buses, which are often decorated with royal portraits. In short, don't mess with the man whose name means "Strength of the Land, Incomparable Power."

THE ELEPHANT

Elephants are the good luck charms of Thailand, and are depicted on the national currency and the national flag. In fact, Thailand is geographically shaped like an elephant's head and trunk. White elephants were historically given to the King as a mark of respect and to ensure the success of his reign, and they have come to symbolize not only the monarchy but also national peace and prosperity. This stems from the story that in the night before giving birth to the Buddha, his mother had a dream in which a white elephant came bearing a lotus flower, the symbol of purity and knowledge. Today, March 13 has been set aside as Elephant Day in the hope of raising Thais' awareness about Thailand's declining elephant population.

THE FLAG

Historians believe that the Thai national flag was raised for the first time in 1608, when the country dispatched its first Thai embassy to the Netherlands. In 1816, Singapore declared that Siamese ships needed a more distinctive flag for trading purposes. King Rama II added a white elephant, because of its connotations of sacred royalty, to the make-shift red flag. Nearly a hundred years later, King Rama IV redesigned the flag, choosing five horizontal stripes in white and red. Being both horizontally and vertically symmetrical, the flag could never be flown upside down. The colors of this Trairong (tricolor) flag are said to represent different aspects of Thailand: red for the nation, white for Buddhism, and blue for the monarchy. The official modern flag, which is raised and lowered in daily ceremonies, was declared as such on September 28, 1917.

CUSTOMS AND ETIQUETTE

WAI NOT?

To show respect, put your palms together at chest level, pointing your fingers away from you, and gently bow your head: this is the Thai traditional greeting, called a *wai*. More than just a way to say (hello) *sawadee*, however, the *wai* is a gesture of respect. The degree to which you should bend your waist while performing a *wai* is determined by your social status relative to the person you are greeting. Older people receive lower, and thus more respectful *wais*. Younger people or those of inferior social standing *wai* first. You should never perform a *wai* to a child; you will only embarrass yourself and make everyone around you uncomfortable. That said, the use of the *wai* by foreigners is generally appreciated by Thais and seen more as respectful than inappropriate. The *wai* is also directed towards inanimate objects, like **spirit houses,** because they are believed to bring prosperity, good luck, and protection to one's family.

 TIP **FARANG, FARANG.** Although the origins of the word are uncertain, any Westerner quickly will become familiar with the label "*farang*." Used to refer to foreigners, *farang* is universally applied to all non-Asians. As it is also the word for the white guava fruit, expect "*farang* eating *farang*" jokes if you happen to purchase any.

TABOOS

According to an ancient Hindu belief (now incorporated into Buddhism), the head is the most sacred part of the body, inhabited by the *kwan,* or the spiritual force of life. However tempting it may be in the event of a height difference, a pat on the head in Thailand is neither playful nor cute—it's simply disrespectful. Conversely, the feet are considered the lowest and dirtiest part of the body. Don't point your feet—or cross your legs—toward an image of the Buddha or toward another person, especially if he or she is older. **Shoes,** which are considered to be even more unclean than feet, are unwelcome in temples and most private homes. Also considered "dirty" is the left hand, used only to clean oneself after bodily functions—so don't eat with your left hand!

While Buddha images are available for sale in countless tourist shops, in the past there are restrictions on taking them out of the country. In general, treat the image of the Buddha respectively: never take photographs with one, and keep the Buddha on a high shelf (definitely above foot level). And be warned: as respectful as Thais are of different cultures, Thailand does **imprison** foreigners for actions considered sacrilegious.

HANDS OFF

Women should never touch a monk or give him anything directly, as this will violate an important part of his vows. The way one dresses is also important: clothing should be modest, and men and women should wear long sleeves and pants or skirts when visiting a *wat* (Buddhist temple). Public displays of affection between lovers are frowned upon. Affectionate same-sex caresses or hugs are commonplace and rarely have sexual overtones.

STAND AND DELIVER

Remember your national anthem? Thais certainly remember theirs. Visitors to Thailand are struck by how citizens respond so patriotically to their national anthem and the national flag. Whether they're in the bus station, on the street, or in the market, Thai people stop what they're doing when they hear the anthem. In some smaller cities, traffic comes to a screeching halt. Thailand's flag is raised each morning at 8am and lowered each evening at 6pm to the accompaniment of the national anthem. If you don't stand still, you will never feel more like a *farang*. Respect Thailand's national custom—be still and stand up anytime the anthem is played.

TABLE MANNERS

Thailand is known for its food, and much of Thai life revolves around eating. Customarily, when dining out with a group in Thailand, many dishes are ordered and food is served family-style, as opposed to one dish per person. The oldest or most successful person at the table pays for the meal. Taking a large portion from a communal dish is frowned upon. Most Thai meals are eaten with a spoon in the right hand and a fork in the left, to help guide the food onto the spoon. Chopsticks are only used with noodle dishes.

FOOD

TIP **HOT STUFF.** Thai cuisine's fascination with the chili pepper has been known to cause stomach discomfort or other unsavory digestive problems for the unaccustomed traveler. To avoid potentially painful dining experiences, stay away from smaller, hotter peppers and learn the phrase *mai pet* ("not hot") or *pet nit noy* ("a little hot").

TRADITIONAL DISHES

Thai food is actually a collection of influences and spices from Asia, India, South America, and Europe. The Chinese brought the technique of frying to Southeast Asia and many Thai dishes originated in India.

Traditional Thai food varies from region to region. Although it is a sea-based cuisine, with many of its ingredients (fish, vegetables, and herbs) taken directly from river regions and oceans, Thailand's staple food, just like its Asian neighbors, is rice. "To eat" in Thai is literally "eat rice," or *kin khao*. Even this staple has variations. Those in Central Thailand usually eat plain rice, whereas the Northern Thai specialty is **sticky rice,** or *khao niaw*, a glutinous grain, which is eaten with everything. A **traditional Thai meal** is composed of a harmony of spices, tastes, and textures. It always includes a fish plate, a vegetable dish, a curry with condiments, and soup. By the time they leave the country, backpackers will inevitably have eaten their weight in **pad**

thai, claimed to be Thailand's national dish. Pan-fried noodles, garlic, bean sprouts, ground peanuts, eggs, dried red chili, and shallots are the defining ingredients in this common dish. Fried and **veggie-stuffed** spring rolls, or *po pia thot*, are similarly ubiquitous. **Green curry,** made of lemongrass, coriander root, garlic, green chilis, and galanga, is mixed with meat or fish for another standard meal. Those new to Thai food often become obsessed with **som tam,** a shredded salad from northeastern Thailand, which contains shredded raw papaya, diced long beans, dried shrimp, and toasted peanuts, combined with palm sugar, lemon juice, fish sauce, and hot chilies.

DRINKS

Most meals are served with drinking water, but Thais will often purchase purified bottled water as tap water in places like Bangkok is generally unsafe to drink. When asking for ice, make sure it is made with purified drinking water. Thai **coffee** (*kaafae thom* or *kaafae thung*), both Indian and Chinese teas, and iced lime juice with sugar (*naam manao*) are quite popular in Thailand. Thais drink most fruit juices with a little salt mixed in, so specify *mai sai kleu* ("without salt") if this sounds unappealing. And don't be surprised if your iced drink is handed to you in a plastic bag; unlike spill-prone plastic cups, the bag is perfect for that motorbike ride through the crowded Thai streets. Thai **beer** and **rice whiskey** are also widely consumed. **Singha beer,** whose original, bitter recipe was developed in 1934 by nobleman Phya Bhirom Bhakdi, is by far the most common. For the very brave, there is "white liquor" (*lao khao*), which is made from sticky rice and contains 35% alcohol. Liquors made from herbs, spices, roots, seeds, and fruits can be found throughout the country, often homemade, but be wary: some illegal concoctions have close to 95% alcohol.

THE ARTS

ARCHITECTURE

HISTORY. Thai architecture encompasses a broad range of influences (including Burmese, Chinese, Indian, Sri Lankan, and Khmer) and forms (including royal palaces, wooden houses, and its most common manifestation, religious structures). By the 20th century, increased contact with Europeans led to the steady decline of traditional Thai architecture. Western styles and materials like concrete were adopted, making Thailand's modern architecture remarkably similar to that of modern Western cities. Some intrepid Thai architects do still study historical styles, utilizing modern materials for construction in traditional forms.

A WAT? Buddhist **wats** are the finest examples of traditional Thai architecture. A compound with separate buildings, each with its own distinct purpose, the *wat* has a variety of social functions, including monastery, school, and gathering place for the community. The **bot,** or main chapel, which often faces east, is a tall, oblong building with a three-level, steeply sloped roof that houses the principal Buddha image and serves as the site of most ceremonies. Similar to the *bot* but often larger, the **wihaan** is more sparsely adorned and functions primarily as a worship hall, utilized for meetings, meditation, and sermons. The **sala** is an open, gazebo-like structure for meditation and preaching. Above some monastic compounds looms a tapered spire-like tower, called a **chedi.** Derived from the Indian *stupa*, the *chedi* serves as a reliquary for the possessions and cremated remains of high priests, members of royalty, and the Buddha. Another tower found in Thai architecture is the **prang,** which is more phallic than the bell shaped *chedi.*

Most are constructed of carved sandstone, later replaced by brick, and their various pieces held together by vegetable glue. In the heavily-forested north, however, wood is the major building material. While the most spectacular example of classical Thai religious architecture is Bangkok's intricate and detailed **Wat Phra Kaew** (p. 110), **Wat Benchamabophit** (see p. 113), built in 1899 in Bangkok's Dusit district, is widely considered to be the most impressive example of modern Thai Buddhist architecture.

VISUAL ARTS

SCULPTURE. Ancient Thai sculpture focused largely on the production of Buddha images, emphasizing the spirituality of the image rather than anatomical details. Rigid artistic rules ensured that a relatively uniform tradition passed from generation to generation. The giant seated Buddha at **Wat Sri Chum** (p. 315) is an example of the artistic achievement of the Sukhothai period.

Since southern Thailand lies along maritime trading routes, it developed unique styles of sculpture influenced by Indian and Khmer culture. Khmer artistic traditions, however, have exerted the greatest influence over the sculpture of the northeast. In Thailand, Khmer art is referred to as the **Lopburi style,** which consists of stone and bronze sculptures, mainly of Hindu gods, Bodhisattvas, and Tantric Buddhist deities. Images of the Buddha often portrayed him seated on a coil of the famous seven-headed mythical serpent Muchalinda. Also significant are the distinctive Khmer **lintels** of northeastern temples featuring detailed carvings from Hindu stories.

WEAVING. Even before it became a cottage industry, weaving was an important part of rural life. A woman spent a great deal of time and energy handweaving the material for her wedding dress. Similarly, for the most important day in a man's life, entrance to the monkhood, his mother prepared his saffron robes. The female head of the household also handwove all of the shrouds to be used at the funerals of each family member. For centuries, village women in the northeast bred silkworms and worked at hand looms to produce bolts of traditional Thai silk. Cheaper fabrics imported from China and Japan however, severely weakened the industry in the second half of the 19th century. Revived by famous American expatriate **Jim Thompson** (p. 115) after World War II, the silk industry thrived off its distinctly Thai character in the international market. Today, the company founded by Thompson at **Pak Thong Chai** (p. 208) is still the largest hand-weaving facility in the world. Each region has its own special style and technique, and the most famous Thai silk is woven in the northeast. The **mud-mee** style of silk weaving, characterized by geometrical and zoomorphic designs, is particularly popular.

LITERATURE

HISTORY. The most enduring work of Thai literature is the *Ramakien,* the Thai version of the Indian epic, the *Ramayana.* Early versions of this lengthy document were lost when Ayutthaya was sacked in 1767. Of the three surviving versions, the most famous was written in 1798 by **King Rama I.** This version, written in conjunction with several courtiers who were close to the king, incorporates uniquely Thai and Buddhist and portrays the rites, traditions, and customs of the Ayutthaya state. Given early Thai literature's focus on religion, poet **Sunthon Phu** (1786-1855) revolutionized the tradition with his portrayal of the emotions and adventures of common people in a common language that all classes could understand. His 30,000-line **Phra Aphaimani** is arguably Thailand's most famous literary work; it tells the story of the physical and emotional journey an exiled prince must complete before he can return victorious to his kingdom.

CURRENT SCENE. Modern Thai literature, shaped both by foreign influences and changing perceptions of the individual's place in society, has increasingly sought to address personal and social problems. Former Prime Minister **M.R. Kukrit Pramoj** wrote prolifically. Among his most notable works are **Si Phandin**, describing court life between the reigns of King Rama V and Rama VII, and **Phai Daeng**, about the conflict between Communism and Buddhism. **Seni Saowaphong**, or Sakdichai Bamrungphong, often writes about class exploitation and the widening gulf between the rural and the urban. Similarly, the protagonist of the late **Suwanee Sukhontha's** most famous novel, **Khao Chu Kan**, is a young doctor with a promising career lined up in a big city who leaves to work in a rural area where the peasants have little access to modern medicine. **Krisna Asokesin** also covers more personal topics, writing extensively about issues such as love and family life. All of the aforementioned authors have been awarded National Artist status in Thailand or Southeast Asian literary awards, which speaks to both the accessibility of their styles and the popularity of their subjects.

MUSIC

INSTRUMENTS. Thailand's musical tradition combines elements of the Indian, Chinese, and Khmer traditions and boasts more than 50 kinds of musical instruments. During the Sukhothai period, Thais developed unique instruments with onomatopoetic names such as the **ranaat ek** (a bamboo xylophone), the **phin** (a small guitar), and the **pii** (a woodwind instrument like the clarinet). In the Ayutthaya period, music was an official part of court life as territorial expansion added musical instruments and styles from neighboring regions such as Myanmar, Malaysia, and Java. During this period, rules defining musical forms were introduced. Songs were composed in a form called **phleng raung**, a suite of melodies. Today, three orchestral types of music are appropriate to different occasions order Thai musical form: piphat is used at ceremonies and in the theater; **kruang sai** is used in performance at village festivals; and **mahori** often accompanies vocalists.

Thai music emphasizes variation in pitch and rhythm, with individual changes in tempo creating a dense layering effect. Also, instead of a five-note scale like that used in many other Asian countries, Thai music works on a **seven-note scale.** The music composed in this unique system has been passed down orally, but today, many fear that the institutional memory of traditional Thai music is fading. Many modern Thai musicians are therefore working to invent a system by which traditional Thai music can be translated into Western musical notation and thus recorded for future generations.

T-POP. Contemporary Thai music takes many forms. Regional folk music, studied less frequently than classical music, is still common; one of the most popular styles is **luk thung** (country music), which, much like American country music, tells tales of woe in daily rural life. *Luk thung* has recently developed upbeat electronic versions. In the 1960s, Thai pop collided with folk to create the genre of protest songs, called *plaeng peua chiwit*, or "songs for life," which focused primarily on criticizing the US military presence in Thailand. The Thai student band **Caravan** filled the musical vacuum of the 70s with pro-democracy songs that fused Western and Thai styles. Caravan inspired other bands to take up causes. The most famous rock band in modern Thailand, **Carabao**, also sings about social issues, such as the AIDS crisis. In the late 1980s, there was a movement to promote ethnic Thai pop music. Today, Thailand unusually is a music market where international labels play a minor role. Instead it is Thailand's local giants like Grammy Entertainment that package attractive bubblegum pop and rock *dara* (stars) for mass consumption. One of the most successful contemporary Thai artists is **Tata Young,** a Britney Spears-esque, pop singer.

FILM

A NASCENT INDUSTRY. While cinemas are common in large cities, about 2000 mobile film units travel from village to village in rural areas of Thailand, offering open-air screenings for large numbers of people. Most of the movies shown are either of the Chinese *kung-fu* or Hollywood variety. Thai films—traditionally low-budget productions packing a sensationalist punch—are less popular, though 2001 seems to have been a turning point for the industry, with Thai movies beginning to gain recognition on the international film circuit. *Tropical Malady*, by director Apichatpong Weerasethakul, won the 2004 Jury Prize at Cannes. Co-directed by the Pang brothers from Hong Kong, *Bangkok Dangerous* is a dramatic thriller set to a frenetic techno beat—a change for Thai audiences, who usually favor upbeat comedies. Many film critics have enthusiastically noted the release of director Nonzee Nimibutr's third film, *Jan Dara* (2001, Buddy Films), as possibly indicating a new stage of maturity for the Thai film industry. Based on a novel by journalist Pramoon Un-hathoop (who writes under the pen name of Utsana Pkleungtham), the movie only passed Thailand's film censorship board after repeated screenings. *Jan Dara* ran into trouble with this official body because of the prevalence of sexual themes throughout: the protagonist is caught in a web of Oedipal lusts and primal urges. Prince Chatreechalerm Yukol's 2001 film, *Suriyothai*, details the life of a young princess as a 16th-century battle for the throne of Thailand rages above her head. It marked a transition for the Thai film industry to big budget blockbusters.

HOLLYWOOD GOES EAST. Thailand has long inspired Hollywood stories (including the Thai-banned 1956 musical *The King and I*) and movie shoots (*Bridget Jones: The Edge of Reason*, for example). The Thai government has begun to actively promote the shooting of foreign films in Thailand because of its economic benefits; however, all scripts have to be approved. Numerous Western productions are expected to film in Thailand annually. The potential environmental damage from the shooting of large commercial films and Western television shows (such as 2002's *Survivor*) is becoming a concern to both the government and local NGOs. Indeed, an uproar arose after Danny Boyle's 2000 film *The Beach* was shot on location on Ko Phi Phi Don, a small island accessible from Phuket (p. 376). The island, once largely unnoticed, filled up with garbage, guesthouses, and tourists so quickly that the government considered closing it down for a year. So far, development has reigned unchecked on the island, which is part of a national park system. A slew of backpacker-friendly businesses and services have cropped up all over the island, irreversibly transforming its once-unspoiled landscape.

SPORTS AND RECREATION

MUAY THAI (THAI BOXING)

Muay Thai is a martial art that was originally used as a way to keep Thai soldiers battle-ready during the 15th and 16th centuries. The first boxer to win historic recognition was **Nai Khanom Tom.** Captured by the Burmese, he won his freedom after dispatching 10 Burmese soldiers one by one in a boxing challenge. *Muay Thai* reached the peak of its popularity in the first decade of the 18th century during the reign of Phra Chau Sua, who promoted it as a national sport. Due to an alarming number of injuries and deaths, though, *Muay Thai* was banned in the 1920s. It was reinstated in 1937, after undergoing a series of regulations that shaped the sport to its present form. Today these fights, full of ritual, music, and blood, are put on display throughout Thailand. Every blow imaginable, with the exception of head-butting, is legal. Fighters exchange blows for five three-minute rounds; the winner either knocks out his victim or takes the bout by points (most bouts are decided in the latter manner). Fights are packed with screaming fans, most of whom have money riding on the outcome. While many provinces have venues, most of the best fighting occurs in Bangkok's **Ratchadamnoen** and **Lumphini Boxing Stadiums.**

TRADITIONAL PASTTIMES

Every year during the hot season, a strong wind lifts handmade **kites** high over Bangkok. **Kite-fighting,** which has been popular for over 700 years, is enjoyed by kings and schoolboys alike. In a more gruesome fight, crowds watch and bet on **Siamese fighting fish.** When let loose in a tank, these fish battle to the death in a flurry of fins and scales. The fish are so aggressive that they will often kill themselves trying to attack fish in nearby tanks. The fighting fish have been raised in Thailand since the Sukhothai period and breeders are constantly developing new varieties. Their international popularity is a great source of pride. Thais also embrace karaoke, beauty pageants (for every shape and size), comedy clubs, and, especially in the countryside, cockfighting.

HOLIDAYS AND FESTIVALS (2009)

The Thai, Buddhist, and international holidays listed below are current as of this book's date of publication. Many of the religious days, whose dates are not determined by a lunar cycle, will be given a date by the Royal Family or religious centers at the beginning of 2009. The listed dates are subject to change. Be sure to check with the Tourism Authority of Thailand before attending one of the festivals or holiday celebrations. Note that on national holidays, most establishments and all banks are closed.

DATE	NAME AND LOCATION	DESCRIPTION
Jan. 1	New Year's Day	International celebration of the passing year.
Jan. 18-20	Bosang Umbrella Festival, Chiang Mai	Spirited fair celebrating Bosang's famous umbrellas, complete with crafts and contests.
Jan. 26	Chinese New Year	Fourth waxing day in the first lunar month. Celebrated by nearly all of Thailand, as many Thais are of Chinese descent. Most businesses close for at least three days.
Jan 29th.	Dragon and Lion Parade, Nakhon Sawan	A Golden Dragon, lion, and ancient deities parade with bands and the Chinese community.
Feb. 7-9	Flower Festival, Chiang Mai	Thailand's floral float and beauty pageant extravaganza.
Feb. 23	Makha Bucha	Full moon of third lunar month. Commemoration of the 1250 disciples of Buddha coming to hear him preach. Public holiday.

Late Feb.	Late Phra Nakhon Khiri Fair, Phetchaburi	9-day local celebration featuring historical monarch processions, cooking demonstrations, and entertainment.
Mar. 13th	National Thai Elephant Day	A day to raise awareness about and commemorate Thailand's national animal.
Mar.-Apr.	Poi Sang Long, Mae Hong Son	Stunning Shan tribal celebration of the ordainment of boys as novice monks.
Apr.	Pattaya Festival, Phuket	Delicious food, floral floats, and fireworks.
Apr. 6	Chakri Day	National holiday to commemorate the acension of the first king of the present dynasty to the throne.
Apr. 13-15	Songkran, Thai New Year	Best in Chiang Mai, the holiday is known for water: washing with scented water and throwing water at everyone.
May	Boon Bang Fai Rocket Festival, Yasothon	Celebration for a plentiful upcoming rain season for rice-planting. Homemade rockets launched.
May 1	Labor Day	Banks, factories, and offices closed.
May 5	Coronation Day	National holiday.
May 11	Royal Ploughing Ceremony, Bangkok	Official beginning of rice-planting outside the Royal Palace, with re-enactments of ancient Brahman rituals. Government holiday.
May 22-23	Visakhabucha	Full moon of sixth lunar month. Birth, enlightenment, and death of Buddha. Holiest holiday, celebrated at every temple with candlelight processions.
May-June	Wai Kru Day	Usually a Thursday, specific date varies from school to school. A day for students to honor their teachers for their important role in children's lives.
June	Phi Ta Khon, Dan Sai, Loei	People dress as spirits and carry Buddha images while monks read the story of the visit of his incarnation.
July 22	Khao Pansa Day: Buddhist Lent begins. Candle Festival, Ubon Ratchathani	Townspeople celebrate the monks' Buddhist Rains Retreat by walking up to the temple with huge ornate candles. A time of giving up indulgences, the first day is commemorated with particular attention by students.
Aug. 1-10	Rambutan Fair, Surat Thani	Anniversary of the first rambutan tree planted in Surat Thani is commemorated with fruit floats and performing monkeys.
Aug.	Cake Festival	Chamber of Commerce holiday for Southern Thailand's yummy pastries.
Aug. 12	The Queen's Birthday, Mother's Day	Best celebration is in Bangkok, where the city is draped in lights. Thais celebrate their queen's birthday by honoring their own mothers.
Sept.	Barbecue Festival	Chamber of Commerce holiday for Thai food.
Sept.	Boat Races, Phichit	Annual regatta down the Nan River.
Oct.	Buffalo Races, Chonburi	Water buffaloes stop work and race each other and farmers.
Oct.	Wax Castle and Boat Racing Festival, Sakhon Nakhon	Procession of beeswax carvings of Buddhist temples to mark the end of the Buddhist Rains Retreat, followed by regatta.
Early Oct.	Vegetarian Festival, Phuket	Chinese festival enjoyed since the 1800s with parades, rituals, and, of course, vegetarian food to honor two emperor gods.
Mid-Oct.	Nakhon Phanom Boat Procession	Evening ritual in which thousands of exquisitely carved boats adorned with lights are launched on the Mekong.

Oct. 23	Chulalongkorn Day	National holiday commemorating the death of King Rama V.
Nov.	Hill tribe Festival, Chiang Rai	Cultural performances and handicrafts.
Nov.	Loi Krathong & Candle Festival	Best in Sukhothai, where it originated, with fireworks and folk dancing. Also good in Ayutthaya and Chiang Mai.
Nov.	Elephant Roundup, Surin	Celebration of the revered animal, with performances by over 100 elephants, even some in costume.
Dec.	World Heritage Site celebration.	Celebration of the past with exhibitions and traditional performances
Dec.	Trooping of the Colors, Bangkok	In the Royal Plaza, the elite Royal Guards, dressed in bright colors, renew their allegiance to the Royal Family.
Early Dec.	River Kwai Bridge Week, Kanchanaburi	Remembrance of the site, with historical and archaeological exhibitions; rides on vintage trains.
Dec. 5	His Majesty's birthday, Father's Day	Thais celebrate the king's birthday by honoring their own fathers.
Dec. 10	Constitution Day	The flag flies prominently among a plethora of bright lights to commemorate the country's transition to constitutional monarchy. National holiday.
Dec. 25	Christmas	Not a public holiday, but celebrated by schoolchildren.

ADDITIONAL RESOURCES

GENERAL HISTORY

The Chastening: Inside the Financial Crisis that Rocked the Global Financial System and Humbled the IMF, by Paul Blustein (2002). A cogent study of the Asian Financial Crisis.

Thailand's Durable Premier: Phibun through Three Decades 1932-1957, by Kobkua Suwannathat-Pian (1996). A biography of Thailand's most controversial and influential political leader, Field Marshal Phibunsongkhram.

The Lands of Charm and Cruelty: Travels in Southeast Asia, by Stan Sesser (1994). A collection of compelling essays originally published in The New Yorker.

Modern Thailand: A Volume in the Comparative Societies Series, by Robert Slagter and Harold Kerbo (1999). A review of contemporary Thai institutions and social change.

Thailand: A Short History, by David Wyatt (1982). An excellent history of Thailand.

CULTURE

When Elephants Paint: The Quest of Two Russian Artists to Save the Elephants of Thailand, by Dave Eggers, Vitaly Komar, and Alexander Melamid (2000). This book tells the artists' story of their struggle to support Thai elephant sanctuaries with profits made by the elephants themselves through the sale of their jumbo-sized artistic masterpieces.

Genders and Sexualities in Modern Thailand, ed. by Peter Jackson and Nerida Cook (2000). Essays interpreting roles and patterns of gender in Thailand since the 1800s.

Peoples of the Golden Triangle: Six Tribes in Thailand, by Paul and Elaine Lewis (1998). A historiography of local hill tribes in northern Thailand, with personal vignettes.

Endangered Relations: Negotiating Sex and AIDS in Thailand, by Chris Lyttleton (2000). Describes the intersection of Thai conceptions of sexuality and public health measures to reverse the nation's infamous AIDS/HIV trend.

The Buddhist World of Southeast Asia, by Donald Swearer (1995). A comprehensive academic text covering Buddhist scripture and tenets, the relationship between Buddhism and the government, and the changes in Buddhism in the past 30 years.

Very Thai: Everyday Popular Culture, by Philip Cornwel-Smith (2005). Great photographs offset colorful text in this book on pop culture in Thailand.

FICTION AND NON-FICTION

Singing to the Dead: A Missioner's Life Among Refugees from Burma, by Victoria Armour-Hilleman (2002). Journal of a missionary working with Mon refugees in an illegal camp.

4,000 Days: My Life and Survival in a Bangkok Prison, by Warren Fellows (1998). True story of an Australian who was caught trafficking heroin and spent 12 years in jail.

The Beach, by Alex Garland (1997). A thrilling narcotics adventure about backpackers in search of paradise. A perfect beach read.

Ban Vinai, by Lynellyn Long (1992). Narrative based on the author's ethnographic research in Ban Vinai, a Thai camp sheltering Lao and Cambodian refugees.

Silk Umbrellas, by Carolyn Marsden (2004). Children's book about a young girl's attempt to help contribute to her struggling family. Contains a small glossary of Thai terms.

Thaksin: The Business of Politics in Thailand (2004). A study of controversial former Prime Minister Thaksin Shinawatra.

Monsoon Country, by Pira Sudham (1988). Personal account of the period of tumult and revolution experienced by Thai culture and politics from 1954-1980. Sudham was nominated for the Nobel Prize for this work. His *People of Esarn* (1987) is highly informative background reading for those traveling to northeast Thailand.

The Force of Karma, by Pira Sudham (2001). The sequel to *Monsoon Country*, depicting the Thai massacres of 1973, 1976 and 1992.

A Fortune-Teller Told Me: Earthbound Travels in the Far East, by Tiziano Terzani (2001). A journalist's trek through Southeast Asia, focusing on myths, religions, and mysticism.

Siam: Or the Woman Who Shot a Man, by Lily Tuck (2000). A novel highlighting cultural misunderstandings and an obsession with a lost American entrepreneur.

FILM

The Bridge on the River Kwai, directed by David Lean, starring Sir Alec Guinness and William Holden (1957). WWII epic based on a true story about Allied POWs forced to build a bridge connecting Thailand to Burma. The film won seven Academy Awards, including Best Picture, and brings hundreds of tourists to flock to Kanchanaburi annually.

The Iron Ladies, directed by Youngyooth Thongkonthun (2000). A comedy about an underdog volleyball team, composed mostly of gays, transvestites, and transsexuals.

Mysterious Object at Noon, conceived and directed by Weerasethakul (2001). Fiction tale crafted by the many people the director encountered as he traveled through the Thai countryside. Documentary film provides a glimpse into Thai traditions and culture.

Ong Bak: Thai Warrior, directed by Prachya Pinkaew (2003). Action film follows a Muay Thai boxer as he tracks down his village's stolen Buddha statue.

Suriyothai, directed by Chatrichalerm Yukol (2001). Historical epic set in the Ayutthaya period that follows events in the life of Queen Suriyothai.

Tropical Malady, directed by Apichatpong Weerasethakul (2004). This surrealist film won the Jury Prize at Cannes in 2004.

TRAVEL BOOKS

Dream of a Thousand Lives: A Sojourn in Thailand, by Karen Connelly (2001). A young Western woman's experience working and studying on a small Thai farm.

Travelers' Tales: Thailand, ed. by James O'Reilly and Larry Habegger (1993). Collection of stories about Thailand, Thai culture, and traveling.

Travels in the Skin Trade: Tourism and the Sex Industry, by Jeremy Seabrook (2001). In-depth look at the relationship between tourism, Western media, and the sex industry.

Thailand: The Golden Kingdom, by William Warren and Luca Tettoni (1999). Photograph-filled travel companion book that details Thai art, history, and culture.

ON THE WEB

Tourism Authority of Thailand (www.tourismthailand.org). Official website of TAT is possibly the best launching pad for information on visiting Thailand, containing travel tips, a constantly updated events list, and a general overview of the country.

Thailand Youth Hostel Association (www.tyha.org). The name says it all: solid budget accommodations. Individual hostel information and Internet booking available.

LIFE AND TIMES

BEYOND TOURISM

A PHILOSOPHY FOR TRAVELERS

HIGHLIGHTS OF BEYOND TOURISM IN THAILAND

STIR-FRY the meanest *pad thai* in Siam. (p. 83).

HIKE through a rainforest on a wildlife rescue mission (p. 77).

VOYAGE through Isaan and teach English at a village school (p. 85).

Sure, hostel-hopping and sightseeing can be great fun, but connecting with a foreign country through studying, volunteering, or working can extend your travels beyond the tourist traps. We don't like to brag, but this is what's different about a *Let's Go* traveler. Instead of feeling like a stranger in a strange land, you can understand Thailand like a local. Instead of being that tourist asking for directions, you can be the one who gives them (and correctly!). All the while, you get the satisfaction of leaving Thailand in better shape than you found it. It's not wishful thinking—it's Beyond Tourism.

As a volunteer in Thailand, you can help out doing everything from rescuing sea turtles in Ranong to building homes in Nakhon Ratchasima. This chapter is chock-full of ideas to get involved, whether you're looking to pitch in for a day or run away from home for a whole new life in Thai activism.

Thailand is also a great place to study abroad. Not only is the experience incredibly valuable, but English courses are a well-established part of Thai education, and more Western students are currently enrolling in Thailand than ever before.

Working abroad immerses you in a new culture and can bring some of the most meaningful relationships and experiences of your life. Yes, we know you're on vacation, but these aren't your normal desk jobs. However, those considering working in developing countries should remember that employment is already scarce for locals, and *Let's Go* encourages you to take work only where your particular knowledge, whether that be English or some other skill, will aid development rather than hinder it.

 SHARE YOUR EXPERIENCE. Have you had a particularly enjoyable volunteer, study, or work experience that you'd like to share with other travelers? Post it to our website, www.letsgo.com!

VOLUNTEERING

Feel like saving the world this week? Volunteering can be a powerful and fulfilling experience, especially when combined with the thrill of traveling in a new place. Thailand is rich in culture and history, but it also has significant concerns related to conservation, development, and health. Luckily, for every problem it faces, there exist a number of organizations actively working to combat that concern. The chance to become a part of their efforts can be challenging but exhilarating.

Most people who volunteer in Thailand do so on a short-term basis with organizations that make use of drop-in or once-a-week volunteers. The best way to find opportunities that match your interests and schedule may be to check classifieds in the *Bangkok Post*, look for listings through universities, or ask at local organizations. Environmental conservation and poverty relief are two of the most popular areas for volunteers, or search the web to find others. As always, read up before heading out.

Those looking for longer, more intensive volunteer opportunities usually choose to go through a parent organization that, for a fee, takes care of logistical details and often provides a group environment and support system. There are two main types of organizations—religious and secular—although there are rarely restrictions on participation in either. Websites like **www.volunteerabroad.com**, **www.servenet.org**, and **www.idealist.org** allow you to search for volunteer openings both in your country and abroad.

I HAVE TO PAY TO VOLUNTEER? Many volunteers are surprised to learn that some organizations require large fees or "donations," but don't go calling them scams just yet. While such fees may seem ridiculous at first, they often keep the organization afloat, covering airfare, room, board, and administrative expenses for the volunteers. (Other organizations must rely on private donations and government subsidies.) If you're concerned about how a program spends its fees, request an annual report or finance account. A reputable organization won't refuse to inform you of how volunteer money is spent. Pay-to-volunteer programs might be a good idea for young travelers who are looking for more support and structure (such as pre-arranged transportation and housing) or anyone who would rather not deal with the uncertainty of creating a volunteer experience from scratch.

ENVIRONMENTAL AND WILDLIFE CONSERVATION

Thailand is known for its beautiful and diverse environment and wildlife; unfortunately, both are currently threatened by development. The organizations below offer volunteer activities related to conservation in Thailand, from preserving elephant habitats to monitoring turtle hatchings.

Earthwatch, 3 Clocktower Pl. Ste. 100, Box 75, Maynard, MA 01754, USA (☎+1-800-776-0188 or 978-461-0081; www.earthwatch.org). Arranges 1- to 3-week programs to promote conservation of natural resources and historical heritage. Offers a few volunteer programs in Thailand. Fees vary based on location and duration; costs average $1500-3000, not including airfare.

Elephant Nature Park (☎053 699 125; www.rejoicecharity.com), 60 km north of Chiang Mai, a sanctuary and rehabilitation center, accpets volunteers for any period of time.

Omprakash Foundation, 112 Rosebrook Rd., New Canaan, CT 06840, USA (☎+1-203-554-0350; www.omprakash.org). Started by college undergraduates, this group provides opportunities to volunteer at rural schools in Thailand.

Wild Animal Rescue Foundation of Thailand, 65/1 3rd fl. Pridi Banomyong Building, Sukhumvit 55, Klongton, Wattana, Bangkok 10110, Thailand (☎02 712 9515 or 02 7 12 9715; www.warthai.org). Recruits volunteers to work with various animal conservation projects throughout Thailand. Projects with gibbons, elephants, and sea turtles.

THAILAND'S AIDS FIGHT

In 1974, Mechai Viravaidya founded the Population and Community Development Association (PDA) to run family-planning programs in rural areas of Thailand. There are now 16 regional centers and branch offices throughout the country. Recently, he has started programs aimed at teenagers, factory workers, and hill-tribe villagers. The modern PDA is focused on the community, tending to every element of the larger picture. Mechai has been a senator, a cabinet member in the Prime Minister's administration, a visiting scholar at Harvard University, and a senior economist for the Southeast Asia region. In 1997, he was given the United Nations Population Award for outstanding contribution to population solutions and questions. He sits on the board of the Narcotics Control Foundation, is a trustee of the International Rice Research Institute, and is the Chairman of the Society for the Prevention of Cruelty to Animals. He is also the "Condom King," a symbol for activism and, of course, safe sex.

Thailand's first AIDS case was discovered in 1984. By the late 1980s, one-third of Thailand's 200,000-400,000 intravenous drug users was infected with HIV. A sex industry had facilitated the disease's rapid spread through the general population. In 1987, using techniques perfected during his family-planning campaign of the 1970s, Mechai Viravaidya and his PDA launched an AIDS prevention campaign.

At an international AIDS conference in Montreal in 1989, Mechai called for a massive public education campaign about AIDS in Thailand. While the government stalled, Mechai continued anti-AIDS activism. PDA staff awarded t-shirts to the winners of condom-blowing contests. They opened popular Cabbages & Condoms restaurants with condom decor and appropriately named dishes. Captain Condom cruised the go-gos in Patpong, Bangkok's red light district, urging customers to practice safe sex. Mechai even crowned a queen in the Miss Condom beauty contest.

The epidemic in Thailand reached a turning point in 1991, when Prime Minister Anand Panyarachun made AIDS prevention a national priority at the highest level. The Prime Minister chaired a National AIDS Committee. The media, government, and non-government organizations (NGOs) promoted 100% condom use in commercial sex. The campaign reduced visits to prostitutes by half, raised condom usage, cut cases of STDs dramatically, and achieved significant reductions in HIV transmission.

In 1991, the number of new HIV infections was almost 150,000 annually. In 2000, that number was less than 30,000. The Ministry of Public Health's epidemiological surveillance system (used to track the progression of a communicable disease) proved a critical tool in generating public awareness and political commitment. Effective pilot projects helped ensure that policy led to the right outcome, and the NGO community played a key role in non-discrimination, respect for human rights, and a political dialogue on AIDS.

With one million infected since the start of the pandemic, Thailand is still one of the world's hardest-hit countries. Today, over 700,000 Thais live with HIV or AIDS—approximately 2% of Thai men and 1% of Thai women. Without heroes like the Condom King, the tragedy would be far worse.

For over a decade, the United States Armed Forces Research for Medical Science and the Atlanta-based Centers for Disease Control have collaborated with colleagues in the Armed Forces in Thailand and the Ministry of Public Health, as well as the private sector, to fight HIV/AIDS. International collaboration has been important since the 1997 Asian financial crisis, when Thailand cut its HIV/AIDS budget by nearly 30%. HIV prevalence among intravenous drug users is approaching 50%. Some Buddhist monasteries take in AIDS sufferers who have run out of money and have nowhere else to go. The task of prevention and care is far from complete and, unless efforts are sustained and sources of infection addressed, the control over the epidemic could be at risk. Still, Thailand's response to the epidemic is one of the world's few examples of an effective national AIDS prevention program. Mechai Viravaidya's condom crusade has helped save millions of lives, both Thai and foreign.

The PDA (www.pda.or.th) is devoted to fighting the AIDS epidemic, and to community involvement and activism. See **Beyond Tourism**, p. 76 for more information.

-Ted Osius

URBAN ISSUES

Although Thailand's urban areas are the first to benefit from economic development and foreign investment, problems like persistent poverty and uneven economic improvement remain. One organization that seeks to address these issues is **The Human Development Foundation,** 100/11 Kae-ha Klong Toey 4, Dhamrongratthaphiphat Rd., Klong Toey, Bangkok 10110, Thailand (☎02 671 5313; www.mercycentre.org). Devoted to the grassroots development of Bangkok's poorest neighborhood, Klong Toey. The founder, Father Maier, constantly needs donations and volunteers for his schools, HIV/AIDS and drug prevention programs, legal aid projects, and infirmaries.

RURAL DEVELOPMENT

From government-instituted programs to the work of non-governmental organizations, Thailand has an array of initiatives working on improving education, health care, and sustainable environmental practices throughout the country.

Lattitude, 44 Queen's Road, Reading, Berkshire RG1 4BB, UK (☎+44 01 189 59 49 14; www.lattitude.org.uk). Formerly known as Gap Activity Projects, organizes volunteer work placements for those aged 17-25 in a "gap year" after secondary education. Programs are 3-6 months in length and cost about US$2400. Financial aid is available. For British, Irish, Australian, Canadian, and New Zealand passport-holders only.

Global Service Corps, 300 Broadway Ste. 28, San Francisco, CA 94133, USA (☎+1-415-788-3666, ext. 128; www.globalservicecorps.org). Programs and internships in education, health care, and service learning (can be specialized) last 2-9 weeks and range US$2200-4700.

Habitat for Humanity International, 121 Habitat St., Americus, GA 31709, USA (☎+1-800-422-4828; www.habitat.org). 253 Asoke Building, 12th Floor, Sukhumvit 21 (Asoke), Klongoey, Wattanan Bangkok 10110, Thailand (☎02 664 0644). Offers extensive opportunities in Thailand and Southeast Asia to live and build houses in a host community.

Institute for Cultural Ecology Internships, P.O. Box 991, Hilo, HI 96721, USA (☎+1-808-577-1743; www.cultural-ecology.com). Offers internships to American and Canadian citizens in fields from journalism to ecology. Positions last from 4 weeks to 1 year.

Peace Corps, Paul D. Coverdell Peace Corps Headquarters, 1111 20th St. NW, Washington, D.C. 20526, USA (☎+1-800-424-8580; www.peacecorps.gov). Opportunities in 71 developing nations, including Thailand and the Philippines. Volunteers must be US citizens age 18+ willing to make a 27-month commitment. A bachelor's degree is strongly recommended.

Voluntary Service Overseas Canada, 844 Eccles Street, Suite 100 Ottawa ON K1R 6S4 Canada (☎+1-613-234-1364 or 888-876-2911; www.vsocan.org). Opportunities to work in Thailand and Southeast Asia on a wide range of projects. Most youth volunteer positions are for Canadian residents and last 6 months; professional overseas volunteer positions by application, for those 21 years or older, last from 7 months to 2 years. VSO covers all expenses; stipend provided.

GoEco, Rozanis 13, Tel Aviv, Israel (☎ +97 20 36 47 42 08; www.goeco.org). Offers volunteer tourism opportunities across the world. In Thailand, their program focuses on educating rural children. English-speaking volunteers welcome. Fees from US$800-2000 cover accommodation and other expenses.

YOUTH AND THE COMMUNITY

Due to widespread poverty and instability, children in Thailand are particularly vulnerable to exploitation, neglect, and abuse. Statistics indicate that anywhere from 60,000 to 200,000 Thai children are involved in prostitution, and 289,000 have been orphaned as a result of AIDS. Many organizations are involved in child welfare in Thailand, especially centers and orphanages that seek to provide children with both nurturing homelife and education.

Baan Kingkaew Orphanage (☎053 275 650, www.baan-kingkaew-orphanage.org), 75 Wualai Rd., 100m southwest of the Chiang Mai Gate. You don't have to call in advance. If you show up around 2:30pm, after the children's afternoon nap, you can play with them until 6pm or so. Most of them are between 2 and 4 years old. Food or toy donations are also welcomed. For any other questions about volunteering, ask at Eagle House in Chiang Mai (See, **Accommodations,** (p. 272)).

Chaiyapruk Foundation, 32/2 Moo 1, Soi Chadsan Thaharnrua, Sukhumvit 103, Bangkok 10260, Thailand (☎02 328 0272; www.geocities.com/chaiyaprukhome). An orphanage run by 2 doctors that maintains a home and school for about 30 children. Volunteers accepted.

Fountain of Life, 3/199 Moo 6 Naklua, Banglamung, Chonburi 20150, Thailand (☎38 361 720; www.fountainoflifepattaya.com). A daycare center that strives to provide children from the slums of Pattaya with health care and counseling.

Pattaya Orphanage Trust, 124 North End House, Fitzjames Avenue, London W14 ORZ UK, (☎+44 020 7602 6203; www.pattayaorphanage.org.uk). The UK-based trust supports orphanages in Pattaya, Rayong, and Nong Khai. The orphanage needs long-term volunteers to undertake responsibilities from taking care of babies to teaching English at the Vocational School for the Physically Handicapped.

Right to Play, 65 Queen Street West, Thomson Building, Ste. 1900, Box 64, Toronto, Ontario, M5H 2M5 Canada (☎+1-416-498-1922; www.righttoplay.com). A Canadian organization that uses sports to enhance child development in 23 countries around the world, including Thailand. Volunteers accepted for 1-year positions.

Tree of Life, 166/23 Na Watpa, Amphur Muang, Changwat, Buriram 31000, Thailand (☎44 617 011; www.treeoflifeorphanage.com). A small home orphanage in northern Thailand. Volunteers welcome.

MEDICAL OUTREACH

Recent estimates suggest that 580,000 people in Thailand are living with HIV/AIDS, including 16,000 children, and this is merely one of the health-related concerns that plagues the country. Additionally, the costs of medical treatment for those not covered by insurance can be staggering. The following organizations all work towards the improvement of health care in Thailand.

Operation Smile, 6435 Tidewater Dr., Norfolk, VA 23509, USA (☎+1-888-677-6453 or 757-321-7645; www.operationsmile.org). 153/3 Goldenland Building, 5th Floor, Soi Mahardlek Luang 1, Rajadamri Road, Pathumwan, Bangkok 10330 Thailand (☎02 6522 8367). Provides reconstructive surgery and related health care. Trains and educates health-care professionals in Thailand, Cambodia, the Philippines, and Vietnam.

Population and Community Development Association, 8 Sukhumvit, Soi 12, Bangkok 10110, Thailand (☎02 229 4611; www.sli.unimelb.edu.au/pda). Programs specializing in everything from environmental research to family planning and AIDS education.

Rejoice Charity, Rejoice Urban Development Project 39/10 Moo 4, T. Suthep A. Muang, Chiang Mai 50200, Thailand (☎05 327 3053; www.rejoicethailand.org). This project brings greatly needed medical welfare resources to those suffering directly and indirectly from AIDS.

STUDYING

There's no better way to break your educational routine than to spend a few months on the other side of the world. And more students than ever are flocking overseas to study nearly every subject imaginable, in universities from Bangkok to Pathum Thani. You're sure to see both Thailand and your studies in a whole new light, no matter which classes you take.

Study-abroad programs range from basic language and culture courses to university-level classes, often for college credit. In order to choose a program that best fits your needs, research as much as you can before making your decision—determine costs and duration, as well as the type of students that participate in the program and what sorts of accommodations are provided.

In programs that have large groups of students who speak the same language, there is a trade-off. You may feel more comfortable in the community, but you will not have the same opportunity to practice a foreign language or to befriend other international students. For accommodations, dorm life provides a better opportunity to mingle with fellow students, but there is less of a chance to experience the local scene. If you live with a family, you could potentially build lifelong friendships with natives and experience day-to-day life in more depth, but you might also get stuck sharing a room with their pet iguana. Conditions can vary greatly from family to family.

UNIVERSITIES

Most university-level study-abroad programs are conducted in Thai, although many programs offer classes in English as well as courses geared toward non-fluent Thai speakers. Savvy linguists may find it cheaper to enroll directly in a university abroad, although getting college credit may be more difficult. You can search **www.studyabroad.com** for various semester-abroad programs that meet your criteria, including your desired location and focus of study. If you're a college student, your local study-abroad office is often the best place to start.

AMERICAN PROGRAMS

AFS International Programs, 71 West 23rd St., 17th fl., New York, NY 10010-4102, USA (☎+1-800-237-4636 or 212-807-8668; www.afs.org). Runs study abroad and community service programs for both students and educators in Thailand. Volunteers live with host families, and programs last from several months to 1 year. Cost varies widely based on program type and duration.

Council on International Educational Exchange (CIEE), 300 Fore St., Portland, ME 04101, USA (☎+1-207-553-4000 or 1-800-407-8839; www.ciee.org). One of the most comprehensive resources for work, academic, and internship programs around the world, including in Thailand.

BEYOND TOURISM

Lexia International, 6 The Courtyard, Hanover, NH 03755, USA. (☎+1-800-775-3942 or 603-643-9899; www.lexiaintl.org). Students live at Pyap University in Chiang Mai, study Thai, and choose a field research project in Thai culture. Application fee US$40.

Where There Be Dragons, 3200 Carbon Place, Suite #1, Boulder, CO 80301, USA (☎+1-800-928-9203; www.wheretherebedragons.com). Runs youth summer programs and short adult trips to Cambodia, Laos, Thailand, and Vietnam. Youth programs cost US$6000-6500. Adult programs cost US$3500-5000. Fee includes food, accommodations, and travel.

THAI PROGRAMS

Most Thai universities that will accept foreign students are in Bangkok and Chiang Mai, although other universities occasionally offer international programs. The universities below offer programs that foreign students can apply to directly and have classes taught in English.

Assumption University, 592 Ramkhamhaeng 24, Hua Mak, Bangkok 10240, Thailand (☎02 300 4553; www.au.edu). This Catholic university runs August, summer, and January sessions.

Chulalongkorn University, Jamjuree 4 Building, 4th fl., Phyathai Rd., Bangkok 10330, Thailand (☎2218 3331; www.inter.chula.ac.th/index.htm). Foreign students can apply directly to the University thorough its Office of International Affairs. Enrollment fees vary by department.

International Association for the Exchange of Students for Technical Experience (IAESTE), 1518 Piboonsongkram Rd., Bangsue, Bangkok 10800, Thailand (☎02 912 2009; www.iaeste.org, www.kmitnb.ac.th/iaeste). Chances are that your home country has a local office; contact it to apply for hands-on technical internships in Thailand. You must be a college student studying science, technology, or engineering. "Cost of living allowance" covers most non-travel expenses. Most programs last 8-12 weeks.

Payap University, Lumpang Rd., Amphur Muang, Chiang Mai 50000, Thailand (☎53 241 255; http://ic.payap.ac.th). Foreign students can enroll either in the Thai and Southeast Asian Studies program or directly into the International College.

Rangsit University, 52/347 Muang-Ake, Paholyothin Rd. Lak-Hok, Pathumthani 12000 Thailand (☎02 997 2200; www.rsu.ac.th). The International College offers international students the opportunity to study alongside Thai nationals in subjects ranging from business to philosophy.

Thammasat University, Dome Building, 2 Phrachan Rd., Phranakorn, Bangkok, 10200 Thailand (☎02 613 2009; interaffairs.tu.ac.th). Offers Thai Studies Program open to International students. All classes are taught in English.

LANGUAGE SCHOOLS

Enrolling at a language school has two major perks: a slightly less rigorous courseload and the promise that you'll learn exactly what those kids in Chiang Mai are calling you under their breath. There is a great variety in language schools—independently run, affiliated with a larger university, local, international—but they rarely offer college credit. These programs are best for younger high-school students out of place among older students in a university program. Some worthy organizations (mostly in Bangkok) include:

American University Alumni Language Center (AUA), 179 Rajatami Rd., Bangkok 10330, Thailand (☎02 528 1703); www.auathailand.org). This respected language center offers different levels of Thai instruction for anywhere between 30-200hr. of study. AUA has locations throughout Thailand.

Baan Phaasaa Thai (Thai Language House), 2 Sukhimvit Rd., Rm. 18-19 Ploenchit Center, Klogtoey, Bangkok 10110, Thailand (☎02 656 7719; www.thailanguagehouse. com). This school offers private tutoring or group sessions 3-5 times per week.

Berlitz Language Center, Silom Complex, 22nd fl., Silom Rd., Bangkok 10500, Thailand (☎02 653 3611; www.berlitz.com). This reputable language center boasts 5 locations in Bangkok.

Union Language Center, 328 Church of Christ Thailand Office Building, 7th fl., Phayathay Rd., Rajchathewi, Bangkok 10400, Thailand (☎02 233 4482). This center's 4-week, 80hr. courses are taught in Thai.

COOKING SCHOOLS

Thai cooking courses can last anywhere from one day to two weeks. The shorter classes usually cover basic curries, while the longer classes coach you through more complex Thai dishes. One-day course 700-900฿; recipe book usually included.

A Lot of Thai, 165 Lampoon Rd., Soi 9, T. Nonghoi Muang, Chiang Mai 50000, Thailand (☎53 800 724; http://www.alotofthai.com). This family-run cooking school runs cooking classes in an intimate environment. 1-day 900฿, short evening class 800฿.

Benjarong Cooking Class, 946 Rama IV Rd., Dusit Thani Hotel, Bangkok 10500, Thailand (☎02 236 6400). Thai culinary classes every Sa 9:30am-12:30pm; taught by the head chef of the hotel's exceptional restaurant. The full program consists of 12 courses, and participants receive a certificate upon completion.

Chiang Mai Cooking Schools, Chiang Mai (see **Cooking Classes, p. 280**).

Samui Institute of Culinary Arts, 46/6 Moo 3, Chaweng Beach, Ko Samui 84320, Thailand (☎53 800 724; www.sitca.net). Cooking classes, vegetable- and fruit-carving classes, and vocational training classes. 1-day lesson 1950-52500฿.

HOMESTAYS AND CULTURAL LEARNING

If you are feeling adventurous, there are a number of Thai homestay opportunities, massage schools, and boxing camps that provide a more unconventional cultural immersion experience; below are just a few options.

Center for Cultural Interchange (CCI), 746 N. LaSalle Dr. Chicago, IL 60610 USA (☎+1-312-944-2544; www.cii-exchange.org). Organizes 1- to 4-week family homestays to promote cultural understanding. US$1000-1500 includes room and board.

Global Routes, 1 Short St., Northampton, MA 01060, USA (☎+1-413-585-8895; www. globalroutes.org). Has high-school programs and college teaching internships throughout the world; all involve homestays. Programs cost around US$4500, not including airfare.

Lanna Kiat Busaba Muay Thai Camp, 161 Soi Chang Kian, Huay Kaew Rd., Chiang Mai 50300, Thailand (☎53 892 102; www.lannamuaythai.com). Learn to box like the pros. 1-day lesson 250฿; prices vary for longer training periods.

The Old Medicine Hospital. (See **Massage Classes,** (p. 281))

Tribal Museum, Ratchamangkla Park, Chang Puak Rd., Chiang Mai 50300, Thailand (☎53 221 933). Helps interested visitors arrange homestays in hill-tribe villages in the area surrounding Chiang Mai.

B E Y O N D   T O U R I S M

WORKING

In general, *Let's Go* discourages working in Thailand, given the country's low employment rate and the arduous process of obtaining a work permit (see **Work Permits,** (p. 11)). If you're brave enough to tackle long-term employment in Thailand, teaching English is the most commonly available job and one of the best ways to give back to Thailand while also getting paid.

VISA INFORMATION. To volunteer, study, or work for less than 30 days, US, Australian, Canadian, European, New Zealander, and South African citizens do not need a visa. If you plan to stay longer than 30 days, you can buy a tourist visa good for 60 days (US$25). If you have set up a job or volunteer placement before arriving in Thailand, you need a 90-day non-immigrant visa (single-entry US$65, multiple-entry US$175), which covers work in medical and educational fields. The Thai government will require a letter from your academic institution, volunteer program, hospital, NGO, or place of work indicating their need for your assistance. It generally takes about 2 weeks to process the application. Extensions can be granted from within the country if you already have a 90-day visa. If you don't, you must either apply for an extension at an Immigration Office or simply cross the border and re-enter the country; this gives you a clean slate and you can now stay another 30 days without visa, as if you had only just come to Thailand. (Visiting countries hostile to Thailand such as Myanmar may slow this process). For those who would like to get an extension, instead, be aware that this process operates on a case-by-case basis, so contact the Thai embassy before your 90-day visa runs out, and before you leave the country in order to find out the most up-to-date procedures.

BEYOND TOURISM

TEACHING ENGLISH

One of the best ways to do work with meaningful, long-term effects for the people of Thailand is to teach English, which opens a whole world of opportunities for the students you teach, who are often trapped in rural poverty. Accordingly, some of the teaching jobs listed here are on the charitable side and forgo a real salary. Even then, teachers often receive some sort of a daily stipend to help with living expenses. Thailand's low cost of living also makes teaching more feasible. In almost all cases, you must have at least a bachelor's degree to be a full-fledged teacher, although college undergraduates can often get summer positions teaching or tutoring.

Many schools require teachers to have a **Teaching English as a Foreign Language (TEFL)** certificate. You may still be able to find a teaching job without one, but certified teachers usually find higher-paying jobs. The Thai-impaired don't have to give up their dream of teaching, however. Private schools usually hire native English speakers for English-immersion classrooms where no Thai is spoken. (Teachers in public schools will more likely work in both English and Thai.) Placement agencies or university fellowship programs are the best resources for finding teaching jobs. Additionally, the *Bangkok Post*'s "Classifieds" section is a good resource for those hoping to teach English in Thailand. The **Australian Center** in Chiang Mai provides a leaflet on working in the area. Alternatively, you can contact schools directly or to try your luck once you arrive in Thailand. In the latter case, the best time to look is several weeks before the start of the school year. The following organizations are extremely helpful in placing teachers in Thailand:

American University Alumni Language Center, Head office, 179 Rajadamri Rd., Lumphini Pathumwan, Bangkok 10330, Thailand (☎02 528 1703; www.auathailand/slc/index.html). Hires teachers-in-training (250฿ per hr.) and teachers under contract. Locations all over Thailand.

Australia Center, 75/1 Moo 14, Suthep Rd., (☎053 810 552; www.insearch.edu/international/accm). This center hires and places volunteers wishing to teach English to all ages.

English and Computer College, 97/11 Rajdamri Rd., Pathumwan, Bangkok 10330, Thailand (☎02 665 1236; www.eccthai.com). Constantly recruits teachers for schools all over Thailand, from the most rural to the most urban. Also offers teaching certification courses, with guaranteed job placement in one of their programs upon completion.

Hasadee School, in Si Chiangmai, accepts volunteers to teach English for grades 7-12 (contact David Peel at peelieorion@yahoo.com). 1-week min. commitment.

International Schools Services (ISS), 15 Roszel Rd., P.O. Box 5910, Princeton, NJ 08543, USA (☎+1-609-452-0990; www.iss.edu). Hires teachers for more than 200 overseas schools, including some in Thailand. Candidates should have teaching experience and a bachelor's degree. 2-year commitment.

Involvement Volunteers Association Inc., P.O. Box 218, Port Melbourne, Victoria 3207, Australia (☎+61 39 646 9392; www.volunteering.org.au). The organization offers a variety of placements in Thailand and around the world for a placement fee of US$268.

Kanchanaburi Catholic School, in Kanchanaburi (☎98 890 050). Teachers receive room, board, and a stipend. School requests 1-month, 3-month, or 1-year commitment. Ask for Orwan.

Office of Overseas Schools, US Department of State, Room H328, SA-1, Washington, D.C. 20522-0132, USA (☎+1-202-261-8224; www.state.gov/m/a/os/). Has comprehensive lists of schools abroad and agencies that place Americans in schools in Cambodia, Indonesia, Laos, Myanmar, the Philippines, Singapore, Thailand, and Vietnam.

Teach in Asia, (www.teach-in-asia.net/jobs). This website posts teaching jobs of all types, giving information about salary and necessary experience for each opening.

FURTHER READING ON BEYOND TOURISM

Alternatives to the Peace Corps: A Guide of Global Volunteer Opportunities, edited by Paul Backhurst. Food First, 2005 (US$12).

The Back Door Guide to Short-Term Job Adventures: Internships, Summer Jobs, Seasonal Work, Volunteer Vacations, and Transitions Abroad, by Michael Landes. Ten Speed Press, 2005 (US$22).

Green Volunteers: The World Guide to Voluntary Work in Nature Conservation, by Fabio Ausenda. Universe, 2007 (US$15).

How to Live Your Dream of Volunteering Overseas, by Joseph Collins, Stefano DeZerega, and Zahara Heckscher. Penguin Books, 2001 (US$20).

International Job Finder: Where the Jobs Are Worldwide, by Daniel Lauber and Kraig Rice. Planning Communications, 2002 (US$20).

Live and Work Abroad: A Guide for Modern Nomads, by Huw Francis and Michelyne Callan. Vacation Work Publications, 2001 (US$20).

Volunteer Vacations: Short-Term Adventures That Will Benefit You and Others, by Doug Cutchins, Anne Geissinger, and Bill McMillon. Chicago Review Press, 2006 (US$18).

BANGKOK

After a day or two in the city, most travelers are amazed that Bangkok, an exhilarating city of teeming millions, of gigantic golden temples and exuberant markets, still remains standing at sunset. Armadas of BMWs and Mercedes meet at intersections famous for infuriating traffic as legions of people battle for territory on the city sidewalks and spill out of every bus. Bangkok wasn't fashioned by city planners; it was hewn from unsuspecting rice paddies by the double-edged sword of Thailand's growing economy. In most ways it is a consummately modern city: 7-Elevens are found on every corner, and modern medicine, education, and technology are givens. But the ancient monasteries and ramshackle food stalls of Bangkok, as well as the omnipresent sex trade, are reminders that this can still be a traditional and poverty-stricken city.

Bangkok is the tourism hub of Southeast Asia, and the vast majority of tourists to the region pass through here, many several times, though some purists claim that visitors to Thailand should spend as little time here as possible. It's true that the traffic, noise, pollution, and crowds make the city unbearable for some. But this urban center of over 10 million people is the center of Thailand's government and economy, and boasts cultural, religious, and historical sights, the revered royal family, mind-boggling shopping markets and malls, an incredibly diverse nightlife, and one-of-a-kind restaurants and entertainment.

All of this gives Bangkok a rare combination of history buffs drooling over the National Museum's treasures, while only steps away, on frenzied, narcotic Khaosan Rd., travel-weary backpackers arrive at their modern mecca. It is a city of constant surprises—no two people know the same Bangkok.

✈ INTERCITY TRANSPORTATION

BY PLANE

All international flights in and out of Bangkok go through **Suvarnabhumi International Airport** (☎02 132 1888). Due to ongoing construction, a few direct domestic flights are still being channeled through Don Muang Airport (see below). Suvarnabhumi consists of two main levels—**departures,** on **level 4** (☎02 132 9324) and **arrivals,** on **level 2** (☎132 9328). Luggage storage is available on both levels (behind exit 4 in the arrivals terminal and near the front of entrance 4 in the departures terminal) for 100฿ per day for up to three months; from three to six months for 200฿ per day (no luggage held more than six months). The departures terminal has a post office, extensive duty-free shopping, and value-added tax refund centers; the arrivals terminal has currency exchange kiosks as well as a bookstore that sells phone cards and other necessities.

To get from Suvarnabhumi to the city center, take one of the metered taxis waiting to the left of the terminal exit (250-400฿; you will have to pay tolls and a 50฿ airport charge) or go to gate 8 on the first floor to catch one of the airport express buses (150฿, 45-60min., 5am-midnight; AE1 goes to Silom, AE2 to Banglamphu, AE3 to Sukhumvit, AE4 to Hualumphong). A free shuttle bus runs from gates 3 and 8 to a terminal a few kilometers away, where you can catch one of many local buses for 35฿. However, this is probably more trouble than it is worth. A goverment bus for Pattaya leaves from gate 8 on the first floor (106฿, daily at 6:45, 9:15am, 1:15, and 5:15pm).

BANGKOK

A   B   C

1

TO NONTHABURI
(20km)

Nakhon Chai Si Rd.

Nakhon Chai Si Rd.

Rama V

Charan Sanitwong Rd.

Krung Thon
Bridge

Samsen Rd.

Sukhothai Rd.

THEWET

Chao Phraya River

14 18
15 76

Nakhon Ratchasima Rd.

Ratchavithi Rd.

88

DUSIT

TO 🚌 SOUTHERN
BUS TERMINAL (1km)

Tha Thewet

35

Tha Thewet
Market

Luk Kuang Rd.

Krung Kasem Rd.

2

74
69

64

50

Rama V Rd.

60

O Thong Rd.

Si Ayutthaya

2

37

Phra Athit Rd.

Chakrapong Rd.

Prachathipatai Rd.

Ratchadamnoen Nok Rd.

Phisanulok Rd.

Royal
Turf Club

Chao Fa Rd.

SEE KHAOSAN ROAD AREA MAP, P. 101

Tha
Phra Athit

Tha
Banglamphu

Phra Sawn Rd.

81

Saw

Phra Pinklao
Bridge

Arun Amarin Rd.

Tha
Thonburi

75

BANGLAMPHU

Khaosan Rd.

Krung Bangkok Nok Rd.

Ratchadamnoen Klang Rd.

Klong Phadung Krung Kasem

1

Tha Thonburi
Railway
Station

Siriraj
Hospital

79

77

84

Ratchadamnoen Rd.

63

Nakhon Sawan Rd.

Lam Luang Rd.

3

TO NAKHON PATHOM
(60km)

86

85

Na Phra That Rd.

Ratchadamnoen
Nai Rd.

Mahachai Rd.

64A

RATCHADAMNOEN

Klong
Taxi Pier

57

Bamrung Muang Rd.

THONBURI

Tha
Chang

Na Phra Lan Rd.

66

Ratchini Rd.

Atsadang Rd.

Tanao Rd.

Dinso Rd.

56A

Boriphat Rd.

Worachak Rd.

Sua Pa Rd.

Charoen Krung Rd.

49

Tha
Tien

Maharat Rd.

52

Saham Chai Rd.

Ti Thong Rd.

Pahurat Rd.

Chakraphet Rd.

Tri Phet Rd.

Yaowarat Rd.

Thieves
Market

Luang Rd.

Rong Muang Rd.

Krung Kasem Rd.

Banthat Thong Rd.

4

Memorial
Bridge

PAHURAT

34

Song Wat Rd.

Ratchawong Rd.

32
31

33
8

39

Song Sawan Rd.

9

59

Hualamphong
Railway Station

HUALUMPHONG

Isaraphap Rd.

Ireland

Tha
Ratchawong SE

CHINATOWN

Khao Lam Rd.

Mahanakhon Rd.

17

Rama IV Rd.

Tha Harbor
Dept.

Si Phraya Rd.

5

Pratchathipok Rd.

Somdet Chao Phraya Rd.

Lat Ya Rd.

Tha Si
Phraya

Public Telecomm
Service Center

GPO

Naret Rd.

Surawong Rd.

Decho Rd.

SILOM &
PATPONG

6

Intharaphithak Rd.

70

Charoen Rat Rd.

Chao Phraya River

Mathesak Rd.

Silom Rd.

83

Pan Rd.

25

M.R.T

SKYTRAIN

Taksin Rd.

King Thonburi Rd.

Charoen Krung Rd.

Tha
Oriental

80

Tha
Sathorn

Taksin
Bridge

SAPHAN
TAKSIN

Surasak Rd.

Pramuan Rd.

Myanin

SURASAK

TO DAMNOEN SADUAK
(109km)

TO SAMUT PRAKAN
(30km)

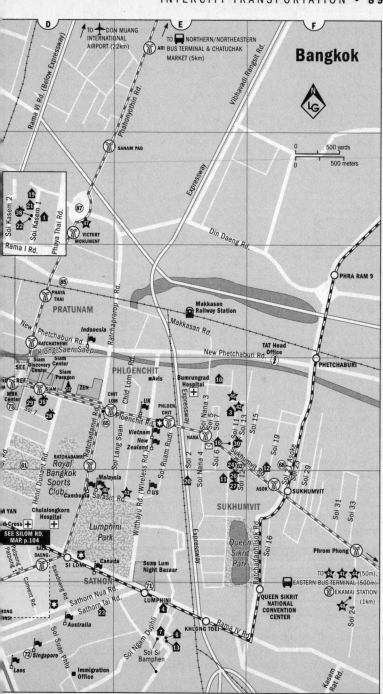

Bangkok
see map p. 88-89

🏠 **ACCOMMODATIONS**

A-One Inn, **1**	D2
Bangkok International Youth Hostel, **2**	B2
Bright City Tower Service Apartments, **3**	E4
Charlie House, **4**	E6
Chinatown Hotel, **5**	B4
Lee Guest House 3, **6**	E6
Lee Mansion 4, **7**	E6
Lub*d, **8**	C5
New Empire Hotel, **9**	B4
P.B. Hotel, **10**	E4
P.S. Guest House, **11**	E5
S.V. Guest House, **12**	F4
Sala Thai Daily Mansion, **13**	E6
Shanti Lodge, **14**	B1
Sri Ayuttaya, **15**	B1
Suk 11, **16**	E4
T.T. Guest House, **17**	C5
Tavee Guest House, **18**	B1
The Bed and Breakfast, **19**	D2
The Atlanta, **20**	E5
Wendy House, **21**	D2
White Lodge, **22**	D2
YWCA, **23**	D6

🍴 **FOOD**

Arirang Restaurant, **24**	E4
Bussaracum, **25**	C6
Cabbages & Condoms, **26**	E5
Crepes and Co., **27**	E5
Coca Noodles, **28**	D4
Doo Dee Shop, **29**	D4
Dosa King, **30**	E4
Hua Seng Hong, **31**	B4
KP Suki, **32**	B4
Jumbo Noodles, **33**	B4
Royal India Restaurant, **34**	B4
Sai Ta Ra Restaurant, **35**	B2

Som Tam Paradise, **36**	D4
Tham Na, **37**	B2
Unnamed Noodle Place, **38**	D2
White Orchid Restaurant and Coffee Shop, **39**	B4

⭐ **NIGHTLIFE**

70's Bar, **40**	D5
808, **41**	F5
Bed Supperclub, **42**	E4
Brown Sugar Jazz Pub and Restaurant, **43**	E5
Flix and Slim, **44**	F5
Q Bar, **45**	E4
Route 66, **46**	F5
Saxophone Pub and Restaurant, **47**	D2
Tokyo Joe's, **48**	F6

🚩 **WATS**

Arun (Temple of Dawn), **49**	A4
Benchamabophit (Marble Temple), **50**	C2
Mahathat, **51**	A3
Patum Wanaram, **52**	D4
Phra Kaew, **53**	A3
Pho, **54**	A4
Ratchabophit, **55**	B4
Ratchanada, **56**	B3
Saket, **57**	B3
Suthat, **58**	B3
Traimit, **59**	C4

⭕ **SIGHTS**

Chitralada Palace, **60**	C2
Chulalongkorn University, **61**	D4
Chuvit Garden, **62**	E4
Democracy Monument, **63**	B3
Dusit Zoo, **64**	C2
Erawan Shrine, **65**	D4
Grand Palace, **66**	A4
Jim Thompson's House, **67**	D4
Kamthieng House, **68**	F4
King Chulalongkorn (Rama V) Statue, **69**	C2
King Taksin Monument, **70**	A5
Lumphini Boxing Stadium, **71**	E6
M.R. Kukrit's Heritage Home, **72**	D6
Mahboonkrong Center, **73**	D4
National Assembly, **74**	C2
National Gallery, **75**	A3
National Library, **76**	B1
National Museum, **77**	A3
National Stadium, **78**	D4
National Theater, **79**	A3
Oriental Hotel, **80**	C6
Ratchadamnoen Boxing Stadium, **81**	B2
Royal Barge Museum, **82**	A3
Ruen Thep, **83**	C6
Sanam Luang, **84**	A3
Suan Pakkad Palace Museum, **85**	D3
Thammasat University, **86**	A3
Victory Monument, **87**	D2
Vimanmek Palace, **88**	C1

A few domestic flights to and from Bangkok go through **Don Muang International Airport,** 171 Vibhavadi-Ransot Rd., 25km north of the city center. Travelers should check beforehand, as the frequency of flights through Don Muang varies. The only terminal currently in use is Domestic Passenger Travel (departure info ☎02 535 1192, arrival info 02 535 1253), which has baggage storage (70฿ per bag per day over three months 140฿ per day; see p. 98).

DESTINATION	PRICE	DESTINATION	PRICE
Chiang Mai	2875฿	Phuket	3330฿
Hanoi	7930฿	Singapore	9945฿
Kuala Lumpur	8040฿	Udon Thani	2385฿
Phnom Penh	5700฿	Vientiane	4405฿

As you exit the terminal, take one of the waiting taxis (250-400฿) or the convenient, comfortable, air-conditioned airport buses, which run four routes into the city center. A1, A2, and A3 run every 30min. 5am-midnight. A4 runs every hour, or when eight people get on, with no service from 3 to 6pm. All buses cost 100฿. A2 goes to Khaosan Rd.

AE1: SUVARNAB-HUMI-SILOM	AE2: SUVARNAB-HUMI-KHAO SAN ROAD	AE3: SUVARNAB-HUMI-SUKHUMVIT	AE4: SUVARNAB-HUMI-HUA LAM-PHONG
Petchaburi Soi 30 (under flyover)	Petchaburi Soi 30 (under flyover)	Sukhumvit Soi 52-50	Victory Monument
World Trade / Central World Plaza	Platinum Fashion Mall	Prakanong Market	Soi Rangnam
BTS, Rachdamri Station	Petchaburi Soi 20	Eastern Bus Terminal	99 Hotel
Lumpini Park	Petchaburi Soi 10	Sukhumvit Soi 38	BTS, Phayathai Station
Saladaeng (on Rama 4 Rd.) Surawong Rd.	Urupong	Sukhumvit Soi 34	Livestock Department
Montien Hotel	Sapan Kao	Sukhumvit Soi 24	BTS, Rachatewee Station
Tawana Ramada Hotel	Thai Airways (Lan Luang)	Sukhumvit Soi 20	Siam Discovery Center
Plaza Hotel	Wat Rachnatda (Temple)	Sukhumvit Soi 18	Maboonkrong (MBK)
Surawong Soi Kamjai Lamsuri	Democracy Monument	Sukhumvit Soi 10 (Bangkok Bank)	Chulalongkorn University
Charoen Krung Soi 47/1, Silom Road	Royal/Ratanakosin Hotel	Sukhumvit Soi 6	Mandarin Hotel
Lertsin Hospital	National Theater	Sukhumvit Soi 2	Bangkok Centre Hotel
Central Silom	Pra A-Thit Rd.	Central Silom, Rachdamri Rd.	Hua Lumpong Railway Station
Silom Soi 26	Phra-sumen	World Trade/Central World Plaza	
Narai Hotel (Silom Soi 18)	Khaosan Rd.	Phetchaburi Soi 25	
Sofitel Hotel (Silom Soi 12)		Phetchaburi Soi 35	
Silom Soi 6 (Bangkok Bank)		Soi Nana	
BTS, Saladang Station			

A cheaper way to get from the airport to the city is to cross the bridge to the Don Muang Train Station, catch an inbound **train** to Hualamphong Railway Station (10-15฿), and then take a **city bus**. Night service is infrequent.

Suffocating and unreliable **public buses** are available on the highway just outside the exit (regular #3, 24, 52; A/C #504, 510, 529; 3.50-16฿).

BY TRAIN

Second only to elephant transport in style, train travel is cheap, efficient, and safe. Four train lines start and end at **Hualamphong Railway Station** (☎220 4334, 24hr. info 1690), on Rama IV Rd., in the center of the metropolis. *Klongs* (canals) and river ferries, coupled with public buses (p. 94), provide the easiest transportation to the station from the city. Metered taxis or *tuk-tuks* at the side entrance of the station are the best ways into town from the station. The MRT **subway** line terminates at Hualamphong. Bus #29 runs from the airport through Siam Sq. to the station. Otherwise, walk down Rama IV Rd. to a bus stop from which A/C bus #501 and regular buses #29 and 34 go to Siam Sq. Walk down Sukhumvit Rd. for regular bus #53 to Banglamphu (Khaosan Rd. area).

Daily ticket booking is left of the main entrance; advance booking is to the right. The first information counter has train schedules; the third is specifically for foreigners and has English-speaking staff. Upper-class seats have bathrooms and A/C; lower-class seats put you right in the middle of many friendly Thai people (and Thai heat and dust). Sleeper berths for long journeys are popular, so buy tickets well in advance. In order of increasing speed, price, and service, the trains are: ordinary (*rot thamada*), rapid (*rot reaw*), express (*rot duan*), and special (*rot pheeset*).

THE PRICE IS RIGHT! Prices listed are ranges of fares. Add 40ʙ for fast trains, 60ʙ for express trains, and 80ʙ for specials. Duration listed is for rapid trains; add 2-3hr. per 10hr. for normal trains.

The end of the station opposite the ticket counters has a **luggage storage center.** (☎02 215 1920. 30-70ʙ per day, depending on bag size. 4-month max. Open daily 4am-11pm.) Other services include: an **information booth;** a **24hr. ATM** near the main entrance; a **police booth** (☎02 225 0300), left of the main entrance; and a **post office** outside. (Open M-F 7am-7pm, Sa 8am-4pm.)

DESTINATION	DURATION	FREQUENCY/TIME	PRICE
CHIANG MAI LINE (NORTHERN)			
Ayutthaya	1.5hr	11 per day 7am-10pm	15-20ʙ
Chiang Mai	12-15hr.	6 per day 8:30am-10pm	271-1353ʙ
Don Muang Airport	1hr.	11 per day 7am-10pm	5-10ʙ
Lampang	13hr.	6 per day 8:30am-10pm	256-1272ʙ
Lopburi	3hr.	11 per day 7am-10pm	28-64ʙ
Phitsanulok	6hr.	10 per day 7am-10pm	219-1064ʙ
UBON RATCHATHANI LINE (NORTHEASTERN)			
Surin	9hr.	10 per day 5:45am-11:40pm	223-1046ʙ
Ubon Ratchathani	12hr.	7 per day 5:45am-11:40pm	245-1180ʙ
Nong Khai	13hr.	daily 6:30,6:40, 8:45pm	258-1217ʙ
BUTTERWORTH LINE (SOUTHERN)			
Hat Yai	17hr.	5 per day 1-10:50pm	339-1494ʙ
Hua Hin	4hr.	12 per day 8:05am-10:50pm	234-922ʙ
Surat Thani	11hr.	11 per day 8:05am-10:50pm	297-1279ʙ
EASTERN LINE			
Pattaya	3.5hr.	daily 6:55am	31ʙ
Aranyaprathet	5hr.	daily 5:55am, 1:05pm	48ʙ

BY BUS

Government buses depart from four terminals:

Eastern Bus Terminal (E): (☎02 391 2504) on Sukhumvit Rd., accessible via the Skytrain's Ekamai Station (local A/C bus #501, 508, 511, or 513, and regular bus #2, 23, 25, 38, 71, 72, or 98).

Northern Bus Terminal (N): (☎02 936 2852) in a new building west of Chatuchak Park. Take the Skytrain's Sukhumvit Line to Mo Chit and a motorcycle taxi or *tuk-tuk* (5min., 30ʙ) from there to the terminals.

Central Bus Terminal (C): (☎02 936 1972) in same building as Northern.

Northeastern Bus Terminal (NE): (☎02 936 3660) in same building as Northern.

Southern Bus Terminal (S): (☎02 435 1199) at Boromrat Chonnani (Pinklao-Nak-honchaisi) Rd., across the river in Thonburi. To get there, take A/C bus #507, 511, or 513 from the Democracy Monument, regular bus #19 from Phra Athit Rd., or regular bus #30 from Sanam Luang. Tickets for government and **private buses** can be bought at the Southern Bus Terminal.

Information on all routes can be found at www.transport.co.th/Eng/HomeEnglish.htm. Most travel agencies around Khaosan Rd. book through private bus companies, which can be cheaper and more convenient, and can offer more modern amenities than government buses. These are, however, more scam- and accident-prone than government buses.

DESTINATION	DURATION	TERMINAL; FREQUENCY	PRICE
Ayutthaya	1hr.	C; every 20min. 5:40am-8:30pm	41-52฿
Ban Phe (to Ko Samet)	3hr.	E; every hr. 7am-8:30pm	124฿
Chanthaburi	4hr.	E; every 30min. 4am-midnight	103-148฿
Chiang Mai	10hr.	N; 74 per day 5:30am-10:20pm	314-625฿
Chiang Rai	11-13hr.	N; 32 per day 7am-9:30pm	264-700฿
Hat Yai	13-15hr.	S; 14 per day 7am-9:45pm	416 -830฿
Khon Kaen	7hr.	NE; 5 per day 2:30-10:30pm	202฿
Krabi	12-14hr.	S; 16 per day 7:30am-9pm	255-710฿
Mae Hong Son	14hr.	N; daily 6pm	569฿
Nong Khai	10hr.	NE; 5 per day 7:50am-9pm	243-545฿
Pattaya	2hr.	E; every 40min. 5am-11pm	90฿
Phang-Nga	12hr.	S; 5 per day 6:30am-7:30pm	389-685฿
Phrae	7-8hr.	N; 6 per day 8:30am-11:30pm	248-495฿
Phuket	12-14hr.	S; 15 per day 5am-8pm	278-755฿
Rayong	3hr.	E; every 30min. 3:30am-7:30pm, every hour 8-10pm	117฿
Si Racha	2hr.	E; every 20-40min. 5am-9pm	70฿
Sukothai	7hr.	N; 10 per day 9am-10:50pm	199-256฿
Surat Thani	9-11hr.	S; 13 per day 8am-11:50pm	211-590฿
Surin	6-8hr.	NE; 8 per day 8am-11:50pm	204-385฿
Trat	5hr.	E; every 1-2hr. 6am-midnight	189฿
Ubon Ratchathani	9-11hr.	NE; 26 per day 4:30am-11:40pm	297-570฿

BANGKOK

■ ORIENTATION

Beyond backpacker-jammed **Khaosan Road** lies a bastion of unclaimed sights and experiences. The north-south **Chao Phraya River** is a worthy landmark and starting point. To the river's east lies **Banglamphu,** the heart of the city. Home to Khaosan Rd., it is immediately north of **Ratchadamnoen/Ko Rattanakosin,** the location of Bangkok's major sights, including Wat Pho, Wat Phra Kaew, and the Royal Palace. Farther north is **Thewet/Dusit,** a backpacker area and the location of the Dusit Zoo and the former royal mansions. Heading southeast along the river leads to **Pahurat** (the Indian district), **Chinatown,** and the **Hualamphong Railway Station.** Farther south is the wealthy **Silom** financial district and its less reputable neighbor, the **Patpong** red light district. East of the Hualamphong Railway Station is **Siam Square,** the hub of the BTS Skytrain and home to colossal shopping malls and cinemas, as well as streets packed with boutiques popular with young Thais. **Rama I Road** slices through the city, connecting Wat Phra Kaew in the west with Bangkok's eastern edge and the **Sukhumvit Road** area, where Thais and *farang* party until the early hours. ■**Nancy Chandler's Map of Bangkok** (180฿) and the **Bangkok Tourist Map** (50฿) are extremely useful and detailed guides.

BANGLAMPHU AND KO RATTANAKOSIN	This area offers the best historical sights in Bangkok within distance of the cheap accommodations of Khaosan Rd.
DUSIT AND THEWET	Quiet and affordable, with less-visited sights and Thailand's largest zoo, this area is a nice break from the chaos that is Khaosan Rd.
CHINATOWN, PAHURAT, AND HUALAMPHONG	Home to Chinese and Indian immigrant populations, this area has a lively street culture, especially at night.
PATPONG	Bangkok's red light district.
SILOM ROAD	Grand hotels, neighborhood cafes, and the serene Lumphini Park make this a great neighborhood for wandering.
SIAM SQUARE	Known for its shopping, this area offers giant malls for the avid consumer, as well as pleasant accommodations that are centrally located and conveniently close to the Skytrain.
SUKHUMVIT ROAD	Expensive restaurants and a thriving nightlife make this the place to splurge. A handful of guesthouses and affordable hotels also make staying here a viable backpacker option.

LOCAL TRANSPORTATION

Trying to maneuver through Bangkok traffic is enough to drive anyone crazy. The Skytrain and subway have helped to decrease traffic, but getting from north to south is still frustrating. Taking canal boats and river taxis means less time sweating on buses and breathing exhaust in tuk-tuks. Travelers hoping to utilize public transportation will love the **Bangkok Tourist Map** (50฿), which has bus, water taxi, and Skytrain routes, as well as sights information.

BY BUS

The bus system, run by the Bangkok Metropolitan Transit Authority (BMTA), is extensive and inexpensive. Red-and-cream and white buses are without A/C (8฿); orange, blue-and-white, and yellow-and-white buses all have A/C (12-26฿). Pea-green **minibuses** (7฿) supposedly run the same routes but are more often subject to traffic delays and the whims of passengers. **Microbuses** cover long distances and stop only at designated places (5am-10pm, 30฿); their higher price guarantees a seat and fewer stops. A/C buses run 5am-midnight, while regular buses run 24hr. Make sure you get on the right type of bus, not just the right route number. Below is a sample listing. There are many, many buses, so for more options, pick up a **free bus map** at any TAT office.

REGULAR BUSES WITH NO A/C (RED-AND-CREAM OR WHITE)

#1: Wat Pho–Yaowarat Rd. (Chinatown)–General Post Office (GPO)–Oriental Hotel.

15: Banglamphu (Phra Athit Rd., Phrasumen Rd.)–Sanam Luang–Democracy Monument–Wat Saket–Siam Sq.–Ratchadamri Rd.–Lumphini Park–Silom Rd.

18 and 28: Vimanmek Teak Museum–Dusit Zoo–Chitralada Palace–Victory Monument

25: Wat Phra Kaew–Wat Pho–Charoen Krung Rd.–Rama IV Rd. (near Hualamphong Railway Station)–Phayathai Rd.–Mahboonkrong Center–Siam Sq.–World Trade Center–Ploenchit Rd.–Sukhumvit Rd. to outer Bangkok.

48: Sanam Chai Rd.–Bamrung Muang Rd.–Siam Sq.–along Sukhumvit Rd.

59: Don Muang International Airport–Victory Monument–Phahonyothin Rd.–Phetchaburi Rd.–Larnluang Rd.–Democracy Monument–Sanam Luang.

70: Democracy Monument–TAT–Boxing Stadium–Dusit Zoo.

72: Ratchaprarop Rd.–Si Ayutthaya Rd.–Marble Temple–Samsen Rd.–Thewet.

74: Rama IV Rd. (outside Soi Ngam Duphli)–Lumphini Park–Ratchadamri Rd.–World Trade Center–Pratunam-Ratchaprarop Rd.–Victory Monument.

115: Silom Rd.–Rama IV Rd.–along Rama IV Rd. until Sukhumvit Rd.

BANGKOK

116: Sathorn Nua Rd.–along Rama IV Rd. (passes Soi Ngam Duphli)–Sathorn Tai Rd.

204: Victory Monument–Ratchaprarop Rd.–World Trade Center–Siam Sq.–Bamrung Muang Rd.

BACKPACKER'S BUS. Regular bus #15 is especially important for those staying around Khaosan Rd. It connects that area with Siam Sq., where passengers can hop onto the Skytrain to access the eastern parts of the city, such as Sukhumvit, Silom, Patpong, and Chatuchak Market. Alternatively, a taxi from Khaosan to Siam Sq. costs 55-80฿.

A/C BUSES (BLUE-AND-WHITE, YELLOW-AND-WHITE, OR ORANGE)

#501: Wat Pho–Charoen Krung Rd.–Rama IV Rd. (near Hualamphong Railway Station)–Phayathai Rd. (Mahboonkrong Center)–Siam Sq.–along Sukhumvit Rd.

508: Sanam Luang–Bamrung Muang Rd.–Rama I Rd.–Ploenchit Rd.–outer Bangkok

510: National Assembly (Ratchavithi Rd.)–Dusit Zoo–Chitralada Palace–Victory Monument–Phahonyothin Rd.–Don Muang International Airport

511: Khaosan Rd.–Phra Sumen Rd.–Democracy Monument (Ratchadamnoen Klong Rd.)–Phetchaburi Rd.–World Trade Center–Sukhumvit Rd.

BY BOAT

Traveling by boat is one of the most pleasurable and unique ways of navigating Bangkok. **■Chao Phraya River Express** ferries (www.chaophrayaboat.co.th; 6am-6:40pm, 10-32฿) are the best way to travel along the murky Chao Phraya river and provide easy access to the Skytrain. Buy tickets at the booth on the pier or from the ticket collector on board. Specify your stop, as boats will otherwise stop only if there are passengers waiting. Disembark quickly and carefully, especially at rush hour. The main stops, north to south, are:

PIER NAME	PIER DESIGNATION	SERVES
Thewet	15	National Library, Dusit guesthouses
Phra Athit	13	Khaosan Rd., Banglamphu
Thonburi Railway Pier	11	Thonburi Railway Station, Royal Barges
Chang	9	Wat Phra Kaew, Royal Palace
Tien	8	Wat Pho
Ratchawong SE	5	Chinatown, Hualamphong Railway Station
Si Phraya	3	GPO
Oriental	1	Oriental Hotel, Silom
Sathorn	Central	Saphan Taksin Skytrain Station

During peak transit times, special rush-hour express ferries with large triangular orange (15฿) or yellow (20-29฿) flags on their roofs (not to be confused with the smaller, yellow, triangular flags marked by the Thai crest carried by all ferries) stop at select piers (hours vary depending on the route, but mostly 6-8am and 4:30-6pm). Each Chao Phraya River Express pier has useful signs detailing which ferries stop at which piers. Small, brown, boxy ferries with bench seats, easily confused with river taxis, shuttle across the river to every major stop (3฿). A small sign identifies each *tha* (pier).

Klongs are small canals that zig-zag through the city's interior. Thonburi, west of Chao Praya, has an extensive network, and Bangkok proper has two useful lines. **Klong Saen Saep** links Democracy Monument near Banglamphu with the area just north of Siam Sq. and the World Trade Center (10min.). Another route links **Klong Banglamphu** and **Klong Phadung Krung Kasem.** From Tha Banglamphu, at Chakraphong and Phrasumen Rd., you can reach Hualumphong Railway

Station (15min.). Boats run 6am-6:40pm every 30min. during peak hours, and every 45min. during off-peak hours and weekends. A single trip costs 7-20฿.

Longtail boat rentals are available at almost every pier, offering transportation to tourist destinations on the river and *klongs*. Agree on a price before setting off. Usual rates are 800฿ for the first hour and 400฿ each additional hour.

BY SKYTRAIN

The **Skytrain** (part of Bangkok Mass Transit System, **BTS**), a monorail train launched on December 5, 1999, to celebrate the king's 72nd birthday, is an air-conditioned relief. Incredibly useful for navigating Siam Sq., Silom, and Sukhumvit, the train has two lines that meet at Siam Sq. The **Sukhumvit Line** runs from Mo Chit (next to Chatuchak Market) past the Victory Monument to Siam Sq., continues through Sukhumvit Rd., and terminates at On Nut, beyond the Eastern Bus Terminal. The **Silom Line** runs from the National Stadium past Siam Sq. and Lumphini Park, and along part of Silom Rd., before ending at Taksin Bridge. All stations have useful maps. Fares are based on distance (15-40฿), and ticket purchase is automated; the machines only accept 5 and 10฿ coins, but every station has a kiosk where you can get change. Trip passes (20/30/40 rides cost 440/600/800฿, respectively) are the most cost-effective for students (22 or younger); just show your International Student Identity Card (with ISIC card 340/450/600฿; passes must be used within 30 days of purchase). Unlimited one-day passes (120฿) are also available. Insert the card at the turnstile to enter the station; **hold onto it and insert it at the turnstile at your destination to exit the station.** The Skytrain operates daily 6am-midnight. There is a BTS information office in the Siam Center stop (☎02 617 7340, open daily 8am-8pm).

BY METRO

The newest addition to Bangkok's public transportation system is the clean, cool underground metro **(MRT).** The metro passes through fewer tourist neighborhoods than the BTS, but is especially effective at connecting the eastern parts of Silom with the city center. The metro runs from Bang Sue in the north in a southeast semi-circle to Hualamphong in the south, passing through Chatuchak Market, Sukhumvit Rd., Lumphini Park, Suan Lum Night Bazaar, and Silom Rd. The Sukhumvit Rd. and Silom Rd. stations are close to BTS Skytrain's Asok and Sala Daeng stations. Tickets (black plastic tokens) are priced by distance (single ride 12-40฿) and can be purchased in the underground stations: tap the token to the reader when you enter the station and insert it when you leave. The metro has stricter security than the Skytrain, and guards perform brief bag checks at the entrance to every station. (☎02 246 6733; www.mrta.co.th. Open daily 6am-midnight.)

BY TAXI

Your lungs will thank you for using Bangkok's extensive taxi system. Taxis are simple and cost-efficient, but overlooked by most travelers. The fare is 35฿ for the first 2km and 2฿ per additional 0.4km, and 2฿ per min. waiting time. Always insist that the driver uses the meter—there is no such thing as a flat rate, unless you are coming from the airport. Fares across Bangkok rarely exceed 150฿. The only official extra fees are expressway tolls (40฿). Try to have correct change, as drivers will occasionally refuse to accept large bills. For women traveling alone, taxis tend to be much safer than *tuk-tuks* or motorcycle taxis.

BY TUK-TUK

Tuk-tuks scour the city pumping out black exhaust and squeezing through the traffic that brings most vehicles to a halt. Negotiation is key: drivers may charge you twice what they would a local. Skillful negotiators can get prices about 30% cheaper than taxi fares, but most fares rarely fall below 40฿, making the far more pleasurable and stress-free taxis a more attractive option. Tuk-tuks are, however, good for short distances; if a *tuk-tuk* tries to charge you more than 50฿, save yourself from exhaust inhalation and the likelihood that you're getting ripped off, and take a taxi.

 TOURIST SCAMMING. Tuk-tuk drivers are often con artists and have been known to harass women travelers. Drivers have also been known to drive off with passenger luggage, push the sex industry, deliver passengers to expensive restaurants, or tell travelers that sights are closed and take them to jewelry and tailor shops instead. To entice *farang*, they offer tours of the city for low rates (10-20฿ per hr.), but all you'll get is a sales pitch and inflated prices at the destinations they suggest. Beware of these words: free, sexy, massage, jewelry, tailor shop, and go-go. Tuk-tuks aren't all bad—just be firm and make it clear that you want to go to your intended destination and nowhere else.

BY MOTORCYCLE TAXI

Motorcycle taxi drivers loiter on street corners in brightly colored vests. Though faster in traffic and slightly cheaper than *tuk-tuks*, motorcycle taxis carry only a single passenger, are quite dangerous, and require calm nerves. Travelers should insist on a helmet, as police will fine riders without one.

BY CAR

Travelers should avoid cars, as driving in Bangkok is dangerous. A passport, driver's license, **International Driver's Permit** (p. 33), and major credit card are required. Rental agencies include **Avis,** 2/12 Wireless Rd. (☎02 255 5300, open 8am-6pm daily), and **Budget Rental,** 19/23 building A, RCA (☎02 203 9294, open daily 7am-6pm). Renting a small sedan costs 1400-2000฿ per day, including collision insurance. Both companies have branches at Suvarnabhumi Airport, near the second floor arrival baggage claim area (Avis ☎084 700 8157, Budget 134 4006). For more information on renting a car in Thailand, see p. 32.

🛈 PRACTICAL INFORMATION

PHONE CODE	The phone code for all of Bangkok is ☎02.

TOURIST AND FINANCIAL SERVICES

Tourist Offices: TAT, 4 Ratchadamnoen Nok Rd. (☎02 283 1555; www.tourismthailand.org). Ratchadamnoen Nok is the broad boulevard that begins at the 8-way intersection east of the Democracy Monument. The office is 500m down on the right, just past the tourist police station. The helpful staff doles out **free maps,** brochures, and advice in English, French, Japanese, and Chinese. Open daily 8:30am-4:30pm. The TAT **head office** is at 1600 New Phetchaburi Rd. (☎02 250 5500). Get there via gate 2 of MRT's Phetchaburi stop. Open daily 8:30am-4:30pm. **Bangkok Tourism Bureau,** 17/1 Thanon

Phra Athit (☎02 225 7612 ext. 4); www.bangkoktourist.com), underneath Phra Pinklao Bridge, provides information on Bangkok's sights. Open daily 9am-7pm.

Tourist Information: (☎02 1672), information line receives calls daily 8am-8pm. Tourist information booths are scattered throughout the city.

Immigration Office: 507 Soi Suan Phlu (☎02 287 3101-10), off Sathorn Tai Rd. 30-day transit visas can be extended for 10 days, 60-day tourist visas for 30 days (1900฿). Bring 4cm by 6cm passport photo. Open M-F 9am-noon and 1-4:30pm, Sa 9am-noon.

Embassies and Consulates:

Cambodia, 185 Ratchadamri Rd. (☎02 254 6630). Consular services around the corner, off Sarasin Rd., on the 1st soi on the left. 30-day visa, 2-day processing 1000฿. Open M-F 9-11am and 1:30-4pm.

China, 57 Ratchadaphisek Rd. (☎02 245 7033). Open M-F 9-11:30am.

Indonesia, 600 Phetchaburi Rd. (☎02 252 3135 40). Take regular bus #2 or 11 or A/C bus #505, 511, or 512. Open M-F 8am-noon and 1-4pm.

Laos, 502/1-3 Soi Sahakarnpramoon (☎02 539 6667). 2-day processing 1900฿, 4-day processing 1600฿. Open M-F 8am-noon and 1-4pm.

Malaysia, 33-35 Sathorn Tai Rd. (☎02 629 6800). Open M-Th 8:15am-noon and 12:45-4pm, F 8:15-11:30am and 2-4pm.

Myanmar, 132 Sathorn Nua Rd. (☎02 233 2237). Consular services on Pan Rd., off Sathorn Nua Rd., 1 block from the Skytrain Surasak Station. 30-day visa 800฿ (24hr. processing. Inquire at embassy for up-to-date status of land crossings). Open M-F 8:30am-noon and 2-4:30pm.

Singapore, 129 Sathorn Tai Rd. (☎02 286 2111). Open M-F 9am-noon and 1-5pm.

Vietnam, 83/1 Witthayu Rd. (☎02 251 5836). 2- to 3-day processing 2050฿. Open M-F 8:30-11:30am and 1:30-4:30pm.

For other embassies, see p. 10.

Currency Exchange: 24hr. ATMs abound. All **TMB, BankThai,** and **Siam Bank** machines accept AmEx/Cirrus/MC/V; others advertise which cards they accept on the sign. You can't throw a stone in Bangkok without hitting a bank, particularly in Silom.

American Express: Branches: at **G.M. Tour and Travel,** 273 Khaosan Rd. (☎02 282 3980 1. Open M-F 9am-7pm, Sa 9am-4pm) and 391 Soi St. Louis 3, South Sathorn 11 (☎02 676 2211).

LOCAL SERVICES

Luggage Storage: The **airport** is most reliable but a bit pricey (100฿ per day). Open 24hr. Also available at **Hualamphong Railway Station,** 10-30฿ per day. Open daily 4am-11pm. Some guesthouses also offer storage, but it may not be as secure.

Books: Kinokuniya Books and **Asia Books,** on the 3rd fl. of the Siam Paragon (p. 119) and scattered elswhere throughout the city, have a vast array of English-language books and international magazines. Open daily 9am-8pm. **Aporia Books,** 131 Tanao Rd. (☎02 629 2552), opposite the end of Khaosan Rd. One of the best bookshops in Bangkok, with new and used books for sale, trade, or rent. Open daily 9am-8pm. **Used bookstores** are very common in the Khaosan area and most hostels have shelves of books left behind by other travelers, free for the taking.

Local Publications: The **Bangkok Post** is a standard English daily sold everywhere (25฿). **The Nation** is a more trenchant, daring paper (25฿). **Daily Express** is a free English daily available in the more tourist-heavy neighborhoods. ▧**Monthly Metro** divulges the trendiest clubbing secrets (100฿). **BK Magazine** (▧**free**) is a weekly publication with similar content. The monthly magazine **Farang** reviews accommodations, restaurants, and the hottest nightlife in Bangkok; also includes entertaining travel articles about various Southeast Asian destinations.

Gay and Lesbian Resources: Monthly Metro (see above) has extensive gay nightlife listings. **Thai Guys** is a gay newsletter and guide to gay life in Bangkok, published 10 times per year and distributed for free at most gay venues.

BANGKOK

EMERGENCY AND COMMUNICATIONS

Tourist Police: Handles tourist-specific complaints. Most useful office located next to **TAT,** 4 Ratchadamnoen Nok Rd. (☎02 282 1144). All other offices will refer you here. **Branches:** 2911 Unico House Bldg., Soi Lang Suan (☎02 652 1721) off Ploenchit Rd., in Siam Sq.; another at the corner of Khaosan and Chakraphonh Rd. English spoken. **Booths** opposite Dusit Thani Hotel in Lumphini Park and at Suvarnabhumi International Airport (☎02 535 1641). Open 24hr.

Pharmacy: Fortune Pharmacy (Banglamphu), a tourist favorite, is in front of Khaosan Palace Hotel on Khaosan Rd. Open daily 9am-2am. **Siam Drug** (Silom Rd.), at the cul-de-sac of Patpong 2 Rd. Open daily 11am-3:30pm. Many pharmacies cluster on Sukhumvit Road between Soi Nana and Soi II., most open daily 8am-late.

Medical Services: Bumrungrad Hospital, 33/3 Sukhumvit Soi 3 (Soi Nana; operator ☎02 667 1000; emergency ☎02 667 2999). BTS stop: Nana. Thailand's only internationally accredited hospital. Open 24hr. **Chulalongkorn Hospital,** 1873 Rama IV Rd. (☎256 4000). Ambulance service. The best public hospital is **Siriraj Hospital** (Thonburi), 2 Pran Nok Rd. (☎02 411 0241). Take regular bus #19 from Sanam Luang. 24hr. ambulance. Cheapest vaccinations at **Red Cross Society's Queen Saovabha Institute** on Rama IV Rd. **Thai Red Cross,** 1871 Rama IV Rd. (☎02 256 4107; www.redcross. or.th). Anonymous clinic, 104 Ratchadamri Rd.(☎02 256 4109), offers HIV/AIDS testing, counseling, and treatment. Open M-F noon-7pm, Sa 9am-4pm.

Telephones: Make domestic calls at "cardphone" booths (5฿ per 3min.) and international calls at yellow "international cardphone" booths. Metal button at upper right connects directly to an AT&T operator. Offices providing 10-15฿ international calls abound on Khaosan Rd. and in Sukhumvit. The **Public Telecommunication Service Center** (☎02 614 2261), next to GPO, offers fax and telex. Open 24hr.

Internet Access: Try Khaosan Rd. and all other guesthouse areas listed. Khaosan rates 40฿ per hr. Elsewhere in Bangkok 20-60฿ per hr.

Post Offices: GPO (☎02 233 0700), in CAT building, on Charoen Krung Rd., near Soi 32. Poste Restante. Mail held for 2 months. Pick-up fee 1฿ per letter, 2฿ per parcel. Open M-F 8am-5pm, Sa-Su 8am-1pm. **Banglamphu Office,** off Khaosan Rd. Turn left onto Tanao Rd. and walk to the corner of Kraisi Rd. Poste Restante. Open M-F 8:30am-5:30pm, Sa 9am-noon. **Patpong Office,** 113/6-7 Thanon Surawong Center. Head up Patpong 1 Rd. and turn left on Surawong Rd. The post office is at the end of the next dead-end soi, on the left. Open M-F 8:30am-4:30pm, Sa 9am-noon. **Sukhumvit Road Office,** 118-122 Sukhumvit Rd. (☎02 251 7972), between Soi 4 (Nana Tai) and Landmark Plaza. International calls 8am-10pm. Open M-F 8:30am-5:30pm, Sa 9am-noon. To track packages, go to www.thailandpost.com.

Postal Code: 10501 (GPO); 10203 (Banglamphu); 10500 (Patpong); 10110 (Sukhumvit); 10112 (Poste Restante).

⬛ ACCOMMODATIONS

Accommodations in Bangkok are as varied as the backpackers, businessmen, laborers, and laundrywomen walking its streets. Abodes range from dirt-cheap flophouses to five-star hotels, with everything in between. Always ask to see rooms to discern differences in quality.

ACCOMMODATIONS BY PRICE

UNDER 120B (❶)		280-480B (❸)	
Bangkok International Youth Hostel	Dusit	Sri Ayuttaya	Dusit
Peachy Guest House	Bang	S.V. Guest House	Sukh
Sitdhi Guest House	Bang	YWCA	Silom
Tavee Guest House	Dusit	**480-800B (❹)**	
T.T. Guest House	China	The Atlanta	Sukh
120-280B (❷)		The Bed and Breakfast	Siam
🔲 Shanti Lodge	Dusit	White Lodge	Siam
Baan Sabai	Bang	A-One Inn	Siam
Lee Guest House 3	Silom	D & D Inn	Bang
Lee Mansion 4	Silom	Mango Lagoon Place	Bang
My House Guest House	Bang	New Siam II	Bang
New Siam Guest House	Bang	New Empire Hotel	China
Sala Thai Daily Mansion	Silom	P.B. Hotel	Sukh
Sawasdee House	Bang	Lub*D Hostel	Silom
🔲 Suk 11	Sukh	Wendy House	Siam
Wild Orchid Villa	Bang	**OVER 800B (❺)**	
Taewez Guesthouse	Dusit	Chinatown Hotel	China

BANGLAMPHU AND KO RATTANAKOSIN

GETTING TO BANGLAMPHU. Chao Phraya River Express stop: Banglamphu Pier. Buses: Airport Bus AB2, regular bus #15, A/C bus #511.

Located within walking distance of Wat Phra Kaew, Wat Pho, the Grand Palace, and the National Museum, this hub of Buddhism and architecture functions as a kind of decompression chamber for international travelers and budget backpackers as they enter Thailand. The heart of the fanfare is just to the north along **Khaosan Road,** a backpacker mecca of cheap accommodations, free-flowing Chang beer, and fake designer clothing. Rooms are often cramped, noisy, and full—reserve in advance by phone. The area just west, between Chakrapong and Phra Athit Rd., is just as popular but less noisy and may have more availability. Khaosan can be inexpensive, but rooms are often little more than beds with white sheets and walls and bear a striking resemblance to prison cells. About as un-Thai as the Diesel shirts and Hollywood movies piled on vendor's stalls, Khaosan is laden with drunken *farang* who haggle with Thais for overpriced goods and swap travel stories over banana pancakes. It's also easy to navigate culturally and offers nearly every service backpackers require. But since Khaosan isn't well connected to either the BTS or MRT, its relatively impractical orientation often increases most backpackers' sense of separation from the rest of Bangkok.

New Siam Guest House, 21 Soi Chana Songkram (☎02 282 4554; www.newsiam.net), on the small soi that connects the *wat* to the river. Though slightly pricier than the competition, this recently renovated guesthouse has a comfortable feel that's worth relaxing your budget for. Very popular, and the sheets have maps of Thailand on them. Internet 1B per min. Guests of New Siam can use New Siam II's pool (see below) for 90B. 24hr. reception. Singles 280B; doubles 295B, with bath 500B, with bath and A/C 590B. ❷

New Siam II, 50 Trok Rong Mhai (☎02 282 2795) New Siam Guest House's sister establishment is a more upscale version of Siam, with luxurious furniture and a small, murky pool. Doubles with fan 720B, with A/C 820B. Low-season 690/790B. ❹

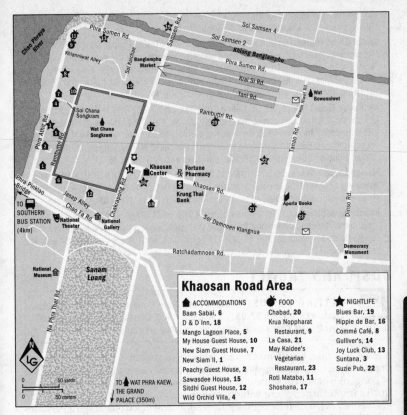

Khaosan Road Area

🏠 **ACCOMMODATIONS**
Baan Sabai, **6**
D & D Inn, **18**
Mango Lagoon Place, **5**
My House Guest House, **10**
New Siam Guest House, **7**
New Siam II, **1**
Peachy Guest House, **2**
Sawasdee House, **15**
Sitdhi Guest House, **12**
Wild Orchid Villa, **4**

🍎 **FOOD**
Chabad, **20**
Krua Noppharat
  Restaurant, **9**
La Casa, **21**
May Kaidee's
  Vegetarian
  Restaurant, **23**
Roti Mataba, **11**
Shoshana, **17**

⭐ **NIGHTLIFE**
Blues Bar, **19**
Hippie de Bar, **16**
Commé Café, **8**
Gulliver's, **14**
Joy Luck Club, **13**
Suntana, **3**
Suzie Pub, **22**

BANGKOK

Wild Orchid Villa, 8 Soi Chana Songkram (☎02 629 4378), across from New Siam. The tasteful earth-tone rooms and ceramic tiles are a welcome change from many of Khaosan's concrete, prison-like guesthouses. Unfortunately, some of the fan rooms don't have windows facing outside. Extremely popular 24hr. restaurant and bar. Pizza 150-250฿. Singles with fan 250฿; doubles with fan 290฿, with bath and A/C 550฿. ❷

Baan Sabai, 12 Soi Rongmai Thanon Chaofa (☎02 629 1599). Slightly away from the busiest tourist areas, Baan Sabai is quieter, less expensive, and better kept than typical Khaosan guesthouses. The shared baths are clean and the lobby has a large plantation-style porch with a garden. Singles with fan 170฿; doubles with fan 270฿, with window 320฿, with bath and A/C 450฿, with hot water and A/C 500฿. ❷

D & D Inn, 68-70 Khaosan Rd. (☎02 629 0526). This upscale guesthouse offers a Khaosan address and spic-and-span but impersonal rooms. Very popular. Book ahead by phone, and ask to stay in the new section. The rooftop pool and bar is party central. Every room has A/C and private bath. Singles 550฿, doubles 750฿. ❹

Sawasdee House, 147 Soi Rambuttri Rd. (☎02 629 3457). From Khaosan Rd., cross Chakrapong Rd. and walk down the soi along the right side of the temple wall; it's halfway down on the right. A socialite's dream—it's practically a backpacker convention. Beautiful restaurant and loads of traditional decor. Rooms are well kept and often full, so reserve in advance. Singles with fan 200฿, with A/C and bath 350฿; doubles with fan 380฿, with A/C 400฿, with A/C and bath 550฿. ❷

Sitdhi Guest House, Rambuttri Rd. Soi 2 (☎02 282 3090), 1 block east of Baan Sabai. Rooms with peach-colored walls are a welcome change from the standard white, bare-bones look of most of the other budget accommodations in the area. Chilly lobby has a popular cafe, large-screen TV, and pool table. Singles with fan and shared bath 150฿;doubles 200฿, with bath 250฿, with A/C 350฿. ❷

My House Guest House, 37 Soi Chana Songkram (☎02 282 9263). From Khaosan Rd., go toward the river and across the temple grounds; it's 50m to the right. Manages to be close to cafes and bars while maintaining a quiet atmosphere. An excellent selection of newly released Western movies keeps crowds transfixed all day. Singles 160฿, with bath 200฿; doubles 250฿, with bath 350฿, with bath and A/C 500฿. ❷

Mango Lagoon Place, 30 Soi Rambuttri Phra Athit Rd. (☎02 281 4783). A little slice of luxury in Khaosan. The cheery rooms are well-furnished and have A/C, hot water, and TV. High-season doubles 700฿, suites 800฿, low-season 600฿/700฿. ❹

Peachy Guest House, 10 Phra Athit Rd. (☎02 281 6471). High ceilings, spacious rooms, and highly polished dark-wood floors give this guesthouse a comfortable feel. No shoes upstairs. Serene garden, Internet cafe (1฿ per 2min.), and bar are bonuses. Singles with shared bath 120฿; doubles 160฿, with shower, toilet, and A/C 400฿. ❶

DUSIT AND THEWET

> **GETTING TO DUSIT.** Chao Phraya River Express stop: Thewet. Regular buses #16, 23, 30, 32, 33, 72; A/C bus #505. One bus from each soi stops near Thewet. Check local listings for complete schedules.

A quiet bus ride, boat trip, or walk from the sights in Ko Rattanakosin and Banglamphu, the guesthouses behind the National Library in Thewet are some of Bangkok's best-kept secrets. Catering to those who wish to escape Khaosan Road's frantic atmosphere without sacrificing affordability and accessibility, Thewet is quiet, with little nightlife. Instead, a laid-back tropical spirit pervades the guesthouses that line the end of Si Ayutthaya Rd. Some taxi and tuk-tuk drivers don't even know where this area is, so be sure to tell them to go to Thewet near Samsen Rd., behind the National Library. Conversely, Dusit is dominated by wide, heavily trafficked avenues and large government buildings and does not have many accommodation options.

 Shanti Lodge, 37 Si Ayutthaya Soi 16 (☎02 281 2497). Billed as "The Oasis of Bang-kok," Shanti is one of the best choices in the city. No smoking or shoes. This place feels like (and is decorated like) a tropical paradise. Impeccably clean rooms, sparkling shared baths, and a restaurant open daily 7:30am-11pm. In high season, reserve 1-2 weeks in advance. Dorms with A/C 200฿; Doubles with fan 400฿, with A/C 450฿; with cold shower 550/650฿, with hot shower 650/750฿. ❶

Tavee Guest House, 83 Si Ayutthaya Soi 14 (☎02 280 1447). Cozy common spaces with wood furniture and a popular restaurant open 24hr. Rooms are clean and tidy. They are also charmingly decorated with warm accents. Dorms 120฿; singles and doubles 300฿, with bath 400฿, with A/C 450฿. ❶

Sri Ayuttaya, 23/11 Si Ayutthaya Soi 14 (☎02 282 5942). Tavee Guest House's street-side, upscale sister establishment gleams with shiny dark-wood furniture. Small Thai restaurant within. Rooms with shared bath and fan 350฿, with cold water and A/C 600฿, with hot water and A/C 750฿. ❸

Taewez Guesthouse, 23/12 Si Ayutthaya (☎02 280 8856, www.taewez.com), next to Shanti. Large, pleasant rooms. Internet 40฿ per hour. Restaurant open 7am-9:30pm. Singles with fan and shared bath 250฿, with A/C and ensuite bath 400฿; doubles with A/C and shared bath 380฿, ensuite 430฿. ❷

Bangkok International Youth Hostel (HI), 25/2 Phitsanulok Rd. (☎02 281 0361). Somewhat out of the way: head south on Nakhon Ratchasima Rd., and turn right on Phitsanulok Rd.; the hostel is 20m down on the right. Colorful murals lead to an open-air lobby. Spacious dorm rooms. Sex-segregated. No alcohol, and smoking limited. HI members only; non-members can buy a year-long membership on the spot for 300฿ or pay 50฿ per night. Dorm-style rooms 100฿, with A/C 120฿; singles with fan 250฿, with A/C and private bath 280฿; doubles with fan 300฿, with A/C and private bath 350฿. ❶

CHINATOWN, PAHURAT, AND HUALAMPHONG

GETTING TO CHINATOWN, PAHURAT, AND HUALAMPHONG. Chao Phraya River Express stop: Ratchawong. Regular buses #1, 4, 25, and 73; A/C bus #501. Boat taxi is easy and enjoyable.

Chinatown accommodations line **Yaowarat Road, Pahurat Road, Chakraphet Road,** and **Rong Muang Road.** Travelers staying here are either evading *farang* hordes or jumping on and off early-morning trains. Chinatown offers few budget rooms that are clean and safe; some are rip-offs, others welcome only Asians, and many are brothels. Stick to those that advertise in English.

T.T. Guest House, 516-518 Si Phraya Rd. Soi Sawang (☎02 236 2946). Exit Hualamphong, take a left on Rama IV Rd., turn right on Mahanakhon Rd., and take the 1st left; it's a 15min. walk or 30฿ *tuk-tuk* ride. Popular in high season (reserve in advance) with clean rooms and a friendly atmosphere. TV room and English library. Lockout midnight. Dorms 100฿, singles 180฿, doubles with window 250฿. ❶

Chinatown Hotel, 526 Yaowarat Rd. (☎02 225 0226; www.chinatownhotel.co.th). One of the few hotels in Chinatown catering to *farang* as well as Asian tourists. The staff wears fancy traditional Chinese uniforms. All rooms have A/C and TV. Restaurant open daily 6:30am-10:30pm. Internet 60฿ per 30min. Doubles with breakfast 1350฿. ❺

New Empire Hotel, 572 Yaowarat Rd. (☎02 234 6990), opposite the Bank of Ayudhya near Wat Traimit. Functional rooms with basic luxuries line dim, cavernous halls at this impersonal hotel. Deluxe rooms are newer and better decorated. All rooms have A/C, TV, and private bath; breakfast included. Standard rooms 720฿, deluxe rooms 800฿. ❹

SILOM ROAD

GETTING TO SILOM ROAD. You can get to Silom Rd. by boat, skytrain, metro, or bus. The stops you need, respectively, are listed here. Chao Phraya River Express: Oriental or Sathorn/Central Pier to access the Skytrain. Skytrain: Saladaeng. MRT: Silom. Regular buses #15, 76, 77, 115. A/C buses #504, 505, 515.

Although lavish hotels dominate **Silom Road,** the surrounding area is home to an astounding variety of neighborhoods. On **Pan Road,** a Burmese community lives between the Burmese embassy and the Hindu temple, while the infamous **Patpong** red light district marks the raunchier side of Bangkok. Some of the cheapest budget establishments in Bangkok are gathered a 2km bus or tuk-tuk ride from Silom Rd., along **Soi Ngam Duphli** and **Soi Si Bamphen** off Rama IV Rd. Silom is also

Silom Rd.

🍴 FOOD
Eat Me!, 5

★ NIGHTLIFE
DJ Station, 8
The Expresso, 7
Lucifer, 1
Luminous, 6
Muzzik Café, 3
Radio City, 2
Tapas, 4

a nightlife center that attracts hip Thais, expats, and tourists alike.

Sala Thai Daily Mansion, 15 Soi Sapankoo (☎02 287 1436). From Rama IV Rd., walk up Soi Ngam Duphli and turn left onto Soi Si Bamphen; take the 1st soi to the left, and then turn right. Tucked away from the traffic of the main road, the alley on which this hotel is located is surprisingly quiet. Interestingly decorated with potted plants and kitschy furniture. Sala Thai features cheerful, sizable rooms with shared bath and a sitting area with cable TV. Also boasts a beautiful, breezy rooftop garden. Singles 200฿, with A/C 300฿; doubles 300/400฿. ❷

Lee Guest House 3, 13 Soi Sapankoo (☎02 679 7045), next to Sala Thai Daily Mansion, offers clean rooms with fan and shared bath. The larger rooms have sinks. Rooms at reasonable prices. Singles 120-160฿, doubles 200฿. Some of the larger rooms are windowless and less pleasant than the small rooms, so ask to see a few before you check in. ❷

Lub*D Hostel, 4 Decho Rd. (☎02 634 7999; www.lubd.com), off Silom Rd. BTS: Chong Nonsi. This newly opened hostel, on a sidestreet close enough to Silom Rd. for convenience but far enough for comfort, is a stunningly hip place. Although it is a tad pricier than the average Bangkok hostel, the mod decor and luxurious amenities make it worth the baht. All the rooms are sparklingly clean and comfortable, with oversize single beds, A/C, free Wi-Fi, and lockers or security boxes. Common "theatre room" with satellite TV and movies. The downstairs bar and cafe are popular with tourists. 8-bed mixed dorm 550฿ per person; ladies' dorm 650฿. Singles 1300฿, doubles 1600฿; all with single-sex shared bath. Double with private bath 1800฿. Book online for a 35% discount. ❹

Charlie House, 36-37 1034 Soi Sapankoo (☎02 679 8330; www.charliehousethailand.com), just south of Rama IV Rd., near the Suan Lum Night Bazaar. 19 hotel-like rooms include luxuries such as A/C, hot water, telephone, and satellite TV. Small attached restaurant serves tasty, inexpensive Thai food (entrees 40-100฿). Singles 450฿, doubles 540฿, oversize doubles 700-750฿. ❸

Lee Mansion 4, 9 Soi Sapankoo (☎02 286 7874). Noisier but closer to the main road. All rooms are clean and bright with small balcony, fan, and shared bath. Small rooms 160฿, large rooms 200฿. ❷

YWCA, 13 Sathorn Tai Rd. (☎02 679 1280), women only. Accessible through the BMW dealership on Sathorn Rd. Small rooms located on a busy road near Lumphini Park, Suan Lum Night Bazaar, and the Silom/Patpong area. Bookstore/giftshop, badminton courts, and restaurant. Singles 750฿, doubles 1000฿; monthly rate 8000/9500฿ includes services and utilities. 5% member discount. 3% credit-card charge. ❺

SIAM SQUARE

GETTING TO SIAM SQUARE. Skytrain: Siam Sq. Regular buses #15, 25, and 204; A/C bus #501.

BANGKOK

In the shadow of Bangkok's ritziest malls, **Soi Kasem San 1** can be found off Rama I Rd., opposite the National Stadium. Quieter than Khaosan and almost free of street vendors, Siam Sq. is filled with returning travelers and expats. Accommodations are higher-priced, but you get convenient location in return. Proximity to the Skytrain makes much of Bangkok's nightlife and the Eastern Bus Terminal easily accessible. Guesthouses can be reached by taking Exit 3 at the National Stadium Skytrain stop, one stop away from Siam Sq.

Wendy House, 36/2 Soi Kasem 1 (☎02 214 1149). This popular guesthouse is clean and simple. Convenience and friendly, English-speaking staff set it apart. All rooms with TV, fridge, complimentary breakfast, A/C, and private hot-water bath. Best to reserve in advance. Laundry (daily 8am-8pm) 55฿ per kg. Internet access 60฿ per hr. Singles 900฿, doubles 1000฿; twins 1100฿. ❹

White Lodge, 36/8 Soi Kasem 1 (☎02 216 8867). Bright, white halls and innumerable windows lend this place the pleasant atmosphere of a solarium. All rooms with A/C, private bath, and telephone. Singles and doubles 500฿. ❸

The Bed and Breakfast, 36/42-43 Soi Kasem 1 (☎02 215 3004). Fairly clean rooms with steel frame beds, all with A/C, phone, and hot shower. Fewer amenities than some of the other hotels on the street, but easier on the wallet. Breakfast included. Reserve in advance Nov.-Feb. Singles 500฿, doubles 600฿, triples 650-700฿. ❸

A-One Inn, 25/13-15 Soi Kasem 1 (☎215 3029). Small, well-kept rooms with large windows. Weekly, bi-weekly, and monthly discounts; no singles. Doubles and twins 700฿, 18900฿ per month; triples 840฿/22680฿; family rooms for 5 940฿/25380฿. Internet access 50฿ per hr. ❹

SUKHUMVIT ROAD

 GETTING TO SUKHUMVIT RD. The stops you need for Sukhumvit Rd. are listed here: Skytrain: Nana or Asok. Regular buses #2, 25, 38, 40, 48, 90; A/C buses #501, 508, 511, 513.

Sukhumvit's accommodations boast proximity to great restaurants, some of Bangkok's trendiest nightlife, and the Skytrain and Eastern Bus Terminal. The actual establishments range from sketchy places that rent rooms "part time" (Sukhumvit hosts a red-light scene second only to Patpong) to some of Bangkok's most luxurious five-star hotels. In between are excellent budget hostels and the delightful **Suk 11.** This district is popular with older expats and is one of the best places to find long-term accommodations.

Suk 11, 1/13 Sukhumvit Rd. Soi 11 (☎02 253 5927; www.suk11.com), 10m down the soi on a side street to the left. A truly beautiful enclave in the heart of Bangkok's nightlife. All rooms (even dorms) have A/C, and are a great place to crash. 2 common rooms with cable TV and DVDs, plus many balconies and sitting areas. All baths with hot water. Laundry service and Wi-Fi available. Complimentary breakfast served daily. Dorms 250฿; singles 450฿, with bath 600฿; doubles 600/750฿. ❷

The Atlanta, 78 Sukhumvit Rd. Soi 2 (☎02 252 6069), at the very end of the road. This budget hotel is full of 60s style and luxury, with large rooms to boot. All rooms with A/C and hot water. The hotel also has a swimming pool, restaurant, and free Wi-Fi. Singles 650฿, doubles 850฿; suites, with bedroom and sitting room, 1020฿. ❸

S.V. Guest House, 19/35-36 Sukhumvit Rd. Soi 19 (☎02 253 3556), near Asok Station. Somewhat disheveled, but good prices, great location, and quiet rooms. Internet 50฿/hr. Reserve in advance Nov-Feb. Singles with A/C and shared bath 450฿; doubles with A/C 500฿, with bath 600฿. ❸

P.B. Hotel, 40 Sukhumvit Rd. Soi 3 (☎02 651 1525). From Sukhumvit Rd., head up Soi 3 (Soi Nana), and turn down the alley across from the Pakistani Embassy; P.B. is on the left. Very large hotel-style rooms with TV, fridge, and marble bath at lower prices than you would expect, but not many other comforts. Doubles 800฿. ❹

LONG-TERM ACCOMMODATIONS

It is not difficult to find long-term accommodation in Bangkok. Sukhumvit, home to a thriving expat community, contains many guesthouses offering weekly and monthly rates. The **YWCA** (p. 104), in Silom Rd., also has monthly rates. **BK Magazine** has an extensive listing of apartments for rent in Bangkok.

P.S. Guest House, 26/1 Sukhumvit Rd. Soi 8 (☎02 255 2309; psguesthouse@hotmail. com). This clean, quiet guesthouse has neat rooms and suites with hardwood floors, and a great location. Monthly rent includes utilities and daily cleaning. Pay extra for laundry service. Bedroom with kitchen 28,000฿ per month, without kitchen 25,000฿. ❹

Bright City Tower Service Apartments, 21/4 Sukhumvit Rd. Soi 11 (☎02 651 0159). Basic but with friendly service. All rooms have A/C, satellite TV, microwave, and refrigerator. Rooms cleaned 6 days per week. 120 pieces of laundry included in monthly rent. Studio 22,000฿ per month; junior suite 25,000฿ per month. ❹

◘ FOOD

Thai cuisine is world-renowned, but no one is more obsessed with or proud of it than the Thais themselves. Food is an integral part of Bangkok culture and plays a central role in nearly every social engagement. The city is home to an internationally diverse selection of foods—everything from superb shawarma to sushi—available within an equally diverse price spectrum. The fusion restaurants where these cultures clash offer some of the more expensive but also the most unique tastes you'll find. Outside of restaurants specifically geared toward *farang*, it's virtually impossible to get a bad meal in Bangkok. Thais are visibly excited by travelers who venture away from banal Westernized fare and eat the way the locals do—right from the street. By far, the most authentic, best-tasting, and cheapest Thai victuals are served from carts and no-name restaurants crowding back alleys; but be careful of the local tap water, which can cause illness in those unaccustomed to its bacteria.

FOOD BY TYPE

THAI		INTERNATIONAL	
Bussaracum	Silom	Chabad	Bang
Cabbages & Condoms	Sukh	Dosa King	Sukh
Coca Noodles	Siam	◙ Eat Me!	Silom
Jumbo Noodles	China	Hua Seng Hong	China
KP Suki	China	La Casa	Bang
Krua Noppharat Restaurant	Bang	◙ Roti Mataba	Bang
Unnamed Noodle Place	Siam	Royal India Restaurant	China
◙ Som Tam Paradise	Siam	Shoshana	Bang
		White Orchid Restaurant	China
WESTERN AND THAI FUSION		Arirang	Sukh
◙ Tham Na	Dusit	Doo Dee	Siam
Crepes and Co.	Sukh	**VEGETARIAN**	
Sai Ta Ra	Dusit	May Kaidee's Vegetarian Restaurant	Bang
All Seasons	Silom		

BANGLAMPHU AND KO RATTANAKOSIN

For good food stalls, stroll down **Soi Rambuttri, Krai Si Road** (in the evening) or **Phra Chan Road** (during the day), opposite **Thammasat University.** The university's cafeteria has good, cheap grub. During the weekday lunch hour, vendors catering to Thai professionals serve a diverse selection of food. On weekends, hawkers hang out around **Sanam Luang. Khaosan Road** bursts with overpriced Thai and Western cuisine. Pra Athit Rd. has more stylish and flavorful restaurants and cafes. One or two blocks north on **Tani Road** and at **Wat Chai Chana Songkram,** food stalls fry noodles and rice dishes all day and into the night.

▨ **Roti Mataba,** at the bend in Phra Athit Rd., where it becomes Phra Sumen Rd. This tiny corner restaurant is home to some of the best Muslim Thai food in the area. The tender chicken curry *roti* (41в) is delicious, and the beef-stuffed *mataba* (25в) will have you asking for seconds. Abundant breakfast *roti* (8-20в). Open Tu-Su 7am-10pm. ❶

May Kaidee's Vegetarian Restaurant (☎02 281 7137). Walk to Tanao Rd. at the end of Khaosan Rd. Take a right, a quick left, and a left again down the 1st soi; it's 75m down. Sit on a streetside stool or indoors on a floor mat and eat sweet Thai specialties like black sticky rice with coconut milk and mango (50в). Dishes 40-150в. May Kaidee has a book of recipes (350в) and offers cooking classes (1000в) that focus on vegetarian cooking. Open daily 9am-10pm. ❷

Shoshana, on Chakrapong Rd. Facing the temple at the end of Khaosan Rd., turn right and right again at the 1st alley. This guesthouse restaurant specializes in delicious Israeli and Middle Eastern cuisine like falafel (50в), shawarma (60в), and large sandwiches and salads (70-100в). Plenty of vegetarian options. Open daily 11am-11pm. ❷

Chabad, 96 Soi Rambuttri. After squeezing past the tight security, you'll find delicious hummus and *baba ghanoush* (30в) being served to a devoted Israeli crowd. Main courses 80-160в. Open Su-Th 10am-10pm, F 10am-3pm. ❸

La Casa, 210 Khaosan Rd. (☎02 629 1627). Fresh pastas (200-250в), salads (160-220в), and creamy gelato are good reasons to stop by this popular Italian restaurant. The extensive menu also includes pizza, risotto, seafood, and meat. Open daily 11am-midnight. ❸

Krua Noppharat Restaurant, 130-132 Phra Athit Rd. (☎02 281 7578). Thais pack in to enjoy an authentic Thai lunch at this award-winning restaurant. Fried rice with pork 50в. Chicken with cashew nuts 80в. Open M-Sa 10:30am-2:30pm, and 5-9pm. ❷

DUSIT AND THEWET

The sidewalk opposite the guesthouses on Si Ayutthaya Rd. bustles with **food stalls,** as does the **market** at the end of the road by Thewet pier. With just about every Thai rice, noodle, and curry dish available at rock-bottom prices (30-40в), these stalls are the best dining option for visitors in this area, especially as there are very few restaurants. Shanti Lodge, Tavee Guesthouse, and Sri Ayuttaya (p. 102) all serve quality Thai food at reasonable prices (60-90в).

▨ **Tham Na,** 175 Samsen Rd., (☎02 282 4979), between Sois 3 and 5. A 10min. walk or short bus ride down Samsen Rd. Small, marvelous vegetarian restaurant with a creative menu full of amazing fusion food (85-120в). Open daily 8am-9pm. ❶

Sai Ta Ra Restaurant, on Si Ayutthaya Rd. at the intersection with Samsen Rd., opposite the National Library. Serves the same dishes as the stalls at slightly higher prices (40-60в). Open daily 7am-10pm. ❶

CHINATOWN, PAHURAT, AND HUALAMPHONG

The center of **Yaowarat Road** is a treasure of outdoor dining, and the sois that branch off it overflow with culinary delights prepared on the spot. Roasted chestnuts and translucent, succulent lychees abound. This area requires adventurous tastes: shark-fin soups and abalone dishes are specialties. Sampling these delicacies on the street is much cheaper than trying them in a restaurant (shark-fin soup in a restaurant runs 2000฿ and up; on the street it's 300-600฿). Further down Yaowarat Rd., cuisine shifts from Chinese to Indian; excellent Indian restaurants are plentiful near **Chakraphet Road** and **Pahurat Road.**

Hua Seng Hong, 371-373 Yaowarat Rd. Look for the cabinet full of pillowy soft barbecue pork buns and the dried shark fins hanging outside. Serves handmade dim sum (25฿) and Chinese dishes, many featuring prawns (100-200฿), to a massive, devoted crowd amidst an all-granite interior. Open daily 9am-1pm. ❷

Jumbo Noodles, 442 Yaowarat Rd., with no English sign across from the White Orchid Hotel. Popular eatery serves up a mean noodle soup (40-70฿) and simple rice dishes. Stainless steel furniture and garage doors that open onto the street set it a notch higher than its food-cart neighbors. Try rice with braised pork rump (50฿), and wash it down with cold chrysanthemum juice (12฿). ❷

Royal India Restaurant, 392/1 Chakraphet Rd. (☎02 221 6565), near the river; look for the sign on the left, on Chakraphet Rd.; it's set back in an alleyway. Menu of delicious Indian dishes (some vegetarian). *Thali*—curry, *masala*, and *naan* menu (185-250฿)—makes your choice easy. Dishes 50-100฿. Open daily 10am-10pm. ❸

White Orchid Restaurant and Coffee Shop, 415 Yaowarat Rd., in the White Orchid Hotel. Famed dim sum (45฿ per dish; buy 5 get 1 free) and nightly all-you-can-eat dinner buffet (6-10pm, 250฿) are delicious. Open 24hr. ❹

KP Suki, 233 Yaowarat Rd. (☎02 222 6573), at the intersection with Ratchawong Rd. This clean, bright restaurant serves a sanitized, *farang*-friendly version of the noodle and soup dishes found on the street. Their specialty is a chicken-broth soup that you cook at your table with meat, dumplings, or veggies. Friendly, attentive service and nice bathrooms. Most dishes 150-200฿. Open daily 10:30am-10pm. ❷

SILOM ROAD

Silom Road is chock-full of expensive restaurants and American chains, particularly near Silom Center. On **Convent** and **Sala Daeng Roads,** however, you'll find a winning mix of Thai food carts with outdoor seating and Western-style cafes, which get busy at lunch when office workers descend from the surrounding skyscrapers. Tourist cafes set up at night on **Surawong Road** opposite Patpong.

☒ Eat Me!, 1/6 Soi Piphat 2 (☎02 238 0931), off Convent Rd., to the left. Creativity and cuisine collide in this stylish fusion restaurant. Servings tend to be small, but are well worth the splurge. Photography and sculpture decorate the downstairs, delicious dishes abound upstairs (340-1200฿). Live jazz F-Su 8-11pm complements the excellent mixed drink menu (240-400฿) that features creations like the fig and ginger martini and mango caipirinha. Open daily 3pm-1am. AmEx/MC/V. ❺

All Seasons Restaurant, 31 Sathorn Tai Rd. (☎02 343 6333; www.allseasons-sathorn.com). The door on the left leads up to the restaurant on the 2nd fl. Sleek and modern, this hotel restaurant (non-guests welcome) hides a surprisingly budget-friendly menu. The Western dishes (burgers, salads, and pastas) are on the expensive side (170-400฿), but the Thai offerings of soups, curries, and fried rice dishes all cost around 150฿. The staff is extremely attentive and formal, adding to the upscale atmosphere. Open daily 11am-11pm. AmEx/MC/V. ❹

Bussaracum, 139 Sethiwan Tower, Pan Rd. (☎02 266 6312), next to the Burmese embassy. The best time to go to this upscale restaurant specializing in royal Thai cuisine is for lunch, when they have an all-you-can-eat buffet of varied spicy salads, rices, fish and meat entrees, and desserts for 220฿. Regular dishes 110-380฿; extensive cocktail and liquor selection 130-200฿. Open daily 11am-2pm and 5-10:30pm. ❹

SPICE UP YOUR LIFE. Thai tables are often cluttered with a vast array of condiments, which vary by region, though fish sauce, dried chilies, sugar, green onions, and peanuts are pretty universal. Thai chefs leave it to you to season your food, so experiment to get that soup just the way you like it—if you don't, the chef might even take offense!

SIAM SQUARE

Siam Sq. is ripe with American fast food, especially in the shopping centers, but Sois 4 and 5 have a number of quirky and decently priced eateries that complement the trendy atmosphere of the neighboring boutiques. In the afternoon and evening, vendors grill up juicy meats in front of the **National Stadium** on Rama I Rd., at the mouth of **Soi Kasem 1,** and along the soi weaving through Siam Sq. The glitzy Siam Paragon mall has a surprisingly affordable and authentic food court in its basement. Sidewalk restaurants pepper **Ratchaprarop Road** and **Soi Wattanasin** opposite the Indra Regent Hotel.

Som Tam Paradise, 392/14 Siam Sq. Soi 5 (☎251 4880). University students come in droves to enjoy flavorful, spicy salads in this hip restaurant. Specializes in northern Thai cuisine with a delicious green papaya salad (60฿), fried chicken (85฿), and steamed sticky rice (20฿). Open daily 11:15am-9pm. ❷

Noodle place (unnamed), Soi Kasem Son 1, between Wendy House and the Reno Hotel. This nameless, bare-bones noodle spot features all your street-side favorites with a place to sit, an English menu, and HBO blaring in the background. Noodle, rice dishes, and soups (40-50฿) can be made with meat or seafood, and are simple and delicious. A good place for those a little intimidated by the food carts to try some authentic street-style food. Open daily 7am-9pm. ❷

Doo Dee Shop, at the end of Soi 4 in Siam Sq. (on the left if you're coming from Rama I Road). Probably as close to a diner as you can get in Thailand, Doo Dee serves up Thai and Korean cooking for crowds of office workers on their lunch breaks. A few dishes go up to 200฿, but most are between 40-70฿. An English menu is available, and will be accompanied with a special set of *farang*-proof condiments (ketchup and a sweet chili sauce) when they see that you aren't Thai. The omelettes (50฿), made with pork or shrimp, are greasy and delicious. Open 9am-9pm. ❷

Coca Noodles, (☎251 6337), at the corner of Henry Dunant Rd. and Soi 7, in Siam Sq. This popular ramen chain has a long menu full of Thai, Chinese, and Japanese dishes, including dumplings, soups, and noodles. Coca also offers *shabu shabu*, a soup made of meats, dumplings, and veggies that you pick out on the spot. Priced from 60-300฿, noodle and rice entrees around 80-140฿. Open daily 11am-11pm. ❸

SUKHUMVIT ROAD

Sukhumvit Rd. brims with expensive restaurants for those who want to burn baht, local eateries for Thai food aficionados, and foreign-themed cafes for travelers longing for a taste of home. If you're in the last category, Sukhumvit has Bangkok's largest selection of foreign cuisines at reasonable prices. Soi 3/1 specializes in Middle Eastern cuisine. **Sukhumvit Plaza,** at the mouth of Soi 12, is filled with Korean barbecue and karaoke joints. Indian restaurants are scattered throughout the area, but are particularly dense around Soi Nana. Japanese restaurants proliferate between Sois 31-53. Finally, there are a number of Italian restaurants and even a German beer house on Soi 11. The

BANGKOK

usual food stalls set up on many Soi (especially 8, 11, and 15) at lunchtime and in the evening to serve up classic Thai dishes (20-40฿).

Dosa King, 153/7 Sukhumvit Soi 11/1 (☎02 651 1700). Serves north and south Indian vegetarian cuisine. Eating one of Dosa King's paper-thin *masala dosas* (130฿) while sipping on a mango *lassi* (80฿) will most definitely transport you to the subcontinent. Open daily 11am-11pm. ❷

Cabbages & Condoms, 10 Sukhumvit Rd. Soi 12 (☎02 229 4610). Founded by an organization that hopes to make birth control as commonplace as cabbages are in local markets, this restaurant serves exceptional Thai food in a beautiful garden hung with lights (indoor A/C seating also available). There is also a small gift store that sells Thai artwork and less traditional t-shirts and souvenirs. Free condom with the bill. Most dishes 150-300฿. Reserve in advance for Sa-Su. Open daily 11am-10pm. AmEx/V. ❹

Crepes and Co., 18/1 Sukhumvit Rd. Soi 12 (☎02 653 3990), past Cabbages & Condoms. Every type of crepe imaginable: dessert-style, Western, Thai—or design your own (120-350฿). Spanish-style tapas 90-130฿. Serene garden, hip French music, and friendly staff make this an ideal place for a leisurely weekend brunch. Open daily 9am-midnight. AmEx/MC/V. ❸

Arirang, Sukhumvit Plaza 1F, Soi 12. With your back to Sukhumvit, Arirang is on the right-hand corner of the plaza. Korean businessmen on golf holidays flock here for vast quantities of alcohol and delicious Korean barbecue. Prices and menus of the many Korean restaurants on this corner are fairly similar: entrees 200-350฿, a bottle of *soju* (Korean rice wine) 300฿. Open daily 11am-2am. ❺

◎ SIGHTS

BANGLAMPHU AND KO RATTANAKOSIN

With its many points of interest, Ko Rattanakosin takes at least an entire day to explore fully. Although very touristed, **Wat Phra Kaew** and the **Grand Palace** are still two of the grandest sights in Bangkok. The Chao Phraya River Express (Tha Chang) and buses (#1, 25, 47, 82; A/C #543, 544) stop near the compound. History and art lovers will be glued to the treasures in the nearby **National Museum.** For the spiritually inclined, a circuit of monasteries is also nearby.

◼**WAT PHRA KAEW** (TEMPLE OF THE EMERALD BUDDHA) **AND THE GRAND PALACE.** Covering over 160 hectares, the Temple of the Emerald Buddha and the Grand Palace complex are as unavoidable as Khaosan Rd., but far more aesthetically pleasing. Thais flock here to pay respects to the 66cm Emerald Buddha, while foreigners are amazed by both magnificent traditional Thai architecture and more modern attempts at 20th-century Western design. The entrance gate at the northern end of the complex faces the glittering **Temple of the Emerald Buddha,** originally the Royal Chapel of the Chakri Dynasty. The virtual kaleidoscope of colors (mainly from the blue, red, gold, and silver mirrors adorning the Temple's walls) and ornate gold-gilded altars are a physical manifestation of Thais' profound devotion to both Buddhism and the Thai royal family. Don't expect a spiritual awakening or serene Angkor Wat-styled temples (although a miniature of Angkor Wat lies to one side of Wat Phra Kaew), but you'll be impressed by the splendor of Thailand's most sacred and culturally intriguing Buddha figure. The actual Emerald Buddha, slightly anti-climactic in size and perched atop a 3m gold-gilded altar, rests inside the *bot.* It was discovered in 1434, when lightning shattered a *chedi* in Chiang Rai and an abbot found a stucco Buddha inside. He removed all the stucco and found the glorious Emerald Buddha, made of precious jade, hidden within. The figure stayed in Lampang until 1468, when it was carted off to Vientiane, Laos. Two hundred and fourteen years later, General Chao Phraya Chakri captured Vientiane and reclaimed the statue. In 1782, King Rama I ascended the throne, moved the capital to Bangkok, and built the Royal Chapel—Wat Phra Kaew—for the Buddha. The frescoes on the walls inside the temple portray scenes from Buddha's life. The impressive back wall shows the Lord Buddha attaining Enlightenment and subduing man. Surrounding the Temple of the Emerald Buddha are shrines of lesser religious import but impressive beauty. Take a look at the frescoes that encircle the compound: the scenes are taken from the ancient Indian epic the *Ramayana.*

Next door to the Temple is the **Grand Palace,** accessible through a gate connecting the two compounds. Once inside the gate, look left; the building behind the gate is **Barom Phiman Hall,** which still houses visiting dignitaries—Queen Elizabeth II and Bill Clinton were recent guests. From this point, turn right and stroll down the path past royal buildings on the left. The first is **Amarinda Vinichai Hall,** which once held court ceremonies. Next is **Chakri Mahaprasad Hall,** the residence of King Chulalongkorn, a hybrid of European and Thai design. Today, the reception areas and central throne hall are used for royal ceremonies and are off-limits to mere mortal backpackers. Farther on is **Dusit Hall,** a symmetrical Thai building with a mother-of-pearl throne inside.

The **Wat Phra Kaew Museum** is inside the Grand Palace (take a right after the gift shop). The first floor displays relics and parts from original buildings that have been replaced, while the second floor contains hundreds of Buddhas and enamel and crystal wares. (☎ *02 623 5500. Entrance off Na Phra Lan Rd., at the northern end of the complex. No pictures allowed inside Wat Phra Kaew, although they are allowed elsewhere. Polite dress required: pants and shirts with sleeves. Sandals are generally acceptable. Shirts, long pants, and shoes are available at the entrance. Complex open daily 8:30am-3:30pm. Museum open daily 8:30am-4pm. 300฿. Admission to Wat Phra Kaew and the Grand Palace includes admission to the Royal Thai Decorations and Coins Pavilion and the Vimanmek Palace in Dusit within 7 days of purchase. Audio guide 2hr., 100฿.)*

 GRAND PALACE, PLEASE. The area around the Grand Palace is full of scam artists who approach tourists, telling them that Wat Phra Kaew is closed for some reason and instructing them to come back in 2hr. Do not listen to these men. Though they are often well-dressed and speak English well, they are lying. The *wat* is not closed, and they are looking to earn commissions on overpriced goods they hope you will buy at their shops. Instead, assume that everything is always open according to the times stated.

WAT PHO (THE TEMPLE OF THE RECLINING BUDDHA). Wat Pho is technically the oldest, largest, and most architecturally spectacular temple in Bangkok. Its grounds are divided by **Soi Chetuphon:** one side is home to the monastery, while the other contains temple buildings. Wat Pho was built in the 16th century during the Ayutthaya period and was expanded by King Rama I. His grandson, King Rama III, built the *wihaan* that houses the spectacular 46m-long, 15m-high Reclining Buddha. Wat Pho is also home to Thailand's first university, originally a monastery that taught medicine, founded a century before Bangkok. A world-famous Thai massage school is its latest development. (*From Wat Phra Kaew, walk around the block and take 3 left turns from entrance.* ☎ *02 225 9595. Open daily 9am-5pm. 50฿.)*

WAT MAHATHAT. Also known as the Temple of the Great Relic, this *wat* houses a large sitting Buddha and was home to King Rama I, who was an abbot before he took up military campaigning. Today, the temple is a center of Buddhist teaching and home to one of Thailand's two Buddhist colleges. The southern

SILKY SMOOTH

With all of the shopping Bangkok has to offer, deciding what to bring back home is a daunting task. While you can find a bewildering number of good deals in Bangkok's many markets, for a luxurious and authentic souvenir from Thailand, one of the best places to go is the Jim Thompson store.

Jim Thompson was an American who revitalized Thailand's silk industry in the mid-20th century; fittingly, his house (p. 115) is a museum dedicated to Thai art and culture. At the stores that bear his name and are the legacy of his original business, you can get silk in every color, shape, and style. Ties are 1300-1800฿, handkerchiefs 300฿, scarves 500-2000+; traditional robes and modern articles of clothing begin at 800฿ for the finest pieces. But the most striking item in the stores is the plain silk itself, in a veritable rainbow of shimmering colors for 570฿ per meter.

The flagship store is at 9 Surawong Rd., near Patpong and the Sala Daeng BTS station. ☎02 632 8100. Open daily 9am-9pm.

part of the complex offers English instruction in meditation. *(Open daily 7-10am, 1-4 and 6-8pm. The wat is between Silpakorn University and Thammasat University on Na Phra That Rd., opposite Sanam Luang. More info on meditation ☎02 222 6011. Open daily 9am-5pm.)*

SANAM LUANG. Sanam Luang is the "royal ground" of Thailand. Once, criminals were lined up and shot here; today, although public executions have been discontinued, summer soccer matches and kite-fighting contests—in which the large "male" kites *(chula)* pursue smaller, fleeing "female" kites *(pukpao)*—have not (see **Traditional Pastimes**, p. 71). Food stalls ring the park in the daytime. *(On Na Phra That Rd.)*

NATIONAL MUSEUM. As Southeast Asia's largest, this is the crown jewel of Thailand's national museum system. King Chulalongkorn (Rama V) founded it in 1874 with the opening of a public showroom inside the Grand Palace to exhibit collections from the reign of his father. The museum has three permanent exhibition galleries: the **Thai History Gallery**, the **Archaeology and Art History Collection,** and the **Decorative Arts and Ethnological Collection.** The Thai History building was recently renovated, and there is now extensive information in English. The section on the monarchy gives great insight into the Western pressures of modernization that the Thai kings have faced. The other two collections have an impressive array of artifacts but have not yet been renovated; the galleries are aged and poorly lit, and there is little information in English. *(On Na Phra That Rd. past Thammasat University. ☎02 224 1333. Open W-Su 9am-4pm; tickets sold until 3:30pm. Free tours in English W and Th 9:30am. 40฿.)*

NATIONAL GALLERY. The National Gallery contains a small collection of classical and contemporary Thai artwork. Rooms upstairs display paintings of scenes from epics and classical plays. Downstairs, works by the novice artist King Rama VI and the considerably more talented King Rama IX are on display, as well as a few rooms of 20th-century Thai art. *(On Chao Fa Rd., opposite the National Theater. ☎02 282 2639. Open W-Su 9am-4pm. 30฿.)*

DEMOCRACY MONUMENT. The monument commemorates Thailand's transition from absolute to constitutional monarchy after the Revolution of 1932. It was the site of bloody demonstrations in May 1992, when students and citizens protested the rule of General Kraprayoon. *(At Ratchadamnoen and Dinso Rd.)*

WAT SAKET. Notable for its **Golden Mount** (an artificial hill topped with a pagoda) soaring 80m high, this popular mount was once the highest point in the city. Today,

Wat Saket's golden *chedi* and panoramic view remain a reward for those adventurous enough to make the trek to the top. *(On Worachak Rd. Open daily 7:30am-5:30pm. 10฿.)*

WAT SUTHAT. This *wat* is famous for its association with the Sao Ching Cha (Giant Swing) directly in front of the temple and for housing Thailand's largest cast-bronze Buddha. In the past, Sao Ching Cha was the scene of several of the more curious Brahmin rituals, including one in which a priest would swing on a rope and use his teeth to try to catch money suspended 25m in the air. The sometimes-deadly feat was a key part of temple life until it was prohibited by a law passed during the reign of King Rama VII. The best part of the complex is the main *wihaan* compound, with marble floors, ornate statues, and impressive murals. The surrounding streets are filled with shops selling religious items like Buddha images and votive candles. *(On Tithong Rd., near the Giant Swing. Open daily 8:30am-9pm. 20฿.)*

DUSIT AND THEWET

The sights of Dusit and Thewet are quieter than those in the heart of the city and make for a relaxing morning or afternoon of sightseeing. The sweeping 20th-century Baron Haussman-esque boulevards, however, can be oppressively expansive and make walking less than pleasurable. Count on taking a few *tuk-tuk* rides to rest your legs (30฿ or less anywhere within the area).

◪VIMANMEK PALACE. This palace was built of golden teak during the reign of King Chulalongkorn (Rama V) and is the largest golden teak mansion in the world. Held together with wooden pegs and filled with Western luxuries, the 72-room structure was the King's favorite palace from 1902 to 1906. The tour gives great insight into the life of the king and his pivotal reign. The museum in Aphisek Dusit Hall houses an impressive collection of silver jewelry, silk, and soapstone carvings. *(Entrance is on U Thong Nai Rd. Bus #70 stops nearby. Shorts and sleeveless shirts not allowed—free clothing rental with 200฿ deposit. Palace open daily 9:30am-4pm, last admission 3pm. Mandatory 45min. English tours every 30min. 9:45am-3:15pm. Museum open daily 10am-4pm. Thai dancing daily 10:30am and 2pm. 100฿, under 5 free; with a Wat Phra Kaew and Grand Palace admission ticket, admission is free. Buy tickets at the entrance to the grounds, before getting to the palace. Admission to the palace includes museum.)*

WAT BENCHAMABOPHIT (MARBLE TEMPLE). This symmetrical *wat's* gleaming white Carrara marble walls went up in 1899 under King Chulalongkorn. The courtyard is lined with 52 bronze Buddhas, while the garden contains sacred turtles given to the temple by worshippers. In February and May, the *wat* hosts Buddhist festivals and candlelight processions around the *bot*. *(On the right of Si Ayutthaya after the Ratchadamnoen Nok Rd. intersection. Enter on Nakhon Pathom Rd. Take bus #72. Open daily 8:30am-5:30pm. 20฿.)*

DUSIT ZOO. Once part of the gardens of the Chitralada Palace, Thailand's largest zoo hosts a collection of regional animals, as well as rare species like white-handed gibbons and white bengal tigers. Most animals are held in depressingly small cages with little room; but the zoo draws large Thai crowds. *(To the right, on U Thong Nai Rd. Other entrances on Rama V and Ratchavithi Rd. ☎ 02 282 9245. Open daily 9am-6pm. 100฿, under 10 5฿.)*

OTHER SIGHTS. Past the Si Ayutthaya Rd. traffic light, Ratchadamnoen Nok Rd. opens onto Suan Amphon, a massive square that is home to a statue of the revered King Chulalongkorn (Rama V). This beloved king, who ruled from 1868 to 1910, is remembered for abolishing slavery, modernizing Thai society (he introduced the first indoor bathroom, among other innovations), and fending off British and French colonialists (see **Life and Times,** p. 58). Patriotic citizens pay homage here on October 23, the anniversary of his death.

Behind the statue, guarded by an iron fence and a well-kept garden, stands the former National Assembly (Parliament Building). This domed building was commissioned as a Royal Palace by King Chulalongkorn in 1908 to replace his old residence. Originally called Anantasamakhom, it was patterned after St. Peter's Basilica in Rome. Following the 1932 coup, the palace became the National Assembly building, but the Assembly has since been moved to Dusit. Past Wat Benchamabophit and Rama V Rd., on the left, is Chitralada Palace, the official home of the Royal Family. The walled compound is protected by a moat and specially trained soldiers. The palace is closed to the public and completely concealed by the trees surrounding the complex.

CHINATOWN, PAHURAT, AND HUALAMPHONG

Chinese immigrants first settled southeast of the royal center along the Chao Phraya River in the 18th century, just after construction of the Grand Palace evicted them from Bangkok's original Chinatown. Today, this area is called **Yaowarat,** after the road that runs through Chinatown, or **Sampaeng,** after the smaller road that runs parallel to Yaowarat, one block south. Sampaeng has the densest concentration of market stalls in Bangkok. The neighborhood's narrow sois and vibrant street life make it worth exploring, especially at night, when the area comes alive. On the western edge of Chinatown is the **Pahurat District,** where the population abruptly turns from Chinese to Indian, and textiles take over as the vendor's ware of choice. **Pahurat Cloth District** is in the area between Pahurat and Chakraphet Rd., where small sois are filled with fabric and retail shops selling cheap clothing.

WAT TRAIMIT. The only major temple in this area, this *wat* is home to the Giant Golden Buddha—a shiny 3m, 5 ton, 700-year-old Sukhothai-style gold statue. Although housed in a rather small and banal 20th-century concrete building, it is nevertheless impressive as the largest pure-gold Buddha image in the world. When the Burmese sacked Ayutthaya in 1767, residents saved the statue by covering it with stucco. It remained occluded until 1955, when the statue slipped from a crane while being transported to Wat Traimit. Cracks developed in the plaster, the stucco was removed, and the Golden Buddha was rediscovered. *(Main entrance on Yaowarat Rd. near Charoen Krung Rd. Smaller entrance on Traimit Rd. Accessible by bus #73. ☎ 02 225 9775. Open daily 8am-5pm. 20฿.)*

SILOM ROAD

M.R. KUKRIT'S HERITAGE HOME. M.R. Kukrit was one of the most colorful characters of 20th-century Thailand. Born in 1911 to a princely family descended from Ramas I and II, Kukrit was part of the last generation to be raised in the Grand Palace during the time of the absolute monarchy, which made him a revered authority on Thai culture and the traditional lifestyle of the Thai upper class. A Renaissance man of sorts, Kukrit was prime minister from 1975-1976 and founder of Thailand's first political party. He was also an amateur actor, dancer, and author (see **Literature,** p. 68). He died in 1995. His old home consists of five traditional Thai houses laid out across two beautiful acres, which have been preserved to appear as they were during Kukrit's lifetime. *(19 Soi Phra Pinit. From BTS: Chong Nonsi, walk south down Norathiwat Rajanakarin, cross busy Sathon Rd., and take the 2nd left; the house is 100m down on the right. ☎ 02 286 8185. Open Sa-Su and holidays 9:30am-5pm; private tours available other days upon request. 50฿. Tour guides who speak some English are available for a free 20min. tour of the buildings. Gift shop on grounds.)*

LUMPHINI PARK. Lumphini Park, Bangkok's largest park and a peaceful, orderly oasis amidst the dirt and bustle of the city, is host to some of the best people-watching in all of Bangkok. In the mornings, Chinese practice tai chi on the lush grass while others rent paddle boats and cruise the park's large pond. During the day, locals and expats relax at cafes along Ratchadamri Rd. The early evening sees a carnival of runners, jazzercisers, and sports enthusiasts crowding the paths. *(The park is bordered by Ratchadamri, Rama IV, Sarasin, and Witthayu Rd. and is accessible from Silom by regular bus #15, 77, 115, or from Siam Sq. and Banglamphu by regular bus #15. Skytrain: Saladaeng. Open daily 5:30am-7pm.)*

SIAM SQUARE

While it is famed for its shopping malls, Siam Sq. does have some worthwhile sights made all the more enjoyable by easy Skytrain access.

▓JIM THOMPSON'S HOUSE. This elegant house was home to American Jim Thompson, who revitalized the Thai silk industry after World War II and later disappeared in 1967 during a trip to Malaysia. Actually a consolidation of six teak buildings, the house is home to one of Thailand's best collections of Ayutthaya- and Rattanakosin-period art. Admission includes a 35min. tour in English (also available in French or Japanese), during which guides discuss the architectural curiosities of Thai houses and share tidbits on Thai culture. Like Jim Thompson's exquisite silk products, his house is a tasteful blend of traditional Thai art and modern Western luxury. A shop that sells lovely silk items (1000฿ and up) and a restaurant are on the premises. Jim Thompson's flagship store, 9 Surawong Rd., is open daily 9am-9pm. *(Soi Kasem San 2, opposite the National Stadium. Take any Rama I Rd. bus. Skytrain: National Stadium. ☎ 216 7368. Tours, every 10min., are mandatory. Open daily 9am-5pm. 100฿, students 50฿.)*

SUAN PAKKAD PALACE MUSEUM. Suan Pakkad's eight traditional Thai houses hold the private collections of Royal Highnesses Prince and Princess Chumbhot of Wagara Svarga. A comprehensive and informative English guided tour takes visitors through rooms filled with artifacts from the Bronze Age Ban Chiang civilization and the Sukhothai, Ayutthayan, and Bangkok periods. Overlooking the pond at the rear of the complex is the beautiful Lacquer Pavilion, filled with Ayutthaya-period artifacts; another of the houses is home to a collection of colorful, intricate Thai dance masks. *(352 Si Ayutthaya Rd. Take regular bus #54, 73, or 204 from Siam Sq. past the Indra Regent on Ratchaprarop Rd. Get off near the corner of Ratchaprarop and Si Ayutthaya Rd., turn down Si Ayutthaya, and it is on the left. Skytrain: Phayathai, take exit 4 from the station. ☎ 245 4934; www.suanpakkad.com. 40min. English guided tours leave frequently. Open daily 9am-4pm. 100฿, students 50฿.)*

CHULALONGKORN UNIVERSITY. Thailand's most prestigious academic institution is worth a visit. The campus consists of a large quadrangle, with modern buildings for the various faculties on three sides, and a cluster of strikingly beautiful classical Thai buildings on the eastern edge. A lovely, nearly *farang*-free place to wander. *(On the eastern side of Phayathai Rd., south of Siam Sq. From the Siam Skytrain Station, walk down Henri Dunant Rd. and the campus will be on your right. From MBK, cross Phayathai Rd. on the footbridge, or take any bus heading south on Phayathai Rd. until you see the campus on the left.)*

OTHER SIGHTS. Opposite Jim Thompson's House is the **National Stadium,** one of the most noticeable landmarks on Rama I Rd. Used for sporting events, the sizeable stadium has a capacity of 65,000. The famous, glittering **Erawan Shrine** is farther on Ploenchit Rd., simply Rama I Rd. renamed further on. After a series of accidents resulted in the deaths of several workers, the Erawan Hotel built this memorial. The shrine was intended to correct the hotel's karma. In

March 2006, a man believed to be mentally ill destroyed the shrine's statue before being beaten to death by bystanders. As it came during the height of the 2005-2006 political crisis, government critic Sondhi Limthongkul charged that Prime Minister Thaksin was responsible for the incident and was using it to retain power through black magic. Thaksin emphatically denied any such involvement. The shrine was rebuilt in May 2006.

SUKHUMVIT ROAD

When Rama I/Ploenchit Blvd. crosses Witthaya Rd., it becomes Sukhumvit Rd., traveling southeast out of the city. This area hosts trendy nightlife, upper-crust hotels and restaurants, and red-light districts, but few tourist sights.

KAMTHIENG HOUSE. This ethnological museum is home to the Siam Society, a cultural organization supported by the royal family. Housed in a beautifully restored teak house, the museum recreates the 19th-century daily life of the matriarchal Lanna culture. Videos and exhibits in English explain cooking, courtship, rice-farming, and water-sharing rituals of Lanna villages. *(131 Soi 21 Asoke, on the left as you walk from Sukhumvit Rd. Near Asok Skytrain station and Sukhumvit MRT station. ☎02 661 6470. 100฿, students 50฿, under 18 20฿. Open Tu-Sa 9am-5pm.)*

CHUVIT GARDEN. Meticulously maintained, this small garden was built by Mr. Chuvit Kamolvisit in the hopes that it might return some serenity to a city so changed by development and globalization. This peaceful spot is graced by tall, leafy trees shading comfortable benches. Come here to escape the madness of Sukhumvit, as many Thais do. *(188 Sukhumvit Rd., in between Sois 10 and 12. Open daily 6am-7pm.)*

THONBURI: WEST OF THE RIVER

WAT ARUN (TEMPLE OF DAWN). Named for Aruna, the Hindu god of dawn, this *wat* was built in the Ayutthaya period and decorated in its current Khmer style during the reigns of Kings Rama II and III. The intricate carvings of the distinctive 79m *prang* are accompanied by inlaid ceramic tiles and porcelain. The best view of the *wat* is from the Bangkok side of the Chao Phraya River in the early morning or in the evening. After a steep climb, the top of the *prang* affords even more gorgeous views. The food stalls to the left of the temple exit (next to the souvenir stands) serve standard street food (chicken fried rice 50฿) at slightly inflated prices. *(In Rattanakosin, from Wat Pho, take a right from Chetupon Rd., onto Maharat Rd. and a left at Tani Wang Rd. This path goes to Tha Tien pier. From an adjacent pier, ferries cross to the wat for 3.50฿. ☎02 465 5640. 50฿. Open daily 7am-6pm.)*

ROYAL BARGE MUSEUM. This museum displays eight long, glittering royal barges and their ceremonial accoutrements. The most impressive barge in the museum is the Suphannahongsa, a 46m long vessel requiring 50 oarsmen, reserved for the King when he makes his annual offering of robes to monks during the Kathin Ceremony. Used only a few times a decade, the barges last cruised the river in June 2006 in an elaborate procession celebrating the 60th anniversary of King Bhumibol's accession. *(On Arun Amarin Rd., under the bridge over Klong Bangkok Noi. Take a river ferry to Tha Pra Pinklao and walk downriver, then follow the signs through the narrow sois to the museum; about a 10min. walk. ☎02 424 0004. Open daily 9am-5pm. 30฿. Camera fee 100฿.)*

▣ ENTERTAINMENT

NATIONAL THEATER

Dedicated in 1965, the National Theater, on Na Phra That Rd., past the National Museum, holds drama and dance shows. The program changes monthly but usually includes at least one *lakhon* dance-drama performance, and a concert by the Thai National Orchestra every Friday. Contact the theater for a schedule. (☎02 224 1342. Open M-F 9am-3:30pm and 1hr. prior to performances. Tickets 40-100฿ for government-sponsored shows.)

THAI CLASSICAL DANCE DINNERS

Missed the National Theater show? Don't worry, many restaurants put on Thai classical dance dinners, featuring half a dozen traditional dances in an hour-long show. Shows usually include *khon* dances from the Ramakien. No shorts, sandals, or tank tops allowed. Reserve at least one day in advance. At **Ruen Thep,** Silom Village, 286 Silom Rd., enjoy a dance dinner in a garden of turtle pools. Performances begin at 8:30pm and include seven dance styles that change monthly. (☎02 234 4581; www.silomvillage.co.th. Open daily 7pm; set Thai dinner 7:30pm. Tickets 450฿. AmEx/MC/V.)

TRADITIONAL THAI MASSAGE

Quality among massage parlors varies tremendously, and many are fronts for prostitution. Pictures of women in the window are giveaways for the latter. Ask other backpackers about their favorites.

Just off of Khaosan Rd., on the tiny soi with Suzie Pub (p. 121), **◼Pian Massage Center and Beauty Salon,** 108/15 Soi Rambuttri, Khaosan Rd., offers high-quality massages in a no-frills setting at unbeatable rates. (☎02 629 0924. Massage 120฿ per 30min., 180฿ per hr. 30hr. certification course 4000฿. Open daily 7am-3am.) At Wat Pho, the **Traditional Massage School** offers massages and a 10-day, 30hr. course. (☎02 221 2974. Massages 350฿ per hr., course 7400฿. Open daily 8am-6pm.) **Bann Phuan,** 25 Sukhumvit Soi 11, offers the traditional triumvirate of Thai, foot, and oil massage. (☎02 253 5963. Open daily noon-2am.) **Marble House,** 37/18-19 Soi Surawong Plaza, one soi up Surawong Rd. from Patpong 2, is one of the few massage parlors in Patpong that doesn't have a VIP room. It has blind masseurs, reputed to be the best in the business. (2hr. Thai massage 330฿. 1hr. head and shoulder massage 280฿.)

MUAY THAI (THAI BOXING)

One of the world's most brutal sports, Thai kickboxing is fought with opponents close together, constantly defending against a kick to the head. With fights occuring daily at two venues, those who don't mind the violence shouldn't miss a match or the fascinating rituals and fervor surrounding it (p. 70).

On Mondays, Wednesdays, Thursdays, and Sundays, the action takes place at **Ratchadamnoen Boxing**

GIVING BACK

NEVER TOO MUCH PDA

The Population and Community Development Association (PDA), founded in 1974, is Thailand's largest NGO (and the organization that runs the well-known Cabbages & Condoms restaurant chain).

Originally designed to promote family planning and birth control in rural Thailand, the organization has since expanded to work in areas from AIDS prevention (where the World Bank estimated the PDA's work had prevented an additional seven million infections) to microcredit financing tied to reforestation efforts to improving water quality and irrigation in rural villages, providing more water storage tanks than all the Thai government agencies combined. They were also extremely active in humanitarian efforts after the 2004 tsunami.

From the beginning, the volunteers dispersed in over ten thousand local villages, especially in Thailand, have been essential to the organization's growth and success. An affiliate, Population Development International, now imparts the experience of the PDA to NGOs and institutions in Laos, Cambodia, and Vietnam. The PDA also welcomes undergraduate and graduate international applicants for internship positions within the organization.

PDA's head office is in Bangkok, at 6 Sukhumvit Soi 12 (☎02 229 4611; www.pda.or.th).

START: Mo Chit Station

FINISH: Shopping heaven

DURATION: 6hr.

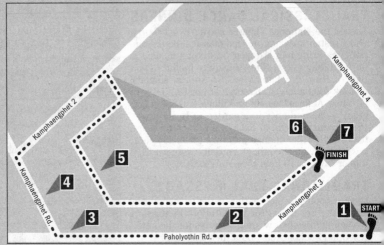

CHATUCHAK MARKET

With over 8000 stalls and 250,000 visitors each weekend, the Chatuchak Weekend Market is a bargain shopper's paradise. Everything from vintage Levi's to flying squirrels can be purchased at this epic market, but crowds, blistering heat, and a labyrinth of streets can make for a less than-pleasurable shopping experience. In order to ensure the most productive and stress-free trip, try to come early to beat the crowds and heat. Numbered sections are organized along a main pathway and maps indicating the various numbered sections are posted throughout the market. Nancy Chandler's Map of Bangkok also has an indispensable guide.

1. BTS SKYTRAIN'S MO CHIT STATION. By far the easiest and fastest way to arrive at the market, a short 5min. walk from its northeastern side.

2. SECTION 5. If you're in the market for vintage Nike hightops or authenticallydistressed jeans, head to the used clothing stalls that fill this section.

3. SECTION 4. Along Kamphaengphet Rd., tucked behind section 4, lie popular, affordable cafes serving authentic and delicious food from across South East Asia.

4. SECTIONS 2 AND 3. If clothes are your thing, it's best to start here, on the southwest end of the market, along Kamphaengphet Rd. Across the walkway, sections 23 and 24 also sport a vast selection of hip, affordable clothing. Witty political t-shirts (about 150†), many by up-and-coming Thai designers, also abound.

5. SECTIONS 23 AND 3. Those with horticultural interests should admire the spectacular orchids lining the main walking path between these sections.

6. SECTION 7. The trees, pleasant art galleries, and quiet cafes on the northeast-ern end of the market offer a welcome respite from Chatuchak's chaos. If you're really feeling decadent, get a Thai foot massage from the serene massage studio at the rear of the section.

7. SECTION 7. For something a little more exotic than t-shirts and mas-sages, the flying squirrels, baby hedgehogs, and enormous lizards in the center of these sections are your best bet. Golden retriever and husky puppies are also on display.

Stadium, on Ratchadamnoen Nok Rd., near the TAT. Take regular bus #70 from Sanam Luang. (☎01 317 9917 or 629 9856. Fights begin at 6:30pm. Open daily 9am-11pm. Foreigner tickets 1000-1500฿, ringside 2000฿.)

On Tuesdays, Fridays, and Saturdays, head to **Lumphini Boxing Stadium** on Rama IV Rd. near Lumphini Park and the night market. Top card is on Friday. (☎02 247 5385. M: Lumphini. Take regular bus #115 from Silom Rd. Fights Tu 6:30pm; Sa 5, 6:30, 8:30pm. Same prices as Ratchadamnoen Boxing Stadium.)

SHOPPING

It doesn't take long to realize that Thais are obsessed with shopping malls. At the heart of this obsession is the area around the Siam Skytrain stop, where four gargantuan shopping centers compete for every last baht. **Siam Paragon,** the newest of Bangkok's malls, houses a 14-theater cineplex, an "Oceanarium" with 30,000 sea creatures, and a 200m cascading waterfall. Simply walking around the eight-story, 300,000 sq. m mall can be exhausting—not to mention the ordeal of having to decide between the newest Prada or Fendi handbag. While most retail shops are beyond a backpacker's budget, Siam Paragon's fantastic **food court** (modeled after Thai street stalls) makes for an affordable and delicious meal (a variety of Asian cuisines served; dishes run 40-80฿).

Next to Paragon, and separated by a very pleasant, well-designed tiled sitting area and water park, lie the confusingly named **Siam Center** and **Siam Discovery Center.** Although successful remodeling has concealed its upscale nature, the shining Siam Center is the place to go for those looking for well-established and cutting-edge Thai clothing designers, who have set up shop mainly on the third floor. Similarly trendy is Siam Discovery Center's fourth floor, which showcases some of Thailand's contemporary interior-design stores.

Across from these three malls, **Siam Square** is the hangout for Bangkok teenagers and students trickling in from Thailand's prestigious Chulalongkorn University. The boutique-lined sois in Siam Square cater to the hip, young Thai crowd looking to set themselves apart from the pack.

Equally colossal, but less pricey, is **Mahboonkrong Center (MBK),** on the corner of Rama I and Phayathai Rd., diagonal to Siam Discovery Center. This mammoth shopping center has seven floors of department stores, arcades, electronics, music stores, and fast-food joints, as well as a cinema. **Amarin Plaza,** at the intersection of Rama I and Ratchadamri Rd., and the **Zen World Trade Center,** once MBK's main competitor for the largest mall, up Ratchadamri Rd. toward Phetchaburi Rd., have similar international shops but are a little less busy.

MARKETS

Talat (street markets) all over the city are sources for knock-off designer watches, clothing (from Ralph Lauren to "Ralph Levis"), and pirated CDs.

CHATUCHAK MARKET. Referred to by locals as "JJ," this weekend market is a bargain-hunter's dream and makes for a great case-study of the chaotic market culture in Southeast Asia. Thousands of enthusiastic vendors sell everything from dalmatians to incense, although the main focus is clothing and plants. Chatuchak has a reputation for being the cheapest of the markets, but come armed with plenty of free time, patience to navigate the crowds, and a readiness to bargain ruthlessly with the relentless vendors. Even the stingiest, most jaded shopper will be hard-pressed to leave empty-handed. *(Skytrain: Mo Chit. Open Sa-Su 7am-6pm.)*

SUAN LUM NIGHT BAZAAR. Between Lumphini Park and Lumphini Boxing Stadium, the Suan Lum night bazaar is one of the best markets in Bangkok. Search for clothing, gifts, souvenirs, and plants, or enjoy an evening stroll amid the bustling but pleasant stalls. Suan Lum houses several nice restaurants, beer gardens, and a food court where live music picks up nightly at 8pm. The best time to go is 6-10pm. At the market, the **Hun Lakhon Lek Joe Louis Troupe** performs daily puppetry shows in the Joe Louis Theater. *(Entrances on Rama IV and Wireless Rd. M: Lumphini. Puppet show 600฿, children 300฿.)*

BANGLAMPHU MARKET. This frenzied market spills onto Chakrapong, Krai Si, and Tani Rd., but the tourist-oriented section is along Khaosan Rd. A late-afternoon affair, the market includes food, souvenirs, leather, and fake designer clothes. Everything is overpriced, but the experience here is priceless.

OTHER MARKETS. **Thewet Market** is on Krung Kasem Rd., along the Chao Phraya River. The selection is not so diverse, but it's the one-stop shopping center for food or garden landscaping. *(Chao Phraya River Express: Thewet.)*

Don't leave out the charming, eye-catching **Pakklong Market,** southwest of the Pahurat District, over Triphet Ave. Take a river taxi to Tha Rachini, and indulge in a relaxing stroll through this wholesale flower market. The best time to go is early in the morning or late at night.

Sampaeng Lane Market runs through the heart of Chinatown, one block south of Yaowarat Rd. If you need cutlery, jewelry, or monk supplies, this is the place to go. Extending northwest from the corner of Yaowarat and Chakrawat Rd. is the **Nakhon Kasea** (**Thieves Market**—so called because stolen goods used to surface here), best known for machinery, ice-cream makers, and ninja weaponry.

Pratunam Market operates daily along Ratchaprarop Rd., opposite the Indra Hotel. Clothes are the main item, but there is also a wide selection of knick-knacks. After nightfall in the Silom area, **vendors** along Patpong 1 Rd. will sneak you fake designer watches, clothing, or pirated Hollywood blockbusters. For something more original, the **stalls** on Silom between Silom Soi 2 and Silom Soi 4 sell a vast array of foreign films and CDs by esoteric European bands.

🔊 NIGHTLIFE

Bangkok's entertainment and nightlife need little introduction. The city's reputation as the epicenter of Southeast Asia's internationalism is rooted in its effortless mix of traditional art and culture and the hip, connected youth who party until dawn. Like other global metropolises, Bangkok offers a wealth of activities, from sophisticated bars and funky discotheques to dance shows and kickboxing—something to entertain and enlighten every type of traveler.

Check out the free *BK Magazine* (available at many bars and restaurants), *Metro* (100฿ at newsstands), or www.bangkokrecorder.com for the latest in "cool." Establishments listed here are not associated with the sex trade.

BANGLAMPHU AND KO RATTANAKOSIN

The best part of nightlife on Khaosan Rd. is the urban carnival that takes place on the street nightly once the road is closed to cars. Market stalls, *pad thai* and spring roll vendors, hair braiders, and impromptu street bars selling 80฿ "very strong cocktails" cover the sidewalks. While Khaosan used to be a scene limited to *farang* backpackers, the area is growing increasingly popular with edgy Thais and curious expats who are drawn in by upscale new bars. For a more artsy experience, head to one of the small bar/restaurants on **Phra Athit Road** near the river. Many have live music, and most are open daily 6pm-1am.

Commé Café, (☎02 329 8151), in the thick of it on Phra Athit Rd. Earth tones, R&B, jazz, and understated art won't get your pulse racing, but this cafe, gallery, and restaurant is a relaxing place to chill with Thais and some *farang*. Cocktails 70-100฿, draft Singha 150฿. Open daily noon-1am.

Hippie de Bar, 46 Khaosan Rd. (☎02 629 3508), 50m from Gulliver's and through a small soi. Tablecloths and the dictionary definition of "hippie," lush banana trees, and a white gazebo provide a funky outdoor atmosphere in which to whittle away hot nights amongst the diverse, pleasant crowd. Drinks 90-150฿. Open nightly 3pm-2am.

Blues Bar, 13 Samsen Rd. (☎02 629 2897), just before the canal where Samsen changes to Chakrapong Rd. Soul, jazz, and Beatles tunes soothe patrons. Beer 60-70฿. Mixed drinks 90-120฿. Live music starts between 9-10pm. Open nightly 7pm-1am.

Suntana, 62 Phra Athit Rd. Hip young Thais pack into this cafe to admire impressive month-long exhibitions and drink the night away. Understated decor with 70s vinyl furniture offers a welcome contrast to the Khaosan debauchery. Open nightly 3pm-1am.

Suzie Pub, 1085-9 Soi Rambuttri (☎02 282 4459), located on a small soi on the eastern end of Rambuttri, just after it curves but before it becomes Bowon Niwet Rd. (also accessible from Khaosan Rd.; look for the neon sign on the left). This large wood-paneled bar conjures up ski-lodge charm with deer antlers hanging from its walls and a case of antique rifles on display. Extremely popular as the night progresses, Suzie offers the closest thing on Khaosan to a club. Drinks 100-150฿. Open nightly 5pm-1am.

Gulliver's, 3 Khaosan Rd., at the corner of Chakrapong Rd., with a life-size *tuk-tuk* over the door. One of the most popular bars on Khaosan Rd., it specializes in Western food and beer in a dark tavern atmosphere. Pool tables and taps don't stop until everyone's forced to go home. Beer 70-80฿. Happy hour (single spirit and mixer for 69฿) until 10pm. Open daily 11am-2am.

Joy Luck Club, 8 Phra Sumen Rd. (☎02 629 4128). One of the many small, hip bar/restaurants on chic Phra Athit Rd. that combines art and atmosphere. Look for the fun, vintage McDonald's toys hidden about. Thai food 70-90฿. Beer 60฿. Vodka 100฿. Johnnie Walker Black Label 1200฿. Open daily noon-1am.

 ID, PLEASE. Most clubs in Bangkok have stringent dress codes requiring closed-toed shoes, long pants, and a valid ID. Be sure to have all 3 things whenever going to a non-Khaosan Rd. nightclub.

SILOM ROAD

Silom's **Soi 4** is ground zero for nightlife in Bangkok. Great bars, restaurants, and clubs abound in the area, as do drunk tourists. Sois 2 and 4 are centers of gay nightlife, although gay establishments are scattered all over the area (for more detailed listings of gay nightlife, see p. 123). Patpong 1 and 2 mark the infamous red light district; hawkers from the various strip clubs will accost you every five feet promising deals for "ping-pong" shows. Patpong 1 also hosts a lively night market that makes navigating the street somewhat difficult.

☒ Tapas, 114/7 Silom Soi 4 (☎02 632 7982). Resident DJs spin house in this extremely popular bar. Sink into a couch or get up for live drum-and-bass beats wherever there's space. Try the outdoor seating for fresh air and entertaining people-watching. Cover 200฿. Beer 120฿. Open nightly 8pm-1:15am.

Luminous, on Silom Soi 4 across from Tapas. Popular with Thai and *farang* alike, this club has something for every musical taste: hip-hop and R&B beats on the ground floor, while DJs spin house and breakbeats on the 2nd. Cover F-Sa 200฿, includes 1 drink. Drinks 120-200฿. Open daily 9pm-2am.

CLUB 808

Though Thailand is in many ways a budget traveler's dream, when it comes to nightlife, Thai prices are comparable to those in the West. A fun night out, especially in Bangkok, can come with a price tag of astronomical proportions; even if you're not splurging on the fanciest bars and clubs, the covers (usually 200-400в) and drinks (120+ for beer, 180+ for mixed drinks) will add up. But nightlife in Bangkok is a sight unto itself and one that can't be missed. You'll rarely see a meeting of East and West as palpable as dancing to the latest American hip hop hits with hundreds of young Thais. So, if you're looking for a way to party as if the exchange rate was a lot more favorable, make your way to the Club 808 on a Friday night, when you can't spend more than 500в—the price of the cover to Open Bar Night. The club will be understandably packed, but the bartenders work quickly and the resident DJ spins great music to keep the crowd moving. Your liver might not thank you, but your bank account certainly will.

(808, Block C, RCA. www.808bangkok. com. Open 9pm-2am.)

Lucifer, on Patpong 1 Rd., next to Radio City, is delightfully and elaborately designed to look like hell. This venue heats up after midnight with trance, dance remixes, and happy house. Drinks 180в. Cover F-Sa 150в, includes 1 drink. Open nightly 10pm-2am.

Radio City and **Muzzik Café,** on the south end of Patpong 1 Rd., on opposite sides of the street. After 9pm, these colorful, popular bars fill with *farang* seeking nightly live music and refuge from the craziness outside. Check out the Elvis Presley (11pm) and Tom Jones (midnight) shows at Radio City, or rock out with live cover bands at Muzzik (starting 9:30pm). Mixed drinks 160-200в. Both open nightly 6pm-2am

SUKHUMVIT ROAD

Often neglected by tourists, Sukhumvit has some of the trendiest nightlife around. **Royal City Avenue (RCA),** a soi that leads off Phetchaburi Rd., about 400m west of Sukhumvit Soi 55's intersection with Phetchaburi Rd., is a new nightlife area with clubs full of young, trendy Thais—and few prostitutes. Most places get busy around 11pm. Other sections are much shadier. **Soi Cowboy** (off Soi 21) has the dubious reputation of being Bangkok's first ever red light district, having served foreign soldiers during the post-Vietnam era. The **Soi Nana** area also hosts a red-light scene, although it is not quite as intense as Soi Cowboy.

- **Bed Supperclub,** (☎02 651 3537; www.bedsupperclub.com), at the end of Sukhumvit Soi 11. Housed in an impressive space-shuttle-like building, this all-white, futuristic club offers one of the hippest experiences in Bangkok. One side has the beds and suppers (bed F-Sa 1390в; M-Th and Su 7:30-10:30pm, 1090в; reserve in advance); the other, the bar and DJs. No shorts or flip-flops. Strict ID policy (20+). Cover M and W-Th 400в; Tu, F, Sa 500в; Su 600в; includes 2 drinks. Open daily 7:30pm-1:45am.

- **808,** Block C, RCA (www.808bangkok.com). Replacing the old Astra club, the already-popular 808 has sleek modern decor and an intimate dance floor with lounge seating on one side. Each night of the week features different music (hip-hop, breakbeats, techno). Saturdays are reserved for some of the best DJs in the world. Cover depends on the night and the DJ, usually no more than 400в. Singha 160в, mixed drinks 200в+ (but most nights have some kind of drink special). Check the website for upcoming events. Open Tu-Su 9pm-2am.

- **Route 66,** RCA (☎02 203 0936). Filled with young Thais, this club, with a distinctly local feel, is split into three giant rooms—one for house, one for Thai pop, and one for commercial hip-hop and R&B—connected by bars. Great for people-watching and drinking. The crowds and tables make dancing a bit more difficult, although the music will certainly get you moving. Drinks, some of the cheapest in the RCA area, are 150฿ and up. No cover. Open nightly 6pm-2am.

Flix and Slim, Block S, RCA (☎02 203 0226). This club consists of 2 colossal, 2-story spaces, each with state-of-the-art sound systems. Flix pulsates with superb, heart-stopping house music, while Slim plays commercial hip-hop and R&B. No cover. Ultra-strict ID policy (20+). Drinks from 180฿. Open nightly 6pm-1:30am.

Q Bar, 34 Sukhumvit Soi 11 (☎02 252 3274; www.qbarbangkok.com). At the end of Soi 11, take a left. Well-to-do expats and even wealthier Thais mix and mingle in this classic fixture of the Bangkok social scene. An upscale place, but the darkness and blacklights give it a relaxed feel. Dance floor downstairs, lounge and terrace upstairs. Food 250-350฿. Mixed drinks 220-400฿. Singha 150฿. Strict ID policy (20+). Cover M-Th 400฿, F-Su 600฿; includes 2 drinks. Open nightly 8pm-2am.

GAY AND LESBIAN

Largely free from any overt discrimination, Bangkok's gays have successfully created a thriving and constantly evolving club scene. The **Silom** area, particularly the gay bar- and club-lined **Silom Sois 4, 2,** and **2/1,** is the most tourist-friendly and enjoyable area in the city to dance the night away. The **Lang Suan** area (meaning "behind the park"), just north of Lumphini Park, attracts swarms of hip Thais. Though the bars in Lang Suan aren't officially gay, they attract many looking for that scene. Even further afield, a cluster of about a dozen clubs in the **Aor Tor Kor** area, on the eastern end of Kamphaengphet Rd., next to the Chatuchak Market (p. 119), entices young university students with cheap whisky sodas and cheesy Thai pop. For more "sophistication," ▨**Bed Supperclub** in Sukhumvit (p. 122) hosts the popular **Think Pink** every Sunday night. Lesbian nightlife in Bangkok has a less noticeable presence, but the ladies-only **Zeta,** in the RCA complex, is undeniably the most popular club in the scene.

70's Bar, 231/15 Sarasin Rd. (☎02 253 4433), 1 of almost half a dozen bars on the northern side of Lumphini Park, where drinking digresses into exuberant dancing as the night progresses, all under red lighting and shimmering disco balls. After a few drinks, catchy Thai pop hits will have you belting out the choruses. From midnight to 1am it's almost impossible to navigate the crowd; arrive early to grab a spot. Beer 150฿. Cocktails 180฿. Open nightly 6pm-1am.

DJ Station, (☎02 266 4029), on Silom Soi 2, is awarded "Best Gay Disco" nearly every year by *Metro*. DJ packs in hundreds of *farang* and Thais who pulsate to the latest pop hits. Features a nightly cabaret (11:30pm). Cover M-Th and Su 100฿, includes 1 drink; F-Sa 200฿, includes 2 drinks. No shorts or sandals. 20+. Open nightly 11pm-2am.

The Expresso, 8/6-8 Silom Soi 2 (☎02 632 7223), directly across from DJ and under same ownership. Before the place gets packed around midnight, the water cascading down the curved wall enclosing this brightly lit bar provides a serene escape from the chaos next door. Be sure to check out the playful and often controversial matching outfits of the 2 DJs. Drinks 200฿. No cover. Open nightly 9pm-1am.

Fake Bar, 359-360 Kamphaengphet Rd., across from the Aor Tor Kor market (MRT: Kamphaeng Phet). More intimate than most of the hip clubs in the area; the trendy purple decor complements the crowds of young Thais who pack into Fake around 11pm to drink and dance, if they can find the space. Drinks 80-150฿. Open nightly 8pm-1am.

Balcony Bar, 86-88 Silom Soi 4 (☎02 235 5891). The sidewalk bar at Balcony is the best place for people-watching on popular Soi 4. Frequent events, such as fancy dress parties, cabarets, and Mr./Miss Silom Soi 4, are always rowdy and welcoming. Drink specials are constantly changing; expect to pay around 150฿ for a mixed drink . Beer 80฿. Open daily 5:30pm-2am.

LIVE MUSIC

Bangkok's most rewarding nightlife centers on jazz establishments with live music and a classy Thai and foreign clientele. Off Ratchadamri Rd., **Soi Sarasin**, north of Lumphini Rd., has establishments that play live music every night. Bands generally start around 9pm, but things get cooking after 11pm.

▨ **Brown Sugar Jazz Pub and Restaurant,** 231/20 Sarasin Rd. (☎02 250 1826), opposite Lumphini Park, is regarded as one of the best in the city, with nightly jazz bands drawing a crowd of well-dressed patrons. Food 90-360฿. Beer 150฿. Mixed drinks 180-200฿. Live music 9:45pm-1am. Open nightly 5pm-1am.

Saxophone Pub and Restaurant, 3/8 Phayathai Rd. (☎02 246 5472; www.saxophone-pub.com), away from Siam Sq., at the southeast corner of the Victory Monument. Another of the city's greatest clubs; several bands play nightly, in a slightly eclectic funk/jazz/blues rotation; check the website for an exact schedule. Best tables downstairs. Thai and Western food (100-250฿) are delicious. Beer from 120฿. Open nightly 6pm-2am.

Tokyo Joe's, 9-11 Sivaporn Plaza, Sukhumvit Soi 24 (☎02 667 0359), opposite the Ariston Hotel (BTS: Phrom Phong). The most intimate of the jazz clubs, with a soulful Su blues special. Generally a whiskey joint (160-180฿), but also has a smattering of sake (200฿) and beer (100฿). Heineken 75฿. Open nightly 5pm-1am.

▶ DAYTRIPS FROM BANGKOK

Travel agencies offer a slew of daytrips to attractions outside Bangkok, but these some sights can be seen more independently, and at a better price.

NONTHABURI

Take the Chao Phraya River Express ferry, from Tha Sathorn (45-60min., 17฿), which ends at the Nonthaburi Pier. From here, take another ferry to the west bank (3฿), and hire a motorcycle (10฿) to Wat Chalerm. Open daily 8am-6pm.

Nonthaburi province straddles the Chao Phraya River 20km to the north of Bangkok. Its sleepy suburban town, on the east bank, is known for its fruit and earthenware. On the west bank of the river, in Amphoe Bangkluai, stands **Wat Chalerm Phra Kiad Wora Wihaan,** known to locals as Wat Chalerm. The temple was built by King Rama III to honor his mother and grandparents, who were from the area. The statues, ceramics, and flowering decorations of the grounds all bear traces of Chinese artistry. A tranquil wander through the grove of the monastery grounds is as pleasant as the breezy ferry ride. Both the eastern and western piers are bordered by **fruit markets,** where you'll find a greater variety of better quality fruit than is available anywhere in Bangkok. An excellent seafood-centered **night market** sets up shop beside the eastern pier around 4pm.

SAMUT PRAKAN

A/C bus #511 runs by Tanao Rd., at the base of Khaosan Rd., and by the Gaysorn Central Chitlum shopping plaza on Phloenchit Rd., on the way to Samut Prakan; save time when returning by getting off the bus at On Nut stop and boarding the Skytrain for the rest of the return trip. Take a #36 songthaew from the center of Samut Prakan to Muang Boran or the Crocodile Farm (9฿ per person). Tuk-tuks and taxis run between the 2 parks (50-60฿). Muang Boran: ☎02 323 9253. Open daily 8am-6pm; last entry 5pm. 300฿, children 100฿. Crocodile Farm: ☎02 703 4891. Crocodile shows every hr. 9-11am and 1-4pm, additional shows Sa-Su and holidays noon and 5pm. Elephant shows 9:30, 10:30, 11:30am, 1:30, 2:30, 4:30pm. Open daily 7am-6pm. 300฿.

The center of Thailand's leather industry, Samut Prakan is 30km south of Bangkok toward the Gulf of Thailand. Since most goods produced here are sold elsewhere, the main reason to come to Samut Prakan is to see two less-industrial attractions: ▦**Muang Boran** and the **Crocodile Farm.** Muang Boran, the "Ancient City," is one of Thai tourism's best kept secrets, a surprisingly lovely open-air museum in the shape of Thailand that contains detailed replicas of 116 (and counting) monuments and sights from around the kingdom, scaled to one-sixth of the size of the originals and set beautifully among streams and trees. Highlights include the Ayutthaya-style **Saphet Prasat Palace,** the **Dusit Maha Prasat Palace,** and **Khao Phra Wihaan,** which sits atop a hill and affords a spectacular view. The best way to explore the park is to borrow a free bicycle and leisurely cruise the park's 15km of paths. The Crocodile Farm houses over 65,000 crocodiles, including, at over 1000kg, the largest Siamese crocodile in captivity. At the "Crocodile Wrestling" show, trainers taunt the toothy behemoths. At the elephant show, the clever pachyderms pluck 20฿ notes from spectators' hands and place them directly into their trainer's pocket. Other attractions include an aviary, snake pits, a dinosaur museum, and go-carts.

DAMNOEN SADUAK

Buses leave from Bangkok's Southern Bus Terminal for Damnoen Saduak and drop passengers off in the thick of the action. The ride is 2hr., and buses depart every 20min., 6am-9pm (87฿). All buses will drop you off along the road lined with piers where locals approach, offering 1hr. boat tours for 600-800฿. The best time to visit is 8-10am. The market is open daily 6am-2pm. Most buses returning to Bangkok leave from this road; otherwise, take a yellow songthaew (5฿) into the center of Damnoen Saduak and wave down one of the buses as it turns around.

Along with ancient *wats* and white-sand beaches, **floating markets** are held by many tourists to be an iconic symbol of Thailand. In reality, however, modern life has rendered most floating markets obsolete, and they now primarily function as tourist theme parks. That said, this floating market, only 109km from Bangkok, does capture the transient canal economy. A boat tour (600-800฿ per hr.) is a must; there are several vendors, so try to find an English-speaking driver with a motorboat. A ride through the actual market is included in any tour. Boats pass on either side, filled with tourists or Thai women selling exotic fruits like *champoo* (rose apple; 50฿ per kg), a red or greenish fruit resembling a bell pepper. Browse through the wood carvings and cowboy hats, then head to the coconut sugar farm and sample some palm flower juice or fresh-from-the-hive honey. Depicted in paintings, postcards, and picture books, the bustling scene has become the picture of traditional Thai life. Some visitors may find the not-so-picture-perfect reality—murky waters, swarming flies, and high-pressure sales techniques—disappointing, but it's a great place to practice bargaining. Bring plenty of cash, as there are no ATMs in the area. Feeding the fish (rendered invisible by the dirtiness of the water) outside the Buddhist temple (5฿ per bag of food) is a popular show of respect for vegetarianism.

NAKHON PATHOM

Nakhon Pathom is 60km west of Bangkok. Buses leave the Southern (Thonburi) Bus Terminal for Nakhon Pathom (1hr.; about every 10min. 4:10am-4pm, less frequently 4-9:30pm; 67฿). The return bus departs from 2 blocks north of the chedi on Thanon Phayaphan, the road bordering the northern side of the canal. From the north entrance of the chedi, walk across the bridge toward the train station and take an immediate left to find the stop for Bangkok buses. If you want to visit both the floating market and Phra Pathom Chedi in the same day, take a bus from Bangkok to Damnoen Saduak early, visit the market in the morning, and stop in Nakhon Pathom on the trip back to Bangkok (last leg 1hr., every 20min.). Nakhon Pathom can make for a pleasant detour on the way to or from Kanchanaburi (32฿), which is 1hr. west of Nakhon Pathom. Nakhon Pathom can also be reached by train from Bangkok, although trains run less frequently than buses. Trains from

Bangkok toward Kanchanaburi (1hr.; 7:45am, 1:55pm; 20฿) and toward southern Thailand (1 hr., 6 per day 8:05am-3:35pm, 20฿) stop here.

For the most part, Nakhon Pathom is a typical, medium-sized central Thai city. Only the massive *chedi* looming over the town offers evidence of its remarkable history. Historians speculate that Buddhist missionaries from India arrived in Nakhon Pathom during the 3rd century BC, establishing it as one of the oldest cities in Thailand—the city's name comes from the Pali words *Nagara Pathama,* which means "first city." By the AD 6th century, when archaeological evidence begins, Nakhon Pathom had begun its 500-year tenure as the center of the flowering Dvaravati kingdom. A *stupa,* first built during the Dvaravati period, has grown larger over the centuries, eventually reaching its current glory as **Phra Pathom Chedi,** the world's tallest Buddhist monument, at 127m. The large golden-brown tiled dome is surrounded by a 7m wide walkway accessible through doors flanked by green stone-carved Chinese soldiers. The caves, temples, statues, and museums that dot the extensive grounds are ripe with exploration opportunities. Dvaravati artifacts, which are of particular note to those interested in the history of Theravada Buddhism or in India's cultural influence on Thailand, have been assembled in the modest but well-organized **Phra Pathom Chedi National Museum,** outside the *wat* gates, near the main ticket booth. Far less orderly is the **Phra Pathom Chedi Museum,** on the southeastern part of the grounds, near the Chinese temple. An eclectic assortment of Buddhist amulets, shadow puppets, and excavated pottery shards—along with such oddities as Hungarian banknotes and rusty guns—overflows in a museum with the organizational clarity of a cluttered attic. (*Chedi* open daily 9am-5pm, both museums open W-Su 9am-4pm. 40฿.)

Another tourist attraction, 2km south of the *chedi,* is the mildly interesting **Sanam Chan Palace.** This complex was constructed in 1907 under the direction of Rama VI and sprawls across 335 impressively manicured acres. The palace is host to an unusual assortment of European and Thai architectural traditions, including a homage to Rama VI's interest in English Tudor style. The palace buildings are used as municipal offices but the grounds are open to the public daily 9am-4pm, and some buildings accept tour groups by appointment.

Nakhom Pathom is best visited during one of its many festivals. A **fruit fair** held every year in conjunction with the Chinese New Year (Jan.-Feb.) showcases the region's agricultural specialties. The **elephant festival** held May 1 at the Samphon Elephant Zoo features a "Jumbo Queen" beauty contest for plus-sized women. During the 12th month of each lunar year (usually Nov.-Dec.), a nine-day, nine-night festival pays homage to Phra Pathom Chedi.

B A N G K O K

CENTRAL THAILAND

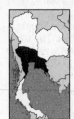

Central Thailand could be a microcosm of the rest of the country. East of Bangkok, the coastal highway follows the progression of economic development; shiny new refineries and power stations dominate the landscape from Si Racha to Rayong, while construction sites and highway traffic yield to groves of *durians* and *mangosteens* farther east. Ko Chang remains a backpacker's favorite despite an onslaught of upscale development, and its surrounding islands provide ample opportunity to escape the crowds. Ko Samet boasts the best beaches on Thailand's east coast. Despite its notoriety for its involvement in the sex trade, Pattaya offers an array of tourist attractions and accessible water activities, while nearby Trat teems with untouched mountains, jungles, and waterfalls. West of the capital, the lush landscapes of the fertile Chao Phraya River Basin stretch from Hua Hin in the south to Nakhon Sawan in the north. In the midst of all this sit the awe-inspiring ruins of Ayutthaya and Lopburi. Southbound buses and trains wind through the beginnings of peninsular Thailand, a preview for the sandy playgrounds farther south.

SI RACHA ☎038

Situated only 2hr. away from Bangkok, Si Racha is a great daytrip for those wanting to get to the coast and dip their toes into water that's a little saltier (and marginally cleaner) than the Chao Phraya River. This fishing village-turned-bustling town draws tourists with a few fabulous *wats*, a not-to-be missed market, and some of Thailand's finest and most traditional seafood dishes. The town is also home to one of Thailand's best zoos. If neither fish nor fowl strike your fancy, make sure to arrive early enough to catch the ferry to Ko Si Chang.

▐ TRANSPORTATION

Buses to **Bangkok** (every 20-40min. 5am-6pm, 60-80฿) and **Rayong** (every 20min. 5am-10pm, 50-70฿) depart across from the mall on Sukhumvit Rd. Infrequent buses to other eastern destinations stop across from the main entrance. To reach the main strip of hotels and restaurants, and the **ferry** to Ko Si Chang, take either a **tuk-tuk** or **motorcycle taxi** (40฿) from the mall or walk for 10-15min. toward the water (you will eventually hit Jermjompal Rd. and should be no more than a block north of Si Racha Nakhon Rd. 3).

✈ ▐ ORIENTATION AND PRACTICAL INFORMATION

Si Racha is laid out in the shape of a square, with the coast and main street, **Jermjompal Road,** running along the western side and the highway to Bangkok, called **Sukhumvit Road,** tracing the eastern side. Intersecting these main roads are **Si Racha Nakhon Road 1,** which forms the northern border, and **Surasak 3 Road,** which constitutes the southern border. Beware of the multiple street names that are identical except for their numbers, such as Si Racha Nakhon 1, 2, and 3. The causeway leading to Wat Ko Loy and the ferry to Ko Si Chang are in the northwest corner, while the stellar fish and vegetable **market** is in the southwest corner. Services in Si Racha include:

Currency Exchange: Siam Commercial Bank, 98/9 Surasak I Rd. (☎038 311 313; open M-F 8:30am-3:30pm), halfway between Sukhumvit and Jermjompol Rd. A second location at 95/1 Sukhumvit Rd. (☎038 770 746; open daily 11am-8pm), between the Pacific Park Mall and Robinson Department Store, with **currency exchange** and **24hr. ATM** (there are other ATMs on Si Racha Nakhon 3 where it meets Jerjompol Rd.)

Police: booth (☎038 311 800), on Jermjompol Rd. near Si Racha Nakhon Rd. 3.

Medical Services: Phayathai General Hospital, 90 Si Racha Nakhon Rd. 3 (☎038 770 200; open 24hr.).

Internet Access: TT Cybernet (☎038 771 164), 3rd fl., Pacific Park Mall, with fax and scanning services (25฿ per hr.; open M-F 10:30am-9pm, Sa-Su 10am-9pm).

Post Office: (☎038 311 202), on Jermjompal Rd., between the Health Park and the causeway to the ferry, with international phones. Open M-F 8:30am-4:30pm, Sa-Su 9am-noon. **Postal Code:** 20110.

▐ ACCOMMODATIONS

There are a smattering of pricey hotels, geared towards the Japanese and Thai tourists that come to Si Racha, around the mall and bus stop, but some cheaper options line the open sea on Jermjompol Rd.

Samchai Hotel, off Jermjompol Rd., across from Surasak I Rd. (☎38 311 134). Offers simple rooms with cable TV. The staff is accommodating, but difficult to communicate with. Singles with fan 260฿, with A/C 400฿; doubles 400/480฿. ❷

Siri Watana, opposite Si Racha Nakhon Rd. 3 (☎38 311 037), perched over the water on a pier jutting out into the ocean, off Jermjompol Rd. The sound of waves will lull you to sleep. Plain rooms with fan. Lacks Western-style toilets and English-speaking staff. Singles 200฿; doubles 300฿.) ❷

FOOD

Si Racha is famous for its seafood, which is often prepared with the famous Si Racha sauce, a spicy red dressing known as "nam prik si racha." The prime location for gorging on local cuisine is **Si Racha Nakhon Road 3,** just one block from Jermjompal Rd. leading away from the water. The road branches in two and the triangle remaining in the middle overflows with food stalls, small restaurants, and larger open-air eateries, allowing diners to stroll through and take their pick. The stalls are mostly open from late afternoon (3 or 4pm) until 10 or 11pm. The larger eateries have English menus. For fresh fruit, vegetables, seafood, or just about any other odd-looking edible in existence, head to the complex of **markets** on the southern end of Jermjompol Rd. where it intersects with Surasak 3 Rd. by the clocktower.

Tik Ka Tow, (☎061 13 4 890), on Si Racha Nakhon 3, under a yellow Thai sign and yellow flags. A festively-lit, open-air restaurant offering an extensive buffet (89฿) of fresh seafood and vegetables that you cook at your table. Singha, Chang, or Leo beer 55-75฿. Open nightly 4pm-midnight. ❸

The Pop, 79 Jermjompal Rd. (☎038 325 712), between Si Racha Nakhon 3 Rd. and the Health Park. Has the best views in town, a jovial atmosphere, live music, and cool ocean breeze. *Pop-phi-rod,* their seafood and chili-curry specialty (139฿), is itself worth the visit. Open nightly 4pm-1am. ❸

SIGHTS

Si Racha's main attraction is the **Si Racha Tiger Zoo,** a rather gimmicky affair 9km east of town. (*Tuk-tuk* from anywhere in the city 25min., 120-150฿.) The zoo claims to host Thailand's largest number of Bengali Tigers, which until recently numbered more than 400. Sadly, over 100 tigers were either put down or died after the bird flu rampaged through the area. But the show goes on; the zoo's Thai-only, kitschy shows range from female performers wrestling live crocodiles to the "Scorpion Queen" covering herself with scorpions. There are several opportunities to get a close look at the many animals, including taking a picture (150฿) with an adorable baby tiger. (☎38 296 556. Open daily 8am-6pm. Several shows per hr. 300฿, children 150฿.)

The town's most touristed temple is **Wat Ko Loi** (Floating Island Temple), next to the ferry port, at the end of the causeway at the top stretch of Jermjopal Rd. Make an offering to the gods or simply wander around the base of the *wat,* where food stalls and trinket shops buzz with the picnicking Thais who relax here on weekends. A shady, well-landscaped **health park** stretches along the waterfront on Jermjompol Rd.

Those with less time can head **Wat Mahasiracha** in town. On Surasak Sa Nguan Rd., just before the market, the *wat* is on the left-hand side of the street. It consists of temples surrounded by monks' quarters.

KO SI CHANG   ☎038

Often overlooked for more picturesque beach locales farther east, Ko Si Chang is a friendly, laid-back island deserving of a second glance. A tourist boom years back encouraged the residents of this fishing village to spruce up their island with new bungalows and English signs and maps. But as the rest of Southeast Asia opened up, more and more visitors headed to the more spectacular Ko Samet and Ko Chang instead. Accordingly, Ko Si Chang remains a pretty island with good tourist services, friendly locals, and hardly a trace of commercialism. While its eastern ocean views are speckled with huge tankers and barges, beautiful, westward-facing Hat Tampang avoids these altogether.

▐ TRANSPORTATION

Ferries to Ko Si Chang depart from Si Racha's main pier at the end of Jermjompol Rd. (45min., every 1-2hr. 8am-8pm, 50฿). **Boats** to Si Racha leave from **Ta Lang Pier** or **Ta Bon Pier,** depending on the tide (every 1-2hr. 8am-6pm); ask your guesthouse owner to verify the location.

Motorized samlor (a motorcycle-drawn variation unique to Ko Si Chang) go anywhere on the island (20-50฿). The best way to see the island is to hire a **tuk-tuk,** regular **samlor,** or **motorcycle taxi** to take you on an all-inclusive tour (150฿). You can also rent a **motorbike** at the pier or from Tiew Pai Guest House (250฿ per day). For the nautically inclined, Tiew Pai also arranges **boat tours** (3-4hr., groups of 10 2500฿) and rents **bikes** (100฿ per day).

✦ ▐ ORIENTATION AND PRACTICAL INFORMATION

Assadang Road, the main road in town, has two different sections. The first is more or less a circle that frames the north part of the island. Heading right from the two central piers, it passes the post office and Chinese Temple, then loops southward and joins its tail end at Tiew Pai Guest House (see below). The other section of Assadang Rd. intersects with its circular counterpart at Tiew Pai's, then runs south to Hat Ta Wang and Hat Sai Kaew and branches off at **Chakra Pong Road** to **Hat Tampang,** the island's best beach.

Kasikornbank, 9-9 Assadang Rd., between the piers, exchanges traveler's checks and has a **24hr. ATM.** (☎038 216 132. Open M-F 8:30am-3:30pm.) The **local police** can be reached at ☎038 216 218. Ko Si Chang's general **hospital** (☎038 216 000) is to the right, up Assadang Rd. from the pier, on the left-hand side. **Internet** access is on Assadang Rd., after the hospital but before the post office, to the right, in a nameless shop. (Printing available. 30฿ per hr.) A 4min. walk from the hospital is the **post office,** on the right side of Assadang Rd. (☎038 216 227. Open M-F 8:30am-4:30pm.) **Postal Code:** 20120.

▐ ACCOMMODATIONS

Pricey bungalows line the beach, and **camping** on the beach is free. You will need to bring your own tent, but decent showers are available at Tampang Beach Resort for 15฿. If you'd like a roof over your head without emptying your pockets, there are a few options.

Tiew Pai Guest House (☎038 216 084), to the left of the pier on Assadang Rd. Cheap, well-kept, with friendly owners who can help arrange your itinerary on the island. Tiew Pai is Ko Si Chang's only real guesthouse. The inexpensive singles leave much to be desired—an upgrade to a bungalow or at least a double is worth the money. Singles with shared bath 200฿, doubles with bath 400฿, small, cozy bungalows with A/C and fridge 600฿, triples and family-sized rooms 750-1000฿. ❷

Tampang Beach Resort (☎038 216 153), right on Hat Tampang. Rooms are basic but clean, and the quick stroll down to the beach makes this option hard to beat, especially for eager beachgoers. A *tuk-tuk* from the pier runs 40-60฿, there are plenty of motorcycles around the beach to get to other parts of the island once there. Singles and doubles 550฿, quads 900-1200฿, 6-person rooms 1500-1800฿. ❸

🍴 FOOD

Taste buds will rejoice on Ko Si Chang, especially at the **noodle and rice vendors** along Assadang Rd. Ask anyone to point you toward the famous "pad thai lady" for a made-to-order bowl of tasty noodles (20฿).

Tiew Pai Guest House's restaurant (see Accommodations, above). Try the full Western breakfast (80฿), or the meals ranging from typical rice dishes (35-50฿) to "fish n' fixin's" (180-200฿). Open daily 7:30am-1am. ❶

Pan & David Restaurant (☎038 216 075), on Assadang Rd., before the turn-off to Tampang Beach, provides well-made meals, including several vegetarian options, and friendly service. The fluffy, homemade pancakes (100฿) and free-range chicken curry (120฿) are memorable. ❸

Unnamed restaurant, on Assadang Rd., before Pan & David and just after Benjaporn Bungalows. Under a blue-and-white awning, patrons enjoy treats like incredible fresh *rotis* topped with condensed milk (20฿). ❶

🏛 SIGHTS

A tour of Ko Si Chang takes just a few hours by motorbike or *samlor* (150-200฿). If you're driving yourself, start at the piers and take a right on Assadang Rd., which winds up and to the right of the **Chinese Temple,** a 163-step climb from the road. The temple houses a golden image of a Chinese god in a natural cave and has a pavilion with views of the ocean. A long and tiring 400 steps farther lies an enshrined **Buddha footprint** whose size makes it a good match for the **Yellow Buddha** on the island's west side. Once there, descend the back stairs for a solitary walk down the hill, but beware the monkeys lurking in the surrounding trees. When you reach the road, walk for 3min. to the left where you will see the first set of stairs. On the road between the Chinese Temple and Yellow Buddha are the striking **Khao Khat Cliffs,** where Rama V built a pavilion to enjoy the horizon and write poetry. The view from the king's seat is stunning and affords views of both the sunrise and sunset. Below the cliffs is a long bridge leading to a path twisting down to the water; sunset here is an awe-inspiring sight.

At the very far end of the second section of Assadang Rd., near the two eastern beaches and past the turn-off for Tampang Beach, are the ruins of King Rama V's **summer palace.** The last economic crisis halted the restoration of this royal residence, but you can stroll around the royal grounds and see pagodas, reservoirs, and European-influenced buildings, while enjoying views of the sea and forests. To get there, continue south on Assadang Rd. through the gate of the Marine Research Institute. 🏖**Hat Tampang,** Ko Si Chang's most swimmable beach, is found by turning off of Assadang Rd. at the sign for Chakra Pong Rd. After climbing over a hill, make a right on Chalerm Prakariat Rd. A number of beachfront restaurants rent out beach chairs (20฿) and serve food and beverages. Kayaks, snorkels, and floating tubes are available for rent (40-100฿).

PATTAYA ☎038

"Welcome to Pattaya—The Extreme City" reads a sign over the road to Pattaya. A blend of the dazzle of Vegas, the sizzle of Amsterdam, and the frazzle of Rio de Janeiro still wouldn't come to close to approaching the overwhelming ethos of hedonism that draws thousands of foreigners to Pattaya every year. Go-go bars filled with Thai women and single—or single enough—foreign men pervade the city. Pattaya has, over the years, garnered a poor reputation for this rampant sex trade, and tourist development-induced pollution. In recent years, however, efforts to clean up the city have made some headway. Diving and snorkeling trips, jet skis, and speedboats make welcome diversions for willing tourists, and Pattaya's many shopping complexes and markets are great places to get inexpensive Western food and clothing. The city's long beaches, slew of activities, and nightlife scene are definitely a draw, but never quite mask the presence of Thailand's overwhelming sex industry.

⌐ TRANSPORTATION

Buses: The main **bus station** is on N. Pattaya Rd., 2 blocks from Sukhumvit Hwy. Buses to **Bangkok's Ekamai Station** (2hr., every 30min. 5:20am-9pm, 128฿) and **Mo Chit Station**

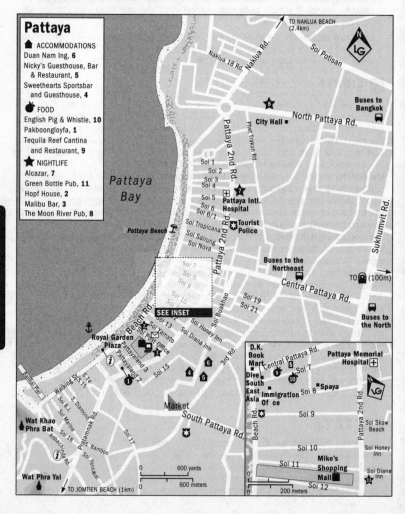

Pattaya

🏠 ACCOMMODATIONS
Duan Nam Ing, **6**
Nicky's Guesthouse, Bar & Restaurant, **5**
Sweethearts Sportsbar and Guesthouse, **4**

🍎 FOOD
English Pig & Whistle, **10**
Pakboongloyfa, **1**
Tequila Reef Cantina and Restaurant, **9**

⭐ NIGHTLIFE
Alcazar, **7**
Green Bottle Pub, **11**
Hopf House, **2**
Malibu Bar, **3**
The Moon River Pub, **8**

(2-3hr., every 30min. 5:40am-7pm, 128฿). Buses to **Si Racha** (1hr., 40฿) and **Rayong** leave from the bus stop on Sukhumvit Rd., near the Central Pattaya Rd. intersection.

Trains: Train station, off Soi 45 on Sukhumvit Rd., north of the intersection between Sukhumvit and Central Pattaya Rd. Trains to **Bangkok's Hualamphong Station** (M-F 2:21pm, 31฿).

Local Transportation: Songthaew (10-50฿) travel up and down most major roads. The routes up Pattaya 2nd Rd. and down Beach Rd. are particularly useful. *Songthaew* also go from the bus station on North Pattaya Rd. and from the train station (40฿) to the beach area, central Pattaya (20฿), and Jomtien Beach (30฿). **Motorcycle taxis** abound and are found on most street corners (20-90฿).

Rentals: Most hotels rent **motorcycles** (200-250฿ per day). Multiple other rental agencies line the beach road, offering anything from scooters to SUVs.

◢ ◪ ORIENTATION AND PRACTICAL INFORMATION

Pattaya's main strip, **Pattaya Beach Road (Beach Road),** runs north-south, parallel to the coast. Toward the southern end of the city, **Beach Road** turns into **Walking Street,** an area closed to vehicle traffic after 9pm and the center of the city's nightlife. **Pattaya 2nd Road (2nd Road)** runs parallel to Beach Rd. **North Pattaya (Pattayanua) Road, Central Pattaya (Pattayaklang) Road,** and **South Pattaya (Pattayatai) Road** all intersect these two streets and form the heart of Pattaya. Small numbered sois, increasing in number to the south, also run between Beach Rd. and 2nd Rd. In northern Pattaya is the quiet neighborhood of **Naklua,** while to the south is **Jomtien Beach,** a burgeoning center of expats, condos, restaurants, and beaches ideal for water sports. Jomtien also exhibits a slightly more family-oriented spirit, as well as nicer beaches than central Pattaya.

Tourist Office: TAT, 609 Moo 10, Soi Pratamnak (☎038 428 750; fax 429 113), on the mountain near Big Buddha at the southern end of Pattaya. Open daily 8:30am-4:30pm. Smaller tourist **booth** at the beginning of the pedestrian section of Beach Rd., next to the more expensive ferry port to Koh Larn.

Immigration Office: (☎038 252 750, ext. 1), in Jomtien Beach, on Jomtien Rd. Soi 5. Extension of stay 1900฿, re-entry 1000฿, multiple re-entries 3800฿. Open daily 8:30am-4:30pm.

Currency Exchange: Krung Thai Bank, on Central Pattaya Rd., 1 block from Beach Rd. Exchanges traveler's checks (33฿ per check). **ATM. Western Union** services at PS Plaza, across the street. Open daily 8:30am-9pm. Other exchanges dot Beach and 2nd Rd.

Books: D.K. Book Mart, 1/61-62 Moo 9, Central Pattaya Rd. (☎038 429 359), a few quick steps away from Beach Rd. Carries a great selection of travel guides, maps, Thai language guides, Thai cookbooks, and popular fiction. Open daily 9am-11:30pm.

Laundromat: On the small soi connecting Sois 7 and 8, across from the Bella Vista. Shirt 15-20฿, pants 15-20฿, shorts 10฿, underwear 5฿. Open daily 8am-8pm. Most hotels and guesthouses offer laundry service for similar prices.

Tourist Police: 2 24hr. stations: 1 branch (☎038 429 371) in north Pattaya, on Pattaya 2nd Rd., just north of Soi Tropicana, and a 2nd to the south, off of South Pattaya Rd. A centrally located main **police station** is on Beach Rd., between Sois 7 and 8 (☎038 424 186 and 420 802).

Medical Services: Pattaya Memorial Hospital, 328/1 Central Pattaya Rd. (☎038 429 422 4). English spoken. Open 24hr. for emergencies. **Pattaya International Hospital** (☎038 428 374), Soi 8 in North Pattaya, is very reputable and has a **24hr. pharmacy.**

Telephones: Many small shops advertise overseas call service. Most in central Pattaya charge 20฿ per min. to call the US, Australia, or Europe. Go a few blocks out from the center and you can find 10฿ shops, like one at the back of Mike's Shopping Center, facing Pattaya 2nd Rd. Small, with A/C and comfy chairs (min. 3min. call).

Internet Access: Similar Internet cafes throughout Pattaya charge 1ᴮ per min; many are open 24hr. **Pattaya Telecommunications Center,** 13/2 Soi Post Office (☎38 710 103), has cheap Internet (20ᴮ per hr.) access and long-distance phone cards.

Post Office: (☎38 429 341). On Soi Post Office. Western Union. Poste Restante. Open M-F 8:30am-8pm, Sa-Su 9am-noon. **Postal Code:** 20260.

ACCOMMODATIONS

Hotels in north Pattaya tend to be a bit quieter and more family-friendly, but also more expensive. Prices drop a bit in central and south Pattaya, and better deals can often be found on Pattaya 2nd or **Pattaya 3rd Rd.,** farther away from the beach. Many travelers feel uncomfortable staying in budget accommodations in Pattaya, as they mainly cater to single males. **Soi Buakhaow,** between Central Rd. and South Pattaya Rd., does host a number of inexpensive but respectable hotels that are backpacker friendly; it's a good place for getting the feel of central Pattaya without seeing go-go bars on every corner. Unless otherwise noted, all hotels in Pattaya have A/C, hot water, and ▨**flushing toilets.**

Sweethearts Sportsbar and Guesthouse, 281/5-6 Soi Buakhao (☎938 724 235), across the road from Nicky's Guesthouse. A welcoming place for weary backpackers. Bright and spacious rooms have DVDs. Ask Danny about low-season discounts on doubles, and book in advance; this guesthouse is often full even in the low season. High-season doubles 650ᴮ, low-season discounts 500ᴮ. ❹

Duan Nam Ing Hotel (☎038 420 119), on Soi Buakhao just before Nicky's Guesthouse. Large, clean rooms with small balconies. The hotel has a luxurious pool, free Internet access, and an adjacent coffee shop that is unusually chic for Pattaya. Wonderfully friendly staff. Doubles 750ᴮ, with pool view 950ᴮ. ❹

Nicky's Guesthouse, Bar & Restaurant, 293/27-28 Soi Buakhao (☎038 723 851; www.nickysbar.com), between South Pattaya Rd. and Soi Lengki. Immaculate, comfortable, dark wood furnished, newly renovated rooms. The bar downstairs is small and welcoming. Spacious doubles with TV and fridge 700ᴮ. ❹

FOOD

Pattaya serves as a clashing point for many cultures, and its food is one area where this is glaringly obvious. Western chains and European pub grub line every street, and Thai cuisine is noticeably sparse, apart from the street vendors that cross the city. The upside of such a selection is the ability to sample all of the chains that aren't so affordable back home but offer far lower prices here. If Western-style food isn't what you're looking for, stick to the **carts** and nameless restaurants peppering the streets. Try **Pattayaland** for lots of cart selection and South Pattaya Rd. for a better diversity of local cuisine. All day Tuesday and Friday, a large covered **market** (open 9am-6pm) is fashioned at the corner of Buakhao and South Pattaya Rd. Although it's mostly full of clothing, music, and jewelry, the strawberry virgin daiquiris are a delightfully cool treat.

English Pig and Whistle, 217/34 Moo 9 Soi 7 (☎038 361 315). The ubiquitous Brits of Pattaya flock to this upstanding restaurant and pub. Also rents rooms (600-750ᴮ, includes breakfast). Full English breakfast 135ᴮ. Open daily 8:30am-1am. ❸

Pakboongloyfa, 325/63-65, Pattaya 2nd Rd. (☎038 429 722), close to its intersection with South Pattaya Rd. Sit outside on Pakboongloyfa's sidewalk patio for inexpensive and generous portions of Thai food and a lot of people-watching. Flip through the massive menu and look for the smaller portions of most dishes; they are even cheaper and still large enough for a meal. Dishes 35-220ᴮ. Open daily 10am-midnight. ❷

Tequila Reef Cantina and Restaurant (☎038 414 035), 50m from Beach Rd., on Soi 7. A clean, colorful atmosphere for enjoying a margarita (130-150฿ per glass; deals on pitchers and bucket-sized "grande" glasses). Sizzling fajitas (315฿) are the house specialty, but the Texas chili con carne (125-155฿) is award-winning. Extensive bar. Burgers 130฿. Thai food 100-120฿. Open daily 11:30am- "late late," around midnight. ❸

📷 SIGHTS

Motor-racing, bungee jumping, bowling, windsurfing, parasailing, tower-jumping, watersliding, or shooting ranges—with so many options, boredom isn't a problem in Pattaya. For something more unique to Thailand, try the **Million Year Stone Park and Crocodile Farm,** at 22 Moo 1, Tamban Nong Pla Lai. The park has a collection of rock gardens, rare plants and animals, and thousands of crocodiles. Several performances are put on (daily 11am, noon, 2:30pm), including crocodile, monkey, magic, and fire-swallowing shows. For a few extra baht, you can ride an elephant or have your picture taken with tame lions, tigers, and bears. (☎038 249 3479. Open daily 8:30am-6:30pm. 300฿, children 150฿.)

The principal event at the **Pattaya Elephant Village** is the elephant show (daily 8:30, 10am, noon, 3pm; 500฿). The Village also offers two half-day elephant treks through the brush. Prices vary depending on where your hotel is, as they pick you up and drop you off at the end of the trek. (☎038 249 818; www.elephant-village-pattaya.com. Off Siam Country Club Rd., a 20min., 100฿ motorcycle ride from central Pattaya.) If you're starting to tire of Thai landmarks, check out **Mini Siam,** at Km 143 on Sukhumvit Hwy., for recreations of famous landmarks from around the world. Alongside the Kwai River Bridge and the Emerald Buddha are icons like the Eiffel Tower, Statue of Liberty, and Leaning Tower of Pisa. Mini Siam is especially popular at night when the miniatures are illuminated. (☎038 727 333. Open daily 7am-10pm. 100฿.)

📷 BEACHES AND WATER SPORTS

The beach in central Pattaya tends to disappoint visitors. While it is not as polluted as it was a few years back, there is very little swimming at Pattaya Beach. For a more idyllic beach experience, head north to the resorts in **Naklua.** For water sports, **Jomtien** is best. The sea isn't clear here, but this doesn't detract from its popularity. Jet skis (800-900฿ per 30min.), boats (1000-1500฿ per 30min.), and sailboats (800฿ per hr.) are all available for rent, though bargaining may be worth your while. Parasailing trips (600฿) are also very popular. Jomtien is the only beach in Pattaya where you can rip it up windsurfing. (600฿ per hr.; 1hr. lesson 100฿ extra).

Scuba diving and **snorkeling** are both popular activities too. Many dive shops in the area offer **PADI certification courses** in scuba diving and daily dive trips to one of Pattaya's islands or to one of the two fantastic shipwreck sites offshore (Ko Larn and the HMS Khran). Visibility is best during the high season (about 15m). There are a number of reputable dive centers around Pattaya. **Mermaid's Dive Center,** on Soi White House in Jomtien, claims to be the only dive school in Pattaya with female instructors. (☎038 232 219. Open-water snorkeling trip 1000฿, basic certification course 4000฿, advanced open-water course 12,000฿.)

Alternatively, stay on dry land and people-watch while lying on one of the thousands of beach chairs (20-30฿ per day) lining the beach. *Touts* and salespeople offering everything from food to massages to tattoos (both temporary and real) make for an exciting and interactive beach day.

🎵 🎤 ENTERTAINMENT AND NIGHTLIFE

Nearly identical massage parlors line the streets of Pattaya. The standard offerings are foot massage (200฿ per hr.), Thai massage (200฿), and oil massage (250฿). Be sure to get a massage in clear view of the shop windows to avoid being uncomfortably propositioned. For an extraordinary experience, try a relaxing massage from a blind masseur at a massage school such as **The Thai Blind Massage Institute,** 413/89 Thappraya Rd., in Jomtien. (☎038 303 418. 1hr. Thai massage 30฿, with A/C 150฿; 1 hr. foot massage 180/200฿; 1hr. oil massage 250฿. Open daily 10am-10pm.)

Pattaya's nightlife is dominated by **beer bars** (open-air pickup joints) and **go-go bars.** The beer bars are all virtually indistinguishable from one another, although many name a country as their patron, attracting male tourists from that region. Beer bars dominate **Sois 7** and **8,** and both beer bars and go-go bars can be found in great numbers along **Walking St.** and the sois that run off it.

Fortunately, not all of Pattaya's nightlife is focused (overtly) on commercial sex, and classier bars dot the city. Gay nightlife is centered slightly north of Walking St. on **Pattayaland 2** (also known as Soi 13/4). One immensely popular form of entertainment in Pattaya is drag-queen cabaret. The most famous of these is at **Alcazar,** 78/14 Moo 9, Pattaya 2nd Rd., which puts on choreographed shows. (☎038 410 224. Shows nightly 6:30, 8, 9:30pm; Sa also 11pm. Tickets 500-600฿.) A less pricey and less professional cabaret is put on at **Malibu Bar,** on Soi Post Office, at the corner of Pattaya 2nd Rd. (Nightly 8pm-1am. Free.)

Hopf House, 219 Beach Rd. (☎038 710 650), between Soi Yamato and Post Office. A good place to meet other tourists. Excellent food and nightly live music in a comfortable interior. Lager and weiss beer (90-150฿) from on-site microbrewery. Weekend dinner reservations recommended. Pizza 160-220฿. Steak 400฿. Open daily 4pm-1am. ❹

Green Bottle Pub, 216/3-9 Moo 10 2nd Rd. (☎038 429 675), between Sois 11 and 12. Laid-back with a good selection of food and nightly live music. Steak 385-435฿. Club sandwich 85฿. Thai food 100-270฿. Singha 80฿. Open daily 11am-1am. ❸

The Moon River Pub, 179/168 Moo 5 North Pattaya Rd. (☎038 370 614), 2 blocks away from the beach. Come here to listen to Thai bands sing about Louisiana. This country-western pub has a loyal local following. Tables even come equipped with cards on which you can make song requests from the band. Tropical drinks 195฿. Draft beer 120฿ and up. Live music Th-Su 8 or 9pm-1am. Happy hour daily 6-7:30pm; drinks ½ price. Open daily 6pm-1am.

🚌 DAYTRIP FROM PATTAYA: KO LARN

There are 2 different ways to get to Ko Larn. At the northern end of Walking St. is a small pier where expensive ferries leave for Tawaen Beach (1hr.; 9:30, 11am, 1pm; return 3, 4, or 5pm. 150฿ round trip). Cheaper ferries (45min.; 7, 8, 10am, noon, 2, 3:30, 5, 6:30pm; return 6:30, 7:30, 9:30am, noon, 5, 6pm; 20฿) leave from the Balihai Pier at the southern end of Walking St. for Naban Port on Ko Larn. At Naban Port, motorcycle taxis (20฿) shuttle you to Tawaen Beach and to more distant beaches (50฿).

Ko Larn, the largest island in the waters around Pattaya, boasts prettier shores and clearer water than the mainland. Its biggest draw is **Tawaen Beach,** a wide expanse of white sand leading to turquoise water. Although beautiful, this is not the ideal place to go for rest and relaxation; it's cluttered with restaurants and beach chairs (30฿). Package tours from Thailand and China fill it up quickly in the high season. A small area is roped off for swimmers, but most of the water is taken up by jet skis (600฿ per 30min.), banana boats (250฿ per 30min.), and speed boats (800฿ per 30min.). There are several other pretty beaches on

Ko Larn, including **Thieu Beach** and **Sanae Beach,** but the coral there makes it difficult to swim. Tiny **Coral Island,** just off Ko Larn's coast, has great snorkeling.

There are no guesthouses on the island geared towards budget travelers; however, in the high season, **tents** can be rented to camp on the beach. (☎015 901 218. 300฿, 350฿ for tent and use of toilet and showers.) There are a number of other **bungalows** for rent around the island, which are advertised at the restaurants and cafes surrounding Naban Port. There is currently **no ATM** on Ko Larn, but ask around for updates.

RAYONG ☎038

The city of Rayong, located halfway between Bangkok and the Cambodian border, does not draw many tourists in its own right. Since it's a major transportation hub, however, travelers headed to or away from Ko Samet will likely spend time here. The city's only claims to fame are its reputation for producing the succulent summer fruits pineapple and *durian* and the dubious distinction of being the *naam plaa* (fish sauce) capital of Thailand. The time-intensive (and extremely smelly) process of producing *naam plaa* involves letting fish decompose for seven months—yum.

TRANSPORTATION. Songthaew leave from **Rayong Bus Station** (☎038 611 379) for **Ban Phe** (45min., every 15min. 6:15am-7:30pm, 25฿). **Buses** go to: **Bangkok** (3hr., every 30min. 3am-8:50pm, 155฿); **Chanthaburi** (2hr., every 30min. 5am-7:30pm, 70฿); **Khorat** (6hr., every hr. 4:20am-9pm, 125-225฿); **Nong Khan** (13hr., every hr. 7am-8pm, 434฿); **Pattaya** (1hr., every 30min. 3am-6:20pm, 60฿); **Si Racha** (2hr., every 20min. 5am-7:30pm, 60฿). To get to **Trat,** go to Chanthaburi and change buses there.

ORIENTATION AND PRACTICAL INFORMATION. Rayong's main street, **Sukhumvit Road,** runs east-west through the center of town. The bus station is two blocks north of Sukhumvit Rd. The ocean lies to the south. Services include: **TAT Office** (☎038 655 420, ext. 1; tourist information line 1672), 7km west of Rayong; **currency exchange** and **24hr. ATM** at the **Bank of Ayudhya,** Sukhumvit Rd. across from Sukhumvit Nakornrayong 39 (☎038 611 534, open M-F 8:30am-3:30pm); **Rayong Tourist Police** (☎038 651 669); **Rayong Hospital** (☎038 611 104), on the corner of Sukhumvit Rd. and Sukhumvit Nakornrayong 45, east of the bus station; free **Internet** access on the second floor of Star Plaza mall, across from the Star Hotel; and the **post office** on Sukhumvit Rd., half a block east of the bus station, across from Sukhumvit Nakornrayong 43. (Open M-F 8:30am-4:30pm, Sa-Su 9am-noon.) **Postal Code:** 21000.

ACCOMMODATIONS AND FOOD. Both hotels and restaurants are scarce in Rayong. The **Burapa Palace Hotel** ❸, 69 Sukhumvit Rd., has large, bright, spartan rooms. (☎038 622 946. Rooms with fan 380฿, with A/C 480฿.) **The Star Hotel** ❺, 109 Rayong Trade Center Soi 4, behind the bus station, is the luxury choice in Rayong, offering bowling, snooker, karaoke, and two pools. (☎038 614 901, ext. 7. Doubles 2000-3000฿.) The Star also has a Japanese **restaurant** ❸ with an excellent lunch buffet. (Buffet 140฿. Open daily 6am-midnight.) The colorful and lively **market** is the highlight of Rayong and, fortunately, only a 2min. walk from the bus station, in the direction of the Star Hotel. Go here to see piles of fruit as tall as people and sample the local fare from vendors cooking inside. Thaksinmajaraj Rd. has numerous noodle, curry, and barbecue **stands** and small areas for sitting and eating.

BAN PHE
☎038

Ban Phe is a small coastal town that serves primarily as a jumping-off point to Ko Samet. **Tarua Phe Pier,** across from the 7-Eleven on Beach Rd., acts as the main point of departure for ferries leaving for Ko Samet, although many of the other piers offer similar services for the same price.

Buses run from Bangkok's Ekamai terminal to Ban Phe (3hr.; 15 per day 5am-8:30pm, return every hr. 4am-7pm; 178-157฿). The **Ban Phe Bus Station** (☎038 651 528) is across from Nuan Tip Pier. To get elsewhere, take a **songthaew** from the street-side stop near the bus station to **Rayong** (45min., every 15-30min. 6:15am-6pm, 25฿) and transfer there, or if heading east toward **Chanthaburi** or **Trat,** take a **motorcycle taxi** to the highway (30฿) and hail a passing bus.

Ferries go to **Na Dan Pier** (every hr. 8am-5pm, 50฿) and **Wong Duan Pier** (9:30am, 1:30, 5pm) on Ko Samet's eastern coast. **Nuan Tip Pier,** across from the bus station, also offers service to the various beaches on Ko Samet. The ferries at Nuan Tip only leave when the boat is full, though, so Tarua Phe may be a more efficient choice. For pricier but easier transportation, **travel agencies** in Ban Phe offer direct **minibus** service to **Ko Chang** (300฿) and **Trat** (250฿); **Chanthaburi** (250฿); **Pattaya** (250฿), and **Bangkok** (250฿). Suriya Tour Service (☎038 651 461), across from Tan Tan Internet, is one such agency.

Other services in Ban Phe include: a **24hr. ATM** outside the 7-Eleven across from Tarua Phe Pier; **Bangkok Bank** (☎038 651 967), 1km west of the piers and a 10min. walk or a 15฿ motorcycle taxi ride from Tarua Phe Pier, which exchanges currency and traveler's checks (open M-F 8:30am-3:30pm); and the **police station** (☎038 651 111), which is midway between the two piers. A surprisingly good selection of English- and foreign-language books can be found at **Blue Sky Books** (☎017 611 388), one block down the side street east of 7-Eleven. Books are both sold and bought here; they have a 2-for-1 trade deal on all books under 200฿, and will buy back any book bought there for half the price. **Internet access** is available at Tan Tan Too, across from Tarua Pier. (☎038 653 671. 1฿ per min., 50฿ per hr. Open daily 7:30am-6:30pm.) Ban Phe also hosts a number of Westerners year-round who take a **TEFL course** in order to earn an English as a Second Language teaching certification. Inquire at **Tristar TEFL** (☎038 653 691; www.english4thais.com), between the piers and the Bangkok Bank.

If you miss the last ferry, there are several lodgings clustered around the piers. The best deal in town can be found at a **hotel ●** lacking an English sign in the same building as HISO Thai Massages, two blocks west of the 7-Eleven on Sukhumvit Rd. Rooms are clean and spacious. (☎038 651 824. Rooms with A/C 400฿.) **Diamond Hotel ❸,** 286/12 Moo 2, Tambol Phe, on the main road, just west of Tarua Phe Pier, has clean, well-maintained rooms for a good price, and a friendly staff. (☎038 651 757. Rooms with fan 350฿, with A/C 500฿.) Satisfy your waiting-for-the-ferry munchies at **Christies Restaurant and Bar ●,** next to the 7-Eleven. (Hamburger and fries 120฿.)

KO SAMET
☎038

Gorgeous white-sand beaches, magical waterside eateries, and Thai rum served by the bucket await you on Ko Samet, one of Thailand's national parks-turned-tourist meccas. Just 4hr. from Bangkok, Ko Samet has become a popular vacation spot for Thais and foreigners alike. Over the past 20 years, beachside bungalows have slowly encroached on much of the shoreline, and loud *farang* pubs and Thai karaoke bars dominate the once-still nights. Development aside, the island still has the best beaches and clearest water on the east coast. A dip in its

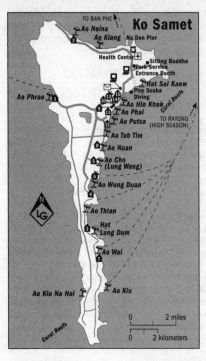

Ko Samet

tranquil waves or a nap on its clean sand will satisfy any traveler seeking good, old-fashioned relaxation.

🏛 TRANSPORTATION

Ferries: Ban Phe has many piers offering ferry trips to Ko Samet. If you arrive via *songthaew* from Rayong, you will be let off at **Tarua Phe Pier**, opposite the 7-Eleven, the main pier that offers ferries at least every hr. to **Na Dan Pier** on Ko Samet (30-45 min., daily 8am-5pm, 50฿). Also goes to **Ao Wong Duan** (45min.; 9:30am, 1:30, 5pm; 70฿) and **Ao Cho** (**Lung Wang**; 45 min.; 10am and 1pm; 65฿). Service from other piers should cost the same but may not be as regular. Buses from Bangkok stop in front of **Nuan Tip Pier** (☎038 651 508), 200m east of Tarua Phe Pier, which offers service to **Na Dan Pier** (40min., round-trip 100฿; 20-person min.). To get to Nuan Tip Pier, walk through the market toward the ocean. Additional boats (7-person min.) are available during peak months to: **Ao Kiu** (round-trip 200฿); **Ao Phrao** (45min., round-trip 120฿); **Ao Wai** (50min., round-trip 200฿); **Ao Wong Duan** (45min., round trip 120฿). **Buses: Ban Phe Bus Station** (☎038 651 548), opposite Nuan Tip Pier on the mainland. To **Bangkok** (3hr., every hr. 4am-7pm, 157-178฿). **Songthaew** to **Rayong** (15-30min., every 15min. 6:15am-6pm, 25฿). **Minibuses** to **Bangkok** (250฿), **Chanthaburi** (250฿), and **Ko Chang** (250฿).

Local Transportation: Songthaew at Na Dan Pier usually wait for 8-10 people before leaving. More remote destinations may require chartering the entire car. From **Na Dan Pier** to: **Hat Sai Kaew** (10฿ per person, 100฿ per vehicle); **Ao Hin Khok, Ao Phai, Ao Putsa, Ao Tub Tim** and **Ao Noina** (20฿ per person, 200฿ per vehicle); **Ao Phrao** (30฿ per person, 250฿ per vehicle); **Ao Wong Duan** (30฿ per person, 250฿ per vehicle); **Ao Wai** (50฿ per person, 450฿ per vehicle); **Ao Kiu** (60฿ per person, 550฿ per vehicle). *Songthaew* returning to the pier or offering taxi service wait at Ao Phai, in front of Silver Sands Resort, and at taxi stands at Ao Wong Duan and Ao Phrao. The island is generally walkable—it's only a 500m stroll from Na Dan Pier to Hat Sai Kaew. However, for beaches beyond Ao Wai, or to get to Ao Phrao, you'll need faster transportation.

Rentals: Shops renting **motorbikes** cluster near Na Dan Pier and along the road to Ao Putsa. (100-150฿ per hr., 300-400฿ per day; passport or 500฿ deposit required.) Bet-

Ko Samet
see map above

🏠 **ACCOMMODATIONS**

Ao Phai Hut, **10**
Baan Praguykaew, **2**
Jep's, **9**
Lima Coco Resort, **1**
Lung Dum Bungalow, **3**
Naga Bungalows, **15**
Nuan Bungalows, **8**
Samet Ville Resort, **7**
Sea Horse Bungalows, **4**
Tok's Little Hut, **14**
Tubtim Resort, **12**
Tutu Bungalows, **11**
Wonderland Resort, **5**

🍎 **FOOD**

Blue Sky Restaurant, **6**
Silver Sands Resort
Restaurant, **13**

ter yet, rent a **4X4** (300-400฿ per hr., 1200฿ per day) to get to the southern and western beaches. Be careful, though: Ko Samet's roads are in an extreme state of disrepair. Many a rider has the scrapes and scars to prove how easy it is to skid off of the road or spin out in the sand. Wear long pants and good shoes for protection.

◼✦ ⁊ ORIENTATION AND PRACTICAL INFORMATION

Two main roads stretch down Ko Samet's 16km length. Most boats disembark at **Na Dan Pier** on the island's northeast corner. A paved road runs south to the Park Service entrance booth, where you must pay a hefty **admission fee** to enter the island, which is a Thai national park (200฿, 10 and under 100฿). After the park entrance, the path forks. Directly ahead is **Hat Sai Kaew**, while the right-hand fork continues south, behind the bungalows of the eastern beaches: **Ao Hin Khok, Ao Phai, Ao Tub Tim, Ao Nuan, Ao Cho, Ao Wong Duan, Ao Thian, Hat Lung Dum, Ao Wai,** and **Ao Kiu.** To get to these beaches, bear left at the fork after Ao Phai. Head straight to go to Ko Samet's only west-coast beach, **Ao Phrao.** Beachside paths and jungle trails link all of the beaches except Ao Phrao and Ao Kiu and are generally easy to walk. The only way to avoid paying the park entrance fee is to stay on one of the northern beaches, **Ao Noina** or **Ao Klang.** To get there, head right from Na Dan Pier down the nice paved road. Some travelers report that though visitors technically should pay the park entrance fee if they want to visit any of the eastern or western beaches, they have been able to avoid this by leaving their luggage at a northern guesthouse; they claim that this prevents the park rangers from distinguishing those who have paid from those who have not. However, the small savings aren't really enough to offset the long walk from the northern to western or eastern beaches, not to mention breaking the law and depriving the park of much-needed funds.

Tourist Office: Visitors center (☎038 644 252), next to the park entrance by Hat Sai Kaew, provides info on local wildlife.

Tours: Many of the larger guesthouses will arrange flight ticketing, domestic **minibus** service, and snorkeling tours. Signs all over the island advertise Ko Samet boat trips, which include a day of fishing and snorkeling (400-500฿). **Night boat trips** are also available for squid fishing (500฿). Check with various vendors for the best deal.

Currency Exchange: There are 2 **ATMs** along the main road, just before the park entrance, next to the 7-Eleven. Good rates for **currency exchange,** traveler's checks, and cash advances can be found at the post office in Naga Bungalows (see p. 141). Another **ATM** can be found in the cluster of stores between the road and Ao Wong Duan.

Books: The post office offers the best book exchange on the island: swap 2 books for 1, swap 1 and pay 100฿ for a new one, or rent a book for 50฿. Some accommodations also offer casual book exchanges or rental libraries (40฿ per week), though most collections are stocked mainly with Thai-language books.

Local Tourist Police: (☎038 644 111). On the mainland, a block east of the market at Nuan Tip Pier. English spoken. Open 24hr. **Police sub-station** on Ao Wong Duan, but it does not have set hours or a direct phone number.

Medical Services: Health Center (☎038 644 123), halfway between Na Dan Pier and the park entrance. Some English spoken. Open daily 8:30am-noon and 1-4:30pm. In emergencies, phone the **hospital** in Rayong (☎038 612 999). Keep in mind that Ko Samet's emergency services are inadequate.

Pharmacy: Samed Pharmacy, near the hospital, on the main road, has some basic supplies. Open daily 9am-10pm.

Telephones: Pay phones are near the visitors center and the pier, and there is another on the road between Ao Hin Khok and Hat Sai Kaew. The unnamed **Internet and calling**

center next to Miss You Coffee Corner (see below) offers international calls starting at 40฿ per min. Post Office sells international phone cards.

Internet Access: The large bungalows at Ao Phai, Ao Phrao, Ao Wong Duan, and Hat Sai Kaew all offer Internet access (2฿ per min.). Fast connections are available at **Miss You Coffee Corner**, just before the park entrance. (☎038 644 060. 2฿ per min. Open daily 7:30am-midnight.) At the post office, Internet access is 2฿ per min.

Post Office: Naga Bungalows (see below) operates the licensed post office next door. Address Poste Restante to: "POSTE RESTANTE, Ko Samet, Ban Phe, Rayong 21160." Open daily 8:30am-9pm. **Postal Code:** 21160.

█ ▐ ACCOMMODATIONS AND FOOD

Lodgings on Ko Samet run the gamut from rustic bungalows to five-star luxury resorts. Most tourists head to eastern beaches like Hat Sai Kaew, Ao Hin Khok, Ao Phai, and Ao Wong Duan, while Ao Nuan, Ao Cho, Ao Wai, and Ao Tub Tim tend to be more isolated and tranquil. Ao Kiu and Ao Phrao cater almost entirely to high-budget travelers and do not offer cheap accommodations. The northern beaches offer a wide range of options, from tents to floating off-shore hotels. Most backpackers head to **Ao Hin Khok**, or the beaches just south of it, for a good balance of affordable prices, proximity to Na Dan Pier and its services, and an abundance of fantastic beach restaurants, noisy bars, and late-night dancing. Many of the accommodations on Ko Samet raise their prices on long weekends and holidays due to the influx of young Thai partiers from Bangkok. Ask about low-season discounts from May to October. **Camping** is available on all beaches, though it may be a good idea to pitch your tent in the vicinity of a beach guesthouse, where **bathrooms** and **showers** can be used for a negotiated fee. No fires are allowed on the beaches, and violators are fined 5000฿.

█ **AO HIN KHOK AND AO PHAI.** A more friendly and welcoming version of Bangkok's Khaosan Rd., █Ao Hin Khok is a backpacker haven. Come here for cheap, quality lodging accompanied by a lively atmosphere and great screenings of English-language flicks; don't come for romantic seclusion or quiet nights. Free of the litter and bobbing boats that plague Hat Sai Kaew and Ao Wong Duan, Ao Hin Khok's white beaches are wide and its waters are good for swimming. Accommodations are plentiful but fill up quickly, so arrive before 3 or 4pm. At the northern end is one of the cheapest accommodations, **Naga Bungalows ❸**, a Ko Samet backpacker tradition that remains the most popular spot on the island. The plainest bamboo bungalows sit on stilts and provide a classic Ko Samet rest under mosquito nets, while the slightly pricier huts with bath have great tiled porches and are less vulnerable to hungry mosquitoes. The comfortable common space is a great place to swap travelers' tales. (☎038 644 035, book exchange and library. Internet 8:30am-9pm; 2฿ per min. High-season bungalows with fan 400฿, with bath 800฿; low-season 200-300/400฿.) Its **restaurant ❸** serves fresh bread, brownies, sundaes, tofu-veggie options, and more. (Dishes 30-250฿. Open daily 8am-10pm.) On-site **Naga Bar** is a friendly and low-key locale for meeting other travelers, and the pool and beer pong tables make the bar especially popular. Drink specials are rampant on the beach, but here they include "12 chin-ups for a free drink." **Tok's Little Hut ❸**, south of Naga, is another good budget option, providing very basic bungalows with fan and bath. (☎038 644 072. Bungalows 200-500฿ depending on proximity to the beach; with A/C 800-1200฿.) Tok's **bar** sits next to Naga Bar and blasts pop music every evening. During Tosser's Hour, toss a coin and call it: guess correctly and the drink is half price. Newer **Jep's ❺**, (☎038 644 112; www.jepbungalow.com) features clean, bright rooms and bungalows with added luxuries, such as extra-large beds and A/C. Its **restaurant ❸** is one of the best on the beach: colorful hanging stars give this place a magical feel. Check out the barbecue with various types of fish on a stick (60-200฿) and *paneer* kebabs. (Open daily 9am-10pm. M-F bungalows with A/C 1200฿, Sa-Su 1500฿.)

On Ao Phai, **Tutu Bungalows ❶** (☎038 644 112; www.tutubungalow.com) sits close to the beach, just over the wooden walkway beyond Silver Sands Resort. Its tidy bungalows, with TV, fridge, and hot water, are a great value, and breakfast is included. (800฿, with A/C 1200฿.) The hillside bungalows at **Ao Phai Hut ❹** are relatively clean wooden huts with private bath. (☎038 644 075. Huts with fan 600฿, with A/C 1200฿; low-season 500/1000฿.) Share a meal with friends in one of the **beachfront restaurants** on Ao Phai. Most have low tables on mats where you can recline on cushions and enjoy a wide variety of cuisines by candlelight. Hours are generally 9am-10pm, although a few can be cajoled into whipping up a quick hamburger if you need sustenance on a long night out. The **Silver Sands Resort restaurant ❷** is a must, not only for its fare (great green curry; 60฿) but also for entertainment including a twirling fire show around 10pm each evening, cheap bucket drinks, and famous as the all-night dance parties.

◪ AO PHRAO.

Ko Samet's only western-facing beach is a smooth, white crescent of sand graced by sky-searing sunsets and some of the island's most luxurious accommodations and fine dining. If you're looking for cheap digs, lively backpackers, and beach frisbee, you're better off staying on the east coast. All but one of Ao Phrao's resorts include both transfers to Ao Phrao from Ban Phe and the admission fee to Ko Samet park (Lima Coco does not include the park fee). If not staying at these hotels, visitors can still travel directly to Ao Phrao on **ferries** leaving Ban Phe's **Seree Pier** (8, 11am, 1:30, and 4pm; 1-way 100฿) and returning from Ao Phrao (10am, 12:30, 3, and 5pm; 100฿). **Lima Coco Resort ❺** is a newer establishment that flaunts a funky, modern style. Although not as swanky as its neighbors, Lima Coca provides a great splurge by offering a touch of luxury without the highest price tag. (☎02 938 1811; www.limacoco.com. Breakfast included. Rooms from 3000฿. Low-season discount 10-20%.)

◪ AO TUB TIM.

This small, pretty beach flanked by low rocks is an easy 5min. walk from Ao Phai and a great option for those who want to be close to the action but far from the noise and bustle of Ao Sai Kaew and Ao Phai. **Tubtim Resort ❹**, on the southern end of the beach, is the one of the best options on the island. The immaculate, stylish thatched bungalows all have private baths, and are far closer to the sea than those at other beaches. (☎038 644 025; www.tubtimresort.com. Smaller doubles with fan and shower from 1000฿, larger doubles with A/C 2000฿.) The **restaurant ❸** offers an extensive menu of European and Thai options (40-300฿) in a well-designed garden patio.

◪ AO NUAN.

Ao Nuan is an unique and rustic place. The best way to get to this beautiful, secluded spot is to take a taxi ride (30฿ per person) from the Na Dan Pier, or walk through a path in a wooded area from Ao Tub Tim. While not the most stunning of beaches, Ao Nuan offers the rare chance to escape the teeming masses. Behind the rocks that form this tiny beach are rustic **🖾Nuan Bungalows ❸**, well-kept wooden huts with mattresses on the floor, and mosquito nets hanging from the ceiling. (Shared outdoors showers and toilets. Usually full Nov.-Apr. Huts 700-800฿. No reservations.) Nuan's **restaurant ❷** is shielded from the sun by a lush garden and is great for relaxing with a drink after a dip in the warm water (Open 8am-8pm. Dishes 30-200฿).

◖ **AO CHO (LUNG WANG).** A daily ferry service leaving Tarua Phe Pier in Ban Phe goes directly to (10am and 1pm) and from (9am, noon, and 3pm; 65ʙ) Ao Cho, a small, secluded, peaceful place with a laid-back feel. The quaint pier on the shore is complemented by a tree swing and flowering bushes on the grounds of the beach's largest accommodation, **Wonderland Resort ❹.** The bungalows with fans are far less nice than the newly refurbished ones with A/C, but the beach will tempt you to spend all your time outside anyway. The resort also includes a **restaurant ❷.** (☎038 644 162; www.lungwang.thie.wthai.com. Laundry. Restaurant open daily 7am-10pm. Snorkel rental 50ʙ per day. Motorbike rental 400ʙ per day. Banana boats and kayaks 100-200ʙ per hr. Doubles with fan 500-900ʙ, with A/C 1200-2500ʙ.)

◖ **AO WONG DUAN.** "Half Moon Bay" is a spacious but mundane beach filled with restaurants, bars, and tour operators. Traffic and congestion make it a noisy place to stay, and the constant roaring of jet skis and ferry departures doesn't foster an atmosphere for swimming or sunbathing. The **Sea Horse Bungalows ❺** complex features amenities like motorbike rental (100ʙ per hr., 400ʙ per day), jet ski rental (1500ʙ per 30min.), boat tours, and some of the best beachside dining on the island. (☎038 653 740. High-season doubles with A/C 800-1200ʙ, low-season 700-900ʙ; extra person 250ʙ.) The **restaurant ❷** serves an impressive range of food. (Dishes 40-100ʙ. Grilled seafood 200-300ʙ or market price. Open daily 8am-1am.) At the far northern end of the beach is the delightful **Blue Sky Restaurant ❹,** perched on the rocks overlooking the entire beach. Although the bill will be higher than at other restaurants right on the beach, the view is worth a meal here. (Thai food 60-300ʙ.) **Internet** access is available in **JR Restaurant,** at the middle of the beach. (2ʙ per min.)

◖ **AO THIAN (CANDLELIGHT BEACH) AND HAT LUNG DUM.** Though these beaches have shorter stretches of sand broken up by longer intervals of rocks, they manage to strike a good balance between seclusion and accessibility, which makes them ideal for those seeking the peace and privacy of their own little cove. To the north, **Ao Thian (Candlelight Beach)** is a lovely area dotted with a few guesthouses and artsy restaurants that look out over the beach. Stretching out across both Ao Thian and Hat Lung Dum, **Lung Dum Bungalow ❹** is both remote and mellow, though still popular. The well-priced but plain bungalows have private baths and ocean-facing patios. (☎016 528 056. M-F doubles with fan 600ʙ, with A/C 1000ʙ; Sa-Su 800/1000ʙ.) Lung Dum's **restaurant ❸** offers inexpensive sandwiches and Thai food. (Dishes 60-200ʙ. Open daily 7am-10pm.)

◖ **AO WAI.** Despite its lovely beach, Ao Wai's remote position on the south of the island keeps most budget travelers away from this destination. **Samet Ville Resort ❺** (☎038 651 681) targets package tourists and dominates the beach with pricey rooms. The **restaurant ❹** serves Thai dishes (40-300ʙ). Snorkeling gear rental is 100ʙ per day but only available to guests of the hotel. (Rooms with fan 1380ʙ, with A/C 1780ʙ. 100ʙ surcharge per person on long weekends. Restaurant open daily 7:30am-9pm.) The resort can arrange for a ferry ride from Ban Phe directly to Ao Wai. Get more info from Koh Kaew Resort in Ban Phe.

◖ **AO NOINA.** Although its views of the mainland are nowhere near as idyllic as those of the eastern and western beaches, Ao Nonia is secluded and beautiful in its own right. **Baan Praguykaew ❸** sits on the water a 20min. walk west of Na Dan Pier and offers the simplest accommodations on Ko Samet, catering mostly to Thai youngsters on a tight budget. (☎096 032 609. Tents in yard 200ʙ; rooms with fan 300ʙ, with A/C 700ʙ.)

👁 🎵 SIGHTS AND ENTERTAINMENT

A thirst for sightseeing can be quenched at the 14m-high **Sitting Buddha** and smaller Buddha images in the nearby temple. A gate next to the **Golden Buddha** borders the road between Na Dan Pier and Hat Sai Kaew; follow its path.

Ko Samet boasts a lively **nightlife** scene on Ao Phai and Ao Hin Khok. The **bar** at Naga Bungalows (p. 141) battles Tok's **bar** next door to attract crowds with nightly promotions. On the weekends, Naga hosts "Fight Nights," where live Thai boxing shows take place in a ring right in the bar, and afterwards "Fight You For a Bucket" lets you challenge a friend to a fight for a drink. Nearby **Silver Sands Resort** (see p. 142), at the southern end of Ao Phai, contains a beachside bar that becomes an impromptu disco when crowds are large enough. On weekends in particular the dance floor is packed with a mix of well dressed, fun-loving Thais (both mainlanders and staff from Ko Samet's restaurants and guesthouses) and a smattering of *farang* out for a night on the town (or, rather, the beach). The other beaches tend to quiet down when their restaurants close. The bars on Ao Phai are famous for serving ■**drinks by the bucket.** These usually consist of the (in)famous local rum mixed with Coke and Red Bull, promising a long night of debauchery along with a long day of aching when the sun rises.

🏄 WATER SPORTS AND RECREATION

With an abundance of coral reefs and clear water, it's no wonder that Ko Samet is popular for **snorkeling.** At Ao Phrao, Ao Kiu, and Ao Wai, reef communities are a 5min. swim from shore. Less-disturbed coral can be found in more remote reaches of the archipelago. Many establishments offer snorkeling tours of Ko Samet and the surrounding islets. There are now several **scuba diving** operations on the island, so it pays to shop around. **Ao Prao Divers,** in the lobby of the Ao Prao Resort on Ao Phrao, runs a PADI-certified **scuba diving school** year-round that makes daytrips around Ko Samet and to Ko Thalu from November to May. (☎038 644 100. Introductory course 3-4hr., 2500฿. 2 dives 2500฿. 4- to 5-day certification course 12,000฿. Specialty and more extensive dives 10,000-13,000฿. Open daily 8am-4pm.) **Ploy Scuba Diving** (☎038 644 112), on Hat Sai Kaew by Ploy Thalay, offers similar services. (½-day snorkel trips 300฿, full-day 600฿. 2 dives 2500฿. Certification course, 2-4 per day, 8000-12,000฿). Open daily high season 8am-8pm, low season 8am-5pm.)

After a few days and nights of dining on Ko Samet, work off some of that scampi at **Naga Muay Thai Boxing Academy** (☎038 644 035; www.nagamuaythai.com). Train for a single session (250฿) or try an entire week (4500฿, accommodations included) with champion instructors. Other package lengths can be arranged with the manager, Gary.

CHANTHABURI ☎039

Chanthaburi, the "City of the Moon," is famous for its gemstones, fruits, and the waterfalls of the parklands around it. Year-round, rubies and sapphires from all over the world are cut and sold right before your eyes in the city's gem district, a hub of the global gemstone market. From May to July, Chanthaburi's fruit market bulges with mouth-watering produce which is also displayed with pride each year at the annual fruit festival. These attractions, in addition to the neighboring national parks and the small-town feel of the locals' warm hospitality, make Chanthaburi a worthwhile visit.

TRANSPORTATION

The **bus station** (☎039 311 299), on Saritidet Rd., sends **buses** to: **Aranyaprathet** (3hr., every hr. 3am-1pm and 7-10pm, 95-133฿); **Bangkok** (4hr., every hr. 2am-midnight, 187฿); **Khorat** (6hr., every 2hr. 2am-10pm, 266฿); **Pattaya** and **Si Racha** (2hr.; 5, 7:30, 8:30, 10:30am, 1, 3pm; 130฿); **Rayong** (2hr., every 40min. 4:20am-7:30pm, 67฿); **Trat** (1hr., every hr. 7am-9:30pm, 57฿). **Motorcycle taxis**, usually clustered near the bus station and around the market, go anywhere in town for 30-50฿.

ORIENTATION AND PRACTICAL INFORMATION

To get downtown from the bus station, turn left onto **Saritidet** (also spelled Sarididech) **Road,** which ends at **Benchamarachuthis Road,** at the Kasemsarn Hotel, a useful landmark. The alley to the left of the hotel leads to **Sukhaphibal Road,** which runs parallel to Benchamarachuthis Rd. along the river. Heading right at the Kasemsarn Hotel leads to the commercial heart of town. **Si Rong Muan Road,** to the right of Kasemsarn, goes to the market. The gem district begins one block past Si Rong Muan Rd., on Kasemsarn, to the right down **Kwang Road** and left on **Sri Chan Road.** Services include:

Tourist Office: (☎039 350 224), in the Municipal Office, 1 block south of the bus station, on Raksakchamun Rd., across from King Taskin Park. Open daily 8am-4pm.

Currency Exchange: Krung Thai Bank (☎039 322 116), next to the post office, on Benchamarachuthis Rd., with **24hr. ATM.** Open M-F 8:30am-4:30pm. The **Bank of Ayudhya** (☎039 312 233), on Kwang Rd., across from the Chai Lee Hotel, with **ATM, currency exchange,** and Western Union services. Open M-F 8:30am-3:30pm.

Police: (☎039 311 111; 039 321 508) a few blocks behind the bus station.

Medical Services: A **clinic** (☎039 321 378), 20m to the left of the bus station, on Saritidet Rd. English spoken. Credit cards accepted.

Internet Access: Fast access on Sri Chan Rd., across from Muangchan Hotel, for 20฿ per hr. Open daily 9am-10pm.

Post Office: Main branch (☎039 311 013) inconveniently located on Thung Dondang Rd., near the Eastern Hotel in the far southeastern corner of town. Poste Restante. Open M-F 8:30am-4:30pm, Sa-Su 9am-noon. **Postal Code:** 22000. The more accessible **Chantani Post Office** (☎039 350 247) is on Benchamarachuthis Rd., across from Kasemsarn Hotel. Open M-F 8:30am-4:30pm, Sa-Su 9am-noon. **Postal Code:** 22001.

ACCOMMODATIONS

Due in large part to the thriving gem-trading market, Chanthaburi has a number of places to rest your head. To reach one budget spot, continue down the alley at the end of Saritidet Rd., on Benchamarachuthis Rd., and turn left onto Sukhaphibal Rd. On the left is the **Arun Sawat Hotel ❷,** which features colorful but basic rooms with small balconies and fan. (☎039 311 082. Doubles with bath 150-200฿.) Turn right at the Kasemsarn Hotel, and follow Benchamarachuthis Rd., which turns into Sri Chan Rd., to the **River Guest House ❷,** 3/5-8 Sri Chan Rd. (☎039 328 211). The well-kept rooms are a pretty good value, but ask for rooms away from the sometimes loud road nearby. (Internet access 30฿ per hr. Rooms with fan 250฿, with A/C 350฿.)

FOOD

Take your grumbling stomach to Chanthaburi's immense **market,** centered on the fountain one block west of Benchamarachuthis Rd., down Si Rong Muang Rd. It is famous not only for its fruit but also for its noodles and selection

CENTRAL THAILAND

of peppers. After sundown, brightly lit food vendors situated on the streets around the market dole out curries and noodle dishes. Chanthaburi's well-known noodles are called *kuay tiow sen jaan*. Ask for *kuay tiow phat pu* for a local speciality that's similar to *pad thai*, but more sweet and spice. On Si Chan Rd., a few blocks from Benchamarachuthis Rd. on the left, is a **restaurant** ❶ advertising Muslim food (no other sign) that serves amazing Indian and Middle Eastern cuisine (*biryani* 35฿; *samosas* 15฿). The riverside **restaurant** ❷ at the River Guest House, has an English menu with breakfast options and sandwiches (50-90฿; open 8am-noon). Air-conditioned and modern **Krua Tah Luang Restaurant** ❸, in the Kasemsarn Hotel, is a nice getaway from street food and street commotion. (Big bowl of muesli and fruit 80฿. Salmon and curry 180฿. Open daily 7am-10pm.) For a relaxing river-side dining experience, head to the **restaurant** ❷ across from Arun Sawat (p. 145). Look for a wooden "welcome" sign and wooden steps leading down to a raised patio. The views are almost as impressive as the extensive menu. Their English menu is a bit more limited, but if you can surmount the language barrier, the cook can whip up any simple Thai dish you want. (Dishes 60฿-80฿. Open daily 10am-midnight.)

👁 SIGHTS

Chanthaburi's more spectacular sights are outside the city limits, but a few treasures within town keep travelers entertained for a day or two. On weekends, shoppers head to **Si Chan Road,** the heart of Chanthaburi's **gem district.** Some 50-60% of the world's rubies and sapphires pass through here on their way from mines in Cambodia, Laos, Myanmar, and even Africa. Though Chanthaburi itself no longer produces as many gems as it used to, the city is still the center for cutting and buying. Tourists can see mounds of gems being inspected and bought. Buyers are sitting at tables; brokers are usually the ones standing and circulating. Those who know what they are doing can get rubies and sapphires at a significant discount, but tourists are discouraged from shopping, as they could be easily swindled into buying low-quality gems.

The impressive **Cathedral of the Immaculate Conception,** across the footbridge, near the southern end of Sukhaphibal Rd., is the largest Catholic cathedral in Thailand and serves the large population of immigrant Vietnamese Christians who fled their native country during the 19th and 20th centuries. The building, whose construction began in 1711, has seen five renovations. The last one (by the French) left it with a decidedly European feel. It has a high Gothic tower, beautiful stained-glass windows, and large statues of St. Joachim and St. Anna inside. (Mass Su 6:15, 8:30am, 7pm and M-Sa 6am, 7pm.)

🎵 NIGHTLIFE

For an unusual night on the town, head to the epicenter of Chanthaburi's nightlife scene at the enormous **Full Moon Pub,** across from the southeastern corner of Taksin Park. Live bands belt out Thai pop while a beautiful, hip young crowd looks on. It rocks all week, but is really packed Fridays and Saturdays. Get here by taxi from the city center for 30฿; taxis may be hard to find for the return journey, but it's only a 15 min. walk back to Benchamarachuthis Rd. (Soda 30฿. Singha 120฿. Open nightly 9pm-2am.) If loud Thai pop isn't your thing, go next door and be treated to loud Thai karaoke at **Delight Bar.** Locals gather in individual karaoke cubicles to battle it out for the title of best amateur singer, perhaps in hopes of one day taking the Full Moon Pub's larger and more popular stage. (Open nightly 6pm-1am.)

🔖 DAYTRIPS FROM CHANTHABURI

Chanthaburi is situated near a number of respected national parks that Thai tourists seeking fresh air flock to by the busload. To save on transportation, arrange **tour packages** with the staff at the River Guest House. A trip to both parks, the temple, Oasis Sea World, and a number of other less interesting sights along the way costs 1200฿ (includes taxi ride; site entrance fees not included). Alternatively, you can combine just Khao Kitchakut and Wat Khao Sukim, or Nam Tok Phliu and Oasis Sea World, for 600฿.

🔖KHAO KHITCHAKUT NATIONAL PARK. Thirty kilometers north of town, on Hwy. 3249 in **Khao Khitchakut National Park**, the **Chanthaburi River** churns down the 13 tiers of **Nam Tok Krathing** (Krathing Falls), the park's most popular attraction. A steep, rocky trail leads up from a Buddha at the mountain's base to tier 9; falls 10-13 are too dangerous to climb to. Falls 5-7 are great for swimming, or simply standing under the spray of the falls. Once you've bathed in cascades beneath enormous vines and golden butterflies, you'll understand why 2000 Thais flock to the falls every weekend. The climb is exhilarating but treacherous. Come prepared with a swimsuit, good shoes, and lots of drinking water.

A small **canteen ❶** stocks a few basic items and prepares simple rice dishes. (20-25฿. Open daily 6am-6pm.) Scrumptious **food stalls ❶** set up on the weekends and during holidays. The **visitors center** has helpful information in English. Bring a tent to **camp ❶** on your own (30฿) or rent one for 150฿. Lodging options here are limited to **bungalows ❹** for two (600฿), six (1800฿), or eight people (2400฿). For weekend stays, call the ranger station at least one week in advance. (*Songthaew leave from the fountain at the market in Chanthaburi for 50-100฿ but rarely go in the direction of Khao Khitchakut. If you're lucky enough to find one, you will be dropped off at the 1.5km access road marked by the number 2511 and a white fleur-de-lis on a red fence post, on the right side of the road. Tell your driver ahead of time that you are going to Khitchakut Park or Nam Tok Krathing, as the signpost is difficult to see coming up on a songthaew. More likely, visitors will have to hire a taxi (250฿, round trip 600฿), depending on the length of time spent at the park. Park headquarters ☎025 620 760, located beyond entrance booth. Open daily 6am-6pm. 200฿, 10 and under 100฿.*)

NAM TOK PHLIU NATIONAL PARK. Welcoming over 80,000 visitors per year, Nam Tok Phliu is one of Chanthaburi's best-known parks and is loved by Thai tourists for its swimmable natural pools filled with carp fish, *pla pluang*, hoping to be fed. To

LOCAL LEGEND

MONASTIC MAVERICK

Travelers making regular visits to wats, especially in southern Thailand, will notice the many framed photographs of the round bespectacled face of Ajahn Buddhadasa Bikkhu, the founder of Wat Suan Mokkha Phalaram. A revered Buddhist monk, Buddhadasa was also a well-known social activist.

After entering the monkhood in 1926, Buddhadasa went to Bangkok to study Buddhism, but was distracted by the corruption there. In 1932 Buddhadasa returned to his home province of Chaiya and founded Wat Suan Mok, an enormous forest wat with meditation spots at every corner.

His belief in one religion—that all religions are part of one dharma—garnered him many supporters. But his critiques on capitalism and materialism, and his association with such figures as Pridi Phanomyong, the left-leaning leader of the People's Party, made him more than just a reformer of Buddhism in the eyes of the government. In the 1970s, Buddhadasa was branded a communist and was nearly forced to leave the brotherhood.

Buddhadasa passed away in 1993, and his ashes were buried at Wat Suan Mok. For greater insight into his teachings, join a 10-day meditation retreat at Wat Suan Mok, north of Surat Thani in Chaiya Province.

experience the fish-feeding frenzy first-hand, purchase a 10฿ bundle of leafy fish food from the stalls outside the park. The most popular falls to visit, **Phliu Falls**, provides tourists with a spectacular waterfall, pools for swimming, and a scenic 1km nature trail circling it. A *stupa* containing the remains of Queen Sunatha, the wife of King Rama V, sits at the bottom of the falls as a memorial for the King's immortal love. Nam Tok Phliu's other falls, **Nam Tok Makok, Nam Tok Klong Nalai,** and **Nam Tok Nong,** offer more seclusion, but are in various parts of the park, each of which must be driven to by car or by taxi. The rest of the park's 135 sq. km of rainforest are bereft of trails. The **Park Headquarters** and **visitors center** (☎039 434 528), on the road leading to the Phliu Falls, have maps with directions to the falls as well as information on camping with your own tent (30฿) or renting a **tent ❷** for two people (270฿) or a **bungalow ❺** for six people (1800฿). Bring a bathing suit and hiking gear if you plan to hike the 1hr. nature trail. *(From Chanthaburi, songthaew (30min., 100฿) leave from the north side of the market's roundabout and stop at the park gate. It may take a lot of luck—or persistence—to find a songthaew containing other people. Alternatively, hire a taxi for 150฿ from the market and negotiate a return fee. Walk the 2.5km to the highway, and catch a passing songthaew from there to save taxi fare, 20฿. Open daily 6am-6pm. 200฿, children 10 and under 100฿.)*

WAT KHAO SUKIM. Perched on a mountainside 20km outside Chanthaburi, Wat Khao Sukim is the pride of local Buddhists. Built as a meditation center, the temple has drawn much attention due to several resident celebrity monks. As a result, it has received impressive donations of Buddhist statues and artwork. Though the temple itself is not spectacular, the display halls, crammed with everything from trees made of colored glass to furniture inlaid with mother-of-pearl, are overwhelming. Amid all these riches, life-like wax replicas of monks sit in meditation. The view from the roof offers panoramas of mountains, a waterfall, and fruit groves, and gives a glimpse of Chanthaburi's natural beauty for those who don't have time for its parks. An enclosure with a number of peacocks, and a lake with tons of sea turtles of varying size, allow visitors to enjoy some fauna amidst all the flora. *(Take a taxi round trip for 400฿, or catch a songthaew for Na Ya-am at Chanthaburi's market, get off at Sathorn, and try get a songthaew to the temple. However, songthaew rarely go there, so a taxi may be your only hope. Open daily 6:30am-5pm.)*

TRAT ☎039

Although Trat is not traditionally a hotspot for tourists, is a surprisingly enjoyable stopover for those bound for Ko Chang or Cambodia. The oldest and quaintest section of town conceals a fantastic array of shockingly low-priced guesthouses geared towards adventurous Western backpackers. Aside from these bargains, there are also opportunities to get laundry cleaned, break for a massage, and sample the delicious local cuisine at the buzzing night market. Trat is also home to Thailand's famous yellow oil ointment *Somthawin,* a cure-all for everything from sore throat to indigestion to bug bites—no visitor's first-aid kit is complete without some.

◧ TRANSPORTATION

Trat's new **bus station** (☎039 534 014) is 2km from the center of town. **Songthaew** (15฿ per person; 50฿ per vehicle) run there from Sukhumvit Rd., next to the market. Four companies operate buses to **Bangkok's Ekamai Station** (5hr., every hr. 8:30am-11pm; second class 207฿, first class 260฿). Buses to Bangkok's **Morchit Station,** near the airport, run less frequently (6hr., 267฿). There are also buses (5, 9:30am, noon, 3pm) to **Pattaya** (4hr., 173฿) and **Rayong** (3hr., 124฿). A slew of **minibuses** departs for various other locations from behind the station;

they leave when full (**Leam Ngop,** 50ʙ; **Khlong Yai,** 60ʙ; **Ban Hat Lek,** 120ʙ). For other destinations, take a minibus to **Chanthaburi** (1hr.; every hr. 8:30am-7pm; 80ʙ from just south of the market, or 70ʙ from old bus station) and change from there.

Two companies operate out of the old bus stops located on opposite sides of Sukhumvit Rd., close to the market and KFC. They will occasionally provide free transportation to the bus station and can book tickets to **Bangkok.**

Some other transportation departs from downtown Trat. **Minibuses** to **Ban Hat Lek** (1hr., every hr. 6am-6pm, 120ʙ), the recommended way to cross the border is to wait on Sukhumvit Rd., two blocks north of the market. Blue **songthaew** going to **Laem Ngop** (7am-8pm, 50ʙ) wait one block south of the market, next to the pharmacy on Sukhumvit Rd., and leave when full. To get around town, rent **bikes** (60ʙ per day) from Friendly Guest House on Lhak Muang Rd.

🔲 🔟 ORIENTATION AND PRACTICAL INFORMATION

The main road in Trat is Sukhumvit Road, which runs north toward Bangkok and south toward Laem Ngop. It has two traffic signals, at its northern and southern ends. Most services lie between or near them. At the northern traffic light, Sukhumvit intersects Wiwattana Road, where the post office, telecommunications office, and police station are all clustered together. The southern light is at the intersection with Lhak Muang Road, the heart of the old town where tourists congregate.

Currency Exchange: Krung Thai Bank, 59 Sukhumvit Rd. (☎039 520 542), opposite the pharmacy and next to the Trat Department Store. Cashes traveler's checks (33ʙ per check). Cirrus/MC/V **24hr. ATM.** Open M-F 8:30am-4:30pm, Sa-Su 9am-3pm.

Bookstore: Tratosphere Bookshop (☎039 523 200), near Ban JaeDee Guest House. French expat and owner Serge knows his stuff—ask him for advice on crossing the border into Cambodia, or for accommodation suggestions. Books in a variety of languages (100ʙ, or bring one to trade).

Police: 13 Samtersook Rd. (☎039 511 239). From Sukhumvit's northern traffic light, walk 3 blocks east on Wiwattana Rd. Open 24hr. Little English spoken.

Immigration Office: The nearest immigration office (☎039 597 261) is in Laem Ngop (p. 151) and grants visa extensions (10-30 days, 1900ʙ). Open M-F 8:30am-4:30pm.

Pharmacy: (☎039 511 356). South of the market opposite the Trat Department Store. Open daily 8am-8pm.

Hospital: Trat Hospital (☎039 511 041) on Sukhumvit Rd., just past the northern traffic light.

Telephones: Telecommunications Office, 315 Chaimongkol Rd. (☎/fax 039 512 599), marked by its radio tower. International phones and fax. Open M-F 8:30am-4:30pm.

Internet Access: Sawadee Guest House on Lhak Muang Rd. (below) has computers with ADSL access on the first floor. 1ʙ per min., 50ʙ per hr. Printing available.

Post Office: (☎039 511 175). Go 3 blocks east on Wiwattana Rd. and turn left on Chaimongkol Rd. just before telecommunications office. Poste Restante. Open M-F 8:30am-4:30pm, Sa-Su 9am-noon. **Postal Code:** 23000.

🮰 ACCOMMODATIONS

There are plenty of excellent guesthouses in Trat, and almost all of these accommodations are in or around the old part of town on Thana Chareun Rd. and Lhak Muang Rd. To get there from the bus and *songthaew* stops, walk south on Sukhumvit Rd. and take a left at the traffic light on Lakmuang Rd.; Thanachareun Rd. is the next left.

Sawadee Guest House, 90 Lhak Muang Rd. (☎039 530 663). Conveniently located close to the market and run by a young family eager to please guests. 5 small but immaculately kept rooms are lovingly decorated. Shared clean bathrooms with hot, pristine showers. Bamboo walls are very thin—snorers and lovers beware. All rooms with fan. Singles 100฿, doubles 200฿, triples 300฿. Computers with Internet (1฿ per min.) and printer on the first floor. ❶

Ban Jaidee Guest House, 69 Chaimongkol Rd. (☎039 520 678). Turn left on Chai Mongkol Rd. from Thana Chareun Rd. and follow the signs. Relaxing common areas filled with friendly cats. The owner's interesting teak wood crafts and warm staff make this beautiful guesthouse feel like a good friend's home. Mattresses on the floor in airy, minimalist rooms. All rooms with fans and double beds. Singles 150฿, doubles 200฿. Luggage storage 10฿ per day. ❷

Residang Guest House, 87/1 Thana Chareun Rd. (☎039 530 103; www.trat-guest-house.com), near the end of the road. Features enormous rooms with large windows. Some rooms with balconies. Strictly enforced lockout: 11pm during the high season, 9pm during the low season. Internet 40฿ per hr. Singles with shared bathroom and cold showers 120฿; doubles with private bathroom, hot showers, and TV 260฿. ❷

🍴 FOOD

There's no excuse for not eating in Trat's markets. During the day, **food stalls** set up on the first floor of the **municipal market building** (soup with meat or fish 20-40฿). At night, the market moves to **the square,** two blocks north, and is packed with rows of vendors, some of which have English menus. With a banner proudly declaring 'Food Safety Street', the night market opens each evening at 6pm and closes down at 10:30pm. Treat yourself to a banana crepe (40฿) from any of the stalls at the market's entrance. If, for some reason, the markets are not your scene, try one of the restaurants below.

Krua Rim Krong (☎039 524 919), off Thana Charuen Rd., before Residang Guest House (above). This tasty Thai restaurant with enclosed garden and refreshing A/C is frequented by young Thai couples on dates and the occasional *farang*. Almost too trendy for its surroundings, boasting flavorful Thai dishes made with the freshest seafood (80-100฿). Delicious mixed drinks 80-100฿. Open daily 11am-10pm. ❸

Orchid Restaurant, 92 Lakmuang Rd. (☎039 530 474), next to Sawadee Guest House. Hang out and chat with Trat's expats. Great place to congregate in the evening for a drink (50-100฿). Breakfast (100-140฿), Thai and Western meals (70-120฿). ❷

Sea House Cafe (☎039 525 577), conveniently positioned on the corner of Lhak Muang Rd. and Sukhumvit Rd., at the southern traffic light. Beachy feel. Tourist information desk and Internet access. Internet 1฿ per min., minimum 15min. Sea House offers good Western meals and tasty fruit smoothies (35฿). Open daily 8am-11pm. ❷

👁️ 🎵 SIGHTS AND ENTERTAINMENT

Although Trat is usually just a stop-over on the itinerary, it provides some great options for the travel-weary. A small parlor near the Chinese temples, just down from Ban JaeDee Guest House (above), has a staff of blind masseuses who give fantastic traditional **Thai massages.** (Full-body, 250฿ per hr.) Closes at 6pm.

Trat also has several language schools, which are often looking for teachers with a variety of language skills. If the charm of this small town takes hold, inquire about teaching English or another language at **TAYF Center,** just beyond the southern traffic light on Sukhumvit Rd. (☎039 531 413).

Though quiet, Trat has a few venues for fun after the sun goes down:

Samkanay Pub, 2 blocks east of the northern set of traffic lights on Sukhumvit Rd., turn left into Sri Suwanpis, Soi 1. Samkay is in the parking lot at the end of the lane; no English sign. This local spot is difficult to find, but worth it if you're looking for a night out on the town with some Trat natives and Thai pop music. Samkanay Bucket mixed drinks 300-500฿, Singha 100฿; no cover. Open nightly 8pm-1am, live music Sa-Su.

Cozy Corner (☎039 512 548), on Sukhumvit Rd. just past the southern traffic lights. For a few quiet beers and late night conversation with other backpackers, head to this mellow bar. Beers 45-75฿. Open 5pm-midnight.

▐◪ DAYTRIP FROM TRAT: LAEM NGOP

Blue songthaew leave from south of the market in Trat (30min.; 50฿ per person, leave when full). Songthaew back to Trat wait at the pier for incoming ferries to arrive.

A quiet village with a chaotic pier, Laem Ngop is the spot to board ferries to Ko Chang. With Trat only a short songthaew ride away, there is no reason to dawdle here and certainly no reason to stay the night.

For **visa extensions** (10-30 days, 1900฿; bring 2 photos and a copy of passport) and official information on visiting **Cambodia,** head for the immigration office on the ground floor of a white building just down the road that leads to the pier. (☎039 597 261. Open M-F 8:30am-4:30pm.) The **TAT** Tourist Information Office, across from the intersection of the main road and the road to the piers, has a friendly and knowledgeable staff. (☎039 597 259. Open daily 8:30am-4:30pm.) Extensive information on and maps of Ko Chang. The **Thai Farmers Bank,** 500m from TAT, on the road to the piers, exchanges traveler's checks. (☎039 597 046. 33฿ per check. Open M-F 8:30am-3:30pm. **24hr ATM)** Laem Ngop's **hospital** (☎039 597 040), on Trat-Laem Ngop Rd., 2km toward Trat, has **malaria medication,** recommended for travelers en route to Cambodia. There's also a **malaria clinic** in Laem Ngop, 800m from the TAT. (Open M-F 8:30am-noon and 1-4:30pm.)

BAN HAT LEK/SIHANOUKVILLE. To enter Cambodia, you must have a Cambodian visa, available at the border at **Hat Lek** for 1200฿, and 1 photo (300฿ extra to return the same day). Shifty border patrol is rumored to change the price at will, so it is best to obtain your visa at the Cambodian embassy in **Bangkok** (p. 98) and pay the more stable US$20. To get from Trat to **Ban Hat Lek,** take a blue *songthaew* from behind the market (1hr., every hr. or when full 6am-6pm) or a minivan from 2 blocks north of the market (1hr., every hr. 6am-6pm). When you exit Thailand at the border, remember to obtain an exit stamp. After crossing the border, you can hire a taxi to cross the newly finished bridge to **Ko Kong.** Most travelers try to avoid spending a night in Ko Kong by getting to the border when it opens at 7am. This way, they can catch the boat to **Sihanoukville** (3-4hr., daily 8am). Stay the night in Sihanoukville or catch a bus to **Phnom Penh** (3hr.). Road travel is also possible, although bumpy and less scenic. Minibuses leave from outside the Cambodian immigration office daily at 9am for Phnom Penh or Sihanoukville—leave Trat by minibus by 7am to catch them.

KO CHANG ☎039

Only 30 years ago, this island paradise, nicknamed "Elephant Island" for the way its high, dark mountains rise from the waters in the shape of an imposing elephant, was primarily a temporary refuge for fishing boats caught in monsoons. In the 70s, a few tourists began staying in simple A-frame homes on Hat Khlong Phrao; ever since, visitors have been pouring in. But the boom came with a downside: inflated prices, piles of garbage, and commercialized resorts. The main road encircling the island is inundated with construction vehicles and noisy motorcycles, making serenity difficult to come by. But pockets of purity remain. The interior of the island bursts with leafy rainforests, towering waterfalls, and abundant natural wildlife; a few isolated beaches and areas of unexplored territory remain on its eastern coast; and the less exploited beaches on the western coast give off relaxing vibes.

TRANSPORTATION

To reach Ko Chang, take a bus to Trat, then a *songthaew* (every 30min. or when full 6am-6pm, 50฿) from infront of the municipal market on Sukhumvit Rd. to a pier with a departing ferry. There are three piers that run ferries to Ko Chang: **Center Point Pier, Ao Thamma Chard Pier,** and **Naval Battle Monumnet Pier** at Leam Ngop. The ferries (30-50min.; 1-way 80-100฿, round-trip 120-160฿) arrive at one of the piers on Ko Chang's northern end. From there, shared **taxis** run frequently down to the west coast beaches (**Hat Sai Khao**, 15min., 50฿; **Hat Khlong Phrao**, 30min., 60฿; **Hat Kai Bae**, 45min., 70฿; and **Lonely Beach**, 1hr., 100฿). Few taxis travel to **Bang Bao**, so take one to **Lonely Beach** and hire a private taxi from there. A new bus service from Trat to eastern Ko Chang leaves from behind Trat Department Store (daily 10am, noon, 3pm; 110฿ includes ferry fare), and goes all the way to **Salak Phet** on the eastern side of Ko Chang. But make sure you actually want to be there—it's a long way from most tourist amenities.

> **Ferries:** Most *songthaew* from Trat (50฿) **will only go to the pier from which the next ferry will depart.** Ferries run from **Naval Battle Monument Pier** at Leam Ngop (1hr.; every 2hr., 6am-5pm; 1-way 80฿), **Center Point Pier** (1hr.; every hr. 7am-7pm; 1-way 100฿, round-trip 160฿), and **Ao Thamma Chard Pier** (35min.; every 45min. 6:30am-7pm; 1-way 100฿, with car 200฿, round-trip 120฿).

> **TIP ROUND-TRIP FERRY TICKETS.** While round-trip ferry tickets to Ko Chang are cheaper than buying two one-way tickets, know that songthaew or taxis will only bring you to a pier where there is a departing ferry. Since tickets purchased at one pier cannot be used at another pier, buying a round-trip ticket could result in you buying two tickets for the same journey.

> **Local Transportation: Songthaew** leave from Lonely Beach on the hour, starting at 8am and running until the last ferry with stops at Hat Khlong Phrao and Hat Sai Khao. *Songthaew* also run between beaches (30-80฿).

> **Rentals: Motorbike** rentals (automatic 150-250฿ per day, manual slightly less; day rental usually requires you to leave your passport or license as a deposit) are available on any of the island's 4 beaches. It is considerably cheaper to rent from the places on the main routes rather than resorts or guest houses. Note that the roads between Hat Sai Khao and the pier and Kai Bae and Lonely Beach are extremely steep and curvy, and very dangerous to ride on—**every year tourists die on the road.** Be sure your bike is in good condition and ask for a helmet (free) when you rent; pull over if it starts to rain, and wear closed-toe shoes with solid soles for extra stabliity. A better option is to ride the local trucks or hire a car. **Don't underestimate the dangers of the roads.**

ORIENTATION

Ko Chang's interior is mostly a trackless rainforest, except for animal paths and national park trails. A well-paved road circles the perimeter of the island, save for the southern part, where a road linking the island's two sides is under construction. From the pier area at the island's northeast end, the road travels south along the east coast, passes waterfall trails, and branches into two

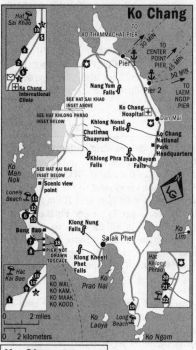

Ko Chang
see map above

♠ ACCOMMODATIONS
Alina Resort, **4**
Boo Guest House, **8**
Cookie Hotel & Restaurant, **10**
K.P. Huts, **20**
Kai Bae Hut, **9**
Magic Resort, **22**
Mam Kaibae Beach Resort, **1**
Nature Beach Resort, **11**
Orchid Resort, **13**
Paloma Cliff Resort, **2**
Paradise Bang Bao Bungalows, **18**
Treehouse Bungalow, **12**
Treehouse Long Beach, **19**

🍴 FOOD
Invito, **5**
Magic Garden Restaurant, **6**
Morgan Restaurant, **14**
O₂ Bar, **16**
Seabird Restaurant, **7**
Tropicana Restaurant, **21**

⭐ NIGHTLIFE
Oodie's, **17**
Paddy's Palms Irish Pub, **3**
Rock Sugar, **15**

roads: a western one ends in the fishing village of **Sa Lak Phet,** and an eastern one ends at sparsely populated **Hat Sai Yao (Long Beach).** Alternatively, a right turn at the pier passes the west coast's four beaches: **Hat Sai Khao (White Sand Beach), Hat Khlong Phrao, Hat Kai Bae,** and **Hat Tha Nam (Lonely Beach).** The road ends in the picturesque fishing village of **Bang Bao.**

🛈 PRACTICAL INFORMATION

Tourist Office: Ko Chang National Park Headquarters (☎039 555 080), in Than Mayom, halfway down the east coast, 20km from Hat Sai Khao. May be helpful for info on Ko Chang wildlife or development. Open daily 8:30am-4:30pm.

Currency Exchange: ATMs (Cirrus/MC/V, some with AmEx) are everywhere—even on the pier far to the south in Bang Bao. Banks offering exchange populate the western beaches. **Ayodya Bank** (☎039 551 431), across from Mac Resort on Hat Sai Khao, has extended banking hours. Open M-F 8:30am-8pm, Sa-Su 10am-8pm.

Books: A number of hotels have small secondhand book selections. Try Ban Pu Resort on Hat Sai Khao and Nature Beach Resort (p. 155) on Lonely Beach.

Laundromat: Laundromats can be found along the main roads at most beaches on the island's west coast. Usually 30฿ per kg.

Police: On the eastern side of the island, just before Dan Mai (☎039 521 657). Irregularly-staffed tourist **police boxes** on Hat Sai Khao, Hat Kai Bae, and Bang Bao (☎039 651 351, in low season ☎081 1522 183).

Hospital: Ko Chang Hospital (☎039 586 131), on the eastern side of the island by Dan Mai Pier. Outpatient 8:30am-noon and 1:30-4:30pm; 24hr. emergency. The more convenient **Ko Chang International Clinic** (☎039 551 151) provides high standards of health care at equally high prices. Open 24hr. Due to the high number of injuries on the roadways, a number of "international clinics" have popped up in imitation of this acclaimed clinic—don't fall for imitators, especially if a health problem is dire.

Telephones: Calls can be made at most bungalows and Internet cafes. A good rate is 40฿ per min. for calls to Australia,

Canada, Europe, New Zealand, and the US. Service fees for collect calls are 10ʙ per min. with a 15min. time limit.

Internet Access: Available throughout the western beaches, even at Lonely Beach; dial-up at **Nature Beach Resort** (first 5min. 2ʙ per min., subsequently 1ʙ per min).

Post Offices: (☎039 551 240), on the main road at Laem Chai Chet just south of Hat Sai Khao. Address Poste Restante to: Post Office, Ko Chang Island, Thailand 23170, Western Union. Also sells international phone cards. Open M-F 8:30am-4:30pm, Sa-Su 9am-noon. **Postal Code:** 23170.

ACCOMMODATIONS

The northern end of the west coast is spiked with soaring cliffs that level off towards Ko Chang's beaches. Upscale development has been squeezing budget travelers farther south and along the east coast of the island. Of the coast's four main beaches, Hat Sai Khao (White Sand Beach) is closest to the pier and the most developed. Hat Khlong Phrao and Hat Kai Bae, 6km and 10km from Hat Sai Khao, respectively, offer more privacy for a pretty penny. Farther south, laid-back Lonely Beach, of Full-Moon Party fame, is still the obvious choice for budget backpackers. Beyond Lonely Beach is the village of Bang Bao, which is seeing substantial development. For less concrete, check out the nearby fishing village of Sa Lek Phet or one of the islands south of Ko Chang (see below).

HAT SAI KHAO

Prices have skyrocketed in recent years at Hat Sai Khao. Oceanside huts are now luxury bungalows, and large hotels increasingly flank the main road. Yet while budget accommodations are virtually nonexistent and the beach is now heavily touristed, Hat Sai Khao does offer the most services on the island. Dive shops, motorbike rentals, bars, restaurants, and Internet cafes are plentiful, though quiet seclusion is rare.

Cookie's Hotel & Restaurant (☎039 551 107), 300m south of Koh Chang Lagoon Resort. Provides renovated rooms with continually rising prices. Their cheapest rooms are on the side of the road far from the beach. All rooms have private bathrooms and A/C. A dip in the luxurious pool comes with an incredible view of the beach. High-season singles 2000-2500ʙ, low season 1300-1800ʙ. ❺

Alina Resort, 9/10 Moo 4 (☎039 551 135; www.alinaresort.com), in the middle of the beach. A mid-range resort trying to appeal to an upscale crowd. 5 bungalows on the beach with private bathrooms and hot water. High-season budget rooms with fan 800ʙ, with A/C 1000ʙ; low-season with fan 600ʙ, with A/C 800ʙ. Other rooms 800-1200ʙ. ❹

Paloma Cliff Resort (☎039 551 119), at the beach's southernmost point, has a pool and bamboo huts overlooking a rocky point. The cheapest 'Cliff Wing' rooms with fan are quirky, but removed from the beach and pool. Huts with fan high-season 1700ʙ, low season 1200ʙ. Other rooms with A/C 2000-2500/1500-2800ʙ.

HAT KHLONG PHRAO

Although not the most remote of Ko Chang's three main beaches, Hat Khlong Phrao is the most serene. Bungalows are widely spaced on broad expanses of sand punctuated by rock outcroppings and creeks trickling from the interior.

K.P. Huts (☎084 133 5995), in central Hat Khlong Phrao. Has cute, rustic, raised bamboo huts which look straight out onto a relatively isolated stretch of beach. Fantastic shared bath with hot water and flushing toilets. High-season doubles with fan 800ʙ, with private bath 1000ʙ; low-season 500/800ʙ. ❷

Magic Resort (☎039 557 075). Sits on a truly stunning stretch of beach and offers clean rooms and amazing snorkeling trips to Ko Yauk. 3hr. snorkeling trips 350ʙ per person. Motorbike rental 250ʙ per day. High-season doubles with private bath and A/C 1300ʙ, low-season 800ʙ. ❹

HAT KAI BAE

Hat Kai Bae has a good selection of restaurants, bars, Internet cafes, and bungalows without the overcrowding and conspicuous consumption found on Hat Sai Khao. The beach, though occasionally covered with dead coral and rocks, also is a good jumping-off point for exploring the island's south side.

Kai Bae Hut (☎01 862 8426). Conveniently located next to the *songthaew* stop. Has clean huts at reasonable prices. High-season doubles with fan 900ʙ, beachside, 4-person bungalows 2500ʙ; low-season 700/2000ʙ. ❹

Mam Kaibae Beach Resort (☎039 557 060), in the center of the beach. This Resort has stunning views and much needed mosquito nets. High-season doubles with fan 900ʙ, with A/C 1500ʙ; low-season 500/800ʙ. ❹

LONELY BEACH

Although this once-secluded beach is now connected to the rest of the world, it is one of the most chilled-out, tailor-made backpacker hideouts in Thailand.

▨ **Treehouse Bungalow** (☎081 847 8215), at the far southern end of the beach, is the place that started it all. Bamboo huts with mattresses on the floor look out onto the water. Treehouse gives off a bohemian vibe that exemplifies the Southeast Asian backpacker experience. Huts with shared bath and bucket showers. High-season singles 120ʙ, doubles 280-300ʙ; low-season 80/150-200ʙ. A second Treehouse for hard-core solitude seekers and lovers of rustic simplicity has been built on isolated Long Beach on the eastern coast (see p. 158). ❶

Nature Beach Resort (☎039 558 027). Boasts beachside bungalows of the well-kept bamboo variety with private bath. Travelers won't be bored here with bicycles (250ʙ per day) and kayaks (80ʙ per hr.) for rent. Nature Beach also has a library filled with books for borrowing. High-season double huts with fan 400-800ʙ, bigger rooms with A/C 1300ʙ; low-season 200-500/900ʙ. ❷

Orchid Resort (☎039 558 139; www.websoldat.at/orchid), in the small community of Bailan located between Lonely Beach and Bang Bao. Orchid is a great place to find solitude and still stay close to the amenities and hippie flavor of Lonely Beach. Bungalows are connected by lovely garden paths leading to the cliffs. Bungalows 250-600ʙ. ❸

BANG BAO

This fishing village turned tourist destination is centered around the main pier, a virtual mini-city with guesthouses, restaurants, dive shacks, and souvenir shops hanging onto its edges.

Paradise Bang Bao Bungalows. (☎089 934 8044). The cheapest place to stay on the pier. A host of tiny rooms hoisted right over the water. Provides comforting mosquito nets to hang over your bed. Rooms 250ʙ. ❷

Boo Guest House (☎09 831 1874), further down on the pier from Paradise Bang Bo, has simple rooms with private bathrooms. Here, too, rooms hang out over the water and are surrounded by colorful fishing vessels moored in the harbor. High-season rooms 500ʙ, low season 300ʙ. ❸

TIP **WALK IT OFF.** If you want to escape the crowds but can't afford the boat transportation to Ko Chang's outlying islands, try walking. Off the southern part of Kai Bae lies a small island where, at low tide, the waters recede, making it possible for you to spend a few hours on your own private island paradise. Mind the rising waters, though!

FOOD

HAT SAI KHAO

Invito, (☎039 551 326), 300m south of Paloma Cliff Resort. Serves delicious oven-baked pizza and pasta in a romantic, intimate setting. Pizza 250-360฿, pasta 390-420฿. Open daily noon-11pm. ❺

Oodie's, right up the road from Cookie Bungalow. If you're looking for live music, Oddie's has it nightly. Mixed drinks 70-190฿. Small beer 60-80฿. Live, rock & roll, blues, and oldies nightly 10pm. Open nightly 4pm-1am. ❷

Paddy's Palms Irish Pub (☎083 851 1174), south of the beach and Invito restaurant. From one island to another, the Irish have made it to Ko Chang. Guinness on tap (200฿ per pint). Happy hour 4-7pm (90฿ pints of Singha; 100฿ pints of Heineken).

HAT KLONG PHRAO

Tropicana's Sea Breeze Seafood Restraunt (☎039 557 122). Eat well before heading home to your bungalow at this resort's yummy beachside restaurant. Thai food 70-125฿. Other dishes 125-315฿. Open daily 6:30am-11pm. ❷

HAT KAI BAE

O2 Bar. With outdoor seating, O2 is a popular place to enjoy delicious and inexpensive Thai food. Serves yummy breakfast. Dishes 40-70฿. Beer 45฿. Mixed drinks 90-140฿. Open daily 8am-midnight. ❷

Morgan Restaurant (☎086 948 9810). Has a varied menu of reasonably priced food and is especially popular for breakfast. Vegetarian options available. Breakfast 35-80฿. Open daily 7:30am-11pm. ❷

Rock Sugar (☎039 557 264). An Italian restaurant with a bumping bar and live music nightly during the high season. Pizza 200-250฿, mixed drinks 90-140฿. ❹

LONELY BEACH

Magic Garden Restaurant (☎662 083 756). A self-proclaimed "psychedelic chill space" where "chillaxing" is required of all customers. Although the neon, furry, chill-out rugs combined with acid jazz music will not be to everyone's tastes, the food likely will. Veggie Reuben 100฿. Nachos 90฿. Open T-Su 10am-10pm. ❸

Nature Rocks, Nature Beach Resort's restaurant, has a breathtaking view of the sunset and an incredible BBQ featuring fresh seafood nightly. Dishes 150-250฿. ❸

BANG BAO

Seabird Restaurant (☎039 558 093), along the pier. With an eccentric expat owner named Jacqui and incredible views to write home about, this restaurant serves up a standard Thai menu. Dishes 50-250฿. Open daily 8am-midnight. ❷

🎣 👁 ACTIVITIES AND SIGHTS

All of the beaches are perfect for relaxation and, of course, swimming. During the rainy season, however, dangerous **riptides** can develop; swimmers should learn current conditions before dipping in. Also, both Ko Chang's east- and west-coast islands have more adventurous activities and attractions.

THE WEST COAST

Diving and **snorkeling** trips are popular and a multitude of tour operators offer everything from day trips to longer excursions to diving certification courses. October through April brings the best visibility for underwater exploration, but check current conditions once you arrive.

There are two wreck sites in the area: a Thai warship sunk by the French Navy in 1941 and the Pak One oil tanker, which sank in 1996 and was dragged to the waters between Ko Chang and Ko Samet.

Most tour operators pick up guests from their hotels and offer similar prices. (Half-day snorkeling from 300฿, scuba-review "fun" dive starting at 500฿, open-water PADI certification starting at 12,500฿.) **The Dive Adventure** (☎017 626 482; www.thedivekochang.com) at Bang Bao and **Ploy Scuba Diving** (014 511 387; www.ployscuba.com), with offices on every beach, are reputable. Most guesthouses can also arrange snorkeling tours to the outlying islands. **Ko Rang** and **Ko Wai** have some of the best coral to explore.

Speedboats, canoes, and **kayaks** are available for rent on all beaches, and as is an islandhopper in the high season (☎08 1865 0610; see **The Outer Islands,** p. 158) takes passengers from Bang Bao to the islands south of Ko Chang. Fishermen take groups fishing or touring for a negotiated rate (about 500฿).

The west coast of Ko Chang also provides some opportunities to see the island's interior. **Khlong Phra Falls** are massively popular and easily accessible. The 150m cascade has pools that are great for swimming. There is a 1km driveway leading up to the falls; the turn-off is on the main road behind Khlung Prao Beach. The falls are just 500m from the national park entrance. (Open daily 8am-4:30pm. 200฿, students with ID 100฿.) **Ban Chang Thai** is another tour operator that conducts tours with adopted elephants who were mistreated by their former owners. (High season 1hr. 500฿, 2hr. 900฿; low season 400/750฿). Real elephant lovers should try the "elephant homestay program" and spend three days and two nights learning how to care for elephants (6000฿ includes full board). Signs promoting these and other tourist activities crowd the island.

THE EAST COAST

The picturesque east coast is short on beaches but big on scenic beauty. Colonnades of rubber trees alternate with rambutan orchards. Several waterfalls are accessible by trails that begin along the road. This opportunity to catch a glimpse of the island's rugged interior shouldn't be missed. The tiny town of **Dan Mai** hides a path to **Khlong Nonsi Falls,** a quick 30min. walk inland. Further along the stretch of highway is the turnoff to **Than Mayom Falls.** Here, clear mountain water gushes over a 7m-high rock into a gorgeous jungle pool. (Accessible in rainy season June-Dec. daily 8am-4:30pm. 200฿, students 100฿; admission covers both waterfalls for a single day.)

Continuing straight at the fork in the road (right branch) leads to the village of **Sa Lek Phet,** a decidedly untouristed town that surrounds a picturesque bay. Two nice waterfalls, **Khlong Nung** and **Khiri Phet,** are a short walk from the road. Continuing further south on the eastern side of the bay, on the west coast of the island's southeast peninsula, leads to the secluded, beautiful, and swimmable Long Beach. This is arguably the most remote place to stay on the entire island, home only to the **Treehouse Long Beach ❶,** with no electricity and simple and clean bungalows. To get there, take a boat from Laem Ngop Pier bound for Koh Wai and get off at Tan Ta Wan Pier, or start at the original Lonely Beach Treehouse and jump on the daily transfer truck to Long Beach (10am, 100฿). Alternatively, take a taxi (100฿ per person, 1000฿ per vehicle) to Long Beach directly from the pier (see **Ferries, p. 152**).

Getting to the rest of the east coast can be tricky. There are no motorbike rentals north or east of Hat Sai Khao, which means that if you plan to take a motorbike you'll be traversing a steep and curvy stretch of road. Try to find a shared taxi from the pier (100฿) heading that way for a safer trip.

🜄 DAYTRIPS FROM KO CHANG: KO CHANG NATIONAL MARINE PARK

Forty-seven other islands in addition to Ko Chang make up the **Ko Chang National Marine Park.** Thirteen have accommodations, some of which cater only to package tourists, and camping is free and legal anywhere, although it's best to check with the locals before unpacking. In the high season, many of these islands are easy to get to and have cheap lodgings; in the low season, most close up shop. Food from island guesthouses is generally overpriced, so stock up on snacks before you leave the mainland.

THE OUTER ISLANDS

Island-hopper boats depart from Bang Bao daily at 9am and noon during the high season and sporadically throughout the rest of the year. They shuttle passengers around the archipelago (arrive in Ko Wai 10am, Ko Kam 10:45am, and Ko Maak 11am). Boats depart from Ko Maak at noon (arrive in Ko Kam 12:20pm, Ko Wai 1pm, and Bang Bao 2pm).

The islands off Ko Chang's southern coast are famous for fishing, coral, rock formations, bird nests, and bat guano. You can scuba dive at **Ko Kam,** home to an abundance of coral, fish, and toothy sharks. **Ko Wai** is surrounded by coral, and is known for its legendary fishing. Crescent-shaped, pure-white beaches make for a picture-perfect daytrip.

KO MAAK

A regular slow boat leaves Laem Ngop pier (3hr., daily 3pm, 300฿ one way) and arrives before sunset. There is also a speedboat that leaves from Laem Ngop pier (1hr.; 11am, 4pm; 450฿ one way). In the high season, boats also depart from Bang Bao (daily 8am and noon) for Ko Maak (returns noon) 350฿ each way. In the high season there's also speedboat service departing from Laem Sok pier, east of Trat (40min., daily 1pm, 400฿).

The most accessible of the outer islands, Ko Maak is quickly following the development pattern of Ko Chang. Rapidly upgraded resorts cater more to Thai package tourists than to budget travelers. The beaches, however, are still immaculate, and there are a few smaller outfits that put up backpackers. There is a **clinic** and a **police box** on the road heading into the island from the pier. Expensive bottled water, toilet paper, and other simple amenities are available at the minimart, which also rents **bikes** and **motorbikes.** There is no official taxi service, so on arrival, but hotels and guesthouses usually send one to meet boats free of charge. For the latest on accommodations on Ko Maak, inquire at **Tratosphere Books** (☎ 039 523 200; see **Practical Information,** p. 149) in Trat. Serge, the owner, is a French expat who knows his these outer islands well.

On the southern side of the island is **Au Kao Resort ❶**. (☎039 501 001. Bungalows 120฿, with fan and private bath 300฿.) The north side ends in a beach with unobtrusive bungalows and calm, coral-strewn waters, bordering a long bay. Beachfront bungalows with private baths, beach chairs, and fans go for 250฿. Up the beach, **Koh Maak Resort ❸** offers high-quality bungalows starting at 1000฿ and increasing the closer they are to the beach. (☎039 599 296.)

KO KOOD

A slow boat leaves from Daan Kaw Pier, east of Trat (☎861 267 860; 5hr.; T, W, F, Su 10am; 250฿). There is also a speedboat from Daan Kaw (1½hr., daily 8:30am, 400฿ one-way, and 9:00am, 550฿). In the high season, boats leave Bang Bao on Ko Chang (☎818 650 610; 600฿ one-way). Speedboats also leave from Laem Ngop pier (2hr.; T, F, Sa 9am; 500฿) for Nam Leuk pier on Ko Kood.

Life on Ko Kood is slow, although commercial development and tourism are surging at an alarming rate. There is currently no public transportation, but some hotels will rent out **motorbikes.** Taking a jungle tour to see **Khlong Chao Waterfall** is a good way to spend a few hours. Better yet, away from the jungle hills lie some of the most pristine beaches in Thailand. Coral reefs just beneath the surface make for world-class snorkeling and diving. The island has a small **clinic** (☎039 521 852) and **police station** on its western side. Accommodations in the low season can be difficult to find. Tratosphere Bookshop in Trat can offer up-to-date information along with photos of various spots. A good option for backpackers is **Ban Pai Ko Kut ❷**. Simple rooms with shared bath 250฿, with separate bath 450฿. Pricier options are easy to find.

BORDER CROSSING: ARANYAPRATHET/POIPET. To enter Cambodia, you must have a Cambodian visa, even if you just want to cross over to get a visa extension. Travelers can obtain visas at the Cambodian embassy in Bangkok for US$20 (p. 98) or pay 1000-1200฿ right at the border. Hotels in town will offer to get you a visa (1100฿) in only 20min., which will save about 5min. at the border but will likely cost 100฿ more. At the border, *Touts* can help you navigate the busy transit areas, but be wary of their advice about onward travel to Siem Reap—they will likely try to get you on a painfully slow bus (5-8hr. depending on road quality, US$10). Instead, find a taxi (2-5hr.; US$10 per person, US$40 per vehicle). The border is open daily 7am-8pm. Arrive early to avoid a long wait. (*Tuk-tuk* from town to the border 60-80฿, motorcycle taxi 50฿). Although a 30-day tourist visa is free for most nationalities at the nearby Thai border, the hassle of crossing to Cambodia can be eradicated by paying 1900฿ for a 30 day extension at the immigration office in Aranyaprathet (p. 159). The Cambodian consulate can be reached at ☎037 421 734 and the TAT office at ☎037 312 282.

ARANYAPRATHET ☎037

Aranyaprathet is the border town for the Cambodia-bound. There's very little to hold one's attention here, and the savvy traveler will arrive early enough to press on without staying the night. The first train from Bangkok arrives in plenty of time for those heading to Siem Reap to reach it on the same day.

▐ TRANSPORTATION

In the center of town, **Mahadthai-Suwannasorn Road** and **Chaoprayabodin Road** intersect at a small purple clock tower. The **train station** sits at the north end of

Suwannasorn Road. Trains (☎037 231 698) go to **Bangkok** (5hr.; 6:40am, 1:55pm; 48฿). The **bus station** is on the west side of town; from there, walk three blocks straight and one block right to reach the clock tower. The ticket booth for government buses (☎037 231 262) to **Bangkok** (4hr., 6:30, 10:30am, 1, 1:30, 3pm; 236฿) and **Sa Gaeo** (every hr., 6am-7pm, 49฿) is located to the left of the bus station, behind the 7-Eleven. Further down to the left of the bus station is the departure point for **Khorat** (6:30, 9am, noon, 3, 5:30pm; 206฿) and has connections for most places in the north and northeast. **Tuk-tuks** and **motorcycle taxis** (30-40฿) putter to hotels from the bus and train stations.

✷ PRACTICAL INFORMATION

Thai Farmers Bank branches are all over town. The one across from Aran Gardern II on Raduthid Rd., has a **24hr ATM** that accepts Cirrus/Maestro/MC/V. **Siam City Bank,** also has an ATM. The **pharmacy,** one block north of the Aran Garden I Hotel has no English sign. Open M-Sa 6:30am-8pm. The **hospital** (☎037 231 010), at the corner by the clock tower; a 24hr. **police station** (☎037 232 492) is one block over from the hospital. The border **market,** on Weruwan Rd, is a colossal mass of clothing, sunglasses, and other inexpensive knick-knacks. A motorcycle ride to the market costs 60฿. Open daily 6am-7pm. The **immigration office** (☎037 231 131) is next to the police office and is open M-F 8:30am-4:30pm. The **Telecommunications Office** (☎037 231 728) is near the corner of Mahadthai and Raduthid Rd., 500m south of the clock tower, has international phones, fax, and Internet. Open M-F 8:30am-4:30pm. **Internet access** is available at **I-net,** 2 Raduthid Rd., one block before Aran Garden I Hotel for 20฿ per hr. Open daily 10am-11pm. Also at **Cyber Workshop,** on Banmrungrad Rd. for 20฿ per hr. Open 8am-10pm. The **GPO,** (☎037 231 006) is next to the clock tower. Sells phone cards 300฿ and 500฿. Open M-F 8:30am-4:30pm, Sa 9am-noon. **Postal Code:** 27120.

⌂ ACCOMMODATIONS

Aranyaprathet's accommodations aren't much to write home about, but they are sufficient for the one- or two-night stay most travelers to Aranyaprathet are looking for.

Aran Garden I Hotel, 671 Raduthid Rd. (☎037 231 105). Walk 500m south from the clock tower to Raduthid Rd. and then 600m east to Chitsuwan Rd.; it's on the corner. Rooms are clean and plain with private bathrooms with Thai-style toilets and cold showers. Single-room with double bed 150฿, with two beds 250฿; with TV 200/250฿. ❷

Aran Garden II, 110 Raduthid Rd.(☎037 231 070), is a virtual clone of its namesake but charges more and and has Western-style flushing toilets. Singles with double beds 250฿, with 2 beds 300฿; two beds with A/C and hot water 370฿. ❷

Siam Guesthouse (☎037 233 126), at the end of Chitsuwan Rd., on the highway to the border, is a good mid-range option with comfortable, motel-like rooms. Siam also has a restaurant that serves Thai and Western fare in a cute open-air hut. Dishes 40-170฿. Rooms with A/C, TV, and bathroom 480฿. ❹

▐ FOOD

Aranyaprathet's small **night market** on Chitsuwan Rd. should be your first stop for a good, low-cost fill-up. The best stalls are at the front of the market. Be sure to also check out the food stalls around the border market on Weruwan Rd. (see **Practical Information,** above). Aranyaprathet also has a couple of good, inexpensive eat-in options.

Ton Khaow Restaurant. Low prices and high level of service. Sing Celine Dion late into the night alongside Aranyaprathet locals. Thai and Western dishes 30-200฿. ❷

Thip Kitchen (☎037 231 627), on Chitsuwan Rd., just down the road from Siam Guesthouse. This eatery's walls are covered with original oil paintings and an English-language menu decorated with the Garfield cartoons. Thai and Western dishes 30-80฿. Open 10am-9pm. ❷

AYUTTHAYA   ☎035

The spectacular ruins of the ancient Thai capital of Ayutthaya are only a few hours from Bangkok, in the middle of a modern town. For more than four centuries, both Thai culture and international trade flourished in this royal city, whose population reached one million by the end of the 17th century. The city raised 33 successive kings and repelled 23 Burmese invasions before the Burmese finally sacked it in 1767. They wreaked such devastation that the Thai capital moved to Bangkok, and Ayutthaya never regained its former glory. Today, this UNESCO World Heritage Site offers visitors all the ruins they could want, right in the midst of the speeding motorcycles, late-night food stalls, and 7-Elevens of a modern Thai town. The ruins are best seen in the evening, when the crowds thin, the heat relents, and floodlights illuminate the *wats*.

▐ TRANSPORTATION

Trains: Ayutthaya Train Station (☎35 241 521), on the mainland east of the island. Take the convenient and pleasant **ferry** from U Thong Rd. (3฿) and walk up the street to reach the station. Otherwise, it's a long walk across **Pridi Damrong Bridge** and up your 1st left (*tuk-tuk* 40-80฿). Trains to: **Bangkok's Hualamphong Station** (1½-2hr., about 20 per day 4:20am-10pm, 15-20฿); **Chiang Mai** via **Phitsanulok** (12-13hr., 4 per day, 161-1253฿); **Lopburi** (1hr., 8 per day, 17฿); **Saraburi** (1hr., 14 per day, 9฿); **Udon Thani** (9hr., 5 per day, 145-306฿).

Buses: Ayutthaya has 3 bus stations.

Naresuan Rd. has a small station 1 block east of Chikun Rd. Fan and A/C buses go to and from Bangkok's **Northern Bus Terminal** (1-2hr., every 20min. 5am-7:10pm, 30-47฿) and the Bangkok airport (1-2hr., 1 per hr. 5am-7pm, 40฿).

Chao Phrom Market, also on Naresuan Rd. A chaotic mess of local buses leaving from the west end of the market to **Saraburi** (#358, 2hr., every 30min. 6am-5:30pm, 40฿), connecting to destinations in the northeast, and **Suphanburi** (#703; 1hr.; every 25min. 6am-5pm; 40฿), connecting with #411 to **Kanchanaburi.**

Mainland bus terminal, 5km east of the island (*tuk-tuk* 70฿). Hub for buses to and from the north. Buses go to: **Chiang Mai** (9hr., 14 per day 6:30am-10:40pm, 283-570฿); **Phitsanulok** (5hr., 10 per day 7am-7pm, 140฿); and **Sukhothai** (6hr.; 9 per day 7am-8:30pm, 169฿; VIP 11:30am and 9pm, 256฿). Buses from this station run regularly to **Chiang Rai, Tak,** and **Nan.**

Ferries: Continuous ferries to the mainland and the train station leave from an alley off U Thong Rd., near the intersection with Horattanachai Rd. **Longtail boats** and **cruisers,** which fit up to 8 people, can be hired at Chantharkasem Palace pier (the island's northeast tip) for trips around the island (1-2hr.; 500฿, with 2 temple stops 600฿).

Local Transportation: Tuk-tuk/songthaew hybrids wheel around the island (between any two points on the island 30-100฿, 150฿ per hr., 700-900฿ per day). Drivers here are less likely to scam travelers. Most guesthouses rent **bicycles** (40-60฿ per day). Bicycle quality varies considerably, so shop around.

✈ 🛈 ORIENTATION AND PRACTICAL INFORMATION

Encircled by **U Thong Road,** the Ayutthaya city center is an island at the intersection of the **Chao Phraya, Pa Sak,** and **Lopburi Rivers.** Buses from nearby cities stop next to the **Chao Phrom Market** at the corner of **Naresuan** and U Thong Rd., near **Khlong Makham Rieng Road** on the island's northeastern corner, while buses from northern Thailand arrive east of the island, 5km beyond the **Pridi Damrong Bridge.** Although *wats* are found all over the island, most tourist attractions cluster north of the **Tourist Information Center** on **Si Sanphet Road.** Guesthouses are concentrated in the eastern part of the island on Soi Pamapro 5, north of the Chao Phrom Market.

Tourist Offices: Tourist Information Center (☎035 322 730), on Si Sanphet Rd., a 5min. walk south of Wat Phra Si Sanphet. Sponsored by **TAT.** Carries timetables and large, handy maps. The refreshingly air-conditioned **Ayutthaya Historical Exhibition Hall** on the 2nd fl. gives insight into the old capital. Another permanent exhibit displays the work of local artists. Office open daily 8:30am-4:30pm.

Tours: A store with a sign that reads "Tourist Information Services," across from Tony's Place (p. 164), right before Ayutthaya Guest House, arranges **bike tours** (80฿) and nighttime *tuk-tuk* tours (180฿ per person) of the *wats*. Open daily 8am-10pm.

Currency Exchange: Many banks along the eastern stretch of Naresuan and the northeastern curve of U Thong Rd. have **24hr. ATMs.** Close to the guesthouses is **Siam Commercial Bank,** next to the Naresuan Rd. bus station. Open M-F 8:30am-3:30pm.

Local Tourist Police: (☎035 241 446 and 035 342 446 115-5), on Si Sanphet Rd. next to the TAT office (not to be confused with the nearby Tourist Information Center). Some English spoken. Open 24hr.

Medical Services: Ayutthaya Hospital, 46 U Thong Rd. (☎035 241 888), at the intersection of Si Sanphet and U Thong Rd. English spoken. Open 24hr. Cash only.

Internet Access: Unnamed store next to the Tourist Information Services (on the main strip of guesthouses) has Internet access for 40฿ per hr. (open 9am-11pm). A few of the guesthouses and Coffee & Tea (next to Moon Cafe) have free, often slow, Internet available.

Telephones: International telephone booths at the GPO and at P.U. Inn (p. 162).

Post Offices: GPO, 123/11 U Thong Rd. (☎035 252 246), on the island's northeast corner. Poste Restante. Open M-F 8:30am-4:30pm, Sa 9am-noon. **Postal Code:** 13000.

🏠 ACCOMMODATIONS

Ayutthaya has many promising budget accommodations, most huddled on a block-long strip on Naresuan Soi 1, north of Naresuan Rd., near Chao Phrom Market bus stop. Most places have laundry and bike rental, and many provide tour services. Rates increase and lodgings become scarce from Nov.-Dec.

Baan Lotus Guesthouse, 20 Pamapro Rd. (☎35 251 988). From the backpacker strip, turn left on Pamapro Rd.; the entrance to Baan Lotus is about 1 block down, on the left. Traditional teak Thai house, with rooms opening onto shared verandas, offering an airy respite from the Ayutthaya heat. The thin wooden shutters and handful of roosters give the place a rural feel, but might make it hard for some travelers to get a good night's sleep. Gracious owner is eager to help with tours and local travel advice. Large rooms 240฿, singles with A/C and bath 500฿, doubles 600฿. ❷

U.P. Inn, 20/1 Soi Thor Korsor (☎35 251 213). From Naresuan Rd., head up the soi opposite the bus station next to the Chao Phrom Market and make a left following the signs. Large, clean rooms and hot showers. All rooms with fan have private bath, but not all have good air circulation. Motorbike rental 250฿ per day. Internet access

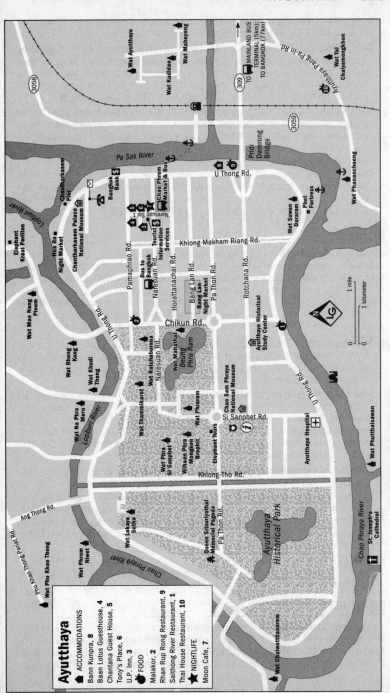

CENTRAL THAILAND

15฿ per min, 60฿ per hr. International phone. Nighttime tours of ruins. Singles and doubles 180-350฿, with A/C 550฿. ❷

Tony's Place, 12/18 Naresuan Soi 1 Rd. (☎35 252 578), across from Ayutthaya Guest House. The heart of *farang* social life, with backpacker prices to boot. Worn but clean rooms. Sprawling hang-out space includes a restaurant, bar, TV lounge, and pool table. Breakfast at 7am. Bar open until midnight. Motorbike rental 250฿ per day; reserve in advance. Dorms 80-100฿; doubles 250฿, with bath 300฿, with A/C 450฿. ❶

Bann Kunpra, 48 Moo 3 U Thong Rd. (☎35 241 978; www.bannkunpra.com), beside the river, between the ferry dock and the bridge. Sumptuously decorated with antiques and showcasing a romantic riverside restaurant—an excellent choice for a splurge. The dorm is lovely. Riverside rooms are quieter than those on the street. 4-bed dorm with shared baths 250฿; singles 300฿; doubles 400-600฿, with A/C 800฿. ❷

Chantana Guest House, 12/22 Naresuan Rd. (☎35 323 200), next to Tony's Place. Quiet, simple, and clean. All rooms have Western toilets and shower; upstairs digs have balconies and are far sunnier than downstairs ones. Reserve in advance. Singles and doubles with large bed 300฿, with A/C and hot shower 400฿. ❸

🍴 FOOD

Ayutthaya is a great town for market eating. **Food stalls** serving 20฿ chicken and rice are interspersed with tables of toys, dried fish, and fruit at **Chao Phrom Market,** one block east of the local bus stop (Open daily 7am-7pm). More stalls line U Thong Rd., particularly on the eastern side of the island, after the post office. For dinner, try the food stalls at the **night markets** such as the **Hua Ro Night Market** (open nightly 4-10pm) and the **Bang Lan Night Market** (open nightly 5-9pm). Most *farang* take many of their meals in Ayutthaya at the local guesthouses.

🥢 **Malakor,** on Chikun Rd., opposite Wat Ratchaburana. Great, cheap local food in a cool bamboo-laced porch with a view of the *wat*. Make anything on the menu vegetarian by substituting tofu for meat. The river fish spicy soup (75฿) is a piquant house specialty. Dishes 40-120฿. Open daily 10am-10pm.

Thai House Restaurant (Ruenthai Maisuay Restaurant), 8/2 Moo 3 Klongsuanplu District, down the road from Wat Yai Chai Mongkhon, around the bend, on the right. Worth the trek from town, or a good place to stop for a snack while *wat*-touring. Wooden boats are moored in mossy gardens at the entrance to this elegant teak house, where patrons enjoy such rarefied dishes such as salted eggs in fish cake (100฿). Dishes 80-250฿. Open daily 10am-10pm. ❸

Bann Kunpra's restaurant, (see Accommodations, above) offers an ambitious Thai-European fusion cuisine on a romantic riverside terrace (prawn skewers 50฿).❷

Saithong River Restaurant, 45 Moo 1 U Thong Rd. (☎35 241 449), close to the intersection of U Thong and Chikun Rd. A classy Thai crowd gathers to sample local delicacies (the "wild" section of the menu includes many frog dishes) and potent curries. Restaurant surrounds a bodhi tree and overlooks the bustling river. Small portions. Dishes 80-180฿. Open daily 10am-9:30pm. ❷

Rhan Rup Rong Restaurant, 13/112 Moo 2 U Thong Rd. (☎35 211 036). One of several restaurants on the river offering dinner on land (dishes 100-300฿) or on a boat (groups of 8 or more, 1-2hr., 1000฿ per person). Open daily 11am-9pm. ❸

👁 SIGHTS

Ayutthaya's crumbling ruins span several dozen kilometers, so a grand tour will take several days. One place to start is **Ayutthaya Historical Park,** which holds Wihaan Phra Mongkhon Brophit and Wats Phra Si Sanphet, Mahathat, Phraram, Ratchaburana, and Phananchoeng. Biking is a good choice for this part of town, as the park has little traffic and a few dedicated bike paths. The **Tourist Information Center** has free maps that locate nearly every site and an exhibit showcasing the city on slick touch screens (exhibit closed W). Make the best of your time by renting a bicycle or motorbike, available at most guesthouses. Otherwise, *tuk-tuk* drivers will take you to the sights and wait while you visit them. The "official" price is 200฿ per hr. or around 700-900฿ per day, but try to bargain for about half that (especially if traveling alone). Most ruins are open until 6pm.

WAT CHAIWATTHANARAM. This ancient royal monastery and cremation site, the most majestic and impressive of all the Ayutthayan ruins, spreads over riverside grounds west of the island of central Ayutthaya. A restored Khmer-style tower and *chedi* reflect the great wealth of King Prasat Thong, who built the *wat* in 1630. The 35m main *stupa* represents Mount Meru, the throne of the gods and center of the cosmos. The four mid-sized and eight smaller *stupas* surrounding it represent the rest of the universe. The wat is particularly beautiful at sunset and is lit up at night. Visitors can climb to the top of the central *stupa* for an excellent view of the surrounding ruins and the river but should remember that the walk down the steps is more precarious. *(To reach Wat Chaiwatthanaram by bicycle, motorbike, or foot from the island, take the bridge from the west end of Ayutthaya Historical Park, following signs for Highway 3263 and Suphanburi. After crossing the bridge, the first road on the left leads to the wat. Open daily 8am-6pm. 30฿.)*

WAT YAI CHAIYAMONGKHON. Wat Yai Chaiyamongkhon is entirely different from most Ayutthaya ruins: this working temple lies on the manicured grounds of a partially restored 14th-century *wat* that has a magnificent giant *chedi* at its heart. Even better, unlike at many Ayutthaya *wats*, the Buddha statues here have their heads and hands, as well as glowing saffron sashes. A large reclining Buddha and a community of Buddhist nuns reside here, and the unique combination of ruin and restoration, historical site and living temple, makes Wat Yai, as it is known locally, well worth the trip from town. *(Southeast of the island on the mainland. 20min. bicycle ride from the island or a 40฿ tuk-tuk ride. To reach the wat by bicycle from the island, cross Saphan Pridi Damrong, the bridge that leads to the train station, then continue straight until the intersection with Ayutthaya Pang Pa-In Rd. Turn right, and the temple is on the left. Open daily 8am-5pm. 20฿.)*

WAT PHRA SI SAN PHET. The charred ruins of three imposing *chedis* mark the old Ayutthaya's

ON THE MENU

SWEET STALLS

A worthwhile stop at any food market is the dessert (*khanom*) stall. There, the adventurous eater will find a colorful assortment of treats, most made from the staple ingredients of coconut (in the form of milk or dried shavings) and rice, usually a cake and paste.

A Thai favorite is bananas in warm coconut milk (*klouay buad chee*), and equally popular is sweet sticky rice (*khao niaw*), often served with mango (*khao niaw mamuang*) or sweetened coconut milk (*khao dom gati*). Beware—these accompaniments can take a savory turn, with such additions as garlic shavings or tiny shrimp, giving a Western dessert enthusiast an unexpected surprise.

Desserts unique to specific locales of Thailand are also worth a try. *Khanom Mor Gaen* is a delicious custard that hails from Phetchaburi. Coconut caramels dipped in sesame seeds are a Ko Samui specialty and are especially tasty when still hot.

While at least one dessert stall can be found in just about any food market, the market at Surat Thani (p. 395) is noteworthy for having a tremendous proportion of dessert stalls.

largest temple, a royal monastery that once hosted Thailand's most sacred rituals and ceremonies. The *chedis*, built in classic Ayutthaya style, once held royal remains, but now lie empty. *(Open daily 7am-6pm. 30฿.)*

WIHAAN PHRA MONGKHON BROPHIT. At 12.45m high and 9.5m wide, the 15th-century Buddha snuggled inside this *wat* is one of the largest bronze Buddhas in Thailand. The gleaming 1956 building that houses the statue offers a sharp visual contrast to the surrounding ruins and displays photos and blurbs that trace the process of the statue's restoration. *(Just south of Wat Phra Si Sanphet. Open M-F 8am-4:30pm, Sa-Su 8am-5:30pm. Free.)*

OFF WITH THEIR HEADS. Ayutthaya ruins contain thousands of Buddha images—but only a handful have heads or right hands. While some of the heads were carted off by European archaeologists, most fell to the swords of the Burmese in 1767. They lopped off heads and right hands to kill the power believed to reside within an intact Buddha image, weakening their enemy.

WAT MAHATHAT. The grounds of Wat Mahathat hold Ayutthaya's most photographed sight, a Buddha head artfully framed by twisting tree roots. You'll have to fight through the crowd for a chance to get a picture, and the camera-toting crowds pay little attention to the rest of Wat Mahathat, a royal monastery that dates to 1374 and now lies in a state of ruin. A Khmer-style *stupa* remains, however, and excavations undertaken in the 1950s uncovered sacred relics hidden in a seven-layer reliquary. The artifacts now reside at the Chao Sam Phraya National Museum. A pleasant bike path snakes through the grounds behind this *wat*. *(At the corner of Chikun and Naresuan Rd. Open daily 8am-6pm. 30฿.)*

WAT RATCHABURANA. A small crypt containing intact mural paintings sets Ratchaburana apart from its neighbors. Fifteenth-century King Chao Sam Phraya built the impressive ruins that surround the crypt on the site of an elephant-mounted duel in which both of his older brothers died, allowing him to ascend the throne. *(North of Wat Mahathat. Open daily 8am-6pm. 30฿.)*

WAT PHANANCHOENG. This *wat* houses a massive gold sitting Buddha. This statue, arguably the largest in Thailand, was created in 1324, before Ayutthaya became the Thai capital. Legend has it that tears formed in its eyes when the city was sacked by the Burmese in 1767. Today the temple is a place of pilgrimage for Thai visitors, who come on weekends to drape the statue in saffron cloth. *(West of Yai Chaiyamongkhon, about 2km farther down the road. A ferry (10฿) from the southeast corner of the island, near Phet Fortress, docks near the wat and allows bicycles onboard. Open daily 8am-5pm. 20฿.)*

WAT PHU KHAO THONG. Rising from rice paddies northwest of Ayutthaya, the stark white *prang* at Wat Phu Khao Thong gleams thanks to restoration in the last decade. Its newly slick appearance, however, belies a turbulent history: a Burmese king built the pedestal to commemorate the sacking of Ayutthaya, but control of the area passed back to the Thais before construction was complete, and King Naresuan crowned the Burmese pedestal with a Thai *chedi*. Today, visitors can climb to the base of the *chedi* for a sweeping view of the island of Ayutthaya. *(Leave the island on Ang Thong Rd. and make a left on Phu Khao Thong-Pariat Rd. The chedi is behind the massive King Naresuan the Great Monument. Open daily 9am-6pm. Free.)*

AYUTTHAYA HISTORICAL STUDY CENTER. One of the most high-tech museums in Thailand, this US$8 million research institute, funded by the Japanese government, features exhibits on the ancient city's political, economic, and social history. Dazzling scale models of villages during the Ayutthaya period give insight into its daily life, and miniature reconstructions of Ayutthaya's most famous *wats* complement the real-life ruins. In addition to the main building, a recent annex focuses on international trade and diplomacy in the ancient city. *(On Rotchana Rd., 2 blocks east of the Chao Sam Phraya National Museum. Open M-F 9am-4-:30pm, Sa-Su 9am-5pm. 100฿, with student ID 50฿.)*

OTHER SIGHTS. Just north of the island sits **Wat Na Phra Meru**, the only *wat* to survive the Burmese sacking unscathed. Highlights include the intricately-carved ceiling of its 16th-century *bot* and the largely intact defensive walls surrounding it. *(Open 8am-5pm. 20฿.)* A short bike ride north of the train station are the impressive **Wat Maheyong, Wat Kudidao**, and the smaller **Wat Ayutthaya.** All three are devoid of tourists and are free. North of the island is **Elephant Kraal Pavilion,** where the king used to watch his elephant army train. The Kraal now serves as a home for abused elephants, and it supports itself in part by making paper out of elephant dung and offering elephant tours of the city's ruins. Visitors are welcome to the Kraal, but shouldn't approach the elephants without talking to the staff first. The elephant tours depart from the northwest corner of the intersection of Pathon and Si Sanphet Rd., south of Wihaan Phra Mongkhom Brophit. *(On Pathon Rd. south of Wihaan Phra Mongkhom Brophit. ☎35 321 982. Open daily 9am-5pm. Elephant tour 20 min. 400฿, 30 min. 500฿. Donations appreciated.)* Ayutthaya is also the site of one of the country's largest **Loi Krathong festivals,** which takes place in November during the full moon. Thais gather at **Beung Phra Ram,** the lake in the center of the island, to see fireworks, watch *likay* (Thai folk dance), and enjoy live music. The *loi* (floating) of *krathong* (lotus-shaped paper boats with candles and incense) takes place at Chantharkasem Pier opposite the Chantharkasem Palace Museum.

♫ 🎭 ENTERTAINMENT AND NIGHTLIFE

After a hard day of *wat*-hopping, treat yourself to a massage at the massage parlor next to Malakor, on Chikun Rd. (2hr. Thai massage 300฿. Foot massage 200฿ per hr. Open daily 10am-10pm.) From 7:30-9:30pm nightly, Wat Phra Si Sanphet, Wat Mahathat, Wat Ratchaburana, Wat Phraram, and Wat Chiawatthanaram are illuminated by floodlights. P.U. Inn (p. 162) and the Tourist Information Services (p. 162) offer night tours of these *wats* (7pm; 180฿). Entering the grounds of the *wats* alone after dark is illegal and dangerous. *Farang* nightlife in Ayutthaya centers around the guesthouses and is largely limited to laid-back pubbing. The popularity of the three or four pubs on a given night is largely dependent on what music each is playing, **Moon Cafe** (☎35 232 501, open nightly 4pm-1am) tends to have old rock 'n roll standards and occasional live shows, while the guesthouse bars across the street have live, earnest singer-songwriters or jazz. Prices at each are fairly standard (large Singha 100฿, cocktails 150-200฿). Next door to and sportier than Moon Cafe, **Tony's Place** often plays soccer games on TV. While usually busy, it tends to close early if the crowd begins to peter out.

LOPBURI ☎036

While many Thai cities have a rich history, rarely is the past as palpable as it is in Lopburi. In the compact old city, remarkably well-maintained ancient *wats* and traces of a 4500-year-old civilization can be found around every corner. For many visitors, however, the real draw is the rowdy monkey population, perched on every *wat*, telephone pole, and ledge, that rules much of Old Lopburi. Both the proximity of Lopburi's sights to one another and the city's location, 153km north of Bangkok along the train line, make it an easy daytrip or overnight stop on the way north to Chiang Mai. The convenience and charm of the tiny town may just persuade you to stay a bit longer.

▣ TRANSPORTATION

Rail is the best way to get to Lopburi as the city is located away from the major north-south highways but lies directly on the northern train line. The train station is in the heart of the old city, while the bus station is inconveniently located in the new city, an area of little interest to tourists. Frequent arrivals and departures to and from Ayutthaya and Bangkok, however, make Lopburi an accessible destination by bus from the south.

Trains: The train station (☎036 411 022) is on Naphrakan Rd., in the southeastern corner of the old city across from Wat Phra Sri Rattanamahathat. Trains to: **Bangkok** (3hr., 15 per day, 28-64฿), **Ayutthaya** (1hr., 19 per day, 14-48฿), **Chiang Mai** (9-11hr., 6 per day 8:55am-midnight, 146-212฿), and **Phitsanulok** (3-4hr., 12 per day, 28-64฿). Tickets to Bangkok on trains coming from cities farther north can only be purchased within 30min. of departure.

Buses: The **bus station** is near New Lopburi on Narai Maharat Rd., the east-west road that connects the old and new cities, 2km from Old Lopburi. **A/C buses** go to Bangkok (2hr., every 20min. 4:20am-8:30pm, 78฿). **Regular buses** make trips to **Ayutthaya** (1hr., every 10min. 4:50am-6:30pm, 28฿) and the closest town on the Bangkok-Chiang Mai route, **Singburi** (45min., every 20min. 5:10am-6:40pm, 13฿). **A/C vans** leave for **Bangkok** (2hr., every hr. 5am-7pm, 100฿) from Old Lopburi on Naphrakan Rd., a 2min. walk toward Narai Maharat Rd. from the train station.

Local Transportation: Blue and green **city buses** line Narai Maharat Rd. between the old and new cities (every 2min. 5am-8pm, 6฿). Blue **songthaew** handle the short north-south routes within Old and New Lopburi (every 5min. 5am-8pm, 5฿). Omnipresent orange-vested **motorcycle taxi** drivers are good for rides within Old Lopburi (20-40฿). **Samlor** can be found at the rail station and on some streets in the old city (within Old Lopburi 10-20฿).

▣▣ ORIENTATION AND PRACTICAL INFORMATION

Lopburi actually comprises two gradually converging cities, centered 2.5km apart along **Narai Maharat Road: Old** and **New Lopburi.** New Lopburi, east of the old town, is the bustling epicenter of regional commerce, but virtually everything of interest to tourists is in Old Lopburi. Here, Narai Maharat Rd. changes to **Wichayan Rd.** The old city's eastern edge is marked by **Naphrakan Road;** past it, you'll encounter the train station, restaurants, the night market, Internet cafes, several sites of historical interest, and tribes of insufferable primates. **Surasongkhram Road** (also called **Surasak Road**) is the other major north-south road in the old city and features banks, hotels, police, day markets, King Narai's palace, and more ancient temples.

Tourist Offices: TAT (☎036 422 768; tatlobri@tat.or.th), on Rop Wat Pharthat Rd. in Old Lopburi, is convenient for tourists. Exit the train station to the right, make the first left onto Rop Wat Pharthat Rd., and walk a block. Staff speaks decent English and dispenses maps, brochures, and transit info. Open daily 8:30am-4:30pm.

Currency Exchange: Krung Thai Bank, at the corner of Wichayan and Surasongkhram Rd., with a **24hr. ATM** in front. Open M-F 8:30am-3:30pm, Sa 9:30am-12:30pm. Many other banks have offices on Surasak and Surasongkhram Rds. with currency exchange and ATMs; hours are typically M-F 8:30am-3:30pm.

Police: (☎036 411 0135), at the corner of Ratchadamnoen and Naphrakan Rd. Open 24hr.

CENTRAL THAILAND

Medical Services: The general **hospital** (☎036 621 537), in the new town on Phahol Yothin Hwy. From the old city, follow Narai Maharat Rd., turn left at the provincial hall, and follow the road for a block. Some English spoken. Open 24hr.

Telephones: An **international telephone booth** located at the CAT office next door to the main post office. Open daily 8:30am-8:30pm.

Internet Access: Online, on Ratchadamnoen Rd., halfway between KFC and Naphrakan Rd., has good connections. 30฿ per hr., after 6pm 15฿ per hr. Open daily 6am-10pm. There are many other Internet spots on Naphrakan Rd. across from the station, with similar prices and hours.

Post offices: The city's **central post office** (☎36 411 011) is on Narai Maharat Rd. on the right just before the bus station coming from the old city. A **branch** (☎036 411 804) on Prang Sam Yod Rd., just past the Prang Sam Yot temple on Narai Maharat Rd. Both open M-F 8:30am-4:30pm, Sa 9am-noon. **Postal Code:** 15000.

█ ACCOMMODATIONS

While Lopburi lacks conventional backpacker accommodations, the Old City has several comfortable and decent budget options, most of which are old-school Thai-Chinese hotels. Most are within walking distance of the train station and sights.

Noom Guesthouse (☎036 427 613), on Phraya Kamjid Rd. across from the park. Rooms are spacious, cheap, and are the closest Lopburi comes to a backpacker spirit. The newly renovated bungalows are a great deal. Rooms with fan and shared bath 200฿, bungalows with fan and bath 350฿. ❷

The Lopburi Asia Hotel, 1/7-8 Surasongkhram Rd. (☎036 618 894). From the train station, turn right on Naphrakan Rd., left on Phraya Kanjit Rd., and right when the road dead-ends onto Narai's Palace. Large rooms: ask to see several, as amenities and states of repair vary. Rooms 250฿, with A/C 350฿. A/C rooms have hot showers and big TVs; fan rooms have cold water and smaller TVs. ❷

Nett Hotel, 17/1-2 Ratchadamnoen Rd. (☎036 411 738), situated in an alley 1 block toward the train station from Lopburi Asia Hotel. Similar to that hotel but with friendler staff. A bit dimmer and grimier, with smaller rooms. Rooms 200฿, with A/C 300฿, with A/C and hot water 400฿. ❷

█ FOOD

There are excellent **day markets** in the small alleys off Surasongkhram Rd. north of Narai Maharat Rd., going away from the train station, with plenty of fish and fresh produce. The smallish **night market** sets up on Naphrakan Rd. near the train station. (Open daily from late afternoon until 10 or 11pm.)

May Ka Mind, on the corner of Naphrakan and Ratchadamnoen Rd., about a 5min. walk from the train station. The English sign on the door reads "Food & Drink & Welcome." Offers tasty Thai dishes in a cheerful setting decorated with art by local schoolchildren. Pointing at other people's dishes may be more fruitful than ordering off the limited English menu. Dishes 45-85฿. Open daily 10am-6pm. ❷

Coffee House, on Ratchadamnoen Rd., a block west of Naphrakan Rd. Far less expensive than its upscale black-wood-and-sepia-photograph decor suggests. Menu keeps it simple and delicious with small bowls of soupy noodles (10฿), real coffee drinks (20-40฿), fresh lime and roselle juices (10-20฿), and Western breakfast (59฿). Open daily 8am-8pm. ❶

Noom Guesthouse Bar & Restaurant, on the corner of Phraya Kamjad Rd. facing the park and White House Garden Restaurant. The relaxed, open-air bar is the only place in town that approaches *farang* nightlife. Good guesthouse-style food (dishes 40-100฿), beer (35-90฿), and a full bar. Singha 35฿. Open daily noon-midnight. ❷

New World Steak House, on Ramdecho Rd. right after Bridge 33, just south of the bus station in the new city. A 40฿ motorcycle ride from the old city will take you to this marvelous restaurant run by an English couple; the menu has steak, ribs, and homemade bread and pies for those longing for a taste of Western home cooking. Handmade hamburgers 60฿, other dishes 40-150฿. ❸

🄖 SIGHTS

Lopburi is built upon twelve centuries' worth of notable ruins and artifacts that span the Dvaravati, Sukhothai, and Ayutthaya eras, all reflecting a strong Khmer influence. Most of the complexes are completely open to visitors, and a pleasant morning or afternoon can be whiled away clambering over the ruins.

KING NARAI'S PALACE. These sprawling ruins, built by King Narai of Ayutthaya in 1666 when military and business affairs prompted frequent trips to Lopburi, contain vestiges of Narai's elephant stables, royal reception hall, harem quarters, and the four throne halls that King Rama IV added to the complex in the 1850s. The massive complex, much of it designed by French and Italian architects, reflects a striking blend of European, Khmer, and Thai styles. Intricate lotus designs appear at every turn. For example, walls of the middle and inner courts have 2000 lotus-shaped candle holders, used to spectacular lighting effect. The Narai throne halls also draw on a fusion of French and Thai architectural motifs.

The French-influenced, pleasantly manicured grounds host a small herd of topiary elephants. The adjacent **Lopburi National Museum** features artifacts dating back to prehistoric times—although with an unfortunate lack of English information—along with biographical artwork depicting King Narai and King Rama IV. Another section of the museum describes the relationships between Narai's court and other notable courts of the day; these rooms have all information available in English. Lastly, the ethnographic section of the museum displays some of the region's famous shadow puppets and a quirky assortment of oddities, like a two-headed snake in a jar. *(On Surasongkhram Rd., 2 blocks behind Wat Phra Sri Rattanamahathat. Open W-Su 8:30am-4pm. 30฿.)*

WAT PHRA SRU RATTANAMAHATHAT. The charming, crumbling Wat Phra Sru Rattanamahat is a partially restored 12th-century, Khmer-style temple, once Lopburi's largest monastery. While most of the monastery lies in serious disrepair, restored *chedis* and towers in both Sukhothai and Ayutthayan styles dot the extensive grounds. The *wat*, across the street from the train station, is worth a visit, even if you only have time for a quick hop from the train. *(Across from the train station, on Naphrakan Rd., in Old Lopburi. Open daily 6am-6pm. 30฿.)*

PHRA PRANG SAM YOT. Situated in the very heart of monkey territory, Phra Prang Sam Yot is a complex of three connected pagodas dating to the 11th century. This site is most celebrated for its well-maintained examples of the Bayon style of Khmer artwork. Visitors to the *wat* are issued a monkey-hitting stick for the duration of their visit. Peanuts to feed the monkeys are sold for 10฿ and should only be given to the primates through the window-bars of the main bulding's monkey-free interior. The ruin hidden beneath the monkeys was originally a Khmer Buddhist temple sacred to members of the Mahayana sect. This group had overt ties to Hinduism, evident in *linga* features at the pagoda's base. King Narai the Great later converted it into a Thai Buddhist temple and constructed a brick assembly hall on the premises. *(Open daily 8am-6pm. 30฿.)*

PHRA KAN SHRINE. Across the railroad tracks from Phra Prang Sam Yot is the Phra Kan Shrine, a large 12th-century square pagoda that sits in ruins. Largely blocked from view by a pavilion built in 1951, its shrine is home to several statues of the Hindu god Vishnu. A particularly notorious gang of monkeys, reputed to attack the cameras and bags of many visitors, lives here as well. *(On Narai Maharat Rd., at Naphrakan Rd. From the train station, follow the road toward the center of town to the major intersection 3 blocks away. Phra Kan Shrine open daily. Free.)*

WAT PRANG KHAEK. Lopburi's oldest historical site, Wat Prang Khaek dates to the 9th century and shows its age. Three brick pagodas lie quietly on a triangular green lawn as traffic zooms by in every direction. The pagodas feature Khmer artwork in the venerable *Phakho* style. The assembly hall and water tank, located opposite each other, were commissioned by King Narai the Great. *(On Surasongkhram Rd., at Wichayant Rd., in the center of Old Lopburi. Free.)*

▶ DAYTRIPS

While most of the *wats* of Lopburi lie in ruin, an active temple a few kilometers from town offers a powerful example of socially engaged Buddhism—and a sobering reminder of the devastating impact of AIDS in Thailand. When a monk named Dr. Alongkot Dikkapanya opened an eight-bed hospice for AIDS patients at this *wat* in 1992, he faced stiff opposition from both the Buddhist establishment and the local community. Local villagers, frightened that the runoff of water from the *wat* would transmit HIV to their crops, even ceased giving alms to the temple. Dr. Alongkot persisted in his project of relieving the suffering of dying AIDS patients, however, and today **Wat Phra Baht Nam Phu** is home to a 400-bed hospice. The *wat* welcomes visitors and has created several exhibits designed for them. The most prominent of these, the Life Museum, displays the mummified bodies and brief biographies of some of the thousands of patients who have died here. Consistent with Buddhist thought, the museum aims not only to raise awareness of AIDS but also to inspire reflection on the fleeting nature of all life. Another exhibit, the Bone Museum, displays the cremated remains of former residents, and a garden holds art made of the bone resin of former patients. These exhibits may be inappropriate for children under 14. *(8km from Old Lopburi. Either take a motorcycle taxi from Lopburi (80-150฿) or take a city bus (7฿) from the corner of Wichayan and Sorasak Rd. and tell the driver you're going to Wat Phra Baht Nam Phu. You'll be let off at the turn-off for the 4km road to the temple. Motorcycle taxis usually wait at this intersection and the trip to the temple will cost 30฿. One of the guards at the front gate can call you a motorcycle for the return trip. Bangkok office ☎02 749 87667; www.aidstemple.co.th. Museums open daily 8am-8pm. Temple gates open daily 8am-10pm.)*

KANCHANABURI   ☎034

The Japanese invasion during WWII immortalized the town of Kanchanaburi and the humble Kwai River, the site of the building of the infamous Death Railway Bridge. The sights that mark this tragic history now draw tour groups by the busload, while backpackers use the city as a base for exploring the surrounding waterfalls, caves, and jungles. Waterfront guesthouses, with their river views and tranquil atmosphere, provide another draw.

◤ TRANSPORTATION

Trains: Kanchanaburi Train Station (☎034 511 285), on Saeng Chuto Rd. next to the Night Market. To: **Namtok** (2hr., 3 per day in each direction, 100฿) via the **River Kwai Bridge** and **Bangkok** (3hr.; 7:19am, 2:44pm, returns 7:45am and 1:35pm; 25฿).

Buses: The **Kanchanaburi Bus Station** (☎034 511 182) is in Ban Nua Village at the southern end of Kanchanaburi. Schedules and prices change often, so get a current copy from the TAT, a 5min. walk from the bus station. To: **Bangkok's Southern Bus Station** (#81; 2nd-class with A/C 2hr., every 20min. 3:50am-7pm, 83฿; 1st-class with A/C, 2hr., every 15min. 4am-8pm, 106฿); **Erawan National Park** (#8170, 1hr., every 50min. 8am-5:20pm, 45฿); **Ratchaburi** (with connections to **Cha Am, Hua Hin,** and **Phetchaburi** #461, 2hr., every 15min. 5:10am-6:20pm, 47฿); **Sangkhlaburi** (VIP bus #8203, 4hr., every hr. 7:30am-4:30pm; 146฿; A/C van #8203, 3hr., every hr. 7:30am-4:30pm; 180฿, departs across from main bus terminal); **Suphanburi** (#411, 1-2hr., every 20min. 4:50am-6:10pm, 45฿) with connections to **Ayutthaya** and **Nakhon Sawan** (last connecting bus to these destinations leaves at 5pm).

Local Transportation: Orange **songthaew** run up and down Saeng Chuto Rd. and stop at the River Kwai Bridge (10฿). **Samlor** go from the train station to TAT (10-30฿). **Motorcycle taxis** to guesthouses from bus station (30-40฿). A **ferry** crosses the river at the end of Chaichumphon Rd. (5฿).

Rentals: The **bicycles** available on Maenamkwai Rd. vary widely in quality: alignment and a comfortable seat may be worth an extra 10฿, and be sure to try out a bike before renting it. 20-50฿ per 24hr. There are **motorbike** rentals all along Maenamkwai Rd., centering around the area near the Jolly Frog (see **Accommodations,** p. 173). Rates are fairly uniform, averaging 150฿ per 24hr. for manual transmission and 250฿ per 24hr. for automatic. Passport deposit required.

✈ ⏱ ORIENTATION AND PRACTICAL INFORMATION

Kanchanaburi is 129km from Bangkok and stretches roughly 5km along the banks of the **Kwai River,** which flows parallel to **Saeng Chuto Road,** the city's busy main thoroughfare. At the north end of town is the famous **Death Railway Bridge,** (also called the **Kwai River Bridge**). Two kilometers south of the bridge is the **train station** and the riverside **guesthouse area,** where *farang* congregate. **Mae Nam Kwai Road** connects the guesthouses to the Death Railway Bridge and is lined with Internet cafes, bike rentals, tour companies, massage parlors, laundry services,and bars. Two kilometers farther south of the guesthouse area is **Ban Nua Village,** the city's main commercial area and home to the bus station. West of the bus station are the city gate, day markets, and river wharf area. Because Kanchanaburi is quite spread out and many sights are outside of town, consider renting a bicycle or motorbike.

Tourist Office: TAT (☎/fax 034 511 200), on Saeng Chuto Rd., a 5min. walk south of the bus station. Friendly staff speaks some English. Excellent regional map and free guidebook. Bus and train schedules. Lenso phone. Open daily 8:30am-4:30pm.

Immigration Office: (☎034 513 325), on Mae Nam Maeklong Rd., 4km from TAT. Follow Saeng Chuto Rd. south away from Ban Nua Village and turn right at City Hall, 1km past the GPO. 60-day visa extension 1900฿; 1-day processing. Bring 1 photo, 2 copies of passport, visa, and departure card. Open M-F 8:30am-noon and 1-4:30pm.

Currency Exchange: Banks are common on the roads from the Kanchanaburi Bus Station. Several have **24hr. ATMs. Thai Farmers Bank** is 1 block from Saeng Chuto Rd., on Luk Moeng Rd., heading toward the bus station. Open M-F 8:30am-3:30pm.

Work Opportunity: Teach English at the local Catholic school. For more info, see **Teaching English,** p. 85.

Tourist Police: (☎034 512 795), 1.5km north of train station on Saeng Chuto Rd., on the right. Free **luggage storage.** English spoken. Open 24hr. Helpful **booths** at the foot of the Death Railway Bridge, on Song Kwai Rd., at Burakamkosol Rd., and on Mae Nam Kwai Rd., 50m past Apple's Guest House toward the cemetery. Open daily 8:30am-6pm.

Medical Services: Saeng Chuto Hospital (☎034 621 129), 500m north of TAT, on Saeng Chuto Rd. English spoken. **Pharmacy** open 24hr. MC/V.

Telephones: Kanchanaburi Telecommunications Office (☎034 514 088), on Soi 38 off Saeng Chuto Rd. Turn left at the post office, and it's 200m up on the right. **International calls** and phone cards. 1st min. 3в, then 0.50в per min. Open M-F 8:30am-4:30pm.

Internet Access: Available all over the city, especially on Maenamkwai Rd., where the *farang*-friendly atmosphere yields prices (25-40в per hr.) that are slightly higher than in the area around the bus station.

Post Office: GPO (☎034 511 131), on Saeng Chuto Rd., 1km south of TAT, on the left. Poste Restante. Open M-F 8:30am-4:30pm, Sa-Su 9am-noon. **Postal Code:** 71000.

ACCOMMODATIONS

Most of Kanchanaburi's best budget accommodations sit along (or in) the River Kwai in the northern part of the city, a 10min. walk from the train station or a 25min. walk from the bus station. Taxi rides from the bus station are 30в, although some guesthouses will arrange free pick-up if you call upon arrival. Guesthouses on Rongheabaoy Rd. are quieter, while those on Mae Nam Kwai Rd. are flooded with *farang*. All establishments listed help arrange tours, and all but Nita Raft House have restaurants attached.

Jolly Frog Backpacker's, 28 Soi China, Mae Nam Kwai Rd. (☎034 514 579; www. jollyfrog.net). A young, lively crowd relaxes on hammocks with excellent river views in the bougainvillea-lined courtyard. Clean, well-maintained rooms decorated in a curious explosion of textures and patterns. Nightly movies selected by guests. Singles with shared bath 70в; doubles 150в, with bath 200в, with A/C 290в; 4-bed bungalow with bath and fan 400в. MC/V. ❶

Nita Raft House, 27/1 Pak Prak Rd. (☎034 514 521). A 10min. walk from the bus station and a 20min. walk south of the main guesthouse area; look for the small sign, in English, 50m past the southern end of Song Kwai Rd. Clean but simple rooms set on delightfully rambling rafts, some with beautiful views down the river. A spirit house is tucked under a side table in the floating lounge area, where all the furniture is low-slung and the DVD collection is impressive. Friendly English-speaking owners Booey and Thip approach this more as a family environment than as a purely commercial enterprise. Due to the proximity of Song Kwai Rd., you may hear some late-night sound from the floating discos. Singles with shared bath 90-100в; doubles 160-180в, with bath 220-250в, with A/C 500в. ❶

Sugar Cane Guest House, 22 Soi Pakistan (☎034 624 520), off Mae Nam Kwai Rd.; turn-off 1 block north from the turn-off to Jolly Frog (see above). Signs reminding guests to "Whisper Only" after 11pm capture the peace-and-quiet spirit. Bamboo and cinder block bungalows cluster around a carefully tended riverfront garden. Restaurant overlooks river. Bungalows 150-250в, raft houses with A/C and hot shower 350-550в depending on size. Second location, 7 Soi Cambodia (☎034 514 988), off Mae Nam Kwai Rd., 1km farther north toward the bridge. Doubles with bath 200в, with hot water 300в; raft doubles with A/C and hot water 550в. ❷

Apple's Guest House and Restaurant, 52 Rongheabaoy Rd. (☎034 512 017), at the juncture with Mae Nam Kwai Rd. Thatched rooms surround a courtyard with a seating area and immaculate garden. The lack of riverside real estate is offset by a constant tranquility. Hospitable co-owner Apple leads a day-long cooking course (950в). Internet 20в per hr. Rooms with bath 250-350в, with A/C 650в. ❷

FOOD

Due to Kanchanaburi's sizable expat population and the constant flow of tourists, Western food is widely available near the main guesthouse area. Some restaurants, including those at the Jolly Frog and Sugar Cane guesthouses, offer a menu of both Western and Thai dishes. Still, the food in the guesthouse neighborhood tends to be more expensive and less flavorful than in other parts of town. To eat as the locals do, head to the food stalls and markets. There are excellent **noodle stands,** some with covered seating areas, across from the bus station in Ban Nua Village and just south of the tourist police booth on Song Kwai Rd. A plate of *pad thai* with pork and fresh herbs is 20-30฿. The **Dalat Kao Market,** bounded by Chao Khunnen and Burakamkosol Rd., offers fresh produce and meat. **Phasuk Market,** across from the bus station near Lak Muang Rd. in Ban Nua Village, sells clothing and accessories. Both open daily dawn-dusk. The **night market** closest to the guesthouses is the haphazard roadside affair just north of the train station, on Saeng Chuto Rd. Open M, Th, Sa-Su 5-10pm.

▨ **Ali Bongo's Taste of India,** 232 Mae Nam Kwai Rd., just north of Beer Barrel. Serving a wide selection of Indian specialties with a warm, low-key atmosphere, Ali Bongo's is a refreshing change from the homogenous guesthouse-area restaurant scene. The menu includes standards like Tandoori Kebab (95-155฿), along with fish (95-105฿) and vegetarian selections (Saag Paneer, 90฿). Post-meal hookahs (250฿ for a group) are available in the adjacent lounge. Open daily 11:30am-11:30pm. ❸

Floating Restaurant (☎034 625 055), down the stairs immediately north of the bridge. Waitstaff in traditional Thai garments serve local river fish on an elegant teak terrace with a view of the bridge. Pictures on the menu help you find delicious options such as the yellow mystus (45฿) and the snake-head fish (200฿). Vegetarians can opt for the local wild mushrooms (350฿). Prices listed per 100 grams; a standard serving is 300 grams. Open daily 8:30am-10pm. MC/V, 500฿ min. ❸

Jolly Frog Backpacker's Restaurant (☎034 514 579), attached to the Jolly Frog Backpacker's (p. 173). Popular with locals and *farang* alike. Offers a fantastic menu in a wide range of categories—Western breakfasts, local fish, pizzas and burgers, vegetarian dishes, and Thai standbys like *pad thai* (30฿) and Pad Siew (30฿). Prices are significantly lower than at most guesthouse restaurants. Open daily 7am-10:30pm. MC/V. ❷

⑤ SIGHTS

With the exception of a number of *wats,* all of the sights in or near Kanchanaburi relate to the region's role in World War II. Along with the Death Railway Bridge and the graves of Allied POWs, the town documents its painful past with war museums that range from excellent to bizarre.

Kanchanaburi's attractions are spread out over more than 10km. To take everything in over a couple of days, rent a bicycle or motorbike—it's faster and easier than walking, cheaper than taking a taxi, and more convenient than trying to catch a bus. Plus, the sugar cane fields, lemon-yellow butterflies, and limestone crags that dot the area around town make for a scenic ride—albeit a harrowing one, as large trucks sometimes barrel past on the narrow road.

▨DEATH RAILWAY BRIDGE (KWAI RIVER BRIDGE). Constructed between 1941 and 1942, the original Kwai River Bridge was the Japanese army's final attempt to complete the 415km Thai-Myanmar railway line (the "Death Railway") for transporting war materials to military camps in Myanmar. Roughly 16,000 Allied POWs and 96,000 local laborers died building the bridge, which was subsequently destroyed by British air raids in 1945. Engineers predicted that it would take five years to construct, but the Japanese forced Allied POWs and local laborers to complete this vital section of the railway in 16 months. The current bridge, although impressive, is a reconstruction built as a memorial to those who lost their lives. In the bridge's immediate vicinity are tourist-oriented shops, a textile market, and an indoor jewelry market. A word of caution: although the bridge is usually thronged with tourists, it is still in use and trains pass over it regularly. Kanchanaburi celebrates the **Kwai River Bridge Week** during the first week of December. Activities include archaeological and historical exhibitions, performances, musical events, and a spectacular light and sound show. *(3km northwest of train station. Take the orange minibus #2 from the Focus Optic shop, 2 traffic lights from TAT, for 10min., 10в. Approx. 2.5km walk north of guesthouses on Mae Nam Kwai Rd. Songthaew to bridge 10-20в. Many local tour companies arrange rides on a train that crosses the Kwai River Bridge.)*

THAILAND-BURMA RAILWAY MUSEUM. As well-organized as it is well-funded, this slick, air-conditioned museum is an excellent place to begin a visit to Kanchanaburi. It offers a clear, detailed historical and geographical context for the Death Railway and uses both models and artifacts to evoke the daily life of POWs. The silk RAF survival map of the region is a highlight, while film footage from the camps' liberators is particularly harrowing. The coffee shop offers a view of the Allied War Cemetery, and a gift shop sells local handicrafts and flowers for visitors to offer at the cemetery. *(73 Chao Kunnen Rd., across from the Allied War Cemetery. ☎034 512 721; www.tbrconline.com. Open daily 9am-5pm. Admission 80в, children 40в. Flowers 20в per bunch.)*

JEATH WAR MUSEUM. Established in 1977 by the abbot of Wat Chaichumphon to honor victims of the Death Railway Bridge, the JEATH (Japan, England, America/Australia, Thailand, and Holland) War Museum sits in a bamboo hut like those that were used to house POWs. The collection of pictures, artifacts, and drawings is modest, yet powerful. Newspaper articles posted on the walls highlight the accomplishments of famous POWs and their efforts to raise awareness of wartime events. The artwork by the POWs is particularly moving. Roosters from the neighboring *wat* provide company. *(500m south of the town gate, on Pak Prak Rd. ☎034 515 203. Open daily 8am-6pm. 30в.)*

KANCHANABURI ALLIED WAR CEMETERY. This is the final resting place for 7000 Allied POWs, most of whom were British and Dutch, and died while working on the Death Railway Bridge. At mid-morning, Western tour groups seem to outnumber the headstones; go in the afternoon for a more quietly reflective experience. *(2km north of the bus station on Saeng Chuto Rd., a 5min. walk from the train station. Free.)*

CHUNG KAI WAR CEMETERY. Farther afield, Chung Kai holds the remains of 1750 Death Railway POWs. This cemerary is on a riverside setting more peaceful than its larger counterpart in town. The majority of those buried here are British Commonwealth soldiers who died of illness in the camp hospital. *(3km from town, cross the bridge at the northern end of Song Kwai Rd. and stay on that road. Free.)*

WATS. Wat Chaichumphon (also called **Wat Dai**), next to JEATH, is most often frequented by townspeople and roosters. The enormous horse-pulled ship on its grounds draws upon Thai mythology to honor a highly revered monk. Many locals avoid **Wat Tham Khao Poon**, 4km beyond Chung Kai War Cemetery, believing it to harbor bad spirits. Indeed, the *wat's* caves have a dark history: a drug-addicted monk murdered a British tourist here in 1995, and local lore holds that the Japanese used the caves to torture Allied POWs. Despite the bad omens, the cave itself is the best in the town's immediate area. A well-marked series of underground Buddhist shrines, overhung with stalactites, takes at least 20min. to explore and comes out above the *wat's* garden. Some passages require you to crouch, and try not to be startled when you encounter the indigenous bat population. *(20в. The sign on the road says "Khoapoon Cave." Cave closes after nightfall.)* On the other side of the river, Chinese-influenced **Wat Tham Mongkon Thong** (Cave Temple of the Golden Dragon) attracts tour buses with its "floating nun," a woman who strikes yogic poses while floating on water; she's the successor to the original floating nun, now dead, who meditated while float-ing. *(10-15min. performance. 200฿, or 10฿ per person with a group of 20 or more. Go early on a weekend morning for the best chance of arriving while a tour group is there.)* A better reason to visit the temple is its enchanting grotto, located halfway up the hillside. A long staircase with serpent-shaped railings leads to the cave entrance. Find a monk to switch on the lights, and you can continue past the initial chamber, walking and crawling through a cramped underground tunnel before climbing a ladder that takes you back outside. A trail leads back to the temple. Bring a friend for safety. *(Motorcycle taxis make the trip for 30฿; by bicycle or motorbike, follow the road out past immigration and over the bridge. After about 4km, you'll see a group of colorful signs next to a tall, ornate gate. Take a left and follow the road for 0.5km.)*

🎵 NIGHTLIFE

Kanchanaburi's nightlife centers on the floating discos off Song Kwai Rd. and the foreigner-targeted bars along Mae Nam Kwai Rd. A recent government crackdown on noise pollution has dampened the disco boat scene, but a few lively bars remain along Song Kwai Rd.

Bar Beer's (☎034 516 919). 2 live bands perform every night as foreigners congregate at this low-key bar. Large Singha 100฿. Open daily 6pm-late.

Snooker Bar (☎034 624 954), on Mae Nam Kwai Rd. Sit and drink with the locals at this awesome sidewalk bar. Large Chang 40฿. Open daily 7am-midnight.

The Wild Life, on Mae Nam Rd., 2 blocks north of the Snooker Bar. This bar continues Beer Barrel's jungle theme but adds 3-story treehouses overlooking a thatched seating area. Beer 60-100฿. Live music. Open daily 6pm-midnight.

🏞 DAYTRIPS FROM KANCHANABURI

Kanchanaburi proves an ideal base for exploring the waterfalls, caves, and parks that stretch all the way to Sangkhlaburi and the Thai-Burmese border. And at just over 2hr. from Bangkok, the area's towering mountains, flat, fer-tile floodplains, and dense, lush vegetation make for an incredibly scenic and accessible escape from the chaos that is Bangkok.

Routes 3199 and **323** bisect the province at the northern end of Kanchanaburi and make good points of reference. 3199 is a well-paved passage to the Erawan waterfalls. Route 323 heads west to Sangkhlaburi and the Thai-Burmese border along Three Pagoda Pass, passing Sai Yok National Park and Hellfire Pass. Public transportation is an option (bus or train), though only leaves time for visiting only one or two attractions per day. Motorbikes are an efficient way to see the sites, but novice riders would be better off using other means of transportation—while the roads are generally excellent, the points of interest are separated by long stretches of highway driving. Between Kanchanaburi and Sangkhlaburi, gas must be obtained in Sai Yok or Thong Pha Phum. The scenic and paved 221km to Sangkhlaburi along route 323 (3-4hr. nonstop) has a steep final ascent that is tiring for both bike and body—make sure you're well rested and have your bike serviced before leaving. Pick up the excellent regional map from TAT for any independent exploration. A well-restored 🚂train also runs from Kanchanaburi to Nam Tok Station and allows for a more scenic and inter-esting alternative to the highway. Traveling by train in the region also provides impressive views of the Kwai River and access to parts of the countryside that are not easily viewed when trapped in a minibus.

For a few extra baht, a very reasonable alternative to independent travel is to use a tour agency. Most guesthouses lead or arrange tours. (120-1000฿, 3-5 person min. Most day tours start at 8am.) Numerous tour companies in

TO SAI YOK NOI WATERFALL (10km),
TO PRASAT MUANG SINGH HISTORICAL PARK (43km),
TO ERAWAN NATIONAL PARK (65km),
TO SRI NAKHARIN NATIONAL PARK (105km),
TO SANGKHLABURI (220km)

Kanchanaburi

ACCOMMODATIONS
Apple's Guest House and
 Restaurant, **10**
Jolly Frog Backpacker's, **7**
Nita Raft House, **13**
Sugar Cane Guest House, **2, 6**

FOOD
Ali Bongo's Taste of India, **5**
Apple's Restaurant, **11**
Floating Restaurant, **1**
Jolly Frog Backpacker's
 Restaurant, **9**
Noodle Stalls, **12**

NIGHTLIFE
Beer Barrel, **8**
Snooker Bar, **4**
The Wild Life, **3**

Death Railway Bridge

Art Gallery and
World War II Museum

Mae Nam Kwai Rd.

Sol Cambodia

England Rd.

Sol Pakistan

Sol China

Rongheabaoy Rd.

Dontuk Rd.

Night Market

323

Thailand-Burma
Railway Center

Mae Nm Kwai Rd.

Kanchanaburi
Allied War Cemetery

Kwai Yai River

Kran Pra Radawang Bo Won Rd.

Thawonwith Rd.

Chinese
Cemetery

Saeng Chuto Rd.

Song Kwai Rd.

Wat
Nua

Ban Nua Rd.

Tessaban Bumroong Rd.

Kratai Thong Rd.

Saeng
Chuto
Hospital

TO
SUPHANBURI
(95km)

Pak Prak Rd.

Hiran Prasas Rd.

Bovorn Rd.

U Thong Rd.

Dalat Kao
Market

Burakamkosol Rd.

Prasit Rd.

Koe Moeng Rd.

Luk Muang Shrine
(City Pillar)

Phasuk
Market

Luk Muang Rd.

BAN NUA
VILLAGE

Night
Market

Song Kwai Rd.

Kam Pang Mueng Rd.

Visutharangsi Rd.

Saeng Chuto Rd.

Thanakain
Hospital

JEATH
War
Museum

Mae Khlong River

Wat
Chaichumphon
(Wat Dai)

Chukkadone
Market

Chaichumphon Rd.

323

N

LG

0   500 yards
0   500 meters

Chung Kal
War Cemetery

Kwai Noi River

City Hall

TO
BANGKOK
(129km)

Mae Nam Maeklong Rd.

TO WAT THAM KHAO PUN (1km)

Wat Tham
Mongkon Thong

TO WAT
THAM KHAO NOI,
WAT THAM SUA
(13 km)

Immigration
Of ce

TO
RATCHABURI

Kanchanaburi clamor for your money, but only 10 are TAT-certified. **B.T. Travel Center,** 44/3 Rong Heep Oil Rd. (☎624 630), 50m down the soi opposite VN Guest House, offer one day sightseeing tours to Erawan Waterfall, Hellfire Pass, and the Death Railway. (Mixed Travel 750฿, Travel Center 690฿; trip with bamboo rafting and elephant riding costs an extra 200฿.) As always, be sure your agency has a TAT license. Many include national park entrance fees and an English-speaking guide, while others only cover transportation costs. The companies also run 2- to 3-day treks (1500-2000฿).

A fourth way to see many of the sites is to charter a boat, as several sites are clustered along the River Kwai. Contact **Safarine Travel** (☎624 140) for more information. Some of the travel companies also arrange boat tours.

ALONG ROUTE 3199:

ⓘERAWAN NATIONAL PARK. The foremost tourist destination near Kanchanaburi is idyllic Erawan ("Three-Headed Elephant") Waterfall. The seven-tiered waterfalls may not be the biggest cascades in the area, but they're certainly the most accessible, and they offer fun opportunities for swimming and hiking. It is best to arrive early to beat the crowd of locals and *farang*. Tiers one, three, and four are the best for swimming, while the nearly vertical cliff above the seventh tier offers the most impressive view. Keep an eye out for brave swimmers using a natural rock waterslide on the fourth tier. The first three levels are a 5-10min. walk from the trailhead. The challenging 1.5km trail to the top (1hr.) leads past enticing, clear-water swimming holes, rewarding the intrepid with greater seclusion. But watch out—the trail at the seventh tier is slippery. Sturdy shoes are highly recommended. Monkeys are constant companions along the trail, but don't get too close or they may become territorial. Another persistent friend is the mosquito, who bites all the way to the top—bring repellent. The visitors center, next to where the Kanchanaburi bus stops, has maps, photos, and a slide show. Accommodations range from **camping** (two-person tent 60฿) to **dorms** (mattresses 10฿, dorms 30฿) to **bungalows** (four beds and bath 250฿ per person or 800฿ per bungalow). National Park Headquarters, opposite the visitors center, handles accommodations and emergencies. *(65km from Kanchanaburi. Take public bus #8170: 1hr.; every 50min. 8am-5:20pm, last bus back at 4pm; 45฿. Open daily 8am-4:30pm. 200฿. Motorbikes 20฿, cars 30฿.)*

Phrathat Cave, also in the national park, 9km from Erawan Waterfall, has impressive stalagmites and stalactites, which remain undisturbed by *farang* due to their remote location. For 20฿, a guide at the park office will take you on a 1hr. tour of the caves. *(From the market at Erawan Waterfall, turn left, and follow the signs to Huay Mae Khamin Waterfall and Phrathat. The journey is over a rough dirt road. It may be possible to charter transport from the market 300-400฿, but it is easier and cheaper if you have your own wheels. Open daily 8am-4pm, but arrive by 3pm to see the caves.)*

SRI NAKHARIN NATIONAL PARK. Sri Nakharin has more animals and fewer tourists than Erawan, but getting to this park demands more time, money, and effort. About 105km from Kanchanaburi, the turquoise waters of **Huay Mae Khamin Waterfall's** nine tiers are best reached from Erawan. Only motocross bikes and 4WD vehicles can traverse the 42km dirt road that runs parallel to the reservoir and leads from Erawan (about 2hr.). Conditions vary with season: the first few kilometers of dirt track are a good indication of the roughness of the road. Service facilities are available along the way, though, so you won't run out of gas. A romantic alternative is to charter a boat (1-2hr., 10-person max., 1000-1500฿) from **Tha (Pier) Kraden,** 13km northeast of the Sri Nakharin Dam, 5km past Mongatet Village. The pier can be reached by a dirt road from Ban Kradan, but boat options may be limited. Continue the rough journey to

Sisawat if this is the case. The National Park at Huay Mae Khamin has **accommodations** ranging from camping (30B per person) to bungalows. *(Park open daily 8am-4:30pm. 200B, children 100B. Motorbikes 20B, cars 30B.)*

ALONG ROUTE 323: BAN KAO AREA

PRASAT MUANG SINGH HISTORICAL PARK. Muang Singh (City of the Lion) is an ancient city dating back to the 13th century. Once part of the Angkor Empire, it features Khmer design and artwork. The ruins sprawl across almost 74 hectares, surrounded by moats, city walls, and the Kwae Nai River. Still, most of the park consists of grass and trees, so the actual ruins can be seen in less than an hour. The most notable structure in the park is **Monument No. 1** (Prasat Muang Singh), which sits at the center of the city and towers above the rest of the park. An interesting exhibition hall near the park office has Buddhist sculptures found at the site. There is also an ancient burial site dating back 2000 years. The park makes for a worthwhile trip, especially for those interested in the Angkor Empire who are not able to go to Cambodia. There is a restaurant and guesthouse onsite. *(Located 43km northwest of Kanchanaburi. If driving, take Rte. 323, then turn off onto Rte. 3455; the turn is about 40km from Kanchanaburi. The park is a well-posted 7km drive southwest on Rte. 3455. Trains from Kanchanaburi (1hr., 3 daily in each direction. 5:57am-4:19pm, 100B) come closer to the park than buses. Get off at Thakilen, and from the train station, walk 1km to the main road, then 1km to the right. Bus #8203 stops 7km from the park, but transportation for the final leg may be hard to find. Return buses are best caught before 4pm. ☎591 122. Open daily 8:30am-4:30pm. 40B. Motorbikes 20B, cars 30B.)*

WAT LUANGTA-MAHABUA FOUNDATION. This foundation runs a tiger conservation project and wild animal rescue park. The grounds of the *wat* contain Indo-Chinese tigers, a leopard, water buffalo, deer, gibbon monkeys, and all kinds of farm animals. The best time to visit is in the late afternoon, when the tigers are brought out of their cages for feeding. If you arrive in the morning, however, the monks will gladly bring the tigers out for photo-ops. The rigors are very tame, having been raised by the monks since birth. The monks will allow you to take photos with the gentle giants. *(Take Rte. 323, and turn off for the Prasat Muang Singh Historical Park. After 5km, a large billboard marks the next turn-off onto a 1.5km dirt road that leads to the wat's impressive green-gated entrance. Most travel agencies in Kanchanaburi organize transportation to the wat. 300B.)*

ALONG ROUTE 323: SAI YOK NATIONAL PARK

Sai Yok National Park is a 500 sq. km park that stretches for almost 70km alongside Rte. 323 and the Mae Nam Kwai River. The first attraction is the Sai Yok Noi Waterfall, 60km from Kanchanaburi; the last is the Hin Dat Hot Springs, 130km from Kanchanaburi. All of the sights, with the exception of Lawa, are easily accessible from Rte. 323. *(Public bus #8203 to Sangkhlaburi leaves Kanchanaburi every 30min. 6am-6:30pm, and returns at similar intervals, 50-100B. Open daily 6am-6pm. 200B, children 100B. Motorbikes 20B, cars 30B.)*

SAI YOK NOI WATERFALL. The *Noi* ("little") Sai Yok Falls are decent, though they are accompanied by food stalls and concrete paths, and are devoid of any real hiking trails. Tours stop here for quick photographs, which is about enough. *(60km from Kanchanaburi. Bus #8203 to Sai Yok Noi. 1hr.; every 30min. 6am-6:30pm, last return 5pm; 35B. Free.)*

LAWA CAVE. This electrically-lit 200m cavern is the region's largest. Unfortunately, the cave is not accessible by public transportation. Hire a longtail boat (45min., 10-person max., one-way 800B; landing is 350m from caves) from Pak Saeng Pier, 2km southwest of Sai Yok Noi. Boats can continue up the river to Sai Yok Yai Waterfall and National Park. Alternatively, complete the 30min. trip on motorbike. After crossing the bridge next to Pak Saeng Pier, turn right past the 3km marker and follow the partially sealed road to the caves. (*75km from Kanchanaburi. Open daily 6am-6pm. National Park entrance fee 200฿, children 100฿.*)

SAI YOK YAI WATERFALL AND NATIONAL PARK ENTRANCE. Celebrated in poetry and song, the Sai Yok Yai Waterfall gushes impressively from July-Sept. One of the world's smallest mammal species, Kitti's Hog-Nosed Bats (p. 54), live in the park's Bat Cave, 2km from the visitors center and accessible by trails. You can get maps and leave gear at the visitors center (3km off Rte. 323). Accommodations include **camping** (30฿) and **rooms** over the river (2-12 people, 500-1000฿). Food vendors set up by the parking lot. (*104km from Kanchanaburi. Bus #8203 runs to Sai Yok Noi; 2hr.; every 30min. 6am-6:30pm, last return 4:30pm; 48฿. Open daily 6am-6pm. 200฿, children 100฿. Motorbikes 20฿, cars 30฿.*)

◾ALONG ROUTE 323: HELLFIRE PASS

In their quest to complete the Thai-Myanmar railway, the Japanese Imperial Army would not let a mere mountain stand in their way. Thousands of oppressed laborers worked for months manually chipping away rock under grueling conditions to create the **Hellfire Pass** (aka Konyu Cutting) so named for the ghostly campfire shadows that would dance on the mountain walls at night. Today, the pass leads down the former railway, creating a stunning 4km circuit. The excellent ◾**Hellfire Pass Memorial Museum** exhibits pictures,

Kanchanaburi to Sangkhlaburi

TO THREE PAGODA PASS (15km)

MYANMAR

Wat Wang Wiwekaram
Sangkhlaburi

Khao Laem Lake

0 ___ 10 miles
0 ___ 10 kilometers

Da Chong Thong Waterfall

Thong Pha Phum
323

Khao Laem Dam

Kwai Noi River

Hin Dat Hot Springs

Huay Mae Khamin Waterfall

Daowadum Cave

SRI NAKHARIN NATIONAL PARK

Sai Yok Yai Waterfall

SAI YOK NATIONAL PARK

323

Sri Nakharin Lake

Sisawat

Lawa Cave

Hellfire Pass

Tha Kraden
Ban Kradan

Sai Yok Noi Waterfall

Phrathat Cave

ERAWAN NATIONAL PARK

Erawan Waterfall

Pak Saeng Pier

Namtok Station

3457

Sai Yok

PRASAT MUANG SINGH HISTORIC PARK

Tha Kilen Station

Kwai Noi River

Kwai Yai River

323   3199

3086

3299

3342

3228

Kwai River Bridge
Kanchanaburi

324

Tha Muang
346

323

3209

Tha Maka

articles, and personal stories of the POWs whose lives were sacrificed in its construction. The 7min. archival video presentation about the pass's construction is especially compelling. Hellfire Pass is a 15min. walk from the museum. (*Between Sai Yok Noi and Sai Yok Yai. Take bus #8203 from Kanchanaburi, and tell the attendant where you want to get off; 1hr.; every 30min. 6am-6:30pm, last return bus at about 4:45pm; 54฿. Open daily 9am-4pm. Free audio guide. No admission but suggested museum donation.*)

SANGKHLABURI ☎ 034

Sangkhlaburi's remote location, high in the mountains near the Thailand-Myanmar border, offers visitors the chance to experience rugged natural beauty alongside friendly, welcoming local culture. The border is a strong influence throughout the town: the Karen and Mon hill tribes have a large presence here, and volunteer opportunities among the local Burmese refugee populations attract a number of foreigners. Most visitors from Bangkok, though, make the day-long journey to Sangkhlaburi for the terrific trekking opportunities in the surrounding mountains and national parks. Those interested in a border crossing are advised to plan ahead, as on-and-off strife results in frequent and unpredictable border closures.

▐ TRANSPORTATION

Public transportation from Sangkhlaburi only runs to Kanchanaburi, sometimes with a transfer in Thong Pha Phum; ask before you depart. There are two **bus** stations both located on the main road north of the market. The main station sits next to the post office west of the main market road, red local buses leave from here (4-5hr., 4 per day 6:45am-1:15pm, 100-150฿). The second station located at the east end of the main market road, has **A/C buses** and **A/C vans** (3-4hr., 8 per day 6:30am-3:30pm, 140-200฿). Bus travel times and frequency between Sangkhlaburi and Kanchanaburi can be very unpredictable, as the stretch of road between Sangkhlaburi and Thong Pha Phum is notorious for slow uphill progress and causes frequent engine trouble. Ask about schedules in either bus station the day before you leave. Transportation also runs to the Three Pagoda Pass by **songthaew** (30min., every 40min. 6am-6pm, 30-35฿) that depart across the street from the post office. **Motorcycle taxis** congregate near the main local bus station, ready to take visitors to guesthouses (10-20฿) or Wat Wang Wiwekaram (50฿). Because Sangkhlaburi is not especially touristed, foreigners are generally not overcharged.

✸ ▐ ORIENTATION AND PRACTICAL INFORMATION

An indoor-outdoor market bustles at the town's center and is open all day and night. The main market road, with a bus station at either end and the JA Internet Cafe in the middle, is directly on the market's north side. Most buses will let you off in the middle of this road. The bank is on the south side of the market, the post office on the west, and the entire area is dotted with convenience stores. To reach the guesthouses, go west on the main market road (toward the buses' parking area) and turn left toward the post office. Once on this road, follow the signs for any of the guesthouses. In order, you'll pass the Burmese Inn, Birdland, and finally the P. Guest House. To get to the wooden bridge from the town center, walk down the road toward the guesthouses, turn right at the first paved intersection and follow the sign for the Burmese Inn. Once past the Inn, you can't miss the bridge.

Other services include: **Siam Commercial Bank** (opposite the market, and the last opportunity to get cash before crossing the border into Myanmar) which has currency exchange and an **ATM**—if it is out of order, go inside and the bank will manually withdraw cash for you (☎034 595 263; open M-F

8:30am-3:30pm); the **police station,** in the small park opposite the east side of the market (☎595 300; open 24hr.; very little English spoken), **the hospital,** located two blocks southwest of the market (☎034 595 058; open 24hr.); and **Internet access** at **JA Computer,** on the market's north side (25฿ per hr.; open daily 9am-8pm). **Bicycles** (70฿ per day) and motorbikes (200฿ per day) can be rented at the P. Guest House (see p. 182). The **post office,** 25m south of the regular bus stop (☎034 595 115; open M-F 8:30am-4:30pm, Sa 9am-noon), has an **international telephone** booth outside. **Postal Code:** 71240.

ACCOMMODATIONS

The Burmese Inn, 52/3 Tambon Nong Loo (☎/fax 034 595 556; www.sangkhlaburi. com), 800m from the bus station. Follow the road that leads to the guesthouses and take a right at the first paved intersection. A motorcycle taxi will take you to the guesthouse from the center of town (10฿). Highlights a stunning view of the bridge from its open-air restaurant, and wonderfully knowledgeable owners Armin and Meo, arrange a plethora of treks. The bungalow-style rooms, all with mosquito nets, are set on a hillside overlooking the bridge. Motorbike rental 200฿ per day. Singles with fan 100฿, with cold water bath 200฿; doubles with fan, warm water bath, and TV 500฿, with A/C 800฿. ❶

P. Guest House, 81/2 Tumbon Nong Loo (☎034 595 061; www.pguesthouse.com), 300m beyond the turn-off to the Burmese Inn. The large, immaculate rooms boast inlaid-stone walls, tiled bathrooms, and views of the lake. This is the only place in town that schedules elephant rides: a 1-day expedition, including a room for the night, is 900฿. Kayaks 150฿ per hr., 600฿ per day; motorbikes 200฿ per day; bicycles 70฿ per day. Rooms with shared bath 200฿; with A/C, private bath, and TV 900฿. ❷

Birdland, past the Burmese Inn, with yellow signs, on the left side of the road, is run by a jovial expat named Jimmy, who has created a little oasis of relaxation. He offers four very basic rooms with baths and hot water, and runs a well-stocked Western bar. His collection of 200 DVDs are fantastic. Internet 1฿ per hr. Singles 150฿, doubles 200฿. ❶

FOOD

Burmese Inn, 52/3 Tambon Nong Loo (☎034 595 556). The Inn's restaurant offers a consistently delicious mix of Thai and Burmese selections served in an attractive open-air seating area. Try the Ono Khao Swe, a traditional Burmese noodle dish with curry sauce, fried egg, fried tofu, and chicken (90฿). Entrees 70-100฿. Soups 70-150฿. Open daily 7:30am-9pm. ❷

Restaurant (unnamed). For a lunch that strikes a balance between food stalls and sit-down, walk 150m past the post office and look for the thatched roof cottage to your right, just off the road. There is no sign and no menu, but if you know the name of a Thai dish, the cook will make it for you. *Pad thai* 30฿. ❷

Baan Unrak Bakery and Vegetarian Restaurant (☎034 595 428), 300m past the Burmese Inn on the left. Proceeds from dishes like stir-fried tofu with potato and cashews (65฿) and chocolate cake (10฿) go toward the Baan Unrak Children's Home. Open daily 7am-8pm. ❷

SIGHTS

Many visitors find more to do in the region surrounding Sangkhlaburi than in the town itself. The longest **wooden bridge** in Thailand, the 400m bridge of the Reverend Auttamo, crosses the massive Lake Khao Laem and connects the city of Sangkhlaburi to the Mon Village. The villagers built this bridge in 1984 after the dam project that created Lake Khao Laem cut them off from the town. The bridge collapsed in 1993, was promptly rebuilt, and has recently been restored. The **Mon Village** itself, not just a tourist attraction but a functioning town, offers travelers a taste of Burmese culture: vendors sell Mon curries in addition to the same range of wooden handicrafts, jade, and fabrics available at the nearby border markets, and villagers wear sarongs and face chalk typical of Myanmar. Although they do not possess Thai citizenship, the Mon people are not quite refugees, as they live under the protection of the Thai government. The elderly, revered spirit Luang Phaw Utama is believed to watch over them, and attracts Chinese and Thai visitors with offerings in tribute to his supposed healing powers. To get to his temple, **Wat Wang Wiwekaram,** also known as Wat Mon, walk uphill from the bridge to until you reach a T intersection. Turn left, follow the winding road, and take a left at the next stop sign. The red-and-gold Wat Wang Wiwekaram sits at the end of the road opposite a handicrafts market, 4km from Sangkhlaburi (30min. walk from wooden bridge; suggested donation 20฿). The wooden bridge is open only to pedestrian traffic, so if traveling by motorbike, head to the highway, turn left, and follow the road over the commuter bridge. At the police box turn left (right heads to Huay Malai village) and take another left in 2.5km at the stop sign. Each year during the first week of March, the wat hosts a spectacular five-day festival in honor of Utama's birthday. It features traditional dance performances, fireworks, and a night market.

During the dry season from November to May, locals swim and raft at **Ban Songkaria,** a river 10km from town. Take a songthaew (20฿) toward Three Pagoda Pass and tell the driver where you want to get off. If driving, stop at the first and only bridge on the way to the Pass. There are food stalls and inner tube rentals on site.

The Burmese Inn books 1hr. **boat trips** on scenic Lake Khao Laem that survey the wooden bridge, the top of the submerged **Old Sangkhlaburi Temple,** and the cliffs at the lake's southern end (1-3 people 400฿, 4-5 people 500฿, large groups 100฿ per person). The Burmese Inn and the P. Guest House also arrange multiple-day trekking trips to **Thung Yai Sanctuary Park** and nearby hill-tribe villages.

▶ DAYTRIPS FROM SANGKHLABURI

Venturing a few kilometers away from Sangkhlaburi, while somewhat of a transportation challenge, is well worth it, yielding a combination of natural beauty, history, and culture

THREE PAGODA PASS. Three Pagoda Pass has been a point of strategic importance on Thailand-Myanmar trade routes for hundreds of years. The Death Railway crossed into Myanmar at this point during World War II. After the war, the railway was dismantled, but strife continued: control of the profitable border crossing flip-flopped between the Karen and Mon liberation armies, both resisting the Myanmar government. Heavy fighting between the Karen and the Mon broke out in the late 1980s. The Myanmar regime took advantage of the strife to seize control of the pass in 1989, and has maintained control ever since. Although the three squat pagodas are unremarkable and not worth the trip on their own, both sides of the border feature markets that offer high-quality teak products, jade, and fabrics at some of the best prices in the region. Daytrips into Phayathonzu are possible, but travelers are not permitted to go more than 1km into Myanmar. Check for reports of border skirmishes before you go, as the area occasionally undergoes periods of instability. The best way to visit Three Pagoda Pass is to combine browsing in the market with a short hike to the nearby Sawan Badan temple and cave. The turnoff, a dirt road on the right, is located 4km before the border. If traveling by songthaew, you can either get off at the border and walk the 3km back, or disembark directly at the turnoff and skip the Pass altogether. Once on the dirt road, follow it for 700m and turn right at the sign marked with flags. A 0.5km walk through a grove of rubber trees will bring you to the temple. The cave is located inside the complex and is closed during the wet season. Bring your own flashlight and enter at your own risk. To get back to town, walk back to the main road and flag down a passing songthaew or motorcycle taxi. *(To reach the pass, follow the highway toward Kanchanaburi for about 4km, passing several immense Buddha statues, then take the left turn-off for the Chedi Sam Ong border gate. This road leads all the way to Three Pagoda Pass. Songthaew travel the 22km stretch from Sangkhlaburi to Three Pagoda Pass from 6am to 6pm (30min., 30-35฿), departing from Sanghklaburi beside the post office. Border open daily 6am-6pm, depending on current political situation.)*

THUNG YAI SANCTUARY PARK. Due to poaching, the elephants, tigers, tapirs, bears, gibbons, and peacocks that inhabit Thung Yai Sanctuary Park, Thailand's largest conservation area, have retreated deep into the forest. Many visitors make the trip into the park to see the Karen villages within its borders, which are easier to find than the animals. Most areas are accessible only by 4WD vehicles, even during the dry season. **Takian Thong Waterfall** in Thung Yai Sanctuary Park is an exception, with fully paved road access. The waterfalls, more accurately described as a river cascade, are a 20min. walk from the park office through dense jungle. Sign in at the park office before beginning the trip. In the rainy season, reaching the falls is often difficult and sometimes impossible. In the dry season, a 30min. walk upriver from the falls leads to bigger ponds for swimming. Ask at the Burmese Inn or the P. Guest House (see **Accommodations**, p. 185) about accessibility, road conditions, and possible jeep rental to other parts of the sanctuary. *(The well-marked turn-off to Thung Yai Sanctuary Park and Takian Thong Waterfall is 18km from Sangkhlaburi along the road to Three Pagoda Pass. This road leads 9km to the park's forestry office. Entrance 200฿. Park open daily 8am-6pm.)*

PHETCHABURI ☎ 032

Few tourists make it to Phetchaburi, commonly known as Phetburi. This prosperous provincial town, bearing a strong Chinese cultural influence, is only a short bus ride south of Bangkok. The town is sprinkled with historic *wats*, a former royal palace, Khao Wang, as well as nearby stalactite and stalagmite-filled caves, and is known throughout Thailand for its delicious desserts. Those with an eye for culture, a taste for sweets, and a yearning to escape fellow *farang* will find Phetchaburi a rewarding place to explore.

▐ TRANSPORTATION

Trains: Phetchaburi Train Station (☎032 425 211), on the northern edge of town, a 15min. walk from the center. To get to town after traveling by train, head left out of the station and, after 1km, take a right at the second big intersection onto Damnernkasem Rd.; continue straight for 100m, and the night market will be on your left. To: **Bangkok** (3-4hr., 3pm, 34฿), **Hua Hin** (1hr.; 10:40am, noon, 4:00, 4:45pm; 13-33฿, depending on train), and other destinations in the south. Buses are more convenient but less scenic.

Buses: There are 4 bus stations in town. A/C buses from **Bangkok** arrive at the intersection of Damnernkasem and Rodfai Rd., southeast of the train station. The biggest station for outgoing buses is on Phetkasem Hwy., about 300m south of the entrance to the Khao Wang cable car; to **Bangkok** (3hr., every hr., 90-120฿) and **Hua Hin** (1hr., frequent, 40-60฿). Orange (non-A/C) buses depart frequently from Photaram Rd., around the corner from Wat Kamphaeng Laeng, to **Cha Am** (50 min., 40฿) and **Hua Hin** (1hr., 50฿).

Local Transportation: The whole city can be traversed on foot. However, it is more conveniently seen by **bike**. Hotel Chom Khao (80฿ per day) and Rabieng Rimnum Guest House (120฿ per day) both rent bikes. For longer distances, **samlor** and **songthaew**

are good options. Hard bargaining will be rewarded: no trip within the town should cost more than 40฿, outside of the town, 60฿.

⚒ 🛈 ORIENTATION AND PRACTICAL INFORMATION

Phetchaburi is best navigated by using the murky brown waters of the **Phetchaburi River** as a point of reference. The river runs south to north, bisecting the city. **Damnernkasem Road** runs parallel to the river on the western bank and intersects at its north end with **Rodfai Road,** which leads west, away from the river, to the hospital and train station. Heading south from Rodfai Rd., Damnernkasem first intersects **Ratchavidhi Road,** which also leads west away from the river to Khao Wang. It next intersects **Cheesain Road,** which leads eastward to several hotels, *wats,* and the **Chomrut Bridge** across the **Phetchaburi River.** Cheesain Rd. becomes **Phongsuriya Road** on the eastern bank of the river. Another main road, which runs parallel to the river on the eastern bank, is called **Phanitcharern Road** south of Phongsuriya Rd. and **Thaywes Road** north of Phongsuriya Rd. In addition to the river itself, **Khao Wang,** the **white prang** of Wat Mahathat, and the **clock tower** at the southern end of Surinruechai Rd. are all useful landmarks.

Tourist Office: (☎032 402 220), at the corner of Ratchavidhi and Phetkasem Rd. Small tourist booth staffed by one woman who speaks decent English. Provides free maps. Open daily 8:30am-4:30pm.

Currency Exchange: Siam Commercial Bank, 2 Damnernkasem Rd. (☎032 425 303). Halfway between the bridge and the Ratchavidhi Rd. intersection. **24hr. ATM.** Open M-F 8:30am-3:30pm. There are other **24hr. ATMs** sprinkled along Damnemkasem Rd. and Phanitcharem Rd.

Police: Phetchaburi Police Station (☎032 425 500), 3 Ratchavidhi Rd., opposite the GPO. Very little English spoken.

Medical Services: Phrachomklao Hospital (☎032 401 2517), 150m north of the train station on the left. Open 24hr. Some English spoken. Cash only. Farther out is the **Petcharat Hospital** (☎032 417 029), on Phetchkasem Hwy. north of town, close to the Khao Wong cable car stop. 24hr. emergency care. Cash only.

Telephones: International pay phones are located in front of all 7-Elevens, including the one on Damnernkasem Rd. across from Wat Mahathat Worarihara. **TOT** phonecards can be purchased in all 7-Elevens.

Internet Access: Playnet8, on Cheesain Rd., near the intersection of Cheesain Rd. and Damnernkasem Rd. Comfortable leather chairs, A/C, and a fast Internet connection. A popular hangout for schoolboys playing computer games. 20฿ per hr. Open daily 9am-10pm.

Post Office: GPO 4 Ratchavidhi Rd. (☎032 425 571), at the intersection of Ratchavidhi Rd. and Damnernkasem Rd. Poste Restante. Open M-F 8:30am-4:30pm, Sa-Su 9am-noon. **Postal Code:** 76000.

⌂ ACCOMMODATIONS

The accommodation situation in Phetchaburi is grim: most places are unclean, unfriendly, or both. Budget guesthouses along the river are friendlier and convenient, but often have low standards of cleanliness; the few mid-range hotels that cluster near the highway are cleaner, but less personal and convenient.

Chom Khao Hotel, 1 Thaywes Rd. (☎032 425 398), opposite corner from the Rabieng Rimnum Guesthouse across the river. When crossing the Chomrut Bridge from the eastern bank, Chom Khao Hotel is the 4-story building on your left with the blue windows.

CENTRAL THAILAND

Offering large rooms with private bath, fan, cold water showers, and somewhat dodgy pillow covers and blankets. Singles 170฿, doubles 250฿. ❷

Petchkasem Hotel, 86/4 Phetkasem Hwy. (☎032 425 581), behind Khao Wang, at the foot of the Phetkasem highway interchange (20min. walk from the town center). English sign visible only from highway direction. *Samlor* should cost 30-40฿ from the town center. The best option for those interested in Khao Wang, the Banda-It caves, or higher standards of cleanliness. Large, clean rooms with private bath, hot water, and Western toilets. Rear rooms escape highway noise. Singles 200฿, with A/C 350฿; doubles 300/450฿. ❷

Rabieng Rimnum Guest House, 1 Cheesain Rd. (☎032 425 707), at the foot of the Chomrut Bridge, on the west bank. The willfully optimistic could see the rooms at Rabieng as having a certain cobwebby-garret charm. Sagging standards of cleanliness, however, are apparent, and loud noises floating up from the street add to this stark guesthouse's peculiar charm. The shared bathrooms leave much to be desired. The laid-back adjoining restaurant is the best thing about the place. Singles 120฿, doubles 200฿. ❷

🍴 FOOD

Phetchaburi is a far better place for eating than for sleeping. The city is known throughout Thailand for its scrumptious Chinese-influenced desserts, most famously *khanom mor gaeng*, a delicate egg custard perfected in Phetchaburi. A number of good **dessert stalls** line Phetkasam Soi Kao Rd. at the base of Khao Wang, near its intersection with Phetkasame Rd. But guard your sweets carefully: this is monkey territory. Both the **night market** (at the corner of Damnernkasem and Ratchavidhi Rd.) and the **day market** (along Surinruechai and Matayawong Rd., south of Phongsuriya Rd.) are excellent introductions to local cuisine. The night market offers the usual range of Thai dishes as well as Chinese items and local desserts. There also are many **noodle stalls** along Damnernkasem Rd., which cook up inexpensive and delicious meals.

Mae Ubon, on the east side of Phanitcharern Rd., 50m south of Suraphon Rd.; no English sign. The best of the town's dessert shops stands out in flavor and in ability to keep bees away. *Khanom mor gaeng* (25฿) is displayed proudly in a case at the front. Open daily 8am-10pm. ❶

Rabieng Rimnum Restaurant, at the Rabieng Rimnum Guest House. The most *farang*-friendly restaurant in town. Frank Sinatra and other classics play in the background as diners looks out onto the river. The owners speak decent English and are very helpful. Affordable Thai dishes (35-85฿) and dozens of varieties of *yum* (spicy salads). If you're feeling adventurous, try one of the several serpent's head dishes. ❷

👁 SIGHTS

With the exception of the Banda-It and Khao Luang caves, all sights are within walking distance of one another, though bicycling is not a bad idea.

PHRA NAKHON KHIRI HISTORICAL PARK AND NATIONAL MUSEUM (KHAO WANG). In the 1850s, King Rama IV, tired of the heat and exhaustion of central Thailand, looked south to build a new royal retreat. His search ended on the hilltops overlooking Phetchaburi, where in 1858 he built **Phra Nakhon Khiri.** A unique mixture of Chinese and Western architecture, the park spreads across the hill's three peaks. While none of the sights are individually spectacular, the fragrant hillside paths and terraces offer nice views, and the experience of wandering among the palace's sights is greater than the sum of its parts. The westernmost peak houses a collection of halls and pavilions that form the **royal residence.** The palace's original furnishings are still on display here.

Phra That Chom Phet, a 49m-tall *chedi*, sits on the middle peak. On the eastern peak is **Wat Phra Kaew,** which Rama IV ordered to be constructed in the same style as the Temple of the Emerald Buddha in Bangkok's Grand Palace (p. 110). In early February, the town celebrates the **Phra Nakhon Khiri Fair (Festivals, p. 72),** which features local art shows, cultural performances, and cart races. Many visitors have complained about the especially aggressive behavior of Khao Wang's monkeys. In order to avoid monkey harassment, don't bring any snacks or sweets with you up the mountain. *(Accessible by a cable car that runs up to the royal residence, or the steep but short footpath from the end of Ratchavidhi Rd.; entrance to cable car is located on an access road just east of Phetkasem Hwy. To reach the cable car, take a samlor (30-40฿) from the town center. Cable car runs 8:30am-4:30pm; 70฿, children 10฿. Cable*

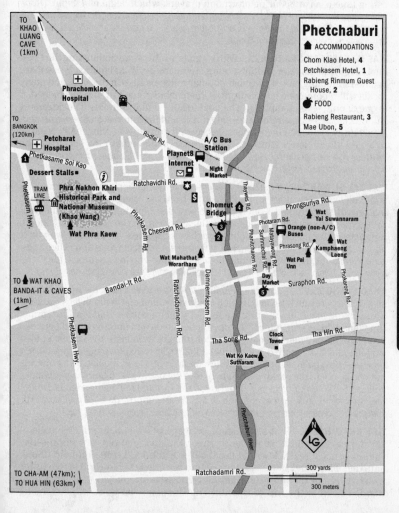

Phetchaburi

⌂ ACCOMMODATIONS

Chom Klao Hotel, **4**
Petchkasem Hotel, **1**
Rabieng Rinmum Guest House, **2**

🍴 FOOD

Rabieng Restaurant, **3**
Mae Ubon, **5**

TO KHAO LUANG CAVE (1km)

Phrachomklao Hospital

TO BANGKOK (120km)

Petcharat Hospital

Phetkasame Soi Kao

Dessert Stalls

Phra Nakhon Khiri Historical Park and National Museum (Khao Wang)

TRAM LINE

Wat Phra Kaew

Rodai Rd.

A/C Bus Station

Playnet8 Internet

Ratchavidhi Rd.

Night Market

Chomrut Bridge

Phetkasem Rd.

Cheesain Rd.

Wat Mahathat Worarihara

TO WAT KHAO BANDA-IT & CAVES (1km)

Bandai-It Rd.

Ratchadamnem Rd.

Dammenkasem Rd.

Phetkasem Hwy.

Thawes Rd.

Phongsuriya Rd.

Photaram Rd.

Wat Yai Suwannaram

Orange (non-A/C) Buses

Phrasong Rd.

Wat Kamphaeng Laeng

Malaywong Rd.

Surinuechai Rd.

Phanichcharon Rd.

Wat Pai Unn

Day Market

Suraphon Rd.

Phokarong Rd.

Tha Song Rd.

Clock Tower

Tha Hin Rd.

Wat Ko Kaew Sutharam

Phetchaburi River

TO CHA-AM (47km);
TO HUA HIN (63km)

Ratchadamri Rd.

300 yards

300 meters

CENTRAL THAILAND

car ticket includes cost of admission to the museum. ☎ *032 428 539. Museum open daily 9am-4pm. Museum admission 40฿. Park open M-Sa 8:15am-4:30pm.)*

WAT KAMPHAENG LAENG. These five impressive laterite-block structures hold Buddha images that were originally part of a 12th-century Khmer Hindu shrine. It is likely that Phetchaburi was once the southernmost outpost of the Khmer empire. Each of the five *prangs* is thought to have been dedicated to one of the five major Hindu deities. In the Ayutthaya period, the temple was reconsecrated to Buddhism, and images of Buddha replaced the Hindu sculptures within two *prangs*. The lavish main shrine contrasts sharply with the older surrounding buildings, reflecting Kamphaeng Laeng's status as the residence of Phra Khruu Yanwitmon, Phetchaburi's most revered monk. Tables and chairs scattered throughout the grounds make an excellent spot for a picnic. An interesting time to visit is during afternoon prayers, which begin at 4:45pm. *(Follow Phongsuriya Rd. east past Wat Yai Suwannaram and turn right on Phokarong Rd. The wat will be on the right after 500m. If the front gate is locked, turn right on the road just after the wat, and enter at the gate on the right. Open 6am-6pm.)*

WAT MAHATHAT WORARIHARA. With its giant white *prang* dominating the Phetchaburi skyline and the Buddhist relics stored inside, Wat Mahathat Worarihara is understandably one of the most popular religious sites in the area, and many locals will recommend it to visitors as Phetchaburi's can't-miss sight. Indeed, it is one of only seven temples in Thailand to have Buddhist relics. The dozens of Buddha images surrounding the main *prang* and the stuccos on the *prang* pedestals draw crowds. The *bot* contains several gorgeous carvings. Ask a monk to access the cloisters (through a small door on the right of the *bot*) to see its endless rows of peaceful Buddhas. *(On Damnernkasem Rd., 1 block south of its intersection with the Chomrut bridge. Open 6am-6pm.)*

WAT YAI SUWANNARAM. This 17th-century religious compound features outstanding examples of art and architecture from the Ayutthaya period. Try asking one of the monks to open the two wooden buildings that contain well-preserved 18th-century murals of mythical angels. In the center of the pond, a monastic library on stilts holds Buddhist scriptures. The library was built above the water to keep the sacred scriptures away from ants and other bugs. Also check out the *bot* surrounded by Buddhas in varying positions. *(On Phongsuriya Rd., a 10min. walk east from Chomrut Bridge away from Khao Wang. Open 6am-6pm.)*

KHAO LUANG CAVE. There are actually two caves: **Khao Luang,** the more impressive of the two, and **Khao Jung,** which is above ground and is much less exciting. Khao Luang has four caverns, the first of which features Buddha's footprints (on your right as you enter). The cave is best seen and photographed between 11am and 2pm, when dramatic shafts of sunlight illuminate the largest golden Buddha and the red-tiled floor. Bring a flashlight to explore the cave's darker recesses, but the most detailed statues are in front. Good English tours operate out of a booth in the parking lot right before the pathways to both caves. Guides will ask for 200฿ per cave as a donation to the *wat* and for their services. Do not feel pressured: give however much or little feel is appropriate. *(20min. bicycle ride from the town center. Motorcycle taxi from town center 50-60฿, round-trip 100-120฿.)*

WAT KHAO BANTA-IT. A set of steps between two elephant statues leads to several caves, which, in terms of sheer Buddha quantity, are impressive. Unless you are really brave, a flashlight is a good aid, and will help illuminate the "Thousand Buddhas" tucked into the crevices. You will arrive (after walking about 60 steps, and battling agressive monkeys) to a large gold Buddha head at the top of the hill. The Buddha head is, as of 2008, being renovated, but the view from the top is quite nice. *(3km from town. Take Bandai-It Rd. west, away from the river, past Khao Wang. The entrance is 100m. past the intersection with Phetkasem Hwy., on the right side of the road, at the group of 3 ornate shelters. No English sign. Go through the archway and up the short road. 20min. bicycle ride from the town center. Motorcycle taxis from town 50-60฿, samlor 60-80฿. Open daily 9am-4pm.)*

▶ DAYTRIP FROM PHETCHABURI

KAENG KRACHAN NATIONAL PARK

60km from Phetchaburi and best reached with your own car. No direct public transport goes to the park from town, but you can take a songthaew from the clock tower at the center of town to Ban Kaeng Krachan village (50฿, 1½hr., 6am-6pm), 4km from the park, and catch a motorcycle taxi from there (30-40฿). Rabieng Rimnum Guesthouse runs 1- and 2-day excursions to Kaeng Krachan for 800-1500฿ per person per day, depending on how many people go and for how long. 4-person bungalows 1500฿, tents 30฿ to pitch your own, 280฿ to rent. You should arrive at the park by 9:30am, as the road leading from the park entrance to the waterfalls becomes one-way in the wrong direction at 10am.

Home to the stunning Pala-U waterfalls, Thailand's largest national park envelops 3000 sq. km of rain forest in the western half of Phetchaburi Province. Its terrain ranges over lush forests, grasslands, caves, and cliffs; tigers, dusky langurs, and gibbons, among many other species of flora and fauna, call it home. Since its opening in 1981, four white elephants, considered symbols of royal prestige and good fortune, have been captured here and presented to the king. The **Phetchaburi** and **Phanburi Rivers** entice rafters, and park rangers occasionally lead hikes. Inquire at the **visitor station** near the park entrance. Spending the night at **Kaeng Krachan Lake**, near park headquarters, is pricey unless you camp. There are two additional **campsites** 30 and 40km to the west, closer to Pala-U waterfalls. However, a drive is still necessary to get to them. Renting a bus to get to these sites costs 1500฿, but you can team up with others to split the cost. Kaeng Krachan Park is not easy to reach or explore, but is worth the effort.

CHA AM ☎ 032

Only a few hours south of Bangkok, Cha Am is primarily a weekend beach destination for Thais. However, foreigners, especially European expats, have also discovered the charms of Cha Am's mile-long whitesand beaches and inexpensive fresh seafood, and middle-aged Norwegians, Germans, and Danes have a particularly visible high-season presence. With flamboyantly painted tour buses from Bangkok driving into town, spirit houses tucked into the trees that line the beach, and Thai rock bands performing at night, Cha Am has a more authentic atmosphere than many of the beaches farther south. Come Monday, though, you and the stray dogs will likely have the beach all to yourselves.

▶ TRANSPORTATION

The Cha Am Train Station, at the west end of Narathip Rd. 2km from the beach, has trains to **Bangkok** (3hr.; 2:30, 3:20, 7:05, 11:50am, and 2:25pm; 40-90฿) and **Chumphon** (4hr.; 2 per day 12:35, 7:43pm; 53฿). The best place to catch a bus out of town is on Phetkasem Hwy., just south of Narathip Rd., in front of the 7-Eleven, where there's a small sign that says "bus stop." Regular and A/C buses stop here on the way to **Hua Hin** (30min., every 20min., 25฿) and **Bangkok** (3hr., every 20-45min., 171฿). To get to **Phetchaburi,** take a Bangkok-bound bus (40min., 40-50฿). A/C buses for Hua Hin and Bangkok also leave from the station on Soi 1 of Chaolai Rd., one short block south of the intersection of Chaolai and

Narathip Rd. Note that only buses whose origin or terminus is Cha Am stop here, so the frequency of service is relatively low. For example, only 3 buses a day go from Cha Am to Bangkok.

Motorcycle taxis will take you from the town center to any destination in the city for 20-30฿. A surplus of outfits along Ruamchit Rd., almost one per block, rent **bicycles,** many sporting a Hello Kitty theme (20฿ per hr.), and motorbikes (100฿ per hr.). Motorbike rental requires a passport deposit.

ORIENTATION AND PRACTICAL INFORMATION

Ruamchit Road, home to most of the hotels and restaurants in town, runs north-south adjacent to the beach; when you're going north, the beach is on your right. The area of Ruamchit Rd. that is most populated by tourists is **Long Beach,** which is about 1km north of **Narathip Road.** Running parallel to Ruamchit Rd, **Chao Lai Road** is a food and lodging center, particularly in the area south of Narathip Road. Narathip Rd. meets Ruamchit Rd. in the middle of Cha Am Beach and leads to **Phetkasem Highway** and the train station. For more information on the city, accommodations, and nearby sights see www.chaambeach.com.

Tourist Information: The regional **TAT** office (☎032 471 005), inconveniently located on the right side of Phetkasem Hwy., 1km. south of Narathip Rd. Open daily 8:30am-4:30pm. More convenient **travel agencies** all over Ruamchit Rd. will likely be able to answer any questions you might have.

Tourist police: In the small booth at the intersection of Narathip and Ruamchit Rd.; they offer free maps of the area. Some English spoken. Open 24hr.

Bank: Siam Commercial Bank, 244/10-11 Ruamchit Rd., just north of Narathip Rd., exchanges currency and has a **24hr. ATM.** Open M-F 8:30am-3:30pm. **Currency exchange** M-F 8:30am-7pm, Sa-Su 10am-7pm in high season; M-F 8:30am-3:30pm in low season. Other 24hr. ATMs are conveniently sprinkled around Ruamchit Rd.

Hospital: Cha Am Hospital (☎032 471 007), on Klongtien Rd., 1km. north of Narathip Rd., northwest of the beach. Some English spoken. 24hr. emergency service.

Telephones: International phones in front of each of the three 7-Elevens on Ruamchit Rd. Calling cards can be purchased at most 7-Elevens.

Internet Access: CV Net, 241/64 Ruamchit Rd., just south of Kaenchan Beach Resort. 40฿ per hr. Open daily 9am-midnight.

Post Office, on Ruamchit Rd. 400m north of Narathip Rd. Open M-F 8:30am-4:30pm, Sa 9am-noon. **Postal Code:** 76121.

ACCOMMODATIONS

Accommodations in Cha Am fall into two categories: mid-range hotels and exorbitant luxury resorts. Within each price range, establishments tend to cater either to Thai or to foreign tourists. On Ruamchit Rd., south of Narathip Rd., most hotels are primarily Thai; *farang* hotels and restaurants cluster farther north near Long Beach.

Manopun House, 222/1 Ruamchit Rd. (☎032 433 507), right before Soi 8 about 800m. north of Narathip Rd. No English sign, but there is a "Room for Rent" sign in front of what appears to be a restaurant. A worthwhile splurge. 400฿ will get you a spacious spic-and-span room fully furnished with a double bed, TV, private bath with warm shower, and private balcony overlooking the ocean. ❸

Prathanchok House, 244/31 Ruamchit Rd. (☎032 471 215), three blocks north of Narathip Rd. under the blue tile facade and the sign that reads "Fisher Pub." Offers the cheapest lodging in town. The shared 4th fl. balcony overflows with flowers and offers excellent sea views. Rooms are sufficiently clean, though small; shared baths have squat toilets. Fan rooms with shared bath 200฿, rooms with A/C and private bath 300-350฿. TV 50฿ extra. ❷

Sam Resort, 246/9 Ruamchit Rd. (☎032 471 197), just north of the post office, 450m north of Narathip Rd. Clean and small rooms with fan and private bath go for 300฿. For another 100฿, you get a bigger room with warm shower. ❸

🍴 FOOD

The best thing to eat in Cha Am is seafood, and the best place to eat it is by the sea, where beachside vendors sell fresh, cheap snack-sized portions (see **Cha Am Chow Down,** p. 191). Arrive at the fishing pier before 7am to watch the day's haul come in and have fish cooked to order for 20-60฿. The pier is located on the north end of town, past Wat Neranchama. Many of Cha Am's food falls into two price ranges: on the beach, vendors offer 35฿ skewers, while on the other side of Ruamchit Rd., restaurants charge 200-400฿ for seafood dishes. Either way, the food is likely to be fresh and delicious.

Kaenchen Beach Hotel Restaurant, 241/4 Ruamchit Rd. (☎032 471 314). A bit pricey, but delicious. The outdoor, lamplit setting is really romantic. Dishes 170-370฿. Fresh soba fish cooked in a banana leaf (160฿). Outdoor dining available from 6-10pm. ❹

Manopun House, 222/1 Ruamchit Rd. (☎032 433 507), also serves tasty Thai standards at reasonable prices. Dishes (30-120฿). Delicious curry with coconut milk (60฿). Open 8am-10pm. ❷

🏖 BEACHES

The mile-long stretch of sand that makes up **Hat Cha Am** (Cha Am Beach) is clean, white, and wide. During the week, when the town is deserted, you need only compete with dogs for control of the beach. On weekends, even in high season, the lovely stretch of beach north of the main strip, near Wat Neramchara, remains refreshingly uncrowded.

There are a number of ways to enjoy the surf and sand. Beach chairs (20฿ per hr.) line the sand. Just find one and sit, and its owner will come find you to collect the rental fee. Banana boats (500-600฿ per hr.) and ponies (200฿ per 30min.) are also available all over the shore.

If you've rented a bike or motorcycle and are wondering where to go, or are looking to take a nice stroll, head north to find traces of the fishing village that preceded the beach resort. At the northern end of Ruamchit Rd., **Wat Neramchara** is home to an unusually large, white, Chinese-style

ON THE MENU
A CHA AM CHOW DOWN

When I arrived at Cha Am beach, I saw just how different beachgoing habits can be: while Europeans were milking the tropical sun for all it was worth, most Thais sat fully dressed under the shade of umbrellas. This Thai propensity for shade reflected a significant cultural difference: as the proliferation of skin-whitening products at any Thai 7-Eleven attests, Thai culture associates pale skin with beauty and elite status. I too made a beeline to the shade, fully aware of my inability to tan. Here I saw that while the foreigners were baking, the Thais were eating. And the food looked great. Where did this food come from?

Before long, my question was answered: a teenager wove through the crowd with a tray of fried prawns and octopus, and I bought a portion for 35฿. Someone else appeared; for 15฿, I was soon munching on crisp watermelon. Minutes later, fish-shaped waffles made a perfect dessert for 20฿, and the bottled water vendor (5฿) took care of my thirst. From noon to nightfall, the best Thai restaurant in Cha Am, it turns out, is the beach itself. Small portions make it easy to sample a variety of flavors, and prices are far lower than at restaurants. To complete the experience, you can enjoy your many-course meal with a full view of the kite-flying, horse-back riding spectacle that is a weekend at Cha Am Beach.

Buddha statue. On the right approaching the *wat* the manicured grounds of the Monument of King Naresuan the Great make for a nice picnic spot.

HUA HIN   ☎032

Long before Phuket and Ko Samui were catapulted into stardom, Hua Hin ("Head Rock") catered to the Thai upper crust. Following the example of King Rama VI, wealthy Thai families vacationed on this long, clean stretch of sand where local fishermen once dried their squid hauls. Today, Europeans have joined in, and high-rise resorts tower above the waterfront. Paradoxically, Hua Hin is by day a family friendly resort town, while revealing a sprawling red-light district at night. It is also a hip city with a real affinity for jazz: every year in June, there is a huge jazz festival on the beach that attracts big name jazz musicians from around the world. Today, though the fishing village is gone, a few traces of the regal turn-of-the-century getaway remain amidst overpriced beachside pony rides and tourist t-shirt shops.

⌐ TRANSPORTATION

Flights: Hua Hin Airport (☎032 522 305; www.huahinairport.com) is out of commission until further notice.

Trains: Train Station (☎032 511 073), at the western end of Damnernkasem Rd., is a tourist attraction in and of itself: the elaborate cream-and-red building beside the station is the former royal waiting room. 10min. walk from town center. To: **Bangkok** (4hr., 12 per day, 94-382฿); **Chumphon** (4hr., 10 per day, 49฿); **Phetchaburi** (1hr., 9 per day, 30-43฿); **Surat Thani** (7hr., 11 per day, 184฿).

Buses: VIP Buses (☎032 511 654) to **Bangkok** leave from the 1st fl. of the Siripetchkasem Hotel on Srasong Rd., near Decharnuchit Rd. (3hr., every 40min. 3am-9pm, 210฿) via **Cha Am** (20min., 35฿). Southbound A/C buses and all others depart from the **regular bus station** (☎032 511 230), a dusty roundabout at the intersection of Liab Tang Rodfai Rd. and Chomsin Rd., about 500m north of the train station. To: **Bangkok** (4hr., every 20min., 180฿) via **Cha Am** (20min., 25฿); **Chumphon** (4hr., 12 per day, 190฿); **Phuket** (12hr., 6 per day 10am-11pm, 295-486฿); **Prachuap Khiri Khan** (1½hr., every hr. 6:30am-4pm, 60฿); **Surat Thani** (8hr.; 10am, 240฿; 11pm, 360฿).

Local Transportation: Samlor go round-trip to Khao Krailas and Khao Takieb (every 15min. 6am-7pm, 60-80฿). Green **songthaew** leave from the motorcycle shop at Decharnuchit and Srasong Rd. to Khao Takieb (every 30min. 6am-7pm, 20฿). **Tuk-tuks** and **motorcycle taxis** can be found on most street corners, particularly on Dechanuchit Rd. No trip within town should cost more than 40฿ by *tuk-tuk* or 30฿ by motorcycle. *Tuk-tuks* and motorcycle taxis may be aggressive; do not automatically believe them if they tell you the place you're walking to is far away. Most guesthouses rent bicycles for 50฿ per day, with 10% discounts for longer than 3-day rentals. Try out the bike before you rent it; not all bikes are created equal. A large number of guesthouses and travel agencies near Dechanuchit Rd. and Naresdanri Rd. rent motorbikes (200฿ per day, with passport deposit).

◼◼ ORIENTATION AND PRACTICAL INFORMATION

Hua Hin is small, walkable, and straightforward. **Petchkasem Highway** runs north-south through town. **Lieb Tang Rodfai Road** runs parallel to a set of train tracks. Both Lieb Tang Rodfai Rd. and the train tracks mark the western edge of the city, while Petchkasem Hwy. runs right through the center. **Damnernkasem Road** leads from the train station to the beach and forms the southern boundary of the town proper, although the beach and resort area extends far beyond to the south. To the north running parallel to each other are **Dechanuchit Road** and **Chomsin Road,** which lead from the beach to Petchkasem Hwy. Most hotels, restaurants, and bars cluster near Naresdamri Road, which intersects Damnernkasem Rd. close to the beach, passes by the Hilton to the northeast, and then curves to the west, running by the water up to the fishing pier. The tourist office, guesthouses, and many restaurants and bars hand out free maps.

Tourist Office: Tourist Information Service Center, 114 Petchkasem Hwy. (☎032 532 433), on the ground floor of the municipal building, at the intersection of Petchkasem Hwy. and Damnernkasem Rd. English spoken. Open M-F 8:30am-4:30pm, Sa-Su 9am-noon.

Currency Exchange: Banks, exchange booths, and **24hr. ATMs** line Naresdamri and Damnernkasem Rd., near the Hilton. Most exchange booths are open daily 11am-7pm. **Siam Commercial Bank,** 77/33 Petchkasem Hwy. (☎032 532 420), is around the corner from the post office on Petchkasem Hwy. Currency exchange window open daily 8:30am-3:30pm. Open M-F 8:30am-3:30pm.

Books: Megabooks (☎032 532 071), 166 Naresdamri Rd., opposite Sofitel Hotel. Open daily 8:30am-10pm.

Tourist Police: (☎032 516 219), 3/2 Damnerkasem Rd. in the little white building on the left side of Damnerkasem Rd. just before the beach. English spoken. Open 24hr.

Hua Hin

🛏 ACCOMMODATIONS
All Nations Guest House, **4**
Memory Guest House, **5**
Pattana Guest House, **3**
Mod Guesthouse, **7**

🍴 FOOD
Dream Cones, **2**
Ket Sa Rin Seafood, **6**
Kuay Tien Rua Nai Beer, **1**
World News Coffee, **8**

★ NIGHTLIFE
Hua Hin Brewery, **9**
Mon Thri Restaurant and
  Mai Tai Cocktails, **10**

TO KLAI KANG WON PALACE (100m);
TO HUA HIN AIRPORT (150m);
TO HUA HIN HOSPITAL (4km)
TO CHA-AM (26km);
TO PHETCHABURI (64km);
TO BANGKOK (224km)

Soi 68
Regular Bus Station
Chomsin Rd.
Naebkehardt Rd.
TO KAENG KRACHAN NATIONAL PARK (55km)
Chatchai Market
Petchkasem Hwy.
Leung Lom Soi
Naresdamri Rd.
Fishing Pier
Dechanuchit Rd.
Night Market
VIP Bus Station
Srasong Rd.
Clock Tower
Wat Hua Hin
Selakam Rd.
Khao Hin Lekfai Viewpoint
Liab Tang Rodtai Rd.
Amnuaysin Rd.
Sunshine Internet Cafe
Poolsuk Rd.
Hilton Hotel
Hua Hin Beach
Soi Bintaban
Thai Boxing Garden
Naresdamri Rd.
Kamnoadvitee Rd.
Petchkasem Hwy.
Soi 59
Soi Kanjanomai
Tourist Police
Railway Station
Damnernkasem Rd.
Srasong Rd.
Red Cross Station
Siam Commercial Bank
Megabooks
Sofitel Central Hotel
Gulf of Thailand
San Pau Lo Hospital
TO SUAN SAN BEACH, KHAO TAKIEB, AND KHAO KRAILAS (6km); TO ROI YOD NATIONAL PARK (40km)

N

0   50 yards
0   50 meters

Medical Services: San Pau Lo Hospital (☎032 532 576), on Phetkasem Hwy., 400m south of the Tourist Center. Credit cards accepted Am Ex/MC/V. Open 24hr. **Hua Hin Hospital** (☎032 520 371), 4km north of town on Phetkasem Hwy. Open 24hr. A **Red Cross station,** 25 Damnernkasem Rd., next door to the municipal building, provides basic services 8:30am-4:30pm.

Telephones: CATPhoneNet, next to the GPO. International phone (22฿ per min. to the US) and fax. Internet access 100฿ for a 3hr. card. Open daily 8:30am-4:30pm. Much cheaper phone cards can be purchased at the 7-Eleven.

Internet Access: Sunshine Internet Cafe, beneath Hotel Thanawit, in a small alley off of Soi 76 (which turns into Amnuaysin Rd. farther west) near Phetkasem Hwy. A rare bargain. Internet with a very fast connection for 20฿ per hr. Open daily 9am-midnight. Closer to the beach, the computers at **World News Coffee** are also a decent deal. 40฿ per hr. Open daily 8am-10pm.

Post Office: GPO (☎032 511 063), opposite the police station on Damnernkasem Rd. Poste Restante. Open M-F 8:30am-4:30pm, Sa-Su and holidays 9am-noon. **Postal Code:** 77110.

ACCOMMODATIONS

Most budget hotels gather around Naresdamri Rd. and the roads and sois that branch off it. While prices can be similar, quality varies, so shop around. Reservations are recommended during the high season. Accommodations on and around Soi Bintaban Rd. and Poolsuk Rd. are located in the red light district.

Pattana Guest House, 52 Naresdamri Rd. (☎032 513 393). Look for the sign pointing down an alley off Naresdamri Rd., 100m south of the pier. This exquisitely refurbished hundred-year-old teak house is set amidst fountains, wood carvings, and a peaceful garden. Rooms are lovely with antique furnishings. Courtyard is also home to several pet turtles. Cheaper rooms share baths; all rooms with fan. Low season singles 250฿, large double 450฿. High season prices rise about 50฿ per room. ❸

All Nations Guest House, 10-10/1 Dechanuchit Rd. (☎032 512 747), about 50m from the intersection of Dechanuchit and Naresdamri Rd. Clean closet-sized rooms, shared baths with hot water, and the closest thing to a backpacker atmosphere in Hua Hin. The bar with pool table in the lobby is open until midnight and has a good selection of beers for 50฿. Upper-level rooms have less noise and better views. Rooms with fan 200-350฿, big doubles with A/C 500฿. ❷

Mod Guesthouse, 116 Naresdamri Rd. (☎032 512 296), on the coast, right next to World News. Mod is friendly and passably clean, but its real draw is the sight and sound of the waves. The guesthouse was built on top of a dock. Furniture and floors are somewhat sea-battered, but the outdoor common area looking out onto the sea is a highlight. All rooms have very small private bath. Rents motorbikes for 200฿ per day. Small rooms with fan 250-350฿; rooms with A/C, hot water, and a great ocean view 450฿. ❸

Memory Guesthouse, 108 Naresdamri Rd. (☎032 511 816), across the street from Mod Guesthouse, 200m south of the pier. Less memorable than most of the other guesthouses; rooms are clean, simple, and padlocked, but very small. Rooms with fan and shared bath 200฿. Larger rooms with fan and private bath 300฿. For 500฿, you can get a decently sized double with A/C. ❷

FOOD

While Hua Hin offers some of the region's best seafood, the local catch is becoming harder to find amid an explosion of Spanish, French, Italian, German, Austrian, Irish, and Mexican cuisine. Even a McDonalds and Starbucks have creeped their way onto the culinary scene of Hua Hin. The seafood restaurants on Naresdamri Rd., just south of the pier, are all excellent, but not budget friendly. **Chatchai Market**, between Srasong Rd. and Phetkasem Hwy. just north of Dechanuchit Rd., is the best place to sample a local foods, including live seafood, pig's heads, and a staggering array of colorful produce. It's particularly lively in the morning, when Chinese doughnuts (10฿ per bag of 10) and sliced fruit (20฿ per small bag) make an excellent breakfast. The **night market** right next door on Dechanuchit Rd. is a has great *pad thai* (25฿) and soup (25฿).

Kuay Tien Rua Nai Beer, at the intersection of Sarasong Rd. and Damnernkasem Rd., without an English sign, but with an English menu. This local lunch spot serves all the delicious Thai classics at good prices. Stir fried beef and basil with rice 50฿. *Tom yum* 50-70฿. Open 8am-8pm. ❷

Ket Sa Rin Seafood, 17/1 Naresdamri Rd. Highly praised by locals. Top-notch seafood. When navigating the epic menu, stick to the chef's recommendations at the front and avoid the Western dishes. Dishes 150-350฿. Open daily 11am-11pm. MC/V. ❸

Dream Cones, in a small stall on the side of the road in front of the Jed Pee Nong Hotel on Damnernkasem Rd. Of the many European cuisines available in Hua Hin, the most climate-appropriate is Italian gelato. 40฿ per scoop. Open daily 4-11pm. ❷

World News Coffee. New York-worthy bagels in a familiar Starbucks-like setting stand out among Hua Hin's other *farang* offerings. The green tea, guava, watermelon, and pineapple smoothie (100฿) is delectable, if pricey. Bagel with cream cheese 60฿. Open daily 8am-10pm. ❷

NIGHTLIFE

The live boxing matches at the intimate **Thai Boxing Garden** in a small alley off of Poonsuk Rd. are a great source of entertainment; the arena holds no more than 100 people. Fights are on Tuesday and Saturday nights at 9pm. Seats for five fights and a free beer 400-500฿ (prices depend on where you sit). If blows and blood aren't your style, head to the streets around the intersection of Sarasong Rd. and Damnernkasem Rd. where amateur **jazz groups** frequently play from 10pm to midnight. At night, the red light district sprawls outwards from its core on **Soi Bintaban**. *Farang* looking to avoid prostitutes should head to the popular bars on **Naresdamri Rd.** in the immediate vicinity of the Hilton.

Mon Thri Restaurant and Mai Tai Cocktails (☎032 532 128), just south of the Hilton, Attracts large crowds of Westerners, who stay until 1am, drinking *Mai Tais* for 90฿ and beers for 55฿ at tables for 4.

Hua Hin Brewery, attached to the Hilton, where a wrecked ship juts out of the wall, has a dancefloor with loud Western pop hits blaring until 2am. Drinks 60-120฿. Often the liveliest place in town, though partially populated by those looking for red light district fun.

SIGHTS

Hua Hin's major attraction is the **Hua Hin Beach,** which rolls along for kilometers in either direction from town. While more scenic beaches can be found farther south, Hua Hin's is cleanest, with soft white sand. The prettiest stretch of the beach begins just south of the entrance to the Sofitel Hotel. If you are looking to get away from the beach bums and vendors who wander the sand offering massages, food, and pony rides (400-600฿ per 30min.), just keep heading south to the more secluded resort beach areas. For those who wish to enjoy the sights and sounds of the ocean without getting sandy or wet, the fishing pier to the north is a nice place to relax.

The Sofitel Central Hotel, 1.5km south of the pier, offers a rare glimpse of Hua Hin's graceful past. Originally known as the Railway Hotel, it was built by

Prince Purachatra, the former Director General of State Railways. It also had a brief stint in cinema as Phnom Penh's leading hotel in the film *The Killing Fields*. The spectacular ⬛**topiary gardens** are not to be missed. Head in through the front gate on Naresdamri Rd., south of Damnernkasem Rd., and head to the left after the front desk. They are pretty strict about only letting guests into the hotel, so you may not make it to the garden but it is worth a shot.

Khao Takieb (Chopstick Hill) and ⬛**Khao Krailas,** both 6km south of Hua Hin, on Petchkasem Hwy, stand in stark contrast of one another. At Khao Takieb, tourists pay exorbitant prices (20฿ per banana) to feed bananas to obese monkeys lolling around the concrete brontosauruses scattered among Buddha images. For a far more tranquil, scenic, and monkey-free experience, skip Khao Takieb and head to neighboring Khao Krailas. There is no English sign; coming from Hua Hin, veer right at the police station where you would veer left for Khao Takieb, then take an immediate right onto the dirt path that leads to the stone staircase up the mountain. Here, the shrines and temples that dot an enchanting hillside are far less crowded. As you reach the top of the initial staircase, head to the right up more stairs. A large Buddha statue and stunning views will greet you at the top.

Suan San Beach, is further south than Khao Krailas, has unbeatable swimming, and a lovely sideview of Khao Takieb. To get there, continue straight after veering right at the fork in the road by the police station. Continue down this road for about 2km and take a left when you can see the ocean. You can also charter a *songthaew* or *tuk-tuk* from Hua Hin (round trip 200฿) or Khao Khalias (round trip 80฿)

▶ DAYTRIPS FROM HUA HIN

KHAO SAM ROI YOD NATIONAL PARK. Stunning limestone hills (the "Three Hundred Peaks") rise from surrounding sea and marshland at this beautiful park, which shelters two unspoiled beaches, a limestone cave system, and a diverse waterfowl population that makes for excellent bird-watching. There are some excellent hikes from headquarters for daytrippers, as well as extensive canals for overnight visitors to explore. The jewel of the park complex is the magnificent **Tham Phraya Nakhon** cave complex, which has huge caverns, stalactites, stalgmites, and a monument commemorating King Rama VI's visit. It is 2km uphill from the headquarters. Watch your step, as the steps can get pretty slippery after rain. **Insect repellent is a must,** as history demonstrates: King Rama IV, who came here in 1868 to observe a solar eclipse that he had predicted, later died of malaria contracted during the visit. A flashlight is handy for exploring the caves. *(The entrance to the park is 40km south of Hua Hin. Difficult to reach and explore without a car; take a bus from Hua Hin to Pranburi (1hr., 45฿), then a samlor or motorbike taxi (40 min., 300฿ round trip) to the village of Bang Pu. Taxi drivers hang out near the bus stop. Expect to bargain a little. From Bang Pu, park headquarters are within walking distance, but one must hike 2km over a mountain with spectacular views to get to the beach where the headquarters (☎032 619 078) are located. You can also hire a boat that can hold up to 10 people to take you around the mountain to the beach for 400฿ per hr. Bungalows accommodate up to 20 (1200฿). Reserve in advance. ☎02 579 0529. Park open M-F 8:30am-4:30pm. Free.)*

PRACHUAP KHIRI KHAN　　　☎032

Flanked by verdant rock formations jutting from the bay, the pretty fishing town of Prachuap Khiri Khan offers travelers a rare treat. Colorful fishing boats fill the harbor, and along the shore you're more likely to see squid drying than fellow *farang* bumming on the beach. With inexpensive hotel rooms and friendly locals, the few tourists who come here are consistently charmed.

The attractive coastline near town, with its beaches, *wats*, and boat-building village, is ripe for exploration by bicycle or motorbike.

TRANSPORTATION

Trains: Train station (☎032 611 175), on Maharaj Rd. right where Kong Kiat Rd ends. To: **Bangkok** (5hr., 12 per day, 168-225฿); **Chumphon** (3hr., 11 per day, 34-358฿); **Hua Hin** (1hr., 12 per day, 49฿); **Phetchaburi** (3hr., 11 per day, 31-165฿); **Surat Thani** (5-6hr., 9 per day, 171-228฿ 2nd-3rd cl.).

Buses: A/C buses to **Bangkok** (4½hr., every hr., 246-266฿) leave from Phitak Chat Rd., between Kong Kiat and Mitringam Rd. Most Bangkok-bound buses stop at **Hua Hin** (1hr., 80฿). The regular **bus station,** on Phitak Chat Rd. across from the Inthira Hotel near the night market, runs buses to **Chumphon** (4-5hr., every hr. 8am-4pm, 140฿). For **Surat Thani,** catch a southbound bus from **Bangkok** (7hr., about every 1½hr., 230฿) on the highway 3km east of Prachuap (motorcycle taxi 50฿), or take a bus to **Chumphon** and transfer there.

Local Transportation: Downtown can be traversed on foot. For longer distances, rent a **bicycle** or **motorbike** or look for **tuk-tuks.** Any trip around town should be no more than 20฿. *Tuk-tuks* to Ao Manao 30฿, to Khao Khan Kradai Cave 40-50฿.

Rentals: There is a small store without a name at the corner of Kong Kiat Rd. and Maharaj Rd., on your right when you reach the train station, that **rents motorbikes** for 200฿ per 24hr., with passport deposit. Open daily 8am-4pm. **Prachuap Suk Hotel** south of downtown also rents motorbikes at the same price and bicycles for 50฿ per 24hr.

ORIENTATION AND PRACTICAL INFORMATION

Prachuap Khiri Khan is extremely easy to navigate. It is laid out roughly in a grid, and the downtown area can be traversed on foot in 15min. The waterfront road, **Chai Thaleh,** runs north-south on the eastern edge of town while **Khao Chong Krajok,** Prachuap's *wat*-topped mountain, rises on the northern edge of the waterfront. Between the train tracks and the waterfront (and running parallel to them) are, from west to east: **Maharaj Road, Phitak Chat Road, Sarachip Road,** and **Suesuk Road.** Perpendicular to these is **Kong Kiat Road,** running from the train station in the west to the pier in the east. **Mitringam Road,** south of Kong Kiat Rd., hosts the day market.

The ◪**Tourist Information Office,** well-marked, 200m north of the pier between Suesuk Rd. and Chai Thaleh Rd., gives out maps, and may be the friendliest, most English-proficient tourist office in Thailand. (☎032 611 491. Open daily 8:30am-4:30pm.) **Bangkok Bank,** on the corner of Sarachip Rd. and Mitringam Rd., has currency exchange and a **24hr. ATM.** (Open M-F 8:30am-3:30pm.) Other 24hr. ATMs are dotted along Sarachip Rd. and Phitak Chat Rd. Other services include: **police,** 15 Kong Kiat Rd. (☎032 611 148), at the corner of Kong Kiat and Sarachip Rd.; **Prachuap Hospital** (☎032 602 060), on the left, three and a half long blocks down Phitak Chat Rd. from Kong Kiat Rd.; **Internet access** at **VIP Internet** (sign is in Thai), on Kong Kiat Rd., half a block east of the train station (20฿ per hr., open 8am-midnight), and at **Yuttichai Hotel** a little farther east on Kong Kiat Rd. (30฿ per hr.). Other Internet stores can be found along Suesuk Rd.; most are open from 8am to midnight. There is a **GPO** at 44 Suesuk Rd. (☎032 611 035), at the intersection of Suesuk and Mitringam Rd., by the market. (Open M-F 8:30am-4:30pm, Sa-Su 9am-noon.) **Postal Code:** 77000.

Prachuap Khiri Khan

⌂ ACCOMMODATIONS
The Inthira Hotel, **2**
Prachuap Suk Hotel, **4**
Yuttichai Hotel, **3**

🍴 FOOD
Ma Prow, **5**
Super Restaurant, **1**

☐ ACCOMMODATIONS

Though Prachuap Khiri Khan has limited selection of accommodations, it does have some excellent budget options for those looking to catch a little shut-eye after a long day at the beach.

Yuttichai Hotel (☎032 611 055), along Kong Kiat Rd., a 2min. walk from the train station, on the right. Everything here is impeccably clean. Pale colors and high ceilings give the spacious rooms an airy feel. Breakfast 15-30฿. Free maps of town. Singles 160฿, with bath 200฿; doubles 220/300฿. ❷

Prachuap Suk Hotel, 69-71 Suesuk Rd. (☎032 611 019). From the train station, go down Kong Kiat Rd. for 300m., turn onto Suesuk Rd., and walk for 3 long blocks, past the market on the left. A small, well-maintained hotel; near the water and in a quieter location than Yuttichai. The rooms are freshly scrubbed and have private bath. Fairly large singles with fan 200฿; doubles with A/C 350฿. ❷

The Inthira Hotel, 120 Phitak Chat Rd. (☎032 611 418). From the train station, go down Kong Kiat Rd., and take the first left; near the night market. This mediocre hotel is conveniently located and has adequate rooms with cold water bath and fan. Singles 200฿, with A/C 300฿, doubles 250/350฿. ❷

☐ FOOD

Cheap, delicious seafood is plentiful in Prachuap Khiri Khan. The **day market** is on Mitringam Rd., close to the post office. In the evenings, the **night food stalls,** in the parking lot area north of the police station, between Sarachip Rd. and Phitak Chit Rd., serve excellent seafood. (Open daily 5pm-midnight.) Look out for roasted hollow sugar cane stuffed with a delicious mixture of sticky rice and coconut (10฿).

Ma Prow Restaurant, 44 Chai Thaleh Rd. (☎032 551 208), 150m. south of the pier. Serves exquisite, decently priced Thai curries and seafood to a mostly *farang* crowd. The *Pad Char* fish (120฿) explains why people rave about authentic Thai food. Great nightime view of the bay from the patio. Open 10am-midnight. ❸

Super Restaurant, on Kong Kiat Rd. across the street from Yutichai Hotel. This immaculate and unexpectedly chic eatery has flat screen TVs and stays open late. The mostly Chinese dishes are reasonably priced (60-100฿). Open 4pm-3am. ❷

◉ ☐ SIGHTS AND BEACHES

Prachuap Khiri Khan affords several secluded and remarkable sights.

KHAO CHONG KRAJOK (MIRROR TUNNEL MOUNTAIN). It is 421 steps through a gauntlet of aggressive monkeys to the golden *chedi* of this hilltop *wat*, which offers a glorious 360° panorama of the surrounding bay and province. Living off the corn and bananas fed to them by Thai tourists, the swarms of brazen monkeys are a real challenge. Regardless, the view from the top (where there are no monkeys) is spectacular. *(On the northern tip of town overlooking the bay. The steps start on Sarachip Rd., opposite the wat. Open 24hr. Free.)*

WAT KHAO THAM KHAN KRADAI AND CAVES. Two impressive cave systems overlook the **Ao Khan Kradai Bay.** About 20 steps up during the initial ascent of the mountain, on the right, is another set of steps. These shell-paved stairs lead to the first and smaller cave that holds several seated Buddha statues. Another superior complex holds two spectacular reclining Buddhas and offers a view of the bay. This cave is a testament to the Thais' ability to put enormous Buddhas into caves of all shapes and sizes. Before heading up the steps, find a monk at the base of the mountain to turn on the cave lights. You won't always be able to find a monk, so a flashlight is a good idea. Beware of bats in these caves. *(8km north of town. Motorcycle taxi 80-100฿ round-trip. If driving, head north of Prachuap past Khao Chong Krajok, cross over a bridge into Ao Noi District, turn right at the blue sign for Ao Noi Seaview Resort, and follow that road until its end. There are no signs for the cave. Free.)*

AO MANAO (MANAO BEACH). Ao Manao is a scenic 2km beach enclosed by cliffs only accessible via the adjoining Thai airforce base. A golf course, campground, and shooting range are all in the vicinity. Chairs under umbrellas are 10฿. Inner-tubes (10฿) are available for visitors, and excellent seafood stalls (25-80฿) are located at the food court. *(6km south of Prachuap Khiri Khan. Follow Sarachip Rd. south from town. Motorcycle taxi 40฿ 1 way. Foreigners must sign in and out of the base.)*

CENTRAL THAILAND

NORTHEAST THAILAND

It's high time everyone knew the truth about the overlooked land mass encompassing nearly one third of the total area of Thailand. The region loosely refers to the area north and east of Bangkok, and shares huge stretches of border and thousands of years of culture with two of Thailand's neighbors, Cambodia and Laos. Isaan, meaning "vastness and prosperity," is at first glance a misleading designation—Isaan is the country's poorest region, with an economy based largely on its agricultural production of rice. The northeast's true vastness and prosperity comes in the form of the sparkling hospitality, warmth, and graciousness of its top natural resource: its people. Intrepid visitors to this tourist-sparse area will be greeted with friendly shouts of "hello!" and "where are you going?" in dazzling urban markets and quiescent, lush farmlands alike. Beyond the human connection lies the historical one. Remnants of the ancient Khmer civilization scattered throughout the region constitute some of best preserved and visually stunning ruins in Southeast

Asia. For skeptics who hold that any statement containing both "Thailand" and "off the beaten path" is oxymoronic, Isaan rises to the challenge.

PAK CHONG   ☎ 044

Primarily a market town, Pak Chong sparks little interest for travelers except as a point of transit for those traveling to Khao Yai National Park (p. 202). The surrounding region is rapidly being developed into a tourist destination to accommodate park visitors and wealthy Thais retreating from the madness and concrete of Bangkok. Although upscale resorts and spas are becoming the norm, a few budget options just out of town make Khao Yai National Park an enjoyable and feasible possibility.

▢ TRANSPORTATION

Guesthouses and resorts between Pak Chong and the park will pick up and drop off guests at the Pak Chong bus or train stations. Call in advance to make reservations. *Songthaew* leave from Pak Chong for the park around the corner from the 7-Eleven, on Tesabarn 19 (every 30min., or when full 6am-6pm, 40฿). The **train station** (☎044 311 534) lies at the end of Tesabarn 15. Trains go to **Bangkok** (4-5hr.; 12:30, 1:30, 2:30, 10, 11:30am, 2, 4:30, 10:30pm, midnight; 36฿) via **Ayutthaya** (23฿), and **Khorat** (1hr.; 12:15, 2:15, 4, 9, 10:50am, 1:15, 3:20, 7:40, 9:35, 10:45pm; 18฿). Get to the station 15min. before scheduled departure. There are three main **bus stations.** One at the **Thai Farmers Bank,** just after Tesabarn 19 and next to the 7-Eleven (☎044 313 750). Buses to **Khorat** (1hr., every 20min., 64฿) and connections to northern and northeastern destinations. On the other side of the Mittaphap (Friendship) Highway, about 1km west and 200m past the overpass, there is a second station (☎044 312 131) with buses to **Bangkok** (2hr., every 40 min. 4am-9:20pm, 157฿) and **Khorat** (1hr., every 30min 6:30am-3pm, every hr. 3-10pm). As of summer 2008, a new bus station is under construction, 50m down Tesabarn 10. In the meantime, buses to **Phitsanulok** (7hr.; 7:20, 10:30am; 249฿) depart from near the construction site; tickets can be purchased at small desk also next to the construction site.

✈🛈 ORIENTATION AND PRACTICAL INFORMATION

Pak Chong's development along transport lines explains its layout, which extends approximately 2km along its main axis, **Mittaphap (Friendship) Highway,** paralleling the railway. Side streets are designated "**Tesabarn Rd.,**" followed by a number. Odd-numbered Tesabarns intersect with the highway on its northern side, while even-numbered Tesabarns intersect on its southern side. Starting at the western part of the highway, the major landmarks are the stoplight at Tesabarn 16/17, the pedestrian overpass, and the Shell gas station at Tesabarn 25.

Bangkok Bank, centrally located near the overpass, gives cash advances, cashes traveler's checks, and has an MC/Plus/V **24hr. ATM.** (☎044 311 361. Open M-F 8:30am-3:30pm.) Other services include: a **Police Station,** about 1km west of the center of town, on the main road (☎044 311 234, open 24hr., some English spoken); **The Bangkok Hospital Clinic,** 1km west of the police station (☎044 316 6115, open 24 hr.), a **supermarket** at the corner of Tesabarn 16, with flashlights, batteries, and toiletries for treks (open daily 8:30am-9:30pm); **laundry,** at Garden Lodge and Greenleaf Guesthouse (30฿); **CAT,** on the corner of Tesabarn 22, which handles faxes, has free Internet, receives collect calls, places domestic and international phone calls (collect calls free; open M-F 8:30am-4:30pm); and the **post office,** directly across from CAT. (☎311 736. Open M-F 8:30am-4:30pm, Sa-Su 9am-noon.) **Postal Code:** 30130.

NORTHEAST THAILAND

◼ ◻ ACCOMMODATIONS AND FOOD

Khao Yai Garden Lodge ❸, Thanarat Rd., on the left side of the road from Pak Chong to Khao Yai. Has a pleasant garden with small pools and lamyai trees and swimming pool. Clean shared bathrooms with hot water. (☎044 365 178; www.khaoyaigardenlodge.com. Doubles with shared bath 350฿, suites with marble bath and A/C 1300-3000฿. Discounts for suites are negotiable.) **Greenleaf Guesthouse ❷**, Km 7.5, Tanarat Rd. Organizes cheap, decent rooms with fan and cement floor. Offers tours of the park. (☎044 365 073; www.greenleaftour.com. Doubles with bath 200฿.)

If you're in Pak Chong in the evening, don't miss the **night market** and its assortment of food, drink, and fruit vendors. The roast pork is a particular favorite among locals. The **day market**, which starts near Tesabarn 21 and extends one block uphill from the main road, also has food stalls. (Open daily 6am-4:30pm.) Restaurant options in town are limited. **Khao Yai Garden Lodge Restaurant ❸** has a busy open-air restaurant serving Thai and German dishes (90-220฿). **Greenleaf Guesthouse Restaurant** also serves meals, and a cheap **noodle vendor ❶** in front of the property has tasty noodle soup (20฿).

KHAO YAI NATIONAL PARK

For travelers hoping to rescue their lungs from the fumes of Bangkok, Khao Yai National Park's 40km of hiking and biking trails offer salvation. A World Heritage Site, Khao Yai displays truly amazing varieties of flaura and fauna, all set in one of the world's largest monsoon rain forests. Only 160km from Bangkok, Khao Yai opend in 1962 and is Thailand's first national park. Its humbling 2168 sq. km range from stark prairies to thick evergreens. The park is inhabited by roaming wild elephants, tigers, and bears (oh my!), though you'll more likely be swatting insects and peeling off leeches than coming face to face with a leopard or Asiatic black bear. You'll also likely get a glimpse of one of the more than 300 species of birds, including the great hornbill, that call the park their home. Khao Yai is most easily reached via Pak Chong (p. 201).

◼ **TRANSPORTATION.** Most traveling to Ko Yai will travel through **Pak Chong.** Songthaew bound for Khao Yai leave from Pak Chong around the corner from the 7-Eleven, on Tesabarn 19 (30min., when full 6am-6pm, 40฿). The **park headquarters** and **visitors center** (☎081 773 127; open 8:30am-4:30pm) are located 14km from the park's entrance. You can arrange pickup from the park headquarters (☎044 297 406). Although *Let's Go* does not recommend it, many travelers hitchhike to the park.

◼ ◻ **ORIENTATION AND PRACTICAL INFORMATION.** The park is open daily from 6am-9pm. It costs 400฿ to enter, 200฿ for children, and vehicles are an additional 50฿. The **park headquarters** and **visitor center** rents bikes (50฿ per hr., 200฿ per day), hands out simplistic trail maps (150฿), and can provide trekking guides (300-800฿ depending on length of trek). The map is sold in the souvenir shop, alongside leech guards (50฿) and other helpful products.

To avoid leeches, don't trek in sandals and steer clear of salty water. Leechguards are a necessity during the rainy season. Unless you're a seasoned trekker, **hiring a guide or taking a tour is highly recommended.** Not only do guides keep you on the poorly designated paths, but they can point out otherwise unrecognizible fauna of the jungle. Many travelers opt for an all-inclusive tour arranged by their hotel. **Greenleaf Guesthouse** and **Khao Yai Garden Lodge** offer similar tours that range from half-day to a 1 and a half day treks. The popular day-and-a-half tour includes a visit to both Buddhist meditation and bat caves, waterfall swims, elephant-trail treks, and jungle hikes. Hotel or guesthouse guide prices usually include entrance fees, transportation, guides, and lunch. Greenleaf Guesthouse's ½-day tour costs 1300฿; 1½-day is 1500฿. For private bird-watching tours, Greenleaf's Bird-Man is your man: after 10-years on the job, he continues to chase after birds with childish glee (private tour 2500฿, groups of 3 2000฿ per person). Khao Yai Garden charges 1500฿ for a half-day;,400฿ entrance fee to park not included.

Khao Yai National Park

ACCOMMODATIONS. The **Royal Forest Department** in Bangkok (☎02 506 2076) can grant permission to stay overnight in the park; it is probably a good idea to try and book by 6pm the day of your stay. There are two campsites within the park: **Lumtakong ❶**, 6km from the visitors center, and **Orchid ❶** (Pha Kluai Mai), 9km from the visitors center; both offer campsites (30฿) and tent rentals (80฿ for 2-person tents, 150฿ for triples; pillows, sleeping bags, and blankets also available for rent). Both campgrounds have bathrooms with cold water showers. Be careful with food as gibbons can be quite forward; bear-bagging is highly recommended. Alternatively, **Suratsawadee Lodge ❷**, 1km from the visitors center, offers dorm beds (100฿). Hardwood-floor space (50฿) is at **Kong Kaew Camp ❶**.

SIGHTS. Once in the park, there are a few sights you cannot miss. The waterfalls are at the top of this list. **Haew Narok** ("awful cliff"), a three-tiered cascade, is the tallest waterfall in the park. Elephants have been known to slip and fall from the surrounding cliffs. **Haew Suwat Falls** was filmed for the popular American movie, *The Beach*. The Haew Suwat Falls also boasts a rope-swing; *Let's Go* definitely does not reccommend you give it a try. **Pha Kluai Mai Falls** (named for the surrounding red orchids) are also noteworthy. To observe the park's wildlife, venture to **Nong Pak Chi Watch Tower,** 11km from the north entrance. This is the place to observe deer, and other, smaller wildlife. **Elephant Crossing** is the spot to view elephants.

NAKHON RATCHASIMA (KHORAT)   ☎044

Known locally as "Khorat" for the plateau on which it rests, Nakhon Ratchasima straddles the main corridor to all other destinations in Isaan. Boasting a population of about three million, Khorat is one of Thailand's largest cities—and has the noise and air pollution to prove it. Designed by French engineers

NORTHEAST THAILAND

for Ayutthayan King Narai, it was once fortified by a wall and surrounded by a moat, the remains of which are still visible. Today, a new world is replacing the old as sprawling malls and sleazy nightclubs multiply. Also populating this northeastern city is Khorat's very own breed of cats—the Khorat cats, which can be worth up to 2,000฿. Beyond shopping and a few interesting temples, Khorat is also a convenient base from which to visit the silk weavers of Pak Thong Chai, the pottery manufacturers of Dan Kwian, and the ruins of Phimai and Phanom Rung. If you happen to be around from late March to early April, you might have a chance of catching the Thao Suranari Festival, a series of parades through the city center to honor local heroine Thao Suranari.

▐▐ TRANSPORTATION

Trains: Nakhon Ratchasima Train Station (☎044 242 044; www.railway.co.th), on Mukkhamontri Rd. From the center of town, the station is 500m west on Mukkhamontri Rd., with an old locomotive out front. A variety of trains depart for Bangkok (4-6hr., 10 per day 8:20am-midnight). Trains also depart for **Ubon Ratchathani** (4 per day, midnight-5:30am, 206-368฿) via **Khon Khaen** (188-297฿) and **Nong Khai**. Call in advance for the day's schedule.

Buses: Khorat has 2 bus terminals. Buses traveling within the region depart from Terminal 1; buses going further afield depart from Terminal 2. Buses for Bangkok leave from both terminals. Prices quoted are for A/C buses. Note that times are only guidelines.

Terminal 1, on Burin Rd. 3companies run buses to **Bangkok,** all with similiar prices and times **Ratchasima Tours,** (☎044 269 234, every 40min. 6am-9pm, on the hour after 9pm; 227฿). Request info for other destinations within the province.

Terminal 2, on Rte. 2, north of town beyond the Takhong River. There are numerous ticket booths, each selling tickets to different places. Ask around for the appropiate vendor for your location. To: **Bangkok** (4hr., every 30min., 227฿); **Buriram** (4hr.; 9 per day 10:30pm-2:30am, 2 buses 1:45pm; 121-236฿); **Chiang Mai** (12hr., 7 per day 6:30am-8:30pm, 643฿); **Chiang Rai** (13hr., 698฿); **Nong Khai** (6hr.; 5am, 2, 5:30, 7pm; 308฿); **Khon Kaen** (3hr., every 30min. 4:50am-11:30pm, 171฿); **Udon Thani** (5hr., 11 per day, 266฿); **Phimai** (1hr., every 30min. 5am-10pm, 54฿); **Surin** (4hr., every 30min., 140฿); **Ubon Ratchathani** (6hr., 4 per day 2pm-1am, 300฿); **Dan Kwian** (40min., every 30min. 25฿).

Local Transportation: Samlor and **tuk-tuks** are omnipresent. **City buses** (6am-8pm, 8฿) are also convenient. Buses #1, 2, and 3 start on Mukkhamontri Rd. (near TAT) and go to town, before splitting on Phoklang (#1), Suranaree (#2), and Jomsurangyard Rd. (#3). Frequent, numbered **songthaew** (8฿).

✈ ▐ ORIENTATION AND PRACTICAL INFORMATION

Khorat is enclosed to the west and north by **Mittraphap Road,** to the east by **Pol Lan Road,** and to the south by the railroad. **Ratachadamnoen Road** and **Chumphon Road,** separated by a narrow park, divide the city into two halves: the quieter western half and the more commercial eastern one. In the middle of this divider, marking the center of the city, stands the dramatic **Thao Suranaree Memorial.** A rectangular moat, a remnant of the city's old fortifications, circumscribes the city's eastern half. **Chomphon Road,** not to be confused with Chumphon Rd., begins behind the Thao Suranaree Memorial and cuts east-west through the center of the old city.

Nakhon Ratchasima (Khorat)

▲ ACCOMMODATIONS
Dr. Guesthouse, **2**
San Sabai Hotel, **6**
Tokyo Hotel, **4**

● FOOD
Cabbages & Condoms, **1**
Chez Andy, **8**
The VFW Cafeteria, **3**

★ NIGHTLIFE
Bar Nana, **5**
The Fun Factory, **7**

NORTHEAST THAILAND

Tourist Offices: TAT, 2102-2104 Mittraphap Rd. (☎044 213 030; www.tat.org.th/north-east1), near Mukkhamontri Rd., next to the Sima Thani Hotel. English spoken. Free brochures and useful maps. Open daily 8:30am-4:30pm.

Currency Exchange: Bank of Ayudhya, 168 Chomphon Rd. (☎044 242 388). MC/V cash advances and traveler's check exchange. Open M-F 8:30am-3:30pm. **24hr. ATM.** Cirrus/MC/Plus/V. Other ATMs line Chomphon Rd.

Books: Klang Plaza II Department Store (☎044 260 436), on Jomsurangyard Rd., has book-stores with limited English-language sections on the 2nd and 3rd fl. Open daily 10am-9pm.

Local Tourist Police: (☎044 341 778). Main office on Mittraphap Rd., across from Bus Terminal 2. A tourist police box is next to the Thae Suranaree Memorial.

Pharmacy: Amarin, 122 Chumphon Rd. (☎044 242 741), behind the memorial, to the left. "Rx" on the glass doors. Some English spoken. Open daily 8:30am-8:30pm. Another location on the lower level of Klang Plaza II.

Medical Services: St. Mary's Hospital, 307 Mittraphap Rd./Rte. 2 (☎044 261 261), 50m south of Bus Terminal 2. Private hospital with English-speaking staff and facilities. **Khorat Memorial Hospital,** 348 Suranaree Rd. (☎044 263 777). From the Thao Surana-ree Memorial, it's past Sri Pattana Hotel on the right. English spoken. Open daily 24hr. V.

Telephones: CAT (☎044 251 138), next to the post office on Jomsurangyard Rd. Inter-national phone, fax, and telex. Open daily 8:30am-4:30pm.

Internet Access: Net Guru, 356 Phoklang Rd. (☎044 267 811), near Yotha Rd. 15฿ per hr. Open daily 9am-10pm.; **AU Net,** 768 Ratchadamnoen Rd. (☎044 260 678), along the moat near the clock tower; 15฿ per hr. Open daily 11am-midnight. **Step Up** (☎044 242 833) is diagonal to Tokyo Hotel (see below). 15฿ per hr., printing 5฿. Open 24hr.

Post Office: 3 post offices within the main city. **Main office** (☎044 264 906), on Assa-dang Rd., near Chainarong Rd. Post Restante. **Chomsurang post office** (☎044 256 670), 48 Jomsurangyard Rd. **Amphawan post office** (☎044 213 840), next to TAT, on Mittraphap Rd. All offices open M-F 8:30am-4:30pm, Sa 9am-noon; main office also open Su 9am-noon. **Postal Code:** 30000.

Rentals: Motorbikes (manual) can be rented from **Euro Khan Chang** (☎044 267 115) next to the Suzuki sign 200m east of San Sabai House (300฿ per day).

ACCOMMODATIONS

Surprisingly for a city of this size, few guesthouses target the backpacker crowd. There are, however, reasonably clean and centrally located hotels that are good for a night or two.

San Sabai House, 335 Suranaree Rd. (☎044 255 144). 1min. walk from Bus Terminal 1. Simply decorated rooms and shiny bathrooms. The best value in the city. Rooms with cable TV and fan 250฿, with A/C and hot water 300-500฿. ❷

Tokyo Hotel, 256-258 Suranaree Rd. (☎044 242 788). Good location and large rooms, for cheap. Rooms upstairs are better quality. Rooms with fan 250฿, with A/C 450฿. ❷

Doctor's Guest House, 78 Suebsiri Soi 4 (☎044 255 846), near the TAT. Though a little further out of town than other accommodations, this guesthouse offers a welcom-ing atmosphere and clean shared bathrooms with hot water and Western flush toilets. Rooms with fan 200฿, with A/C 350฿. ❷

FOOD

Mouth-watering cuisine is plentiful in and around Khorat. The **day** and **night markets** (6-10pm) are fine places to sample regional specialties such as *sai klog* (grilled pork sausages stuffed with rice; 5฿), *kanom bueng* (small, taco-shaped, coconut-stuffed crepes; 1฿), and *pad mee Khorat* (fried noodles with vegetables and pork; 20฿). If you are up for the trek, a larger **night market** sits just south of town on Mitraphap Rd. (5pm-10pm) The **food courts** in Klang Plaza II, are highly recommended by locals to those looking for good authentic Isaan food, cheap Chinese-Thai dishes (20-35฿), or hybrid pizza crepes (20฿). Purchase food coupons before ordering. (Open daily 10am-9pm.) In the evenings, stroll east along Mahadthai Rd. beyond the night bazaar to reach boisterous open-air restaurants serving a variety of Thai dishes.

Suan Pak (SPK), 154-158 Chumphon Rd. (☎044 255 877), just east of the Thao Suranaree Memorial, on the corner. Upbeat, popular cafe serving cakes and an extensive Thai, Chinese, and Western menu. Dishes 45-160฿. Open nightly 4pm-midnight. ❷

Cabbages & Condoms, 86/1 Sueb Siri Rd. (☎044 253 760), just past Soi 4 and before the train tracks. The to-the-point name reflects the belief that birth control should be as easily accessible as vegetables in a market. C&C offers a nutritious and "safe" meal. Vegetarian options 55-65฿. The bold can try the "condom salad" (100฿). Live music nightly 7pm. Open daily 10am-11pm. ❷

The VFW Cafeteria (☎044 253 432), adjacent to Siri Hotel on Phoklang Rd. An attempt to reconstruct an American diner, VFW offers a simple menu with a variety of inexpensive steak meals (sirloin steak 75฿) and other Western items. Cheeseburger 30฿. Fries 10฿. Open daily 10am-9pm. ❶

🔍 SIGHTS

Khorat's handful of sights can be visited in a single afternoon. A good starting point is the **Thao Suranaree Memorial.** The copper statue depicts a governor's wife who led an attack against invading Laotian forces in 1826. This folk heroine turned demi-god is hailed as inspiration for people from the region, and many make a pilgrimage to this sight, constructed in 1934, to pray for strength and good luck. The city celebrates her life each year (Mar. 23-Apr. 3) with cultural shows. In the city's northeast corner is **Wat Sala Loi.** The *wat* is shaped like a Chinese ship to represent the various sagas of Buddha's life as the ebb and flow of the sea. Inside the main pavilion is the plaster figure of Thao Suranaree (who commissioned the *wat*) prostrating herself in front of the Buddha.

Wat Phra Narai Maharat, on Prajak Rd., between Assadang and Chompon Rd., inside the city moat, contains a sandstone image of the Hindu god Narayana and a *shiva linga* (phallic pillar). The *wat* is open to the public for a short while at 6am and again at 6pm.

🎵🎭 ENTERTAINMENT AND NIGHTLIFE

Competitive and popular **Muay Thai matches** are held on the third floor of the **Mall** on Mittraphap Rd. (Th 5-8pm). Call in advance to ensure tickets (☎037 231 000, 50-100฿). The Mall also features an indoor, Olympic-sized **swimming pool,** a **bowling alley,** and a top-notch **movie theater** playing Thai and Western movies (120฿, open daily 10:30am-8pm). If singing isn't your cup of tea, dance at some of Khorat's best clubs.

Bar Nana (☎044 458 461), next to the Grand Hotel on Mitraphap Rd, has dance floors, live music, and plenty of whiskey to go around. Locals flock to this trendy nightclub and let loose among the high tables scattered across the floor. No cover. Bottles of whiskey 450-1299฿, singha beer 90฿. Open 9pm-2am.

The Fun Factory, on Jomsurangyard Rd., across from Klang Plaza II, is another sprawling dance mega-complex. Live music and hip-hop dance floor F-Sa. 20+. 1 drink min. Open nightly 9pm-2am.

DAYTRIPS FROM KHORAT

DAN KWIAN VILLAGE. Tiny Dan Kwian Village, 15km southeast of Khorat, was once the crossroads for traders traveling in bull-cart caravans between Khorat and Khmer. Villagers have collected dark clay from the Moon River for years, which gives their renowned pottery its distinctive, rusty color. The geometric-patterned work is beautiful, though heavy and fragile. Browse through the vendors on the right hand side of the road, but don't miss out on the actual village, where most of the pottery is made. *(Buses depart from Bus Terminal 2. 20min., every 30min. 6am-6:30pm, 20฿. Alternatively, head to the southeastern side of the city, and jump on a songthaew from Kamhaeng Rd. Disembark when the small road forks into 3 lanes. To return to Khorat, wait on the left side of the road. When the bus comes, gesticulate wildly. Last bus 6pm.)*

PAK THONG CHAI. Pak Thong Chai, 32km south of Khorat, was once a traditional silk-producing village but is now dominated by factories, from which tourists can purchase silk in a variety of qualities and colors. Two of these, **Matchada,** 118/1 Moo Suebsiri Rd. (☎044 441 684), and **Radtree,** 442/1 Pak Thong Chai Rd., arrange free tours through their facilities and allow visitors to observe the silk production cycle. *(Take a bus from Khorat's Bus Terminal 1. 45min., every 30min. 5:30am-8:30pm, 17฿. Both factories open 9am-5pm. Call in advance for tours.)*

PHIMAI ☎044

Phimai's historical park, an ancient sanctuary dating from the 11th century, was once connected by a road to Angkor (in present-day Cambodia) and exhibits many of the same Khmer-style features as its world-renowned relative. Aside from the impressively maintained ruins, this cordial little town has a few comfortable budget accommodations and enough nearby attractions to warrant a few days of sightseeing mixed with a dollop of general laziness. Rent a bike to travel the town and its surrounding farms and rice paddies at your own pace.

TRANSPORTATION

Buses to **Phimai** depart from **Khorat's Bus Terminal 2** (1hr., every 30min. 5am-10pm, 54฿). They first drop passengers off at the center of town, after crossing Moon River. **Buses** continue to **Phimai Town bus station** in a housing development outside of Phimai proper. To get to the center of town from the Phimai Town bus station, take a red **songthaew** (5฿), or take a right from the bus station and walk down Sra Kaew Rd. for 1km. For most destinations, travel to Khorat and change there. Buses depart Phimai for **Khorat** across from the clock tower or from the bus station (every 30min. 5:30am-7pm, 37-50฿). There are a limited number of A/C buses; ask on the day of travel for their schedule. To head north **to Khon Kaen, Nong Khai,** or **Udon Thani,** get off at **Talad Khae** (12฿), 10km away from Phimai, and ask someone where to wait. Those moving on east to **Buriram, Surin,** or **Ubon Ratchathani** may bypass Khorat and save considerable time by taking a *songthaew* from the Phimai bus station to the **train station** at **Hin Dat** (30min., M-F 8am-4:30pm, 30฿). From there, catch an east-bound train (7am, noon, 5, 10:30pm; 13-23฿).

ORIENTATION AND PRACTICAL INFORMATION

Khmer ruins crown the northern end of the town's main thoroughfare, **Chomsudasaget Road.** It is at these ruins that Chomsudasaget Rd. meets **Anantajinda Road,** which runs along the front of **the park.** About 300m away from the park,

Chomsudasaget Rd. intersects **Haruethairome Road.** The town's **clock tower** sits at the southeast corner of the park, at the intersection of Anantajinda Rd. and **Songkhran Road;** this is also where buses often stop for passengers to disembark. Services in Phimai include: the **Kashikornbank,** 248 Chomsudasaget Rd., which has an AmEx/Cirrus/MC/V **ATM** and exchanges traveler's checks (☎044 471 352; 30฿ per check; open M-F 8:30am-3:30pm); **Phimai Hospital** (☎044 471 288, emergency 044 481 908), 2km northwest of town on Route 206; a **tourist police booth** (☎044 341 778, open 8am-6pm), located next to the park entrance, and a good place to go for tourist information and maps; **Internet** at the **Agfa Film Shop** 100m down from the entrance to the park, on the corner of the alleyway leading to Old Phimai Guest House (☎044 471 423, 20฿ per hr.); and a **post office,** 123 Wonprang Rd., along the western border of the park; when facing the park gate, take a left onto Anantajinda Rd.; Wonprang Rd. is the first right, and the post office is 150m down on the left. (☎044 471 342. Open M-F 8:30am-4:30pm, Sa 9am-noon.) **Postal Code:** 30110.

ACCOMMODATIONS

Phimai is more backpacker friendly than most places in the northeast, with dorm rooms and English signs in the town's guesthouses. Most accommodations are situated around Chomsudasaget Rd., which runs south, starting at the park entrance.

Boonsiri Guest House, 228 Moo 2 Chomsudasaget Rd. (☎044 471 159), has clean rooms and offers the best value in town. The second floor communal patio is nice for a meal or post-ruins relaxation. The owner rents bicycles (30฿ per hr., 80฿ per day) and hands out town maps. Dorms with fan 180฿; doubles with TV 400฿, with A/C 500฿. Discounts readily given. ❷

Old Phimai Guest House, 214 Moo 1 Chomsudasaget Rd. (☎044 471 918), 2½ blocks down Chomsudasaget Rd. from the bus station, on a small soi to the right (look for a sign). Budget rooms overseen by an English-speaking family. All rooms have shared bath. Tours to Prasat Phanom Rung and Prasat Muang Tam available 940฿ per person with 3 people. Laundry service 5-15฿. Singles 150฿, doubles 180฿; A/C extra. ❶

FOOD

Your first option for eats in Phimai has to be the **markets.** Gathered near the clock tower, stalls serve up fresh, hot *khanom kroks*, bite-sized coconut treats, for 10฿ a box. The **night market,** also close to the clock tower, serves up treats like Phimai's *phad mee* (similar to *pad thai* but without eggs and peanuts) starting at 25฿. **Khru Pom Restaurant ❷,** 276 Moo 2 Thanon Naimuang, is at the end of a small soi, just beyond the 7-Eleven on Anantajinda Rd., in front of the park entrance. There's no English-sign, so look for a sign that says "restaurant" and "fresh coffee." Khru Pom has an English menu and some fantastic Isaan specialties. Try the "money bags," filled with pork and onions (60฿), or the fresh fruit punch. (☎044 285 304. Punch 30฿. Open 8am-10pm.)

NIGHTLIFE

Nite Bar, on the corner of Chomsudasaget and Anantajinda Rd., across from the clock tower. An eclectic nightspot that's good for a drink, although the grubby interior and stale odor may not agree with everyone. It has a Thai menu (35-100฿) and serves drinks (30-80฿). Live music nightly 9pm. Open until 1am.

Rabing Mai (☎081 760 9642), on Samairujee Rd., 1 block north of the clock tower and opposite Phimai Paradise apartments, without an English sign. A great place to grab a beer while listening to live music. Dishes 40-180฿. Open 5pm-midnight.

NORTHEAST THAILAND

WHERE'S THE BE IN BC? You may wonder why Thai historical markers seem to date the fall of Angkor to the same year as the end of the Vietnam War. Many Thai brochures and historical markers use the traditional Buddhist Era (BE) calendar, marking year 1 as the year of Buddha's death. To convert from Buddhist (BE) to Gregorian (BC), subtract 544 from the BE year.

SIGHTS

PRASAT HIN PHIMAI HISTORICAL PARK. Phimai's main attraction is the stately Khmer ruin of **Prasat Hin Phimai Historical Park,** smack in the middle of town. At its zenith, the Khmer empire covered much of the mainland of Southeast Asia, and evidence of its power and wealth lingers in the form of hundreds of temples that still dot the region. The central white sandstone tower of Phimai's Khmer temple and the red sandstone-and-laterite antechambers and walls that surround it were built in the late 11th century in a style similar to that of the Angkor Wat. The entire site was created with its central artistic features facing Angkor to the southeast, whereas most other *wats* in this region face east. Faded sandstone lintels are to the right of the stone causeway, while *naga* balustrades and four ceremonial ponds mark the corners of the outer courtyard. The temple is dedicated to Buddhism, but many lintels depict scenes from the epic Ramayana, evidence of the Hindu tradition that preceded the spread of Buddhism. (☎ *044 471 568. Open daily 7am-6pm. 40฿.*)

During the second week in November, Phimai hosts a huge festival which ends in a boat race and involves a light and sound show at the Khmer ruin. If you miss it, however, there is a smaller light and sound show on the last Saturday of each month. (*800฿ per person, with a Thai banquet dinner included. Ask at the TAT in Khorat for specific times and infomation.*)

PHIMAI NATIONAL MUSEUM. The Phimai National Museum (in a white building with a red-tiled roof) includes an extensive collection of Khmer and Dvaravati art from all over the lower northeast, as well as exhibits documenting the social, political, and economic history of the Isaan region. Head here after the ruins to see some of the more intricate relics from the area or, alternatively, for an A/C break. The second floor exhibits the development of the northeast from prehistoric to modern times, the ground floor shows some of the archaeological and historical aspects of Phimai's own development, and the outside exhibition displays some of the sandstone objects found in and around the region's Khmer ruins. If you don't want to be stuck indoors, explore the pond out front and the outdoor displays of numerous lintels depicting Hindu gods. (*The museum is 500m down Song-khran Rd., which runs past the eastern perimeter of the temple complex. Facing the park, take a right onto Anantajinda Rd., then take the first left. ☎ 044 471 167. Open daily 9am-4pm. 30฿.*)

OTHER SIGHTS. For a fairy-tale experience, visit **Sai Ngam** ("area of splendid Banyans"), the largest banyan tree grouping in Thailand. Walking under Sai Ngam's thick green canopy is like entering a J.R.R. Tolkien-inspired underworld. Wizened old men will read your palm for a few baht, or you can (temporarily) purchase fish, snakes, or birds (10-20฿) in order to "give freedom to the birds and fish for luck and long life." At the center, a small pagoda houses the spirit of the 360-year-old area. (*On the banks of Moon River, 2km east of town on Anantajinda Rd., past the clock tower; stick to the main road and follow the signs. It's about a 10min. bike ride or 20-30฿ motorcycle jaunt from town.*)

BURIRAM ☎044

The capital of one of the most populated provinces in the northeast, Buriram is a typical soundscape of urban Isaan life, where the constant din of motorbike engines and chattering students masks the quiet decay of the surrounding Khmer-era ruins. Buriram serves as a regional transportation hub for northeastern Thailand, but also sports an active nightlife catalyzed by the large university in the city. Buriram is also home to a large number of Western expats. Buriram's most impressive quality is its proximity to one of the most visually stunning Khmer sites in all of Thailand: Phanom Rung Historical Park. An annual festival makes March or April in Buriram a good time to visit.

TRANSPORTATION

Trains: Buriram Train Station (☎044 611 202), across from the clock towers at the northern end of Romburi Rd. To **Bangkok** (3-8hr., 13 per day 6am-11pm,177-655฿) via **Khorat** (1-2hr., 12 per day, 24-54฿) and **Ubon Ratchathani** (2-4hr., 13 per day, 40-90฿) via **Surin** (1hr., 9-29฿) and **Si Saket** (3hr., 29-59฿).

Buses: The **bus station** (☎044 612 534) is at the west end of town, 2km from the center of town and the train station. To: **Bangkok** (5hr., 14 per day 7:30am-10:30pm, 259-333฿); **Rayong** (9hr., 14 per day, 354-455฿); **Pattaya** (9hr., 14 per day, 531฿); **Chang Mai** (6 per day, 547-821฿); **Khon Kaen** (5hr., every hr. 4:45am-4:15pm, 176฿); **Khorat** (2hr., every 20-40min. 4:30am-7pm, 120฿); **Surin** (1hr., 8:30am-5:30pm, 40฿); **Ubon Ratchathani** (5hr., every 30min., 170฿).

Local Transportation: Tuk-tuks (40-60฿) congregate at the bus station and in the center of town around Romburi Rd. **Motorbikes** (30-40฿) are more common than *tuk-tuks* and are the most convenient way to get around. There are no city buses.

ORIENTATION AND PRACTICAL INFORMATION

Most activity in Buriram centers around the train station and **Romburi Road.** The **station** and **tracks** form the northern and western edges of the city. An oval-shaped **moat** to the east of Romburi Rd. encompasses an area that includes the post office and police station. Two upscale hotels flank the city's eastern and western edges off **Jira Road,** a mainfare running east-west. The bus station is on the western end of town, a few blocks north of **Buriram Ram Ratchaphat University,** in an area with a number of inexpensive eateries patronized by students.

Tourist Office: Info is available at the **TAT** in Khorat. **The Buriram Cultural Center** (☎044 611 221), behind the gates of the university on Jira Rd., offers some assistance, but not much English. Displays exhibits on the province's geological and cultural history. Open M-F 8:30am-6pm, Sa-Su 8:30am-3:30pm.

Currency Exchange: Banks line Romburi Rd. and Sunthorn Thep Rd. **Bangkok Bank** (☎044 612 718) is on the corner of Sunthorn Thep Rd. and Thani Rd., with AmEx/Cirrus/MC/Plus/V **ATM.** Open M-F 8:30am-3:30pm.

Books: Dokya Bookstore, 25-25/1 Thani Rd. (☎044 621 264), across from Bamboo Beer Bar (see below). The largest bookstore in town. Has a rack of current, English-language books. Open daily 8am-8:30pm.

Police: Buriram Police Station (☎044 612 240), on Jira Rd., 50m east of Romburi Rd. Open 24hr.

Medical Services: Buriram Hospital (☎044 615 002), on Na Sathanee Rd. Exiting the train station, take a left; the hospital will be on your right.

Internet Access: PT Center (☎044 613 3778), centrally located on Thani Rd., 2 blocks east of Romburi Rd. and 10m west of Palad Muang Rd. 12฿ per hr. Open daily 8am-9pm.

Mr. P Internet (☎044 620 177), on a small street off Jira Rd. Internet for 15ʙ per hr. Other Internet cafes are near the Wong Thong Hotel, on the same street as Book n' Bed (p. 212).

Post Office: Buriram Post Office (☎044 611 142), on Lak Muang Rd. From the train station, walk down Romburi Rd., and take a left onto Jira Rd. Walk past the police station, make a left onto Lak Muang Rd., and it's 1 block up. Open M-F 8:30am-4:30pm, Sa-Su 9am-noon. **Postal Code:** 31000.

ACCOMMODATIONS

Buriram has a handful of hotels catering to the budget crowd, along with a few options that offer a higher level of comfort for a few more baht.

Thai Hotel, 38/1 Niwas Rd. (☎044 611 112), diagonally across from the train station on Romburi Rd. (despite mailing address). Typical Thai hotel rooms with basic amenities in a characterless building. Friendly staff. Good choice for those wanting to hit up Buriram's nearby night scene. Doubles with fan and squat toilet 180ʙ; with TV, Western flush toilets, and hot water 220ʙ.; with A/C 320ʙ. ❷

Fhean Fha Palace Hotel, 240/9 Jira Rd. (☎044 617 112), on a small side street off of Jira Rd., behind City Hall, on the western side of town. This new hotel has become popular for its modern amenities and clean rooms. Well worth the extra baht. Rooms with A/C, cable TV, hot water 400ʙ; slightly bigger rooms 450ʙ. ❸

Grand Hotel, 137 Niwas Rd. (☎044 611 089). At the end of Romburi Rd., take a left onto Niwas, and it's 50m down on the left. Look for the turquoise building. Decent rooms, but may be best left as a second option after the more affordable Thai Hotel (see above) up the street. Doubles with fan 220-260ʙ, with A/C 360ʙ. ❷

FOOD AND NIGHTLIFE

The **day market** on the south side of Jira Rd., just off Romburi Rd., overflows with *mangosteens* (3-18ʙ per kg) and fatty pork leg over rice (25ʙ). Buriram also has an array of good restaurant choices. Palad Muang Road, between Thani Rd., Niwas Rd., and Bulamduang Rd., is loaded with open-air restaurants frequented by locals, and devoid of English signs. Within Buriram city proper lies a raging nightlife scene in a large parking lot off Romburi Road, near the train station, where a number of bars and discos can be heard.

Laan Ta, Romburi Rd., about 50m south of Bamboo Bar, on the other side of the road, makes a mean cappuccino. Yummy salads and sandwiches (55-80ʙ). Cool down with a scoop of homemade frozen yogurt (25ʙ) or a banana split (70ʙ). Coffee 35-45ʙ. Open M-Sa 9am-10pm. ❷

Book n' Bed, 524/13 Jira Rd. (☎044 601 6713), close to the Vongthong Hotel, is Buriram's other coffee shop, serving ice cream treats, refreshing fruit shakes, and a friendly local crowd. Open daily 7:30am-9pm. MC/V.

Restaurant, attached to Vongthong Hotel; beautiful outdoor dining area, serving Chinese and American dishes. Amazing steamed seabass in brown sauce (150ʙ). Other dishes 45-150ʙ. ❷

Bamboo Beer Bar, 14/13 Romburi Rd. (☎044 625 577), on the corner of Romburi Rd. and Thani Rd. Drink a beer in this expat hangout while sitting on cushioned bamboo furniture. Add your cat to the growing wall in the back. Western breakfast 90ʙ. Thai food 80-100ʙ. Most importantly, large Chang beer 50ʙ. Open daily 8am-midnight. ❸

Speed, 24/4 Romburi Rd., is a zany, 2-floor outer-space extravaganza. Get cosmic with a live band, and float among the glowing stars. Singha or Heineken 70ʙ. No cover. Open nightly 9pm-2am. ❷

SIGHTS

Buriram serves as a convenient base for daytrips to the **Khmer ruins** at Phanom Rung, about 120km south of the city. The most impressive sights closer to the city are the **Khao Kradung Forest Park** and the **Kradong Reservoir**, both only 6km from Buriram. The centerpiece of the park is a large white **statue** of Phra Suphatbohit Buddha, a figure sacred to the people of Buriram. It sits atop **Khao Kradung**, an extinct volcano, and is accessible by a 265m-high staircase or a paved road lined with Buddha statues. The reservoir below provides an ideal picnicking spot and has a great view of the large Buddha on the mountain above. *(To get to the park, catch a songthaew, a motorcycle taxi (1-way 60฿), or a bus heading toward Prak Hon Chai.)*

DAYTRIPS FROM BURIRAM

Catch a bus from Khorat (Bus Terminal 2) or Surin, and get off at Ban Ta-Ko (2hr., 53-74฿), which is marked as the turn-off for Phanom Rung (16km). If you're just going to Phanom Rung, you may be able to catch a songthaew heading right to the base (around 30฿), but you'll more likely have to take one to Ban Don Nong Nai (Tepek), which is 6km closer to Phanom Rung. Alternatively, bus #522 from Buriram heading to Chanthaburi passes by Ban Don Nong Nai (1hr., every hr. 5:30am-2pm, 60฿). From Ban Don Nong Nai, motorcycle taxis will take you the 12km to Phanom Rung and back (120-150฿, includes 1hr. at the ruins). This is the best option during the low season and on weekdays, when transportation is unpredictable. To return by bus to Khorat (80-220฿) wait on the northern side of the highway; for Surin (70฿), Ubon Ratchathani (220฿) or Buriram (60฿) wait on the southern side. Buses come about every 30min. Get back to Ban Ta-Ko before 5pm, as buses run less frequently after that. Returning to Ban Ta-Ko by motorbike is an additional 30฿. From Ban Don Nong Nai you can pick up the Buriram-bound bus if you arrive before 2pm.

PHANOM RUNG

Prasat Hin Khao Phanom Rung Historical Park is home to one of the largest surviving Khmer monuments in the region, a majestic **temple** that was built here between the 10th and 13th centuries. Standing atop an **extinct volcano** 383m above sea level, it commands dramatic vistas of the surrounding plain, broken in the southeast by the Dongrek Mountains of Cambodia. Inside the complex, three terraced platforms lead up to the robing room, a partially reconstructed stone structure on the right, where the king prepared himself before performing religious ceremonies. The 160m promenade lined with lotus bud shaped pillars leads to the main complex and its stairway, guarded by five-headed *nagas* (mythical snakes). The stairs that follow lead to the main temple. At the top is a second bridge and the main gallery. Once you're through the hallway of the gallery, you'll be on the third bridge, facing a portico of the chamber leading to the main sanctuary. The lintel above this entrance, the **Phrai Narai Lintel**, depicts a Hindu creation myth featuring Lord Narayana, an *avatar* (incarnation) of Vishnu. It was once stolen, resurfaced in the Art Institute of Chicago, and then returned in 1988. A perfect time to visit the park is during the **Climbing Up Khao Phanom Rung Festival**, usually held in late March or early April. During this time people flock to the park to climb up the hill and pay tribute to the Buddha images at the top. *(☎044 631 746. Open daily 6am-6pm. 40฿. Tourist information center open daily 9am-4pm.)*

SURIN ☎044

For one week each November, hordes of Thai and *farang* flood Surin to watch dancing, bejeweled, soccer-playing pachyderms on parade at the Surin

Elephant Roundup. The other 51 weeks of the year, Surin remains a rare stop on itineraries, as most travelers press on to the Mekong River. Their loss is your gain. This peaceful town, boasting one of the niftiest night markets around, is a handy jumping-off point for the many small Khmer ruins and traditional villages that dot the surrounding countryside. Only 50km from the Cambodian border, Surin reflects the province's unique mixture of Lao, Khmer, Thai, and indigenous Suay cultures.

TRANSPORTATION

Trains: Surin Train Station (☎044 511 295) is conveniently located beside the elephant statue on Tanasan Rd., in the center of town. To **Bangkok** (8-9hr., 13 per day, 599-1146฿) via **Khorat** (2-3hr.,82฿) and **Buriram** (1hr., 39฿), **Ubon Ratchathani** (3hr., 14 per day, 81-150฿).

Buses: Surin Bus Station (☎044 511 756), on Chit Bam Rung Rd. From the train station, go 2 blocks east (left when facing away from the station) and half a block to the right; the station is down an alley on the left. To: **Bangkok** (7-8hr., every 30min. 6am-11:30pm, 248-495฿); **Chiang Mai** (15hr., every hr. 4:15-9:15pm, 532-925฿); **Khorat** (4hr., about every 20min. 4:15am-7pm, 86-167฿); **Rayong** (9hr., frequently 7pm-10:30pm, 355-664฿); **Ubon Ratchathani** (4hr.; every hr. midnight-8:30am, 4:40pm.; 110-206฿); **Si Saket** (2hr., 6am-4:30pm, 50฿).

Local Transportation: Samlor around town 20-25฿; **tuk-tuk** 30-40฿.

ORIENTATION AND PRACTICAL INFORMATION

Provincial capital Surin is 452km from Bangkok and easily reachable by bus or train from Bangkok, Khorat, or Ubon Ratchathani. Surin has few English street signs. The main street, **Tanasan Road,** runs north-south. At its north end is the train station, which faces an elephant statue. Several blocks down Tanasan Rd. from the train station is a **traffic circle.** Both the post office and the hospital are found on the street to the right of the traffic circle. One block past the traffic circle on Tanasan is the intersection with **Krung Sri Nai Road,** which alternates between a day market and a night market (beginning at 6pm), transforming part of the road into a walking lane. **Tesabarn Sam Road** forms the western border of town and crosses the train tracks in the direction of Pirom-Aree's House. **Sanit Nikonrut Road** forms the eastern border, which runs from the train tracks past the bus station, and intersects with Krung Sri Nai Rd. to the south. To reach the traffic circle from the bus station, exit to the left, pass the soi with the sign for the Petchkason Hotel, and take the next right. Tanasan Rd. is at the first intersection.

Tourist Office: Brochure and Surin map available at **TAT** in Khorat. **The Surin City Hall** (☎044 516 075), on Lakmuang Rd., offers tourist info. Open M-F 8:30am-3:30pm. Mr. Pirom at Pirom-Aree's House (see below) is an invaluable English-speaking resource.

Travel Agency: Sarren House Travel Agency (☎044 520 174), 100m from the police station on Lak Muang Rd. Open M-Sa 8:30am-6pm, Su 9am-noon.

Currency Exchange: Bangkok Bank, 252 Tanasan Rd. (☎044 512 013), just past the traffic circle on the right. **24hr. ATM.** AmEx/MC/Plus/V. Open M-F 8:30am-3:30pm. Several other banks and ATMs also lie along Tanasan Rd.

Police: Surin Police Station, 765 Lak Muang Rd. (☎044 521 500). Walking from the train station down Tanasan Rd., take a left; it's on the 2nd block, on your left.

Pharmacy: Kayang Chelan Pesat, 294 Tanasan Rd. (☎044 513 055). On the corner with Krung Sri Nai Rd.; look for a green awning and sign. The English-speaking pharmacists are extremely helpful. Open daily 8:30am-9pm.

Medical Services: Surin Hospital, Tesabarn 1 Rd. (☎044 511 523). Facing away from the train station. Open 24hr.

Internet Access: Cyber Game, 219/4 Tesabarn Sam Rd. From the traffic circle, walk past the hospital and take the 1st right past the KFC. 15฿ per hr. Open daily 2pm-10pm. Alternatively, try **Gift Online** (☎044 539 001) on Lak Muang Rd. Internet 10฿ per hr. Open 9am-midnight.

Post Office: Surin Post Office (☎044 511 009), on Tanasan and Tesaban 1 Rd. International phones. Open M-F 8:30am-4:30pm, Sa-Su 9am-noon. **Postal Code:** 32000.

♦ ACCOMMODATIONS

Surin's accommodations run from the luxurious to the slightly expensive and luxurious. During the Elephant Roundup, rates can soar by 50-100%, and finding a room is nearly impossible. Book as far in advance as possible.

Pirom-Aree's House, 55-326 Soi Arunee, Thungpoh Rd. (☎044 515 140). Take a right when exiting the train station and walk to the end of the road. Take another right over the train tracks, and make the first left onto Thungpoh Rd. After 1km, look for the sign on the left. Alternatively, hire a *tuk-tuk* (50-60฿) from the train or bus station. This lovely little home is a decent hike from town, but the upside is the tranquility and beauty of the surrounding farmland. Mr. Pirom also offers tours in his SUV (from 750฿ per day) as well as more expensive tours of sights in the area (from 1200฿ for groups of 4-6; includes lunch). Doesn't take advance bookings during the Elephant Roundup. Laundry 5-20฿. All rooms with shared bath and mosquito nets. Singles 120฿, doubles 200฿. ❷

The Song Thong Hotel, about 20m south of the roundabout, directly opposite the post office. A fantastic urban alternative with unique rooms. The cheapest rooms, with shared bathroom and cold water, are on the top floor and provide spectactular views of the city. Rooms 80-500฿, rooms with A/C, hot water, and cable TV are more expensive. Prices increase by about 300฿ during the Elephant Roundup. ❶

◪ FOOD

Surin has some of the best Isaan food around, especially at the **markets** along Krung Sri Nai Rd. (From the train station, walk 1 block past the traffic circle.) At the **night market,** try *hoi tod* (fried sea mussels in crispy batter over bean sprouts flavored with sweet-and-sour sauce; 30-40฿); ask around for the "hoi tod lady." Other Isaan specialties worth a try include *lab* (chopped meat with sticky rice) and *tom sep* (Isaan-style soup). Wash it all down with one of the many different juices or smoothies (20-30฿). If markets aren't your scene, try some of the other restaurants and cafes around town.

Phai Lin, 174 Tanasan Rd. (☎044 513 586), on the right side of Tanasan Rd. when walking away from the train station, serves up some scumptious curry dishes. Try the filling, tasty *khao num phrik goong* (rice with shrimp in a red curry and coconut milk sauce, 60฿). Open daily 8am-8pm. ❷

Coca Restruant, (☎044 512 390), diagonally across from Phetchkasen Plaza on Tesabarn 1, to the east of the roundabout. Without an English sign; small 'Coca' sign over the welcome desk. A popular local hang-out. Try the Oyster Hot Pot (120฿) or one of the other delectable dishes (40-220฿). Open 11am-10pm. ❷

◙ ♫ SIGHTS AND ENTERTAINMENT

Surin's must-see event is the **Elephant Roundup,** which is usually held during the 3rd weekend in November (check with TAT for exact dates). The stars of this festival honoring Thailand's national animal are the 200 pachyderms who awe audiences with feats of strength and skill. Highlights include a battle reenactment, a staged "elephant hunt" exhibiting traditional Suay techniques, and a tug-of-war between man and beast. The finale features a soccer match. Tickets (100-500฿) can be bought in advance from City Hall or at the gate if tickets remain.

BORDER CROSSING: CHONG JIAM/CAMBODIA. To enter Cambodia, you need a Cambodian visa, which can be obtained at the Cambodian embassy in Bangkok (p. 98) for the best rate (US$20). Visas can also usually be obtained at the border for 1000-1300฿. The border crossing is about 70km from Surin and is open daily 8am-4pm. Buses from Surin depart from the bus station (1hr., 5 per day 5:50am-1:40pm). It is possible to get from Surin to Siem Reap in 1 day if you reach the border by noon and catch a *songthaew* or bus to take you the 172km. Check with the Cambodian embassy or local authorities for current border conditions before you go.

DAYTRIPS FROM SURIN

SILK WEAVING VILLAGES. The landscape surrounding Surin is dotted with rural villages still dedicated to the traditional practice of weaving silk. A few villages that are particularly esteemed for their high-quality silk production—**Ban Chan Rom, Ban Sawai,** and **Ban Khaosinarin**—have become well-known tourist destinations. Every visit is slightly different depending on the cycle of the silk worms, so consider yourself lucky if you catch the stage when the silk is being spun from the cocoon. Anyone can visit, but the communication barrier and wary villagers make learning about the silk making process difficult for the average traveler. Luckily, Mr. Pirom (of Pirom-Aree's House, see above) can act as a go-between. (*To visit the villages solo, take a songthaew from the bus station, or walk toward the train station on Tanasan Rd. After the traffic circle, enter the 2nd alley on the left. From here, trucks (about every hr. 7-9am, 25฿) bring visitors the 20km. Return early to avoid a wait or an overnight stay in the village.*)

KHMER RUINS. Surin is also famous for its proximity to the oldest Khmer sanctuary in Thailand. As in the case with the silk weaving villages, there are a number of different spots in the Surin area to visit some spectacular ruins. A pre-arranged tour is a great way to take in these sites and learn some information about the area. **Prasat Ban Phiai, Prasat Ban Phluang,** and **Prasat Sikhoraphum** are all in the vicinity of Surin but generally require a private vehicle to visit.

OTHER SIGHTS. Mr. Pirom's tours also venture to places like **Ban Ta Klang,** a Suay village 60km north of Surin featuring elephants that are trained and kept as pets. An elephant show (Sa 9-11am, 200฿) is held at the **Elephant Education Center.** Contact the **Surin Elephant Village** (☎019 665 284) for more information. (*To reach Ban Ta Klang solo, catch a songthaew from beside the information window at the bus station, every 40min 7am-5pm, 50฿. Alternatively, take a Roi Et-bound bus until Km 36. Make sure you tell the bus driver your destination before boarding. There are 2 bus routes to Roi Et: one drops you off close to the village; the other requires you to transfer to a songthaew or, although Let's Go doesn't recommend it, hitchhike 22km along the road to the left.*)

SI SAKET ☎045

Vignettes of daily Isaan life abound in this small provincial capital. Locals come together to share a meal and some local gossip every evening at the lively night bazaar. This daily routine is briefly interrupted by the Lamduan

Festival, held during the first weekend of March, which celebrates the blooming season of the province's official flower, and the Rambutan-Durian Fair in May or June, when lines of Ram Danawasi dancers don elaborately carved golden headdresses amid fragarant fruit stands. Although relaxation may be one of the prime selling points of Si Saket, for the more spry visitor, the city can be a launching point to explore some of Isaan's natural beauty. Waterfalls flow in abundance following the rainy season, and Khao Phra Wihaan National Park is dotted with Khmer ruins along the border.

TRANSPORTATION

Trains leave from the **train station** (☎045 611 525) in the center of town on Konrotfai Rd. and go to Bangkok (10hr., 9 per day 7:45am-8pm, 314-962฿) via Surin (1hr., 20-130฿), Khorat (3hr., 48-198฿), and Ubon Ratchathani (45min., 11 per day 3am-7:30pm, 13฿). **Buses** depart from **Si Saket Bus Station** (☎045 612 500) in the south of town. From the train station, walk down Kwangheng Rd. for 4 blocks, toward the city hall; **the bus station** will be on your right. Buses go to Bangkok (8-9hr., 10 per day 7am-9:15pm, 337-430฿), Chiang Mai (15hr., 350-685฿), and Rayong (7:40am, 8 per day 4:50-8:50pm; 260-620฿) via Khorat (5hr., 420฿). **Samlor** around town cost 10-25฿, **tuk-tuks** 20-40฿.

ORIENTATION AND PRACTICAL INFORMATION

Si Saket is laid out in an irregular grid pattern: the railway runs from the west to east and divides the city into two north-south sections. The main street in the northern section of the city, **Si Saket Road,** stems from the train station and heads north. Along it are a few hotels and the landmark **traffic circle,** two blocks from the train station. The main street in the southern part of the city is **Khunkhan Road,** beginning just east of the train station and heading south past the bus station. The tourist service center, post office, and police station are all located on **Tepa Road,** in the north, which runs east-west and intersects with Si Saket Rd., **Lakmuang Road, Paladmonthol Road,** and **Wijitnakhon Road,** from west to east. South of the railway, Khunkhan parallels **Kwangheng Road** until they intersect one block past the bus station. **Ubon Road** is the major east-west road in the south, running parallel to the train tracks, three blocks to the south.

ON THE MENU

OODLES OF NOODLES

For most, Thai cuisine brings two words to mind: *pad thai.* Naturally, the *pad thai* eaten in Thailand is a far cry from the imitations served up in the West, but even in its native country there's a huge amount of variation.

Some restaurants serve pad thai with thicker noodles, others with thicker sauce; some with dried shrimp, some with fresh. The basic ingredients are rice noodles, tamarind sauce, fish sauce, lime juice, bean sprouts, fried egg, and some kind of protein, usually chicken, shrimp, or tofu. Most restaurants in Thailand leave it up to the customer to season their noodles themselves with chilis and chili oil. Even if you don't like too much spice, don't shy away from adding just a tiny bit to your plate; it is essential to this staple's unique flavor. Pad thai is also one of the few dishes that's acceptable to eat with chopsticks (most Thai dishes are eaten with fork and spoon).

No one can agree on where to get the best pad thai; start at the food stall outside your hotel and work your way from there.

Tourist Office: The Tourist Service Center (☎045 611 283), at the intersection of Tepa and Lakmuang Rd., can offer some information about the province. Limited English. Open M-F 8:30am-4:30pm. Brochures and maps of Si Saket are available at **TAT** in Khorat.

Tours: Aspara Tours (☎045 622 444), right at the traffic circle on Si Saket Rd. Can arrange tours of the nearby attractions and offers an affordable way to see the sights with 4 or more people.

Bank: Bangkok Bank, on Khunkhan Rd., across from the Kessiri Hotel. Has an AmEx/MC/Plus/V **ATM.** Open M-F 8:30am-3:30pm. Several other banks and ATMs also line Khunkhan Rd.

Police: Police Station (☎045 612 732) on Tepa Rd.

Pharmacy: several pharmacies on Khunkhan Rd.

Hospitals: Pracharak Hospital (☎045 616 380) on Ubon Rd., in the south of town between Lakmuang and Paladmonthol Rd.

Internet Access: Free **Internet** access is available at the **CAT,** located on Tepa Rd., between Lakmuang and Paladmonthol Rd. Open M-F 8:30am-noon and 1-4:30pm. A number of **Internet shops** can be found in the south of the city, particularly near the Prompinam Hotel (see below).

Post Office: The **post office** (☎045 612 421) is next door to the CAT. Open M-F 8:30am-4:30pm, Sa-Su 9am-noon. **Postal Code:** 33000.

ACCOMMODATIONS

Si Saket won't win any awards for its accommodation offerings, but there are a few budget hotels in town as well as some upscale ones that drop their rates significantly in the low season.

Thai Siem Thai Hotel, 147/5 Si Saket Rd. (☎045 611 458) From the train station, walk past the traffic circle on Si Saket Rd.; it's on your right before the intersection with Tepa Rd. Has some of the only budget rooms in town. Doubles 160฿, with A/C and TV 260฿. ❷

Prompinam Hotel, 849/1 Lakmuang Rd. (☎045 612 677). From the train station, cross the train tracks and turn right, and look for the white 5-story building on the left. This mid-range hotel has recently upgraded many of its rooms, which are quite large. Singles and doubles with A/C and TV 440฿. MC/V. ❸

FOOD

The best place to eat in town is the bustling **night market,** right behind the train station. Try the *tom yum kung* (spicy prawn and lemon grass soup with mushrooms, 60฿) Alternatively, get your sugar fix from the huge snow cones topped with bread, jelly candies, and condensed milk (10฿). Finding an English-language menu in Si Saket is a challenge.

Khun, 1877 Ubon Rd. (☎045 611 235). From Khunkhan Rd., walk west 2 blocks; it's on the left side of the street. Fun-loving groups cook their own dinner over a boiling hot-pot at this open-air restaurant. You can get a hot-pot for 1 (from 49฿) or for larger parties for 99฿ and up. Live music on the weekends. Open nightly 5pm-midnight. ❷

PS Steak House, 820/14-16 Ubon Rd. (☎045 613 718), 1 block west of Khunkhan Rd., offers inexpensive Western and Thai food and has an English menu with pictures of some key menu items. Spaghetti 35฿. Seabass steak 65฿. ❷

SIGHTS AND ENTERTAINMENT

While there's little to do in town, *wats* and waterfalls dot the surrounding landscape. One option is **Prasart Srakamhaeng Yai,** an 11th-century ruin that consists of three towers erected on the same base. The tops of the towers have collapsed, but the lintels over the doorways remain, displaying intricately carved images of Hanuman giving a ring to Sita and the god Indra riding Airavata, his elephant. From Si Saket, take a bus or *songthaew* heading to Surin via Uthumpornphisai. The ruins are also accessible by train from Uthumpornphisai. A quick 2km walk from the train station will bring you to the ruins.

Huai Chan Falls is a group of waterfalls popular with weekenders. To get there, take a bus to Kunhan (every hr. 6am-6pm, 25฿), and hire a motorcycle taxi (50฿) to take you the remaining 24km to Huai Chan. The 8m **Sum Rong Khiat Falls** (a.k.a Pisat Falls) are 26km from Kunhan. Hiring a motorbike is the best way to get there (100฿). The waterfalls are most impressive during their peak flows (Sept.-Feb.); otherwise, they're timid trickles. Also in Kunhan is **Wat Lan Khuad,** or the **"Wat of 1000 Bottles"**—a product of religious inspiration, grassroots environmentalism, and thousands of beer bottles. After seeing local drunks litter the roadsides with beer bottles, a monk was inspired to build a temple out of them. Local citizens donated their own bottles—emptied of liquid, of course.

⚡ DAYTRIP FROM SI SAKET: KHAO PHRA WIHAAN NATIONAL PARK

One of Thailand's best monuments is actually in Cambodia, 1km over its contested southern border. **Khao Phra Wihaan** is a temple complex built between the 10th and the 12th centuries by the Angkor kings, probably as a retreat and pilgrimage site for Hindu priests. It rises 800m up a steep grade overlooking the Cambodian plains to the south, and its principal chapel is on the peak of a great cliff, 600m high. Although officially opened to the public in 1991, it was closed two years later because of violent skirmishes between the Khmer Rouge and the Cambodian government and didn't reopen until August 1998. Today, a ripped-up helicopter pays homage to the last government siege that captured the mount. The region has since stabilized; nevertheless, don't stray from the well-trodden path. The area may still contain land mines.

Apsara Tours in Si Saket and Mr. Pirom (see **Accommodations and Food,** p. 215) in Surin both arrange tours of the park. If you journey there alone during the week, the grounds will be empty, and transportation will require some creativity. Whenever you go, start the 98km haul early for a smoother trip. Catch a bus or *songthaew* to Phum Saron (10km from the ruins) from the bus station in Si Saket (1hr., infrequently 6am-6pm, 30฿). Buses and *songthaew* can also be taken to Katharalak (1hr., every hr. 6am-6pm, 30฿), where you'll have to catch another *songthaew* to Phum Saron. From there, some travelers choose to ignore the motorcycle taxis, and, although *Let's Go* does not recommend hitchhiking, some travelers hitch a ride for the remaining 10km south on the highway. From Ubon, buses go to Kantaralak, where you can return to Si Saket. (*Park open daily 8am-4pm. 200฿ to enter in Thailand, another 200฿, plus a 5฿ fee to photocopy your passport, to gain temporary entrance to Cambodia.*)

UBON RATCHATHANI ☎ 045

The trading and communications hub for the northeast corner of Thailand, Ubon Ratchathani (or simply "Ubon") attracts few travelers until its stunning Candle Festival draws thousands in July. This "royal city of lotuses" was formed only 200 years ago, and the well-planned roadway grid is evidence of its relative modernity. There are, nevertheless, a few fine *wats* to visit, and a great central park offering an escape from the concrete streets. Ubon is famed for its silk and cotton cloth, and great shopping awaits tourists, while those interested in monastic Buddhism can visit many of the region's secluded forest monasteries. Not far downstream, the Moon River flows into the "emerald triangle," where Laos, Cambodia, and Thailand converge in the lush jungle.

▣ TRANSPORTATION

Readily accessible by air, bus, or train, Ubon is also the last stop on the northeastern branch of the national rail network. To go farther east or north, travelers must rely on the sometimes-daunting bus system.

Flights: Ubon Ratchathani International Airport (☎045 244 073), on Thepyothi Rd. **Thai Airways,** 364 Chayangkun Rd. (☎045 313 340), 2km north of the river, on the right. Open M-F 8am-5pm. **Ubon Takerng Tour Co.,** 425 Promrach Rd. (☎045 242 400), in the center of Ubon, also books flights with Thai Airways or Air Asia. Open daily 6:30am-8:30pm. Flights to **Bangkok** (M-Sa 6:30am, 2:35, 6:35pm; Su 6:30am, 3, 6:35pm). **Air Asia** departs for **Bangkok** (daily 8:10am and 3pm). Prices vary considerably depending on when you purchase tickets.

Trains: Train Station (☎045 321 276, advance ticketing ☎045 321 004), on Sathani Rd., Warin Chamrap District. **Songthaew** #2 runs to the station from Upparat Rd., and #1, 3, and 6 head to Ubon from a few short blocks away from the train station (8฿). To **Bangkok** (9-12hr., 7 per day 7:05am-7:15pm, 158-741฿) via **Si Saket** (13-50฿), **Surin** (31-152฿), and **Khorat** (58-313฿); additional trains to **Khorat** (6:15am and 12:25pm) via **Si Saket** and **Surin.**

Buses: Ubon has 2 main bus stations. Ubon's main station is efficient and should generally be used as the departure point for most destinations. Some **local buses** and **songthaew** depart from the station in Warin Chamrap market (near the train station) but are less regulated and structured than departures at Ubon's main bus station. Multiple companies operate, and all offer varying bus classes and prices, so shop around.

Ubon bus station: (☎045 316 089), at the north end of town. Take **songthaew** #1, 2, 3, 10, or 11 (8฿) or a **motorcycle taxi** (60-80฿) from central Ubon. There is a new bus route offered from Ubon to **Pakse** in Laos (See **Border Crossing,** p. 223). To: **Bangkok** (8-12hr., 11 per day 7-11am and 7-11pm, 506-590฿); **Buriram** (4hr., 95-200฿); **Chiang Mai** (18hr., every hr. noon-6pm, 644-1027฿); **Nakhon Phanom** (4-6hr., 5 per day 6am-2pm, 132-238฿); **Mukdahan** (2hr., 12 per day 5:30am-5pm, 119-153฿); **Rayong** (13hr., 10 per day 6:30am-7:30pm, 237-1027฿) via **Pattaya** (12hr., 290-630฿) and **Khorat** (6hr., 145-455฿); **Sakhon Nakhon** (10:30am and 3pm, 120฿); **Surin** (3hr., 16 per day, 75-200฿); **That Phanom** (3hr., 91-130฿); **Udon Thani** (5-6hr., 14 per day 6am-4:30pm, 266-342฿) via **Khon Kaen** (4hr., 18 per day, 5:30am-3pm, 120-216฿); **Yasothon** (1hr., every hr. 3:50am-7:30pm, 66฿). Tickets for these buses can be purchased at the kiosks in the terminal. For destinations within the province, **buy tickets on the bus.** To: **Det Udon** (every 30min. 6:30am-5pm, 20฿); **Kantaralak** (every 20min. 5:30am-6pm, 35฿); **Khong Chiam** (6, 10:30am, noon, 2:30pm; 60฿); **Na Cha Luai** (2hr., 4 per day 9:30am-12:30pm, 47฿); **Phibun** (1hr., every 30min. 5am-6pm, 40฿).

Warin Chamrap Station: south of the Moon River, is a good place to depart from for destinations south of Ubon. Take **songthaew** #1, 3, 6, or 9 (8฿). To: **Na Cha Luai** (2½hr., every hr. 9am-3pm, 100฿); **Phibun** (every 20min. 5am-7:40pm, 40฿); **Si Saket** (1½hr, every 45min. 6am-6pm, 45฿).

Local Transportation: City buses (numbered songthaew) run 5am-6pm (10฿). City maps that outline all routes are available from TAT and the train station. **Tuk-tuks** and **samlor** roam the streets (up to 90฿ from the Moon River to the main bus station).

Rentals: Thai Yont, 300-316 Khuanthani Rd. (☎045 243 547), across from the Ratchathani Hotel (p. 221), rents reliable, well-maintained, and well-serviced **motorbikes** (300฿ per day). Most bikes are manual, so book in advance for an automatic. Open M-Sa 8am-5pm, Su 8am-3pm. **Ubon Rental Cycle,** 115 Sinarong Rd. (☎045 242 813), across from Krungtong Hotel, rents **bicycles** (20฿ per hr., 100฿ for 5-24hr.). Overnight rental available. Open M-Sa 8am-5pm.

✈️ 🛈 ORIENTATION AND PRACTICAL INFORMATION

Ubon's main thoroughfare, **Upparat Road,** stretches north-south for 12km; at its north end it is called **Chayangkun Road.** It's southern end it crosses the **Moon River** into the **Warin Chamrap District,** home to the train station. Songthaew #1, 2, 3, and 6 go near there from Ubon proper. North of the river, Upparat Rd. passes the riverside market and intersects **Khuanthani Road,** two blocks up. The hospital and museum are here; TAT is to the right. The large university and the main bus station are situated northwest from the center of town, and the airport is to the northeast.

Tourist Offices: TAT, 264/1 Khuanthani Rd. (☎045 243 770). Turn right onto Khuanthani Rd. at the National Museum. TAT is on the left, 2 blocks down. Free, useful maps. Open daily 8:30am-4:30pm.

Currency Exchange: Bangkok Bank, 13 Ratchabut Rd. (☎045 262 453). AmEx/MC/Plus/V **ATM.** Open M-F 8:30am-3:30pm. Banks also line Upparat Rd.

Local Tourist Police: (☎045 244 941), at the corner of Suriyat and Thepyothi Rd., near the airport. English spoken.

Pharmacy: Chai Wit, 87 Promathep Rd. (☎045 254 077). From TAT, walk 2 blocks toward the river. Chai Wit is 1 block to the left—look for the yellow and green sign across the street. Open M-F 7am-7:30pm, Sa 7am-noon.

Medical Services: Saphasithiprasong Hospital, 122 Sappasit Rd. (☎045 244 973). Open 24hs.

Internet Access: Ubon provides some of the fastest and cheapest places to surf the web in northeast Thailand. **Kitty Internet Cafe** (☎087 655 1161) is 100m east of TAT and is chock-full of Hello Kitty paraphernalia. Internet 12฿ per hr. Open 8am-10pm. Other options line Khuan Thani Rd. and offer similar prices without all the pink.

Post Offices/Telephones: GPO, 145 Sinarong Rd. (☎045 260 465). From the museum, walk past TAT, and turn left on Luang Rd.; it's on the corner. Open M-F 8:30am-4:30pm, Sa-Su 9am-noon. **Other branches:** 159-163 Phadaeng Rd., between Suriyat and Sapasit Rd., and Warim Chamrap, 88 Tahar Rd. (☎045 324 333). **Postal Code:** 34000.

🛏️ ACCOMMODATIONS

In Ubon, a good night's sleep can come at a relatively good price unless you're planning to visit during a festival. If that does happen to be the case, be sure to call ahead and make reservations.

Aree's Mansion, 208-212 Phadeaeng Rd. Fantastic value with large, basic rooms with fan, hot water shower, cable TV, and Western flush toilets. Laundry machines and dryers (20฿ each) are available near reception. Rooms with fan 250฿, with A/C 300฿. ❷

Tokyo Hotel, 360 Upparat Rd. (☎045 241 739), is another decent budget option set back from busy Upparat Rd. There are 2 buildings: a new one with slightly more modern rooms, and an older one with decent but tired-looking rooms. Prices vary by building. Rooms with fan from 220-350฿, with A/C from 300-600฿. ❷

Ratchathani Hotel, 297 Khuanthani Rd., 1 block from the National Museum. Renovated lobby and bright, clean rooms with daily cleaning service. Located in the heart of the Candle Festival action, which means that in July a decent night's sleep may require earplugs. Rooms with fan 400฿, with A/C 650฿ and up. AmEx/MC/V. ❸

🍴 FOOD

The **riverside market** is a round-the-clock affair, but is most lively in the morning. A **small night market** sets up around 5pm. As you cross the bridge into Ubon, the market is immediately to the right of Upparat Rd. A **better night market** sets up just north of the main market in stalls lining Ratchabut Rd., east of the museum and park. Fried chicken, fruit shakes, and crepes, easily make a full meal. Ubon is a good place to try Isaan's famous *som tom* (25-30฿).

🍽 **Uthayam Booniyom,** on the corner of Sinarong and Thepyothi Rd., is more than just a vegetarian restaurant—it's a vegetarian heaven. Hard-working women affiliated with a nearby Buddhist temple create delicious vegan delicacies full of soybean derivative that are crafted to look, taste, and feel like real meat. Line up to fill a heaping plate at the buffet (15฿) or try individual dishes (10฿). Open daily 6am-2pm. ❶

Chiokee Restaurant, 307-317 Khuanthani Rd. (☎045 254 017), diagonally across from the National Museum. Wooden screens opening onto the street make for great people-watching. Friendly owner recommends *kaeng pa kai* (red curry with bamboo shoots, 40฿). Other dishes 30-160฿. Open daily 6am-7pm. ❷

Indochine Restaurant and Intro Pub (☎045 245 584), on Sapasit Rd., between Phadaeng and Nakhonbant Rd. Vietnamese food with a creative twist. Beautiful teak surroundings add to the chilled-out atmosphere. B*an khao* (crispy pancakes filled with minced pork, shrimp, and bean sprouts 40฿. Open daily 9am-6pm, lounge open 6pm-2am. ❷

👁 SIGHTS

Wat Nong Bua, off Thammawithi Rd., near the bus station, is a breathtaking, 56m replica of the Great Chedi of Buddhagaya in India, the site of Buddha's enlightenment. The exterior reliefs depict the four postures of Buddha: birth, achievement of enlightenment, first sermon, and passing. The greenery growing from the stark grey *chedi* augments the striking stature of the *wat*. Take *songthaew* #10 to get there. **Wat Ban No Muang,** northeast of town, features a modern, 50m tall three-headed elephant statue. Take *songthaew* #8 to get there.

The **Ubon Ratchathani National Museum** is in the heart of the city. To get there, heading toward the bus station, take a right off Upparat Rd.; it's on the left, on Khuanthani Rd. The museum documents the region's history and culture and features a 2100- to 2500-year-old bronze kettle drum, a 9th-century Dvaravati boundary stone, Khmer lintels, and local crafts. The exhibition is mostly in Thai; unless you're a real museum buff, the 30฿ might be better spent elsewhere. (☎045 255 071. Open W-Su 9am-4pm. 30฿.)

Two spots on the Moon River provide relaxing diversions for locals. **Ko Hat Wat Tai** is an island surrounded by huts on stilts above the water. Locals order food from restaurants on the island and picnic in the huts during the dry season (Jan.-Apr.). Open daily 11am-6pm. Take *songthaew* #1 to the end of Khuanthani Rd. and walk toward the river and across the concrete bridge, where a set of stairs descends to the island. Highly recommended, **Hat Khudua,** is located 12km west of town. *Songthaew* #9 from Warin Chamrap bus station will take you there. (Open daily 8am-5pm, depending on demand; open as late as midnight in high picnicing season.)

Wat Thon Si Muang, on Luang Rd., has one of the best-preserved wooden scripture halls in Thailand. Raised on piers in the center of a pool, the hall was designed to prevent ants and termites from destroying the scriptures. In the convocation hall, wall paintings depict everyday life in the 19th century. The **July Candle Festival,** which celebrates the Buddhist Lent, takes place in the park that shares a name with the *wat*, encompassing an entire city block north of the National Museum. For those who miss the festival, the park houses an impressive permanent wax sculpture which will give you a taste of this local art.

ENTERTAINMENT AND NIGHTLIFE

Ubon's nightlife is concentrated north of the river along Chayangkun Rd. The **Nevada multiplex,** past the intersection of Upparat and Ratchathani Rd., shows the latest Hollywood flicks (80฿) dubbed into Thai.

U-Bar, 97/8-10 Phichitrangsan Rd. (☎045 265 141), between Thepyothi and Luang Rd. Currently Ubon's most popular discotheque for the younger, 20-something clubbers dressed up and ready to party. 20+. Open nightly 7pm-1am.

The Rock, 207 Chayangkun Rd. (☎045 280 999), in the basement of the Nevada Grand Hotel. Some nights it becomes a venue for screeching, wannabe pop stars to strut their stuff in front of a live audience; other nights, the place morphs into a pumping disco. Large Chang 60฿. No cover. Open nightly 9pm-2am.

> **BORDER CROSSING: CHONG MEK/VANG TAO.** There are 2 ways to get to Laos from Ubon. Travelers can enter Laos at the village of **Chong Mek,** 44km from Phibun. From the village of Vang Tao on the Laotian side, it is 1hr. to **Pakse,** an excellent springboard for exploration of southern Laos. Other than the border crossing itself, there is little of interest for travelers here except a Sa-Su market, featuring baskets, *sarongs,* frogs, and military fatigues, that springs up on both sides of the border. From Ubon, take a bus from the **Warin Chamrap station** to **Phibun** (every 20min. 5am-7:40pm, 40฿). At the Phibun market, locals can direct you to *songthaew* heading to **Chong Mek** (1hr., every hr. 7am-5pm, 40฿). A new option is more expensive, but also easier and faster: a bus runs from the Ubon bus station and takes passengers all the way to **Pakse** (3hr.; 7, 9:30am, 2:30, 3:30pm; 200฿). This bus returns to Ubon (daily 7, 8:30am, 3:30, 4:30pm). Travelers can purchase a 15-day visa on arrival for US$30 or a heftier 1500฿ (1 passport photo required). 30-day visas are available from the Lao embassy in Bangkok or the consulate in **Khon Kaen** (3-day processing 1100฿, expedited processing up to 1400฿). Before crossing the border, you must officially register your departure from Thailand at the **immigration office,** 30m before the fence, on the right. Once in Laos, present visas to immigration officials, just beyond the border, on the right. From Vang Tao, *songthaew* can drive you to Pakse (10฿). Border open daily 8:30am-4pm. The Laotian entry tax varies, but as of Aug. 2008 stands at 50฿.

MARKETS

Ubon is famous for silk and khit-patterned cotton cloth. **Maybe Cotton Hut,** 124 Sinarong Rd., is near Ratchawong Rd. and sells inexpensive cotton clothing in some unique styles and patterns, all of which are locally made. (☎045 254 932. Open daily 7:30am-9pm.)

Those looking for world-famous Isaan silk should try the **Women's Weaving Cooperative** in the village of Ban Pa Ao, 21km north of Ubon, on Rte. 23. **Ban Pa Ao** is a 200-year-old village famous for its bronze and silk wares. Their traditional *mudmee* silk is available in an array of colors and patterns; prices (from 650฿ per meter) run into the thousands. Weavers perform demonstrations on request. From the Ubon bus station, take a *songthaew* heading to Keang Nai (30min., every hr. 8am-4pm, 12฿), then walk 400m into the village. To return to Ubon, flag down any bus heading south to the city, or catch a *songthaew* directly from the village. For more information, contact the town leader, **Apichat Phanngoen** (☎045 313 505).

For a more general selection of local handicrafts, try ⚑**Punchard,** 56 Phadaeng (☎045 265 751; www.punchard.net), which sells local silk, *mawn khuan* (traditional axe pillows), fish traps, rice containers, and bronze trinkets. The larger of the two showrooms is located across from Hanza Pub. (Open daily 9:30am-8:30pm.)

A few meters south of Punchard, on Phadaeng Rd., is the equally excellent **Khampun Shop,** which sells its famous silk, produced locally, at a unique village southwest of Ubon. Visitors to Ubon during the Candle Festival have a rare opportunity to visit the village, Baan Khampun, where this sought-after silk is produced for the 10 days leading up to the festival (contact TAT for more info). The rest of the year, its production is kept under wraps. To get to the village, take *Songthaew* #9.

▶ DAYTRIPS FROM UBON RATCHATHANI

FOREST MONASTERIES. Northeast Thailand is known for its meditation. Forest *wats* are home to *dudtong* (serious and ascetic) monks who keep strict vows—they limit food to one meal per day and ask for alms daily. Members of the even stricter Santi Asok sect are only allowed to walk barefoot. When visiting the monesteries, visitors should wear proper dress (preferably white tops and bottoms for men, white tops and black bottoms for women; no shorts) and enter quietly, as silent meditation is often in session.

⚑**Wat Pa Nanachat** has the unique mission of training primarily non-Thai Buddhist students in the ancient practice of forest-dwelling monasticism. English is the primary language, and those studying meditation and Buddhism (as well as those with a healthy curiosity) are welcome to visit. It is recommended that visitors arrive before 8am to partake of the daily meal and offering with all practitioners and to have the chance to speak with the abbot and get a tour of the facilities. Modesty should be observed, and women and men are normally discouraged from conversing. Serious students may be able to arrange an overnight or several-week stay, but must write in advance (address letter to "The Guest Monk," Wat Pah Nanachat, Bahn Bang Wai, Warin Chamrab, Ubon Ratchathani 34310, Thailand). The *wat* is a branch of nearby **Wat Nong Pa Pong,** known principally for meditation teacher Ajahn Chah, who passed away in 1992 and was famed for his discipline and forest-dwelling form of asceticism. Both *wats* have more than 20 acres of forest, providing a pleasant place to spend some time. A major branch of the controversial Santi Asok sect resides 6km to the east of town; ask in town for details. (*Wat Pa Nanachat is behind a rice field, off the highway to Si Saket, near Bung Wai village. Catch a Si Saket-bound bus or songthaew from Warin Chamrap Station, and ask to get off at Wat Pa Nanachat (every 45min. 6am-6pm, 13km, 15฿). Alternatively, head 200m west to the songthaew stop near the clocktower where the number 219 songthaew begins its route. The songthaew are sometimes faster than the bus and leave more regularly (20฿, every 30min. 7:30am-5:30pm). The wat is located about 500m from the road, inside a walled, forested compound. Wat Nong Pa Pong temple is 10km south of Ubon and off the road to Katharalak. Ask for directions at Pa Nanachat.*)

KHONG CHIAM ☎045

The tranquil hamlet of Khong Chiam, 60km east of Ubon Ratchathani, rests securely on the map of major tourist destinations in the northeast due to its interesting location at the confluence of the Moon and Mekong Rivers. During the wet season—when the rivers are in full force—their two distinct colors create a unique vision as they meet and mix for the first time. Khong Chiam won't hold your attention for too long, but with an array of top-notch accommodations and a couple of national parks nearby, it's a great way to break up the journey between Thailand and Laos and a relaxing get-away from the everyday.

TRANSPORTATION

Take a bus from the **Warin** or **Ubon Ratchathani bus stations** to **Phibun Mangsahan** (1hr., every 30min. 5am-6pm, 40฿). From the Phibun market, take a **samlor** (20฿) or walk to the **songthaew station** on the Moon River. From the bus stop, head towards the market. Turn right onto Thiboon Rd. and walk three long blocks. At the traffic signal, take a left, and walk until you reach the river. **Songthaew,** in a parking lot on your right, go to Khong Chiam (45min., every hr., 30฿).

Transport out of Kong Chiam is variable and it is best to move out in the early morning. The bus station is the carpark next to the market about 50m west of Mongkong Guest House. *Songthaew* run to **Phibun** (leave when full; daily 6am, 9am; 40฿). From there you can get buses to **Ubon Ratchathani** (every hr. 5am-7pm, 40฿), **Bangkok** (7:30am and 2:30pm, 392฿) or **Chong Mek** (every hr. 6:30am-5:30pm, 40฿). Buses also depart from Kong Chiam to **Tagarn** (2hr.; 6:30, 10am, 1pm). From Tagarn, limited connections can be made to other towns in the northeast, including **Mukdahan** (130฿); you need to arrive in Tagarn as early as possible. Tell the driver your final desitation as soon as you board the bus in Kong Chiam.

If you get stuck in Phibun, either on the way to or from Kong Chiam, **Hotel Phibun ❸**, 65/1 Thiboon Rd., opposite the Kashikornbank, is on the way from the bus stop to the *songthaew* station along the river. This hotel, on the right, has immaculate rooms and an extremely friendly, English-speaking owner. (☎441 201. Rooms with fan 200฿, with A/C 300฿.)

ORIENTATION AND PRACTICAL INFORMATION

Khong Chiam is a peninsula shaped like a long acute triangle: its two main roads come together in a point near where the **Moon** and **Mekong** rivers, that flow on both sides of the town, come together. **Klaewpradit Road** runs from the market and bus stop through the center of town (on the Moon River side). **Rimkheng Road** runs along the Mekong River parallel to Klaewpradit Rd. until the two roads meet at the *wat*. On Rimkheng Rd., a stone tablet identifies Khong Chiam as Thailand's easternmost point.

Services include: **the immigration office** (☎045 351 084) on Klaewpradit Rd., which can give visa extensions (30 days 1,900฿; requires a copy of your passport and 1 photo); Khong Chiam's **bank, Krung Thai Bank,** on Klaewpradit Rd., which exchanges currency and traveler's checks (☎045 351 123; open M-F 8:30am-4:30pm); the **police station** (☎045 351 023), located opposite the stone tablet on Rimkheng Rd.; **Khong Chaem Hospital** (☎045 351 331), 1.5km above town, on the Khong Chiam-Phibun Rd.; a small **pharmacy,** at Klaewpradit and Ratsadonytid Rd., a few meters beyond Mongkhon Guest House (☎045 351 245; open daily 6am-8pm); **Internet access,** at a small shop (☎045 351 417) on Klaewpradit Rd., 100m east of Mongkong Guest House; computers are slow but they work (Internet 20฿ per hr.); and the **post office,** on Klaewpradit Rd., with international phone. (☎045 351 016. Open M-F 8:30am-4:30pm, Sa 9am-noon.) **Postal Code:** 34220.

ACCOMMODATIONS

Surprisingly, tiny Khong Chiam is packed with comfortable guesthouses.

Mongkhon Guest House, 595 Klaewpradit Rd. (☎045 351 352; www.mongkhon.com), 30m up from the bus station, has beautiful teak bungalows and cheaper double rooms. Rooms, all with bath and TV, are impeccably clean and a great value. Laundry available at 10฿ per pant or shirt. Also rents motorbikes for 200฿ per day. Doubles 200฿, with A/C 350฿; newer bungalows 500-800฿. ❷

Apple Guest House, 267 Klaewpradit Rd. (☎045 351 160), past the bank and opposite the post office, is less charming than the others but has clean and affordable rooms. Rents motorbikes 200฿ per day. Singles and doubles 150฿, with A/C 300฿. ❷

FOOD

Khong Chiam also lacks the market flair of most small towns in the northeast, but makes up for it with charming restaurants that literally float on the rivers. Also, be sure to hit up the great *som tam* (20฿) maker across from Mongkhon Guest House.

🍴 **Arraya Restaurant,** 200 Rimkhong Rd. (☎045 351 015), sits right on the water, down a steep staircase from the road—about as close as you can get to the Mekong without actually going for a swim. English menu. Dishes 40-150฿. Mixed vegetables in oyster sauce 50฿. Open daily 10am-8pm. ❷

Krua Phai San Cuisine, on Klaewpradit Rd. opposite the post office. Void of the scenery available at other restaurants, Krua Phai San still offers great food at low prices. Vietnamese and Thai dishes 30-80฿. ❶

> **! ENDANGERED ANIMALS.** Restaurants in Thailand serve up many varied and delicious meals—but some may contain the meat of endangered animals. Look out for any restaurant serving Giant Mekong Catfish, *Plaa Buek*, softshell turtle, barking deer, clouded leopard, and certain species of bear, among other animals. Check out www.animalinfo.org or www.wwfthai.org for updated information on endangered species and environmental concerns.

🔍 SIGHTS

PHA TAEM NATIONAL PARK. Khong Chiam is known for the *mae nam song si*, the convergence of the "Two-Color" River, an effect created by the different levels of silt suspension from blue Moon River and brown Mekong River. In the dry season, this effect is not as stunning, but the low water level makes it so travelers can nearly reach Laos. The end of Klaewpradit Rd., through the temple grounds, leads to a pavilion with a pleasing view of the two rivers.

About 20km north of Khong Chiam is **Pha Taem National Park** and its stunning 200m long cliff, which offers truly spectacular views of the surrounding area. The rock face of the cliff is covered with colorful 3000-year-old rock paintings; some archaeologists believe they were made by prehistoric soothsayers and shamans in trance-like states. A pleasant 3km path takes you down past the viewing platforms at the paintings to some incredible lookouts. A trailhead can be found next to the visitor's center. While at the park, also visit **Sao Chaliang,** an area where erosion has created interestingly shaped rock formations. Camping (30฿, if you have your own equipment) is possible; tents can be rented (2-person 150฿) and sleeping bags (30฿), mattresses (20฿) and pillows (10฿) are also available. A number of in-park bungalows (6-person with fan 1200฿, 5-person with A/C 2000฿) can be rented in the park for an overnight stay. *(Contact ☎045 246 332 or write to Pha Taem National Prak, P.O. Box 5, Tambon Huayphai, Khong Chiam, Ubon Ratchathani 34220 to make reservations. Or, book online at www.dnp.go.th; make your payment beforehand at any Khrung Thai Bank in Thailand. Tuk-tuks (1-way 200-250฿, round-trip 300-350฿) can take you to the park, or you can rent a private car from the bus station (350฿). ☎045 249 780. Open daily 6am-6pm. 400฿, children 200฿.)*

MUKDAHAN ☎ 042

Although a small town at heart, Mukdahan exhibits a certain international flair thanks to its prime location along a river stemming from the far-away Himalayan Mountains. The 1893 demarcation of the Mekong River as an international boundary politically separated Mukdahan from Savannakhet, Laos, but the region remains unified by its culture, food, and lifestyle. French-Lao golden baguettes are sold by street vendors and in shops. Annual boat races in October are enjoyed by all from both sides of the river. In 2007, Mukdhan declared itself the "Gateway to Indo-China" as the impressive bridge across the river to Laos was opened. Now, the modern **Mudkahan Tower** (20฿) provides impressive views of the region. Although there isn't too much to keep travelers occupied in Mukdahan itself, it serves as a calm place to decompress after a trip through Laos, and a good base for the nearby pleasant Mukdahan National Park.

▐ TRANSPORTATION

The **main bus station,** 33 Chayangkong Rd. (☎042 671 478; baggage storage available for 20฿ per day), is 3km away from the main part of town. Yellow **songthaew** (10฿) travel to town when full, and **tuk-tuks** (20-40฿) go to the river. To **walk** into town, take a left out of the terminal and a right at Wiwitsurakan Rd., the first major intersection, 500m ahead. Follow this street as it merges to the right. Make a left at Phitak Phanomket Rd., and walk 0.5km into the heart of town (about 30min.) Different companies run **buses** to **Bangkok** (☎042 630 793; 10-12hr 8:30am, 5:30, 7:20, 8, 8:15pm; 437-870฿); **Khorat** (☎042 630 1156, 6hr; 5 per day 6:30am-4pm, 238-330฿), **Pattaya** (646฿); **Rayong** (10-14hr., 6 per day 6am-7pm, 718฿); **Khon Kaen** (4hr., every 30min. 3:30am-5pm, 165฿); **Nakhon Phanom** (2hr., 4 per day 9am-2pm, 55-99฿); **That Phanom** (1hr., 8 per day 8:30am-4:30pm, 30-53฿); **Ubon Ratchathani** (3hr., 14 per day 8am-5:30pm, 85-153฿); **Udon Thani** (5hr., 8 per day 8:30am-5:30pm, 135-207฿). With the new bridge, you can now catch the **Thai-Lao International Bus** across the border (12 per day 8:15am-7pm, 45฿). Be sure to have your Laos visa before you board, obtainable at the Lao embassy in Bangkok or the consulate in Khon Kaen. (See **Border Crossing,** p. 229.)

▟ ▐ ORIENTATION AND PRACTICAL INFORMATION

Mukdahan is laid out on a grid, with streets running roughly parallel (north-south) and perpendicular (east-west) to the **Mekong,** the town's eastern border. Along the river bank is **Samron Chaikhong Road,** site of the Indochine Market, the *wat,* and the pier. Parallel to Samron Chaikhong Rd., heading from the river, are **Samut Sakdarak (Mukdahan-Domton) Road** and **Phitak Santirad Road.** Perpendicular to these are **Song Nang Sathit Road,** which runs from the pier past the Huanum Hotel to the night market, and, to the south, **Phitak Phanomket Road.** The **traffic circle** is located at the intersection of Phitak Phanomket and Phitak Santirad Rd. The bus station is on the main highway, **Chayangkong Road (Route 212),** 3km northwest of the main area of town.

There is an irregularly staffed **Tourist Information Center** on Pitakphomket Rd. next to the traffic circle (☎042 632 700; open M-F 8:30am-4:30pm), and you can also obtain your maps and brochures at the **TAT** in Ubon Ratchathani. A few **travel agencies,** including **Orchid Travel,** 14 Pitak Phonomket Rd. (☎042 633 144), line Phitak Phanomket Rd. and can book tours and international airline tickets. **Bangkok Bank,** 33 Song Nang Sathit Rd., two blocks up the road from the pier and one block past Huanum Hotel, has an AmEx/MC/V **24hr. ATM** and exchanges currency and traveler's checks. (☎042 611 554. Open M-F 8:30am-3:30pm.)

NORTHEAST THAILAND

Other services include: the eclectic **Indochine Market,** which sets up every day at the waterfront and sells trinkets like mini disco balls, Buddha images, and dinnerware; **bike rentals** at the Huanum Hotel (100฿ per day); **Sa-art Laundry,** 77 Samut Sakdart Rd., one block from the traffic circle toward the river and a couple of blocks right from there (☎042 613 647, t-shirts and pants 10฿); the **Mukdahan Immigration Office,** 2 Song Nang Sathit Rd., across from the ferry pier, which provides visa extensions (☎042 611 074; bring 1 photo and 1 passport copy for a 30-day visa extension, 1900฿; open M-F 8:30am-4:30pm); the **police station,** 83 Phitak Santirad Rd. (☎042 611 333), between the traffic circle and Song Nang Sathit Rd.; **Nguam Hong Osoth Pharmacy,** 38 Samut Sakdarak Rd., opposite Huanum Hotel (☎042 611 850; open M-Sa 6am-8pm, Su 6am-noon); **Mukdahan Hospital,** 24 Samudsukdaruk Rd. (☎042 611 285), just west of the traffic circle; **Internet,** at 44 Phitak Phanomket Rd., 400m from the traffic circle, heading away from the river, past the Ploy Palace Hotel (15฿ per hr.; open daily 9am-11pm) and at the more central Huanum Hotel (20฿ per hr.); and the **post office,** 18 Sribooruang Rd. (☎042 611 065. Open M-F 8:30am-4:30pm, Sa-Su 9am-noon.) **Postal Code:** 49000.

ACCOMMODATIONS

Mukdahan accommodations are nothing special, but are perfect for the traveler on a tight budget.

Huanum Hotel, 36 Samut Sakdarak Rd. (☎042 611 137), on the corner of Samut Sakdarak and Song Nang Sathit Rd., 1 block from the pier. Well-priced rooms with fan. The shared bathrooms are clean and have hot water and Western flush toilets. Has a small, bright cafe in the lobby. Internet 20฿ per hr. Bike rental 100฿ per day. Doubles with shared bath 120-200฿, with A/C 280-320฿. ❷

Ban Lim Suan Mansion, 18 M Kdahan-Dontan Rd. (☎042 632 980). From the traffic circle, walk 1 block toward the river, turn right, and walk another 600m. Rooms are a fantastic value and very well kept. Free Internet in the lobby. Rooms with A/C and TV 330฿. ❸

Sansook Bungalows, 136 Phitak Santirad Rd. (☎042 611 214). From the traffic circle, head south away from the tourist center. Thai sign. Provides fairly standard, air-conditioned rooms with TV, set around a parking lot. Rooms 280-350฿. ❸

FOOD

Given that Mukdahan is a crossroads of culture, and it is home to a vast array of food from China, Laos, Vietnam, and, of course, Thailand. The **night market** along Song Nang Sathit Rd. is especially good (closes around 9pm). Clean, well organized stalls serve spicy *som tam* and *larb sod* (tangy, and very spicy minced pork). *Paw pia thawt* (Vietnamese spring rolls) come *sot* (fresh) or *thawt* (fried). But Mukdahan is especially famous for its *kanom tuay* (roasted pork served with sticky balls of rice, 25฿) and tasty *naam* (raw pork wrapped in a banana leaf and left to turn into sausage, 20-60฿). Packed in single-serving plastic bags, an entire meal totals an astounding 20-30฿. In the mornings, **street vendors** sell fresh baguettes, some filled with minced pork (*kun chiang*) to make tasty sandwiches (6-20฿). French-Lao bakeries also vend rolls, cakes, eclairs, and more.

Pith Bakery, 703 Phitak Santirad Rd. (☎042 611 990), opposite the police station, serves some of the best brownies this side of the Mekong. The gregarious English-speaking owner dispenses sound travel advice. Coffee 15-16฿. Open daily 8am-8pm. ❶

Mac's Cafe, 30 Soi Sasimong (☎042 614 571). Heading toward the roundabout from Sansook bungalows, take the first right; it is the soi directly next to the big Buddha at Wat Gow Siweechai. Head here for a good cup of coffee. Western and Thai food 30-120฿, Western breakfasts 70-80฿. ❷

◎ SIGHTS

A larger-than-life golden Buddha contemplates the Mekong from **Wat Gow Siwee-chai**, on Samron Chaikhong Rd. Further down the road, across from the immigration office, lies **Wat Si Mongkan Tai**, which is particularly revered by Laotians. Look for the high gables and the unique face and short body of the Buddha—all are characteristics of Lao-style Buddhist art. Accompanying the completion of the new bridge between Thailand and Laos in 2007, a new observation tower, the **Mukdahan Tower**, was built 2km to the south of the town center. On Mukdahan Rd., this tower boasts spectacular views of the new bridge, the town, and the winding Mekong. Open daily 8am-5pm, 20฿. If you happen to arrive at the end of Buddhist Lent (in late fall), you can catch **boat races** on the Mekong.

> **BORDER CROSSING: MUKDAHAN/SAVANNAKHET.** Purchase a 15-day visa on arrival for US$30 or a heftier 1500฿ (1 passport photo required). 30-day visas are available from the Lao embassy in Bangkok or the consulate in Khon Kaen (3-day processing 1100฿, expedited processing up to 1400฿). From Mukdahan, take the Thai-Lao International Bus (45฿, 12 per day 8:15am-7pm). The Lao entry tax varies (currently 50฿).

▶ DAYTRIP FROM MUKDAHAN

MUKDAHAN NATIONAL PARK. Known for its rock formations and caves, Mukdahan National Park also boasts prehistoric rock art, wildlife, and cliff-top views of the Mekong. The collection of huge, oddly shaped rocks at the main entrance is the chief crowd-pleaser. The undersides of many overhanging rocks are decorated with faded prehistoric paintings. Trail maps are available from the **park office** at the entrance. Trails are marked in Thai, and arrows pointing straight ahead direct hikers along the main 2km hike to the **Buddha Cave Waterfall**. During the dry season, the falls shrink to a trickle. Rickety wooden stairs lead to the **Buddha Cave**, lined with thousands of wooden Buddha images, a likely clue to the existence of an ancient community in the area. Look for the peculiar statue of two twin monks standing back to back. (*The park can be reached from Mukdahan by buses and songthaew leaving from Phom Phet market, by the river on the southern side of town. One occasionally leave from in front of the hospital near the traffic circle and goes straight to Dontan. From Phom Phet, change songthaew for one heading to Dontan, and ask to get off at the park (2 per hr. 6am-6pm, leaves when full; 20฿). The entrance is a 15min. walk down a small paved road, on the right. This journey can be arduous and time consuming, so your best bet may be to hire a tuk tuk (around 400฿) for a return trip.* ☎ 042 601 753.; www.dnp.go.th; Camping fee 20฿. Open daily 8am-6pm. 200฿.)

THAT PHANOM ☎ 042

Most travelers would follow the Mekong right past this tranquil town if it wasn't home to one of Thailand's most sacred pilgrimage sites, Wat That Phanom. Towering nearly 60m high, the Lao-style (gem-encrusted, gold-gilded) *chedi* is revered by Thais and Laos alike. The energy of the visitors that flock in homage to this formidable tower is palpable. The its radiant Buddha images have even been covered in gold foil by faithful worshippers.

▐ TRANSPORTATION

That Phanom, midway between Nakhon Phanom and Mukdahan, is easily reached by either **bus** or **songthaew** (30฿), which stop along Chayangkun Rd. (Hwy. 212) and at a small bus station (☎042 547 247) south of town. Buses leave for **Ubon Ratchathani** (3hr., 14 per day 6:30am-2:30pm, 121-197฿) via **Mukdahan** (1hr., 27-47฿), and **Udon Thani** (5hr., 9 per day 9:30am-6pm, 115-195฿) via **Sakhon Nakhon** (1hr., 35-52฿). Several companies run to **Bangkok,** including **government buses** (11hr., every 30min. 7-9am and 4-6:30pm, 400-620฿). Buses and *songthaew* to **Nakhon Phanom** (1hr., 7 per day, 26-40฿) leave from a stop 150m north of the *wat*, across from the gas station.

▣ ▐ ORIENTATION AND PRACTICAL INFORMATION

Wat That Phanom is on **Chayangkun Road (Highway 212),** the main thoroughfare through town. Running parallel to Chayangkhun Rd., along the **Mekong River,** is **Rimkhong Road,** where many restaurants and hotels are situated. **Kuson Ratchadamnoen Road** runs straight out from the *wat* under the **Lao Arch of Victory** and all the way to the river.

Siam Commercial Bank, 359 Chayangkun Rd., diagonally across from the *wat*, has an AmEx/Cirrus/MC/V **24hr. ATM.** (☎042 525 784. Open M-F 8:30am-3:30pm.) The **Lao Market,** on the far end of Rimkhong Rd., sells wood products from Laos and other trinkets and wares. (Open M and Th 6am-noon.) Other services include: the **police station** (☎042 541 266) and **That Phonom Hospital** (☎042 541 256) are both about 2km out of town on the Chayangkun Rd.; **Internet access,** at **Jan Internet,** 45 M1 Phranongphrarak Rd., across the road from the Arch of Victory; (open daily 8am-9pm, 20฿ per hr.); and the **GPO,** 373 Chayangkun Rd., past the bank and *songthaew* stop, which also has international phones. (☎042 541 169. Open M-F 8:30am-4:30pm, Sa 9am-noon.) **Postal Code:** 48110.

▐ ACCOMMODATIONS

Accommodations fill up fast during the February festivals, so when possible, make reservations ahead of time.

Niyana Guest House, 65 Moo 14 Soi Weethree Sawrachin. From the Arch of Victory, head to the pier, and take the 1st right onto Soi Weethree Sawrachin. A fantastic inexpensive option. Rooms have comfortable mattresses, mosquito nets, and polished wooden floors. Niyana speaks great English and hands out helpful maps of That Phanom. Singles 120฿, doubles 160฿. ❷

Kritsada Rimkhong Resort, 90-93 Rimkhong Rd. (☎042 540 088; www.ksresort. com). From the pier, walk north along the river front past Niyana Guest House. It's 6 sois on the left, across from the *wat*. Expansive 2-room suites with fridge, TV, and A/C are available at this friendly and well-managed accommodation. Includes free breakfast, free Internet, bicycles for the borrowing, and even occasional fishing lessons (100-200฿) on the Mekong. Suites 400-600฿. ❸

Rimkhong Bungalows, 130M 14 soi Brembuchanee Rd. (☎ 086 642 1910). If Niyaya is closed and the prices at Kritsada Resort are outside your budget, you may be forced to try a night or 2 in these Bungalows. With fan 250฿, with A/C 350฿. ❷

▐ FOOD

At **food stalls** on Chayangkun Rd., 20฿ buys savory roast chicken, sticky rice, or a bowl of Vietnamese *pho*. A good **night market** sets up off Chayangkun Rd., across from the school, and dishes up tantalizing cuisine like *pad mun sen* (pork and bean vermicelli. Most dishes 20-30฿. Open until around 9pm.) A number of riverside restaurants hang precariously over the Mekong, giving them some of the best views around.

Kritsada Rimkhong Restraunt (☎042 540 088), directly in front of Kritsada Resort, is one of the best places to eat in town. Some of the items on the Thai menu have been translated into rough English. Try the spicy fish salad (120฿). Other dishes 60-150฿. Open 10am-11pm. ❷

Mai Srirat, 162 M 13 Chayangkool Rd. (☎042 541 394), without English sign, about 200m north of the *wat*. Come dance to live Thai folk music with the locals. Thai menu only, but the English-speaking owner can help you. Try the *tom yam pra* (100-150฿) or a fish salad; other dishes 40-150฿. Live music nightly 8pm. ❷

👁 SIGHTS

Wat That Phanom is the most sacred religious structure in northeast Thailand. Legend says it was built to house one of the Buddha's clavicle bones, transported all the way from India. Topped by a 110kg gold spire, the shrine has been restored seven times since its initial construction, most recently in 1978, after heavy rains in 1975 collapsed the 57m tall *chedi*. The *wat* is surrounded by a cloister housing dozens of golden Buddha images. Depending on whom you ask, it's between 12 and 26 centuries old. Look for the raised platform in front of the *chedi* with a large golden Buddha sitting under an ornate umbrella. On the platform, there are groupings of seven Buddhas, each one representing a day of the week, starting on the left with Saturday. People commonly donate a few baht and pray to the Buddha representing the day of the week on which they were born.

Upon entrance, most visitors make a small donation and pick up a bundle with three sticks of incense, a candle, some gold pieces of paper, and a couple of roses. Light the incense and place it in an incense holder; do the same with the candle. The flowers are usually left near the foot of the tower, and people sometimes attempt to stick the gold flakes of incense onto the Buddhas situated around the *chedi* in hopes that wealth and wisdom will be bestowed upon them. You can also get your fortune read behind the *chedi*. Give a small donation, then pick up the cup full of sticks and shake until one falls out. It will have a number on it which will correspond to a fortune on one of the pieces of paper in front of th small Buddha. For more luck, free a turtle, some birds, fish, or snakes (100฿ each) at one of the vendors to the right of the *chedi*. Afterwards, check out the informative museum with interesting relics and information boards detailing the region's religious history.

A particularly good time to visit is at the beginning of February during the annual **Phra That Phanom Homage Fair,** when thousands come to pay their respects and emulate the journey that the Buddha himself took to this important location thousands of years ago. There's no set date for the fair—it takes place from the 10th day of the waxing moon to the day of the full moon in the third lunar month. (*Wat* open 5am-8pm daily.)

About 15km northwest of That Phanom is the silk-weaving village of **Renu Nakhon.** Visitors to the **Renu Nakhon Wat** can enjoy Isaan music and dance, sporadically performed during the winter and holidays. Contact TAT in Nakhon Phanom for more information. To get there, take any Nakhon Phanom-bound *songthaew* to the Renu Nakhon junction 8km north of town. From there, hire a *tuk-tuk*.

NAKHON PHANOM   ☎042

Nakhon Phanom, "the city of mountains," presents an amazing panorama of the jagged green limestone outcroppings across the river in Laos. The picturesque vista of these stunning hills dominates the city and creates a dramatic backdrop for ordinary life. At sundown, the riverside promenade comes alive with women sweating to aerobic workouts and young teens gossiping while the occasional elephant ambles casually by. Nakhon Phanom does attract a fair number of travelers, but its laid back atmosphere is perfect for whiling away a day or two along the meandering Mekong.

⬛ TRANSPORTATION

Nakhon Phanom Airport (☎042 587 444) is 15km from town. **P.B. Air** (☎042 587 207) has flights to **Bangkok** (70min.; M, W, F, Su 7:45am; Tu, Th-F, Su 5:15pm; Sa 8:45pm). **Tuk-tuks** (60-90฿) go to the airport. The **Nakhon Phanom Bus Station** (☎042 511 403), on Piya Rd., is in the southwest corner of town. Buses to: **Bangkok** (11-12hr., every 30min. 7-8am and 4:30-6:30pm, 472฿); **Khon Kaen** (7hr., 6 per day 7:30am-4pm, 160-252฿); **Mukdahan** (2hr.; 6, 7, 7:30, 8:30am, 2pm; 55-99฿) via **That Phanom** (1hr., 29-52฿); **Udon Thani** (4hr.,every 30min 4am-3:10pm, 175฿) via **Sakhon Nakhon** (2hr., 66฿); **Nong Khai** (7hr., every 30min. 6am-11am, 140-190฿). **Tuk-tuks** gather near the night market on Aphibanbuncha Rd. and go around town (20-30฿). **LA Bicycle**, at the clock tower on Sunthon Wichit Rd., rents **bicycles.** (☎042 478 480. 10฿ per hr., 50฿ per day. Open daily 8am-5pm.) With help from TAT's tourist map, bicycling is a great way to view the city.

⬛ 🛈 ORIENTATION AND PRACTICAL INFORMATION

Two main roads run parallel to the river, connected by smaller perpendicular roads. **Sunthon Wichit Road,** adjacent to the river and lined with a promenade, houses TAT, the post office, and the police station. Farther south, past the intersection with **Fuang Nakhon Road,** Sunthon Wichit Rd. leads to the **clock tower,** the immigration office, and the intersection with **Nittaya Road,** where most buses enter and exit the city. The bus station is just north of Nittaya Rd., 1km from the river. **Aphibanbuncha Road,** with the hospital and the day market, runs parallel to Sunthon Wichit Rd., three blocks inland from the river.

The local **TAT,** 184/1 Sunthon Wichit Rd., one block north of the post office, provides an excellent map of Nakhon Phanom with a bicycle route of all the major tourist sites. (☎042 513 490. Open daily 8:30am-4:30pm.) **Bovorn Travel,** 85 Nittaya Rd. (☎042 512 494), one block away from the river, is the easiest place to book flights. **Bangkok Bank,** on Si Thep Rd., behind the Indochine market, exchanges currency and has an **ATM.** (☎042 511 209. Open M-F 8:30am-3:30pm.) Other services include: **Nakhon Phanom Police Station** (☎042 511 266), on Sunthon Wichit Rd., one long block north of the clock tower; **tourist police** (☎042 515 773), a little farther south on Suthon Witchit; the **pharmacy, Sawang Fhama,** 478/80 Aphibanbuncha Rd., where Aphibanbuncha intersects Fuang Nakhon Rd. (☎042 511 141; some English spoken; open daily 7am-8pm); **Nakhon Phanom Hospital** (☎042 511 422), on Aphibanbuncha Rd., a few blocks north of its intersection with Fuang Nakhon Rd.; **Internet access** at **Carp Internet,** directly across from the Grand Hotel, on Si Thep Rd. (15฿ per hr.; open daily 8:30am-10pm); and **Nakhon Phanom Post Office,** 341 Sunthon Wichit Rd., next to the police station. (☎042 512 945. Poste Restante. Open M-F 8:30am-4:30pm, Sa-Su 9am-noon.) **Postal Code:** 48000.

ACCOMMODATIONS

Nakhon Phanom doesn't really have a guesthouse scene, but some decent mid-range hotels do drop their prices during much of the year. Rates skyrocket during the famous Illuminated Boat Festival, in late October at the end of the Buddhist rains retreat. If you plan on visiting at this time, book well in advance.

Windsor Hotel, 272 Bamrungmuang Rd. (☎042 511 946). From Aphibanbuncha Rd., walk toward the river on Fuang Nakhon Rd. and take a right; the hotel is on your right. Rooms are well kept, with a professional feel. Some rooms have a view of the Lao mountains. The lobby is welcoming and the staff is attentive. Singles with TV 250฿, with A/C 350฿; doubles with A/C 400฿. ❷

KS Mansion (☎042 516 100), on the corner of Aphibanbuncha and Salaklang Rd., across from the imposing yellow French-colonial building, has spotless modern rooms, each with a small balcony, fridge, and cable TV. Very little English spoken. Internet 20฿ per hr. Rooms with fan 280฿, with A/C 350฿. ❸

Grand Hotel, 2210 Si Thep Rd.(☎042 511 526), a few blocks south of the clock tower. Nothing too grand here, but the rooms are comfortable enough. Singles 180฿, with A/C 320฿; doubles 280/380฿. ❷

FOOD

Get a 20฿ bowl of noodles at the **night market,** or, better yet, sample some of Isaan's famous chopped pork (*lab*) or salted Mekong fish on **Fuang Nakhon Rd.** There is also a popular **food court** above the Indochine market, where locals congregate to sip bottles of whiskey mixed with soda at all hours of the day and night. Thai food (25-80฿) is available as well. Riverfront restaurants dominate Nakhon Phanom's culinary scene. A few open-air restaurants line Sunthon Wichit Rd. south of the immigration office.

Nakhon Phanom Riverview Hotel Restaurant, 9 Nakhon Phanom-That Phanom Rd. For great river views, stroll 1-2km south along the river promenade toward the Nakhon Phanom River View Hotel. The hotel boasts a fancy restaurant with ample A/C and phenomenal food to justify the splurge. Dishes 80-350฿. Live music nightly. ❸

View Khong, 527 Sunton Witchit Rd. (☎042 522 314), an open-air riverside eatery with a stunning view of mountains in Laos. Has an extensive menu with fish (50-169฿) fresh from the river. Open daily noon-midnight. ❷

Meringue Bakery, 203 Sunthon Wichit Rd. (☎042 514 237), across from the clock tower, makes a great place for a midday coffee break. Bakes an impressive selection of brownies. Baked goods 10-30฿, coffee 20-45฿, shakes 25-30฿, small selection of Thai food 30-80฿. ❶

SIGHTS AND ENTERTAINMENT

By far the best way to experience Nakhon and see the sights is to rent a bike from **LA Rentals** (see above) and get a map from **TAT** that clearly marks out a fantastic bicycle route throught city, surrounding rice fields, and *wats*. **Wat Okatsibuaban,** adjacent to the promenade south of the clock tower, houses two highly revered images of the Buddha in a brightly painted and immaculately kept *wat* complex.

Thai-Vietnamese Friendship Village and **Ho Chi Minh House** are a few kilometers from town, off the highway toward Sakhon Nakhon. There is an interesting museum displaying artifacts and information about Thai-Vietnamese relations during the last century. Of particular interest is Nakhon Phanom's link with Ho Chi Minh, who stayed in Thailand for much of 1928-1930 and planned his return to Vietnam to bolster support for his Communist Party of Vietnam and pending revolution.

Near the Friendship Village is the rustic home where Ho Chi Minh actually stayed, surrounded by rice paddies and nibbling cows. Some of Ho Chi Minh's belongings have been preserved as they were when he lived here. An amusing sign points to a coconut alm that Ho Chi Minh supposedly grew. Bring water and be prepared for a real workout if you choose to bike (30min.). Alternatively, negotiate with a *tuk-tuk* driver to take you (10min., 50-80฿) and wait. Ask the groundskeeper to turn on the lights and some kitschy Communist music will pipe up. (Free entrance to displays; small box for donations as you enter.).

If all this *wat*-hunting and pleasure-strolling has worn you down, recharge with pumping MP3s and an ice-cold Singha (small 50฿) at the **Duck Pub**, on Nitayo Rd., one block toward the city center from the bus station. A younger crowd sits around high tables and listens to local rock bands. The dancefloor gets going later in the night. No cover. Live music at 10:30pm and again at midnight. Open nightly 8pm-1:30am. There are also a number of music venues and drinking spots along Nitayo Rd. near Duck Pub, very close to the river. Crowds pick up around 9pm, and some spontaneous karaoke is known to break out from time to time. If you're looking for a more low-key evening, **Livingroom Pub and Bar** has acoustic music and a more relaxed environment. Open 6pm-midnight.

BORDER CROSSING: NAKHON PHANOM/THA KHAEK. Travelers can purchase a 15-day visa on arrival for US$30 (1 passport photo required). 30-day visas are available from the Lao embassy in Bangkok or the consulate in Khon Kaen (3-day processing 1100฿, expedited processing up to 1400฿). Before crossing the border, obtain an exit stamp from the immigration office, just opposite the Indochine Market, on Sunthon Wichit Rd. (☎042 511 235. Open M-F 8:30am-4:30pm.) A boat behind the office shuttles passengers to Tha Khaek (every 15min. 8am-6pm, 60฿). The Lao entry tax varies, but currently stands at US$1.

SAKHON NAKHON ☎042

Once a small farming town on the banks of Nong Han Lake, the largest lake in northeast Thailand, Sakhon Nakhon has evolved into a hectic industrial city laced with a maze of crooked *sois* and the occasional city-planned, wide-avenued roadway. Visitors come to Sakhon Nakhon mainly to revere the attractive Phra That Choeng Chum, an elaborate *stupa* built to cover the Lord Buddha's sacred footprints left on the land beneath. In late October, at the end of the Buddhist rains retreat, the city also plays host to the annual Wan Phra Jao Phanom, which invigorates the city with a flurry of *wat* offerings and boat races. Take a quiet stroll around the lakeside park, chill out in Phu Phaan National Park, or visit the Khmer sanctuary of Phra Thad Phu Phek. No matter what you choose, you will not get bored in Sakhon Nakhon.

 TRANSPORTATION

The **Sakhon Nakhon Airport** (☎042 713 919) is 6km northwest of town. **PB Air** flies to **Suwannabhum airport** in **Bangkok** (70min.; M,W, F, Su 8:40pm; Tu, 7:40am; Th 7:40am, 8:40pm; Sa 7:40am, 5:20pm; 3115฿). There is no public transport to the airport, and taxis can cost up to 200฿. Buses to **Bangkok** (11hr; nightly 6:30, 7, 7:30pm; 531-620฿) from a small office (☎042 711 737) 50m to the right of the bus station. Sakhon Nakhon's **bus station** (☎042 712 860) is at the southern end of Ratpatana Rd. From the post office, take a left onto Ratpatana Rd.; the terminal is about 1km down, on the left. Buses to: **Maha Sarakham** (4hr; 10 per day 8am-

9:30am and 5pm-7pm, 150-170฿); **Kalasin** (3hr.; 5 per day 7:30am-2pm, 59-89฿); **Khon Kaen** (4hr., 6 per day 8am-5:30pm, 176฿); **Nakhon Phanom** (2hr; approx. every hr. 7:30am-7:15pm, 70฿); **Udon Thani** (3hr., 14 per day 5:45am-5:20pm, 115฿); **Ubon Ratchathani** (5hr., 8 per day 6:30am-5:30pm, 134-241฿). **Tuk-tuks** are hard to find, but **samlor** (30-50฿) are everywhere.

◼ 🔧 ORIENTATION AND PRACTICAL INFORMATION

Sakhon Nakhon is 647km from Bangkok and 93km from the **Mekong River.** Most buses traveling from the northeastern edge of Thailand will pass through on their way to Bangkok in the south or Udon Thani in the west. The streets are fiendishly complicated, with twisted, connecting sois that add character and confusion. The western border of town is marked by **Ratpatana Road,** and the bus station is at its southern end. To the north, **Charoenmuang Road** runs east-west and is lined with hotels. The post office is at its western end. **Sukkasem Road** connects these two roads, forms the eastern boundary, and makes a truncated trapezoid within which most of the city clusters. A useful city map is availabe from reception at Dusit Hotel.

Services include: **Phu Sakon Travels,** 332/3 Sukkasem Rd. (☎042 712 259), between Kamjadphadi and Charoenmuang Rd., which can book PB Air, Air Asia, Thai Air, and Nok Air flights; **Bangkok Bank,** 1324/20 Sookkasem Rd., at the intersection with Primprida Rd., with a currency exchange and **24hr. ATM** (☎042 711 501; open M-F 8:30am-3:30pm); **laundry machines** in a random shed on the corner of Thanon Charoenmuang and Thanon Prempreeda about 50m north of L.P. Mansion (40฿); the **Sakhon Nakhon Police Station,** 75 Jaiphasook Rd. (☎042 716 506), two blocks north of the traffic circle; **Sakhon Nakhon Hospital** (☎042 716 565), on Charoenmuang Rd., east of the traffic circle; the **Yathongchai Drugstore (pharmacy),** 1891/2 Sookkasem Rd., near the night market (☎042 732 678; open daily 8am-9pm); **Internet access,** at **Com.,** 1608/3 Primprida Rd. (☎042 736 204), just south of Kamjadphadi Rd., toward the bus station (20฿ per hr.; fax available; open noon-10pm); and **the post office,** 224 Charoenmuang Rd., at Ratpatana Rd. (☎042 711 049. Poste Restante. Open M-F 8:30am-4:30pm, Sa-Su 9am-noon.) **Postal Code:** 47000.

▮ ACCOMMODATIONS

Quiet Sakhon Nakhon has a plethora of comfortable and affordable places to get some shut-eye.

L.P. Mansion, 303 Prempreeda Rd. (☎042 715 356), between Chareonmuang Rd. and Kam Jad Phai Rd., about 1m north of the bus station. A new hotel with crisp, clean, well-maintained modern rooms. Little English spoken. Rooms with fan and private bath 250฿, with A/C 350-400฿. ❷

Dusit Hotel, 1784 Yuwapatana Rd. (☎042 711 1989; www.dusitsakhon.com), near Robmuang Rd. Pleasant rooms with spic-and-span bathrooms and excellent service. Free Wi-Fi. Rooms with hot water, A/C, and TV 360-500฿; larger rooms with breakfast 400-650฿. Discounts occasionally granted. ❷

Somkait Hotel, 1348 Kamjadphadi Rd. (☎042 711 044), sits between Sukkasem and Primprida Rd. Offers simple, clean rooms with squat toilets and TV. Rooms 200฿, with A/C 350฿. ❷

▮ FOOD

Between trips to the *wats* around town, sample Sakhon Nakhon's fabulous cuisine.

Willy Nam Nueng, 1301/6 Sookkasem Rd. (☎042 731 120), north of Wat Jaeng, with some of the best Vietnamese food in the city. Try the yummy springtime sandwiches for

NORTHEAST THAILAND

a lettuce-wrapped pork-and-egg snack (20฿) or freshly-made vegetarian springrolls for (50฿). Open daily 7am-8pm. ❷

Lan Som Dao, (☎080 186 7191), opposite the entrance to Somdej Phra Srinakarin's garden on Sa-Pan Thong Rd. No English sign or menu. Heap your plate at the buffet (179฿) and cook your meal yourself on a small hot plate in the middle of your table while listening to live music in this fantastic open-air restaurant. Live music nightly. Open 5pm-10:30pm. ❸

Tongdee Steak House, 1310 Kum Jad Phai Rd. (☎042 711 817). Serves large steaks with garlic bread, salad, and boiled vegetables (220-550฿) in an eclectic setting: cuckoo clocks, Princess Diana paraphernalia, and log cabin walls. Thai dishes 80-250฿. Open daily 10:30am-9pm. ❸

Noodle-and-Rice Joint Clearwon, on Jaiphasook Rd., next to the Chareonsook Hotel, serves generous portions of noodles with pork strips for 30฿. Open daily 8am-7pm. ❷

👁 🎭 SIGHTS AND NIGHTLIFE

Wat Phra That Choeng Chum ("place of gathered footprints") is one of the most sacred shrines in all of Issan. Located on Reuang Sawat Rd., at the intersection with Charoenmuang Rd., it houses a 24m, gold-and-white, Lao-style square *chedi* shaped like a lotus bud. According to the legend of Urangkathat, the four incarnations of Buddha have all traveled here to place their footprints in the soil. The *chedi* houses their impressions. To the left of a *chedi* is a small *wat* decoated with ornate wooden carvings and thousands of small pieces of colored glass. The annual wax castle procession, featuring a collection of miniature beeswax Buddhist temples and shrines, celebrates the end of Buddhist Lent (usually in mid-Oct.) and takes place at the *wat*. Behind the *wat* on the shores of Nong Han Lake is the **Somdej Phra Srinakarin's** garden, created in honor of the king's mother. Accordingly, it is kept in beautiful condition and its interconnectiong ponds and walkways make for a fantastic stroll at sunset. Steer clear of the water, though: the lake is infested with liver flukes, freshwater parasites that infect fish and treat human skin as if it were an amusement park. Don't swim in the lake, and don't eat undercooked fish, especially in Sakhon Nakhon. Several **open-air bars** line Tor Patana Rd., off Ratpatana Rd. A local favorite is **Suan Rak.** (Small Singha 60฿. Open nightly 4pm-midnight.) Next door, **Golden Pond** offers live rock and pop bands nightly at 9pm.

🎭 DAYTRIP FROM SAKHON NAKHON

PHU PHAAN NATIONAL PARK. A hideout for communist guerilla forces in the 1970s, the 645 sq. km of low-lying mountains and forests are now home to deer and monkeys, as well as the occasional black bear and elephant. Its few short hiking trails can be a welcome respite from dusty Isaan towns. (30฿ camping fee, 50฿ tent rental. Dorms 100฿, bungalows 500-600฿.) The **park headquarters** is located 25km from Sakhon Nakhon, on Rte. 213 to Kalasin. Most of the small waterfalls and viewpoints are only 3km off the road.

The incomplete Khmer sanctuary of **Phra Thad Phu Phek,** located on a hill 544m high, is in the opposite direction as the park, and offers a spectacular view and some decent ruins. It is best visited by private car or by hiring a motorcycle taxi (700฿ to take you there, wait, and then drive you back) from Sakhon Nakhon. Alternatively, if you are in a group and planning to visit both Phu Phaan an Phra Thad Phu Phek, you might consider hiring a private truck and driver from the bus station (☎087 949 0040, 1200฿ for a day, 600฿ for ½ day). Finally, although Let's Go does not reccommend it, hitchiking may be an effective strategy. (*To get to the park from Sakhon Nakhon, take a Kalasin bound bus for 15km (20min., 20฿) or a songthaew* *from behind the bus station (when full 8am-3pm, 20฿) and ask to be let off at the park. To return, walk out to the road, and gesticulate furiously at every bus on its way to Udon via Sakhon Nakhon. Alternatively, hire a motorcyce taxi to drive you there, wait until you're done, and drive you back (500฿). ☎ 042 703 044. Open daily 8:30am-4:30pm.)*

UDON THANI   ☎042

With the largest expat population in northeast Thailand, Udon Thani has a palpable international presence. An array of restaurants, pubs, and accommodations cater to a variety of Western tastes and desires, but dig a little deeper and the richness of the local culture is easily uncovered. Wander around Nong Prajak Park and its natural lake in the early evening as friendly locals exercise in the health park or munch on street cuisine, then turn back time and get a glimpse of life as it was thousands of years ago in the village of Ban Chiang, a UNESCO World Heritage Site. With its 100,000+ population, Udon is not only a pleasant place to visit, but also a genuinely intriguing Thai city.

◨ TRANSPORTATION

Flights: Udon Thani Airport (☎042 246 254), on the Udon Thani-Loei Hwy., 5km southwest of the city. **Air Asia** (☎02 515 9999) flies to Bangkok (5:40pm, 1980฿). **Thai Airways** also flies to **Bangkok** (1hr.; 11:10am, 3:05, 7:45pm; 2590฿). **Nok Air** (www. nokair.com) flies to **Bangkok** (1hr.; 7:30am, 2, 6:30pm; 2360฿) and **Chiang Mai** (1hr., 7:35pm, 1550฿). **Skylabs** run between the airport and the city (100฿).

Trains: Train station (☎042 222 061), at the east end of Prajak Rd. Booking office open daily 6am-8pm. To: **Bangkok** (10-11hr.; 6:47am, 6:40, 7:20, 8:10pm; 245-1177฿) via **Khon Kaen** (2hr., 25-50฿) and **Ayutthaya** (8hr., 257฿), the train at 6:40pm also stops at **Khorat** (5hr., 64฿) and **Pak Chong** (7hr., 83฿); **Nong Khai** (1hr.; 4:11, 6:34, 7:53am; 15฿). Walk 500m in front of the train station to catch *songthaew* #7, 9, or 14.

Buses: There are **2 bus terminals** in Udon. **Terminal 1** is located near the train station in the east of town and dispatches buses to most destinations. **Terminal 2** is located on the southwest border of town and sends buses to destinations north and west of Udon. Buses to **Nong Khai** can be taken from either terminal, but buses from both will stop at Rangsima Market in the northwest of town. Catch a bus right from this market for the most frequent and efficient service (Udondutsadee Rd. 100m before you reach Ring Rd.; 1hr., approx. every 40min. 7:30am-8pm, 41฿).

    Bus Terminal #1 (☎042 222 916), near Charoensri Shopping Complex, off of Sai Uthit Rd. To: **Bangkok** (9-10hr., every 30min. 6am-11pm, 368-750฿) via **Khorat** (4hr., 207฿) and **Khon Kaen** (2hr., 85-104฿); **Sakhon Nakhon** (3hr., every 40min. 6am-5:20pm, 115฿) via **Ban Chiang** (45min., 50฿); **Ubon Ratchathani** (6hr., 10 per day 5:52am-2pm, 190-324฿); **Mukdahan** (4hr., 8 per day 5:45am-12:50pm, 181-236฿); **Nong Khai** (every hr. 11am-7pm (except 4pm), 60฿); **Ban Pang** (5 per day 6:20am-2:20pm, 120-160฿).

    Bus Terminal #2 (☎042 247 788), 2km west of town, on the ring road, has northbound buses to: **Chiang Mai** (12hr.; 7:30, 8pm; 601-701฿); **Chiang Rai** (14hr.; 3:50, 7, 8:30pm); **Loei** (3hr., every 30min. 4am-8pm, 66-105฿); **Rayong** (11hr; 8:30am, every hr. 4-11pm; 599-930฿); **Phitsanulok** (6hr.; 5 from 7:30am-3:30pm, every 30min. 6:20-8:30pm). *Songthaew* #6, 7, and 15 go by the station.

Local Transportation: Songthaew go anywhere in the city (8฿). #7 runs between bus terminals #1 and #2; #6 along Udondutsadee Rd. from the fountain north to Rangsima Market and bus station #2; #14 from the train station to TAT; #9 and #15 from Charoensri Shopping Complex down Srisuk Rd. Larger **yellow buses** (10฿) run from the train station down Posri Rd. and up Phoniyom Rd., passing the Orchid Farm (p. 240). Free *songthaew* route maps available from TAT. Plenty of **samlor** (20-30฿) and **tuk-tuks** (20-50฿) run around town; haggling with the drivers is necessary unless you want to pay twice the normal amount for a ride. **Car** and **motorcycle** rental shops line the streets near the shopping complex. Try **Santisook Car Rental,** 546 Posri Rd. (☎042 246 087), on the corner close to the Sarorn Hotel, opposite the *songthaew* stop. Manual motor-cycle 200ʙ per day, automatic 250ʙ; car 1200ʙ per day.

📲 🚻 ORIENTATION AND PRACTICAL INFORMATION

Udon Thani lies between Khon Kaen and Nong Khai, along the railroad line and Friendship Highway. Navigating the city can prove tricky, so carry a map. A num-ber of hotels and bars are clustered in the southeast corner of town near the **Charoensri Shopping Complex,** the train and bus stations, and the night market. **Prajak Road** and **Posri Road** run to the west from this area to the other side of town, near **Nong Prajak Reservoir** in the northwest. Each road sports a traffic circle where it diagonally intersects **Udonutsadee Road,** the main north-south artery. The airport and bus terminal #2 are on the far side of the reservoir, west of the town center on **Ring Road,** which circles the town. The university is just south of the shopping complex, on the other side of Posri Rd. The largest night market is located just outside of the train station entrance at the east end of Prajak Rd. Thai Issan Mar-ket is on Sai Uthit Rd. Rangsima Market sets up on Udonutsadee Rd.

Tourist Office: TAT, 16/5 Mukkhamontri Rd. (☎042 325 406), at the edge of the reser-voir. Enter from Tesa Rd. Open daily 8:30am-4:30pm. **On Time N.E. Co.,** 539/72 Posri

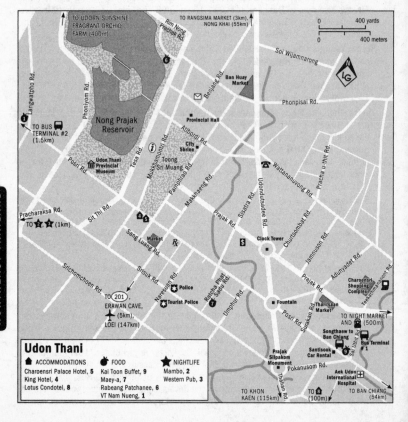

Udon Thani

🏠 ACCOMMODATIONS
Charoensri Palace Hotel, **5**
King Hotel, **4**
Lotus Condotel, **8**

🍴 FOOD
Kai Toon Buffet, **9**
Maey-a, **7**
Rabeang Patchanee, **6**
VT Nam Nueng, **1**

⭐ NIGHTLIFE
Mambo, **2**
Western Pub, **3**

NORTHEAST THAILAND

Rd. (☎042 247 792), is an efficient travel agency that books flights to Bangkok and Chiang Mai. Open M-Sa 8am-5pm, Su 8am-2pm.

Currency Exchange: Bangkok Bank, 154 Prajak Rd. (☎042 221 505). **24hr. ATM. Currency exchange** open daily 8:30am-5pm. Bank open M-F 8:30am-3:30pm.

Local Tourist Police: 55/55 Naresuan Rd. (☎042 211 291), south of the regular police station, has English-speaking officers. Open 24hr.

Police: (☎042 211 077), at Srisuk and Naresuan Rd. Has an old computer with free Internet. Open 24hr.

Pharmacy: 194 Posri Rd. (☎042 222 478). Well stocked pharmacy is accredited by the Pharmacy Council of Thailand. Pharmacist speaks English. Open daily 8am-10pm.

Medical Services: Aek Udon International Hospital, 555/5 Posri Rd. (☎042 342 555, emergency number ☎042 341 555; www.geocities.com_aekudon/). One of the best hospitals in the northeast. English-spoken. **24hr. pharmacy.** AmEx/MC/V.

Telephones: CAT, 108/2 Udondutsadee Rd. (☎042 348 474). North of the clock tower, before Wattananuvong Rd. Open M-F 8:30am-4:30pm.

Internet access: Cafes crowd the area near Bus Terminal #1 and the shopping complex. Fast service is also available at many shops near the university, particularly along Soi Thongkham Uthit. Usually 15-20ß per hr.

Post Office: GPO, 2 Wattananuvong Rd. (☎042 222 304), behind the provincial wall. Poste Restante. Open M-F 8:30am-4:30pm, Sa-Su 9am-noon. **Postal Code:** 41000.

ACCOMMODATIONS

There's no backpacker scene here, but due to a growing economy, a number of new hotels have recently been built, widening the range of accommodations from aging and cheap to modern and expensive.

Lotus Condotel, 43/4 Roumjit Rd. (☎042 212 221), is accessible by Thepburi Rd., 1 block beyond the Paradise Hotel. Lotus gets high points for its location near the mall and the bus station and for its well-priced, clean rooms. All rooms with A/C, a small balcony, and cable TV. Doubles with private bath 279-399ß. ❷

Charoensri Palace Hotel, 60 Posri Rd. (☎042 242 611), at the corner of Posri Rd. and Parnphrao Rd. Recommended by locals as the best budget place around, its rather old rooms have cable TV, and comfy beds. Friendly staff cleans rooms daily. Singles or doubles 360ß, with fridge 450ß; suites 600ß. Discounts sometimes available. ❸

King Hotel, 57 Posri Rd. (☎042 221 634), set back from the street on the same block as Charoensri Palace Hotel. Possibly the first hotel built in Udon for American GIs, it should be nominated for the kookiest architecture award. Basic rooms get little light but are well priced and cleaned daily. Singles 190ß, with A/C 220ß; doubles 230/270ß. ❷

FOOD

Ban Huay Market, at the north end of Udondutsadee Rd., where a network of vendor-lined sois surrounds a huge covered area with tons of delicious goodies. In a city heavily influenced by Western culture, the following affordable restaurants, which serve traditional Thai dishes, are a special find.

Kai Toon Buffet, 539/14 Posri Rd. (☎042 343 966). For starved stomachs and wallets. 60ß buys all-you-can-eat Thai food, a salad, and dessert. Open daily 9am-11:30pm. ❷

VT Nam Nueng, 345/1-3 Phosri Rd. (☎042 347 111; www.vtnamnueng1997.com). *Songthaew* #9 runs past here. A Vietnamese hotspot with a sit-down section and drive-through to-go area. Its famous dish is also its namesake: *nam nueng* (pork balls roasted over an open fire and served with fresh veggies and wrapping papers that you transform into your own springrolls, 90-165฿). ❸

Maey-a, 81 Ratcha Phat Sadu Rd. (☎042 223 889), 4 blocks south of Posri Rd. Walking toward the reservoir from the fountain, take the second left; it's on the second block on the left. A multi-story family restaurant bursting with hoards of hungry Thais here for the giant menu and yummy desserts. 7-scoop sundae 88฿. Thai, Chinese, and Western dishes 40-260฿. Open daily 9:20am-10:30pm. AmEx/MC/V. ❷

Rabeang Patchanee, 53/1 Bannon Rd. (☎042 241 515), offers a more scenic experience. At the northern end of the park, this large restaurant has a open-air terrace that looks out over the lake and bridge. Try the steamed curried fish and cuttlefish in a kanomkok plate (90฿). Thai dishes 50-180฿. ❷

👁 SIGHTS

UDORN SUNSHINE FRAGRANT ORCHID FARM. About 2km northwest of town, the small Udorn Sunshine Fragrant Orchid Farm is a veritable botanical talent show. The recently deceased Mr. Pradit Kampermpool devoted a decade of his life to developing the first orchid perfume, aptly named "Miss Udorn Sunshine," which is naturally available for purchase (300-1000฿ per bottle). Before seeing the orchid, visitors are treated to a rather uninspiring video explaining the farm and its botanical wonders. Next, guests are led to the orchid enclosure, where the orchid itself can only be smelled in the mornings before 2pm; afterwards, it appears to be a pretty, yet rather normal flower. The next enclosure over, where *Desmodium gyrant* makes its home, is even more fascinating. These unremarkable-looking plants perk up and shimmy to the vibes of music or human voice. Thanks to Mr. Kampermpool's years spent cross-breeding, the plants respond almost instantaneously, as opposed to their more lethargic wild counterparts. These plants are reputed to have psychological healing powers related to meditation: by focusing on the plants, patients are relieved of worry. Some make a strong tea out of the plant's leaves which many claim can prevent and cure stomach cancer or intestinal problems. *(To get to the farm, take Posri Rd. past the reservoir and bear right on Phoniyom Rd. After the 1st stoplight, take the turnoff for the farm, 100m ahead on the left. Farm is another 100m on your right. Songthaew #16 and #5 pass by the turnoff. 127 Nongsamrong Rd. ☎042 242 475; www.udon_sunshine.com. Open daily 8am-5pm.)*

UDON THANI PROVINCIAL MUSEUM. This museum, easily accessed via Posri Rd., was built in 111 days and opened on January 18th, 2004, to commemorate the 111th anniversary of Udon province. Covers topics including geology, archaeology, and ethnology. The museum does an impressive job of summarizing thousands of years of Udon's past. *(Open M-F 8am-4:30pm, Sa-Su 8am-4pm. Free.)*

NONG PRAJAK RESERVOIR. This beautiful reservoir, in the northwest section of town, is full of benches, pavilions, and footbridges. Join mothers, children, and sweethearts feeding the catfish, or work up a sweat with the joggers who circle the paths every evening for some exercise. The best part of this area is the night massage vendors that arrive daily around 5pm and offer superb hour-long Thai foot massages. *(1hr. Thai massage 120฿, 1hr. foot massage 100฿, 30min. foot massage 60฿. Open 5am-8pm)*

🎵 🎭 ENTERTAINMENT AND NIGHTLIFE

The **theater** at the top of the **Charoensri Shopping Complex** screens Thai films (70฿). **Bowling** on the same floor. (60-90฿, plus 30฿ shoe rental. Open 11am-12:30am.) Udon's nightlife is surprisingly hopping. To get to **Mambo,** 572 Pracharaksa Rd., in the Napalai Hotel, head west toward the reservoir on Srisuk Rd., turn left where Pracharaksa Rd. branches off Srisuk, and walk 1km. Alternatively, a *tuk-tuk* from downtown should cost 70-80฿. Bathe yourself in fluorescent blue light and the pounding beats of the local DJs and rock bands. (☎042 346 547. Mixed drinks 100-150฿, Heineken and Singha 80฿. 20+. Open nightly 9pm-2am.) Across the road from Mambo is **Western Pub,** 420 Pracharaksa Rd., where the staff, the band, and much of the clientele are dressed in head-to-toe Western digs, complete with cowboy hats and plaid shirts. Order a BBQ steak (100฿) and a bottle of Jack Daniels (1400฿). Live Western music all night. (Open nightly 7pm-1am.)

▶ DAYTRIPS FROM UDON THANI

BAN CHIANG

Orange songthaew leave from Posri Rd. for Ban Chiang, (1hr.; M-F 4 per day 6:30am-5pm, infrequent Sat and Sun., leave when full, 50฿). On Sai Uthit Rd., walk past the bus station on your left and make a right onto Posri Rd. You'll see the songthaew on the right side of the road, opposite a small supermarket. In the case that none are going, take a bus from the nearby bus station headed to Sakhon Nakhon, (every 40min. 6am-5:20pm.) Buses drop off at the turnoff in Pulu (50฿). From here, take a tuk-tuk the remaining 6km, (60฿ per person, 100฿ per vehicle). Buses and songthaew return to Udon from the museum entrance every hr. until 2pm, (80-130฿). If you miss these, hire a tuk-tuk to the main road; there are frequent buses from Sakhon Nakhon to Udon. Alternatively, rent a motorcycle in town (see above) and drive yourself, following the clearly marked English signs. Look closely for the turnoff, just past a mysterious set of traffic lights in Pulu.

Ban Chiang, 54km east of Udon Thani, is one of Southeast Asia's most significant **archaeological discoveries** and was recognized as a UNESCO World Heritage Site in 1992. The story of its discovery begins in 1966, when Stephen Young, then a junior at Harvard College and son of the ambassador to Thailand tripped over a large root while doing research for his senior Anthropology thesis in Ban Chiang. Catching himself, he found the rim of a partially unearthed pot staring him in the face. Upon closer scrutiny, he found that the area was littered with half-buried pottery. By the time excavation began in the mid-1970s, many valuable artifacts had been sold to collectors in trading centers worldwide.

The skeletons and numerous bronze artifacts found here have shed light on the lives of the inhabitants of the area from 3000-1000 BC. They also indicate that the civilization possessed knowledge of metallurgy much earlier than originally estimated, casting doubt on the theory that the practice came to Thailand from China. The **national museum** documents the unearthing of Ban Chiang. Information in English (including some of Stephen Young's original notes and a copy of his thesis) can also be viewed at the national museum. The second-floor exhibits have comprehensive captions in English. (☎042 208 340. Open daily 8am-4pm. 30฿.) In contrast to the museum, the **dig site,** at **Wat Phosi Nai,** is anticlimactic. Still, it displays a well-preserved burial site with intact artifacts. (Exit left from the museum; the excavation site is 600m down on the right. Admission included in the price of museum ticket.)

Ban Chiang's local **homestay program** provides a glimpse of authentic village life. You can stay with a local family and share in three meals and daily activities like the early morning alms-giving ceremony (300฿ per day). Call Anoy (☎083 145 8026), in advance to arrange for pickup from Udon airport or city and transfer to Ban Chiang.

NONG KHAI ☎042

Nong Khai is a town that knows how to multi-task. As a border town, it hosts the daily ebb and flow of Laotian shoppers, expats on visa runs, and travelers on Indochine border crossings that give this small city an international flavor. Nong Khai boasts the most *wats* per capita in all of Thailand, but also knows how to put on a show; thousands of visitors make their way here every year for a number of worthwhile festivals, including the unexplainable Mekong fireballs that mysteriously appear at the end of the Buddhist rains retreat. When your visa has been stamped, the temples have been toured, and the fire balls have disappeared high into the sky, you'll know it's time to leave.

TRANSPORTATION

Trains: Nong Khai Train Station (☎042 411 592), on Hwy. 212, 1.5km west of town. Trains to **Bangkok** (11hr.; 6am, 6:20, 7:15pm, 388-1217) via **Udon Thani** (1hr., 11฿), **Khon Kaen** (3hr., 35฿), and **Ayutthaya** (9hr., 242฿). Booking office open daily 7am-7pm. *Tuk-tuk* ride from Rimkhong Rd. 40-60฿.

Buses: Nong Khai Bus Station, off Prajak Rd., at the east end of town. To: **Bangkok** (12hr.; 10am, every 30min. 6:30pm-8pm;, 402-800฿) via **Khon Kaen** (122฿), **Khorat** (320฿), and **Udon Thani** (41-91฿), **Nakhon Phanom** (5-7hr., 6 per day 6:40am-10am, 156-189฿) via **Beung Khan** (3hr., 120฿); **Udon Thani** (1hr., every hr. 6am-6pm, 41฿). Green buses to **Rayong** (12hr., 10 per day 6am-6:30pm) and **Loei** (6-8hr.; 11am, 2:30pm; 120฿) via **Si Chiangmai** (1½hr., 40฿), **Sangkhom** (2-3hr., 55฿), and **Pak Chom** (5hr., 84฿). To get to **Chiang Khan,** switch buses at **Baan Tat.** For **Chiang Mai,** go to **Udon Thani** and change buses. Buses to **Vientiane, Laos** (2hr.; 7:30, 9:30am, 12:40, 2:30, 3:30, 6:30pm; 55฿) are available only if you already have a Laos visa.

Local Transportation: Motorcycle taxis and **tuk-tuks** (30-70฿) shuttle all over town.

Rentals: Bicycle rental at **Mut Mee Guest House** (43฿ per day, see **Accommodations,** p. 243), and at **Ruan Thai Guest House** (30฿ per day, see p. 243). **Motorbike** rentals (250฿ per day) at Ruan Thai Guest House. Test ride all rentals before you pay.

ORIENTATION AND PRACTICAL INFORMATION

Nong Khai is a major border crossing to Vientiane, Laos. **The Friendship Bridge** crosses over the **Mekong River,** joining the two countries. To the north, Nong Khai is bordered by the Mekong River, while **Highway 212** marks the town's southern boundary. Parallel to Hwy. 212, from south to north, are **Prajak Road, Meechai Road,** and **Rimkhong Road.** The train station, on Hwy. 212, 2.5km west of the town center, is a bit of a hike. The bus station is off of Prajak Rd., southeast of the main tourist area. The nearest airport is in Udon Thani. Some guesthouses offer detailed tourist maps of Nong Khai and of the surrounding area, and the town is small enough that bicycling is an ideal way to get around and see the sites.

Tourist Information: TAT, 2 Mitraphap Rd. (☎042 427 326), in the Mekhong Center of Quality Goods and Tourism Services, just off the highway between Nong Khai and Udon Thani. Has a useful map, but is a fair trek from the guesthouses and center of town. Open daily 8:20am-4:30pm.

Tours: Rapport Travel Service, 169/8 Moo 4 (☎042 465 6889), books domestic and international flights. Open M-Sa 8:30am-5pm.

Immigration Office: 106 Moo 7 Chalermprakiet Rd., on the road heading towards the bridge to Laos. Issues visa extensions (1900฿, 1 photo, 1 copy of passport, and evidence of intended departure required).

Currency Exchange: 372 Soi Srisaket (☎042 412 675). Open M-F 8:30am-3:30pm.

Books: Hornbill Bookshop, 1121 Kaeworawat Rd. (☎042 460 272), on the soi to Mut Mee Guest House (p. 243), buys and sells used books. This is the only bookstore of its kind in Isaan, so stock up if heading deep into the region. Also has Internet for 30฿ per hr. Open daily 10am-7pm.

Police: (☎042 411 612), 813 Meechai Rd., facing the hospital. **Tourist police** (☎042 460 186) are right next door. Open daily 8:30am-4:30pm.

Pharmacy: Tong Tong Pharmacy, 382/2 Meechai Rd. (☎042 411 690). Exit left from the post office and it's on the corner. Open daily 7:30am-8pm.

Medical Services: Nong Khai Hospital, 1158 Moo 3 Meechai Rd. (☎042 411 504), near the city hall, opposite the police station.

Internet Access: Internet will likely find you before you find it. 20-30฿ in many guest-houses. **P+W Com,** 888/12 Phochai Rd. (☎042 412 536), is a cheap cafe on the small soi leading to Wat Po Chai (10฿ per hr.). Open daily 10am-10pm. **Oxynet,** 569/2 Meechai Rd., is a more central cafe. 25฿ per hr. Open daily 9am-midnight.

Post Office: 390 Meechai Rd. (☎042 411 521). International phone. Poste Restante. Open M-F 8:30am-4:30pm, Sa-Su 9am-noon. **Postal Code:** 43000.

ACCOMMODATIONS

Mut Mee Guest House, 1111/4 Kaeworawat Rd. (☎042 460 717; www.mutmee.com). The place to be in Nong Khai: a riverside restaurant, oodles of tourist info, and a steady stream of travelers. Garden patio and cleverly-designed rooms feel like an oasis. Fantastic western breakfast served at restaurant (60-85฿). Dorms 90฿; singles with shared bath 140฿; doubles with shared bath 160-260฿, with private bath 290฿, with A/C 530฿ and up. ❶

E-Sarn Guesthouse, 538 Moo 7, Soi Wat Srikunmuang (☎042 412 008), is a quiet retreat with only a few rooms surrounding a lovely green garden. Traditional Thai rooms with a homey feel are very clean and have beautiful, polished wood floors. The shared bathrooom has hot water and a Western toilet. Singles with fan 150฿; doubles 250฿, with private bathroom and A/C 450฿. ❷

Mekong Riverside, 519 Rimkhong Rd. (☎042 460 431). Rooms with comfy bed, TV and private bath. More expensive rooms with killer location over the river. Singles with fan 250฿, doubles 350฿; with A/C 400/500฿. More luxurious rooms available for 800฿ with breakfast included. ❷

Ruan Thai Guest House, 1126/2 Rimkhong Rd. (☎042 412 519). From the market, walk 3 blocks toward Wat Haisok. Rooms are clean and decently priced. Full American breakfast 80฿. Laundry service 30฿ per kg. Rents bikes (30฿ per day) and motorbikes (200฿ per day). Rooms with fan and shared bath 150฿, with bath 200-300฿, with A/C 400-500฿. ❷

FOOD

Good, inexpensive Thai food can be found at small local **street vendors,** like the ones that gather every evening around the intersection of Prajak and Chuenjit 1 Rd., creating an informal **night market** with the usual produce and meats. On Sunday evenings, a vibrant **market** takes shape off Hwy. 212, one block west of the highway to Udon Thani, towards the train station. Food, clothing, and the usual odds and ends are sold for bargain prices. (Open nightly 6-9pm.) The **Indochina market** (Taa Sadej Market), along Rimkhong Rd., has a few Thai eateries with excellent views of the river. (Open daily 9am-5:30pm.) For the homesick traveler, *farang*-runestablishments along the Mekong provide some Western comfort.

Dang Nam Neung, 526 Rimkhong Rd. (☎042 411 961), is an old favorite, with a comfy terrace looking out over the Mekong. It still serves amazing *nam neung* (make-your-own Vietnamese spring rolls). 90฿ per person or 165฿ for 4 buys a platter of greens, starfruit, green banana, cucumber, sausages, and rice-paper wrappers. Open daily 8am-8pm. Other dishes 35-90฿. ❷

Yota Vegetarian, along the river on Kaeworawat Rd., is a faux-meat eatery that will make vegetarians and vegans jump with glee. Heaping plates of Thai favorites sans meat 15-20฿. Excellent fried seaweed 12฿. Pork rind crisps—minus the pork, of course—15฿. Open daily 7am-1pm. ❶

Dee Dee's (☎411 548), at Prajak Rd. and Soi Vientamnuson. Serves up inexpensive Thai food that's popular with locals. Dee Dee's is also in the center of the evening action. Most dishes 40-100฿. Open nightly 2pm-midnight. ❷

⚑ SIGHTS

⬛**SALA KAEW KU** (WAT KHAEK). The city with the most *wats* per capita, Nong Khai can boast another superlative, as it is home to one of Southeast Asia's most unique sculpture parks. Towering concrete statues of Hindu and Buddhist figures are the artistic creations of Luang Poo Boun Leua Sourirat, a Laotian artist-turned-spiritual guru, who fled his Communist homeland in 1975 seeking the freer shores of Thailand to sculpt his larger-than-life work. The concrete structures, some towering seven stories high, represent various levels of Hindu and Buddhist cosmology: the good and the evil, the mundane and the fantastic, the innocent and the freaky. Most of the temple's gravity-defying figures are gods, goddesses, demons, and Buddhas found in the Indian pantheon of mythical deities. Towards the back of the park, you can walk through a mouthed penis and out of a massive vagina, a concrete representation of *samsara*, the Buddhist belief in the endless life cycle of rebirth and suffering. A series of sculptures arranged in a circle represents the events of the life cycle. An amusing map of the cycle is available from Mut Mee Guest House and can help explain some of the eccentricities. The skeleton lovers are also a little odd, but they don't even compare to the artist's mummified body and personal remains that are displayed on the third floor of the main building. Through a corridor covered with creepy portraits of the artist himself, Luang Poo Boun Leua Sourirat's body lies inside of a plastic dome drapped with holiday lights. *(4km outside of town. Head east on Rte. 212, past "St. Paul Nong Khai School," on the right; Sala Kaew Ku is 2 turnoffs later. 15-20min. by bike. Tuk-tuks 100-120฿ round-trip. Open daily 8am-5pm. 20฿.)*

WAT PO CHAI. This *wat* houses a small Buddha statue with a unique history. As you enter on the right, monks will bless you by sprinking water on you, and tie a colored string around your wrist for good luck. Stunning murals on the inner walls of the *wat* illustrate the story of how this gold and bronze Buddha image, known as **Luang Pho Phra Sai,** sank into the Mekong after the raft that was transporting it from Laos capsized. Twenty-five years later, it resurfaced; many believe this was a miracle. *(Off of Prajak Rd., down Prochai Rd. Open daily 7am-7pm. Donations accepted and appreciated.)*

VILLAGE WEAVER HANDICRAFTS. Those looking for handwoven *mudmee* fabrics can visit Village Weaver Handicrafts. This 24-year-old project promotes local industries and offers lucrative work to Isaan women in an attempt to provide them with the means to become self-sufficient. Ask to see the small workspace in the back where talented seamstresses tailor outfits at warp speed, which are then shipped all over the world. *(1151 Soi Jittapunya. ☎042 411 236; www.villageweaver.net. Open M-Sa 8am-5pm. Mostly cotton items are sold here; a 2nd store at Prajak and Haisok Rd. sells mostly silk products. Open 8:30am-4:30pm.)*

HAT JOMANEE. On the far side of the Friendship Bridge, just before the Mekong Royal Hotel, is this natural, fine-white-sand Mekong beach. This play area is only accessible from late January to April, when it magically emerges as the water drains out of the river. Try your luck at the local fishing park, where poles can be rented and locals will get a hoot out of watching *farang* trying their hardest to pull fish out of the pond.

DAYTRIP FROM NONG KHAI

WAT PHU TOK AND BEUNG KHAN

From the Nong Khai Bus Station, take a bus to Beung Khan (7hr., every 30min. 6am-11am, 140-190ʙ). From the Beung Khan bus stop across from the Kasikorn Bank, catch a bus to Ban Similai (40min., approx. every hr. 4:50am-3:40pm, 35-54ʙ). From Ban Similai, negotiate with a tuk-tuk driver to take you the 20km to Wat Phu Tok and ask them to wait (300ʙ). Alternatively, hire a jumbo (large tuk-tuk) from Bueng Khan clock tower directly to Wat Phu Tok and negotiate a return rate including several hours at the wat (about 650ʙ). On the return journey, buses depart from Ban Similai to Bueng Khan from a small shelter near the police box, approx. every hr. 9am-9pm. From Bueng Khan, buses depart for Nong Khai (2½hr., approx every hr. 6am-3:30pm) and Nakhom Phanom (5hr., every 40min. 8am-12:30pm, 140ʙ).

Although it is one of northeast Thailand's most spectacular sights, ▨**Wat Phu Tok** ("single mountain") remains untouristed because of its remote location. The shrine stands on a red sandstone outcropping rising seven levels, each representing a stage of enlightenment. Level five has a sanctuary built into the cliff while thick bamboo groves cover the paths at level seven. On the opposite side of the mountain, a hermitage on a pinnacle nestles under a boulder. Along the way, huts and platforms are used for meditation. Reaching the top involves climbing stairs to a maze of paths that cut into the rock and wooden platforms—while traversing the platforms, be careful of the gaps between the lower planks. The journey itself is intended to be physically arduous, representing the spiritual challenges of attaining Nirvana. The view of the Isaan plains is incredible, though during the rainy season, **the rocks and paths can become very slippery.** Take extreme caution. It is always a good idea to climb with a buddy.

Considering Wat Phu Tok distance from Nong Khai and Nakhom Phanom, you'll probably want to spend the night in **Beung Khan**, on Hwy. 212, and the only place between Nong Khai and Phu Tok where an overnight stay is possible. Hwy. 212 becomes **Thaisamok Road**, home to a small bus stop, a rotary, and clock tower. **Maenam Hotel ❸**, through the rotary on Thaisamok Rd. and left on Chasin Rd., is your best bet for a restful night's sleep. Modern rooms with soft bed, A/C, large TV, and private bath start at 400ʙ. (107 M1 Chasin Rd. ☎491 0512; www.maenamhotel.com.) The hotel also has a **restaurant ❷** with an English menu.. (☎491 037; Thai dishes 60-100ʙ.) A bunch of other small eateries can be found on Chasin Rd. There is a **hospital** at 255/1 Maesongnang Rd. (☎491 161), and the **Bueng Khan Police Station** (☎491 354) is 200m further at 395 Maesongnang Rd. A few **Internet cafes** are on Prasatchai Rd.

> **BORDER CROSSING: NONG KHAI/VIENTIANE.** 30-day Laotian tourist visas are issued on the Friendship Bridge for US$30 (1 passport photo required—available at Pro Studio in Nong Khai). 30-day visas are also available from the Laotian embassy in Bangkok (p. 98) or from the consulate in Khon Kaen, but there is little reason to get one ahead of time except to take the direct bus from Nong Khai bus station to Vientiane (see **Transportation,** p. 242). Ask at Mut Mee Guest House (see **Accommodations,** p. 243) for the latest info. A tuk-tuk from Nong Khai to the bridge should cost 40-60ʙ. A bus shuttles people across the bridge (15ʙ). On the other side, public buses go 25km to Vientiane (#14, 15ʙ); you can also take a taxi (100-150ʙ) or wait for a group to take a songthaew (50ʙ per person). The Laotian entry tax varies, but currently stands at 50ʙ. Border open daily 6am-10pm.

PHU PHRA BAT HISTORICAL PARK

Not far from the dusty village of Ban Phu, Phu Phra Bat Historical Park covers about 5.5 sq. km of mountains in the Phu Pan Range. Famous for pre-historic rock paintings dating back to 1500 BC, the caves and mushroom-like rock towers are truly captivating. Over a dozen excavations are scattered along a shady, well-marked path that takes several hours to meander around. Buddhas abound in **Tham Phra** (Cave of Buddha Images). At the top of the mountain, the 800m path yields an astounding vista of **Pha Sadet Cliff**, with a perfect picnic area overlooking the Laotian mountains. *(The best way to get to the park is by motorbike. Take Rte. 2266 next to the post office. At Ban Klang Yai, 29km away, head towards Ban Tiu for 8km; signs will direct you the remaining 4km. Although longer, in the rainy season it may be better to take the main highway to Ban Tha Bo, follow signs to Ban Pheu, and continue to Ban Tiu.* ☎042 910 107. *Open daily 8:30am-sunset. Camping fee 20฿. Tent rental 50฿, bungalow rental 400฿ per person. 30฿.)*

SANGKHOM   ☎042

A little town on the banks of the Mekong, Sangkhom's proximity to several picturesque waterfalls makes it a pleasant stop en route to Nong Khai or Loei. While it has retained some of its jungle-village charm, wooden and concrete-block houses have replaced most of the bamboo and straw-thatched huts, now regulated to the domain of tourist bungalows. The town's drowsy pace is still welcoming, as is a stroll through streets filled with the aroma of frying banana chips, a local specialty.

▛ TRANSPORTATION

Sangkhom lies on Rte. 211, between Nong Khai and Pak Chom. Transportation can be sporadic due to rising gasoline prices. Flag down **buses** along the main street near DD Guest House (see **Accommodations**, p. 247). On the southern side of the road, buses go to **Pak Chom** (1hr., approx. 3 per day 7am-5pm, 42฿), where there are connections to many other destinations. On the northern side of the road, they depart for **Nong Khai** (2hr.; 7, 9am, 5pm; 56฿) via **Si Chiangmai** (1hr., 20฿). Buses for **Bangkok** (6:30pm, 571฿) leave from a small office on the main road at Soi 8. They travel via **Nong Khai** (100฿), Udon (130฿), and **Khon Kaen** (255฿). For **Chiang Khan**, transfer to songthaew (1hr., 7am, 25฿) at **Pak Chom**. Alternatively, **samlor** will take you there for 350฿.

✸ 🄝 ORIENTATION AND PRACTICAL INFORMATION

Sangkhom is essentially a one-street town. **Ming Muang Road** forms the spine from which numbered sois branch, increasing in number as you head west, in the direction of Pak Chom. Entering Sangkhom from Nong Khai, you'll pass by the hospital; 1km farther is the center of town, home to the police station and the market.

Services include: **police** (☎042 441 080), opposite DD Guest House in the center of town.; a **pharmacy** (☎081 369 2000), 289 M 4 Ming Muang Rd., diagonally across from Buoy's Guesthouse (see below), toward the market (open daily 6-7am and 4:30-8pm); **Sangkhom Hospital** (☎042 441 029), 72 Moo 3 Ming Muang Rd., 1km east of town; **Internet access** at a shop without an English sign, diagonally opposite DD Guest House (30฿ per hr., open daily 7am-8pm); **Krung Thai Bank,** near soi 8 with a **24hr ATM** MC/V/AmEx/Cirrus (open M-F 8:30am-3:30pm); and the **post office,** 43 Moo 1, 1.5km from the market, after the second bridge. (☎042 441 069. Open M-F 8:30am-4:40pm, Sa 9am-noon.) **Postal Code:** 43160.

▛ ACCOMMODATIONS

Most accommodations in Sangkhom provide rooms with great views of the quiet Mekong River. Though they may cost a little extra, these rooms are well worth it.

■ **The Buoy Guest House,** 87/4 Ming Mueng Rd., between Sois 8 and 9, 500m before the GPO. 4 thatched-roof huts, with private porch, fan, and mosquito net, rest in quiet seclusion on a small plot of land on the water's edge. The shared bathroom has Western-style toilet and cold shower. Motorbike rental 200฿ per day. Bungalows with shared bath 150฿, with private bath 200฿. Hot shower in main house 30฿. ❷

The Bungalow Cake Resort, 116 Moo 2 (☎042 441 440), beyond the second bridge and 50m before the GPO. Has—in addition to a charming name—small white cottages, with clean private bathrooms and TVs. Some have a river view. Doubles with fan 250฿, with A/C and hot water 500฿. ❷

DD Guest House (☎042 441 332), on the river, diagonally across from the police station. Has 3 clean, wooden rooms behind its restaurants' second floor terrace. Singles 100฿, doubles 200-300฿. ❶

⬤ FOOD

Unfortunately, the town's **market,** opposite the police station near DD Guest House, is rather small. Fortunately, the accommodations in town have attached restaurants that serve up some tasty treats.

■ **The Buoy Guest House Restaurant** (☎042 441 065). Mr. and Mrs. Toy, owners and chefs of the guesthouse's restaurant, prepare Thai and Laotian specialties and are a great source for info on the local area. Jungle curry 50฿. Restaurant open 7am-10pm. Kitchen closes 8pm. ❷

The Bungalow Cake Resort Restaurant, with a commanding terrace view, serves vegetarian dishes on request. Dishes 35-100฿. Open daily 7am-11pm. ❷

DD Guest House, one of the best places to eat in town, with an extensive English menu and soothing atmosphere. The English breakfast is particularly good (100฿). Other dishes 30-180฿. Open daily 7:30am-10pm. ❷

⬤ SIGHTS

The jungle surrounding Sangkhom is dotted with caves, *wats*, and waterfalls. The impressive **Than Thip Falls** are a 15min. motorbike ride west of town. Take any bus or *songthaew* heading toward Pak Chom or Loei for 13km. Get off between Km 97 and 98, take a left, and go down the road for 3km. And bring your bathing suit—the second tier has a swimming hole.

Just as relaxing, though not as grand, are the **Than Thong Falls,** just off the road between Km 72 and 73, 12km east of town. A Nong Khai-bound bus can also take you there. Than Thong Rd. leads 4km up to **Wat Pha Tak Seu,** a temple with a commanding view of the Mekong. Wat Pha Tak Seu can also be reached via a 2km series of steps and trails leading up from the river road, 4km east of town. It is not advisable to take this path during the rainy season (May-December).

Wat Hin Maak Peng, 20km east of Sangkhom, is halfway between Sangkhom and Si Chiangmai, at Km 64. Any Si Chiangmai-bound bus or *songthaew* (10฿) will drop you off. The exteriors of these grand, modern buildings are set among richly landscaped grounds and bamboo groves. *(Gates open daily 6am-7pm.)*

NORTHEAST THAILAND

CHIANG KHAN ☎042

Tucked behind the Mekong River north of Loei and west of Nong Khai, Chiang Khan is not to be missed. It offers the same beautiful scenery and slow afternoons as other border towns, but steps it up a notch with relative seclusion and spectacular guesthouses. Life remains fairly slow and isolated here along the meandering Mekong. With a soothing atmosphere and few sights to distract you, you're free to kick back, enjoy the cultural enrichment, and rejuvenate.

⌐ TRANSPORTATION

Pak Chom and Loei serve as Chiang Khan's connection to the rest of the world. **Songthaew** leave from Rte. 201. Wait opposite the Shell gas station, for *songthaew* going **Loei** (1hr., every 30min. 5:30am-5:30pm, 40в). There is one direct **bus** to **Pak Chom** each day (1hr., 3:30pm, 40в); otherwise, catch a bus to Loei and ask to get off at **Ban Tat** (20в). From there, buses to Pak Chom leave more frequently (60в). From Pak Chom, buses run infrequently to **Nong Khai** (#507, 2 per day 8am-3pm, 140в) via **Sangkhom** (42в) and **Si Chiangmai** (78в). However, if your final destination is Nong Khai, you are better off traveling via Loei. A small orange office (☎086 011 2540), one block south of the market on Soi 9, sells tickets for buses to **Bangkok** (10-11hr.; A/C buses 6:30pm, 795в; 2nd cl. 6:40pm, 398в) via **Loei** (83в).

⊿ 🔁 ORIENTATION AND PRACTICAL INFORMATION

Chiang Khan sits on a particularly stunning stretch of the **Mekong River** in Nothern Loei Province. It is 50km from Loei city, the provincial capital. The two main roads in Chiang Khan, parallel to each other and to the river, are **Chai Khong Road**, which is closer to the water, and **Sri Chiang Khan Road**, connected by Sois 0-28. **Route 201** merges with Chiang Khan Rd. between Sois 6 and 7. Buses stop at a Shell petrol station on route 201, 500m south from this intersection. As of Summer 2008, a boardwalk is under construction along the river's edge.

Tours: Mekong Culture and Nature Tours, whose main office is 1.5km west of town on Sri Chiang Khan Rd. Runs biking, kayaking, hiking, and boat tours to nearby sights (including the rapids) and visits to small local farming villages. A smaller, but more convenient office (☎042 821 530), is located opposite Chiang Khan Guest House (see **Accommodations, p. 249**) on Chaing Khong Rd., near Soi 19. Kayaking tours 1500в per person, bike tours 1000в per person; 4-person min. Open M-F 8:30am-5:30pm.

Immigration office: (☎042 821 911), on Chai Khong Rd., at Soi 26. 30-day visa extension 1900в. open M-F 8:30am-4:30pm.

Bank: Krung Thai Bank ATM on the corner of Route 201 as it intersects with Sri Chiang Khan Rd. Open 24hr. Cirrus/MC/V.

Police: (☎042 821 181), 300m east of the immigration office just off Chai Khong Rd., near Soi 28.

Chiang Khan Hospital: 427 Sri Chiang Khan Rd. (☎042 821 101), across from Soi 25.

Pharmacy: (☎042 822 351). On Soi 9 just before the market. Open daily 6am-8pm.

Internet access: U.U Net, on Sri Chinag Khan Rd., near Soi 13. Internet 15в per hr. Open 8am-10pm.

Post Office: Chiang Khan Post and Telegraph Office, 50 Chai Khong Rd. (☎042 821 011), on Soi 26, enter from Sri Chiang Khang Rd. as there are no signposts for *sois* greater than Soi 17 on Chai Khong Rd. International phone. Poste Restante. Open M-F 8:30am-4:30pm, Sa 9am-noon. **Postal Code:** 42110.

🏠 ACCOMMODATIONS

For a small town with few noteworthy attractions, Chiang Khan has a surprising number of quality guesthouses.

Loogmai Guest House, 112 Chai Khong Rd. Soi 5 (☎042 822 334), is modern and chic. The owner is an abstract artist and, together with his wife, has created one of the best designed guest houses in the northeast. There are only 3 rooms, but each one is spectacular. All rooms with fan. Small rooms 300฿; single room with private bath 400฿. ❹

Chiang Khan Guest House, 282 Chai Khong Rd. (☎042 821 691), between Sois 19 and 20, has homey, wooden rooms with shared bath. The friendly owner, Pim, speaks English and has loads of information about the surrounding area. For large groups, the guest house will whip up an all-you-can-eat feast (280฿) and can arrange live Isaan music and dance performances (2000฿). Pim is also happy to give you free cooking lessons. Bicycle rental 50฿ per day, motorbikes 200฿ per day. Doubles 200-300฿. ❷

Ton Khong Guest House, 299/3 Chai Khong Rd. Soi 10 (☎042 821 871), has small, snug rooms with fan and polished wooden floors. The rooms on the second floor with shared bathroom are considerably nicer. The downstairs restaurant serves excellent Thai food, including a number of vegetarian options. Dishes 40-80฿. Western breakfast 70-120฿. Bike rental 50฿ per day, motorbikes 200฿ per day. Singles 150฿, doubles 240-450฿. ❷

🍴 FOOD

During the day, a small **market** with a few small food stalls opens up one block south of Sri Chiag Khan Rd. between Sois 9 and 10 (open 5am-8pm). Chiang Khan doesn't have many restaurants, so choices are especially limited in the evening, when the market shuts down.

Rabieng (☎042 821 251), on Chai Khong Rd. between Sois 9 and 10, churns out tasty Chinese food. Soup with minced pork 80฿. Dishes 70-90฿. Open daily 8am-10pm. ❷

Look Kochana, on Soi 9 (no English sign). Its *pad thai* (25฿) and morning glory vine in garlic bean sauce (50฿) satisfy even the pickiest taste buds. Open daily 7am-10pm. ❶

🔆 SIGHTS

About 3km east of town, towards Nong Khai, a turnoff leads left to **Kaeng Khut Khu Rapids,** where picturesque rock piles interrupt the Mekong's seaward journey. Follow the sign to Wat Thakhaek, and continue for 1km. A row of covered picnic areas are great for watching the rapids (Feb.-May). *Songthaew* (10฿) and *tuk-tuks* (round trip 50฿) leave from Chiang Khan Rd. On weekends, and occasionally during the week, vendors set up stalls selling local goods and cooking up fresh fish and shrimp dishes. Along the river by the Kaeng Khut Khu (Kaeng Kood Ku), the local specialty, *kung den* (tiny live shrimp that dance around your plate; about 40฿), and *kung tot*, the same shrimp but deep fried and crunchy, are especially popular. (Ferry service 30min., 400฿; 1hr., 700฿.)

The kayaking tours run by **Mekong Culture and Nature Tours** offer a more hands-on way to experience the rapids (see **Practical Information,** above). Trips can also head upstream to the Hueng River. They will often visit **Phra Yai** (Phu Khok Ngra), a 19m Buddha statue located on a 315m hill overlooking the Mekong, about 23km from Chiang Khan. **Chiang Khan Guest House** can arrange boat trips to both Kaeng Khut Khu (200-250฿ per person) and the Hueng River (900฿).

A convenient viewpoint for the Buddha statue at Phra Yok is at **Phu Tok.** About 3.5km in the direction of Nong Khai, 0.5km past the Wat Thakhaek turnoff, another turnoff leads right. Follow that narrow paved road for 3km until the road forks, then bear right. Before you go, make sure your bike's brakes are in very good condition, as it is a steep descent.

LOEI ☎042

Loei province's spectacular mountains, national parks and welcoming towns make it a must on any traveler's itinerary. At the end of June, the three-day rain-making Phi Ta Khon Festival in Dan Sai transforms the western district into a shamanistic orgy of brightly colored costumes and masks, parading spirits, and dancing fueled by shots of *lao khao* ("white spirit"), culminating in a final day of Buddhist sermons at the *wat*. Absent from most tourist itineraries, Loei city, the capital of Loei province, is a hidden gem relatively untouched by visitors. This city is the most convenient locale from which to venture into the cloud-frosted mountains in search of hermit caves, or to Thailand's version of the vineyards of southern France—the Chateau de Loei Vineyards. Loei's quiet, fountain-filled streets and friendly residents also make it the perfect place to unwind after a day spent exploring the countryside and national parks.

TRANSPORTATION

Buses: All buses leave from the main bus station (☎042 833 586), off Maliwan Rd., south of the city center. Buses depart for **Udon Thani** (3hr., every 40min. 4am-5:30pm, 75-105฿) from platform #11. If you are heading to **Nong Khai**, take a bus to Udon Thani and transfer there. For **Si Chiangmai** and **Sangkhom**, follow the same route to Nong Khai and catch a bus from there. Buses also run to **Bangkok** (10hr., every hr. 6am-1:30pm and every 30min. 6:30-9:20pm, 492-690฿), **Lom Sak** (3hr.; 9am, noon, 2pm; 120฿), **Chiang Mai** (10hr.; 11am, 9:30, 10pm; 601฿), and **Chiang Rai** (11hr.; 6:30, 10, 11pm; 630฿). Chiang Mai and Chiang Rai buses travel via **Phitsanulok** (4hr.; 10am, 2:20pm; 160฿). Long distance buses may be full upon arrival, but you can reserve a seat by buying a ticket at the bus station counter. **Songthaew** to **Chiang Khan** (1hr., every 30min. 5:30am-6pm, 40฿), **Pak Chom** (2hr., 10 per day 6am-5pm, 60฿) leave from behind the main bus station.

Local Transportation: Samlor and **tuk-tuk** 20-40฿. The bike shop (☎042 811 377), behind a green storefront on Sathon Chiang Khan Rd., 20m north of the traffic circle, rents **motorbikes** (200฿ per day, new bike 250฿ per day; passport copy required). Sugar Guest House also rents motorbikes (200฿ per day).

ORIENTATION AND PRACTICAL INFORMATION

Loei city is a tangled mess of streets on the **Loei River's** western bank. Four large streets converge at the fountain traffic circle in the downtown center. **Sert Si Road** leads south past the artificial lake and intersects at its end with **Charoen Rat Road,** which runs the length of the river beginning near the bus station, at the market. **Chum Saai Road** is home to several hotels and leads east from the traffic circle, while **Nok Kaew Road** extends west from the traffic circle. **Sathon Chiang Khan Road** runs north from the center and intersects **Ruam Jai Road,** a major east-west thoroughfare. Western-style pubs line **Rhuamphattana Road.** Walking west on Nok Kaew Rd. toward the highway, Rhuamphattana Rd. is the first right after the traffic circle. **Maliwan Road (Highway 201)** forms the town's western border.

Tourist Office: TAT (☎042 812 812), in the parking lot on Charoen Rat Rd., opposite the GPO. Excellent maps and brochures of Loei province. Open daily 8:30am-4:30pm.

Currency Exchange: Bangkok Bank, at the intersection of Oua Aree and Charoen Rat Rd. **24hr. ATM.** AmEx/MC/Plus/V. Open M-F 8:30am-3:30pm.

Police: (☎042 811 254), on Pipat Mongkon Rd., the city's northern border.

Tourist Police: (☎042 861 164), 23/23 Maliwan Rd., near the intersection with Pipat Mongkon Rd.

Medical Services: Muang Loei Hospital, 32/1 Maliwan Rd. (☎042 811 541), 100m north of the intersection with Nok Kaew Rd.

Pharmacy: Bun Jung Pesat Pharmacy, 83 Charoen Rat Rd. (☎042 830 634), on the corner of Ruam Jai Rd. Open daily 3am-9pm.

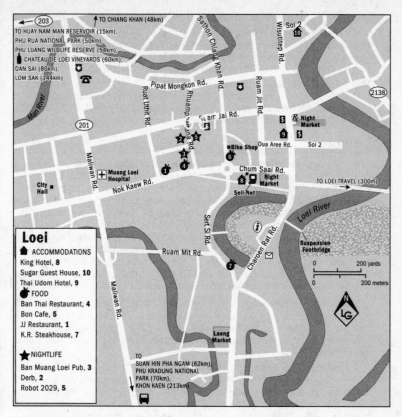

Loei

🏠 ACCOMMODATIONS
King Hotel, **8**
Sugar Guest House, **10**
Thai Udom Hotel, **9**
🍴 FOOD
Ban Thai Restaurant, **4**
Bon Cafe, **5**
JJ Restaurant, **1**
K.R. Steakhouse, **7**

⭐ NIGHTLIFE
Ban Muang Loei Pub, **3**
Derb, **2**
Robot 2029, **5**

Internet Access: Several Internet shops are on the soi adjacent to the Royal Inn on Chum Saai Rd., halfway between Ruam Jit Rd. and Sathon Chiang Kahn Rd. One prominent spot is **Seli Net,** 50m east of King Hotel on Chum Saai Rd. (☎042 830 729. 15฿ per hr. Open 10am-10pm.)

Telephones: International phone at **CAT,** on Maliwan Rd., just south of the bridge to Hwy. 203. Open M-F 8:30am-noon and 1-4pm.

Post Office: GPO (☎042 812 0222), on Charoen Rat Rd., between the footbridge and the night market. Open M-F 8:30am-4:30pm, Sa-Su 9am-noon. **Postal Code:** 42000.

🏠 ACCOMMODATIONS

Unsurprisingly for a town overlooked by foreign tourists, Loei only has one guesthouse. Modern hotels with little atmosphere are in the center of town.

Sugar Guest House, 4/1 Wisuttiep Rd. (☎042 812 982), down Soi 2, on the right. English-speaking owner Pat and her dog Popeye welcome travelers to clean rooms with comfortable beds and polished wood floors. Shared bathroom with Western toilet is immaculate and has hot water. Laundry 20฿ per kg. Bike rental 30฿ per day, motorbikes 200฿ per day. Singles 150฿; doubles 200฿; with A/C and private bath 350฿. ❷

King Hotel, 11/8-12 Chum Saai Rd. (☎042 811 701), is a modern hotel with spotless rooms that surround an open air garden. Those on the higher floors have sweeping views of the city. All rooms with A/C, TV, and hot shower. Doubles 420-450฿, suites 850฿. MC/V. ❸

Thai Udom Hotel, 122/1 Charoen Rat Rd. (☎042 811 789), the bright orange building at the intersection of Charoen and Oua Aree Rd. Thai Udom has decent, clean rooms with Western toilets, hot showers, phone, and TV. Double with fan 200฿, with A/C 300฿; VIP room 600฿. ❷

🔲 FOOD

Some of the best places to eat are the open-air restaurants in front of the movie theater on Sathon Chiang Khan Rd., between the traffic circle and Ruam Jai Rd. Pyromaniacs can order *pak boong fai daeng* (flaming morning glory vine), leafy water spinach that the chef sets on fire before hurling towards your plate. A fantastic **night market** sets up on Chum Saai Rd., across from Ruam Jit Rd. (Open nightly 5pm-10pm.) Another **market,** at the northern end of Charoen Rat Rd., opposite the 7-Eleven, sells produce and sells to grilled meats and largely useless plastic items for the rest of the day. The **Laeng market** is primarily an evening market and sets up at the southern end of Charoen Rat Rd. Six tin-roofed rows of stalls offer the usual meat and produce. Outdoor garden restaurants scattered throughout the city are popular with locals.

JJ Restaurant, 32/106 Nok Kaew Rd. (☎042 812 819), 2 blocks west of the traffic circle, away from the river. This huge open-air bonanza is packed with locals enjoying the grill buffet's impressive selection of Chinese and Thai dishes (99฿). Some dishes you cook yourself on a communal, tabletop hotplate in the table. Open nightly 4pm-midnight. ❷

K.R. Steakhouse, 58/1 Sert Si Rd. (☎042 861 672), near the intersection with Charoen Rat Rd. Known for its grill, K.R. offers Thai and Chinese dishes accompanied by a view of the fountain-filled artificial lake from its terrace. Spicy green mango with fried shrimp 100฿. Most dishes 80-120฿. Open daily 11am-midnight. MC/V. ❸

Ban Thai Restaurant, 17/33 Nong Kaew Rd. (☎042 833 472), has an English menu with pictures of their mainly western specialties. International flags line the walls. Fresh pizzas 119-330฿, Western dishes 80-220฿, Thai dishes 60-100฿. Open 10am-11pm. ❷

Bon Cafe, 35/52 Maliwan R. (☎042 830 038), serves up fresh coffee in a hip, modern environment with plenty of A/C. Coffee 25-45฿, ice-cream 15-45฿. Free Internet. Open daily 9am-10pm. ❶

🔲 NIGHTLIFE

Most serving whiskey, some themed, the bars on Rhumphatta Rd. in Loei promise interesting entertainment late into the night.

Derb (☎081 860 3558; no english sign) is the place to be. A great inexpensive place to try and get to know some locals. Large Singha 69฿, bottle of whiskey 250-729฿. Open 6pm-midnight.

Ban Muang Loei Pub (☎081 717 4908), across the road from Derb, with live Thai country music and Thai pop blasting late into the night. Large Singha 80฿, bottle of whiskey 250-110฿. Open nightly 6pm-1am.

Robot 2029, 9/7 Rhuam hattana Rd. (☎042 812 581), with 2 robot statues near its glowing spaceship entrance. Live rock bands complete with backup dancers keep the neon-lit hall bumping late in the night. Small beers 60-80฿, Smirnoff Ice 100฿. Open 9pm-2am.

📍 DAYTRIPS FROM LOEI

CHATEAU DE LOEI VINEYARDS. One of Thailand's first wine-producing vineyards, Chateau de Loei is large by any standard. After surviving a long process of securing permits to import foreign grapevines into Thailand, a thriving vineyard now stands in the middle of Loei's mountains. A 6km loop leads through the vineyard and ends at the winery, where you can observe the wine-making process and actually taste the Syrah and Chenin Blanc. Though Thailand is not known for the quality of its wines, a walk through the vineyards is pleasant and offers views of marching rows of grapes, and a small reservoir. *(Take a bus bound for Lom Sak, (1hr., 60km, 40฿). Get off when you see the blue metal gate with an English sign. The Chateau will be on your left. The vineyard shop sells fresh grapes, organic produce, local crafts, souvenirs, and, of course, bottles of wine. White wine 300฿, red 670 or 1010฿. The actual vineyard is 2km down the road, beneath the sign. Ask at the shop about wine tastings and tours of the vineyard. ☎042 809 521. Open daily 9am-5pm.)*

PHU KRADUNG NATIONAL PARK. The bell ringing that could be heard every week on Buddhist Day inspired the name of this popular sanctuary ("Bell Mountain"). Trails criss-cross the 60 sq. km plateau's pine forests and grassy meadows. The 5km hike from the mountain base to park headquarters on the plateau rim is facilitated by bamboo stairways. Porters can tote your gear for 10฿ per kg. Visitors who reach Pha Lom Sak or Pha Daeng are rewarded with views of the sunset. *(Pick up a detailed booklet on the park from the tourist office in Loei. To get to the park, take a bus to Khon Kaen (70km, 50฿) and ask to be dropped off at the Amphoe Phu Kradung Administrative Office. From there, take a minibus (20-25฿) to the National Park Office (☎042 871 333). The park is packed on weekends and holidays, but closes from June-Sept. Camping 30฿ per person. Tents 225฿ for 3 people, 445฿ for 6 people. Limited mountaintop lodging from 1600฿ for a 4-person lodging to 2400฿ for an 8-person. Reservations should be made 30 days in advance with the National Park Division of the Forestry Department in Bangkok, (☎02 561 4292; ext. 724; online at www.dnp.go.th. Park open Oct.-May daily 9am-5pm. 400฿.)*

PHU RUA NATIONAL PARK. The majestic centerpiece of this park is a 1365m mountain. Personal vehicles can travel to the top, where a large Buddha surveys the scene below. Routes up include a 2.5km trek to a waterfall, 5km from the peak. The park office arranges accommodations. *(Camping 30฿ per person. Tents for 3-person 450฿, 6- person 810฿. 4- to 6-person bungalows 2000-3000฿.)* Contact the National Parks Division in Bangkok (☎02 561 4836) for reservations or book online at www.dnp.go.th. There are a number of small nurseries that cultivate a rainbow of flowers along the road near the turnoff to Phu Rua National Park. Each year in Janurary they are highlighted in a flower show. *(The park can be reached by a #14 bus from Loei to Lom Sak (1hr., every hr. 5am-5pm, 35฿) via Phu Rua. A bus from Udon bound for either Chiang Mai or Pitsanulok or a bus from Nakhom Phanom heading for Chiang Rai can take you to the park. In each case, let the driver know you want to get off at Phu Rua National Park. If are dreiving the 50km from Loei youself, watch for the large English sign on the right, and take the 3rd U-turn after the sign; on the other side, look for the small, wooden sign on your left. Headquarters, (☎042 801 716, open daily 5am-8pm), is 3.5km from the main road. Chartered songthaew go there for 300฿. 200฿.)*

HIGHWAY 203. Loei's real attractions lie outside the provincial capital in the surrounding mountains. The first is 📍**Huay Nam Man Reservoir,** about 15km from the city center. Rent a bamboo raft (150฿) for a lazy afternoon of floating about. A small flag is provided to signal to food-filled boats to come serve you a bowl of noodles or a bag of fruit (30-60฿). Further along the highway, 35km from Loei, on the left, is the turnoff for the **Phu Luang Wildlife Reserve** (☎01 221 0547, open daily 8am-4pm), which contains thick jungles, grasslands, and pine forests. Those wishing to tour the area should contact the sanctuary office first to arrange guides. *(Transportation is somewhat difficult to arrange, as no songthaew travel this far out of the city, and distances are impractical for a tuk-tuk. However, a bus to Lom Sak runs along Hwy. 203, from which these sights are accessible. Watch the decreasing Km markers (distance from Phu Rua) on your right. After the Km 36 marker, turn right onto a small road marked by a multi-tude of Thai signs; it's another 3.5km to the reservoir. The turnoff for the Phu Luang Wildlife Reserve is in Ban San Tom. Songthaew travel the remaining 18km to the park checkpoint when it's open.)*

LOM SAK ☎ 056

Located between the Phang Hoei and Luan Prabang mountains, Lom Sak serves as a transit point between Khon Kaen and Phitsanulok. This small town is also a convenient base for exploring Nam Nao National Park, which offers a stark verdant contrast to Lom Sak's dusty streets and crumbling facades.

▐ TRANSPORTATION

The **bus station** is located 5km west of town, at the intersection of Samakeechai Rd. and Rte. 12. Most buses will also stop in the town center. Accordingly, tickets to some destinations can also be purchased from smaller stalls in town for the same buses, departing slightly earlier. From the **main bus station** (☎056 912 270), buses go to: **Chiang Mai** (9hr., 5 per day 6:20am-11am, 371-477฿) via **Pitsanulok** (2hr., 98฿) and **Sukhothai** (4hr., 137฿); **Chiang Rai** (9hr., 6 per day 1:30pm-11pm, 363-466฿); **Khon Kaen** (4hr., 22 per day; 146-177฿); **Loei** (4hr.; 8am, 2pm; 120฿); **Pitsanulok** (2½hr., every hr. 5:20am-5:30pm, 95฿); **Bangkok** (6hr., every hr. 5am-11pm, 262-337฿). The same buses to Khon Kaen, Chiang Mai, and Chiang Rai can be caught from a small stall in the carpark near the police station on Soi Suriyasa opposite the 7-Eleven on Wajee Rd. Buses to Bangkok can also be met at **Phet Tours** (☎056 701 164), 6 Soi Suriyasa, off Wajee Rd., opposite the police station.

▐ ORIENTATION

The town's main intersection is where north-south **Kotchasanee Road** becomes **Soi Pirit Road,** after crossing **Ronnakij Road** to the east and the multilane **Samakeechai Road** to the west; it is marked by a shiny digital clock tower. **Wajee Road** runs parallel to Kotchasanee, and sois branch off both of these roads. The fenced municipal grounds are two blocks north of Ronnakij Rd., between Kotchasanee and Wajee Rd. Running between these two roads, next to the municiple grounds, is **Soi Suriyasak.** It houses the in-town bus stations. Parallel to and one block south of Ronnakij Rd. is **Tesabarn 2 Road.** Another block south is **Tesabarn 3 Road,** which borders the day market.

▐ PRACTICAL INFORMATION

Currency Exchange: Bangkok Bank (☎056 701 413), across from New Sawan Hotel (p. 255) on Samakachai Rd.; **24hr. ATM.** Cirrus/MC/V. Open M-F 8:30am-3:30pm.

Police: (☎056 704 717), 103 Wajee Rd., in the municipal complex on Soi Suriyasa Rd., adjacent to the bus stop.

Pharmacy: 340 Wajee Rd. (☎056 701 629), just south of Soi 2. Open 8am-9pm.

Hospital: Lom Sak Hospital, 15 Samakee Chai Rd. (☎056 704 1201), 500m south of the main intersection. Take the first right after the overpass; it's 150m down the road on the right. English spoken.

Internet access: Starnet, 118 Ronnakij Rd. (☎056 702 439), 2nd block to the left, when walking away from the main intersection. 20฿ per hr. Open daily 10am-10pm.

Telephones: CAT, behind the post office. Open M-F 8:30am-4:30pm.

Post Office: (☎056 701 103), on Wajee Rd., past Soi 20. Open M-F 8:30am-4:30pm, Sa 9am-noon. **Postal Code:** 67110.

ACCOMMODATIONS

As a transit point, Lom Sak's accommodations are what you'd expect: nothing too special, but good enough for a quick stopover.

The New Sawan Hotel, 47/6 Samakeechai Rd. (☎056 702 545), is the lime-green building at the main intersection. Rooms are clean and kept ship-shape by a friendly staff. Each has a TV and a private bathroom Western toilets and hot water. Singles with fan 300฿, with A/C 400฿; doubles 350/450฿. ❸

Baan Kaew Guesthouse, 18/4 Prauttaboth Rd. (☎083 007 4065), is on a quiet side street. From the in-town bus stalls, walk south on Wajee Rd. and take a left on Soi 3. Baan Kaew is set around a parking lot behind the wooden pub to your right. Its rooms are well-priced and have private bathrooms with squat toilets. Rooms with fan 250฿, with TV 300฿, with A/C 350฿. ❷

FOOD

At night, **food stalls** set up at the bus stations near the municipal grounds. (Grilled pork chops 20฿, side of sticky rice 5฿. Open daily 5pm-9pm.) On Tesabarn 3, off Wajee Rd. south of the main intersection, a covered **day market** makes way for a small **night market** when the sun goes down.

Duang Ta, 132 Wajee Rd. (☎056 701 781). Find the bus station to Bangkok on Soi Suriyasak near the police station. To the right of it is a small carpark. At the back of the carpark is Duang Ta on a small soi. Helpful, English-speaking owner Ekapol serves up a small selection of Thai and Western dishes. American Breakfast 80฿. Thai curries 50฿. Fish and chips 160฿. Most dishes 30-80฿. Open daily 9am-7:30pm. ❷

Puang Choom Restaurant (☎056 745 0216), at the Grand Hotel, serves Thai, Chinese, and Western dishes from an extensive English menu. "Fried Chicken Maryland" 120฿. Flame Re-Fried Water Mimosa Watercress 60฿. Most dishes 60-120฿. Open daily 6am-1am. ❷

Muang Lome, 22/14 Samakeechai Rd. (☎056 701 105), the beige building after the Caltex gas station, specializes in Chinese and Thai food. The extensive English menu does not list prices. Frog with garlic and pepper 80-120฿. Dishes 80-180฿. Open daily 10am-10pm.

DAYTRIP FROM LOM SAK

Nam Nao National Park (*nam nao* means "cold water") stretches for 1000 sq. km at the junction of Loei and Phetchabun provinces. Hwy. 12, between Khon Kaen and Lom Sak, winds through the park's high mountain passes and spectacular forest. The park headquarters are on this road, 55km from Lom Sak and 103km from Khon Kaen. The park's sandstone hills and sandy plains make it ideal for hiking. Along the 6-7hr. ascent to the park's highest peak, **Phu Pha Chit** (1271m), a landscape of low shrubs and small yellow flowers rolls down the mountain. The park also has bamboo forests, and some mildly interesting caves and waterfalls. The **camping** fee is 30฿ per person. Tent rental for one to three people 250฿. Resorts line Hwy. 12 near the park but are quite expensive. *(Take a Khon Kaen-bound bus and get off at park headquarters on the left (1hr., 50฿). As most trailheads start from this road, buses to Lom Sak or Khon Kaen can help traverse the long distances between trailheads. ☎056 729 002. Park admission 400฿.)*

KHON KAEN ☎043

Unlike other Isaan cities, Khon Kaen feels like a major urban center, thanks to its notable, albeit small, skyline, and its large and well-planned grid system of roadways. The presence of Isaan's largest university, with its thousands of vibrant students, also sets the city apart from its neighbors. Like other northeastern cities, Khon Kaen lacks a big tourist attraction and is often overlooked. Nevertheless, its festive nightlife, open-air markets, and efficient transportation system give visitors the means to enjoy themselves. It also serves as a handy base for trips to the silk village of Chonabot and Phu Wiang National Park.

⌗ TRANSPORTATION

Khon Kaen is 450km from Bangkok and is accessible by plane, bus, or train.

Flights: Khon Kaen Airport (☎043 246 774), 8km west of town off Maliwan Rd. **Thai Airways,** 9/9 Prachasamran Rd. (☎056 227 701), inside the Sofitel Hotel, flies to **Bangkok** (2340฿). Open daily 9am-4:30pm.

Trains: Khon Kaen Train Station (☎043 221 112), where Ruen Rom Rd. ends at Darunsamran Rd. To: **Bangkok** (9hr.; 8:37, 8:11am, 9:05, 10:16pm; 379-679฿); **Khorat** (3hr.; 1:38, 3:54pm; 30฿); **Nong Khai** (3hr.; 9:40am, 2:10, 4:15, 5:42pm; 35฿) via

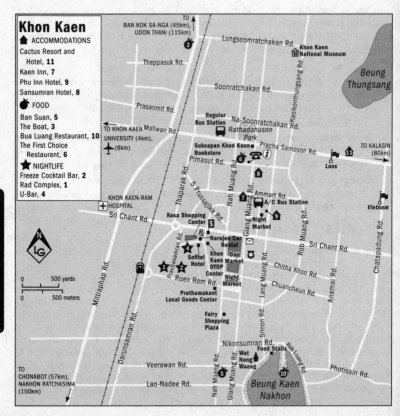

Khon Kaen

🏠 ACCOMMODATIONS
Cactus Resort and
Hotel, **11**
Kaen Inn, **7**
Phu Inn Hotel, **9**
Sansumran Hotel, **8**

🍎 FOOD
Ban Suan, **5**
The Boat, **3**
Bua Luang Restaurant, **10**
The First Choice
Restaurant, **6**

⭐ NIGHTLIFE
Freeze Cocktail Bar, **2**
Rad Complex, **1**
U-Bar, **4**

Udon Thani (2hr.; 4:20, 7pm; 25฿). Advanced booking office open daily 6am-6pm. *Songthaew* #3, 11, 12, 14, and 17 run past the train station.

Buses: Khon Kaen has **2 bus stations.** The regular bus station serves more destinations, while the A/C bus station has a central location but more expensive bus service.

Regular bus station (☎043 237 472), on Pracha Samoson Rd., by the pedestrian overpass. To: **Bangkok** (7-8hr., 12 per day; 6:30am-5:30pm, 294฿) via **Khorat** (3hr., 133฿); **Chiang Mai** (12hr.; 6, 8, 9:30am, 1, 5:45pm; 503฿) via **Pitsanulok** (6hr., 231฿); **Loei** (3hr., every 30min. 3:40am-6:30pm, 146฿); **Mukdahan** (5hr., every 30min. 4am-6:30pm, 146฿); **Ubon Ratchathani** (5hr., 9 per day 5:20am-4pm, 192฿); **Nong Khai** (3hr., every 30min. 5am-6:30am, 120฿); **Udon Thani** (2hr., every hr. 5am-4pm, 85฿); **Surin** (6hr., every hr. 4am-3pm, 187฿); **Roi Et** (2hr., every hr. 6am-6pm, 83฿); **Rayong** (12hr., 6 per day 10am-9:30pm, 392฿) via **Pattaya** (10hr., 346฿); **Chiang Rai** (13hr.; 5 per day 10am-7:30pm; 494฿).

A/C bus station (☎043 239 910), on Glang Muang Rd. To: **Bangkok** (6hr., every hr. 6:30am-12:15am, 378-585฿); **Khorat** (4hr.; 8am, 1pm; 171฿); **Chiang Mai** (13hr.; 6, 8, 9pm; 578฿) via **Phitsanulok** (5hr., 297฿); **Chiang Rai** (14hr.; 6, 8, 9pm; 635฿); **Nong Khai** (4hr.; 9am, noon; 157฿) via **Udon Thani** (2hr., 110฿); **Ubon Ratchathani** (5hr.; 9, 11am, 1, 2pm; 247฿).

Local Transportation: Look for **samlor** (30-40฿), **tuk-tuks** (30-60฿), and **songthaew** (8฿). *Songthaew* #4 runs along Nah Muang Rd., #11 runs from Khon Kaen Train Station to TAT, #17 runs from TAT to the National Museum and #13 runs down the east side of Beung Kaen Nakhon. *Songthaew* route numbers are also listed on signs at the numerous stops throughout the city. Routes are always subject to change, so ask the driver before you get on.

◢◤ ⚡ ORIENTATION AND PRACTICAL INFORMATION

The main north-south thoroughfares, **Nah Muang Road** and **Glang Muang Road,** are lined with hotels, restaurants, and the A/C bus station. Farther south, they cross **Sri Chant Road,** home to the best nightlife. Past Sri Chant Rd., on Glang Muang Rd., the post office, police station, and day market lead to **Ruen Rom Road.** A right turn onto Ruen Rom from Nah Muang Rd. leads to the train station. The regular bus station and TAT office are on **Pracha Samoson Road,** which intersects with Nah Muang Rd. and Glang Muang Rd. on the north side of the city. The university and airport are northwest of the center, and the reservoir, Beung Kaen Nakhon, is southwest.

Tourist Office: TAT, 15/5 Pracha Samoson Rd. (☎043 244 498). A brown and white building several blocks from the regular bus station. Offers maps and guides of Khon Kaen and surrounding provinces. Open daily 8:30am-4:30pm.

Tours: Kaen Inn Travel (☎043 234 5734; kaeninnhotel@yahoo.com), inside the Kaen Inn Hotel, can book transportation, accommodations, and tours. Open M-F 9am-4pm. AmEx/MC/V.

Consulates: Laos, 171 Pracha Samoson Rd. (☎043 242 856). Fees for 30-day visas vary by nationality. Most range 1200-1700฿. Same-day service available for 200฿. 1 photo required. Open M-F 8am-noon and 1-4pm. **Vietnam,** 65/6 Chatapadung Rd. (☎043 242 190). 15-day visas US$25, 30-day visas US$40. 1 photo required. Open M-F 8-11:30am and 1:30-4:30pm. *Songthaew* #10 runs to both consulates.

Currency Exchange: Many banks and ATMs are on Sri Chant Rd. **Bangkok Bank,** 254 Sri Chant Rd. (☎043 225 144), next to Charoen Thani Princess Hotel entrance. **24hr. ATM.** Open M-F 8:30am-3:30pm, currency exchange open Sat-Su 9am-5pm. **Krung Thai Bank** is next door. Open M-F 9am-4:30pm.

Books: Suksapan Khon Kaen Bookstore, 23 Pracha Samoson Rd. (☎043 237 005; www.suksapan-kk.com), on the corner of Glang Muang Rd., down the yellow-colored alley. Open M-Sa 8am-8pm, Su 8am-6pm.

Rentals: Motorbikes and **cars** can be rented from shops around the Sofitel Hotel, off Sri Chant Rd. One is **Narujee Car Rent,** 178 Soi Kosa (☎043 224 220), just off Sri Chant

Rd., in the underpass near Kosa Hotel. Motorcycles 200ʙ, cars 1200-1800ʙ. Copy of passport required. Open daily 7am-7pm.

Tourist Police: 149 Mittraphap Rd. (☎043 236 937), south of Khon Kaen, 300m before Lotus supermarket, on the righthand side. *Songthaew* #3-6, 10-12, 17, 19-20 go by. Open 24hr.

Pharmacy: Phon Phesad (☎043 228 260), just off Sri Chant Rd., near the Bangkok Bank. Open daily 8am-midnight.

Medical Services: Khon Kaen-Ram Hospital, 193 Sri Chant Rd. (☎043 333 800), near the intersection with Mitraphap Rd. English-speaking doctors. Open 24hr. *Songthaew* #2, 14, 19, 20 go by.

Internet Access: Numerous Internet cafes on Glang Muang Rd., north of Ammart Rd. (15ʙ per hr.) Those near the university shopping plaza open 24hr. **CAT,** 18/13-14 Phimpasut Rd. (☎043 241 560), sells calling cards (100min. card for 7ʙ per hr.) and offers Internet service. Open M-F 8:30am-4:30pm.

Post Office: GPO, 153/8 Glang Muang Rd., just south of Sri Chant Rd. Poste Restante on ground floor. Open M-F 8:30am-4:30pm, Sa-Su 9am-noon. **Postal Code:** 40000.

🏠 ACCOMMODATIONS

Khon Kaen is a large city with plenty of accommodation options. Most budget travelers opt for one of the cheaper places in the heart of town, between the two bus stations. There are also inexpensive hotels around the university, many of which offer major rate reductions. Thanks to the city's convenient *songthaew* service, all accommodations are within an 8ʙ ride.

Phu Inn Hotel, 26-34 Sathityutitham Rd. (☎043 243 174), has an ideal location. For a reasonable price you get an excellent room. Each has a large cable TV, comfortable bed with clean sheets, couch, and private bathroom with hot water and Western toilet. Doubles with A/C 350ʙ. ❸

Cactus Resort and Hotel, 171/38-39 Pracha Samosan Rd. (☎043 244 888), across from the Laos Embassy, off *songthaew* routes #10 and 11. The chic rooms and sparkly, colorful tiled bathrooms create a real oasis in the middle of Isaan. Rooms with A/C, minibar, cable TV, and free Wi-Fi 550ʙ. MC/V. ❸

Sansumran Hotel, 55-59 Glang Muang Rd. (☎043 239 611). The closest thing to a backpacker vibe in Khon Kaen. Small rooms 170ʙ; larger rooms 200ʙ. ❷

Kaen Inn, 56 Glang Muang Rd. (☎043 245 42031), at the intersection with Ammart Rd. and opposite the A/C bus station. Apart from the suites, only rooms with twin beds are available. They are a little dark, but comfortable with large cable TV and carpeted floors. Breakfast included. Karaoke bar, restaurant, and airport transfers (60ʙ per person). Rooms with 2 twin beds 660ʙ, suites with 1 large bed 1400ʙ. AE/MC/V. ❹

🍽 FOOD

There's no need to go hungry in this gourmand-friendly city. Options range from upscale and atmospheric (around Beung Kaen Nakhon Reservoir) to ultra-cheap (clustered on Phimpasut and Ammart Rd.). A sizeable **day market** selling fruits, vegetables, and pig heads hides behind storefronts along Nah Muang and Glang Muang Rd., and stretches south to Ruen Rom Rd. (Open daily 5am-6pm.) Cheap Isaan meals like *sup nau mai* (shredded bamboo-shoot salad) tempt hungry passersby at **night markets,** on Lang Muang and Ruen Rom Rd. Look for *pad mee khon kaen,* fried noodles similar to *pad thai,* but with a slightly sour taste, unique to this city (20ʙ). Rumor has it that the best place to taste it is from is the small **cart** on Sathityutitham Rd., across from the night market. And for those on a budget, you can't beat the dirt cheap meals at the university joints throughout campus.

Ban Suan, 539/3 Nah Muang Rd. (☎043 227 811). Exiting Fairy Plaza, take a left, and walk for 1km. *Songthaew* #9, 19, and 20 go by. Chinese, Thai, Isaan, and outdoor Korean BBQ. Stuff yourself to your heart's content with cook-your-own food (109฿). If you come alone, 99฿ will only buy you the precooked food (still an impressive selection). You will have to pay for the equivalent of 2 people (218฿) to do cook-your-own at your table. Open nightly 4pm-2am. ❸

Bua Luang Restaurant (☎043 222 504), at the end of a piece of land that juts out into Bua Luang Reservoir. Listen to the water lapping up against the pilons below while you eat your meal. The English menu has a small selection of tasty meals. Try the prawn with coconut palm heart (80฿). Most dishes 80-150฿. Open daily 10am-11pm. ❸

The Boat, 243/79 Mittraphap Rd. (☎043 239 943), north of the city. Khon Kaen's famous restaurant and jazz club. On certain nights, Thai pop makes way for a live jazz band. Braised duck with vegetables 100-180฿. Music starts around 7pm. Most dishes 80-150฿. Open daily 11am-10:30pm. ❷

The First Choice Restaurant, 18/8 Phimpasut Rd. (☎043 332 019), opposite Khon Kaen Hotel. A chill backpacker space perfect for reading the paper and chatting with other travelers while snacking on numerous vegetarian options. Serves up a hefty selection of Western favorites. Owner also runs a travel agency. Western breakfast 80฿. Thai dishes 50-100฿. Open daily 7:30am-10pm. ❷

◉ SIGHTS

In the southeast corner of Khon Kaen is ◻**Beung Kaen Nakhon,** a lakeside recreational area enclosed by four *wats*. Numerous food stalls line the northern shore. At dusk, youngsters compete in games of table tennis and couples holding hands as they walk along the lake's shoreline. Every year in the middle of April, the lake also plays host to the **Dok Khoon Song Kran Festival,** which features Isaan music, floral processions, and dances. On the southwest shores of the lake is **Wat Nong Waeng,** where you can climb to the top of the 9-story *chedi* to meditate or take in panoramic views of the city. Monks and laypeople walk up each layer of the *chedi*, gaining good karma while burning calories.

The well-presented **Khon Kaen National Museum** (Phiphitthaphanthasathan Haeng Chat), at Lungsoomratchakan and Kasikonthungsang Rd.,

FROM THE ROAD

BOUND TOGETHER

Part way through my route as a researcher this summer, I was invited to a Thai wedding. I had just arrived at another small town in northeast Thailand when my guesthouse owner, Nimowarat, insisted that I join her family the next day in Khon Kaen for a wedding. I threw my inhibitions to the wind and agreed to go.

Buddhist weddings in Thailand are extravagant affairs. As the only *farang* at the wedding, I watched each elaborate step wide-eyed. A monk chanted Theravada Buddhism's Three Refuges and Five Precepts. Then, the couples' parents were called upon to connect the newlyweds by placing conjoined twin loops of rope on their heads. Later, the couple presented offerings to Buddha, and lit incense at the top of a small tree.

Toward the end of the ceremony, small pieces of cotton were handed out to the assembled crowd. A toothless old man at the back demonstrated how to assemble a small donation in the cloth, and then how to attach it to the wrists of the newlyweds. Though I fumbled my gesture horribly, I have never felt so welcomed by a group of strangers in my life.

We feasted and drank long into the night. I attempted to sing some Thai songs, and enjoyed the incredible food. I finished the night sitting quietly amazed at another incredible experience in Thailand.

—Jeff Overall

documents the history of central northeast Thailand. The second floor has articles from the olden days, while the first floor is devoted to prehistoric times. Particularly impressive are the *semas*, or carved boundary stones. (☎043 246 170. *Songthaew #12, 17, and 21 go by. Open W-Su 9am-4pm. 30฿.*)

About 4km northwest of town, **Khon Kaen University** (Mahawitthayalai Khon Kaen) is a student city built over almost 6000 *rai* of land. *Songthaew* #8 drives through the campus. Hop off at the 7-Eleven next to the shopping plaza and wander around the shops and cheap eateries to get a feel for student life. The university is also home to a small art and cultural **museum** (☎043 332 035), near the university gate on Maliwan Rd. It has temporary exhibits and Isaan music. There's also a finearts department on campus. If you're lucky, friendly students may give you a tour and show you their artwork. *(Open daily 10am-7pm. Free.)*

■ NIGHTLIFE

Khon Kaen's nightlife centers around Prachasamran Rd., near the upscale Sofitel Hotel. The area gets infused with the energy and style of Khon Kaen's young hipsters, who dance the night away at the bars and clubs that constantly close and reopen with a fresh lick of paint.

U-Bar, 222/2 Prachasamran Rd. (☎043 320 434; http://ubarkk.hi5.com), just off to the side of the Sofitel Hotel. Great local bands and a sleek, young atmosphere draw lines outside the door on nights. 20+. Small Singha 80฿. Bacardi Breezer 100฿. No cover. Open daily 8pm-2am.

Rad Complex, 321/2 Prahasamran Rd. (☎043 225 988), has different themed rooms and bands: **Rad Alive** cranks out variety and rock, **Rad Society** moves to indy and hip-hop, and **Freak Out** bumps to techno. Singha 100฿. No cover. Freak Out open 1am-4am, all others 9pm-2am.

Freeze Cocktail Lounge, 141 Prachasmran Rd. (☎043 224 444; www.freezepub. com), 100m up from the Rad Complex, is the place to go for a quieter evening. Built like a giant icecube with frosted glass walls, Freeze Cocktail has A/C and sleek modern furniture. Both floors serve scrumptious mixed drinks (150฿). Stella Artois 140฿. Open nightly 10pm-2am. V/MC.

■ SHOPPING

Sample some of the local crafts and silk at Khon Kaen's stores.

OTOP Center, 250-252 Sri Chant Rd. (☎043 320 320 ext. 2007), in the underpass near Kosa Shopping center and leading to Kosa Hotel. Open 9:30am-8:40pm.

The Kosa Shopping Center, a large, rather generic mall with an excellent food court. On the top floor. **Prince Cineplex** (☎043 389 024) screens Hollywood movies dubbed in Thai. 80฿ per person. First movie starts at noon, the last around 10pm. On the same floor is **Kosa Bowl** (☎043 389 160), with 30 bowling lanes. 55฿ per game, 100฿ for 3 games. Shoe rentals 25฿. Open daily 11am-midnight. V.

■ DAYTRIPS FROM KHON KAEN

PHUWIANG NATIONAL PARK. If you're interested in ancient reptiles, swing by Phuwiang National Park, home to the largest dinosaur fossils in the country. Fossils dug up from the nine quarries discovered in the area in 1976 have added weight to the theory that Tyrannosaurus Rex first lived in Asia before crossing the Bering Strait to North America. Paleontologist wannabes will love the dinosaur trail, which connects the excavation sites. Although the first dig site is within walking distance of the entrance office, the park is large and the different sites are best explored by car. There is also camping available in the park. To get to the dinosaur trail without a car, hire a *tuk-tuk* (250-280฿) from the Phuwiang bus station and negotiate a price for a return trip. *(Buses to Phuwiang (50฿) leave daily before 1:30pm from the regular bus station. From Phuwiang Station, hire a tuk-tuk for the remaining 20km (130฿). Camping 30฿, 2-person tent 120฿, large bungalows 1200฿. Open daily 8:30am-4:40pm. Park 200฿.)*

CHONABOT. This remote town is the capital of hand-made Thai silk, especially *mudmee* (traditional tie-dyed) silk. Locals skillfully produce incredible patterns and material on ancient, manual weaving machines. Most weaving occurs in private houses; however, the town has three "factories." Most have stores attached, and are more than willing to give you a free guided tour explaining the whole process. Go early in the morning to watch the dying process. One such factory is **Ruenthai Maithai.** *(From Khon Kaen's regular bus station, catch any bus heading in the direction of Khorat. Ask to be let off at Ban Phai (40min., 12 per day 6:30am-5:30pm, 40฿). From there, buses and songthaew to a variety of destiations run the extra 11km to Chonabot. Alternatively, hire a motorbike. Follow the signs to Nakhon Ratchasima. Ban Phai is 37km along the highway. The turnoff for Chonabot is clearly marked. The last bus back leaves from in front of Chonabot police station at around 5pm. ☎ 043 287 229. Pure silk scarfs 500-650฿. Open daily 8am-5pm.)*

ROI ET   ☎ 043

This charming city sits smack-dab in the middle of Thailand's agricultural heartland. Built around a peaceful lake and park, Roi Et is watched over by the tranquil gaze of the world's tallest blessing Buddha. This enormous figure is aptly situated in a city meaning "101," which was likely created in remembrance of Roi Et's former prosperity. Intense flooding has since destroyed much of the city and only one gate remains from the glory days. Today, Roi Et is still a beautiful and charming city, well off the beaten path, that produces some of the best jasmine rice in the world. Beyond rice, the city is a great place to taste *sup nau mai* (bamboo shoot curry), browse *mudmee* (tie-dyed silks) and *khaens* (Isaan panpipes), and visit impressive *wats*.

⌐ TRANSPORTATION

Flights: Roi Et's **airport** (☎ 043 518 246) is 13km from town on the Roi Et-Pon Thong Rd. **PB Air** (☎ 043 518 572; open daily 9am-4pm) flies to **Bangkok** (1hr.; M and F 7:20am; W, and Sa-Su 10:20am).

Buses: Roi Et's **bus station** (☎ 043 511 939) is 2km west of town, towards Maha Sarakham on Jangsanit Rd. Either walk—from the post office, turn right onto Jangsanit Rd. for 2km—or take a *tuk-tuk* (40-50฿). Different companies can run buses to the same destination, so check around. Buses to: **Bangkok** (8hr.; every hr. 6am-1pm except 10am, every 30min. 7pm-8pm; 335-665฿) via **Khorat** (4hr., 175-345฿); **Kalasin** (1hr., every hr. 6:20am-5:20pm, 36฿); **Surin** (3hr., every hr. 5am-7pm, 104฿); **Ubon Ratchathani** (3hr., 11 per day 8am-2:30pm, 122฿) via **Yasothon** (1hr., 53฿); **Udon Thani** (4hr., every hr. 5am-4pm, 100-130฿); **Khon Kaen** (2hr., every 20min. 5am-6:30pm, 80฿); **Buriram** (3hr., every hr. 5:45am-4:45pm, 80฿). **Samlor** (20-40฿) and **tuk-tuks** (30-60฿) will take you around town.

🛈 ORIENTATION

Roi Et is centered around the **Beung Phlan Chai Lake. Sunthornthep Road** encircles the lake, before joining **Suriyadet Bamrung Road** in the east. Most stores and hotels are east of the lake, on **Peonjit Road. Rattakitkhlaikhla Road,** to the south, and **Haisok Road,** to the north, bisect the city. The bus station is located on the western end of the main east-west artery, **Jangsanit Road,** which becomes **Thewapiban Road** in the east. The hospital, tourist center, and other government buildings are centered around a traffic circle where Rattakitkhlaikhla and **Rachakrandamnean Road** intersect, south of the lake.

⚡ PRACTICAL INFORMATION

Tourist Office: The **tourist information center** (☎043 519 310), is on Rachakrandamnean Rd., near the traffic circle, across from the Chamber of Commerce. Offers Thai language maps. Limited English spoken. Open M-F 8:30am-4:30pm.

Bank: Bangkok Bank, 27 Suriyadet Bamrung Rd. (☎043 514 591), at Sukkasem Rd., exchanges currency and has a Cirrus/MC/V **24hr. ATM.** Open M-F 8:30am-3:30pm.

Police: 123 Suriyadet Bamrung Rd. (☎043 511 177), next to CAT.

Pharmacy: Chai Rat Pharmacy, 68 Suriyadet Bamrung Rd. (☎01 670 3344), with English-speaking pharmacists. Open daily 9am-8pm.

Hospital: Roi Et Hospital (☎043 511 336), 111 Ronnachaichanyut Rd., away from the lake, past the traffic circle and moat on Rattakitkhlaikla Rd., on the left across from the 7-Eleven.

Internet Access: Pop Net, 6/7 Peonjit Rd. (☎043 514 050), across from the large "Adidas" sign on the sporting goods store. 15฿ per hr. Open daily 10am-8pm.

Telephones: CAT, 119 Suriyadet Bamrung Rd. (☎043 511 600), next to the post office. International calls and faxes. Internet 6฿ per hr. Open M-F 8:30am-4:30pm.

Post Office: GPO, 117 Suriyadet Bamrung Rd. (☎043 511 306), at the intersection with Suriyat Rd. Open M-F 8:30am-4:30pm, Sa-Su 9am-noon. **Postal Code:** 45000.

🏠 ACCOMMODATIONS

Roi Et has, at best, a paltry selection of budget accommodations. Rooms are commonly shared with mosquitoes and the occasional cockroach. They're manageable for a couple of nights, but a few extra baht can be well spent on a hotel upgrade.

▣ Petcharart Garden Hotel, 404 Kotchapalayuk Rd. (☎043 519 0009; www.petcharartgardenhotel.com), 1km north of town. Pretend you're a movie star here, as you lounge around the large resort-style pool with plenty of deck-chairs, and the pool-side bar. Cable TV, free Wi-Fi, and a breakfast buffet for 2. Doubles 540฿, with bathtub 580฿. ❶

The Saitip Hotel, 95 Suriyadet Bamrung Rd. (☎043 511 742), situated around a large parking lot, a block away from the night market. Decent rooms with private bathrooms. Rooms with fan 240฿, with A/C 330฿. ❷

🍴 FOOD

The best Isaan food is at **roadside stalls** throughout the city, or at the clean and friendly **night market,** one of the largest in Isaan. This market sets up off Peonjit Rd., between Sukkasem and Suriyat Rd. The **day market** is at the intersection of Haisok and Phadung Phanit Rd., north of the lake. Watch for the stir-fry man who cooks up spicy veggie and meat stir-fry with flames shooting up meters into the air. There's also an early morning **fresh market** in the same building as the night market, with fruit, veggies, fish, and meat. (Open daily 6-9am.)

Korean BBQ Joint (Sat Hong Ngeu Yang Kao Lee), 2/13 Robmuengdamai Rd. (☎043 513 407), just north of the moat, on the road leading to Petcharat Garden Hotel (above). Locals love to gorge themselves here with the all-you-can-eat buffet (99฿), which includes meat, seafood, and vegetables that you cook yourself over your own

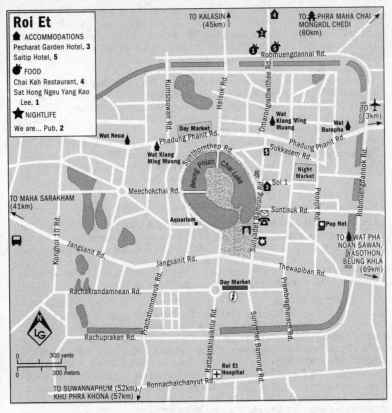

Roi Et

ACCOMMODATIONS
Pecharat Garden Hotel, **3**
Saitip Hotel, **5**

FOOD
Chai Kah Restaurant, **4**
Sat Hong Ngeu Yang Kao
Lee, **1**

NIGHTLIFE
We are... Pub, **2**

grill or hot pot. Request your favorite Thai pop tune from the band that kicks off at 7pm. Open daily 11am-midnight. ❷

Chai Kah Restaurant, 67 Damrongrathwithee Rd. (☎043 523 158). Just south of the BBQ, on the other side of the moat. Serves portions of Isaan, Thai, and Chinese food in a peaceful garden area. Chai Kah has one of few English menus in town. A popular dish is *plaa chon loei suan* (fish with vegetables, 150-180฿). Most dishes 60-80฿. Open daily noon-11pm. ❷

SIGHTS AND ENTERTAINMENT

Roi Et is centered around **Beung Phlan Chai Lake** and its well-maintained park, whose pathways and footbridges dot the lake. It is the perfect setting for an afternoon stroll. Stop to feed the fish at the water's edge (5฿), or rent a paddleboat (30min., 30฿). The park can be accessed from one of its footbridges. A small **aquarium** is located on the southwest shores of the lake. Cool off in the aquarium's air-conditioning and stroll through its walk-through tunnel displaying Thailand's northeastern aquatic life. (☎043 511 286. Aquarium open W-Su 8:30am-4:30pm. Park open daily 4am-9pm. Free.)

Wat Burapha, off Phadung Phanit Rd., is in the northeast corner of town. From Peonjit Rd., turn right onto Phadung Phanit, and it's 500m to the left—keep looking up, you can't miss it. The largest structure at this *wat* isn't a pagoda, it's the world's tallest Buddha, in a blessing posture, towering over the city at 67.8m. Known locally as **Luang Pho Yai,** the Buddha was constructed from 1973-1979 giving it little historical significance. Nonetheless, it is a spectacle to behold. Climb the set of stairs running up behind the Buddha to get a nice view of Roi Et. (Open 9am-5pm daily.)

In contrast, the 200-year-old monastic hall at **Wat Klang Ming Muang,** on Pha-dung Phanit Rd., dates back to the late Ayutthaya period, when it was used as a site to pledge official allegiance to the King. The *wat* houses mural paintings, and has a climbable three-story bell tower. *(From the lake, take a left onto Phadung Phanit Rd.; the wat is on the left. Open 8am-4pm.)*

Roi Et's limited night scene is concentrated along Ratchapalayuk Rd. The helpfully named **"We are...Pub",** 410 M 14 Ratapalayuk Rd., directly opposite Petcharat Garden Hotel, gets the beats going at 10pm each night. (☎081 779 1919. Singha 75฿. Live music starts at 10:30pm. Open 9pm-2am.)

▶ DAYTRIPS FROM ROI ET

PHRA MAHA CHAI MONGKOL CHEDI. Phra Maha Chai Mongkol Chedi ("the great, victorious, and auspicious pagoda") lives up to its name. It's on 101 *rai* of land and is 101m in width, length, and height. You can walk along the wall that encloses a 7000 sq. m forest. The temple is located 80km away from Roi Et. *(From Roi Et bus station, catch a mini-bus to Nong Phok (every 20min. 5am-2pm, 40฿). From there, catch a 30฿ songthaew that going to Phra Maha Chai Mongkol)*

WAT PHA NOAN SAWAN. Located along the road to Yasothan, Wat Pha Noan Sawan, a melange of Hindu and Buddhist culture. Two giant tortoises and two towering pagodas resembling pinecones are at this temple's entrance, which is shaped like the mouth of Hanuman (from the *Ramayana*). As a result, this *wat* looks like a cross between a sacred space and an amusement park. Yasothon-bound buses will drop you off 4km from the *wat* (15฿). Farther away from Roi Et, on Yasothon Rd., is Beung Khla, a lovely **reservoir** is frequented by locals. Food stalls serve a range of Thai meals. *(Buses heading in the direction of Yasothon can drop you off at the resevoir (15min., 11 per day 8am-2:30pm, 10฿). Alternatively, charter a tuk-tuk to take you there, wait, and bring you back, for 180-200฿.)*

NORTHERN THAILAND

Northern Thailand's mountains constitute the lowest crags of the Himalayan foothills. Its Salawin River flirts with Myanmar before flooding into the Bay of Bengal, and its northeastern border is formed by none other than the mighty Mekong River. The former Lanna kingdom attracts adventurous travelers eager to trek through hills and visit Karen, Hmong, Yao, Lahu, Lisu, and Akha hill-tribe villages. A home of Burmese refugees, Chinese immigrants, and nine hill tribes, and subject to ongoing influence from Laos and Myanmar, northern Thailand is perhaps the most culturally diverse region in the country. Chiang Mai, Thailand's second largest city, forms the central hub of the region and introduces foreigners to Lanna culture, cuisine, meditation, and massage. Northeast of the bustling metropolis, calmer brother Chiang Rai sits on the scenic Kok River, dotted with elephant camps and hill tribes. To the east of Chiang Mai is the Mae Hong Son Loop, renowned for its treks, though many travelers never make it past the charming riverside village of Pai. The north is an great escape from the beach crowds of the south; a haven of mountain villages where you can enjoy the famed hospitality of the Lanna people.

CHIANG MAI   ☎ 053

The sighting of several good omens convinced King Mengrai to establish the seat of his great Lanna Kingdom in Chiang Mai in 1296—an auspicious beginning for a city that has become Thailand's second-largest. Thousands of *farang*, drawn by the promise of adventure and a cooler climate, clog the narrow streets of the "Rose of the North." Many have settled here, adding to the sizable expat community. While the increasing number of tourists raises both environmental and cultural preservation concerns, Chiang Mai has retained its cultural uniqueness. A distinctive dialect, Burmese-influenced art and architecture, and an abundance of sticky rice (a northern specialty) prove that the city is not about to surrender its heritage anytime soon.

⊠ INTERCITY TRANSPORTATION

The monthly magazines **Welcome to Chiang Mai and Chiang Rai** and **Guidelines Chiang Mai,** available at travel agencies, guesthouses, and hotels throughout the city, have comprehensive transportation schedules.

BY PLANE

Chiang Mai International Airport, on Sanambin (Airport) Rd., 3km southwest of the city center, is accessible by **tuk-tuk** (100฿) or **songthaew** (20฿ on the street, 80฿ from a guesthouse). **Thai Airways,** with an air-conditioned office at 240 Phra Pokklao Rd. (☎ 053 211 044; open daily 8am-5pm) and at the airport (☎ 053 270 222), flies to **Bangkok** (7 per day 7am-9pm, 2165฿); **Mae Hong Son** (10:10am and 4:10pm, 1260฿); **Phuket** (6 per day 7am-9pm, 3410฿); **Kunming, China** via **Bangkok** (2:25pm, 7000฿); **Phnom Penh, Cambodia** (2:40 and 9pm, 7700฿). **Bangkok Airways** (☎ 053 281 519), on the second floor at the airport, flies to: **Bangkok** (1-2 per day, 2300฿) via **Sukhothai** (940฿); **Jinghong** (Tu, Th, Sa, Su 4:10pm; 4445฿). **Lao Airlines** (☎ 053 223 401) flies to **Vientiane** (Tu and F 12:50pm; Su 3:40pm; 4340฿) via **Luang**

Prabang. Air Mandalay, 148 Charoen Prathet Rd. (☎053 818 049), flies to **Mandalay** (Tu 6:05pm, Th 2:20pm; 3500฿) and **Yangon** (F 8pm, Su 2:20pm; 3400฿). **Silk Air,** 153 Sri Donchai Rd. (☎053 276 459; open M-F 8:30am-5pm, Sa-Su 8:30am-1pm), at the Imperial Maeping Hotel, flies to **Singapore** (Tu-W, and F 11am, Su 6pm; 7500฿). A branch of **STA Travel, Trans World Travel Service Co., Ltd.,** 259/61 Tha Pae Rd. (☎053 272 416), may offer cheaper student tickets than carriers. You'll need a student card (200฿ with passport and proof of student status). All international flights are subject to a 500฿ departure tax (cash only).

BY TRAIN

The **Chiang Mai Railway Station,** 27 Charoen Muang Rd. (☎053 244 795), on the eastern outskirts of the city, is accessible by **songthaew** (30฿) and **tuk-tuk** (50-70฿).

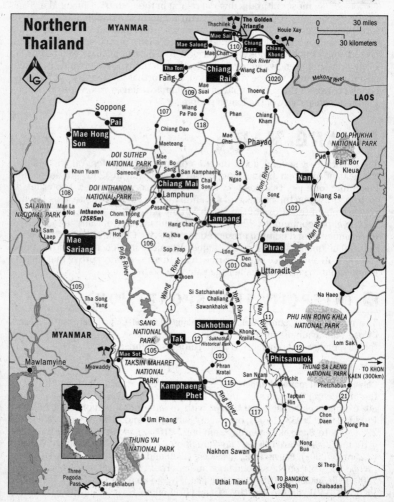

Northern Thailand

Trains run to **Bangkok** (11-14hr., 7 per day 6:45am- 9pm, 231-1353฿). All Bangkok-bound trains also stop in **Lampang** (2hr., 23-53฿), and some stop in **Phitsanulok** (7hr., 215-440฿). Many more options are available for an extra charge. Reserve sleeper tickets in person and well in advance. (Refund 80% 3 days before travel, 50% up to 1hr. before travel. Ticket window open daily 6am-8pm.)

BY BUS

Tuk-tuks (50-90฿) and **songthaew** (60฿) shuttle between the old city and **Arcade Bus Station** (☎053 242 664), 3km to the northeast. The main room of the bus station has ticket offices for buses to **Bangkok** and **Khorat** (window #12), as well as the **Green Bus** ticket office, which runs buses to **Chiang Rai, Chiang Khong, Lampang, Mae Sot,** and **Nan.** Ticket offices for **Phitsanulok, Sukhothai, Khon Kaen,** and **Mae Hong Son** are behind the main building. **NCA,** the ticket office for Ubon Ratchathani, is across the parking lot from the other ticket offices. **Chang Phuak Bus Station** (☎053 211 586), on Chang Phuak Rd., 500m north of the city, runs buses within the province.

Guesthouses sell tickets for **Aya Service's** A/C **minibus** to **Pai** (3hr., every hr. 8:30am-4:30pm, 150฿) Some organize minibuses to **Mae Sai** (600฿) and **Chiang Khong** (300฿). Minibuses are a faster option than regional buses, because they do not make stops along the way.

DESTINATION	DUR.	FREQUENCY/TIME	PRICE
ARCADE BUS STATION Bangkok	10hr.	every hr. 6:30am-9pm	374-745฿
Chiang Rai	3hr.	11 per day 6am-12:15pm	225฿
Khon Kaen	12hr.	13 per day 5am-5:30pm	260-524฿
Khorat (Nakhon Ratchasima)	12hr.	12 per day 3:30am-8:30pm	430-510฿
Lampang	2hr.	every 30min. 6am-4pm	80฿
Mae Hong Son	8hr.	6:30, 8, 11am, 8, 9pm	145-216฿
Mae Sariang	5hr.	7 per day 6:30am-9pm	78-140 ฿
Mae Sot	6hr.	11, 11:45am, 1:10, 1:30pm	134-241฿
Nan	6hr.	10 per day 6:15am-10:30pm	117-230b฿
Pai	3hr.	7, 8:30, 10:30, 11:30am, 12:30, 4pm	60฿
Phitsanulok	6hr.	10 per day 6:30am-8pm	120-216฿
Sukhothai	5hr.	12 per day 5am-8pm	177฿
Ubon Ratchathani	17hr.	6 per day 12:15-6pm	225-685฿
CHANG PHUAK BUS STATION Chom Thong	1hr.	every 20min. 6:30am-4pm	50฿
Lamphun	1hr.	every 10min. 6:20am-6pm	30฿
Tha Ton	4hr.	6 per day 6am-3:30pm	90฿
Fang	3hr.	every 30min. 5:30am-5:30pm	100฿

✦ ORIENTATION

Chiang Mai is 720km north of Bangkok. Most of the action centers in the beautiful **old city,** roughly 1.5km across and surrounded by a square-shaped **moat.** Many of the tree-lined streets within the moat are limited to pedestrians and motorbikes only. The **northeast corner** of the old city, with inexpensive guesthouses and restaurants, is a hub of backpacker activity. The **southeastern corner** has a similar, slightly less touristy vibe. The **western edge** of the old city, only a few blocks west of the central **Phra Pokklao Road,** exudes a more local feel, as many tourists never make it there. The highest concentration of foreigner activity occurs around the **Tha Pae Gate area,** in the middle of the old city's eastern edge. Guesthouses here aren't quite as nice as they are in other parts of the

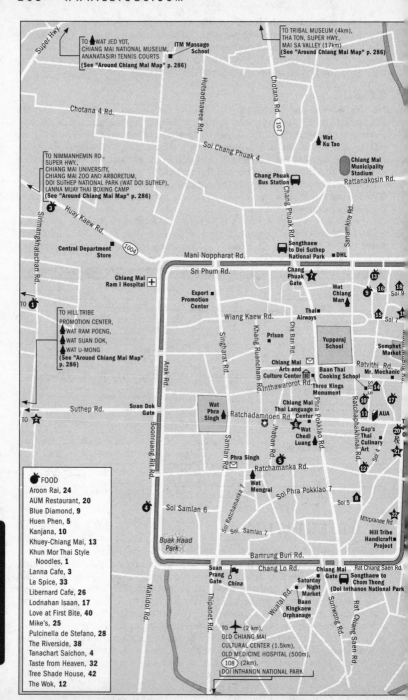

TO WAT JED YOT, TRIBAL MUSEUM (4km),
CHIANG MAI NATIONAL MUSEUM, THA TON, SUPER HWY.,
ANANATASIRI TENNIS COURTS MAI SA VALLEY (17km)
(See "Around Chiang Mai Map" p. 286) (See "Around Chiang Mai Map" p. 286)

ITM Massage School

Super Hwy.

Chotana 4 Rd.

Hutsadisawee Rd.

Chotana Rd. (107)

Wat Ku Tao

Soi Chang Phuak 4

Chang Phuak Bus Station

Chiang Mai Municipality Stadium

Rattanakosin Rd.

TO NIMMANHEMIN RD.,
SUPER HWY.,
CHIANG MAI UNIVERSITY,
CHIANG MAI ZOO AND ARBORETUM,
DOI SUTHEP NATIONAL PARK (WAT DOI SUTHEP),
LANNA MUAY THAI BOXING CAMP
(See "Around Chiang Mai Map" p. 286)

Chang Phuak Rd.

Sanamkira Rd.

Huay Kaew Rd.

Songthaew to Doi Suthep National Park

DHL

Sirimangkhalachan Rd.

(1004)

Central Department Store

Mani Noppharat Rd.

Chang Phuak Gate

Sri Phum Rd.

Wat Chiang Man

Wat 7

Chiang Mai Ram I Hospital

Export Promotion Center

Wiang Kaew Rd.

Thai Airways

13

9 16 18
Soi 9

TO 1

TO HILL TRIBE
PROMOTION CENTER,
WAT RAM POENG,
WAT SUAN DOK,
WAT U-MONG
(See "Around Chiang Mai Map" p. 286)

Singharat Rd.

Cha Ban Rd.

Khang Ruancham Rd.

Prison

Yupparaj School

15
Soi 7

Somphet Market

Ratvithi Rd.
Mr. Mechanic

Chiang Mai Arts and Culture Center

Baan Thai Cooking School

Three Kings Monument

Soi 5

14

Suthep Rd.

Arak Rd.

Suan Dok Gate

Wat Phra Singh

Ratchadamnoen Rd.

Inthawarorot Rd.

Chiang Mai Thai Language Center

Phra Pokklao Rd.

Ratchaphakhinai Rd.

10

17

TO

Boonnuang Rit Rd.

Jhaban Rd.

Wat Chedi Luang

11 AUA

Gap's Thai Culinary Art

20 R
21

Samlan Rd.

Phra Singh

Ratchamanka Rd.

Soi 4

12

Soi Ratchamanka 7

Wat Mengral

Soi Phra Pokklao 7

Soi 5

8

Soi Samlan 6

Soi Samlan 7

Mitrpranee Rd.

22

Buak Haad Park

Bamrung Buri Rd.

Hill Tribe Handicraft Project

Mahidol Rd.

Thipanet Rd.

Suan Prang Gate

China

Chang Lo Rd.

Saturday Night Market

Chiang Mai Gate

Songthaew to Chom Thong
(Doi Inthanon National Park

Rat Chiang Saen Rd.

Baan Kingkaew Orphanage

Wualai Rd.

Surwong Rd.

Rat Chiang Saen Rd.

TO (2km),
OLD CHIANG MAI
CULTURAL CENTER (1.5km),
OLD MEDICINE HOSPITAL (500m),
(108) (2km),
DOI INTHANON NATIONAL PARK

🍴 FOOD

Aroon Rai, **24**
AUM Restaurant, **20**
Blue Diamond, **9**
Huen Phen, **5**
Kanjana, **10**
Khuey-Chiang Mai, **13**
Khun Mor Thai Style Noodles, **1**
Lanna Cafe, **3**
Le Spice, **33**
Libernard Cafe, **26**
Lodnahan Isaan, **17**
Love at First Bite, **40**
Mike's, **25**
Pulcinella de Stefano, **28**
The Riverside, **38**
Tanachart Saichon, **4**
Taste from Heaven, **32**
Tree Shade House, **42**
The Wok, **12**

N LG

| 0 | | 400 yards |
| 0 | | 400 meters |

Chiang Mai

ACCOMMODATIONS

Ben Guest House, **41**
Daret's House and
    Restaurant, **23**
Eagle House, **30**
Good Will Guesthouse, **39**
Julie Guest House, **8**
Kristi Guest House, **14**
Lamchang House, **15**
Libra Guest House, **18**
Pun Pun Guest House, **36**
Rendezvous Guest House, **11**
Royal Guest House, **31**
Supreme House, **16**

★ NIGHTLIFE

The Gallery, **35**
The Garden, **6**
The Good View, **37**
Inter, **29**
North Gate Jazz Co-op, **7**
Pornping Tower Hotel, **34**
Mandalay and Star Planet, **22**
Rooftop Bar, **27**
Tapas Bar, **19**
WarmUp Cafe, **2**
The Zest, **21**

Fa Ham Rd.
India

Rama IX Bridge
36

Doi Saket Kao Rd.

TO PAYAP
UNIVERSITY

Chetuphon Rd.

McCormick
Hospital

Muang Samut Rd.
Wangsingkham Rd.
Ping River

Wat
Chetuphon

Kaew Nawarat Rd. 118

Bamrung Rat Rd.

UK

Witchayanon Rd.
US

Nakhon Ping Bridge

Sithiwong Rd.
Ratchawong Rd.

Taiwang Rd.
Wichayanon Rd.

els

30

TO ARCADE
BUS STATION (800m),
CHIANG RAI (140km),
(See "Around Chiang Mai Map"
p. 286)

Mon Tri Rd.

Thung Hotel Rd.

Lanna
Thai
Massage
School

Chiang Moi Rd.

Wat Ou Sai
Kham

Warorot
Market

Wat
Saen
Fang

Lanyal
Market

Backstreet Books
Gecko Books

Tha Pae Rd.
29 Trans World
Travel Service,
Co., Ltd.

Charoen Raj Rd.

35

Songthaew
to Bo Sang

37
38

Thai Farmers
Bank

Nawarat Bridge

Nawatket 1 Rd.

Thewi Uthit Rd.

Charoen Muang Rd. 1006

TO BO SANG (10km),
SAN KAMPHAENG (15km),
SUKHOTHAI (175km),
PHITSANULOK (200km)

The Peak Adventure

Soi 3

Soi 1
40
Chiang Mai
Green Tour and
Trekking Soi 2
39 41 42

GPO
Aya Service

Loi Kro Rd.

31

Night Bazaar
Chiang Klan Rd.

34
33 Kalare
Food
Court

Avis

i
Osathapan Rd.

Nai Phon Rd.

Kawila
Boxing
Stadium

Kong Sai Rd.

Imperial
Mae Ping
Hotel

Anusan
Market
Soi 8

Tasatoi Rd.

Sannalung Rd.

Rot Fai Rd.

Sri Dornchai Rd.

Chiang Mai
Plaza Hotel

France

Chiang Mai-Lamphun Rd.

Ra Kaeng Rd.

Mae Kha Canal

Alliance
Française

Rat Uthit Rd.

Chiangmai
Gymkhana
Club

phaeng Din Rd.
Prachasamphan Rd.
Changklan Rd.
Charoen Prathet Rd.

TO LAMPHUN (26km)

city, but there is no shortage of restaurants. The busy **Moon Muang Road** runs north-south on the inside edge of the moat and intersects **Ratchadamnoen Road** at the Tha Pae Gate. The area east of the Tha Pae Gate, between the moat and the Ping River, is a popular dining and drinking area. The famous **Night Bazaar** along **Chang Klan Road** is a sight in and of itself and is always packed. Past the Night Bazaar and across the **Nawarat Bridge,** to the east the Ping River, is another lively area, with restaurants, bars, and guesthouses. To the west of the old city lies trendy **Nimmanhemin Road** and the **Chiang Mai University district,** home to a large expat community. Chiang Mai's main tourist attraction, Wat Doi Suthep, is 16km northwest of the city, past the university.

Guesthouses, the TAT, and other tourist-geared establishments stock free copies of **Guidelines Chiang Mai** and **What's on Chiang Mai,** which offer useful and often amusing practical info. Keep an eye out for **City Life Chiang Mai,** the local expat monthly, with announcements, classifieds, and expatriate horror stories. For more information see www.chiangmainews.com.

▐ LOCAL TRANSPORTATION

Local Buses: Buses (approx. every 15min. 6am-10pm, 10-15฿) run along 5 routes in greater Chiang Mai. More information on the routes available at TAT.

Songthaew, Tuk-tuk, and Samlor: Songthaew (15-30฿) go anywhere in the city, but cost more to the airport or bus station. Already-occupied *songthaew* are cheaper than empty ones, which usually cost as much as *tuk-tuks*. **Tuk-tuks** and **samlor** cost 40฿ within the old city, 40-80฿ for trips across the city, and 400-700฿ per day. Rates are more expensive at night. Taxi service (☎053 201 307) can also be arranged during the day.

Bike Rentals: Bicycle and motorbike rental shops line both sides of the moat along Moon Muang Rd., centering on the Tha Pae Gate area. All require a deposit and a photocopy of passport. **Bicycles** 30-60฿ per day. **Motorbike** rental is typically 150฿ per day for 100cc and 200฿ for 125cc, with an additional 50฿ for insurance. Discounts for long-term rental. Because prices are similar throughout Chiang Mai, base your decision on the quality of a shop's bikes and the service it provides in the event of a breakdown. The 3 shops of **Mr. Mechanic,** 4 Moon Muang Rd. Soi 5 (☎053 214 708), get high marks in both categories and have comprehensive insurance. 110cc motorbike 80-120฿, insurance 50฿; a full range of additional options 300-700฿ per day.

Car Rentals: Avis, at the Royal Princess Hotel, 112 Chang Klan Rd. (☎053 281 033), and at the airport (☎053 201 574), rents Toyota Vios (1550฿ per day) and Toyota 4Runner 4WDs (2720฿ per day). Open daily 8am-5pm, airport location open daily 7am-9pm. Near the old city, **North Wheels,** 70/4-8 Chaiyamphum Rd. (☎053 874 478), rents a similarly wide variety of cars for 850-1900฿ per day. Open daily 7am-9pm. There are plenty of other car rental shops in the Tha Pae Gate area.

▐ PRACTICAL INFORMATION

TOURIST AND FINANCIAL SERVICES

Tourist Office: TAT, 105/1 Chiang Mai-Lamphun Rd. (☎053 248 604 or 053 258 607), 500m south of Nawarat Bridge. On the 2nd fl. of a traditional house. Full of maps, transportation schedules, and brochures. English spoken. Open daily 8:30am-4:30pm.

Consulates: Australia, Canada, China, France, India, UK, and the US offer visas and consular services. See **Embassies and Consulates,** p. 10 for contact info.

Visa Services: Travel agents around town can organize visas, though prices vary from agent to agent. **Laos:** 30-day visa 1650฿, 2-day processing.

Immigration Office: 21 Moo 3 Sanambin (Airport) Rd. (☎053 277 510). Visa extensions: 1-day processing 1900฿. Bring 2 passport photos, 2 copies of passport photo page, visa, and arrival/departure card. Open M-F 8:30am-4:30pm, Sa 8:30am-noon.

Currency Exchange: Banks line Tha Pae Rd. and are easy to find throughout the city. **Thai Farmers Bank,** 169-171 Tha Pae Rd. (☎053 270 151). Cirrus/MC/Plus/V **24hr. ATM.** Open M-F 8:30am-3:30pm. Currency exchange booths in the night bazaar on Chang Klan Rd. Open daily until 10pm.

Work Opportunities: Rejoice Urban Development accepts volunteers for projects providing medical and social support to local villages. **The Elephant Nature Park** is a sanctuary and rehabilitation center that accepts volunteers for any period of time. **Australia Center** hires English teachers. For more information on these opportunities and others, see **Beyond Tourism,** p. 76.

LOCAL SERVICES

Luggage Storage: At the railway station: 10฿ per piece per day for the first 5 days, 15฿ per additional day, max. 20 days. Open daily 4:50am-8:45pm. At the airport: ☎053 277 782. 30฿ per day, max. 14 days. Open daily 6am-5pm. Most guesthouses store luggage for free, although security is questionable. Never leave passports or credit cards in luggage.

Books: The best used bookstores, **Gecko Books** (☎053 874 066) and **Backstreet Books** (☎053 874 143), both open daily 9am-9pm, sit next to each other on Chang Moi Kao Rd., at the Tha Pae Gate. **The American University Alumni Language Center (AUA) Library,** 24 Ratchadamnoen Rd. (☎053 211 973), offers library service with a large selection of English books and videos. Free 1-day pass. Membership mandatory for subsequent visit: 150฿ per month, 400฿ per year; students 200฿ per year. Open M-F 8:30am-6pm, Sa 9am-1pm.

EMERGENCY AND COMMUNICATIONS

Ambulance: ☎1669.

Tourist Police: (☎1699), on Fa Ham Rd., before the superhighway. Open 24hr.

Pharmacy: Pharma Choice 2 (☎053 280 136), 29/2 Moon Muang Rd., just south of Tha Pae Gate. Open daily 9:30am-9:30pm. MC/V.

Medical Services: The modern **Chiang Mai Ram I Hospital,** 9 Boonruang Rit Rd. (☎053 224 861), has ambulance service and a **24hr. pharmacy.** English-speaking doctors. MC/V. Another hospital the other side of town, 1 133 Kaew Nawarat Rd. (☎053 262 200), has similar services.

Telephones: Internet cafes and tour agencies around town offer collect and international calls (7-30฿). Most Internet cafes have Skype installed.

Internet Access: Internet cafes line the major streets of the old city and the area around the Night Bazaar. They're concentrated in highly touristed areas and near guesthouses, and logically, rates tend to be higher (40-60฿ per hr.) in these places. For cheaper rates, head to places that tourists don't go. The lower ½ of Phra Pokklao Rd., between soi 5-7, has a number of inexpensive Internet and gaming cafes catering to locals (20-30฿ per hr.). Additionally, many guesthouses and cafes provide free Wi-Fi.

Post Offices: GPO (☎053 245 376), on Charoen Muang Rd., 150m toward the old city from the train station. Poste Restante and fax. Open M-F 8:30am-4:30pm, Sa-Su 9am-noon. **Phra Singh Post Office** (☎053 814 062), on Samlan Rd., south of Wat Phra Singh. Open M-F 8:30am-4:30pm, Sa 9am-noon. Other post offices are scattered throughout the city and marked on the map. To send packages, try

GIVING BACK

BAAN KINGKAEW ORPHANAGE

While there are plenty of long-term opportunities to volunteer in Thailand, there are relatively few options for those who wish to give their time on a day-by-day basis. The Baan Kingkaew Orphanage in Chiang Mai is the exception. Here, volunteers are encouraged to drop by and play with the children any time. There's no need to call ahead and volunteers can stay for as long or as little as they'd like.

The Baan Kingkaew Orphanage was established in 1966, and today it houses 50 children, the youngest of whom is only 3 months old. The orphanage provides education and healthcare to these displaced children.

While volunteers are welcome at any time, the best time to show up at Baan Kingkaew is at 2:30pm, after the children have taken their afternoon nap.

Baan Kingkaew Orphanage (☎275 650, www.baan-kingkaew-orphanage.org), 75 Wualai Rd., 100m southwest of the Chiang Mai Gate. Food and toy donations are greatly appreciated. No photographs are allowed.

DHL Express International, 168/1 Mani Noppharat Rd. (☎053 418 501), east of the Chang Phuak Gate. Open M-Sa 8:30am-6pm.

Postal Code: 50000 (GPO); 50200 (Phra Singh Post Office).

◪ ACCOMMODATIONS

Guesthouse signs sprout from almost every *soi* entrance within a 1km radius of **Tha Pae Gate.** Be sure to make a reservation during festival periods (see **Holidays and Festivals,** p. 71), the largest of which are the three-day **Flower Festival** in early February and the four-day **Songkran Water Festival** (Thai New Year) in mid-April, when certain guesthouses inflate their prices. Each neighborhood in the city hosts a number of comfortable and inexpensive accommodations. The area around Tha Pae Gate is close to everything, although the drone of traffic and bar tunes can be distracting. Heading north from Tha Pae Gate on Moon Muang Rd. leads to Soi 7 and 9 in the old city; both are quiet at night and packed with budget choices. The pace near the night bazaar is frenetic, and it's difficult to find budget lodgings. More affordable accommodations lie along quiet soi near the Ping river, 10min. away from the night bazaar. Expensive guesthouses will often give sizeable discounts on long-term accommodations. For large groups staying for extended periods of time, this can be significantly more cost-effective than staying in guesthouses.

WITHIN THE MOAT (THE OLD CITY)

▨ **Libra Guest House,** 28 Moon Muang Rd. Soi 9 (☎/fax 053 210 687). With a convenient location and large rooms arranged around a courtyard, this family-run guesthouse is one of the best options in Chiang Mai. The staff is especially helpful and friendly. Quiet hours after 8pm. Consistently praised treks organized (1-3 days; 2-day 1500฿-2500฿, max. 12 people). Cooking school 700฿ per day. Laundry service 25฿ per kg. Free Wi-Fi. Reservations recommended. All rooms with fan and private bath. Rooms 200฿, with hot water 300฿; with both hot water and A/C 380-420฿; triples 400฿, with A/C 480-540฿. ❷

▨ **Julie Guest House,** 7/1 Soi 5 Phra Pokklao Rd. (☎053 274 355; www.julieguesthouse.com). Walk south on Ratchaphakhinai Rd. and take a right at the English sign on Soi 5. Cheap, colorfully painted rooms and rooftop hammocks make this place very popular with backpackers. The cheery lounge and restaurant (open daily 8am-1:30pm and 4-8:30pm) downstairs has a pool table, and TV. 1-7 day trekking tours available.

5-bed dorm 70฿; singles and doubles 100-140฿, with private hot shower 130-200฿; higher-quality "stylish" rooms with private hot shower 250-350฿. ❶

🏠 **Lamchang House,** 24 Moon Muang Rd. Soi 7 (☎053 210 586). The 8 rooms on the 1st fl. of this traditional Thai house stay cool during the heat of the day, and always fill up quickly. Call ahead for reservations. The shaded sitting area out front is particularly attractive. All rooms with shared bath. Singles 100฿, doubles 200฿, triples 300฿. ❶

Kristi Guest House, 14/2 Ratchadamnoen Rd. Soi 5 (☎053 418 165). The hotel-like building has rooms that are practically luxurious, with hot water, TV, and bathtubs. Laundry 20฿ per kg. *Khantoke* dinner tickets available here. Low-season rooms 250฿, with A/C 350฿; high-season 300/400฿. ❷

Supreme House, 44/1 Moon Muang Rd. Soi 9 (☎053 222 480), 100m from Libra Guest House (see above). This is another solid budget option. The spare but tidy rooms have private baths with hot water, and on the higher floors, open onto terraces. Library and book exchange. Singles 150-180฿, doubles 200-220฿, triples 250-300฿. ❶

Rendezvous Guest House, 3/1 Ratchadamnoen Rd. Soi 5 (☎053 213 763), 50m to the north off Ratchadamnoen Rd. Sparkling, comfortable rooms with bath, TV, and small balcony. Laundry 30฿ per kg. Free Wi-Fi. Visa service for Myanmar, China, Laos, and Vietnam. Safety deposit box. Rooms 300-360฿, with A/C 500฿. ❸

EAST OF THE OLD CITY

BETWEEN THE MOAT AND THE RIVER

🏠 **Eagle House,** 16 Chang Moi Kao Rd. Soi 3 (☎053 874 126; www.eaglehouse.com). Walk east on the soi adjacent to the northernmost bridge on Chaiyaphum Rd., and take a right immediately after the ruined *chedi*. Rooms here an excellent value, and owners Annette and Pon provide great travel advice. Fully TAT-licensed, they pride themselves on "eco-sensitive tours". Annette arranges volunteer placements in the area. Restaurant in the garden courtyard. Treks 800฿ for 1 day, 2390฿ for 4 days; not including 200฿ national park entrance fee. All rooms have baths. Smaller rooms 150-180฿, larger rooms 200-240฿; with A/C 290-360฿. ❷

Daret's House and Restaurant, 4/5 Chaiyaphum Rd. (☎053 235 440), opposite Tha Pae Gate's north end. Considering their prime location, the simple rooms here are incredibly low-priced. The top-notch restaurant downstairs is consistently packed at dinnertime. Internet 30฿ per hr. Trekking tours available. All rooms with bath. Low-season singles and doubles 140-160฿, with hot water 180฿; triples 300-320฿. Prices rise in the high season. ❷

Royal Guest House, on Kotchasarn Rd. Soi 4 (☎053 282 460). Heading east on Loi Kro Rd. from the moat, turn right at Soi 1 and then take the next right onto Kotchasarn Rd. Soi 4. It's 50m ahead on the right. Although the cheapest rooms are all the way on the 7th fl., this family-friendly guesthouse's excellent location, onsite trekking, Internet services (40฿ per hr.), and swimming pool make it worth the inconvenience. Rooms with shared bath 150฿, with bath 250฿, with hot water 300฿, with A/C 500-1000฿. ❷

EASTERN BANK OF THE PING RIVER

Ben Guest House, 4/11 Chiang Mai-Lamphun Rd. Soi 2 (☎053 244 103; www.ben-guesthouse.com). Look for marked signs leading to this guesthouse. Its 16 rooms, with bath, hot shower, and unusually comfortable beds, are located in a quiet neighborhood near the river. Behind the house is a garden courtyard with a restaurant and lounge. It's a 30min. walk from here to the old city, but the Night Bazaar is only 10min. away.

Free Wi-Fi. Motorcycle rental 150฿, with insurance 200฿. TAT-licensed trekking available. Laundry 40฿ per kg. Rooms 250฿. ❷

Good Will Guesthouse, 8/2 Chiang Mai-Lamphun Rd. Soi 2 (☎053 242 323), next door to Ben Guest House. The rooms and prices are almost identical to those at nearby Ben's. In place of a garden, however, Good Will has a communal rooftop kitchen. 3-bed dorm with shared bath 100฿, rooms with bath and hot shower 250฿. ❷

Pun Pun Guest House, 321 Charoen Rat Rd. (☎053 246 180), just south of the Rama IX Bridge. For those who prefer local flavor to the bustle of the city center, this guest-house is a perfect solution. The neighborhood directly across the river is full of roadside markets and rarely visited by tourists. Rooms are in a main building or in bungalows near the river, with a restaurant-bar onsite. Motorbike 200-230฿ per day. Bicycles 50฿ per day. Rooms with shared bath 275฿, with bath 375฿, with A/C 425฿. ❸

🔲 FOOD

Chiang Mai has exceptional culinary diversity, with everything from quick mar-kets to elaborate eateries. Thanks to the large number of expats in the city, you can find Western dishes around Tha Pae Gate, but the culinary highlight of Chiang Mai is its northern Thai food. Dishes are served with sticky rice, and regional curries, characterized by a lack of coconut milk, are generally spicier. Try heading to the area west of Phra Pokklao Rd. in the old city, where you can't go a block without seeing low-key, traditional Thai restaurants populated almost exclusively by locals. Another regional specialty is coffee. The hills of the North have proven ideal for coffee plantations, and the delicious results of that process are readily available in Chiang Mai.

MARKET FOOD. Somphet Market, on Moon Muang Rd. between Soi 6 and 7, serves fried noodles (20-40฿) and *kuay tiaw lu chin plaa* (fishball noodle soup; 20฿). It is open all day until midnight, but food stalls don't get going until after 7pm. During the day, the **produce market** has a larger variety of local food. Other **night food stalls** line the moat to the south of the old city, near Wualai Rd. The **Night Bazaar** is another popular destination for late-night eats, but while there are some good restaurants in the area, prices are generally high. **Anusan Market,** in the southern part of the Night Bzaar between Chang Klan Rd. and Charoen Prathet Rd., is an overpriced nocturnal snack zone. Dining is cheaper at the **Kalare Food Court** in the middle of the Night Bazaar, where food booths surround a dining area and a stage with nightly entertainment. In the evening, the road that runs between **Warorot Market** and **Lanyai Market,** on the west bank of the Ping River, is crammed with food stalls.. Freshly sliced fruit (10฿) is available at all of the markets. The mango season (Mar.-May) brings 🍴 **khao niaw mamuang** (mangos and sweet sticky rice), a Thai delicacy.

KHANTOKE. For a memorable culinary experience, try a *khantoke* dinner. At this formal meal, diners sit on the floor and use their hands to eat rice, two meat dishes, and two vegetable dishes from bowls placed on a *khantoke,* a low tray table. The **Old Chiang Mai Cultural Center,** 185/3 Wualai Rd. (☎053 275 097), 1.5km south of the old city, offers vegetarian and Muslim versions. State prefer-ences when calling for the necessary reservation. The 3hr. affair, accompanied by traditional dancing, begins nightly at 7pm (320฿, includes transportation).

WITHIN THE MOAT (THE OLD CITY)

🍴 **Huen Phen,** 112 Ratchamanka Rd. (☎053 814 548), 300m west of Phra Pokklao Rd. Look no further than this restaurant, packed all day long, for northern Thai dining at its finest. Locals come for the spicy *num phrik* (chili paste with meat, 35฿) and other traditional northern entrees (20-50฿). Portions are small, but with exquisite flavor. Young jackfruit curry 50฿. Fruit juices 20-35฿. Open daily 8:30am-4pm and 5-10pm. ❶

The Wok, 44 Ratchamanka Rd. (☎053 208 287), east of Ratchaphakhinai Rd. The owner, a well-known Thai chef who hosts a television show, also runs the **Chiang Mai Thai Cookery School** (see **Cooking Classes,** p. 280). The creative "special Northern style food" is served in an airy outdoor patio. Spicy Chiang Mai sausage 79฿. Thai-style fishcakes 79฿. Chiang Mai curry 89฿. Banana cake 40฿. Open daily 3-10pm. ❸

Blue Diamond, 35/1 Moon Muang Rd. Soi 9 (☎053 217 120). Follow the soi west until the sign on your left. This bakery and restaurant, with seating indoors or alongside a well-kept garden, is well known in Chiang Mai for its vegetarian food and huge portions. Seasonal avocado menu. Most dishes 40-80฿. Health food ingredients available for sale. Open M-Sa 7am-8:30pm. ❷

Khuey-Chiang Mai (☎081 8838 662), on Mani Noppharat Rd. at the northern edge of the old city. Walking west from the northeast corner of the old city, pass the first bridge across the moat and you'll see it on the left. Another local favorite, Khuey-Chiang Mai has an inexpensive menu of northern Thai cuisine and a wide, high-ceilinged patio. Entrees 55-75฿. Open daily 6am-late. ❷

AUM Restaurant, 65 Moon Muang Rd. (☎035 278 315), just south of the Tha Pae Gate. Another of Chiang Mai's best all-vegetarian restaurants, AUM's menu high-lights regional dishes from the Chiang Mai area. Try the delicious *kausoi*, soft and fried egg noodles in curry and coconut milk (40฿). Upstairs from the tiny, intimate dining room is a secondhand bookstore. Entrees 40-50฿. Fried bean sprouts with mushrooms and tofu 40฿. Open daily 8am-5pm. ❷

Lodnahan Isaan (☎087 1790 096), 50m up the first soi to the right as you walk west on Ratchadamnoen Rd. from Tha Pae Gate. No English sign. It is on the right side of the street and recognizable by blue awnings and blue chairs. Despite being only steps away from the center of Chiang Mai's tourist activity, this hole-in-the-wall eatery doesn't see much *farang* traffic. The local dishes here come at amazingly low, almost market-level, prices. Entrees 30฿. Open daily 11am-9pm. ❶

Kanjana, 7/2 Ratchadamnoen Rd. Soi 5 (☎053 418 368), just north of Rendezvous Guesthouse. This dependable restaurant serves straightforward Thai dishes on a blue-tiled patio. Set breakfast 60-110฿. Entrees 40-80฿. Open daily 8am-9pm, closed 2nd and last Sa of every month. ❷

EAST OF THE OLD CITY

BETWEEN THE MOAT AND THE RIVER

▨ **Aroon Rai,** 45 Kotchasarn Rd. (☎053 276 947), south of the Tha Pae Gate and before Loi Kro Rd. Aroon Rai is starting to look well-worn from the crowds of *farang* and Thais who eat here every day. Rumored to have "The best curries in town," Aroon Rai lives up to its reputation. Curries 45-55฿. Frog dishes 80฿. Open daily 8am-10pm. ❷

▨ **Le Spice,** Charoen Prathet Rd. Soi 6 (☎053 234 983). From Charoen Muang Rd., turn south onto Chang Klan Rd. (the Night Bazaar) and take the 2nd left. Le Spice, one of the best Indian restaurants in the city, can be hit-or-miss; but even when it misses, the food remains well above average. And when it hits? Watch out. Entrees 70-160฿. Set menu with rice, *papadom*, and 3 dishes 99-129฿. Open daily 11am-11pm. ❸

▨ **Libernard Cafe,** 295-299 Chaiyamphun Rd. (☎053 874 377), down a narrow alley south of the intersection with Chang Moi Rd. Hidden off the road in a courtyard lined with tall bamboo, this small cafe has some of the best fresh-roasted coffee in Chiang Mai (45-50฿).

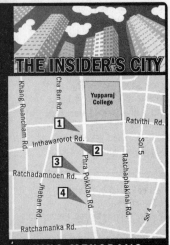

Khang Ruancham Rd.
Cha Ban Rd.
Yupparaj College
Ratvithi Rd.
1
Inthawarorot Rd.
Soi 5
2
Phra Pokklao Rd.
3
Ratchadamnoen Rd.
Ratchaphakinai Rd.
Jhaban Rd.
Soi 4
4
Ratchamanka Rd.

KING MENGRAI'S PILGRIMAGE

Today there are numerous pilgrim-age sights in Chiang Mai dedicated to the city's founder, King Mengrai of the Lanna kingdom.

1. Three Kings monument: Mengrai consulted King Ramkhamhaeng of Sukhothai and King Ngam Muang of Phayao about the site of his new city.

2. Wat Inthakin: The Temple of the City Navel is on the site of the former Sao Inthakin, Lord Indra's pillar, which guards the city and brings fertility to its soil.

3. King Mengrai's Shrine: This small but ornate shrine was erected here in 1975 because the original shrine was located too far away for people to pay homage to the city's founder.

4. City Pillar: Moved here after the Burmese occupation of Chiang Mai, this teak pillar is underground in a small shrine opened only during the annual City Pillar Ceremony in May.

Scrambled eggs, toast, orange juice, and coffee 120฿. Whole-wheat banana pancake with cappuccino 110฿. Open M-Sa 8am-5pm, Su 8am-2pm. ❸

Taste from Heaven, 237 Tha Pae Rd. (☎053 208 803), 100m past the Tha Pae Gate on the right. The newest vegetarian restaurant in Chiang Mai joins an already crowded field but more than holds its own. In addition to the food and friendly staff, diners here will appreciate the weekly specials, small garden in the back, A/C, and free Wi-Fi. *Mussaman* curry 50฿. Entrees 50฿. Open daily 8:30am-10pm. ❷

Pulcinella da Stefano, 2/1-2 Chang Moi Kao Rd., off Tha Pae Rd. As far as Italian restaurants in Thailand go, this one is very good. The air-conditioned dining room, a welcome respite from the heat, is both elegant and family-friendly. Pizza 120-200฿. Pasta 140-200฿. AmEx/MC/V. Open daily 11:30am-10:30pm. ❸

Mike's (☎084 6086 661), on Chaiyaphum Rd., 300m north of the Tha Pae Gate. This roadside fast-food joint specializes in delicious late-night burgers. If you don't want to sit at the counter, there are benches nearby along the moat. Combo with burger, fries, and drink 110-150฿. Open daily 9am-3am. ❸

EASTERN BANK OF THE PING RIVER

▨ **Tree Shade House** (☎302 899), on Tasatoi Rd. directly across from the fire station. This cheery lunch spot is in a traditional wooden building overhung with plants. A predominantly local crowd comes here for the inexpensive, tasty food. Noodle and rice dishes 30-50฿. Open daily 9am-9pm. ❶

The Riverside, 9-11 Charoen Rat Rd. (☎053 243 239). From Nawarat Bridge, take a left on Charoen Rat Rd.; it's 50m ahead on the left. The intimate, romantic candlelit setting has live music every night starting at 9:30pm. Memorable dinner boat ride down the Ping River. Across the street is a more modern complex, under the same ownership, with a bar and artificial waterfall. Boat leaves nightly at 8pm. 90฿ per person, not including food. Dishes 80-200฿. Open daily 8am-1am. ❸

Love At First Bite, 28 Chiang Mai-Lamphun Rd. Soi 1 (☎053 242 731). This garden cafe specializes in freshly baked cakes and pies (50-70฿ per slice). Limited food menu, primarily quiches and pot pies. On weekends, cheeseburgers are barbecued outside. Open Tu-Su 10:30am-6pm. ❷

WEST OF THE OLD CITY

Thanachart Saichon, 2/1 Mahidol Rd. (☎053 808 642), on a vast covered platform at the southern end of Boonruang Rit Rd., approximately across from Soi

Samlan 6; the English sign advertises "variety buffet." The all-you-can-eat pricing of this typical hot-pot establishment, combined with the wide variety of dishes available, makes it very popular with locals. Price includes individual grills. Adults 130฿, children 65฿. Live music nightly at 7pm. Open daily 5pm–midnight. ❸

Lanna Cafe, 81 Huay Kaew Rd. (☎053 225 862; www.lannacafe.org), before Sirimang-khlachian Rd. Established by a Japanese NGO to export coffee beans grown by hill tribes to Japan. Coffee 30-50฿. Roasted coffee beans 150฿. Sandwiches 45-75฿. Free Wi-Fi. Open daily 8am-5pm. ❷

Khun Mor Thai Style Noodles, 10/1 Nimmanhemin Rd. Soi 17 (☎053 226 378). Well-known among locals, this noodle shop is a budget oasis in the middle of a traffic-ridden expensive neighborhood. Small English menu. Noodle soup 25-40฿. Chicken with cashew nuts 50฿. Open daily 7am-9pm. ❶

👁 SIGHTS

WITHIN THE MOAT (THE OLD CITY)

▧WAT CHEDI LUANG. The gigantic pyramidal remains of **Wat Chedi Luang,** Chiang Mai's largest *chedi,* tower over its neighboring buildings. Built by King Saen Suang Ma in 1401, it once spiraled 86m toward the sky before it was destroyed by an earthquake in 1545. A *naga* staircase adorns the *wihaan,* which houses a standing gold Buddha and 32 Jataka "story panels" depicting scenes from the Buddha's life. You can't climb to the top, unfortunately, but the Buddha is visible from the ground. Legend holds that Wat Chedi Luang was home to the Emerald Buddha during the statue's stay in Chiang Mai. The *wat* also houses the city pillar, marking the center of Chiang Mai. As you walk in the entrance, look for the tables on the right, which host ▧**Monk Chat,** a unique opportunity for tourists to talk to monks about Buddhism, monastic life, and more. *(From Tha Pae Gate, head west on Ratchadamnoen Rd., and turn left onto Phra Pokklao Rd. Wat Chedi Luang is on the right, opposite the Yamaha music store. Monk Chat open M-Sa 9am-6:30pm. Free.)*

WAT PHRA SINGH. This *wat's* chief attraction is the bronze **Phra Singh Buddha** in **Vihara Laai Kam,** behind the main *wihaan* and to the left. Experts aren't sure if this is the genuine Phra Singh Buddha, as there are identical statues in Bangkok and Nakhon Si Thammarat. The image is the focal point of Songkran festivities, when incense is lit and offerings are made to the Phra Singh Buddha, which is cleansed with holy water. To the right of the entrance, on a stuccoed stone pedestal, stands a beautiful red scripture repository. *(On the western side of the old city, at the end of Ratchadamnoen Rd.)*

WAT CHIANG MAN. The oldest *wat* in the city, Chiang Man was built by King Mengrai in 1296. With its low-sloping roofs and intricate facade, the temple is a classic example of northern Thai design. The *wihaan* on the right contains two small Buddha images: **Phra Setangamani (Crystal Buddha),** thought to have come from Lopburi 1800 years ago, and **Phra Sila (Stone Buddha),** imported from India some 2500 years ago. *(At the northern end of Ratchaphakhinai Rd. Open daily 6am-5pm.)*

OUTSIDE THE MOAT

WAT OU SAI KHAM. The main attraction in this 300-year-old *wat* is the **largest jade Buddha in Thailand,** standing 41in. tall and weighing 900kg. Visitors can view jade carvings in progress in the *wat* courtyard. Murals in the *vihara* depict tales from Buddha's former life. *(Chang Moi Kao Rd., immediately before the intersection with Chang Moi Rd. ☎053 234 210; www.jadebuddha.net.)*

WAT JED YOT. King Tilokaraja built this shrine in 1455. In 1477, the Eighth World Buddhist Council met here to revise the Tripitaka scriptures of Theravada Buddhism. The *wat's* seven *chedis* were deserted in the 17th and 18th centuries; their ruins are the main attraction of the temple. The two **Bodhi trees** are said to be descendants of the one Gautama sat under during his enlightenment. *(On the superhighway, 1km from Huay Kaew Rd.)*

WAT U-MONG. Another remnant of King Mengrai's building spree, this peaceful forest temple has serene footpaths that wind through the trees. Sculptures dot the extensive grounds, and the most notable is the emaciated image of **"Our Lord Buddha before realizing that this wasn't the path to enlightenment."** The sculpture is at the back of the confine before the pagoda representing the four noble truths (suffering, cause of suffering, path leading to cessation, cessation) and after the turnoff to the derelict farm. Tunnels leading into the hill at the site of the original *wat* are lined with niches housing Buddha figures. Other points of interest on the grounds are the Herbal Medicine Garden, a handicapped vocational training center, and the *wat's* library (open daily until 4pm). If you plan ahead, you can enjoy an informal discussion with a *dhamma*. *(Off Suthep Rd., on the outskirts of town. Follow Suthep out of town, then turn left on Soi 4. Look for a blue sign with the wat name. It's 2km farther down the road. Discussions held M, W, F 9-11am and Su 3-6pm.)*

WAT SUAN DOK. King Ku Na constructed the "Temple of Flower Gardens" (also known as Wat Buppharam) in 1383. The enormous Chiang Saen-style bronze Buddha inside the *bot* dates from 1504. Inexpensive Buddhist amulets and literature are sold at nearly every *wihaan*. Originally, the grounds served as a pleasure garden for the first kings of Chiang Mai, but they later became a cemetery for their remains. Suan Dok hosts **Monk Chats:** follow the signs to the building in the back. *(On Suthep Rd., after the Hill Tribe Promotion Center. Monk chats M, W, F 5-7pm; most people arrive around 6pm. www.monkchat.net. Meditation retreat Tu-W.)*

CHIANG MAI NATIONAL MUSEUM. Northern Thailand's definitive museum on Lanna history and culture features art and artifacts collected from Northern Thai royalty, commoners, and hill tribes. Chronological dioramas depict the rise and fall of the Lanna Kingdom (Lanna, referring to the region of northern Thailand, literally means "a million rice fields"). At its peak in the 13th and 14th centuries, the kingdom encompassed modern-day northern Thailand, eastern Myanmar, and western Laos. The modern Lanna region is comprised of Phrae, Nan, Phayao, Mae Hong Son, Lamphun, Chiang Rai, and Chiang Mai. *(☎053 221 308. On the superhighway, 500m past Wat Jet Yod on the left side of the road coming from Huay Kaew Rd. Open daily 9am-4pm. 30฿.)*

TRIBAL MUSEUM. These polished exhibits, collected by the Tribal Research Institute, explore the daily life, language derivation, gender roles, and traditional dress of various hill tribes in northern Thailand. The second floor documents the development of the hill tribes, most notably in introducing cash crops, new technology, and education. The nine-sided building—representing the nine hill tribes of Thailand—makes a great stop for those interested in hill tribe culture and history or for those about to go trekking to local villages. *(☎053 210 872. On Chotana Rd., in Ratchamangkhla Park, 4km north of Chang Phuak Gate, the same entrance as the Chiang Mai Shooting Club. Open M-F 9am-4pm. Suggested donation 20฿.)*

CHIANG MAI UNIVERSITY. Though architecturally uninspiring, the university's 725 verdant acres are a bustling center of activity. The library is in the center of the grounds, just south of the central roundabout. Part of the university district, Nimmanhemin Rd., is home to the university's Art Museum, which often hosts major exhibits. Nimmanhemin Rd. and its soi are also filled with

galleries, coffee shops, cafes, restaurants, and bars. *(Museum ☎053 218 280; 239 Nimmanhemin Rd., 3km northwest of the old city, off Huay Kaew Rd.)*

CHIANG MAI ZOO AND ARBORETUM. The Chiang Mai Zoo houses animals from koalas to zebras along a network of poorly organized roads. Unfortunately, it is difficult to choose which animals to visit, since the paths are confusing and exhausting to walk, and the map is less than helpful. The star attraction in the zoo is the Giant Panda exhibit, introduced in late 2003. Next door, the Huay Kaew Arboretum provides a shady respite, or an invigorating workout if you opt to use the fitness track. *(Zoo ☎053 358 166. On Huay Kaew Rd., at the base of Doi Suthep, after Chiang Mai University. Bicycles 1ʙ, motorbikes 10ʙ, cars 50ʙ. Open daily 8am-6pm. Last tickets sold 5pm. 100ʙ, children 50ʙ; additional 100ʙ to see the pandas.)*

CHIANG MAI ARTS AND CULTURE CENTER. Located in the old Provincial Hall, this well-funded museum has 15 rooms of exhibits documenting the history and culture of Chiang Mai and northern Thailand. The museum is geared more towards local youth, but the slick exhibits will be just as interesting to older visitors. *(☎053 217 793. Located just behind the Three Kings Monument on Phra Pokklao Rd. Open Tu-Su 8:30am-5pm. 90ʙ, students 40ʙ.)*

◪ TREKKING

Chiang Mai has over 200 companies itching to fulfill the trekking desires of eager *farang*. The TAT provides a 50-page booklet with all registered offices in Chiang Mai, Lamphun, Mae Hong Son, and Lampang. Three-day, two-night treks (4-person min.) average 1800ʙ per person to the **Maeteang, Phrao, Sameong, Doi Inthanon,** or **Chiang Dao** areas. Extra days can be negotiated. These five are the only legal trekking areas around Chiang Mai, and with 200 companies tromping through, there is no such thing as a non-touristed area. Many agencies guarantee "private areas" to which they have exclusive access, but this does not guarentee complete seclusion. Maeteang, featuring bamboo rafting, attracts the most trekkers.

Some Chiang Mai-based companies also run treks to **Mae Hong Son** and **Pai.** If either of these locales sounds appealing, it's better to hop on a bus and book from there, where a three-day trek will cost 1500-1800ʙ and won't have a 3-4hr. drive on either end. Mae Hong Son and Pai see fewer trekkers because Pai's rivers are too low to raft in the hot season and the rivers around Mae Hong Son become too rough to navigate in the rainy season. Mae Hong Son also neighbors the troubled border with Myanmar.

All guesthouses either run their own treks or have an affiliated partner (usually TAT certified) that they recommend. It's important to understand exactly what their price includes—ask about sleeping bags, backpacks, and food. Treks run by **Libra Guest House** and **Eagle House** (see **Accommodations, p. 272**). **Chiang Mai Green Tour and Trekking,** 31 Chiang Mai-Lamphun Rd. (☎053 247 374), donates a portion of its proceeds to a conservation program and offers nature and bird-watching tours, as well as the more conventional ecotourism variety.

Travelers looking for adventure can go **rock climbing,** regardless of experience. Most trips go to Crazy Horse Buttress. **The Peak Adventure,** 302/4 Chiang Mai-Lamphun Rd. (☎01 716 4032; www.thepeakadventure.com), runs great trips and has a 15m rock climbing wall at the night market near Tha Pae Rd.

Mountain Biking Chiang Mai (☎01 024 7046; www.mountainbikingchiangmai. com) runs mountain biking tours to Doi Suthep and Doi Inthanon National Parks. One-day tours start at 1250ʙ and include equipment and lunch.

◎ SPORTS

Chiang Mai has plenty of opportunities to watch or participate in sports, such as **Muay Thai** (Thai Boxing), **bowling, ice skating, jogging, cycling,** and **tennis.**

As Thailand's national sport, Muay Thai boxing is very important to locals in Chiang Mai. It attracts significant crowds of tourist as well, who come to experience the spectacle. There is a fight almost every night of the week at one of the city's two arenas. The best time and place to go is on Fridays at ⊠**Kawila Boxing Stadium,** 1km to the east of the Ping River. A *tuk-tuk* from Tha Pae Gate is 50в. Tickets are cheapest (350в) if bought in advance at most guesthouses. At the stadium they're 400в, or 600в for ringside seats. A night of fighting typically starts at 9pm and consists of 8-10 individual bouts in varying weight classes. A three-piece band plays music along with the ebb and flow of the action. It's brutal, exciting, and a genuine taste of Thai culture that should not be missed. The other stadium, **Thapae Stadium,** is more touristy but easier to access, 50m south of the Tha Pae Gate on Moon Muang Rd. It is a large covered space lined with bars, and is a different but equally fun experience. Come early for the best seats. For information on learning how to box, see **Beyond Tourism,** p. 76.

There is a **fitness track** at Huay Kaew Arboretum on Huay Kaew Rd. A better **fitness park** is on Nimonaha Min Rd. at the University Arts Museum. The track is set around a concrete moat (330m) with concrete logs and an archaic wooden bench press. (Open daily 5am-8pm.) **Buak Haad Park,** in the southwestern corner of the old city, is a hidden oasis. Cool off in one of the several hotel pools that open for public use for a nominal fee. (Open daily 5am-10pm.)

Golf and **tennis** can be played at the **Chiangmai Gymkhana Club,** in the southeastern corner of town off the Chiang Mai-Lamphun Rd. The club was founded in 1898 by 14 Englishmen who worked in Chiang Mai as traders but whose true passions were racing, polo, and tennis. Today, club membership is 60% Thai. Nine holes on the course cost 300в. Caddies (100в) are compulsory. (☎053 241 035. Office open daily 9am-5pm. Golf club rental 300в, driving range 25в for one bucket of balls.) **The Anantasiri Tennis Courts,** 48/5 Superhighway (☎053 222 210), across from the National Museum, have lighted courts at night.

▦ COURSES AND FORUMS

Chiang Mai offers several popular courses to tourists, specifically Thai cooking, massage, meditation, and language. (See **Beyond Tourism,** p. 76.)

COOKING CLASSES

The most popular cooking courses last from one to five days and include six dishes, a trip to the market, materials, and a recipe book. Many guesthouses have their own courses and will let you store and reheat the remaining food after your course.

The Chiang Mai Thai Cookery School, 47/2 Moon Muang Rd. (☎053 206 388; www. thaicookeryschool.com). Run out of The Wok (p. 275) by Sompon Nabnian, who has hosted cooking programs on Thai television, this school is the most widely known in Chiang Mai. Comprehensive course: 1-day 990в, 2-day 1900в, 3-day 2800в, 4-day 3700в, 5-day 4600в. Office open daily 8:30am-6:30pm.

Chilli Club Cooking Academy, 26 Rathwithi Rd. Soi 2 (☎053 210 620; www.eagle-house.com). Run by the Eagle House (p. 273), this cooking school runs custom courses targeted at all ages and levels of expertise, from children to professional chefs. Reserve a day in advance. 1-day 900в.

Baan Thai Cooking School, 11 Ratchadamnoen Rd. Soi 5 (☎053 357 339; www. baanthaicookery.com). Apart from the standard morning course (900฿), Ban Thai also runs shorter 3hr. evening courses, in which students cook 4 dishes (700฿), and intensive 1-day classes (1200฿).

MASSAGE CLASSES

Massage classes are quite popular. Most also offer foot reflexology. A course cycle usually starts on Monday.

Old Medicine Hospital, 238/8 Wuolai Rd. (☎053 201 663; www.thaimassageschool. ac.th), opposite the Old Chiang Mai Cultural Center, is one of the most respected massage schools in Chiang Mai, and offers massage courses in traditional Thai medicine taught by experts. 10-day certified course 5000฿.

International Training Massage, 17/6-7 Morakot Rd. (☎053 218 632; www.itmthai-massage.com), about 1km northwest of the old city. Introductory 5-day courses proceed sequentially through the fundamentals of Thai massage (3500-4000฿). Students receive a certificate for Thai Massage. Overseen by Thailand's Ministry of Education. Open house and free demonstration F 10am-noon and 1-3pm. Open daily 9am-4pm.

Lanna Thai Massage School, 47 Chang Moi Kao Rd. Soi 3 (☎053 232 547 or 03 869 672), across from the Karinthip Resort. Supervised by the Thai Ministry of Education. 5-day Thai massage course 4500฿. 10-day foot massage reflexology course 3500฿.

MEDITATION COURSES

Most meditation programs last at least 10 days. Some programs, especially those taught by monks, won't require fees and will accept donations instead.

▨ **Meditation Retreat Workshop** (☎5380 8411 ext. 114; www.monkchat.net), at Wat Suan Dok, 1km west of the old city. Run under the auspices of MCU Buddhist University and functioning entirely on donations, this is a rare opportunity to spend 2 days meditating and learning directly from monks. The program begins around lunchtime on Tu and ends on W. The website provides a suggested list of what to bring. Suggested donation around 200-1000฿ per night.

Tai Chi Chuan (☎01 706 7406; www.taichithailand.com). The 10-day Tai Chi and meditation training program comes highly recommended. Classes begin on the 1st and 16th of each month (10,000฿, with accommodation 12,000฿).

Northern Insight Meditation Center (☎053 278 620), at Wat Ram Poeng, near Wat U-Mong. Offers 10-day retreats and 26-day meditation courses. Payment by donation.

LANGUAGE COURSES

A major step toward cultural immersion is taking a language course like the ones offered at the AUA or Payap University.

Payap University (☎053 241 255; http://ic.payap.ac.th), offers 60hr. practical language courses for all levels, as well as rigorous semester-long courses. 7000฿ fee, includes use of language lab.

Chiang Mai Thai Language Center, 131 Ratchadamnoen Rd. (☎053 277 810; www. chiangmai-adventure-tour.com). Run by Petchara, a former English instructor for Peace Corps Volunteers. The center runs 18-day courses (3000฿) and can arrange homestays with Thai families for its students.

CULTURAL FORUMS

Insights into Buddhism are available through informal discussions about the Buddhist faith held in the Chinese Pavilion at **Wat U-Mong** (Su 3pm), and Monk

Chat at **Wat Suan Dok** and **Wat Chedi Luang** (p. 277). The **Northern Thai Discussion Group** is a forum in English on cultural aspects of Asia and meets (usually the 2nd Tu of each month, 7:30pm) at the **Alliance Française,** 138 Charoen Phrathet Rd. (☎053 275 277). See *Chiang Mai Newsletter* for upcoming speakers.

☐ SHOPPING

Avid shoppers and casual browsers alike will find plenty to enjoy in Chiang Mai. Many will have heard of the famed **Night Bazaar** on Chang Klan Rd., which showcases a variety of antiques, silver jewelry, hill-tribe embroidery, Thai textiles, pottery, designer clothing knock-offs, and pirated DVDs. Haggle down the inflated tourist prices, which can be twice the fee you finally settle on. The Night Bazaar is one of Chiang Mai's top tourist destinations: most nights, the crowds stretch shoulder to shoulder for several blocks. It is an impressive sight even if you don't intend to buy anything.

More unique souvenirs can be purchased at the **Saturday night market** (open nightly 6-11pm) south of the old city on Wualai Rd., where local merchants sell their products alongside more tourist-geared merchandise. The market is especially famous for its silver products. The **Sunday night market** (open 6-11pm), near Tha Pae Gate, is a similar affair, but on a bigger scale. Ratchadamnoen Rd. and its crossroads are closed to traffic and both locals and *farang* flood the streets. *Wat* courtyards along Ratchadamnoen Rd. are turned into food courts, featuring everything from papaya salad to *roti* to doughnuts. Both markets have lower prices than the night market, but bargaining is less effective.

Warorot Market is a multi-story expanse containing dried foods, spices, produce, textiles, clothing, and cosmetics. The higher in the complex you go, the lower the prices. At **Lanyai Market,** across the street on the river side, ubiquitous flower stalls spill out onto the road. A popular keepsake is the *poung ma lai* (festive flower necklace, 5฿). At night, Lanyai is full of food stalls.

The Hill Tribe Handicraft Project, 1 Moon Muang Rd., in a brick building at the southeastern corner of the old city, sells Karen, Lisu, Akha, Lahu, Yao, and Hmong village quilts, bags, pullovers, and sculptures. (☎053 274 877. Open M-F 9am-4:30pm.) The better-known **Hill Tribe Promotion Center,** 21/17 Suthep Rd., next to Wat Suan Dok, has a greater selection of traditional and innovative crafts. (☎053 277 743. Embroidered bag 200฿ and up. Karen dress 1100฿. Open daily 9am-5pm. MC/V.) Both government-run stores seek to shift tribal economies away from opium cultivation by providing alternative means of income. The **Export Promotion Center,** 29/19 Singharat Rd., opposite Cathay Pacific Airways, showcases high-quality Thai products for export. The manufacturer's business card is included with each display, so if you like what you see, it's possible to track each product down. (☎053 216 350. Office open M-F 8:30am-4:30pm. Shop open M-F 8:30am-5:30pm, Sa 9am-6pm.)

If you're interested in high-end antiques, grab a copy of *Art & Culture Lanna*, available in guesthouses, at the TAT, and online at www.artandcultureasia.com. The brochure lists many of the studios and galleries in Chiang Mai.

♫ ENTERTAINMENT

There are three big festivals in Chiang Mai. The **Flower Festival** is held during the first weekend in February, when flower-covered boats float down the Ping River. The weekend features flower exhibitions and a beauty contest. The **Songkran Festival** (New Year) is celebrated April 12th-15th and involves the pouring of sacred water over Buddha images. The full moon in September marks the **Loi**

Kra Thong Festival, when thousands of candles are set cruising down the river on handmade rafts. Check www.chiangmainews.com or the bi-weekly *City Now* brochure for upcoming events in town.

Major Cineplex, 2 Mahidon Rd., in the Central Airport Plaza, is the largest and newest cinema in Chiang Mai. (☎053 283 989; show listings at www.movieseer. com. M-Th 80-100฿, F-Su 100-120฿.) The **Central Department Store** has a **Vista Movie Theater** on the fourth floor that shows newly-released movies. (☎053 894 415. M-Th 70฿, F-Su 90฿.) For live music outside of the bar scene, the **Kalare Food Center,** 89/2 Chang Klan Rd. (☎053 272 067), in the night bazaar, features various acts on a rotating schedule between two stages.

☒ NIGHTLIFE

Chiang Mai's nightlife scene is constantly changing. Nimmanhemin Rd., near Chiang Mai University, is home to the classiest, newest bars and discos. Several popular bars lie on the Ping's east bank, just north of Nawarat Bridge. The 60฿ *tuk-tuk* from Tha Pae Gate is well worth it. Farang pubs with cheap beer line the old-city streets near Tha Pae Gate, and extend north and south on both sides of the moat. Those immediately at Tha Pae Gate attract backpackers, while those to the south on Loi Kro Rd. are sketchier. There are very few outright go-go bars in Chiang Mai. In their place, not-so-thinly disguised "karaoke" bars fill the void. The night bazaar hosts some relaxed gay bars. Updates on gay nightlife in Chiang Mai can be found at www.utopia-asia.com/ thaicm.htm. There isn't much nightlife in the center of the old city. Instead, most of it is near the eastern edge, along Moon Muang Rd.

THE OLD CITY

■ **North Gate Jazz Co-op** (☎085 5992 861), just east of the Chang Phuak Gate, is another place to hear live music. Some patrons watch from atop the city wall across the street. Music nightly at 9:30pm, with a jam session Tu. No cover. Open nightly 6pm-midnight.

The Garden (☎084 8098 768), on Ratchadamnoen Rd., one of the few nightlife destinations in the center of the old city. Live bands take the stage every Su 8pm, and open jam sessions Tu at the same time. Mixed drinks 110-150฿. Open daily 7am-10pm, and until midnight Tu and Su.

Tapas Bar (☎053 419 011), just south of the Kafe, is one of the most romantic nightspots in the old city, with a cushioned area lit by flickering candlelight. Mixed drinks 160-250฿. Tapas 60-90฿. Open daily 9am-midnight.

The Zest (☎053 904 364), a 5min. walk south of the Tha Pae Gate. Has an outdoor patio and, inside, a nightclub upstairs. Large Singha 100฿. Bar open 7am-1am. Club open 11am-late.

Mandalay Bar (☎053 208 395), near the southern end of Moon Muang Rd., long past the point where bars have become karaoke establishments. A 2-club complex that attracts a mixed gay and straight crowd and charges a steep 300฿ cover for foreigners. Cover includes 1 drink. Open nightly 10pm-late.

EAST OF THE OLD CITY

BETWEEN THE MOAT AND THE RIVER

This is where to go for the most easily accessible and exciting nightlife in Chiang Mai. Bars cluster around the Tha Pae Gate, the Night Bazaar, and everywhere in between.

■ **Rooftop Bar** (☎086 7293 583), a Chiang Mai institution that shows up again and again in backpackers' stories. Replete with a bamboo floor, a friendly atmosphere, and low tables that overlook the city, it deserves its good reputation. Expect it to be crowded late.Large beer 100฿. Open nightly 5pm-2am.

Inter (☎053 276 653) on Tha Pae Rd., has 3 live bands nightly from 7:30pm-1:30am. Large beer 140฿. Open daily 1pm-2am.

Pornping Palace Hotel, 46-48 Charoen Prathet Rd., near the Night Bazaar. Houses 2 popular, mixed gay and straight discos. Both are quiet during the week, but crowds arrive F-Sa around midnight. One of them, futuristic **Space Bubble,** has a real dance floor—a rarity in Thailand. Drinks 100฿. Cover 100฿, includes 1 free drink. Open daily 9pm-2am. The other, more traditional **Hot Shot,** has colorful disco lights. No cover. Large beer 120฿. Mixed drinks 120฿.

EAST OF THE PING RIVER

The Ping's riverside bars, mostly located on Charoen Rat Rd. between the two bridges, cultivate a romantic atmosphere.

The Gallery (☎053 248 601), on Charoen Rat Rd., has a rustic theme, with seating in a classy riverside patio and garden. Mixed drinks 120฿. Entrees 90-200฿. Open daily 1pm-midnight. AmEx/MC/V.

The Good View (☎053 241 866), welcomes a more lively crowd to its gargantuan covered patio and multiple bars. Live music nightly 6:45pm-1am. Large beer 120฿. Mixed drinks 170฿. Open daily 10am-1am.

WEST OF THE OLD CITY

Another popular nightlife area in Chiang Mai is the university-oriented Nimmanhemin Rd. It's a hefty 3km walk from the old city, so it might be easiest to get there in a *tuk-tuk.*

WarmUp Cafe, 40 Nimmanhemin Rd. (☎053 400 677; www.warmupcafe1999.com). Guests can start with dinner in the courtyard restaurant before moving to the lounge, the dance floor, or one of the covered bars.

DAYTRIPS FROM CHIANG MAI

DOI INTHANON NATIONAL PARK

To get from Chiang Mai to the summit of Doi Inthanon using public transportation, 1st go to Chom Thong, then to Mae Klang Waterfall, and then to the summit. Chom Thong is 58km from Chiang Mai and the summit is another 48km from Chom Thong. To get to Chom Thong, take either a bus from Chang Phuak Bus Station (1hr. every 20min. 6:30am-4pm, 50฿), or a yellow songthaew from Chiang Mai Gate (30฿, leaves when full). If you're driving, the turnoff to Hwy. 1009 and Doi Inthanon National Park lies before Chom Thong off Hwy. 108. Take either Triparet Rd. or Wualai Rd. out of Chiang Mai to get on Hwy 108. Using private transportation to get to the summit is strongly advised, as it is much quicker, although the roads are steep and curvy. Even if you're using private transportation, you should leave early in the morning in order to return to Chiang Mai before dark. Relying on public transportation will probably result in an overnight stay in the park. Park office ☎053 268 550. Office open M-F 8:30am-4:30pm. Park and facilities open daily 6am-6pm. Park admission 400฿. Motorbikes 20฿, cars 50฿.

Doi Inthanon National Park is located about 60km southwest of Chiang Mai. One of Thailand's best national parks, Doi Inthanon is 482 sq. km, and boasts the country's **highest peak** (2585m), the **most bird species of any site in the country** (400), several beautiful **waterfalls, scenic vistas,** and **well-paved roads** to the summit. Pick up a **map** from the **vehicle checkpoint** (500m after the turnoff to Mae Klang Waterfall), the **visitors center** (1km from the vehicle entrance on Hwy. 1009), or **park headquarters** (at Km 31 of Hwy. 1009). The visitors center has exhibits on local animal life, notably the nocturnal pangolin, a creature similar to the armadillo. It can also arrange guided tours to **Borichinda Cave,** accessible by a 1km path just before the visitors center.

Mae Klang Waterfall, near the park entrance, is the first stop for most visitors. The 1km path above the falls leads to the visitors center. The powerful **Wachiratan Waterfall** is the next stop, 20.8km in. After the initial 40m cascades are a few pools suitable for swimming. The elegant **Siriphum Waterfall** can be found 31km in. The lane leading to it winds through the park's Royal Project, where hill tribes are encouraged to supplant opium production with coffee, strawberry, and flower cultivation. At 41km in, take a left to reach the **Royal Family's twin chedis..** The King's *chedi* is higher, though the Queen's is more ornate and made of purple stone, her favorite color. In clear weather, the view from the terrace of the *chedis* is stunning. (20฿.)

The road ends at Doi Inthanon's summit (usually obscured by mist), 48km from Chom Thong, where a *stupa* holds the ashes of King Inthanon. Nearby, a large sign proclaims the "Highest Point in Thailand." At the summit, there is a visitors center with information about the wildlife in the park. There are also two worthwhile trails, the brief **Aangka Nature Trail** and the 4km **Ki Mae Pan Nature Trail.** Mae Pan is closed during parts of the rainy season and you must get clearance at park headquarters (☎053 268 550) 31km in.

The cool season (Oct.-Feb.), when the temperature in the park averages 12°C (50°F), is the best time to visit. Bring raingear and warm clothing, especially if you intend to hike. The clearest weather is in January. The park has **camping** (30฿), tents (275-300฿), **guesthouses** (from 1000฿ for 3 people), and a **restaurant** at park headquarters, just past Siriphum Falls.

WAT DOI SUTHEP AND DOI SUTHEP NATIONAL PARK

The national park is 16km northwest of Chiang Mai. Songthaew leave when full from Chang Phuak Gate (6am-5pm, 50฿) and the Chiang Mai Zoo (6am-5pm, 30฿), located on Huay Kaew Rd. at the base of the mountain. After Wat Suthep, the songthaew continue to Bhubing Palace (additional 50฿) and Doi Pui, a Hmong village (80฿). Motorbikes make a death defying 30min. trip up the mountain to see the wat. While the road is well-paved, it has sharp turns and it gets crowded during the day. Past the Bhubing Palace, the last 4.5km of the road to the Hmong village is unpaved. The park headquarters (☎053 295 117), 1km past Wat Phra That Doi Suthep, provides trail maps and accommodations. Camping 10฿ per night. Rent 2-person (200฿) or 5-person tents (500฿), or cabins (2-person 200฿, 10-person 2000฿). Reserve at least 1 week in advance. National park admission 200฿.

If you only have time to visit one of Chiang Mai's 300 *wats*, Wat Phra That Doi Suthep, built in 1383, one of Thailand's most sacred pilgrimage sights, should be it. According to legend, King Kuena of Chiang Mai placed Buddha's relics on the back of a white elephant, which then walked without stopping until it reached Doi Suthep and died of exhaustion. The glint of the 20m high golden *chedi* is visible from the city's limits, and the sweeping view of the city from the temple's observation deck, 1676m high, is sublime. Upon reaching the *wat*, visitors have the option of ascending via cable-car (20฿) or by conquering the 306 steps. (Does not require national park admission. *Wat* admission for foreigners 30฿.) An extensive **market** on the way up to the temple sells food and handicrafts. The **International Buddhist Center** at the *wat* offers information (open daily 9-11am and 1-5pm), holds **monk chats** (daily 1-3pm), and allows visitors to participate in chanting (5:30am and 6pm).

Encompassing a 261 sq. km area surrounding Wat Suthep, **Doi Suthep National Park** contains an amazing range of natural life. A project started in 1987 by a Chiang Mai University professor has thus far collected over 2000 species of plants in the park—more than in all of the UK. While the wildlife is being

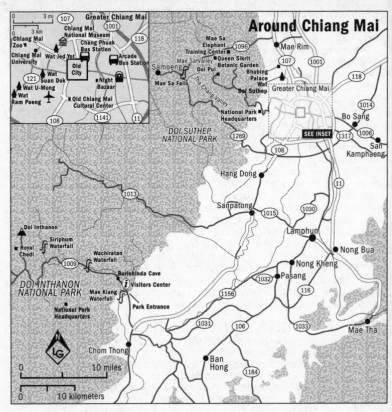

forced up the mountain as Chiang Mai expands, the park still has much to offer. **Waterfalls** line Huay Kaew Rd. (Hwy. 1004), which leads up the mountain; keep an eye out for their well-marked turnoffs. A nature trail leads from the accommodations office and passes **Sai Yok Waterfall** (2km) and **Monthatarn Waterfall** (3km). The standard national park fee applies even if you intend only to see one waterfall. After you reach Monthatarn Waterfall, follow the 2km access road to Huay Kaew Rd., where *songthaew* will shuttle you to Chiang Mai.

Bhubing Palace, 4km up the mountain from the *wat*, is the Royal Family's residence from January to March. For the remainder of the year, the palace and its sprawling rose gardens are open to the public. (☎053 223 065; www.bhubingpalace.org. Open daily 8:30am-4:30pm. Tickets sold 8:30-11:30am and 1-3:30pm. Trolley cart rental with driver 300฿ for 50min., 3-person max. Admission 50฿. Modest dress required; appropriate garments can be rented on-site.)

LAMPHUN

The most convenient way to get to Lamphun from Chiang Mai is to take the blue songthaew that leaves from Chiang Mai-Lamphun Rd., south of the TAT (1hr., every 20min. 5am-6pm, 30฿). Songthaew back to Chiang Mai depart from just south of the museum on Inthayongyot Rd., 30฿. Regular buses to Lamphun leave from the Chang Phuak station in Chiang Mai and from just south of the footbridge near Warorot Market (1hr., every 10min. 6:20am-6pm, 20฿). Get off as the bus passes through the walled city; the Lamphun bus station, where buses arrive and depart for Chiang Mai (every 30min. 6am-6pm), is 2km south of town.

Charming Lamphun, 26km southeast of Chiang Mai, is a small town with a long history. The 12th-century **Wat Phra That Hariphunchai** is considered to have one of the seven most sacred *stupas* in Thailand. The *wat*, Lamphun's chief landmark, sits on Inthayongyot Rd. in the town center; it is the first temple on the left after you enter the city from Chiang Mai. Grassy grounds and a *wihaan* surround the main *stupa*, which is crowned with a nine-tiered golden umbrella reaching 46m into the air. (Open daily, roughly dawn-dusk. 20฿.) A block away is the **Hariphunchai National Museum,** exhibiting a small collection of Buddhas, historical artifacts, and local treasures. With your back to the *wat* on Inthayongyot Rd., it's to the left. (☎053 511 186. Open W-Su 9am-4pm. 30฿.) With your back to Chiang Mai, take a right after the museum onto Mukda Rd.; when the road becomes Chamma Davi Rd., continue 2km to reach **Wat Chamma Davi.** This step-pyramid *chedi* once had a gold coating, but thieves stripped it off, giving the temple its other name, Wat Ku Kat ("pagoda without top").

Lamphun hosts a number of festivals every year. The most exciting is the **Lum-Yai Festival** in August, which celebrates the ripening of the *longan* (a fruit similar to the *lychee*) with theatrical performances, floating carved fruit, and a beauty contest. The **Wine and Sausage Tasting Festival** continues in a similar vein, celebrating the sweet wine made from the *longan*. This mid-January celebration features local performances, games, sampling booths, and live music.

Wat Phra Phut Ta Bat Tak Pah, 21km south of Lamphun, is a scenic hillside shrine dedicated to the renowned monk Luang Pu Phromma, who is commemorated with a lifelike wax statue sitting in meditation posture. The *wat* is a busy place, home to a large community of monks who study Luang Pu Phromma's teachings. The *wat*'s two major points of attraction—a Buddha footprint near the stairway up the hill and an imprint of the Buddha's robe—aren't particularly impressive, but are well-known in the region. To get to the *wat*, take a light blue *songthaew* to Pasang (30min., 15฿) from the south side of the Hariphunchai National Museum (see above), just off Inthayongyot Rd., and ask the driver to take you the additional 9km past Pasang to the *wat* (15-20฿ surcharge).

BO SANG

Located 9km east of Chiang Mai on Hwy. 1006, Bo Sang is easy to reach. White songthaew at the flower market on the west bank of the Ping River make the 15-20min. trip regularly during the day (20฿), as do those at the Chuang Phuak bus station (20฿). ☎053 338 324. Factory and shop open daily 8:30am-5pm.

According to local legend, a Buddhist monk once went on a pilgrimage to the Burmese border and spent time in a village that specialized in umbrella-making. Having studied the villagers' techniques, he returned and shared what he had learned with the residents of Bo Sang. They began to make umbrellas, which soon became so popular, they became the town's main source of income.

Today, this is still the case, even though the nuts and bolts of umbrella construction are now surrounded by some gaudy commercialism. A common first stop is the **Umbrella Making Centre,** on the right directly after the large red town gate. Visitors can observe firsthand the labor-intensive techniques involved in umbrella construction, after which they can buy their own umbrella in a gift shop (50฿ and up). Beware: prices in Bo Sang are generally higher than they are at Chiang Mai's Night Bazaar. Near the gift shop is an area where artists offer to paint designs on whatever object you present to them for 50฿.

Although tourism pervades Bo Sang, there is a town beneath the price tags. The best way to find it is to walk away from the main tourist area, which is concentrated around the Umbrella Making Centre. Try exploring the soi on either side of the main street, where you'll find craftsmen at work, out of range of the tour groups. Most won't mind if you observe and will be happy to answer your questions. To reach the **Saa Paper Factory,** which does have a formal gift shop but is far less touristed than the stores along the main street, take a left on Soi 5. If you keep walking on the main street past Soi 5, you'll find an **instrument maker's shop** on the right, between Sois 14 and 16. The elderly owner will gladly demonstrate a few songs for you.

The best time to visit Bo Sang is during the 3rd week of January, when it hosts the **Umbrella Festival,** which includes a parade and a beauty pageant.

PAI ☎053

Tiny Pai may be one of the few places in Thailand where pedestrians outnumber cars. This bohemian town has attracted a diverse range of artists and musicians, who draw inspiration from the astoundingly picturesque surroundings. The locals, a harmonious melange of cultures and ethnicities, are particularly friendly. Some tourists grow to love Pai so much that they don't leave for weeks. Behind the scenes, however, a clandestine heroin and opium culture has come to the attention of local authorities, who are starting to crack down on nefarious activities in the area.

▐ TRANSPORTATION

Buses: The **station** on Chaisongkhram Rd. has buses to **Chiang Mai** (3-4hr.; 7, 8:30, 10:30am, noon, 2, 4pm; 72-150฿) and **Mae Hong Son** (3-4hr.; 7, 8:30, 11am, 1, 4pm; 72-150฿) via **Soppong** (1-2hr., 50฿). **Aya Service** (below) runs **minibuses** to **Chiang Mai** (3hr., every hr. 8:30am-4:30pm, 150฿).

Motorcycle Taxis: At the corner of Chaisongkhram and Rungsiyanon Rd. They travel to the hot springs (90฿) and waterfall (100฿).

Rentals: Many shops along Chaisongkhram Rd. rent **motorbikes** for 100-150฿ per day. **Aya Service,** 21 Chaisongkhram Rd. (☎053 699 940). Turn left out of the bus station—it's 50m down on the left. Rents motorbikes (115cc automatic 100฿) and **bikes** (30-40฿). It's possible to return motorbikes at Aya Service's **Chiang Mai office,** 10/4 Rot Fai Rd. (☎09 556 6700), near the train station. Open daily 7am-11pm.

✦? ORIENTATION AND PRACTICAL INFORMATION

Pai is 136km northwest of Chiang Mai and 111km northeast of Mae Hong Son. **Highway 1095** cuts through town, turns into **Ketkelang Road,** and forms the town's western border. Parallel to and one block east of Ketkelang Rd. is **Rungsiyanon Road,** where the night market, police station, and numerous restaurants are located. The two roads merge at the southern end of town. The two main east-west roads are **Chaisongkhram Road,** home of the bus station and trekking shops, and **Ratchadamrong Road,** two blocks to the south, which crosses **Pai River** to the town's east side and is a popular guesthouse area.

Currency Exchange: Krung Thai Bank, 90 Rungsiyanon Rd. (☎053 699 028). Cirrus/ MC/Plus/V **24hr. ATM.** Open M-F 8:30am-4:30pm.

Police: 72 Rungsiyanon Rd. (☎053 699 217), 500m south of the bus station. **Tourist Police,** toward Chiang Mai, after Ketkelang and Rungsiyanon Rd. merge.

Medical Services: Pai Hospital (☎053 699 031), on Chaisongkhram Rd., 500m west of the bus station. English spoken. Open 24hr.

Pharmacy: On Rungsiyanon Rd., near Chez Swan. Open daily 6am-9pm.

Internet Access: Most locations on Chaisongkhram and Ratchadamrong Rd. are 1฿ per min. and have computers with headsets and Skype. Open until 11pm. The best prices you'll find in town are about 30฿ per hr. **Ideas Net** (☎053 699 829) is 20m east of Aya Service along Chaisongkhram Rd. Internet 30฿ per hr. Skype available. Open daily 9am-midnight.

Post Office: 76 Ketkelang Rd. (☎053 699 208), south of the day market. Poste Restante. Open M-F 8:30am-4:30pm, Sa 9am-noon. **Postal Code:** 58130.

ACCOMMODATIONS

The immense popularity of the town has increased the number of guesthouses in Pai exponentially in recent years, though prices have stayed surprisingly low. Some of the best deals can be found along the smaller lanes within the area bordered by Chaisongkhram Rd. and Ratchadamrong Rd.

Baan Pai Village, 88 Taseban 1 Rd. (☎053 698 152; www.baanpaivillage.com), 20m from the intersection with Chaisongkhram Rd. The pebbled paths and bamboo bungalows make Baan Pai Village one of the most gorgeous places to stay in town. Even better, each bungalow comes with a fan, floor cushions, mosquito net, drinking water, and a private bath with hot shower and Western toilet. Internet 30฿ per hr. Laundry 25฿ per kg. Low-season smaller bungalows 200฿, high-season 500฿; low-season larger wooden bungalows 250-350/650-850฿; large bungalows with river view 400/1300฿. ❷

Tayai's Guest House (☎053 699 579). Look for the sign on Ratchadamrong Rd.; it's 200m down a soi across from the school. New tiled rooms with private hot shower, TV, and balcony won't come any cheaper in Pai. The quiet garden setting adds to the already terrific value. Singles and doubles 200฿. ❷

Pai Treehouse Resort (☎081 911 3640), 5km from Pai along the road to the hot springs. Every child's dream hotel. The 3 rooms perched perilously in a tree—along with a shared bath and sink—are impressive enough that they're worth a look even if you have no intention of staying here. Also on the grounds, the luxurious (albeit earthbound) riverside bungalows have jacuzzi and flat-screen TV. Low-season Treehouse rooms 600฿, high-season 1000฿; low-season riverside bungalows 800-1000/4000฿. ❹

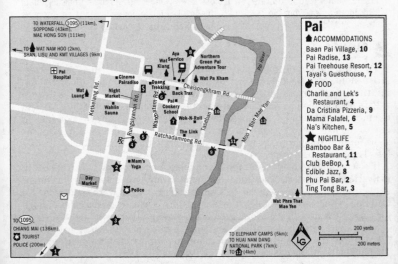

Pai

▲ ACCOMMODATIONS
Baan Pai Village, **10**
Pai Radise, **13**
Pai Treehouse Resort, **12**
Tayai's Guesthouse, **7**

🍴 FOOD
Charlie and Lek's Restaurant, **4**
Da Cristina Pizzeria, **9**
Mama Falafel, **6**
Na's Kitchen, **5**

★ NIGHTLIFE
Bamboo Bar & Restaurant, **11**
Club BeBop, **1**
Edible Jazz, **8**
Phu Pai Bar, **2**
Ting Tong Bar, **3**

PaiRadise, 98 Moo 1 Ban Mae Yen (☎053 698 065; www.pairadise.com). Turn left after the bridge; it's 200m farther on the right. Thoughtfully decorated bungalows with pristine bathrooms surround a swimmable pond lined with palm trees. Owners Kathrin and Pin bake fresh bread daily. The larger bungalows have sitting rooms and are especially suitable for families. Low-season 2-person bungalows with hot water and Western toilet 400-700฿, high-season 800-1500฿. ❸

🍴 FOOD

Pai's culinary scene is exceptional in both its variety and in its quality. Organic, Italian, Indian, and Middle Eastern restaurants can all be found near the center of town. Unlike most other places in Thailand, the market scene here is not especially busy. In the evenings, there is a small **night market** between Chaisongkhram and Ratchadamrong Rd. The more popular **day market** is on Ketkelang Rd., south of Ratchadamrong Rd.

▨ **Charlie and Lek's Restaurant** (☎081 951 3422), on Rungsiyanon Rd., 50m south of the intersection with Ratchadamrong Rd. The owners serve a delicious menu of healthy food, much of it grown at their own local organic farm. Eat outside in their quiet garden patio. The freshness of the ingredients, along with the delicious brown rice, breathes new life into well-trodden standards like sweet and sour chicken (60฿). Vegetarian specials 25฿. Entrees 50-80฿. Open daily 11am-2pm and 6-10pm. ❶

▨ **Na's Kitchen** (☎01 387 0234), on Ratchadamrong Rd., 50m east of the intersection with Rungsiyanon Rd. When simple meals are this good and this inexpensive, people take notice. Na's Kitchen is a local Pai favorite that consistently lives up to its strong reputation. Stir-fried bean sprouts with chicken 40฿. Entrees 30-60฿. Shakes 20-25฿. Open daily 2-11pm. ❶

Da Cristina Pizzeria (☎086 948 5676), on the right just before the bridge. The sign proudly proclaims that this restaurant is "owned and managed by Italians" and it tastes like it. The pizza margherita (110฿) is the most delicious in town, and among the cheapest. The pasta (95-250฿), though relatively expensive by Thai standards, is similarly authentic. Open daily noon-4pm and 5-11pm. ❸

Mama Falafel (☎089 632 6915), 1 block down Wanchatern Rd. from Chaisongkhram Rd. Tucked away from the main road, this low-key falafel restaurant has an extensive menu of Middle Eastern fare. Falafel (pita or plate) 70฿. Open daily 10am-10pm. ❷

👁 SIGHTS

Pai's beautiful countryside is home to waterfalls, hot springs, and caves. Most sights are best accessed by motorbike, as is made clear by the multitudes of *farang* jetting around town.

Pai's notable temple, **Wat Phra That Mae Yen,** has sublime views of the town and the mountains behind it. A Sunset here on a clear day is quite memorable. To get to the *wat*, head east on Ratchadamrong Rd., and cross Pai River; follow signs for the "Temple on the hill." The 360 steps to the *wat* are 1km up on your left. There is also an easier paved route.

If you continue past the Mae Yen River, there are **hot springs,** 7km from town, in **Huai Nam Dang National Park.** Relaxing in the springs is tougher than you might expect, since the water reaches 60°C at the source. Signs warn visitors to "No Boil Egg." Downstream, though, the temperature is usually manageable enough for a soak. (☎053 248 491. Admission 200฿, students 100฿.)

For a more affordable but less authentic experience, try the local resorts (2km before the hot springs), which pump the spring water to their grounds. Thapai Spa Camping has large pools. (☎053 693 267. 50฿).

About 2km before the hot springs (5km from town), numerous **elephant camps** offer rides. The biggest one is **Thom's Pai Elephant Camp,** 200m towards the hot springs from Thapai Spa Camping, which also runs 1- and 2-day elephant treks. (Pai office 5/3 Rungsiyanon Rd., across from Bangkok Bank. ☎09 851 9066; www.yellowpai.com. Treks around 1000฿ per day.)

TREKKING AND RAFTING

Trekking outfitters in Pai offer everything from hiking and rafting to elephant rides (400฿ per hr.). **Back Trax,** 27 Chaisongkhram Rd., one of the town's original trekking outfits, leads groups around the Pai and Soppong areas and donates 15-20% of its proceeds to the villages. Owner Chao, a member of the Lahu tribe, speaks excellent English. (☎053 699 739 or 01 035 2235. Treks 750฿ per day. Open daily 8am-10pm.)

Bamboo rafting is possible from November to May; Pai's rivers become too rough in the rainy season. Whitewater rafting in rubber boats fills the void in the wet season, although by February the water level drops too low for whitewater rafting. **Thai Adventure Rafting** (☎053 699 111) leads adventures down the Khong and Pai rivers. By the time you've finished paddling, you're in Mae Hong Son. (2-day trips including 1 night in a campsite 2000-2200฿; 2 person min.)

ENTERTAINMENT

There are two main cooking schools in Pai. **Wok-N-Roll,** on a soi off Tesaban 1 Rd., has character and a relaxed atmosphere. Its one-day course teaches three dishes plus the basics of cooking many others, and includes a trip to the market, breakfast, a cookbook, and your tasty creations. Added perks include a free dinner invitation for your friends and free use of the kitchen to practice the next day. (☎06 114 9921; www.imerworld.de/bebe. 1-day course 750฿.) A more traditional cooking course is offered by **Pai Cookery School.** Walking from the bus station, turn right on Wanchaterm Rd., and take the first left. (☎01 706 3799. 3 rotating courses; 5 dishes 750฿.) Across the road, "Mam" teaches yoga to those with or without experience. (☎09 954 4981. 4hr., 500฿.)

NIGHTLIFE

Pai's nightlife is vibrant and revolves around live music, which you'll find almost everywhere. In short, it's one of the best scenes in northern Thailand.

Edible Jazz, down the road next to Wat Pa Kham. Many people start their nights here with an early acoustic set. Low tables with floor cushions under a thatched canopy. Live jazz starts at 9pm. Open daily 2pm-1am.

Phu Pai, on Rungsiyanon Rd. Listen to some local jazz at tables outside on a covered patio. Large beer 100฿. World music and jazz bands play nightly, starting at 9:30pm. Open daily 6pm-midnight.

Club Bebop, past the southern end of town on Ketkelang Rd., is regionally renowned as a live music venue, and has a killer house blues band. First band at 9pm, house band at 10pm. Open nightly 8pm-1am.

Bamboo Bar and Restaurant (☎089 554 6404), on the left just after the bridge. The place to go after all of Pai's other bars have closed, this bar is built on a bamboo platform overlooking the river. Serves food all night long. Entrees 40-70฿. Large beer 90฿. Open daily 6pm-5am.

Cinema Pairadiso, 99/1 Chaisongkhram Rd., across from All About Coffee. Come here for a quieter night and enjoy the 3 rooms with DVD players. Also has a large selection of

DVDs. 1-person room 150฿, 2-person 200฿, 4-person 250฿. Last showing 10pm. Best to reserve room several hours in advance.

▓ DAYTRIP FROM PAI

▓THAM LOD (LOD CAVE) IN SOPPONG

Soppong is 43km from Pai and 66km from Mae Hong Son. Ideally, rent a motorbike in Pai and drive to the cave and back along the scenic Hwy. 1095. Public transportation is possible, but unpredictable and expensive. Buses stop in Soppong at a parking lot halfway between Little Eden and Jungle Guesthouse on their way to and from Mae Hong Son (2hr., 5 per day 8:30am-5:30pm, 60฿) and Pai (1½hr., 6 per day 9am-6pm, 45฿). To get to the cave from the Soppong bus stop without private transportation, you'll have to hire a motorcycle taxi to take you both ways (150฿).

Soppong stretches over 4km of Hwy. 1095, and the turnoff to Tham Lod (Lod Cave) is at the end closest to Pai. Follow the 9km road to its end to reach the entrance of the cave, where you must hire a guide to take you through the three gigantic underground caverns. (1-4 people 150฿.) You'll need to charter a raft, too, at the same gazebo where you charter the guide. (Raft for 1-3 people round trip 400฿.) It's possible to navigate the first stretch of the cave by foot, but to see the best parts you'll need a raft. The full tour begins with a ride on the river into the gigantic mouth of the cavern. The interior formations are stunning. In the final chamber, there are prehistoric coffins, small chunks of fossilized food, and faded ancient paintings on a section of the cave wall.

The best time to visit the cave is about 1hr. before closing, so that your tour can conclude with the aerial display put on by 300,000 swifts as they return to the cave. Alternatively, sunrise provides a clearer view of the vortex that forms in the cave before the birds' exit. At some points in the rainy season, the cave is impassable, but bamboo rafts (20฿) will take you into the first chamber. Bring a group to reduce costs. (Park office ☎053 617 218. Cave open daily 8am-5pm.)

From the bus stop in Soppong, renting your own transportation can be difficult, though Little Eden (below) can sometimes arrange motorbike rental (200฿). The most probable option is to catch a **motorbike taxi** (70฿) and arrange a return trip. Other services in Soppong include: a **police box** near the bus stop; the **police station** (☎053 617 173) about 2km from the bus station, in the direction of Mae Hong Son; **Pangmapha Hospital,** directly after the police station (☎053 617 154, limited English spoken); an **international phone** by the bus stop; **Tribal Cafe and Connection,** across the street from Little Eden, with **Internet access** (1฿ per min., 50฿ per hr.); and **the post office,** between the bus station and Jungle Guest House. (☎053 617 165. Open M-F 8:30am-4:30pm.)

Although Soppong's proximity to Pai makes it unnecessary stay overnight, some visitors to the cave prefer to stay the night to remain closeby. The popular ▓**Cave Lodge ❶,** 500m before Tham Lod, has small bungalows scattered down a hillside overlooking a river that leads to the caves. It also provides laundry service. The Lodge's Australian-born owner provides detailed info on local caves and hiking routes, and organizes hiking, caving, and kayaking trips, as well as longer three-day treks. The attached restaurant bakes fresh muffins daily. (☎053 617 203; www.cavelodge.com. Treks 450-650฿ per trip, 3-day treks 1700฿, 4-person min. Dorms 70-90฿, doubles with shared bath 200฿, bungalows with bath 350-450฿.)

MAE HONG SON ☎053

Lush valleys, rocky streams, and forested mountains dotted with hill-tribe villages and temples—some of the most beautiful scenery in northern Thailand—have visitors flocking to Mae Hong Son. *Farang* tourists come for some of

Thailand's best trekking, and Thai tourists come to soak up the rural lifestyle. During the Bua Tong Blossom Festival from the beginning of November, the local wild sunflower turns hillsides golden. During the rest of the year, between hikes and trips to Karen villages, travelers can relax in the sun on the banks of Jong Kham Lake, surrounded by this town's impressive *wats* and restaurants.

▐ TRANSPORTATION

Flights: Mae Hong Son Airport (☎053 611 367 or 612 057), on Nivit Pisan Rd. Turn left at the hospital at the east end of Singhanat Bumrung Rd. **Thai Airways,** 71 Singhanat Bumrung Rd. (☎053 612 220; open M-F 8am-5pm) flies to **Chiang Mai** (35min.; 11:55am, 5:05pm; 1500฿). **Nok Air** (☎053 612 057, ext. 106), with offices at the airport, flies to **Chiang Mai** (35min.; M-Th and Sa 4:15pm, F and Su 11am). In high season, **PB Air** flies to **Bangkok** (1hr., 4000฿).

Buses: The new **bus station** (☎053 611 318) is about 1.5km south of town on a new road that runs parallel and to the west of Khunlum Praphat Rd. It's easiest to take a **motorcycle taxi** (40฿) to and from town. To **Chiang Mai** (7-8hr., 5 per day 6am-9pm, 187-337฿) via **Mae Sariang** (4hr., 6 per day 6am-9pm, 96-173฿) and **Khun Yuam** (2hr., 45-75฿), or to **Chiang Mai** (8hr.; 8:30, 10:30am, 12:30pm; 145-200฿; A/C minibus 8 per day 7am-2pm, 250฿) via **Pai** (3hr.; 150฿) and **Soppong** (2hr., 100฿).

Local Transportation: Songthaew leave for points north of Mae Hong Son from the day market, on Punit Watana Rd. **Motorcycle taxis** and **tuk-tuks** (30-80฿) wait at the bus station, airport, and around the day market.

Rentals: Numerous places around the traffic light on Khunlum Praphat Rd. rent **motorcycles. Highway,** 67/2 Khunlum Praphat Rd. (☎053 611 620), opposite Thai Farmers Bank, south of the lights, has 100cc motorcycles and good service facilities. High-season 200฿ per day, low-season 150฿ per day; 500฿ deposit and passport photocopy required. Open daily 8am-6pm. **Friend Tour,** 21 Phadichonkam Rd. (☎053 611 647), despite occasionally surly service, rents motorbikes (200฿ per day).

▐▌ ORIENTATION AND PRACTICAL INFORMATION

Mae Hong Son is 348km from Chiang Mai via **Mae Sariang** (Hwy. 108, the southern route) and a meandering 274km via **Pai** (Hwy. 107 and 1095, the northern route). From the bus station, walk north for about 1.5km, merge onto Sirimongkol Rd., and take your first right after you pass the turnoff for Wat Phra That Doi Kongmu. The main street, **Khunlum Praphat Road,** is home to restaurants, trekking outfitters, and banks, and runs north-south through the center of town. Toward the southern part of downtown along Khunlum Praphat Rd., the post office is a recognizable landmark. If you go down the road to the **post office's** left (eastern) side, you'll reach **Jong Kham Lake,** which glistens with reflections of *wats* and *chedis*. Guesthouses surround the lake, especially on **Udom Chao Nithet Road,** on the lake's north side.

Tourist Office: TAT (☎053 612 982), on Khunlum Praphat Rd., 200m south of the traffic light, opposite the post office, distributes tourist brochures and detailed regional maps. Open daily 8:30am-noon and 1-4:30pm.

Immigration Office (☎053 612 106), off Hwy 1095, 1km north of the bus station, on top of a hill. 10- or 30-day visa extensions, depending on visa. Departure card, visa, 2 photos, and 2 copies of passport are required. 1900฿. Open M-F 8:30am-4:30pm.

Currency Exchange: Bangkok Bank, 68 Khunlum Praphat Rd. (☎053 611 275). Open M-F 8:30am-3:30pm. AmEx/MC/Plus/V **24hr. ATM.**

Ambulance: ☎1669.

NORTHERN THAILAND

Local Tourist Police (☎053 611 812). At the corner of Rachadamphitak and Singhanat Bumrung Rd.

Pharmacy: 37 Singhanat Bumrung Rd. (☎053 611 380). Open daily 6:30am-9pm.

Medical Services: Srisangwal Hospital (☎053 611 378), at the end of Singhanat Bamrung Rd. English-speaking doctors. 24hr. emergency care.

Telephones: Mae Hong Son Telecommunications Office, 26 Udom Chao Nithet Rd. (☎053 611 711), just west of Khunlum Praphat Rd. International phones and fax. Open M-F 8:30am-4:30pm. Lenso phone at post office and in front of 7-Eleven.

Internet Access: Mae Hong Son Internet (☎053 620 028), 1 block north of the post office along Khunlum Praphat Rd. on the left. Internet 30฿ per hr., 10฿ min. Skype available. Open daily 8am-11pm.

Post Offices: Mae Hong Son Post Office, 79 Khunlum Praphat Rd. (☎053 611 223). Open M-F 8:30am-4:30pm, Sa-Su 9am-noon. **Postal Code:** 58000.

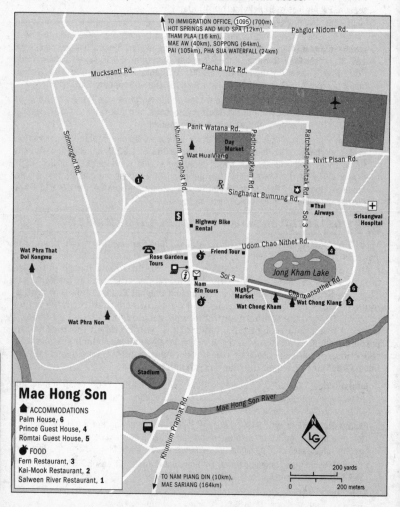

NORTHERN THAILAND

ACCOMMODATIONS

The center of town, especially near the lake, has the best places to stay. The area boasts scenic views and there are a number of good restaurants within easy walking distance. Standard hotels line Khunlum Praphat Rd.

Romtai Guest House (☎053 612 437), just off the eastern end of Chamnansathet Rd., next to Palm Guest House. The bungalows out back, in the midst of a verdant garden, are good deals, but you get even more bang for your baht with the immaculate hotel-style rooms in front. All have private bath, hot shower, and TV. Rooms with squat toilet 200฿, with Western toilet 250฿; bungalows with A/C 400฿. Prices rise in high season. ❷

Palm Guest House, 22/1 Chamnanchathit Rd. (☎053 614 022), just southeast of the lake. The hotel-style rooms in this guesthouse are comparable to those at neighboring Romtai, but their presentation is not quite as polished. All, however, have amenities such as private bath with Western toilet, TV, and hot shower. Low-season rooms 250฿, with A/C 400฿; high-season 300/500฿. ❷

Prince's Guest House (☎053 611 136), north of the lake on Udom Chao Nithet Rd. The simple rooms are part of an old house overlooking the lake, with quality increasing significantly with price. Free Wi-Fi. Plywood-walled rooms with fan and shared bath 150฿, singles and doubles with bath 200-250฿. ❷

FOOD

The sprawling **day market** is on Panit Watana Rd., next to Wat Hua Viang. **Roadside stalls** sell fruits and vegetables, while the covered market sells produce, meat, dried foods, and flowers. The nearby sois contain stores selling housewares, backpacks, and hill-tribe wares. At night, **food stalls** set up along Chamnansathet Rd. on the southern side of the lake. With choices like fried banana and sticky rice, papaya tempura, and fresh spring rolls (10-20฿ each), a mix-and-match dinner is inexpensive and delicious. The busy restaurant scene is similarly varied. In order to satisfy increasing demand, Mae Hong Son has diversified its food options and now most restaurants offer Western specialties alongside northern Thai dishes.

Salween River Restaurant, 3 Singhanat Bumrung Rd. (☎053 612 050). Follow Singhanat Bumrung Rd. west past the intersection with Khunlum Praphat Rd., and it's on the corner as the road curves to the right. This restaurant has fresh, expertly cooked food, where even standard dishes rise above the norm. Breakfast (130฿, includes coffee) is especially tasty, with some of the best homemade bread in town. Book exchange. Thai dishes 50-80฿. Open daily 8am-9:30pm. ❷

Fern Restaurant (☎053 611 374), on Khunlum Praphat Rd., just south of the post office. Locals and families pack this popular traditional restaurant, which has been around for over 20 years. The cavernous inner room, with nightly live music, is perfect for large groups, and the low-key front room creates a more intimate mood. Fried chicken in fragrant leaves 80฿. Entrees 70-150฿. Open daily 10:30am-10pm. ❸

Kai-Mook Restaurant, 23 Udom Chao Nithet Rd. (☎053 612 092), just east of Khunlum Praphat Rd. Despite the cloth napkins and elegant decor, the food here is relatively inexpensive. And considering how good it tastes, it's a value worth seeking out. Entrees 60-120฿. Noodle and rice dishes 30-40฿. Open daily 10am-2:30pm and 5-10pm. ❷

SIGHTS

Wat Phra That Doi Kongmu, 474m above town, has a panoramic view of the city. This Burmese-style temple is Mae Hong Son's most important *wat*, famous for its two white *chedis* built in 1860 and 1874. Nearby, **Wat Phra Non** houses a 12m

reclining Buddha and the ashes of Mae Hong Son's kings. To get to the *wats*, head west on Udom Chao Nithet Rd., and turn left at the end. On the right, at the base of the hill, is Wat Phra Non. Drive up the road just past Wat Phra Non, before the stadium, to reach Wat Phra That Doi Kongmu.

A jogging track circles **Jong Kham Lake** (park open daily 7am-10pm). On the lake's south side are two *wats*. **Wat Chong Klang** is on the right, with Buddhist glass paintings and wooden dolls brought from Myanmar in 1857. (Open daily 8am-6pm.) Next door is the elegant **Wat Chong Kham**, with delicate silver trim.

TREKKING

Several Chiang Mai-based treks can be found in Chaing Mai. In the surrounding hills there are villages of Lisu, Lahu, Hmong, and Karen tribes, as well as Shan and Kuo Min Tang (KMT) zones. During the low season, putting together your own trekking group can lower prices. For those heading to the sights by themselves, try to find a copy of the old edition of the official TAT map (20฿), available at some tour agencies. Guesthouses and tour agencies can also provide a decent free map of the area.

Rose Garden Tours, on Khunlum Praphat Rd. near the intersection with Udom Chao Nithet Rd., leads treks in both the nearby mountains and in more isolated areas. With variable difficulty levels and extensive English documentation, it is easy to find a trek that suits your needs. (☎053 611 681. Easier treks 1200฿ per day, more difficult treks 1500฿ per day. Open daily 8am-10pm.) **Nam Rin Tours,** next to the post office, leads a five-day trek to Pai through the intervening jungle that includes overnight stays, food, and porters. Dam, the charismatic owner—whose business card advertises "Good trek…bad jokes"—also organizes more traditional treks, though he caters primarily to those seeking a strenuous experience. (☎053 614 454. Strenuous treks 15000฿ per person, more traditional treks 800฿-1000฿ per day. Open daily 8:30am-7pm.)

DAYTRIPS FROM MAE HONG SON

NAM PIANG DIN (LONG-NECKED KAREN VILLAGE). Travelers can't make it as far as Mae Hong Son Province without hearing about the Burmese refugees, who make this region their home. At the age of five, the girls in this subset of the Karen tribe can choose to be fitted for their first brass neck rings. By adulthood, the rings have compressed the women's collarbones and rib cages so that their necks appear stretched. The experience of visiting the villages is highly commercial, with a 250฿ entrance fee, and streets that have been turned into little more than long souvenir stands.

There are three long-necked Karen villages in the vicinity of Mae Hong Son: **Nam Plang Din, Nai Soi,** and **Huai Sau Tao.** The easiest to access is Huai Sau Tao, only 12km from Mae Hong Son. Drive south on Khunlum Praphat Rd.; look for the well-marked signs for Ban Huai Sau Tao and "Long-Necked Karen Villages." To get to Nam Plang Din, you'll need to charter a boat. Ask the local TAT for directions to Huai Dau boat landing in Phuang Di. (30min., 500฿ per boat, 6 people max.) The farthest and least accessible Karen village is Nai Soi. It is 15km northwest of Mae Hong Son, and the last section of the road is sometimes impassable in the rainy season. *(This trip is best attempted with private transportation. Alternatively, organize the trip through a tour agency.)*

HIGHWAY 1095 AND ENVIRONS. Some of Thailand's most stunning, rugged scenery graces Hwy. 1095 between Pai and Mae Hong Son (111km). There are numerous options for experiencing this area's sights. A motorbike is reccommended for everything except the Fish Cave, which you can reach via the bus to Pai. The most ambitious daytrip is a journey to the KMT village of Mae Aw, which is on a mountaintop about 40km north of Mae Hong Son, straddling the Burmese border. For those loking for something closer, a number of impressive sights are located off the same road, so you can decide how far you want to go. Before you leave, get a regional map from the TAT.

Starting from Mae Hong Son, drive north on Khunlum Praphat Rd. (Hwy. 1095). After 16km, you'll reach ◪Tham Plaa, also known as the Fish Cave. This beautifully landscaped pond is attached to a small crevice, where thousands of fish struggle to swim up an underground stream. Mysteriously, very few ever come out. The Shan villagers who look after the fish never catch them, believing that the spirit of the mountain guards the fish from harm. As a result of their protected status, they grow to be quite large, with some more than 80cm long. Food stalls at the park's entrance make a nice lunch spot. (Visitor center open daily 8am-4pm. Free)

From the Fish Cave, turn right on Hwy. 1095 and drive 1km back toward Mae Hong Son. Take the first right, with signs marked for the ◪Pha Sua Waterfall. You'll reach it after about 7.5km. The 60m series of waterfalls is extremely impressive, especially during the wet-season. A short trail leads down to the base of the main cascades and continues downstream for a few 100m before returning to the parking area. If you turn left at the bottom of the main cascades, you can follow another trail up to the top of the waterfall. It continues for 1km along the river before coming out onto the main road.

From the Pha Sua Waterfall, follow the road up the mountain for another 5km or so until you reach the **Pang Tong Palace** and the **Queen's Royal Gardens.** This carefully landscaped mountaintop park is rarely visited by tourists. If you follow the road past the gardens, you'll come to an animal exhibition area. Most of the buildings contain birds, but if you walk 50m past them to the cages on the hill, you'll find a clouded leopard.

Head back to the main road, turn left, and continue to Mae Aw, taking a right at the fork after Ban Na Pa Paik. Follow the roadside signs for **"Ban Rak Thai,"** Mae Aw's Thai name. The village entrance is marked by a large gate emblazoned with Chinese script.

MAE SARIANG   ☎053

Mae Sariang, a peaceful town nestled on the eastern bank of the muddy Yuam River, is off the beaten path from Chiang Mai, Pai, and Mae Hong Son. Trade of teak and rice across the border with Myanmar has fueled a small building boom, and the town is prepared for an overflow of tourism from Mae Hong Son: information markers clutter every street corner. But the tourist flood has yet to materialize, and the construction hasn't managed to disrupt Mae Sariang's small town aura. With a relaxing downtown and a charming countryside, Mae Sariang holds hidden rewards for those who venture off the tourist track.

▶ TRANSPORTATION

The **bus station** (☎053 681 347) is on Mae Sariang Rd., 100m north of the traffic light, opposite the gas station. Buses run to **Chiang Mai** (4hr.; 7, 9, 10:30am, 12:30, 3pm; 100-200฿) and **Mae Hong Son** (4hr.; 7, 10:30am, 12:30, 3:30pm; 100-200฿). **Sombat Tour** (☎053 681 532), 100m north of the bus station, coordinates buses to **Bangkok** (12hr., every hr. 4am-7pm, 444-57฿). **Songthaew** head to **Mae Sot** (6hr., every hr. 6:30am-12:30pm, 200฿). Most of the guesthouses along the river, including the **Northwest Guest House,** rent **motorbikes** (150-250฿ per day) and bicycles (50-80฿ per day).

🛈 ✈ ORIENTATION AND PRACTICAL INFORMATION

Mae Sariang is bordered by the **Yuam River** to the west and **Highway 108** to the east. **Mae Sariang Road,** which runs north-south, hosts the bus station and some shops. One block to its west, **Langpanit Road** runs parallel to the river and has the best guesthouses. Perpendicular to these is **Wiangmai Road,** which stretches from the river to Hwy. 108 and intersects Mae Sariang Rd. in the town center at the traffic light. **Saritpol Road,** site of the morning market, connects Mae Sariang Rd. and Langpanit Rd., one block south of the light. Two blocks south of the traffic light, **Wai Suksa Road** leads west out of town to Mae Sam Laep across the town's southern bridge.

Services in Mae Sariang include: an **immigration office,** 300m north of the hospital on Hwy. 108 (☎053 681 339; open M-F 8:30am-4:30pm); **Krung Thai Bank,** on Langpanit Rd., 100m south of Wiangmai Rd., with a Cirrus/MC/Plus/V **ATM** and a currency exchange (open M-F 8:30am-4:30pm); **police** (☎053 681 308), on Mae Sariang Rd., 150m south of Wiangmai Rd.; a **pharmacy,** on the corner of Saritpol and Langpanit Rd. (open daily 7am-7pm); the **hospital** (☎053 681 027), on Hwy. 108, 200m toward Mae Hong Son from Wiangmai Rd.; **Internet access** at the air-conditioned **C & O Internet,** on Mae Sariang Rd., 50m north of the traffic light (15฿ per hr. Open daily 10am-midnight); and the **post office,** 31 Wiangmai Rd., 400m east of the traffic light and just before the town gate. (☎053 681 356; open M-F 8:30am-4:30pm and Sa-Su 9am-noon.) **Postal Code:** 58110.

♦ ACCOMMODATIONS

The most comfortable budget lodgings in Mae Sariang are the guesthouses on Langpanit Rd. along the Yuam River. Most are located within a two-block area. To get to this area from the bus station, make a left onto Mae Sariang Rd., take the first right, and then another right onto Langpanit Rd. You'll be opposite the Salawin Guest House, and the others are only a few meters north.

Northwest Guesthouse (☎089 7009 928), on Langpanit Rd. between the Riverhouse Hotel and the Riverside Guest House, on the opposite side of the street. Saloon-themed lobby contains a restaurant, laundry, and tour service. Large wood-paneled rooms with shared bath are the best deals in Mae Sariang. The English-speaking owner can help with travel advice and has regional maps. Automatic motorbike rentals 200฿ per day. Internet 30฿ per hr. Singles with shared bath 150฿; doubles 200฿, with A/C 300฿. ❷

Riverside Guest House, 85 Langpanit Rd. (☎053 681 188), 200m north of the intersection with Wiangmai Rd. The cheapest rooms are in the damp, dark basement, while the cozy, more expensive rooms open onto balconies overlooking the river. Low-season singles with hot shower and Western toilet 200-300฿, high-season 300-400฿; doubles 250-350/350-450฿, with A/C 450-500/550-600฿. ❷

Riverhouse Hotel, 77 Langpanit Rd. (☎053 621 201; www.riverhousehotels.com), 2 doors south of Riverside Guest House. Not to be confused with the Riverhouse Resort, which is further south on Langpanit Rd. The luxurious wooden rooms with bath, shower curtains, balcony, and TV, are some of the nicest in town. An open-air lobby downstairs also functions as a restaurant. Motorbike rental available. Rooms with fan 550฿, with A/C 750฿, with breakfast 850฿/950฿. In high season (including breakfast) 950฿/1000฿.

Salawin Guest House (☎053 681 690), at the intersection of Langpanit Rd. and Wiangmai Rd. A great bargain in the low season, the tiled rooms here come with bath, fan, and free fruit from the kind owner Sakchai's garden. It's also possible to rent a larger bungalow (for bigger groups) down the street (600฿ per night for 1-2 people, 1500฿ for 6; 6000฿ per month). Singles 300฿, doubles 480฿. Prices rise in high season. ❸

🔘 FOOD

Mae Sariang isn't market-centered when it comes to meals. There is a small neon-lit **night market** on Wiangmai Rd., 200m east of the traffic light, but it is more focused on carnival rides than it is on culinary diversity. The **morning market** on Saritpol Rd. sells produce, meat, and ingredients. The best restaurants are along the river.

Renu Restaurant, 174/2 Wiangmai Rd. (☎053 681 171), 50m toward the highway from the traffic light. Standard, straightforward Thai fare doesn't get much better than this in Mae Sariang. The comfortably dim interior is decorated with traditional crafts and photos of the King. Entrees 50-70฿. Fish entrees 70-80฿. Open daily 8am-10pm. ❷

Sawaddee Restaurant and Bar (☎081 075 0706), on Langpanit Rd. across from Northwest Guesthouse. Choose from a vegetarian-friendly menu as you sit on a terrace overlooking the river. On the other side of the room is a raised lounge area with floor cushions. Entrees 40-80฿. *Laab* (traditional minced meat with vegetables and rice, eaten without utensils) 60฿. Large Singha 75฿. Open daily 8am-midnight. ❷

Ban Rao Food and Drink (☎053 681 743), 300m north of Riverside Guest House on Langpanit Rd. Although it's somewhat removed from the downtown area, Ban Rao is worth visiting for its covered river patio and indoor lounge area, both of which are meticulously decorated and cared after. Entrees 60-120฿. Marinated minced pork 50฿. Open daily 5-10pm. ❸

Intira Restaurant (☎053 681 529), on Wiangmai Rd. across from Renu Restaurant. The menu at Intira Restaurant is almost identical to its neighbor's across the street. Given its neighbor's quality, that isn't a bad thing. The biggest difference here is an air-conditioned room that can accommodate large groups. Entrees 50-70฿. Stir-fried beef with jalapenos 60฿. Open daily 8am-9pm. ❷

🔘 SIGHTS

The country around town, dotted with hill-tribe villages, is perfect for walks or bike rides. It is 5km to 🔲**Pha Maw Yaw (Pha Mo Lo),** a particularly scenic and isolated picturesque Karen village set among the green rice paddies. To get there, take Langpanit Rd. north from the guesthouse area. Follow the road when it veers left and continue over the bridge. It leads directly into tiny Pha Maw Yaw, which is well marked with English signs. The road forks in the middle of the village. To the left is a narrow road that leads through rice paddies, with great views on either side. To the right is the village's **Wat Chom Mon.** After the fork, continue on the road as it crosses the main road. The *wat* is 200m further under an ornate gate. You can walk up the serpent-lined stairways or follow the path to the right to eventually reach the top of the hill. The view of Mae Sariang is partially obstructed by trees, but a gorgeous one nonetheless.

On the other side of town, the **Big Buddha** is an intriguing sight. The 10m tall statue overlooks a panorama of Mae Sariang with blue-green mountains in the distance. To get there, follow Wiangmai Rd. out of town and, just before the highway, turn right onto the road to Tak (Hwy. 105). After crossing the bridge, take a left on the first main road, which meets Hwy. 105 at an acute angle. The *wat* is up the road marked by the large gate.

Because Mae Sariang's countryside hasn't yet been overrun by crowds of tourists, it remains a wonderful place for trekking. **Salawin Tours,** next to the Riverside Guest House, organizes trips that include elephant rides, bamboo rafting, hill-tribe villages, and waterfalls. (☎ 085 7089 824. Open daily 7am-10pm. Full-day treks 700-1400฿ per person, 3-day treks 2500-3000฿ per person). Some guesthouses, including the Northwest Guest House (p. 298), also organize

NORTHERN THAILAND

THE BIG SPLURGE

TREKKIN' WITH NAM RIN

Most tourists come to Northern Thailand to explore the beautiful scenery. But the treks they take, often considered the quintessential Thai wilderness experience, are not always as rugged as advertised. It is difficult to get fully in touch with nature when you're whisked from one "local experience" to another.

Enter **Nam Rin Tours'** (see **Mae Hong Son**, p. 292) 5-day walking expedition from Mae Hong Son to Pai. Sure, some comforts—porters—are provided, as well as necessities like food and lodging. But aside from that, it's a jungle adventure all the way.

The 15,000฿ per person price tag is hefty. Still, there are few other ways to have an experience like this one. You'll encounter hill-tribe villages and scenic vistas as you rough it with fellow *farang* along the trail.

At least Dam, the owner of Nam Rin Tours, is honest. As he advertises on his business card: "Good trek, good tour guide, good food, bad sleep, bad jokes."

Nam Rin Tours (☎053 614 454) is located next to the post office in Mae Hong Son. Strenuous treks cost 15000฿ per person, and more traditional treks run 800฿-1000฿ per day. Open daily 8:30am-7pm.

treks. Ask to see any outfit's TAT license before you sign up. For an activity that stays closer to town, **Kanchana's Bicycle Tours** (☎01 952 2167) organizes trips to nearby hill-tribe villages and temples. (½-day 500฿, full-day 1000฿, includes bike, helmet, and lunch. 4-person max. Call in advance for reservations.)

⛰ DAYTRIPS FROM MAE SARIANG

There are several daytrips within easy reach of Mae Sariang, but they must be undertaken with private transportation or through a tour agency.

THE KAEO KOMON CAVE. This calcite cave, 35km north of Mae Sariang, burrows 120m into a mountainside. Calcite caves, which resemble tunnels surrounded on all sides by delicate crystals, are extremely rare and this one is among the most beautiful of its kind in Thailand. Don't come expecting the grand scale of Tham Lod in Soppong, or you'll be disappointed; a visit here takes no longer than 20min. Still, the intricate beauty of Kaeo Komon's interior makes it well worth a visit. *(Hwy. 108 north from Mae Sariang in the direction of Mae Hong Son. In Mae La Noi look for the well-marked English signs for the cave and turn right under a structure that says "Calcite Cave" on the top. Follow the signs for 5km along back roads. National park building on the right, cave farther up the mountain. Open daily 8:30am-4:30pm. Ticket to the cave 80฿, (includes a guide).)*

MAE SURIN NATIONAL PARK. Contains the **Mae Surin Waterfall.** Located about 120km north of Mae Sariang and 45km northeast of Khum Yuam, this is Thailand's tallest cascade. Though the chances of you seeing any are slim, Malayan sun bears, wild boars, pythons, cobras, and other animals reside in this 397 sq. km park. *(To get to the park, hop off when the Mae Sariang-Mae Hong Son bus stops in Khun Yuam. Catch a songthaew for the remaining distance in front of Ban Farang, 100m toward Mae Sariang from the bus stop, at the curve in the main road. But be warned: this less-traveled route might set you back 500-700฿ for a private songthaew ride or leave you waiting for days. Ask the local TAT for more information before departing.)*

OTHER SIGHTS. Mae Sawan Noi waterfall and the **Mae Um Long hot springs** are both gorgeous and wonderful places to unwind. (Drive about 15km east along the highway to Chiang Mai, where you'll first see a turnoff on the left for the hot springs, about 15km away, and then, a few kilometers later, another turnoff for the waterfall, 5km away.)

If you're waiting for the bus in Khum Yuam, the **Japanese WWII Museum** is worth a quick look. It's not much more than a collection of artifacts (guns, uniforms, photos, etc.), but the English-language articles provide an insightful look at the Japanese occupation in the area.

MAE SOT ☎ 055

Mae Sot (also called Mae Sod) is a small do-gooder's paradise 7km east of Myanmar. With the influx of refugees and Internally Displaced Persons (IDPs) fleeing Myanmar and arriving in and around Mae Sot, foreign NGO workers have flocked to the scene to try to improve the situation for the Burmese on both sides of the border. As a result, an abundance of volunteer opportunities for foreigners are available. Moreover, each resident of this cozy city has an interesting story to tell, and the cultural mix makes for an exciting scene. Mae Sot's vibrant day market is a sight to behold; here, "Union of Myanmar" currency notes, hill-tribe headdresses, and precious gems mingle with the usual pig heads and mangos.

 MYANMAR: TO GO OR NOT TO GO? Tourist dollars in Myanmar often go toward propping up one of the world's worst military regimes, so whether or not to travel to Myanmar becomes a difficult ethical question. Those who argue that foreign travelers should venture into Myanmar cite the fledgling tourist industry as a way for the desperately poor Burmese people to earn money outside of the government-controlled economy. Informed travelers who avoid state-sponsored tours and establishments can, to a certain extent, direct their money to Myanmar's people. Additionally, some argue that contact with the outside world is inherently uplifting to the Burmese people, and travelers who witness the political situation will tell others about it, increasing international pressure on the military regime. Be aware, however, that both the Burmese opposition movement and many international human rights advocates strongly refute these arguments and urge travelers to boycott Myanmar. Human rights groups have documented the use of forced labor on recent tourism development projects. Furthermore, foreign visitors are unlikely to witness the reality of life for the Burmese, as the government strictly controls what tourists are allowed to see and works hard to display the illusion of a happy society. Finally, it is not possible to visit Myanmar without giving money to the regime—in such a poor country, even the $10 tourists pay to cross the border has a impact on the national economy and is one of the regime's only sources of hard currency. Likewise, most hotels and tour agencies are controlled by the government. Should you decide to travel to Myanmar, know that Burmese citizens have disappeared or been beaten severely for discussing politics with foreigners. Avoid discussion of politics, and educate yourself about how to avoid empowering the military junta. The choice to travel to Myanmar is yours. *Let's Go* only asks that you make it an informed one.

⌫ TRANSPORTATION

Buses: There are 5 bus stations in town, in a confusing constellation all within 1km of town center. The **main station** (☎055 532 949), 1km west of the town center at the intersection of Asia Highway and Intharakhiri Rd., has buses to **Bangkok** (9-10hr.,

NORTHERN THAILAND

11 per day 8:00am-10:00pm, 307-610в) and **Chiang Mai** (6hr., 6, 8am, 146-263в). Ticket office at bus station open daily 9am-5pm.

Songthaew and minivans: Orange *songthaew* to **Mae Sariang** (6hr., every hr. 6am-noon, 180в) leave from behind the covered market area 2 blocks north of the police station. Orange-and-white minivans headed to **Tak** (1hr., every 30min. 6am-6pm, 56в) gather on the east side of the same market. Blue *songthaew* to **Um Phang** (4hr., every hr. 7:30am-3pm, 120в) cluster just east of the market on the first road south of Prasatwithi Rd. White vans to **Phitsanulok** (4hr., every hr. 7am-3pm, 136в) via **Sukhothai** (2hr., 110в) leave from the southern end of the market. These destinations may be easier to reach through Tak. Lastly, blue *songthaew* to the **Myanamar border** (10min., every 15min. 8am-5pm, 10в) leave from the western end of Prasatwithi Rd. opposite Bank of Ayudhya near the intersection with Intharakhiri Rd.

Local Transportation: The same blue *songthaew* that go to the Myanmar border also go to the Moei River Market (see afbove). During the day, **motorcycle taxis** (20-40в) go around town, but most visitors rent bicycles or motorbikes.

Rentals: Guesthouses rent **bikes** (40-50в per day) and **motorbikes** (150в per day). Motorbikes can also be rented for 150в at 127/4-6 Prasatwithi Rd., next to the big Honda store (☎055 532 099; open daily 8am-5pm). To keep your passport for Myanmar, pay the US$100 deposit and take an old motorbike.

◼︎◼︎ ☌ ORIENTATION AND PRACTICAL INFORMATION

Mae Sot is 165km west of Sukhothai and 7km east of Myanmar. The two main roads run east-west: **Intharakhiri Road,** with traffic heading east, runs roughly parallel to **Prasatwithi Road,** with traffic heading west toward the border; the two roads converge near the guesthouse neighborhood on the western side of town. **Asia Highway (Rte. 105)** bypasses the town a few blocks north of these major roads, but converges with Intharakhiri Rd. near the Chiang Mai/Bangkok bus station. Free maps with varying degrees of accuracy are available at guesthouses. The most comprehensive free map is offered at Green Guesthouse.

Tours: Go to Um Phang to book a trek. To book in Mae Sot, **Southeast Express Co.** (☎055 547 048) offers guided day and overnight treks for 1200-2200в per day. Many guesthouses also offer guided tours.

Immigration Office: (☎055 563 003), next to Friendship Bridge. For visa extensions, see **Border Crossing: Moei/Myawaddy,** below. Open daily 8:30am-4:30pm.

Currency Exchange: Banks line Prasatwithi Rd., all with **24hr. ATMs.**

Markets: The bustling **gem and jade market,** on Prasatwithi Rd., stretches east from the Siam Hotel (185 Prasatwithi Rd.). Open daily noon-4pm. **The Moei River market,** at the border 7km west of town, next to Friendship Bridge, 200m past the entrance to the border, sells Burmese fabrics, gems, and spices, alongside electronics, snacks, jewelry, and skincare products.

Laundry: All guesthouses have laundry service (30-40в per kg). Ban Thai Guesthouse offers a deal of 1 month of unlimited laundry for 80в.

Local Tourist Police: Near the Myanmar border, also immediately next to the Friendship Bridge. Very little English spoken. Open 24hr.

Medical Services: Pawo Hospital (☎055 544 397), south of town, 1 block south of the vans to Sukhothai. Some English spoken. Hospital and **pharmacy** open 24hr. MC/V.

Telephones: Net4All Internet, 517 Intharakhiri Rd. (☎055 534 153), across from the Bai Fern Guesthouse. International calls via the Internet for 2в per min. Open daily 9am-10pm. **Maesot Telecommunications Office,** 784 Intharakhiri Rd. (☎055 533 364), a 10min. walk west of guesthouses. Collect calls 33в. Open M-F 8:30am-4:30pm.

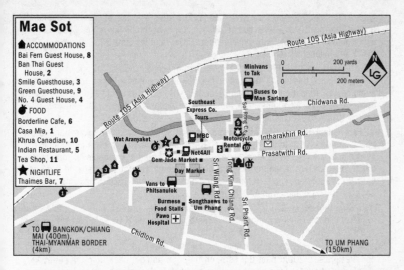

Mae Sot

ACCOMMODATIONS
Bai Fern Guest House, 8
Ban Thai Guest
  House, 2
Smile Guesthouse, 3
Green Guesthouse, 9
No. 4 Guest House, 4

FOOD
Borderline Cafe, 6
Casa Mia, 1
Khrua Canadian, 10
Indian Restaurant, 5
Tea Shop, 11

NIGHTLIFE
Thaimes Bar, 7

Route 105 (Asia Highway)

Minivans to Tak
Buses to Mae Sariang
Chidwana Rd.

Southeast Express Co. Tours

Wat Aranyaket
MBC
Net4All
Gem-Jade Market
Day Market
Motorcycle Rental
Intharakhiri Rd.
Prasatwithi Rd.

Vans to Phitsanulok
Burmese Food Stalls
Songthaews to Um Phang
Pawo Hospital

Sai Rong C.
Tong Kim Chiang Rd.
Sri Wiang Rd.
Sri Pharit Rd.

TO BANGKOK/CHIANG MAI (400m), THAI-MYANMAR BORDER (4km)
Chidlom Rd.

TO UM PHANG (150km)

0   200 yards
0   200 meters

Internet: Net4All Internet (above) has fast Internet for 15฿ per hr. with Skype installed on all of the computers. Open daily 9am-10pm.

Post Office: GPO (☎055 531 277), on Intharakhiri Rd. on the eastern side of town. With your back to the police station, head left; it's 250m down the road on the right. *Poste Restante.* Open M-F 8:30am-4:30pm, Sa-Su 9am-noon. **Postal Code:** 63110.

BORDER CROSSING: MOEI/MYAWADDY. A 7km *songthaew* ride from Mae Sot, this Thai-Myanmar border crossing is a hassle-free way to extend your Thai visa. Blue *songthaew* leave from Prasatwithi Rd., opposite the Bank of Ayudhya (10min., every 15min. 8am-5pm, 10฿). Show up at the Friendship Bridge between 6am and 4pm, present your passport to the Thai authorities to get an exit stamp, walk over the bridge, present 500฿ and your passport to Burmese officials, and then walk back over the bridge and receive your new visa. If you want to see Myawaddy, just leave your passport with Burmese officials and be sure to return by 4pm to get back to the Thai border booth on time. Myawaddy's main attractions are a sumptuous gold-laden temple called Shwe Muay Wan and a fairly typical market. Burmese touts, desperate for foreign currency, are even more relentless than Thai ones—be prepared to have unwanted "guides" on your trip. The market on the Thai side of the border sells similar goods at decent prices in a more hassle-free environment. Get updated on the political situation in Myanmar before crossing the border (**Myanmar: To Go or Not To Go?**, p. 301).

ACCOMMODATIONS

Travelers have a lot of choice when it comes to guesthouses in Mae Sot. Most are at the west end of Intharakhiri Rd. and cater primarily to long-term guests who volunteer at NGOs in the region.

Ban Thai Guest House, 740 Intharakhiri Rd. (☎055 531 590), 25m west of No. 4 Guest House. Sun-filled, simple, clean rooms with fan nestled amidst a serene, manicured garden. The patio at the front with free Wi-Fi fosters a sense of friendly community among the mostly long-term guests. Bike rental 50฿, motorbike rental 150฿. Singles with shared bath 250฿, with private bath 350฿; doubles 350-550฿. Discounts (10-20%) for longer stays. ❷

Green Guesthouse (☎055 533 207), on Intharakhiri Rd., down an alley behind the police station. A basketball net outside this flower-draped, teak house adds to the family-homestay atmosphere. The friendly owner is a wealth of information. Basic 3-bed dorm downstairs. All rooms have fans, private baths, and come with free breakfast. Dorms 100฿; singles 150฿; doubles 200฿. ❶

Bai Fern Guest House, 660 Intharakhiri Rd. (☎055 531 349). With your back to the police station, 400m to the right. Though the rooms are a admittedly a little small, this guesthouse is conveniently located near the center of town and attracts all sorts of visitors. A popular local restaurant is attached. All rooms with fans and shared hot-water bath. Wi-Fi access 50฿. Bike rental 50฿ and motorbike rental 150฿. Small singles 150฿; doubles 200฿; doubles with A/C 250฿. ❷

Smile Guesthouse, (☎851 299 293), on Intharakhiri Rd., next to Ban Thai. Simple, aged rooms of variable sizes, all with fan. Bike rental 40฿. Singles 100฿, with private bath and A/C 150฿, doubles 150/200฿. ❶

No. 4 Guest House, 736 Intharakhiri Rd. (☎/fax 055 544 976; www.geocities.com/no4guesthouse), 200m past Bai Fern, on the right and set back from the street. Very simple teak house, containing bare rooms with fan. Dorms with futons on hardwood floors, with mosquito net and fan 50฿; singles with cold shower 120฿; singles with hot shower 150฿; doubles with hot shower 250฿. ❶

FOOD AND NIGHTLIFE

Catering to its wide array of occupants, Mae Sot has it all: from Thai to Burmese to Indian and Italian. The day market, which stretches south from Prasatwithi Rd. on either side of the Siam Hotel, and the night markets have a huge selection of cheap eats. There are also a number of restaurants at the southern end of the market that showcase delicious, authentic Burmese curries for less than 30฿. Those feeling adventurous should try *Mohinga*, a spicy fish stew that is the traditional Burmese breakfast.

Indian Restaurant, 565/3 Intharakhiri Rd. (☎087 309 182), 50m. west of where Intharakhiri Rd. meets Prasawithi Rd. The Burmese owners, originally from Nepal, cook up truly delicious authentic Indian food at especially low prices. Indian curries 30-55฿. The samosas, which are out of this world, go for 20฿ a pop. Open 8:00am-10:30pm. ❶

Khrua Canadian, on the corner opposite the police station at the intersection of Soi Rang Chak and Intharakhiri Rd. The Canadian owner Dave imports Western ingredients and serves up large helpings of *farang* fare as well as local food. Northern Thai style curries (40-60฿) are as much a specialty as the burgers. Satellite TV and fair-trade hill-tribe coffee. Cheeseburger 50฿. Fries 40฿. Western style steak 250-350฿. Also offers a free map of nearby attractions. Open daily 7am-9pm. ❷

Borderline Cafe (☎055 531 016), on Intharakhiri Rd. near Wat Aranyaket, tucked behind the affiliated Borderline Shop. Excellent local specialties like Burmese tea leaf salad (30฿) in a relaxing outdoor garden. The salted lime juice (20฿) and the chickpeas with flat bread (30฿) are tasty. Open Tu-Sa 10am-6pm and Su 2am-6pm. ❷

Casa Mia, (☎087 204 4701), on Don Kaew Rd. Take a right on the first road heading west past the Ban Thai Guest House. A popular favorite among NGO workers, the Thai and Western food here is good and cheap. It also is the hangout of local celebrity artist Maung Maung Tinn. Thai curries 45-70฿, banana flower salad 40฿, slices of freshly baked pies 20฿. Open 8am-10pm. Delivery available. ❷

Tea Shop, opposite the mosque, is a delicious nook with an English menu that serves up tasty Indian-influenced samosas (5฿), roti (10-20฿), and curries (30฿). The masala tea (10฿) is absolutely incredible. Open daily 6am-7pm. ❶

Thaime's Bar, 634 Intharakhiri Road, just west of the Bai Fern Guesthouse. With tons of seating and a pool table in the back, it is the NGO after-hours hotspot. Trivia night Tu around 9pm, 100฿ per person. Beer 50-80฿. Lychee Martini 100฿. Open 4pm-midnight, or until the last customer leaves. ❷

TAK   ☎ 055

All roads lead to Tak, but for most visitors, they lead out just as quickly. Whether your route is Bangkok-Chiang Mai, Sukhothai-Ayutthaya, or Khorat-Mae Sot, you'll likely pass through this provincial capital. Despite TAT's attempts to paint it as a destination in its own right, there's not much to do. Far more noteworthy than anything in the city are the nearby national parks, Lam Sang and Taksin Maharat, for which Tak serves as a convenient gateway.

TRANSPORTATION

The **bus station** (☎ 055 511 057), near the intersection of Hwy. 1 and 12, 500m northeast of town, is probably the reason you're here and serves: **Bangkok** (6-7hr., every hr., 337-510฿); **Chiang Mai** (4hr., every hr., 130-160฿); **Kamphaeng Phet** (1½hr., every 1½hr., 50-62฿); **Sukhothai** with connections to **Bangkok** (1hr., every hr., 43-58฿). Orange-and-white non-air conditioned **minibuses** go to **Mae Sot** (1hr., every 30-60min. 5am-6pm, 56฿). **Motorcycle taxis** and **tuk-tuks** run from the bus station into town (30-40฿); to **walk** to town, turn left on the main road exiting the bus station. Cross the Hwy. 1 interchange, continue straight down this road for about 1.5km, then turn left onto Chompon Rd. (your fourth left after Hwy. 1), and continue straight down this road for about 1km until you have reached the market at the center of town.

ORIENTATION AND PRACTICAL INFORMATION

Tak's four main roads run roughly parallel on the east side of the **Ping River,** which flows north to south. Closest to the river and farthest from the bus station is **Kitticarjon Road,** then **Chompon Road** with its night-market food stalls. Next are **Taksin Road** and **Mahattai Bamruang Road.** On the town's eastern edge, right next to the bus station, **Highway 1** crosses **Highway 12,** heading north to Chiang Mai or south to Bangkok.

Tourist Office: TAT (☎ 055 514 3413), 500m west of the bus station on Charot Vithi Thong Rd. (the name given to Hwy. 12 near the Tak city center) heading toward town, has a friendly staff. Good English. Dispenses useful maps, and helpful info about national parks, trekking opportunities, and the border situation. Open daily 8:30am-4:30pm.

Bank: Bangkok Bank, 683 Taksin Rd., a little south of the Sa Nguan Thai Hotel, with a **24hr. ATM.** Open M-F 8:30am-3:30pm; AmEx/MC/Plus/V. Other banks and 24hr. ATMs can be found on each of the main roads.

Police: (☎ 055 511 354), on Mahatthai Bamruang Rd., near the pond, about 500m southwest of TAT.

Pharmacy: 231/2-3 Mahatthai Bamruang Rd. (☎ 055 621 973), next to Mae Ping Hotel. Open daily 8am-8pm.

Hoapital: Taksin Hospital (☎ 055 511 0245), on Hwy. 1, in the southern part of town, near Wat Mani Banphot, about 1km southwest of the bus station.

Post Office: (☎055 511 140), across an athletic field, to the left of TAT, with international phones. Open M-F 8:30am-4:30pm, Sa-Su 9am-noon. **Postal Code:** 63000.

ACCOMMODATIONS

There is a spectrum of accomodation options in Tak, ranging from inexpensive and grungy to expensive and classy.

Kaoloy Golden Park Hotel, 75/26 Nong Luong (☎055 517 4612). Facing the road market, with your back to Mae Ping Hotel, head right, take the first right at the intersection, then the first left with the lake in front of you. The hotel is on your left inside a gated area. There is no English sign at its entrance, so look for the coffee store on its. Clean, airy rooms, and spacious bathrooms. Breakfast included. Singles and doubles with A/C and hot water bath 490฿. ❹

Mae Ping Hotel, 231/4-6 Mahatthai Bamruang Rd. (☎055 511 807), across the road from the market. Aging rooms with hard mattresses await the hardcore budget traveler. Singles without A/C 130฿, singles and doubles with A/C 250฿. ❷

The Viang Tak Riverside Hotel, 236 Chumphon Rd. (☎055 512 5078), is the poshest hotel in the province, but the prices are still fairly reasonable. All rooms in this high-rise have soft beds, satellite TVs, A/C, and private bath with hot water. Also has overpriced Internet access (1฿ per min.), and a decent restaurant. Breakfast buffet and swimming pool access included. Singles with river view 800฿; doubles 650-950฿. ❹

FOOD

Tak's only conventional restaurant is the restaurant attached to the **Viang Tak Riverside Hotel,** which serves decent but pricey Thai-Chinese dishes in notably large portions. (Dishes 100-200฿. Burgers 80-100฿. Western breakfast 120฿. Open daily 8am-10pm.) The **shops** and **stalls** near the police station are a much better option, as is the **day market** on Taksin Rd. or the **night market** on Chompon Rd. All specialize in simple but delicious Thai curries and noodle dishes (25-40฿).

SIGHTS

The paved riverside path and the **Bangkok Bicentennial Bridge,** a small suspension footbridge, have fabulous views of the mountains to the west and are the most scenic way to spend your time in Tak. The bridge is at the north end of town, and visible from the night market. Five-hundred meters west of TAT on Charot Vithi Thong Rd. you"ll find the rather unimpressive **shrine** of King Taksin (1734-1782). Many Thais make the pilgrimage here to light incense and pay their respects to their old king.

Lansang National Park is a small park 17km west of Tak on Hwy. 105, the road to Mae Sot. Several waterfalls cascade from the craggy granite hills at the park's center. If you ask the driver, the bus to Mae Sot will drop you off at the **park entrance** on the highway. It is a 5km walk to the **visitors center.** The journey from Tak takes about 1½hr. At **Lansang Waterfall,** 150m from the visitors center, clear water cascades down rocky ledges. Linger on the shady observation deck. Thai tourists flood the lower falls on weekends, turning them into a makeshift water-park, but leave the upper falls, **Pha Peung** (750m walk) and **Pha Tae** (2.2km walk), deserted. As the bathing crowd is mostly Thai,wear modest swimming attire. **Free maps** available at TAT and the visitors center. **Camping** in the park is permitted, though only in certain designated areas. To leave the park, head back 5km towards Hwy. 105 and hope the Mae Sot-Tak buses, which go back and forth between the two cities every 30min., come by soon. *(Park open daily 6am-6pm. Camping 250ß, tent rental 35ß. Bungalows 800-4000ß. One-day admission to both parks: 400ß, children 200ß.)*

KAMPHAENG PHET   ☎055

The defensive walls that give Kamphaeng Phet ("diamond wall") its name once formed the strategic front line of the Sukhothai kingdom. These days, the ancient fortifications enclose a UNESCO World Heritage site that attracts a smattering of daytrippers from Sukhothai, 77km to the north. While there's little to see here apart from the weathered but impressive ruins, the city itself is a pleasantly quiet northern provincial town.

▐ TRANSPORTATION

The **bus station** is 2km west of Kamphaeng Phet, across the wide bridge over the Ping River. As the halfway point between Chiang Mai and Bangkok, Kamphaeng Phet is a transportation hub, and **buses** heading in both directions stop here frequently during the day. Buses go to **Bangkok** (6hr., 140-302ß), **Chiang Mai** (6hr., 145-307ß), and **Phitsanulok** (56ß). **Songthaew** run to Sukhothai (45ß) from the bus station. Upon arrival, ask to be dropped off on the east side of the river, for convenience. In the likely case that you end up at the bus station, a red *songthaew* (20ß) runs across the river to town (every 15min. 6am-6pm). **Samlor** leave from here to the city. (40-70ß depending on where you are going and whether it is after 6pm.) Many hotels provide free or cheap transportation to the bus station. Within the city, a *samlor* will take you anywhere around town for 20-40ß. Otherwise, Three J Guesthouse (below) rents out **bicycles** (50ß) and **motorbikes** (200ß with passport deposit) for the day.

✸ ORIENTATION

Kamphaeng Phet is situated 338km from Bangkok and 337km from Chiang Mai. A large bridge along **Kamphaeng Phet Road** unites the west bank of the **Ping River**, home to the bus station, with the east bank, home to historical parks, accommodations, and restaurants. At the foot of the eastern entrance of the bridge, there is a rotary where Kamphaeng Phet Rd. intersects **Tesa 1 Road**, a one-way road headed north. Tesa 1 Rd. turns into the busiest part of town 1.5km south of this intersection. Running north of the rotary, Tesa 1 becomes **Tesa 2 Road** and leads to the old city walls and historical sites. **Ratchadamnoen Rd.** runs parallel to Tesa 1 and is a one-way road headed south.

🛈 PRACTICAL INFORMATION

Tourist Office: Although there is no official tourist office in Kamphaeng Phet, the **Chamber of Commerce** at the intersection of Tesa 1 and Bamrungrat Rd. provide free maps and answers general questions. Open M-Sa 8:30am-5:00pm.

Bank: Bangkok Bank, at the southwest corner of Ratchadamnoen and Charoensuk Rd., with a **24 hr. ATM** and **currency exchange**. Open M-F 8:30am-3:30pm. There are numerous other 24hr. ATMs on both Tesa 1 Rd. and Ratchadamnoen Rd. near the city center.

Police: On Tesa 2 Rd., 200m north of the rotary, just outside of the old city walls in the west.

Hospital: (☎055 714 223), on Ratchadamnoen Rd., 1km south of Charoensuk Rd.

Internet Access: At an unnamed Internet cafe, on Tesa 1 Rd., just south of Tesa 1 Soi 11 10ß per hr. **B-Net,** near Three J Guesthouse on Ratchavithi Rd., also has Internet. 10ß per hr. Open daily 8am-10pm.

Kamphaeng Phet

▲ ACCOMMODATIONS
Phet Hotel, **5**
Three J Guest House, **3**

● FOOD
Lee La Restaurant, **2**
M&P Coffee Corner, **4**
Tasty Cafe, **1**

Post office: Tesa 1 Soi 1. 200m south of the rotary. Open M-F 8:30am-4:30pm, Sa-Su 9am-noon. **Postal Code:** 62000.

ACCOMMODATIONS

Friendly owners, reasonable prices, and great amenities make an overnight stay in Kamphaent Phet quite enjoyable.

Three J Guest House, 79 Ratchavithi Rd. (☎055 713 129), about 2km northwest of the center rotary. Run by the incredibly kind, English-speaking Charin family. Twelve clean, small, rooms cluster around a teak terrace and verdant garden. Mr. Charin's breakfasts of fruit salad covered in yogurt (45฿) and toast with a poached egg (45฿) are a highlight. Laundry, and telephone available. Also offers agro-tourism homestay in a truly beautiful and relaxing house in the mountains 50km away for 800-1300฿ per night. Free transportation to the bus station upon departure. Internet 30฿ per hr. Rooms with fan and shared bath 200฿, with private bath 300฿, with hot shower and A/C 400฿. ❷

Phet Hotel, 189 Bamrungrat Rd., (☎055 712 8105) three hundred meters east of Ratchadamnoen Rd., across from the 7-Eleven. The fanciest and most popular choice in town. The spacious, well-equipped rooms show their age, but the karaoke lounge, pub, and 2 restaurants help to tip the scales. American breakfast included. Expensive Internet 50฿ per min. Singles 500฿; doubles 650/750฿. ❹

FOOD

The town's **day market,** off Bamrungrat Rd. at Vijit Rd., features rows of fresh produce and fish. For after-dark fare, Kamphaeng Phet's enclosed **night market,** just south of the Chamber of Commerce on Tesa 1 Rd., is a particularly raucous good time with a lot of delicious food stalls.

Tasty Cafe, 115-119 Tesa 1 Rd., between Tesa 1 Soi 11 and Tesa 1 Soi 13. No English sign—look for "Food, Ice Cream, Beverage" on the window. Reminiscent of an old-time American diner, Tasty Cafe serves snack-sized portions of rice dishes, noodle dishes, and ice cream to a crowd mostly made up of local families. English menu available. Dishes 45-65฿. Chocolate sundae 45฿. Open daily 10:30am-10:30pm. ❷

M&P Coffee Corner, across the street from Wat Bang, has a colorful feel and a lengthy English-language food and coffee menu. Cappuccino 50฿. Thai dishes 35-100฿. Open M-F 11am-10pm. ❷

Lee La Restaurant, 125 Tesa 1 Rd., 2 doors down from Tasty Cafe. No English sign—look for the cabin-like building seemingly carved from a giant block of wood. With small lamps, cow skeletons mounted on the wall, and live music most nights, Lee La is the place to go for a night out in Kamphaeng Phet. Dishes 50-120฿. Beer 75-95฿. Open daily 5pm-1am. ❷

SIGHTS

OLD CITY. Both a moat and the partially visible remains of a fort wall encircle the ruins of old Kamphaeng Phet on the northern edge of the modern town. The main attractions of the Old City are **Wat Phra Kaew** and **Wat Phra That,** situated right next to each other in a beautifully maintained park. Around the 16th century, Wat Phra Kaew was the biggest temple in Thailand, of such importance that it supposedly housed the Emerald Buddha (now in Bangkok, p. 110). Centuries of weather have worn down much of the structure, but the remaining Buddha images, columns, and bell-shaped *chedi* display a striking smoothness of form. The square faces, joined eyebrows, and almond-shaped eyes of the two sitting and single reclining Buddha statues suggest the U Thong

LOCAL LEGEND

MAUNG MAUNG TINN

Many artists and writers over the past 20 years have attempted to capture the plight of the displaced Burmese in Thailand. Few have succeeded as beautifully and poignantly as Mae Sot's local painter, Maung Maung Tinn.

Tinn fled Myanmar in 1994 and began working as a cook at Dr. Cynthia's Mae Tao Clinic for refugees. In his spare time, he painted pictures of those suffering around him and would give his work the volunteers at the clinic. Having had only one summer of formal training, Tinn was startled when people showed interest in purchasing his works.

Now, Tinn's art is known world-renowned. Tinn's supporters claim he is able to capture the emotions of his subjects, and that the textures of his pieces are unique for water color. A collection of Tinn's paintings have been exhibited in art museums across Europe since 2007. He now spends a good portion of every day painting; he spends the rest of the day volunteering at Dr. Cynthia's Mae Tao Clinic for refugees.

Linn's dream is to return home to a liberated country and open an orphanage for Burmese children, where he would teach painting.

Maung Maung Tinn is a regular at Casa Mia restaurant, where his postcards and book, *On the Border*, are available for purchase. A short biography and many of his works can be seen at his website, www.burmesepaintings.org.

style of the early Ayutthaya period. Wat Phra That, just southeast of Wat Phra Kaew, is a similarly preserved temple made of laterite and brick. *(Open daily 8am-6pm. Entrance booths at the north and south of the park in the Old City; you can buy tickets to both the Old City and the Arunyik Temples for, 40฿ and a good map, 15฿, at all booths.)*

ARUNYIK (FOREST) TEMPLES. This tranquil forested area, only a few hundred meters behind Wat Phra Kaew, houses more than a dozen temples built by Sukhothai-era monks. These temples were originally constructed in the woods to foster the monks' meditative practices; today the area remains a relaxing and majestic environment for a leisurely walk or bike ride. The first big site on the left as you enter into this park is **Wat Phra Non,** once home to a pavilion housing a massive reclining Buddha. Today, only a lion sculpture, colossal laterite pillars, and traces of the temple's bathrooms remain.

A little north of Wat Phra Non is **Wat Phra Si Iriyabot** and its better-preserved four Buddha images. The square structure in the middle was designed to support a roof, which, in turn, protected the four niches, each containing a different Buddha: walking, reclining, sitting, and standing. Today, the standing figure is in the best condition. A few hundred meters down the road is the jewel of the Arunyik Temples: 68 stucco sculptures of elephants surrounding the lower base of a large, well-preserved temple, **Wat Chang Rawp.** The uppermost section of the temple has been completely destroyed, but climb up anyway for a great view of the area. *(To get to the Arunyik Temples from the Old City, head north on Hwy. 101 out of the Old City and take the left road when the Hwy. splits just outside the Old City walls, about 7km outside ot town. Two-hundred meters further is the Arunyik entrance. Open daily 8am-6pm. Old City and Arunyik Temples 40฿.)*

KAMPHAENG PHET NATIONAL MUSEUM. In other respects, a typical provincial Thai museum, this museum's most interesting artifact is its 500-year-old, 2.1m bronze Shiva statue. The statue's original location, which now features an exact replica, is 300m to the left as you exit the museum. Although Shiva is a Hindu deity, the Buddhist locals continue to venerate the statue. *(Next to the Regional Museum. Open W-Su 9am-4pm. 30฿.)*

KAMPHAENG PHET REGIONAL MUSEUM. A charming group of traditional teak buildings on stilts houses this endearing little museum, where difficult-to-understand push-button interactive displays introduce visitors to the ethnology of the region's hill tribes, as well as the history, archaeology, and architecture of the Kamphaeng

Phet area. (*To the southeast of Wat Phra That, inside the Old City but outside of the historic park. Open daily 9am-4pm. 10฿.*)

SUKHOTHAI   ☎055

Sukhothai is not one city but two. New Sukhothai is notable for little other than a lively market, an excellent selection of guesthouses, and some of the hottest weather in Thailand. Only 12km away, Old Sukhothai holds the spectacular ruins of the ancient kingdom where many Thais consider their nation to have been born. Sukhothai, or "Dawn of Happiness," grew and flourished in the 13th century and created the distinctive architecture and statuary that the city's ruins harbor today. The separation of Old from New Sukhothai—as well as the vast size of the ancient city—enables a visitor to be more fully immersed in the past than in other ancient Thai cities like Ayutthaya or Lopburi.

▛ TRANSPORTATION

Flights: The airport (☎055 612 448) is 26km out of town and privately owned by **Bangkok Airways** (☎055 613 075), at the Pailyn Hotel, on the road to the old city. Flights to **Bangkok** (2300฿). Departure tax 200฿. Shuttle bus from Sukhothai Travel Service to airport 90฿.

Buses: New **bus station** (☎055 614 529), 1.5km north of town, on Bypass Rd. White, red, and blue *songthaew* run along Bypass Rd. to town (daily until 6pm, 40฿). **Tuk-tuks** to town 50฿. Buses to: **Bangkok** (6-7hr., 21 per day 7:30am-11pm, 200-374฿) via **Ayutthaya** (5hr., 169฿); **Chiang Mai** (6hr., 12 daily 7:15am-8:15pm, 122-220฿) via **Tak** (1hr., every hr. 7:30am-6:15pm, 40-60฿); **Chiang Rai** (7hr.; 6:40, 9, 11:30am; 250฿); **Phrae** (4hr.; 8:40, 11:40am, 1:40, 4:10pm; 150฿); **Phitsanulok** (1hr., every 30min. 6:20am-8pm, 70฿). **Minibuses** to **Mae Sot** (3hr., 7 per day 8:30am-4pm, 150฿) leave from a traffic triangle off Charot Withi Thong Rd., west of the bridge.

Local Transportation: Tuk-tuks 20-40฿. **Samlor** 10-30฿. On Charot Withi Thong Rd., 200m west of the bridge, red-, white-, and blue-striped **songthaew** run to Old Sukhothai (every 20min. 6am-6pm, 30฿). A **bus** to Si Satchanalai runs from the bus station (every 30min. 7am-4:30pm, 50฿).

Rentals: Bicycles at the Historical Park 20-30฿ per day, at Si Satchanalai 20฿ per day. Tha-nin Motorbikes, 112 Charot Withi Thong Rd. (☎055 613 402), 20m past the Thai Farmers Bank, with 24hr. service, rents **motorbikes.** (Open daily 7am-8pm; 150-250฿ per day.)

✦ ▛ ORIENTATION AND PRACTICAL INFORMATION

New Sukhothai, 12km east of the old city and 427km north of Bangkok, spreads out along an L-shaped bend in the Yom River. **Charot Withi Thong Road** and **Singhawat Road** run parallel to the river (about 3 blocks east of it), and converge at Sukhothai's largest intersection, near the bend in the "L." From there, Charot Withi Thong Rd. crosses **Praruang Bridge** and continues to the old city. The road directly along the river, on the east side, is **Nikorn Kasaem Road,** while **Pravet Nakhon Road** runs along the west bank. **Highway 101** bypasses the town at its northern end.

Tourist Information: No tourist office in town. The best advice comes from the guest-houses, especially the helpful English-speaking staff at Ban Thai. Transportation schedules can be found at the bus station.

Tours: Sukhothai Travel Service, 327/6-7 Charot Withi Thong Rd. (☎055 613 075), books domestic and international flights. Open daily 8am-5pm.

Books: S.T. Bookstore, 41/2-3 Nikorn Kasaem Rd. (☎055 612 272), 100m from the bridge. Most books are in Thai, but the **Michael Map** (39฿) of Sukhothai is a practical, glossy souvenir. Open daily 8am-9pm.

Currency Exchange: Most banks that line Singhawat Rd. change currency and traveler's checks. **Thai Farmers Bank,** 134 Charot Withi Thong Rd. (☎055 611 932), west of the end of the bridge, has a Cirrus/MC/Plus/V **24hr. ATM.** Open M-F 8:30am-3:30pm.

Police: 263 Nikorn Kasaem Rd. (☎055 613 110), 250m beyond the post office. There is also a 24hr. **police booth** (☎613 112) downtown at the intersection of Charot Withi Thong Rd. and Ban Muang Rd., across from the northern end of the day market.

Medical Services: Patanavej Hospital, 89/9 Singhawat Rd. (☎055 621 502), 200m from the intersection of Singhawat and Charot Withi Thong Rd., on the right. Some English spoken. V. **Pharmacy** in hospital. Hospital and pharmacy open 24hr.

Telephones: The **CAT Telecom** office is 3km from town along Charot Withi Thong Rd., toward Old Sukhothai. Open M-F 8:30am-4:30pm, Sa 9am-noon. There are international payphones along Charot Withi Thong Rd. to the east of the bridge, and **Lenso phones** in front of the numerous 7-Elevens.

Internet Access: Net and Play, across from the night market, has a fast connection for 20฿ per hr., a rate among the cheapest in town. Min. 10฿. Open daily 10am-11pm.

New Sukhothai

🏠 ACCOMMODATIONS
Ban Thai Guest House, **7**
JJ Guest House, **4**
Riverhouse, **8**
TR Guesthouse, **5**
Vitoon Guesthouse, **1**

🍎 FOOD
Ban Thai Restaurant, **6**
Coffee Cup, **2**
Dream Cafe, **9**
Thai Noodles Sukhothai 2, **10**
⭐ NIGHTLIFE
Chopper Bar, **3**

Post Office: GPO, 241 Nikorn Kasaem Rd. (☎055 611 645), 1km south of the bridge. Poste Restante. Open M-F 8:30am-4:30pm, Sa-Su 9am-noon. **Postal Code:** 64000.

ACCOMMODATIONS

High-quality guesthouses cluster near the unseemly Yom River in New Sukhothai. All are located within easy walking distance of the town center. Those interested only in the ruins may find it easier to stay at one of the guesthouses across the street from the Historical Park in Old Sukhothai. Most of these fill up during Sukhothai's long tourist season (June-Feb.)—be sure to call a few days in advance.

Ban Thai Guest House, 38 Pravet Nakhon Rd. (☎055 610 163), on the west bank of the river in New Sukhothai. Impeccably clean, stylish rooms. Guests can retreat from the heat into the inviting restaurant, where they are treated as one of the family. Gleaming shared baths with hot water. The guesthouse's friendly English-speaking owners share a wealth of info and run excellent bike tours. Singles and doubles 200฿; bungalows with bath 300฿, with A/C 500฿. ❷

TR Guesthouse, 27/6 Pravet Nakhon Rd. (☎055 611 663; www.sukhothaibudgetguest-house.com), on the road behind the Thai Farmer's Bank. The 20 simple, well-maintained rooms in this converted apartment building all have private baths, and the beautiful new bungalows in the back are a particularly good deal for 2 people. Amenities includes a restaurant (open daily 7am-9pm), free Wi-Fi, motorbike rentals (150-250฿ per day), and free car parking. Rooms with fan 200฿, with hot water 250฿; with A/C 350-400; bungalows with fan, bath, and hot water 350฿. ❷

JJ Guesthouse, 122 Soi Maeramphan (☎055 620 095). Leaving the west end of the bridge, take the second right and walk to the end of the road; you'll see the sign to the left. Take a *tuk-tuk* after dark. This welcoming complex of large tiled rooms, in both bungalows and a larger mansion house, contains a restaurant, pool, and small garden, making it an excellent option for families. Rooms with fan, hot water, and baths 300-350฿; with A/C 450-500฿. Larger mansion rooms with fan, bath, and terrace 500-600฿. Bungalow with fan and TV 700-800฿, with A/C 800-900฿. ❸

Riverhouse, 7 Soi Kuhasuwan Rd. (☎055 620 396), 150m north of the Thai Farmers Bank. Visitors to this freshly scrubbed, traditional teak house will get a firsthand taste of Thai life in the old days. Mattresses on the darkwood floors have overhanging mosquito nets. The bungalows outside are nice but not as enchanting as the main house. Restaurant downstairs (open daily 6:30am-10pm). Motorbike rentals 150-250฿ per day. Massage 200฿ per hr. Free pickup from bus station when you call ahead. Doubles with fan and shared bath 200-250฿, bungalows with A/C and bath 400฿. ❶

Vitoon Guesthouse, 49 Moo 3 (☎055 697 045). Directly across from the Historical Park in Old Sukhothai. There are 2 separate establishments with the same name; the one slightly nearer to New Sukhothai has better prices. Staff is friendly and the blue tiled rooms are comfortable and clean. Bicycle rental (30฿ per day), Internet (30฿ per hr.). Rooms with private bath and fan 300฿, with A/C 500฿. ❸

FOOD

Much of central New Sukhothai is essentially a 24hr. market: the **day market** kicks off so early and the night market runs so late that the two almost converge. Day and night, there are **food stalls** along **Charot Withi Thong Rd.** on either side of the bridge, offering dinner and dessert. Try the *pad thai* (20-30฿)—it's a point of pride for the people of Sukhothai. In the area around the day market, vendors move onto the streets to sell a staggering variety of fresh fruits and vegetables. Because there is so much good street food in Sukhothai, there is little need to visit the restaurants unless you're seeking additional comfort and a more refined ambience.

■ **Thai Noodles Sukhothai 2,** 139 Charot Withi Thong Rd. (☎055 621 882). 300m past the school on the right, before the turnoff to Ruean Thai. Look for the hanging vegetation in front and a "2" on a sign in all-Thai script. Worth the considerable walk from town, this spacious restaurant serves inexpensive traditional Thai dishes in a relaxing environment. The specialty is *kuay tiaw sukhothai* (noodle soup with pork, green beans, coriander, and chili; 25฿). The top ½ of the Thai menu is noodles, the bottom is rice dishes. Open daily 7am-4pm. ❶

■ **Ban Thai Restaurant,** 38 Pravet Nakhon Rd., at Ban Thai Guest House. The communal seating makes this a great place to meet other travelers. Daily specials for the adventurous; traditional dishes are rewarded with imaginative presentation. Lemon-mint shakes 25฿. Vegetarian options. Open daily 6am-9pm. ❷

Coffee Cup, (☎055 633 480), next to Vitoon Guesthouse, across the street from the Historical Park in Old Sukhothai. Arrive early to enjoy the Western breakfasts (120-150฿) and excellent coffee (30฿). The menu is *farang*-oriented, but Thai dishes like traditional curries (80-100฿) are as tasty as the Western entrees (hamburger 80฿). Internet 30฿ per hr. Open daily 7am-10pm. ❷

Dream Cafe, 96/1 Singhawat Rd. (☎055 612 081), on the right side of the street with a prominent English sign. Crammed with Thai antiques, the moody interior of the Dream Cafe exudes a classy ambience. Order from the extensive Western and Thai menu, or try one of 9 different herbal elixirs promising to improve anything from strength to sexual desire—perhaps through their high alcohol content ("Buffalo race" and "tiger strength" 35฿ per shot). Dishes 80-220฿. Open daily 10am-11pm. MC/V. ❸

👁 🎵 SIGHTS AND ENTERTAINMENT

▨OLD SUKHOTHAI HISTORICAL PARK

To reach the park, located 12km west of New Sukhothai, take the striped red, white, and blue songthaew that leave from the side of Charot Withi Thong Rd. 200m west of Praruang Bridge (20min., every 20min. 6am-6pm, 30฿). Park ☎055 611 110. Open daily 6am-7pm, but most individual wats close at 4:30pm. Old City Entrance pedestrian 40฿, bike 50฿, motorbike 60฿, car 90฿; North, West, and South Entrances 70/80/90/120฿. Museum ☎055 612 167. Open daily 9am-4pm. Combined pass 150฿, includes all of Old Sukhothai's and Si Satchanalai's attractions, and is good for 30 days.

Old Sukhothai is one of Thailand's most revered sites. Sukhothai was the first definitive capital of Siam and reached its peak of power and wealth around AD 1300. The Sukhothai era has often been treated as Thailand's "golden age": art, architecture, and Buddhism flourished at Sukhothai, taking on distinctively Thai forms, and King Ramkhamhaeng devised the first Thai alphabet here.

The Historical Park itself is a vast expanse of grass, trees, and ponds, interspersed with the remains of the ancient city's *wats*. You'll want to rent a **bicycle** or **motorbike** to see everything, especially if you plan to explore the area outside the city walls (available across the street from the park entrance; bikes 20-50฿, motorbikes 150-250฿). Still, even if you have your own transportation, there are enough sights here to occupy the better part of a day.

Those taking a motorbike may want to consider a scenic alternate route from New to Old Sukhothai, which replaces 12km of highway driving with quiet roads surrounded by rice fields and farmhouses on both sides. Leaving New Sukhothai from the west end of the bridge, turn left at the first traffic light. After about 6km, turn right at the sign for the Tham Me Ya waterfall. Drive along this road until you see a four-way intersection with a stop sign, and take a right. After about 10km, you'll T-intersect with the highway from New to Old Sukhothai. A left turn will bring you to the Historical Park.

Four Saturdays a year from June-September there is an impressive light and sound show, which includes fireworks and classical performances. Call the Sukhothai Tourism Business Association for reservations (☎055 647 225).

MAIN ENTRANCE AND RAMKHAMHAENG NATIONAL MUSEUM. To the left of the east gate should be every visitor's first stop, the impressive and informative **Ramkhamhaeng National Museum.** It traces the chronology of ancient Sukhothai, exhibits Buddha images found in the excavations, and displays a replica of Ramkhamhaeng's Thai script. *(Songthaew from Sukhothai arrive at the east gate, which is the main entrance. Museum sells excellent brochures for 3฿. Nearby bike rentals 20-30฿.)*

INSIDE THE OLD CITY WALL. Once the religious and political heart of the royal city, 13th-century **Wat Mahathat** is Sukhothai's largest temple. The main *chedi* is famed for its lotus-bud shape, a distinctive Sukhothai architectural feature that recurs in the 198 *chedis* scattered across the temple grounds. Many of the ornate carvings around the *wat* remain in stellar condition. Nearby **Wat Sri Sawai,** a south-facing temple with three large *prangs* in the Lopburi style, is the only Sukhothai ruin that doesn't face east—a legacy of its Hindu origins. Indeed, fragments of Hindu images remain in the *wat*. **Wat Sra Sri,** located north of Wat Mahathat, is one of the most picturesque locations in the park. Its *chedi* and Buddha occupy a small island surrounded by a palm-lined lake. The small gazebo, with views across the water, is a prime spot for a picnic.

NORTH OF THE OLD CITY WALL. North of San Luang Gate, secluded *Wat Phra Phai Luang* sits on an island encircled by a moat. On one of the *wat*'s three towers, well-preserved plaster reliefs depict the life of the Buddha, and the Khmer-inspired architecture offers evidence of cultural contact between Sukhothai and the Khmer empire. Spectacular ◪**Wat Sri Chum,** arguably the highlight of the entire park, rests just above the northwest corner of the city walls. Its *mondop*, a cone-shaped structure, houses the must-see 15m "talking" Buddha. As the legend goes, the great King Ramkhamhaeng gathered the troops he was assembling for war in front of the massive Buddha image at the *wat*. In a terrifyingly supernatural display, he compelled the image to speak and urge the soldiers to fight bravely. (Since those days, a hidden staircase has been discovered that leads to an opening behind the Buddha's mouth.) The now-blocked tunnels, on your right and left as you enter the temple, served as escape passages for the king. The *wat* is worth visiting for its storied history and stunning visuals. It is one of Thailand's most photographed sites for good reason.

WEST OF THE OLD CITY WALL. In the area west of the city wall, ruins mingle with rice fields, cows, and traditional farmhouses on stilts. Most of the ruins here, although well-marked with English signs and not far off the road, are in varying states of decay. Still, the proximity of the jungle can make this area more rewarding to explore than the manicured park within the city walls. A **bicycle** or **motorbike** is an absolute necessity, however. At **Wat Mungkorn,** with its distinctive circular *chedi*, the road splits, and to the left lies **Saritphong (Phra Ruang Dam),** an earthen dam 487m long and 4m wide, which today can hold up to 400,000 cu. m of water. The water was piped to the city in Sukhothai's glory days. The road to the right of Wat Mungkorn leads back to the main road between Sukhothai and Tak, but not before passing the long laid-stone staircase up to **Wat Saphan Hin,** 200m up the hill. The *wat* contains a towering Buddha in a standing position, known as **Phra Attharot,** and offers a striking view of the area. *(If you're approaching this western area from the northwest corner of the park, or from*

Wat Sri Chum, take the road toward Tak and turn left at the sign for the Sukhothai Boyscout Camp. After a few km, you'll see Wat Saphan Hin on the right.)

OTHER SIGHTS AND ENTERTAINMENT

Most visitors stick to the Historical Park, but the region surrounding Sukhothai also has a number of interesting attractions. Daily bicycle tours led by the friendly English-speaking staff of the Ban Thai Guesthouse are a great way to see the area. Options include tours to **Wat Thawet,** rice-farming villages surrounding Sukhothai, and the old city's historical park. Both evening and day-long tours (250-650฿ per person) are available.

The **Sangkhalok Museum** displays 700-year-old Lanna pottery and is only worth the trek from town if you're an aficionado of Sukhothai-period pottery. *(It is 1.5km outside of town. Follow Singhawat Rd. out of the city as it turns into Hwy. 12 (toward Phit-sanulok. Turn left at the 1st major intersection. Hwy. 101; the museum is 100m on the left. ☎ 055 614 333. Open daily 8am-5pm. 100฿, children 17 and under 50฿.)*

A popular nightspot for tourists and Thais alike is the **Chopper Bar,** 101 Charot Withi Thong Rd., down the street from the **TR Guesthouse** and just past the block with the Thai Farmer's Bank. A balcony overlooking the street and décor comprised of mixed and matched American motifs—flag, antlers, nautical gear—somehow comes together in a friendly, low-key environment. Live music during the high season. Try the trio of drinks that includes the Gimlet, Vimlet, and Rimlet. *(☎ 055 611 190. Open nightly 4-10pm. Mixed drinks 60-65฿. Large Singha 70฿.)*

◤ DAYTRIP FROM SUKHOTHAI: SI SATCHANALAI AND CHALIANG

Old Si Satchanalai is 56km north of Sukhothai, and the park entrance is 1km west off Hwy. 101. Take a public bus from Sukhothai bus station (1hr., every 30min. 7am-4:30pm, 38-45฿). Make sure the driver knows you are getting off at the old city (muang kao), as new Si Satchanalai is 8km farther north. Last bus from Hwy. 101 returns before 5pm. ☎ 679 211. Park open daily 8am-5pm. 40฿. Admission to Chaliang is included in Si Satchanalai admission; its park hours are the same. Kilns open daily 8am-4:30pm. 30฿.

During its golden age in the 13th century, Si Satchanalai rivaled neighboring Sukhothai in wealth and sophistication, but when Ayutthaya rose to preeminence in the late 14th century, it sank into anonymity. A World Heritage Site, the historic park here has excellent tourist facilities, including an **Information Center** marked by signs from the roads entering the park. The **park entrance** has brochures and maps. Near the entrance, you can rent bikes (20฿), sleeping bags (20฿), and tents (80฿). Despite its historical significance and impressive Sukhothai-style ruins, Si Satchanalai doesn't receive many visitors. Locals like to say that Old Si Satchanalai and Old Sukhothai are two beautiful women—but only Sukhothai is dressed up. The park's *wats* lie within a moat beside the Mae Nom Yom River, and the town of Chaliang, also the site of significant excavations, lies 2km downriver.

The bus drops you off along the main road, south of Chaliang. You can rent a bicycle here (20฿) or at the park entrance. From the bus dropoff, walk through the elaborate gate and across the suspended footbridge. After crossing the bridge, you'll find yourself in Chaliang, with clear English signs marking the way to Si Satchanalai. The major ruins in Chaliang, **Wat Phra Si Rattana Mahathat,** have their own separate admission fee (10฿). This fifteenth-century *wat* holds an excellent example of the distinctive Sukhothai-style walking Buddha. Continue toward Si Satchanalai from the *wat* to a turn off 500m past the *wat*, the site of an archeological excavation where human remains confirm the presence of a community predating the Sukhothai period.

Houses, minor ruins, and food stands line the road to the park entrance. Inside the Si Satchanalai park, **Wat Chang Lom** is the city's central *wat* and remains in good condition, with bas-relief elephant heads encircling the *stupa*. According to ancient inscriptions, King Ramkhamhaeng ordered the temple's construction in 1287. Across the road, **Wat Chedi Chet Thaew** contains *stupas* in a mix of northern, southern, and local styles. The largest of these is a copy of Sukhothai's Wat Mahathat. Farther on, Sinhalese-style **Wat Nang Phaya** is notable for its magnificent stucco reliefs on one wall of the *wihaan*. On the hill overlooking Wat Chang Lom, **Wat Khao Phanom Phloeng** has preserved a nice *chedi* and seated Buddha; from here, the layout of the ancient city can be seen.

A 5km bicycle ride north of the historic park, the vast **Sawankhalok Kilns** are remnants of the many riverside pottery kilns that filled this area during the Sukhothai era. The kilns produced advanced celadons (ceramics known today as *sawankhalok* or *sangkhalok*) for export to countries as far away as the Philippines. The Siam Cement Company has spent 2-3 million baht making a few of these kilns accessible to tourists; two of these, kilns #42 and 123, are 5km northwest of Si Satchanalai, along the river.

LAMPANG ☎054

Lampang's history dates back to the 7th-century Dvaravati period, when it played an integral role in the Lanna Kingdom. Today, it's a typical mid-sized Thai town, with sprawling, congested streets that are full of activity all day. The riverside is a peaceful contrast, especially as dusk falls. Because Lampang is within easy range of several noteworthy sights, it's a convenient stop on the way to or from Chiang Mai.

▣ TRANSPORTATION

Flights: Airport on Sanambin Rd., 2km south of the town center. **Thai Airways** has flights to **Bangkok** (W 10:45am, 7pm; 2660฿). Purchase tickets from **Lampang Holiday** (☎054 310 403) on Chatchai Rd., next to the clock tower. PB Air, at the airport (☎054 226 238; open daily 8:30am-5pm) flies to **Bangkok** (daily 10:45am, 5pm; 2725฿).

Trains: Lampang Train Station (☎054 318 648), on Prasanmaitri Rd., 2km southwest of the clock tower. To reach the station, flag down a westbound *songthaew* (25฿). Trains to **Bangkok** (10-12hr., 6 per day, 216-1272฿) via **Phitsanulok** (5hr., 48-942฿) and **Ayutthaya** (9hr., 205-1220฿), and **Chiang Mai** (2hr., 8 per day, 23฿).

Buses: Bus station (☎054 227 410), off Asia 1 Hwy., 2km southwest of the clock tower. To: **Bangkok** (8hr., every hr. 7:30am-9pm, 347-446฿); **Chiang Mai** (2hr., every 30min. 5am-9pm, 67-87฿); **Chiang Rai** (5hr., every hr. 5am-5pm, 101-143฿); **Khorat** (10hr., 9 per day 5am-9:30pm, 271-488฿); **Nan** (4hr., 11 per day 8am-midnight, 107-295฿); **Phitsanulok** (4hr., every hr. 5am-4:30pm, 138-248฿) via **Sukhothai** (3hr., 116-162฿); **Udon Thani** (9hr., 6 per day 9am-9pm, 252-454฿) via **Loei** (8hr., 191-351฿).

Local Transportation: Blue **songthaew** go anywhere in town from the bus and train stations (30฿). **Samlor** 30-50฿. **Num's Tourism**, 235/1 Boonyawat Rd. (☎05 037 5431), rents **motorbikes** (250฿ per day). **Riverside Guesthouse** (p. 318) rents motorbikes (200฿ per day with passport deposit) and **bicycles** (40-60฿ per day).

✦ ▨ ORIENTATION AND PRACTICAL INFORMATION

The town center is roughly between the post office and clock tower. **Boonyawat Road,** the town's main commercial road, runs east-west, passing hotels, banks, and shops. **Thipchang Road,** another commercial avenue, runs parallel to Boonyawat Rd. **Talad Gao Road,** a block north of Thipchang Rd., hugs the **Wang**

River and houses popular guesthouses and restaurants; it is a lot quieter than Boonyawat Rd. and Thipchang Rd. The busy **Chatchai Road** leads southwest from the clocktower to the bus station, on **Jantsurin Road,** and the train station, on **Prasanmaitri Road,** both about 2km away.

Tourist Office: (☎054 218 823), on Boonyawat Rd., 1 block past Praisanee Rd. Set back 50m from the road. English spoken. Offers a free tourist brochure also available from guesthouses or the bus station. Open M-F 8:30am-4:30pm.

Tours: The **horse-cart stands,** 1 opposite the police station on Boonyawat Rd. and several near the clocktower, arrange tours—a unique but expensive way to see the town (15min. 150ℬ; 30min. 200ℬ; 1hr. 200-300ℬ).

Currency Exchange: Banks line Boonyawat Rd. **Bangkok Bank,** 36-44 Thipchang Rd. (☎054 228 135). AmEx/Cirrus/MC/Plus/V **24hr. ATM.** Open M-F 8:30am-3:30pm.

Markets: Tesaban Market 1, near the city hall, at Boonyawat and Rajawang Rd., sells primarily fruit and clothing. Open daily 6am-7pm. On Sa-Su evenings from 6-10pm, Talad Gao Rd. is closed to traffic and it becomes an extensive market.

Police: (☎054 217 017), on Boonyawat Rd., opposite city hall.

Pharmacy: (☎224 333), on the corner, at Boonyawat and Praisanee Rd. Open daily 8am-9pm.

Medical Services: Khelang Nakorn-Ram Hospital, 79/12 Phaholyothin Rd. (☎225 100). English-speaking doctors. Open 24hr. AmEx/MC/V.

Telephones: Lampang Telecommunication Center, 99 Phaholyothin Rd. (☎054 221 700), 500m before the hospital, heading to the bus station. International phone, fax, and Internet access. Open M-F 8:30am-4:30pm.

Internet Access: Monkey Jump Online, 50m east of Tip Inn on Talad Gao Rd. 15ℬ per hr. Open daily 9am-10pm.

Post Office: GPO (☎054 224 069), on Thipchang Rd., at the intersection with Praisanee Rd. Poste Restante. Open M-F 8:30am-4:30pm, Sa-Su 9am-noon. **Postal Code:** 52000.

▟ ACCOMMODATIONS

Lampang isn't a tourist destination in its own right, so guesthouses can be hard to find. The best are along the river.

Riverside Guest House, 286 Talad Gao Rd. (☎054 227 005). At the western end of Talad Gao Rd. From the antique-decorated riverside lobby to the large, tasteful rooms, Riverside Guesthouse exudes elegance and charm. The garden that weaves its way from the front of the building to the back is especially beautiful. Laundry. Bike rental 60ℬ per day, motorbikes 200ℬ per day. ½-day tours of surrounding sights 350ℬ per person, 900ℬ min.; full-day tours 500/1200ℬ. Singles with shared bath 250ℬ, doubles 300ℬ, riverside 400ℬ, suites 600ℬ. ❷

Tip Inn, 143 Talad Gao Rd. (☎054 221 821). From Suandok Rd., take a right on Talad Gao Rd.; Tip Inn is on the right. On the bottom floor are a restaurant and lounge, and upstairs are the spacious rooms, with cheery red walls. Internet 30ℬ per hr. Rooms with shared bath 150ℬ, with private bath 250ℬ. ❷

9 Mituna, 285 Boonyawat Rd. (☎054 217 438), in a parking lot near the western end of Boonyawat Rd. before it reaches the clock tower. The newly painted rooms in this multi-story concrete building don't have much character, but they're a good value. Rooms with A/C also have bathtubs and Western toilets. Singles with bath and squat toilet 143ℬ, doubles 204ℬ; with A/C 265ℬ. ❷

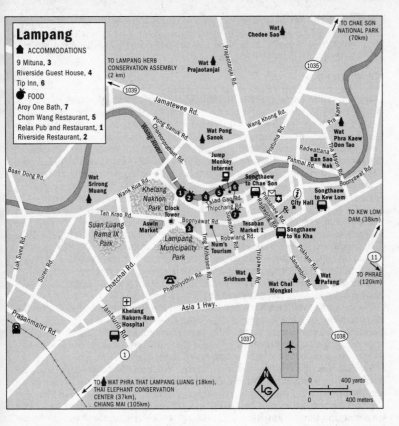

Lampang

⛺ ACCOMMODATIONS
9 Mituna, **3**
Riverside Guest House, **4**
Tip Inn, **6**
🍎 FOOD
Aroy One Bath, **7**
Chom Wang Restaurant, **5**
Relax Pub and Restaurant, **1**
Riverside Restaurant, **2**

🍴 FOOD

There are plenty of affordable places to eat in Lampang. **Aswin Market,** in the soi off Tah Krao Rd., has cheap eats. Open daily 4pm-midnight.

Riverside Restaurant (☎054 221 861), on Thipchang Rd., just around the corner from Riverside Guest House, which is under the same ownership. The cozy outdoor terrace is softly lit and overlooks the river below. The food is good enough that it attracts locals as well as *farang*. Northern dishes 60-90฿. Pizza Tu-Th and Sa-Su 100-150฿. Live music begins nightly at 8pm. Open daily 11am-midnight. ❸

Aroy One Bath (☎081 5948 333), on the corner of Suandok Rd. and Thipchang Rd. This local favorite gets packed after dark, when families eat regional specialties on the outdoor patio. Entrees 20-40฿. Open daily 4pm-midnight. ❷

Chom Wang Restaurant, 276 Talad Gao Rd. (☎054 222 845), 100m east of Riverside Guest House along Talad Gao Rd.; turn down the soi with the Coca-Cola sign. Local and Chinese dishes served on a leafy outdoor deck. Baked lemon-flavored shrimp in hot pot 100฿. Burmese pork curry 80฿. Fried chicken in banana leaves 60฿. Open daily 11am-midnight. ❸

Relax Pub and Restaurant, adjacent to the Riverside Restaurant. The currently popular hotspot for young and trendy locals, with indoor and outdoor seating. The menu includes fried rice with meat (45฿) and seafood soups (60-80฿). Band starts at 8pm. Open daily 5pm-midnight. ❷

👁 SIGHTS

Despite its rather stodgy name, the 🏠**Lampang Herb Conservation Assembly** (☎054 350 787; www.herblpg.com) is one of the most fascinating destinations in Lampang. Though it's only a few kilometers outside of town, its off-the-beaten-path location makes public transportation difficult, so private transportation is the best option. Once you arrive, this spa and research center, set in a lush garden, has the remedy for whatever ails you. There are 116 herbal products for sale, designed to do everything from promote appetite to improve sexual potency. A catalogue in English explains properties of the products. This place claims it is sitting on a gold mine if the "medicinal plant for AIDS immunity" works—but *Let's Go* begs you not to count on it. A much more practical buy is **Porng Karn Yoong Tar Klai Hom** (#104), a citronella oil-based insect repellent (20-60฿). The body-cleansing options are extensive (herbal vapor bath 100฿, herbal bath 150฿, face scrub 50฿, body scrub with herbs 200฿), and massages (100฿ per hr., with herbal oil 300฿) are also available.*(To get there, drive west on Jamatawee Rd. (Hwy. 1039) for approximately 2km. When you see signs for the center, turn right on the street across from the 7-Eleven, go down it for 400m, and then turn left on the road just before the bridge; the center is 200m down on your left. Open daily 8am-7pm.)*

The beautiful **Wat Phra Kaew Don Tao** housed the Emerald Buddha during the 32-year reign of King Anantayot. The 50m *chedi* contains a hair of the Lord Buddha, while a building to its left holds a large golden reclining Buddha. The *wihaan* is open to visitors only on Buddhist holidays. *(Cross the river and turn right after you see signs for the wat. Wat open daily 6am-6:30pm. 20฿.)*

Ban Sao Nak, the "House of Many Pillars," is a large teak structure that sits north of the Wang River. Mentioning this restored masterpiece conjures up significant pride for the people of Lampang, as the Crown Prince and Princess Consort honored this spot by having lunch here on a bright day in 1977. The owner at that time, Khunying Valai Leelanuj, whose grandfather built the house in 1895, has since passed away, and the house is now open to the public as a museum. The history of the house is engaging, but a visit will be most memorable to those interested in traditional Lanna architecture. Most artifacts and exhibits have no labels, but there is a small English brochure. *(6 Ratwattana Rd. ☎054 221 808; www.baansaonak.com. Open daily 10am-5pm. 50฿, includes free soft drink.)*

▓ DAYTRIPS FROM LAMPANG

WAT PHRA THAT LAMPANG LUANG. About 18km southwest of Lampang, in the town of Ko Kha, sits **Wat Phra That Lampang Luang,** one of northern Thailand's finest displays of religious architecture. Its giant *chedi* and low wooden buildings also hold Lampang province's most sacred Buddha. Through the main gate lies the central *wihaan*, an open-air Lanna-style structure supported by 46 laterite columns. Constructed in 1486, the chapel houses two important Buddha images: **Phra Jao Lan Tang,** cast in 1563 and enclosed in a golden *mondop* near the rear of the temple, and **Phra Jao Tan Jai,** which sits behind the *mondop*. Directly behind the *wihaan*, the *chedi* houses relics of the Buddha. **Wihaan Naamtaen,** to the right of the *chedi*, displays murals dating from 1501, while a 700-year-old Buddha image rests inside **Phra Phuttha Wihaan,** to the left of the *chedi*. Inside, to the left of the entrance, there is a mesmerizing demonstration of how sunlight is reflected off the golden *chedi* and onto a white screen. An indistinct Buddha footprint lies within **Haw Phra Phutthabat,** a white building constructed in 1149 that only men can enter.

Beyond the back wall, a shrine showcases the temple's most valuable Buddha image, a jade Buddha from the Chiang Saen period (1057-1757). In April, during the Thai New Year, the image steals the limelight in a procession through the streets of Lampang. On the way to the jade Buddha are several small museums that house an eclectic mix of artifacts sans labels or information. *(Songthaew to Ko Kha leave from the bus station and Robwiang Rd., 1 block west of Praisanee Rd. (30฿). The wat is 3km north of Ko Kha—negotiate with a motorcycle taxi in Ko Kha (30-50฿). If driving from Lampang, take Asia Hwy. 1 south and take the exit for Ko Kha (Hwy. 1034), then look for signs to the wat on your left. If arriving from the Thai Elephant Conservation Center or Chiang Mai, there's no need to backtrack all the way to Lampang; from Hwy. 11, look for signs for Hwy. 1034 leading to the wat and Ko Kha.)*

THAI ELEPHANT CONSERVATION CENTER. The Thai Elephant Conservation Center, 37km west of Lampang, is on the highway between Chiang Mai and Lampang, outside the Thung Kwian Forest. Elephants begin training here at age five and continue under one master until age 71, when they retire from their job. The center was established to employ elephants and their *mahouts* (handlers) in new pursuits, given their decreasing importance in traditional industries such as logging and construction. Shows feature the animals walking in procession, skillfully maneuvering teak logs, *wai*-ing the crowd, and creating modern masterpieces with brushes dipped in brightly colored paint. Afterward, you can take a ride on your own elephant. (10min. 50฿, 30min. 400฿. Rides daily 8am-3:30pm.) The center also has a homestay program that lets you stay and work with mahouts.

The conservation center includes a government-sponsored elephant hospital, but the site is more famous for its **Friends of Asian Elephant (FAE) Hospital.** After the turnoff for the conservation center, bear right at the fork, and follow the signs for 200m. Founder Soraida Salawala helps treat injured and sick elephants from around the region. The hospital's most famous patient was the three-ton Motola, who stepped on a Burmese landmine in August 1999, losing her front left foot. After an agonizing three-day trek to safety, Motola arrived at the hospital, where doctors immediately pumped her full of elephant-strength painkillers. The operation to amputate her injured limb earned the hospital a citation in the 1999 Guiness Book of World Records for the most number of vets involved in one procedure: 30 vets helped mend Motola. Vets later fitted Motola with a metal prosthesis. *(Take a Chiang Mai-bound bus and ask to be let off at the Center (35min., 35฿). Shuttle buses travel the 2km to the show ground. If driving, the center is located on Hwy. 11, 37km west of Lampang. ☎054 247 876; www.thailandelephant.org. 30min. Shows daily 10 and 11am, and 1:30pm on weekends. Elephant bathing 9:45am and 1:15pm. 70฿, includes shuttle bus.)*

CHAE SON (JAE SORN) NATIONAL PARK AND KEW LOM DAM. This award-winning national park boasts modern facilities and **hot springs.** The springs' main draw is not the bubbling sulfurous pools that reach temperatures of 70-80°C, but rather the luxurious private baths (50฿) or shared baths (20฿). A less private but still satisfying option is to plunge into the river where the water from the hot spring merges pleasantly with the river water. **Chae Son Waterfall,** plummeting 150m over six tiers, lies 1km farther up the road. The engineering feat that is the concrete staircase leading to the fall's source is more imposing than the waterfall itself. An easy 3km nature trail along the river links the two sites. The **Kew Lom Dam** is a relaxing spot favored by Thai and *farang* alike. Packed during the holidays, the island can be reached by boat (100฿). Make bungalow reservations with the Royal Irrigation Department (☎02 241 4806) or Wang Kew Lom

Resort (☎054 223 733). *(To catch a songthaew to Chae Son Falls, 70km from Lampang, go to the dirt parking lot next to the soi running between Thipchang and Talad Gao Rd., across from the intersection with Rajawong Rd. (1hr., 90฿). The first songthaew leaves around 10am. Returning will be difficult; Let's Go does not recommend hitchhiking, but families visiting Sa-Su may offer rides. If driving, take Pratum Rd. (Hwy. 1035) north from Lampang. Camping permitted, 30฿. Tent rental for 2 people 180฿, for 3 people 250฿. 4- to 40-person bungalows 900-4000฿. Park open daily 6am-6pm. Park admission 200฿, students 100฿. Waterfall 200฿. Songthaew to Kew Lom Dam run from Phaholyothin Rd., 400m east of the intersection with Prasinee Rd., past the school, but you may have to charter one or use private transportation. If driving, take Asia Hwy. 1 north, then follow the signs for the turnoff. Kew Lom Dam is 38km north of Lampang. Open daily 8:30am-5pm.)*

THA TON   ☎053

Tha Ton is little more than a few buildings huddled along the side of the road, without even a 7-Eleven to its name. Most of the year, it lies dormant, with a 30 ft. white Buddha guarding its rest. Then, in November and December, boatloads of tourists descend upon it to see the hill-tribe villages and natural treasures lining the shores of the Kok River. While there's little to do in town, an afternoon on the beautiful terraces of Wat Tha Ton showcases stunning views of the surrounding countryside.

▐ TRANSPORTATION

Buses: Leave from the north side of the bridge. Orange buses to **Chiang Mai** (4hr., 6 per day 6:30am-2:30pm, 120฿) depart from a lot 100m north of the river, behind the Tha Ton Chalet. The bus from **Fang** to **Mae Sai** (2½hr., arrives in Tha Ton daily at 3pm, 80฿) passes through town; flag it down when it checks in with the unmarked police box just beyond the bus lot. For **Chiang Rai,** take a Mae Sai-bound bus to **Mae Chan** (1hr., 30฿) and wait for a connecting bus (45min., 20฿).

Songthaew: Yellow **songthaew** head to **Fang** (45min., every 10min. 5:30am-3pm, 25฿) and to **Kiew Satai** (45min., every 30min., 30฿) from a lot north of the bridge, around the bend. From Kiew Satai, yellow *songthaew* run to **Mae Salong** (1hr., every hr., 40฿) and **Mae Chan.**

Boats: Longtail boats leave from the pier on the river's south bank for **Chiang Rai** (4hr. with a 20min. stop in Ruammit, 12:30pm, 350฿), on the soi just south of the bridge. Reserve a seat at the **Tha Ton Boat Office,** by the pier. (☎053 459 427. Open daily 8am-6pm.) Chartered private crafts (seat 6-8, 1900฿) won't leave after 3pm, since the ride is dangerous in the dark. In the high season, put together your own group of 6 so you can combine a trip on the river with stops in the villages.

✦ ? ORIENTATION AND PRACTICAL INFORMATION

Tha Ton's main road is Route 1089, which continues northeast across the river 62km to Mae Chan. Mae Salong is 43km away, Chiang Rai 92km, and Chiang Mai 175km. Tha Ton has **no banks or exchange booths.** The nearest **ATM** is in Mae Ai, 9km south of town. The closest **hospital** (☎459 036) is also in Mae Ai. In an emergency, call your guesthouse for transportation—ambulances are slower.

Tha Ton's services include: a **tourist police box,** just before the pier (☎07 804 9182; open daily 8:30am-4:30pm; 24hr. emergency); a **pharmacy,** in the convenience store next to the morning market (open daily 8am-8pm); **Tha Ton Internet,** across from the pier on the south side of the bridge, which also offers international phones (open daily 10:30am-8pm; 30฿ per hr.); and the newspaper stand, 100m south of the market, opposite the entrance to Wat Tha Ton, which acts as the **local post office** (open M-F 8am-noon and 1-4:30pm). **Postal Code:** 50280.

ACCOMMODATIONS

Most of Tha Ton's accommodations, including the amusingly out-of-place Thaton Chalet, are targeted to the high-season tourist crowds. But there are a few excellent budget options, all located north of the bridge, down the first road on the left. The nicest is **Garden Home ❷**, 200m down the road and 100m past the Tha Ton Garden Riverside. Bamboo bungalows are scattered across a huge tropical fruit garden, complete with riverside beach and waterfront restaurant. Trekking services and motorbike rental are available. (☎053 495 325. Rooms with fan and hot shower 200฿, bungalows with hot shower 300฿, larger bungalows closer to river with A/C 600฿, massive stone bungalows on river 1300-1500฿. Prices increase Nov.-Dec.) **Tha Ton Garden Riverside ❷**, on the way to Garden Home from the main road, has bungalows in a garden along the river, with a restaurant overlooking the rushing water. The setting is less exotic but it's another fine option, nonetheless. (☎053 459 286. Singles with cold shower 150฿, with hot shower 200฿; doubles with hot shower 300฿; nicer bungalows with A/C and TV 500฿.)

FOOD

Most guesthouses in Tha Ton have their own restaurants. The best option is **Tha Ton Garden Riverside's restaurant ❷**, which has an english-menu and good *tom yum* soup with shrimp (50฿, open daily 7am-10pm). Local restaurants without names or menu line the main road on both sides of the bridge. The **small restaurant ❷**, across from the boat pier next to Tha Ton Internet, has a small English menu and serves cheap Thai fare. (Minced chicken with basil 50฿. Open daily 7:30am-7:30pm.) For a morning espresso, try **Coffee Mug ❷**, on the other side of Tha Ton Internet. (Latte 45฿.) There are **food stalls** just south of the river, and a **morning market** sets up 200m south of the bridge. (Open daily 5:30-7:30am.)

SIGHTS

Wat Tha Ton dominates the hillside south of the river. The temple features life-size representations of figures from Hindu, Buddhist, and Chinese mythology scattered on hillside terraces and in manmade caves, but the true gem is the fantastic view of the town and river. The easiest route up the hill begins at the arch across the road from the post office. When you reach the fork in the path marked by a large figure, turn left for the golden dragon-headed Buddha or right for the 12m tall white Buddha. Follow the road from the golden dragon-headed Buddha at the top to reach the stunning new temple complex.

The **Kok River**, which originates in the mountains of Myanmar's Shan states, enters Thailand above Tha Ton and flows 200km to meet the Mekong River in Chiang Saen. **Phatai** is a Black Lahu village on the north bank. **Jakue** has a Catholic missionary school and numerous Lahu products for sale. **Pha Khang** boasts a backdrop of picturesque mountains, and **Pha Keau** features rapids. The stop everyone makes is at **Ruammit,** 45min. from Chiang Rai, a large Karen village that now resembles a traveling circus, complete with elephant rides (500฿ per hr.), photos with boa constrictors, and endless rows of souvenirs. From there, it's another 20min. to the **Temple Cave. Tha Ton Tour,** before Chankasem Guest House, 50m. from the boat pier, offers treks to Chiang Rai. (☎053 373 143. 2-day raft and boat trek 1800฿ per person, 3-day Akha and Lalu village trek and boating 2500฿ per person; elephant rides extra. All prices assume at least 4 participants. Open daily 9am-7pm. Hours vary in low season.)

NORTHERN THAILAND

MAE SAI ☎ 053

One of Thailand's main links with Myanmar, Mae Sai is a melting pot of transient guests, from Burmese workers, to retired expats on visa runs, businessmen involved in the gem trade and tourists collecting passport stamps and pirated DVDs. Town life revolves around border crossing, and Mae Sai turns into a ghost town in the evening when the border shuts down. Today, it's hard to imagine it, but just five years ago the border closed for four months when a full-scale, three-way battle broke out between Shan, Thai, and Burmese troops, killing Thai civilians in the shelling (see **Thai-Burmese Relations,** p. 64). Aside from the border crossing, travelers can find impressive caves and national parks near Mae Sai.

▐ TRANSPORTATION

Buses: Mae Sai Bus Terminal (☎053 646 403), 4km south of the bridge off Phaholyothin Rd. To: **Bangkok** (12hr.; 7am, 4:20, 4:30, 4:50, 5, 5:20, 5:30, 5:40, 5:45pm; 554-1105฿); **Chiang Mai** (4-5hr., 8 per day 6:15am-3:30pm, 134-375฿); **Chiang Rai** (1hr., every 20min. 5:45am-6pm, 30-50฿) via **Ban Pasang** (45min., 20฿); **Nakhon Ratchasima** (14-15hr., 6 per day 5:15am-6pm, 582-874฿); **Rayong** (16-20hr., 4 per day 12:30-3:45pm, 727-1025฿) via **Pattaya.** South of Thai Farmers Bank, blue *songthaew* go to **Chiang Saen** (1hr., every hr. 7am-2pm, 40฿) via **Sop Ruak** (40min., 20฿). **Yellow songthaew** run to **Ban Pasang** (40฿) via **Ban Huai Khrai** (20฿)

Local Transportation: Motorcycle taxis and **samlor** pepper Mae Sai. Rides within the city 20-40฿. From guesthouses to bus terminal 40฿. Red *songthaew* (10฿) go up and down Phaholyothin Rd.

Rentals: The Honda Shop (☎053 731 113), on Phaholyothin Rd., nearly opposite the Bangkok Bank, rents 100cc **motorbikes** for 150฿ with passport deposit.

▐ ✦ ORIENTATION AND PRACTICAL INFORMATION

Mae Sai is 61km north of Chiang Rai, 68km northeast of Mae Salong, and 35km northwest of the Golden Triangle. Hwy. 110 turns into **Phaholyothin Road,** and runs north to the border crossing (marked by the new gate) and the **Friendship Bridge.** Phaholyothin Rd. hosts a dusty carnival of *farang*, Thai, and Burmese who browse, bargain, and beg at the street stalls, banks, and shops surrounding it. **Silamjoi Road** follows the river, heading west from the Friendship Bridge toward guesthouses.

Immigration Office: (☎053 731 008), on Phaholyothin Rd., 2km south of bridge. 10-day visa extension 1900฿. 1-month visa extension for 60-day tourist visas. Bring 2 photos and 2 photocopies of passport. Open daily 8:30am-4:30pm. For a cheaper option, see **Border Crossing: Mae Sai/Thachilek.** See the Immigration Office at the border (☎053 733 261) for up-to-date information. Border open daily 6:30am-6:30pm. Tourists are asked to cross back by 5pm.

Banks: All along Phaholyothin Rd. **Thai Farmers Bank,** 122/1 Phaholyothin Rd. (☎053 640 786). Open M-F 8:30am-3:30pm. Cirrus/MC/V **24hr. ATM.**

Markets: Before 5pm, stalls line Phaholyothin Rd. Check out the base of the bridge for herbs, gems, teak, and flowers. 200m south, level with and opposite to the police station, is "ruby alley." Jade fills the stands of a covered market east of the bridge. The market extends west down Silamjoi Rd. The market in Thachilek, just across the bridge, peddles pirated CDs, cigarettes, and standard regional market fare, as well as numerous illegal items like guns and jaguar skins. Thai baht is the only accepted currency.

Ambulance: ☎053 731 300 or 731 301.

Police: (☎053 731 444), on Phaholyothin Rd., 200m south of bridge. There is also a police box near the end of Silamjoi Rd., before the Mae Sai Guest House.

Pharmacy: There is a drugstore next to the police station. Owner speaks some English. Open daily 8am-8pm.

Medical Services: Mae Sai Hospital, 101 Moo 10 Pomaharat Rd. (☎053 751 300), 2km south of the bridge off Phaholyothin Rd. Turn right after the overpass into the soi, 400m down.

Telephones: Mae Sai Telecommunications Center, next to the post office. Fax. Open M-F 8:30am-4:30pm. International phone at 7-Eleven south of the bridge.

Internet Access: Love-Net (☎053 733 906), 50m west of Uncle John's on Silamjoi Rd. 20฿ per hr. Open daily noon-10pm.

Post Office: Mae Sai Post and Telegraph Office, 230/40-41 Phaholyothin Rd. (☎053 731 402), 3km south of the bridge and on a street running west from the main road. Poste Restante. Open M-F 8:30am-4:30pm, Sa-Su 9am-noon. **Postal Code:** 57130.

ACCOMMODATIONS

Although the overwhelming number of one-night stays has lowered the standards for much of Mae Sai's accommodations, there are a few nice guesthouses along the river on Silamjoi Rd.

Mae Sai Guest House, 688 Wiengpangkam Rd. (☎053 732 021). A hefty walk 800m west of the border gate; turn right when the road forks, and bear left at Mae Sai Riverside Resort, after the police box. This idyllic escape is worth the walk for its riverside location and terrific views of nearby Myanmar. The cheapest rooms go fast, so reserve in advance. Curfew 10pm. Laundry. Bungalows with cold shower 200฿, with hot water and river view 300-400฿. ❷

Bamboo House, 135/5 Silamjoi Rd. (☎053 733 055), 200m west of the border gate. Located right near the action, this charming, small hotel is built into a hillside, with beautiful rock formations visible past the main staircase. Restaurant downstairs. Singles 150฿; doubles with cold shower and squat toilet 200฿, with hot shower 250฿, with TV 300฿, with A/C 350฿. ❷

Chad Guest House, 52/1 Soi Wiengpan (☎053 732 054), off Phaholyothin Rd., 1km to the south of the bridge. Coming from the bus station, turn left at the sign. Quiet, simple rooms, guesthouse run by an English-speaking family. Singles with shared toilet and hot shower 100฿, doubles 150฿. ❶

Northern Guest House, 402 Timphajom Rd. (☎053 731 537), on the way to Mae Sai Guest House, just after the road forks. Some of the simple rooms are in a larger building and the rest are in a row of rustic huts. Ask the owner about acupressure massage. No hot water in low season. Rooms with bath 120-150฿, high season 250฿. ❶

FOOD

The meager **night market** along Phaholyothin Rd. has dishes on display; a quick point will get you what you want. Some travelers may find the broad, deserted thoroughfare unnerving by dark. (Open daily 7-10pm.) Going down the soi directly opposite Thai Farmers Bank leads to a series of **stands** with tables that specialize in *pad thai* (20฿).

Uncle John's Restaurant and Bar (☎053 732 815), 100 west of the border gate on Silamjoi Rd., stays open late and serves food as movies play on the big-screen TV in the back. Chicken with cashews 120฿. Open daily 8am-midnight. ❸

Unnamed noodle shop, on Silamjoi Rd., next door to Uncle John's, caters mostly to locals but has a very helpful picture menu of noodle soups (20-25฿) and fruit shakes (20฿). Open daily 7am-6pm. ❶

Rabieng Kaew Restaurant (☎053 731 172), 150m south of the bridge on Phaholyothin Rd., just before the police station, is a good option. Their minced pork and coconut in chili paste (50฿) is a spicy treat, though not enough for a full meal. Specials 60-150฿. Coconut ice cream 20฿. Open daily 9am-10pm. ❸

🔆 SIGHTS

There aren't many tourist sights in Mae Sai itself. Instead, the real excitement comes from observing the bustling border markets and exploring the roads near the river. There is, however, a small cave known as **Tham Pha Jom** that is within walking distance of the border gate. Follow Silamjoi Rd. west, and bear left instead of right at the fork leading to Mae Sai Guest House. Turn left at the end of the street, and the entrance to the cave lies at the back of the *wat*. Bring your own flashlight. The *wat*'s staircases and terraces cover the hillside. Climb the serpent staircase for a great view.

🔳 DAYTRIPS FROM MAE SAI

THAM PLAA (FISH CAVE) **AND THAM LUANG** (GREAT CAVE). There are a number of caves located south of Mae Sai along Highway 110. The most noteworthy of the lot are **Tham Plaa** and **Tham Luang.** If you rent your own transportation, or if you're willing to sign up with a tour agency (300-700฿ per day), you can easily visit them both in one day.

The most visitor-friendly is 🔳**Tham Plaa** (Fish Cave), more commonly called "Monkey Cave" because of the gamboling primates. They're everywhere, so hold onto small children and belongings. Bananas and peanuts are for sale on-site, but feed the monkeys at your own risk. *(Tham Plaa is about 12km south of Mae Sai along Hwy. 110 and 3km west of the main road. Samlor along the highway will take you for 30฿. Immediately after the police checkpoint, turn right under the arch labeled Tham Sao Hu, turn right again at the next intersection, and then take a left.)*

Tham Luang, while a larger cave, is more of a self-directed enterprise, with little tourist infrastructure and no official guides. Its chambers burrow 200m deep into the mountain, although some locals claim they continue all the way to Chiang Mai. Ask in Mae Sai before attempting to explore it. In the rainy season, it's impassable. You might consider hiring a guide (200-400฿) in town and riding out to the cave together. Some guesthouses, including the Mae Sai Guest House, can organize groups. *(There are 2 marked entrances to Tham Luang on Hwy. 110, about 8km south of Mae Sai—take the well-paved one. After the 3-headed dragon, continue straight for Khun Nam Nang Non (Sleeping Lady Lagoon), or take the 1st right, then the next left (about 1km) on paved roads to Tham Luang. Open daily 8:30am-4:30pm.)*

THE ROYAL VILLA AND DOI TUNG. The Royal Villa, located in Doi Tung, is 32km from Mae Sai and was the home of the Princess Mother (mother of King Rama VIII and King Rama IX) from 1988 until 1994, when she passed away at the age of 94. The palace, constructed of recycled pinewood crates at her request, combines traditional Lanna architecture with elements of a Swiss chalet. There is also an exquisite carving of the zodiac in the grand reception hall. Attendants will be happy to guide you through the villa and answer questions about the Princess Mother. Visitors to the royal palace are asked to dress conservatively. If a visitor's clothing is inappropriate—tank top, shorts, or miniskirt—officials will provide a denim garment that's best left in the 80s.

The enormous 🔳**Mah Fah Luang Gardens,** a beautiful blend of Thai and European garden styles, flows down the hill from the Royal Villa. Most of the peaceful arrangement is in bloom year-round. The recently constructed Princess Mother Commemorative Hall is located at the entrance to the gardens. While most of the signs are only in Thai, the Hall captures the deep respect that Thais have for the Royal Family. *(All open daily 6:30am-5:30pm. Ticket sales end 30min. before closing. Royal Villa 70฿, gardens 80฿, Commemorative Hall 30฿; all three 150฿.)*

About 8km past the Royal Villa is the peak of **Doi Tung** (1980m), and **Wat Phra That Doi Tung** and its twin *chedi*. Upon climbing the 153 steps, you'll have a beautiful view over the valley. There is a stunning back route to Doi Tung from Mae Sai, which weaves its way along the border and between police checkpoints. Ask at your guesthouse for current info about the border situation. The route leading from Hwy. 110 to Doi Tung is heavily touristed and generally safe to travel. *(To reach Doi Tung, take a yellow songthaew from in front of Thai Farmers Bank (20฿), or a Chiang Rai-bound bus to Huai Khrai (15฿). From Huai Khrai, purple songthaew take visitors the other half of the trip, but it's a good idea to come in groups, since the songthaews are often not full enough to leave. Chartered songthaew start at 400฿.)*

MAE SALONG ☎ 053

Fifty years after the Chinese Nationalists' 93rd Division fled China in the wake of the Communist victory to settle in this mountaintop village, Mae Salong maintains its Chinese identity. Chinese characters adorn door frames, red lanterns decorate tea houses, and the dialect of China's southern province, Yunnan, is just as common as Thai. Due to its location in the mountains, the village offers numerous hiking opportunities that yield some of the most spectacular views in all of northern Thailand. The best time to visit is in January, when the cherry blossoms are in bloom.

▣ TRANSPORTATION

Songthaew run frequently early in the morning and leave when full; if the wait is unbearable, you can pay the full fare (500฿). To get to **Chiang Rai**, take a light blue *songthaew* from 7-Eleven to **Ban Pasang** (1hr., 8am-3pm, 60฿), and then flag down a passing **bus** (1hr., every 30min. 6am-6pm, 40฿). To get to **Mae Sai**, take the light blue *songthaew* to Ban Pasang, then catch a bus (45min., every 20min. 7am-7pm, 40฿) or *songthaew* (stops close to the border, 40฿) heading north. Yellow *songthaew* to **Tha Ton** (1hr., every hr. 8:20am-1pm, 80฿) leave from the turn off to Mae Salong Resort. The main road through Mae Salong stretches 2.5km and is a continuation of roads from Tha Ton (Rte. 1234) and Ban Pasang (Rte. 1130). Khumnaipol Resort marks the end of Rte. 1234, and Mae Salong Villa marks the end of Rte. 1130.

▨ PRACTICAL INFORMATION

The town center is near the guesthouses and a 7-Eleven. The morning market is the first left off the road to Mae Salong Resort. A day market lies 1km out of town, just past the bank, and features locally grown tea and Akha wares. **Thai Military Bank**, opposite Khumnaipol Resort, has an AmEx/Cirrus/MC/Plus/V **24hr. ATM**. (☎ 053 765 159. Open M-F 8:30am-3:30pm.). There is a **police booth** (☎ 053 767 7109 or 01 603 17 53) near Mae Salong Villa. The nearest **hospital** (☎ 771 056) is in Mae Chan, and there are **no international phones** in Mae Salong.

▤ ACCOMMODATIONS

Lodgings are scarce in Mae Salong, but the few options are uniformly good ones.

Shin Sane Guest House (☎ 053 765 026), just past the turnoff to the Mae Salong Resort, has well-kept bungalows with minimalist decor and bright blue sheets. The cheaper rooms on the overhead bridge are the best value in town. The sociable English-speaking owner distributes maps (10฿) and arranges 1-day horse treks to hill-tribe villages (4hr. trek 400฿). Singles with shared bath 50฿, doubles 100฿, bungalows with Western toilet and hot water 200-300฿. ❶

Golden Dragon Inn (☎053 765 009), on the main road between the Mae Salong Resort and Akha Guest House, has simple rooms with bath and hot shower, some with great views from the balcony. Singles 200฿, doubles 400฿. ❷

Akha Mae Salong Guest House (☎053 765 103), next door to the Shin Sane Guest House, is run by members of the Akha hill tribe and has 4 huge rooms with wood floors and common bath. Singles and doubles 100-250฿ . ❶

🍴 FOOD

Yunnan-style noodle shops abound in Mae Salong. Tea shops provide a relaxing ambience, and a kettle of soothing Mae Salong tea costs 30฿. **Mini ❶**, 400m toward Tha Ton from the Golden Dragon, serves *kanom jiin naam ngiaw* (*Yunnan*-noodle soup; 25฿), the town specialty. Ask for vegetarian options. The store also rents motorbikes for 200฿ per day. (Lao beer 60฿. Open daily 7am-9pm.) Six hundred meters past Golden Dragon Inn, toward the bus station, is a **restaurant ❶** with a covered bamboo tent and breathtaking view. Popular with locals, it serves northern Thai dishes outdoors. (Minced pork with basil 25฿. Grilled fish 40฿. Open daily noon-midnight.)

👁 SIGHTS

Area hill tribes include Akha, Lahu, Lisu, and, in smaller numbers, Yao. There are no organized trekking groups, but the intrepid can set off alone. Pick up a map at Shin Sane Guest House (10฿). In the past, the drug trade has spurred clashes between Khun Sa's Shan United Army and the Wa National Army. The area is generally safe, but you should ask in town about the current situation before you leave. The foot-weary can inquire about 4hr. horseback riding treks at Akha Mae Salong or Shin Sane Guest House (400฿ per person).

CHIANG SAEN   ☎053

King Saen Phu founded this small town in 1328 as the capital of the Chiang Saen Kingdom. In subsequent centuries, it became an important military outpost. Remnants of Chiang Saen's former Lanna glory are mixed with modern buildings along the tree-lined main street. Informative signs and a new visitors center are indicators of the town's interest in its history. And while those ruins are the city's main tourist attraction, the banks of the Mekong River make for pleasant evening strolls. Chiang Saen also makes a convenient and relatively un-commercialized base for exploring the Golden Triangle.

🚌 TRANSPORTATION

Buses: to **Chiang Mai** (5-6hr., 7:15am, 118฿; with A/C 8:30am, 212฿) and **Chiang Rai** (1½hr., every 30min. 5:15am-5pm, 30฿) via **Mae Chan** (45min., 20฿) leave from a stop on the southern side of Phahonyothin Rd., 50m west of the river. (Booking office behind bus stop open daily 6:45am-noon, 1-2:45pm, and 4-5pm.) To catch a bus to **Bangkok** (12hr.; 7am, 3:30, 5pm; 511-750฿) take a left in front of the Immigration Office; the stop is 100m down on your left, directly in front of the booking office at 822/1.

Songthaew: Blue songthaew go to **Mae Sai** (1hr., every 40min. 7am-2pm, 60฿) via **Sop Ruak** (20min., 30฿) from Phahonyothin Rd., across from Siam Bank. **Green songthaew** to **Chiang Khong** (2hr., leaves when full approximately every 2hr. 7am-1pm, 100฿) wait on Rimkhong Rd., 150m south of Phaholyothin Rd.; switch *songthaew* halfway to Chiang Khong. The long wait in low season makes it more convenient to go through the larger city of Mae Chan.

Boats: Longtail boats (☎099 977 913), leaving from the T intersection between Rimkhong and Phaholyothin Rd., head up and down the Mekong to **Chiang Khong** (1hr.; 8:30am-6pm; 2000฿ per boat, round-trip 2500฿; up to 6 people) and **Sop Ruak** (40min., 8:30am-6pm, 500-600฿).

Local Transportation: *Tuk-tuks* (30฿) at stands on the river and along Phaholyothin Rd.

Rentals: You can rent **motorbikes** and **bicycles** at **Visconfondi Rentals** (☎053 650 143), 30m west of the Honda dealership on Phahonyothin Rd. and on the opposite side of the street. No explicit English sign, but there are motorbikes parked on the sidewalk with visible "For Rent" signs. Motorbikes (automatic) 200฿ per day. Bicycles 40฿ per day. Open daily 8am-5pm.

◢◪ ORIENTATION AND PRACTICAL INFORMATION

Chiang Saen's two main roads intersect at the **Mekong River,** which separates Thailand from Laos to the east. **Rimkhong Road** runs north-south along the river. and has a riverfront promenade. **Phahonyothin Road,** where buses arrive, runs east-west from the river. Heading north on Rimkhong Rd. leads to Sop Ruak and Mae Sai; heading south leads to Chiang Khong; going west on Phahonyothin Rd. leads to Chiang Rai. The old city walls and moat surround the city at a 1km radius from its center. Most of Chiang Saen's facilities are scattered along Phaholyothin Rd., all within easy walking distance.

Tourist Information: The brand new **tourist office** (☎053 777 084) is located across from the National Museum, about 0.75km away from the river along Phaholyothin Rd. Housed in a beautiful traditional structure, it gives out free town maps and pamphlets about the region's history. Open daily 6:30am-4pm. You can find travel and trekking information at **Gin's Tour** (☎053 777 335), run by Gin's Guesthouse but located downtown. With your back to the river, take a left at the first soi after the bus stop. It offers treks, bike and motorbike rentals, general tourist information, and arranges Chinese visas and boat tickets. Open daily 8:30am-5:30pm.

Bank: Siam Commercial Bank, 773 Phahonyothin Rd. (☎053 777 041), with a Cirrus/MC/Plus/V **24hr. ATM** and currency exchange. Open M-F 8:30am-3:30pm.

Pharmacy: On Rimkhong Rd., 100m north of the boat pier. Open daily 8am-9pm.

Police station: (☎053 777 111), at intersection of Rimkhong and Phahonyothin Rd.

Hospital: Chiang Saen Hospital (☎053 777 017), 1km from the river past the old city walls, on the way to Chiang Rai.

Immigration Office: (☎053 777 118), walk west on Phahonyothin Rd. from the river; it's on your left at the first intersection. Open M-F 8:30am-4:30pm.

Internet Access: (☎053 650 315), a few doors west of the Honda dealership along Phahonyothin Rd. 20฿ per hr. Open daily 8am-9pm.

Post Office: (☎053 777 116), 600m from the river on Phaholyothin Rd. Also offers international phone service. Open M-F 8:30am-4:30pm, Sa-Su 9am-noon. **Postal Code:** 57150.

◤ ACCOMMODATIONS

J.S. Guest House, 303 Moo 2 (☎081 304 0370). From the river, walk west for 500m on Phahonyothin Rd. and turn right before the post office. You'll see it 100m farther on the right. The simple, tiled rooms surround a courtyard with a garden and a small pool. They're well worth the low prices, and even in a town with few other accommodation options, the J.S. Guest House is an excellent first choice. Free coffee provided.

Bike rental 25฿ per day. Breakfast 10-20฿. Dorms with shared bath 100฿; singles and doubles 150฿, with bath 250฿. ❶

Sa Nae Charn Guest House, 641 Moo 2 Nhongmoon Rd. (☎053 651 138). Walking north along the river on Rimkhong Rd., take a left immediately after the *wat*. Run by Mr. Cheng, a retired police interpreter with excellent English, these 18 spotless hotel-style rooms have fans, TV, and private baths with Western toilets and hot water. Singles 200-250฿, doubles 250-300฿; triples 400฿, with A/C 450. ❷

Gin Guest House (☎053 650 847), 1.5km north on Rimkhong Rd. from the intersection with Phahonyothin Rd. This guesthouse's main drawback, a hefty walk from town, is partially offset by the attractiveness of its grounds, with gnarled tree roots reaching past the main office. Families will want to consider the especially large rooms upstairs, with 2 double beds, a private bathroom with pebbled floor, and an outside sitting area. Restaurant/bar and offers tour information. Internet 50฿ per hr. Bicycle and motorbike rentals. Doubles with bath 200-450฿, depending on size. Family rooms 500-700฿. ❷

🍴 FOOD

Locals here don't eat at formal restaurants, perhaps because Chiang Saen has only a handful of them. Instead, they head to the **food stalls** for breakfast, lunch, and dinner. During the morning and early afternoon, the best food is near the **day market,** which is under a large covered area next to the 7-Eleven, 100m away from the river on Phahonyothin Rd. (soups 15-25฿, rice and noodle dishes 15-30฿). As dinnertime approaches, try the *paw pia thawt* (spring rolls, 20฿) from the stalls outside 7-Eleven. The arrival of dusk shifts the scene to Rimkhong Rd., where locals eat at low tables on the riverside terrace. Most of the stalls have limited English menus. Meanwhile, in the area near the main intersection, tents offer open-air massages with great views of the river. (Thai massage, 110฿ per hr. Open approx. 5pm-8pm.)

If you need shelter from the rain, try **Fah-Mai Restaurant** ❷ (☎089 636 0683), on Rimkhong Rd. Soi 3, 100m past the *wat* on the left side. It has a deck overlooking the river and serves standard traditional dishes (30-40฿), along with fresh coffee (espresso 30฿).

👁 SIGHTS

The **Chiang Saen National Museum** is on Phahonyothin Rd., 150m past the Post Office, just before the city walls. Along with a life-size model of a *plaa buek* (Giant Mekong Catfish), the small museum displays 15th- and 16th-century Lanna artifacts, Buddha images from the region, and hill-tribe costumes. For a town the size of Chiang Saen, it's an impressive museum. (☎053 777 102. Open W-Su 8:30am-4:30pm. 30฿.)

Most people come to Chiang Saen to see its ruins. Some are still well-preserved, and helpful English signs explain each *wat*'s significance. Next door to the museum, a 13th-century brick *chedi*, the tallest Lanna monument in Thailand at 58m, marks **Wat Chedi Luang.** Just outside the old city walls, down a path to the right off Phahonyothin Rd., lie the remains of 14th-century ◪**Wat Pa Sak.** The *wat*'s ornate *chedi*, which reflects Chinese, Khmer, Pagan, and Sukhothai influences, stands in the middle of an airy teak forest. (Open daily 6am-6pm. 30฿.)

To reach **Wat Chom Kitti,** 1.5km out of town, follow the road along the moat next to Wat Pasak and take a left when the city walls curve. Its hilltop location gives it compelling views of Laos and the Mekong. Still more impressive, the gleaming white **Wat Phra That Pha-Ngao** lies 4km southeast of town on the road to Chiang Khong and overlooks Chiang Saen itself.

Chiang Saen Lake, a bird-watching site with the largest variety of water fowl in Southeast Asia, is a 7km ride southwest of town, past a turn-off marked on the way to Chiang Rai.

CHIANG KHONG ☎ 053

Until recently, the quiet border town of Chiang Khong had been a major backpacker hangout as travelers patiently waited here for their visas to Laos. Today, with visas available at the border, few backpackers linger longer than one night before hopping on a boat to Luang Prabang. Those who stay to explore the scenic surroundings can take advantage of Chiang Khong's worthy restaurants and lodgings overlooking the majestic Mekong River.

▐ TRANSPORTATION

Transportation in Chiang Khong seems rarely to correspond to a fixed schedule. Buses or *songthaew* to different locations leave from numerous points along the main road, and there's no central transportation hub or information source. Your best bet is to ask at your guesthouse or at one of the many **travel agencies** near Soi 1-3 the day before you want to leave. Check at many places, ask plenty of questions, and you'll quickly get a sense of how to get to your next destination. As a guide, here is a rough summary of Chiang Khong's transportation options. While prices and times are vulnerable to change, the bus stops and street locations tend to remain constant.

Buses go to **Chiang Mai** (green bus; 7hr., 6am, 200฿; with A/C 9am, 300฿; 11:40am, 250฿). Government buses through the **Travel Company** go to Bangkok (12-13hr.; 7am, 3:30, 3:45pm; 493-634฿). The **booking offices** for bus tickets to **Chiang Mai** (☎053 655 732) and **Bangkok** (☎053 791 004) are next to each other, between the bridge and the Esso gas station. Guesthouses run a faster but less comfortable **minibus** to **Chiang Mai** (5hr.; 10:30am, 6:30pm; 250฿), by the pier. **Sombat Tours,** opposite the Chiang Mai booking office, runs private buses to **Bangkok** (☎053 791 644; 7:25am, 3:05, 4pm; 493-887฿), as does **Siam-First** (3:45pm, 634-739฿), opposite the Thai Farmers Bank. Buy a seat in the morning to guarantee an

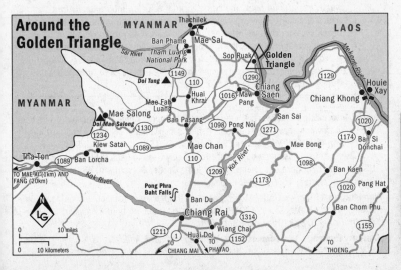

afternoon bus. Buses to **Chiang Rai** (3hr., every hr. 5:30am-5:45pm, 90฿) leave from the day market behind the 7-Eleven. **Songthaew** to **Chiang Saen** (2hr., periodically 7am-noon, 100฿) gather near Soi 3, just south of the post office.

For transportation in and around Chiang Khong, **Ann Tour** has **motorbikes** for rent (200฿ per day), and most guesthouses rent **mountain bikes** (80฿ per day).

ORIENTATION AND PRACTICAL INFORMATION

Chiang Khong is 144km northeast of Chiang Rai and 55km southeast of Chiang Saen. The town is essentially one long main street, **Saiklang Road**, which runs roughly 2km northwest to southeast, parallel to the **Mekong River**. Odd numbered soi head to the river, though the street signs can be faded and hard to read. **Soi 13** is at the southeast end of Saiklang Rd. near the bridge. The day market and most bus stops lie 100m south of this bridge and just north of an Esso station. **Soi 1,** home to several guesthouses and bars, is a 20min. walk to the northwest from Soi 13, on the upper end of town. Continuing northwest past Soi 1 leads to the cargo pier, the turnoff to Chiang Saen (Rte. 1129), and the ferry pier serving Laos.

> **BORDER CROSSING: CHIANG KHONG/HOUIE XAY.** The ferry (20฿) across the Mekong leaves from the old pier and takes less than 15min. Frequent daily departures 8am-6pm, but visas are not issued at the border after 4:30pm. As of June 2008, 15- and 30-day visas are obtainable on arrival in Houie Xay for 1500฿. Check in with the immigration office by the pier to get your Thai departure stamp and then board the ferry. It is a good idea to check with Chiang Khong Immigration before you leave. In the near future, Laos may stop issuing 15-day visas. The cheapest option is to get the visa in Bangkok. If in Chiang Khong, try Ann Tour. 30-day visas are 1500฿ for same-day service, and significantly cheaper ($30) if you pay in US dollars. Most guesthouses have a similar deal. Once in Houie Xay, catch a speedboat (6hr.; 1 or 2 boats 10:30am; 1450฿, 1400฿ at Easy Bar) or a slow boat (2 days, 10:30am, 850฿) to Luang Prabang. If you choose the latter, pack food, water, and a good book. The cramped boat will stop intermittently for cargo and stretching before overnighting in Pakbeng. As Lao currency fluctuates, check current exchange rates next to immigration as you enter Laos. While it is often cheaper to cross the river and then buy tickets, you will have to take a taxi from the arrival pier to the slow boat pier, and the boats may fill up. It is more convenient and not significantly more expensive to arrange the trip through your guesthouse or a tour agency.

Tourist Information and Tours: There is no official tourist office in town, but a number of helpful travel agencies between Sois 1 and 3 can answer questions and give travel advice. **Ann Tour,** 166 M.8 Saiklang Rd. (☎053 655 198), just south of Bamboo Riverside Guest House, has same-day service for 30-day visas to Laos (1500฿, or a cheaper US$30) and boat tickets to Luang Prabang (see **Border Crossing**, p. 332). Sells maps. Open daily 7:30am-7pm. Limited English spoken.

Immigration Office: (☎053 791 332), next to the ferry pier to Laos. Issues departure stamps and visa extensions (1900฿) and has information on border crossing. See **Border Crossing, p. 332**. Open daily 8am-6pm.

Currency Exchange: Thai Farmers Bank, 20m south of Soi 7. AmEx/Cirrus/MC/Plus/V **24hr. ATM.** Open M-F 8:30am-3:30pm. Other major banks line the lower section of the main road.

Markets: Every F 6am-1pm the **regional market,** hawking everything from bathing suits to pottery, spills out onto the main road around the bridge. Sat. brings the **night market** to town (4-9pm), on the main road around Soi 2. A karaoke stage and bar are set up on the lawn across from the Baan Fai Guest House. On Tu evenings, there is a small **Lanna market** near the police station. Another **market,** favored by locals, sets up on W afternoons from 1-9pm, near Soi 19, a 10min. walk south of the bridge on the main road. Vendors here sell both clothing and food, including the popular *geng hun lei* (BBQ pork).

Police: (☎053 791 426), next door to the immigration office, just north of the bridge.

Pharmacy: Boonchai Pharmacy (☎053 791 013), opposite Soi 7. Also has a **gym** (40฿ per hr.). Open daily 7am-8pm.

Medical Services: Chiang Khong Hospital, 354 Moo 10 (☎053 791 206), 3km outside of town. Go due south on Hwy. 1020 toward Chiang Rai. Some English. Open 24hr.

Telephones: In front of the Post Office and at Ann Tour (see above).

Internet Access: Satang Internet (☎053 791 146), across from Soi 1 and between Ann Tours and Lomtawan Restaurant, has high-speed access on new computers. Skype available. 30฿ per hr., 10฿ minimum. Open daily 8am-10pm.

Post Office: (☎053 791 555), near Soi 3. Open M-F 8:30am-4:30pm, Sa-Su 9am-noon. **Postal Code:** 57140.

▚ ACCOMMODATIONS

As a border town, Chiang Khong has no shortage of similarly-priced accommodations, all located by the Mekong River. The *farang* population rises sharply with each incoming bus load, around 5pm in the high season. By then, the town's best accommodations are at their saturation point, so call in advance to reserve.

▨ **Baan Rimtaling,** 99/4 Sobsom T. Wieng (☎053 791 613; www.baanrimtaling.com). Walking south from the bridge, turn left at the Esso station, then left onto Soi 15. Once at the river, turn right; it's on the left 100m ahead. Although far from bars and restaurants, this hidden gem is well worth the walk. A beautiful restaurant and lounge area overlook the river, with cozy rooms perched on the hillside below. Free services include Wi-Fi, bicycles, and pickup and dropoff at port or bus station. Restaurant open daily 7:30am-11pm. Curfew 11pm. 4-bed mixed dorms with bath 80฿; doubles with shared bath 160฿, with balcony and bath 350฿; bungalows with bath, fan, and TV 450฿. ❶

Baan Fai Guest House, 108 M. 8 T. Wiang (☎053 791 394), just off the main road between Sois 1 and 3. A small, charming house in the backyard has 8 traditionally decorated rooms. Laundry services available. Bike rental 80฿, motorbike rental 200฿. Internet 30฿ per hr. Singles with fan and shared bath 80฿; doubles 100฿, with tiny private bath 150฿. ❶

Boom House (☎053 791 310), 175m north of Soi 1, next to 999 Bar. The new tiled rooms in this centrally located guesthouse have high ceilings, fans, and private baths. Cheaper singles in the larger main house have shared baths. A restaurant in back extends on a deck toward the river. Rooms with shared bath 150-200฿. Newer rooms with bath 250-350฿; with river view, TV, and A/C 400฿. ❷

PJ Guesthouse (☎053 791 134), 225m past Soi 1 and the closest guesthouse to the pier. Turn right at the signs for Namkhong and T.N.K. Guesthouse. Easily recognizable pink walls contain 2 stories of simple rooms with baths. The upstairs rooms open onto a small roof deck and overlook the river. Laundry 5฿ per item. Singles and doubles with bath 150฿, with river view and TV 250฿. ❷

THE BIGGEST CATCH

Chiang Khong is notable not only for its beautiful sights along the winding Mekong, but for a massive one that swims in it: the *Pla Beuk*, or giant catfish.

Growing up to 2m and 150-250kg, these fish are rarely sighted and almost never captured. But this doesn't stop dedicated enthusiasts from trying. Every year in April and May, Chiang Khong, Chiang Saen, and other towns on the Mekong River host huge festivals whose main goal is to capture these lucky fish.

After asking Buddhist spirits for permission to catch the giant catfish, Thai and Laotian fishermen take turns trawling the river. Only a few *Pla Buek* are caught each year. They are briefly put on display in the river, and then the meat is divvied up among the townspeople.

For a sense of how gigantic these fish are, check out the life-size model on display at the Chiang Saen National Museum, with pictures from past festivals. Or, plan your visit to northern Thailand between April and May, during one of the festivals along the Mekong.

FOOD

Most restaurants in town are affiliated with guesthouses, and are positioned for terrific views of the river. Noodle and rice shops of varying quality line Saiklang Rd. Start your day with a morning treat from the **day market,** south of the bridge, with *kanon ton kanon niaw* (rice flour balls with coconut filling; 5฿).

Lomtawan Restaurant (☎053 655 740), near Soi 1, next door to Satang Internet. The intimate deck overlooking the old city wall is consistently packed with locals for good reason: it has the best food in Chiang Khong. From the intricately carved drink coasters to the soft play of candlelight on the tables, Lomtawan is exquisite down to the last detail. Curries 70-100฿. Special dishes 80-120฿. Open daily 10am-midnight. ❸

Green Tree Restaurant and Bar (☎089 952 1730), between Soi 1-3, across the street from Baan Fai Guest House. Lounge on floor cushions on the leafy terrace, and choose your dinner from a canvas scroll menu which includes a variety of vegetarian options. It's especially fun on Sa nights from 7pm-midnight, when the restaurant offers a view of the karaoke stage. Fried baby corn with chicken 45฿. Entrees 30-55฿. Fully stocked bar: mixed drinks 90-150฿. Open daily 7:30am-midnight. ❷

Baan Tammila Restaurant, 113 Soi 1 (☎053 791 234), connected to the Baan Tammila Guesthouse. Plants and vines shade the small terrace overlooking the river. Aside from a thoughtful, extensive selection of vegetarian food (40-60฿), this restaurant is notable for its homemade baked goods and fresh coffee (30฿). Drinks available until 10pm. Open daily 7am-6:30pm. ❷

Rimnam Restaurant, 166 Soi 7-9 (☎053 655 680). Turn down Soi 9; it's part of the guesthouse at the end. The roomy, high-ceiling deck area gives you a panoramic view of the river, with food that is more than worth the price. Chinese broccoli with oyster sauce 80฿. Rice and noodle dishes 30-40฿, stir fry 80-120฿. Open daily 7am-9pm. ❷

SIGHTS AND ENTERTAINMENT

Many visitors never notice the lovely riverside walkway that parallels the water. Benches, a rarity in Thailand, are scattered along its length. The river views are especially striking as the sun sets. One place to access the walkway is past the guesthouses near Sois 7-9.

Sights are scattered throughout the immediate vicinity of Chiang Khong. In high season, Baan Tammila guesthouse organizes bike rides to **Hmong villages,** though they may prove inaccessible in the rainy season (3hr.; 3:30pm; 150฿, includes bike and guide.) Those with their own bikes can enjoy a scenic ride to the **dam,** 5km away. (Coming from the bridge, take a right at the Esso station and follow the little blue signs down back roads.)

See Don Chai, a Lu handweaving village, is 14km south of the city. Showrooms are scarce and hours fickle, but politely poke your head into any house and ask if you can watch for a while. (Take a motorcycle taxi or a blue *songthaew* (30฿), which leave from the main road, just south of the Esso station. Alternatively, take a Chiang Mai/Chiang Rai-bound bus, and tell the driver where you want to get off.)

Since most visitors wake up early the next morning to catch a ferry to Laos, nightlife in Chiang Khong is fairly relaxed. Backpackers gather to sip beers, play pool, and watch American movies at the **Easy Bar and Restaurant,** 175m north of Soi 1 and across from the Boom House. (☎053 655 069. Entrees 30-90฿. Large Tiger beer 90฿. Open daily 7am-1am.) 100m toward Soi 1 from the Easy Bar, the **Car Jom Bar,** or "teepee bar," is an unusual experience. The thatched teepee functions as both a bar and home to its owner. (Small Chang beer 40฿. Mixed drinks 120฿. No fixed hours, usually open from lunchtime until late.)

CHIANG RAI ☎053

Chiang Rai has always played second fiddle to its southern neighbor, Chiang Mai. The rivalry between the two cities began when King Mengrai, who built Chiang Rai in 1262 and used it as his central headquarters for three decades, switched allegiance to Chiang Mai, abandoning his original capital city. Today, besides offering quality accommodations and glimpses of the surrounding mountains, Chiang Rai features a hill-tribe museum and a night market stocked with tribal handicrafts. You'll leave here having experienced authentic Thai city life without the hassles and tourist traps of most popular destinations.

TRANSPORTATION

Flights: Chiang Rai International Airport (☎053 798 202), 9km out of town, on Hwy. 110. To **Bangkok** (1hr., 7 per day, 3345฿). **Thai Airways,** 870 Phaholyothin Rd. (☎053 711 179), 1 block south of Teepee Bar. Open M-F 8am-noon and 1-5pm.

Buses: Chiang Rai Bus Station (☎053 711 224), on Prasopsuk Rd., 1 block east of Phaholyothin Rd., next to the night market. To: **Bangkok** (12hr., 21 per day 8am-8pm, 452-900฿; private companies also run buses to Bangkok for the same prices at similar times); **Chiang Khong** (2-3hr., every hr. 6am-5pm, 53-90฿); **Chiang Mai** (3hr., 20 per day 6:30am-5pm, 94-260฿); **Chiang Saen** (1hr., every 15min. 6am-6:30pm, 32฿); **Mae Sai** (1hr., every 15min. 5:50am-6:30pm, 30฿); **Mae Sot** (12hr.; 7:35, 9:20am; 336-425฿); **Nakhon Ratchasima** (12hr.; 6:15, 11:15am, 1:15, 3:20, 5:30, 7pm; 473-710฿); **Phitsanulok** (6hr.; 7:30, 8:30, 9:30, 10:30am; 274฿); **Nan** (6hr., 9:30am, 117-164฿); **Sukhothai** (7hr.; 7:30, 8:30, 9:30, 10:30am; 244฿).

Ferries: Leave from the pier (☎053 750 009), on the north bank of the Mae Kok river, next to the Mae Fah Luang Bridge, 1km northwest of the city. To **Tha Ton** (5hr., 10:30am, 200฿) via **Ruammit** (45min., 80฿). Round-trip cruises to Ruammit and hill-tribe villages 700-1900฿. Max. 8 people.

Local Transportation: Songthaew, tuk-tuk, and **samlor** cluster on Uttarakit Rd. around the day market and on Phaholyothin Rd. near the night bazaar in the evening. Fares within the city 10-40฿. Transportation from the bus station to a river guesthouse 40฿. Within 10-15km radius of pick-up, *songthaew* and *tuk-tuk* should cost around 90฿.

Rentals: Soon Motorcycle, 197/2 Trairat Rd. (☎053 714 068), seems to have monopolized **motorbike** rentals in Chiang Rai, as it supplies the rentals available at nearly all guesthouses. Consequently, prices are locked in, though free pickup and dropoff are provided. New motorbikes 200-300฿, secondhand 150฿; 4WD Suzuki Jeep 1000฿, with insurance 1500฿. Discount for 1-week rental 10%. Passport deposit required. Open daily 8am-6pm. Bicycle rental through **Fat Free**, 542/2 Baanpragarn Rd. (☎053 752-532; www.fatfreebike.com). City bikes 50-80฿, mountain bikes 200฿. Open daily 9:30am-6pm. Photo ID deposit. **North Wheels Rent a Car**, 591 Phaholyothin Rd. (☎053 740 585; www.northwheels.com), has car rentals for 780-2000฿ per day. Open daily 8am-5pm.

◼ ▣ ORIENTATION AND PRACTICAL INFORMATION

Despite some irregularities in street naming, Chiang Rai is a perfect walking city. Its *wats*, markets, and busy thoroughfares invite strolls both day and night. The **Mae Kok River** flows west to east, forming Chiang Rai's northern border. **Singhaklai Road,** site of TAT and guesthouses, skirts the river. The northern part of town lies between the river and **Baanpragarn Road,** which is 500m south of and parallel to Singhaklai Rd. The most helpful landmark, the **Haw Nariga** (clock tower), stands in the middle of Baanpragarn Rd., forming a chaotic roundabout. **Jet Yod Road,** full of bars and laundries, leads south from there. One block east, a portion of **Phaholyothin Road** runs parallel to Jet Yod Rd., while the upper half curves around above the bus station. North of the intersection with Baanpragarn Rd., Jet Yod Rd. becomes **Suksathit Road** and leads to the second clock tower, just two blocks north, at the intersection with Uttarakit Rd. More regional info is available online, at www.chiangraiprovince.com.

Tourist Offices: TAT, 448/16 Singhaklai Rd. (☎053 717 433). Offers detailed free maps (with bus schedules), brochures, a list of approved trekking centers, and info on hotels and restaurants in the area. Open daily 8:30am-4:30pm.

Bank: Thai Military Bank, 897/7-8 Phaholyothin Rd. (☎053 715 657). Open M-F 1pm, Sa-Su 8:30am-9pm. **24hr. ATM** (AmEx/Cirrus/MC/Plus/V). Currency exchange booth (☎053 715 657) on Phaholyothin Rd., next to the night bazaar. Open daily 1-9pm.

Books: ▨**Orn's Bookshop,** 1051/61 Jet Yod Rd. (☎081 022 0818). Walking from the clock tower, turn right in front of Wat Jet Yod and again at the T-intersection. Located on the 2nd fl. of the owner's house, the 2 rooms of this shop are packed with a large selection of books in a dozen languages. You'll find everything from conspiracy theories to *The Secret Life of Bees.* Book exchange. Open daily 8am-8pm.

Ambulance: ☎053 711 366.

Tourist Police: (☎053 740-249), 586/5 Phaholyothin Rd. English spoken. Gives background checks on tour agencies. Open 24hr.

Pharmacy: Boots Pharmacy, 873/78 Phaholyothin Rd., a thoroughly Western-style pharmacy with aspirin, Tylenol®, and antihistamines. Open daily 10am-11pm.

Medical Services: Overbrooke Hospital, 444/3 Singhaklai Rd. (☎053 711 366), 250m west of TAT. **24hr. pharmacy.** MC/V.

Telephones: Telecommunications Office (☎053 716 738), on Ngam Muang Rd. Fax and international calls. Open M-F 8am-noon and 1-4:30pm. MC/V. International credit card operated phone outside Thai Airways (p. 335). There are also payphones next to the bus station and along Phaholyothin Rd.

Internet Access: Connect Cafe, 868/10 Phaholyotin Rd. (☎053 740 688), on the same block as Thai Airways, has Wi-Fi, fax service, overseas calls, and homemade baked goods. 40฿ per hr., 20฿ minimum. Open daily 9am-10pm.

Post Office: 486/1 Moo 15 Uttarakit Rd. (☎053 711 421), 200m south of TAT and 300m north of the clock tower. Poste Restante. Open M-F 8:30am-4:30pm, Sa-Su and holidays 9am-noon. **Postal Code:** 57000.

TO MAE SAI, CHIANG SAEN, (9km)

Wat Pranorn

King Mengrai's Shrine

Sriboonruang Rd.

Sigerd Rd.

Wat Si Koet

Prasopsuk Rd.

TO CHIANG MAI

Sanpanard Rd.

Sankorgchang Rd.

Wat Sriboonrrong

Singhaklai Rd.

Uttarakit Rd.

Wisit Wuang Rd.

PDA Hill Tribe Museum

Thanalai Rd.

Phaholyothin Rd.

North Wheels Rent a Car

Connect Cafe

Night Market

Phaholyothin Rd.

Koh Loi Rd.

Sanirach Rd.

Rattanakhet Rd.

Wat Klangwiang

Fat Free Bicycle Rental

Clock Tower

Pamavipat Rd.

Thai Airways

Jet Yod Rd.

Wat Jet Yod

Satharn Payabarn Rd.

TO (2km)

Dusit Island

Mae Kok River

Thaluang Rd.

Wat Phra Singha

Suksathit Rd.

Day Market

Clock Tower

Ruang Nakhon Rd.

Itsaraphap Rd.

Sanambin Rd.

Orn's Bookshop

Overbrooke Hospital

Soon Motorcycle

Sankhongnoi Rd.

Government Office and Town Hall

Sangkaew Rd.

Wat Phra Kaew

Trairat Rd.

Thanalai Rd.

Wat Ming Muang

Baanpragarn Rd.

Kraisorasit Rd.

Arjanmuay Rd.

Wat Ngam Muang

Ratdetdamrong Rd.

Ngam Muang Rd.

Uttarakit Rd.

Rayotha Rd.

Soi 4

Sankhongnoi Rd.

TO RUAMMIT, THA TON

Wat Dol Thong

Wat Thong

Winitchaikul Rd.

TO MAE FAH LUANG BRIDGE (1km), THAMPU

500 yards
500 meters

Chiang Rai

▲ ACCOMMODATIONS
Akha River House, **3**
Baan Bua Guest House, **6**
Chat House, **1**
Chian House, **11**
Mae Hong Son Guest House, **9**

◆ FOOD
Cabbages & Condoms, **10**
Mae Preeya Noodle Shop, **2**
Nakon Patom, **8**

★ NIGHTLIFE
Cat Bar, **4**
Par Club, **5**
Teepee Bar, **7**

ACCOMMODATIONS

Dozens of guesthouses and hotels have opened since Chiang Rai's tourist boom began. Most are near the river or in the vicinity of the town center (marked by the clock tower). Call in advance in high season to reserve accommodations. All guesthouses have luggage storage, and most can arrange treks and motorbike rentals.

Baan Bua Guest House, 879/2 Jet Yod Rd. (☎053 718 880; www.baanbuaguesthouse. com). 3 blocks south from the clock tower, down a gravel road on the left. It is only steps away from restaurants and bars, but hidden within a quiet, peaceful garden. Rooms with fan, Western toilet, and hot water. 1- to 3-day treks organized, 1200-3400฿ per person. Tiled rooms with bath 200-300฿, larger rooms 300-400฿, with A/C 350-500฿. ❷

Chian House, 172 Sriboonraung Rd. (☎053 713 388). From the TAT, walk east past Rattanakhet Rd. Take the first left onto Koh Loi Rd., cross the bridge, and follow the signs. Despite the 15-20min. walk from the city center, the ample facilities—swimming pool, Internet access, international calls, and a restaurant—make the family-friendly Chian House a relaxing destination once you arrive. The tiled rooms are set around a large shaded courtyard, where guests lounge poolside or read in hammocks. Bike and motorbike rental. 1- to 3-day treks, 1500-3500฿. Doubles 150-180฿, larger rooms with bath and hot water 200-300฿, with veranda 250-300฿; bungalows with A/C 400-500฿. Ask about low season discounts. ❶

Chat House, 3/2 Sangkaew Rd. (☎053 711 481), down the soi directly across from Overbrooke Hospital, off Trairat Rd. The cheap, quiet rooms take up 2 floors of an old house, with a newer addition on 1 side of the small central garden. Laundry, restaurant, and trekking service onsite. Internet 30฿ per hr. Bicycle and motorbike rental. Singles 80฿; doubles 180฿, with bath 250฿, with A/C 400฿. ❶

Akha River House (☎053 715 084), on the banks of the Mae Kok River's upper branch. Cross the bridge next to the TAT, take the first right, and 150m later, walk down the wide dirt path next to the bridge construction area (construction is unobtrusive and rarely noisy). The entrance and sign are near the end, to the left. The Akha River House, with a thatched lounge area and simple rooms in a converted dorm building, is worth considering for the wonderful opportunity to visit the Akha hill tribe villages. A free shuttle leaves daily at 4:30pm for the **Akha Hill House,** where guests can stay in traditional dwellings with great mountain views (rooms 150-250฿, bungalows 200-500฿). The River House is also one of the best places in Chiang Rai to book treks. Manager Nu, an Akha tribesman, has been organizing trips for years, and 10% of the profits benefit educational programs in Akha villages (1- to 2-day treks, 1500-2500฿). Singles and doubles 100-150฿, with bath 150-200฿. ❶

Mae Hong Son Guest House, 126/21 Sanirach Rd., (☎053 715 367). From the TAT, walk east on Singhaklai Rd. and take the 2nd left (at Rattanakhet Rd.) onto Sanirach Rd. Follow the road 400m to the far end. The small, colorfully decorated rooms are housed in a central building on stilts, in Lanna style. Friendly manager Tom keeps guests entertained in the bar out back. Laundry 45฿ per kg. Trekking service and cooking class available. Singles and doubles 150-200฿, with bath and Western toilet 200-250฿; triples with shared bath 300฿. ❷

FOOD

Chiang Rai's culinary activity is concentrated in the neighborhood bounded by Jet Yod Rd., Baanpragarn Rd., and Phaholyothin Rd. Menus catering to Western palates cram the entrance to the night bazaar on Phaholyothin Rd. The **day** and **night markets** both serve a stellar variety of cheap food. The **food stands** outside the day market on Suksathi Rd., between the two clock towers, are the cheapest places to get great dishes before 7pm. Another option is inside the southwestern corner of the day market itself, where you'll find a white-tiled area with a wide selection of food counters. For the less adventurous, most guesthouses have affordable restaurants with Thai and Western cuisine.

▨ **Mae Preeya Noodle Shop,** on Baanpragarn Rd, 50m west of the clock tower and on the northern side of the street. No English sign, but you can recognize it by the low wooden counters and traditional art on the walls that are open to the street. This elegant yet inexpensive noodle shop sticks to authentic regional recipes. An English menu explains what you're eating. The Shan style noodles consist of minced pork, dried cotton tree flowers, and steamed pig's blood. Less intimidating dishes are also available. Noodles and soup 20в, dessert 10в. Open daily 9am-6pm. ❶

Nakon Patom, 869/25-26 Phaholyothin Rd. (☎053 713 617), across the street from Nova Restaurant, caters mostly to a Thai working crowd with fast service and large portions. No English sign, but the staff wears distinctive red aprons. Try the *khao moo dang* (barbecue pork with rice, 30в). Noodle soups 30-50в. Open daily 8am-3pm. ❶

Cabbages & Condoms, 620/25 Thanalai Rd. (☎053 740 657), on the ground floor of the Hill Tribe Museum. The food in the PDA's public-benefit restaurant, served in a classy indoor dining area, is expensive but for a good cause: "Making condoms as easy to get as cabbages." Chicken in pandanus leaves, 90в. Entrees 80-200в. Condoms come free with the bill. Open daily 10am-midnight. AmEx/MC/V. ❸

◪ MARKETS

Chiang Rai's must-see ▨**markets** go above and beyond the norm, giving a sense of the city's lifeblood without catering overtly to tourists.

The **day market** is a massive, covered affair encompassing an entire block, the northeast corner of which borders the post office on Uttarakit Rd. Stalls with vegetables and fresh fruit (pineapple 10в) are on the north end along Uttarakit Rd. Inside is a winding maze of glistening sea life, patterned backpacks, hand saws, blenders, puppies, and almost anything else you can imagine. Food vendors move to the streets surrounding the market at night—go there for delicious, cheap dining before 7pm.

The lively **night market,** with two music stages, hill-tribe craft vendors, and dessert stands, is Chiang Rai's primary nightlife destination. It takes place in the area just north of the bus station. The hill tribe products (including Akha wares) are primarily sold on the soi leading to the bus station off of Phaholyothin Rd. Following it leads to a wider variety of tapestries, intricately carved boxes, handbags, instruments, headdresses, and Hello Kitty lights. A great selection of food counters (fruit shakes 15в, spicy papaya salad 20в) surrounds a vast courtyard at the end of the soi. The focal point of the courtyard is a large stage that hosts performances of traditional hill-tribe music and Thai dance. A smaller stage, accessible from the soi off Phaholyothin Rd., lies in a courtyard with an outdoor bar and an overpriced restaurant. (Nightly performances on both stages 8-10pm.)

♫ ◪ ENTERTAINMENT AND NIGHTLIFE

For locals and foreigners alike, the real crux of Chiang Rai's nightlife is the Night Bazaar. Still, the area around Phaholyothin Rd. and Jet Yod Rd. has some good options for a night out, including an endless row of bars with comparable music and atmosphere. Beware: as the night goes on, bars on the soi linking Jet Yod Rd.'s northern end with Banphaprakan Rd. drop the pretense of karaoke and become solely go-go bars.

▨ **Teepee Bar,** 542/4 Phaholyothin Rd. (☎053 752 163), just south of Baanpragarn Rd., is worth seeing for the sheer absurdity of its decor. 2 rabbits roam free among the bike wheels, tiger-print rugs, and sewing machines. And the guitars aren't just for looks: customers are encouraged to participate in impromptu jam sessions. Open daily 6:30pm-1am, though patrons often stay much later. Small Singha 60฿.

Cat Bar, 1013/1 Jet Yod Rd. (☎089 557 8011), continues this fun musical tradition, adding a drum set and keyboard to the mix. Other patrons play pool or watch movies at the bar. Small Chang 50฿. Open daily 2pm-1am. Music after 10:30pm.

Par Club, in the Inn Come Hotel, 172/6 Ratbumrong Rd. (☎053 717 850), accessible by *tuk-tuk*. Quite possibly the most popular disco in town. Cover 50฿, includes free drink. Open daily 9pm-2am.

◎ SIGHTS

According to local lore, the *stupa* of ◪**Wat Phra Kaew,** originally known as Wat Pa Yier, was struck by lightning in 1434 and revealed an Emerald Buddha, and the temple's name was subsequently changed to "Wat of the Emerald Buddha." Today, the original Emerald Buddha is Thailand's most important Buddha image, and sits in Bangkok's Wat Phra Kaew (p. 110). A new image, commissioned in China in 1991 and carved from Canadian jade, sits in its place. (At the west end of town on Trairat Rd., opposite Overbrooke Hospital. Open daily dawn-dusk.)

At the west end of town, from Trairat Rd. past Chat House on Sang Kaew Rd., **Wat Ngam Muang** rests atop the hill of the same name. Its *stupa* contains King Mengrai's ashes and relics. Directly east from Wat Ngam Muang, where Singhaklai and Uttarakit Rd. intersect Hwy. 101, is **King Mengrai's shrine,** home to a multitude of bronze and wooden elephants resting at the King's feet. Many make the pilgrimage to the site and light incense and candles to pay their respects and draw strength from Chiang Rai's honored founder. **Wat Phra Singha,** on Singhaklai Rd. near TAT, dates from the 14th century and houses a copy of the famous Phra Singh Buddha image of Chiang Mai.

The **PDA Hill Tribe Museum,** 620/25 Thanalai Rd., 3rd fl., 300m east of Pintamorn Guest House, is interesting, though not nearly as informative as the one in Chiang Mai. The museum focuses on opium issues, sells local handicrafts, and arranges treks (p. 341). A recent addition is an exhibit on the importance of bamboo for hill-tribe culture. The 25min. slide show on the region's different tribes is given in five different languages. (☎053 740 088. Open M-F 9am-6pm, Sa-Su 10am-6pm. Admission 50฿.)

Chiang Rai's city sights are all easily and quickly accessed by bicycle. The determined can continue to **Thamtupu,** outside of town, where Buddha images sit inside caverns and protrude from the limestone cliff faces. The dirt road from Thamtupu is in good condition and makes for great, flat mountain bike rides between jagged rocky peaks interspersed with corn and banana plantations. (The turnoff to Thamtupu is on the left, 700m after Mae Fah Luang Bridge (pier to Tha Ton), traveling north from Chiang Rai. The cave is 1km further on a partially closed road.)

◪ TREKKING

Chiang Rai's bucolic province, home to a plethora of hill tribes, contains trekking routes less traveled than those to the south. As always, trek prices should include food, transportation, and an informed guide. Typical treks run three days and two nights (2-4 people 3000฿ per person, 5-7 people 2500฿ per person), but they can be as short as a day or as long as a week. Many companies have access to horses, elephants, rafts, and mountain bikes. Consider which hill tribes you'd like to visit and mix and match. Finally, make sure you are comfortable with your guide, because your life will be in his hands. If considering a company not listed below, check its status with TAT, which publishes a helpful brochure listing all registered guides in the area. Akha River House, Ben's Guest House, Chat House, Chian House, and Mae Hong Son Guest House all run flexible treks with guides who are registered with TAT.

If you decide to sign up for a trek, some options are more culturally sustainable than others. The Akha River House donates 10% of trekking profits to educational initiatives in Akha villages. The **Population and Community Development Association (PDA)**, 620/25 Thanalai Rd., which funds rural development, family planning, and HIV/AIDS education, treatment, and prevention programs for hill tribes, offers treks and one-day tours (p. 80). The PDA has daytrips to **Ruammit** (the Karen elephant camp), which stop at a waterfall, and some to Yao and Akha villages. Company treks are pricier than those run out of guesthouses, but their profits make their way into the above aid programs. PDA also accepts volunteers for many of its health-related projects. Most of the volunteers are selected through the Bangkok office, although occasionally the Chiang Rai office will accept applications directly. Thai language skills are strongly favored. If you're interested, bring a resume and plan to wait a week. (☎053 740 088; www.pda.or.th/chiangrai. 3-day, 2-night trek to Lahu and Akha villages includes elephant and longtail boat rides. 3700-4500฿ per person, 2-person min. Daytrips to the Golden Triangle 1500฿ per person, 2-person min. Prices reduced for larger groups. Max. group size 12.)

If you don't mind paying for your volunteer experience, **Greenway** runs excellent work camps where volunteers live in a hill-tribe community. To volunteer, you must complete an application in your home country. For more information on volunteer opportunities, see **Beyond Tourism**, p. 76.

NAN
☎054

Sharing a name with the province to which it belongs, the city of Nan was founded in 1369. Hidden amidst the mountains on the outskirts of the Lanna Kingdom, Nan developed a unique culture and history, remaining a semi-autonomous principality until 1931. During the 1960s and 1970s, the city's isolation made it a haven for smugglers. Today, Nan's seclusion provokes nothing more threatening than frequent shouts of "Hello" from children unfamiliar with *farang*. Mural-bedecked *wats* and colorful boat races distinguish Nan province from other regions of Thailand; Nan city is undoubtedly a microcosm of its province.

▛ TRANSPORTATION

Flights: Nan Airport (☎054 771 308), on Worawichai Rd., 4km north of town. **PB Air** (☎054 710 729; open daily 9am-3pm) flies to **Bangkok** (M-Tu and F-Sa 1:30pm, 2600฿).

Buses: The **bus station** is just off Chao Fah Rd. (Hwy. 101) as you enter town, 200m north of the Nan River. To: **Chiang Rai** (5hr., 9am, 200฿); **Phayo** (5hr.; 7:30, 9am, 1:30pm; 180฿); **Phitsanulok** (6hr.; 7:45, 9:45, 11am, 12:30, 1:35, 7:15pm; 250฿) via **Uttaradit**; **Phrae** (green bus, 2hr., every hr. 5:30am-5pm, 81-150฿); **Pua** (orange bus, 1hr., every hr. 5am-6pm, 70฿); **Chiang Mai** (6hr., 7 per day 7:30am-8:15pm, 206-255฿) via **Lampang** (4hr., 150฿); **Bangkok** (10hr., 6 per day 8-9am and 6-7pm, 388-770฿). Private companies, such as **Sombat Tours** (☎054 710 122; ticket counter 7) run buses to **Bangkok**.

Rentals: Oversea, 490 Sumon Thewarat Rd. (☎054 710 258), at Mahawong Rd., rents **mountain bikes** (80฿ per day). Open daily 8:30am-5:30pm. Passport deposit required. Rent **motorbikes** directly from the Yamaha dealership (☎054 710 062) a block north on Sumon Thewarat Rd. Open daily 8am-5pm. Motorbikes with automatic transmission 150฿ for a ½-day, 200฿ for 24hr.

🔧📋 ORIENTATION AND PRACTICAL INFORMATION

Nan is bordered on the south and east by the **Nan River.** All buses arrive at the station off **Chao Fah Road,** in the southwestern corner of the city. The downtown area is walkable and contains most of the important sights, accommodations, and food. The main roads are **Anonta Worarittidit Rd.,** which runs east-west and connects the markets, banks, and pharmacies; and **Sumon Thewarat Rd.,** which runs north-south and leads to the upper part of the ciy. There, the streets are less busy and less commercialized. You'll want to rent a bicycle or motorbike to visit this area, though, as it's a long 2-3km walk from downtown.

Tourist Information: The new **tourist information pavilion** (☎054 710 216) is located directly across from Wat Phumin, and gives out free maps and small guidebooks for the area. (Open daily 8:30am-4pm.) Another good source of information is **Fhu Travel** 453/4 Sumon Thewarat Rd. (☎054 710 636; www.fhutravel.com), which primarily organizes city tours and treks in the surrounding countryside (see **Daytrips** from Nan, p. 345). Open daily 8am-6pm.

Currency Exchange: Bank of Ayudhya (☎054 772 584), on Anonta Worarittidit Rd. across from the Sukasem Hotel, has a Cirrus/MC/Plus/V **24hr. ATM.** Open M-F 8:30am-3:30pm.

Police: 52 Suriyaphong Rd. (☎054 751 681), opposite the city hall. There is also a **police booth** (☎054 710 216) in the tourist information pavilion.

Pharmacy: Across from the Ayudhya Bank on Anonta Worarittidit Rd. (☎054 210 031). Open M-F 8am-9pm. Many others on Sumon Thewarat Rd. and Anonta Worarittidit Rd.

Medical Services: Nan Provincial Hospital (☎054 710 138), on Worawichai Rd., at the bend in Sumon Thewarat Rd., 3km north of downtown. Some English spoken. *Songthaew* and motorcycle taxis leave from the area around the intersection of Anonta Worarittidit Rd. and Sumon Thewarat Rd (30฿). 24hr. emergency care and pharmacy.

Telephones: Telecommunications Office (☎054 773 214), Mahayod Rd., 2km outside town. International phones and fax. Open M-F 8:30am-4:30pm.

Internet Access: Kan Internet is down an alley off Mahayod Rd., 30m south of the intersection with Anonta Worarittidit Rd. English sign on the street says "Wireless Internet." 10฿ per hr. Open daily 8am-10pm.

Post Office: GPO, 70 Mahawong Rd. (☎054 710 176). Poste Restante. Open M-F 8:30am-4:30pm, Sa-Su 9am-noon. **Postal Code:** 55000

🏠 ACCOMMODATIONS

The guesthouses and hotels downtown are only a 15 or 20min. stroll from the bus station, and within walking distance of Nan's major sights. The guesthouses in the upper part of the city have a more tranquil atmosphere, but their remote location will probably require a bicycle or motorbike rental if you want to spend time downtown (and you will, because there isn't much to do in the northern neighborhoods).

🏚 **Nan Guest House,** 57/16 Mahaphrom Rd. (☎054 771 849), a 15min. walk from the bus station. Follow Chao Fah Rd., then take a right on Mahaphrom Rd.; the English sign will be on your left, about 500m away. In the middle of a network of small open alleyways, Nan Guest House has a great location near the bustle of downtown, but not within earshot of it. Spotless rooms and shared baths, with a remodeled lounge and sitting area in the main house. English co-owner Ralph is an excellent source of information about the town and surrounding countryside. Laundry 5-10฿ per piece. Internet 20฿ per hr. Singles with shared bath 160฿, doubles with private bath 230฿. ❷

Amazing Guest House, 25/7 Soi Snow White (☎054 710 893). Going north on Sumon Thewarat Rd., take a left after the school onto Prempracharaj Rd. and go down the second soi on your right. Feels as though you're a guest in a friend's home: tastefully decorated bedrooms with towels provided, clean shared baths with hot water, and delicious meals with the family (around 60-80฿). Chores are optional. Newer private bungalows in the back are in the middle of a well-tended garden. Bicycle rentals 30-50฿ per day. Motorbikes 150-200฿ per day. Free pickup from bus station upon request. Singles with fan 90-130฿; doubles 180-200฿; triples 210-250฿; bungalows with private bath and fan 250-330฿, with A/C 350฿. Discount for 1 week 10%, 1 month 25%. ❶

Nanfah Hotel (☎054 710 284), on Sumon Thewarat Rd., next to the significantly more ostentatious Dhevaraj Hotel. Spacious rooms with attractive interiors fill up this two-story hotel. The hallways, stay cool during the sweltering heat. Open-air common areas overlook the street below. All rooms have Western toilets, A/C, hot water, and cable TV. Singles 350฿, doubles 600฿, triples 700฿. ❸

🔲 FOOD

The highest concentration of restaurants is near **Anonta Worarittidit Rd.,** with some staying open until well after dark. The **day** and **night markets** are excellent places to find inexpensive rice and noodle stands (see **Markets,** below).

Nan

🏠 ACCOMMODATIONS
Amazing Guest House, **4**
Nan Guest House, **7**
Nanfah Hotel, **2**

🍴 FOOD
Do.Re.Mi Restaurant, **3**
Ruenkaew Restaurant, **1**
Tanaya Diner, **5**
Pizza Da-Dario, **6**

Tanaya Diner, 75/23-24 Anonta Worarittidit Rd. (☎054 710 930), across the street from the 7-Eleven. The friendly owner offers an English menu with vegetarian options and a delicious Indian curry with chicken (45฿). Lunch noodle and rice dishes 35-45฿, dinner 60-80฿. Open daily 10am-3:30pm and 5-8pm. ❷

Do.Re.Mi. (☎081 027 5965), on the right after you enter the parking lot of the Nara Department store on Sumon Thewarat Rd. Look for a large seating area with communal tables. Popular with locals and families, this barbecue restaurant offers an all-you-can-grill dinner buffet (99฿). Pick and choose fresh meat and seafood and cook your meal at your table on the *mugata,* a traditional grill. Live music. Open nightly 6-11pm. ❷

Ruenkaew Restaurant, on Sumon Thewarat Rd., the last restaurant before the bend 3km from town, just before the hospital. No English sign. Serves mostly Thai dishes from a simple English menu. The main draw here, however, is the terrace overlooking the Nan River. Live music nightly at 7pm. Fried chicken with ginger 80฿. Dishes 50-140฿. Large Singha 80฿. Open daily 10am-9pm. ❷

Pizza Da-Dario, 262/3 Mahayod Rd. (☎087 184 5436), 100m north of the intersection with Mahawong Rd. The clientele for this Italian-American restaurant is more mixed than one might expect, with locals joining *farang* in the intimate dining room and at the tables outside. The "maitre'd steak" (150฿) is particularly good, but expect up to a 1hr. wait for the namesake pizza (110-150฿). Open daily 10am-10pm. ❸

▮ MARKETS

A spacious **produce market,** also referred to as the evening market, sets up on **Jettabut Rd.** just past the Honda dealership, and is active from early to late afternoon. The **night market,** the largest and most comprehensive market in Nan, and certainly worth visiting. Several counters feature more than 20 dishes; a simple point at the bag you wish to purchase will get you a meal for 10-15฿. The northern half of the market sells **non-food items** like belts, handsaws, and motorcycle helmets. The best time to go is 3-6pm.

Anonta Worarittidit Rd. hosts markets along its sidewalks in the morning and at night. The **morning market** sells everything from pineapples to small turtles. The **night market,** primarily a row of food stalls next to the road, starts around 6pm, on Anonta Worarittidit Rd. outside the 7-Eleven, and extends around the corner on **Pha Kong Rd;** it's open until around 9pm.

◉ SIGHTS

The **Nan National Museum,** in the beautiful white palace at the intersection of Suriyaphong and Pha Kong Rd., features informative exhibits in English on Nan's history and hill tribes. Upstairs, Buddha images and a black elephant tusk are on display. (☎054 710 561. *Entrance off Pha Kong Rd. Open daily 9am-4pm. 30฿.*) Nan's ornate, detailed *wats* are among the most beautiful in northern Thailand. All are free, and open from dawn until late afternoon. Two of the most striking *wats* are within easy walking distance of the downtown area. Across from the musuem on Pha Kong Rd. is **Wat Phra That Chang Kham,** which is famed for its walking Buddha made of gold and an elephant-supported pagoda. The 400-year-old **Wat Phumin,** also on Pha Kong Rd., south of the museum, contains murals depicting Lanna culture. The circular building on the right houses bizarre statues depicting humans being tortured in hell.

You'll have to leave town to visit some of the most famous *wats.* Charter a *songthaew* or motorcycle taxi (40-150฿), or rent transportation of your own. The distinctive *chedi* of **Wat Phra That Chae Haeng** shines 2km beyond the Nan River bridge. Constructed nearly 700 years ago, the *wat* is the oldest in the region. Southwest of town, the serene **▨Wat Phra That Khao Noi** has a standing

Buddha surveying the valley below. The tiled terraces of the *wat* offer spectacular views. Don't miss the intriguing stone figures on the hillside directly below the *wat*, alongside the immense serpent-lined staircase to the top.

The attraction at **Wat Phaya Wat** is the slightly lopsided old pagoda that leans parallel to the bending coconut palm. *(Go west on Suriyaphong Rd. to Hwy. 101 and turn right soon after the bus station, immediately after a green sign for Phra That Khao Noi. Wat Phaya Wat is on the plain, while Wat Phra That Khao Noi is 2km up the road, on top of a hill.)*

Back in town, the **Thai Payap Project** sells hill-tribe **handicrafts** from 15 villages in the **Hattasin Shop** on Mahawong Rd., across from the post office. The project also arranges **homestays**, during which travelers may live and work with a family in one of two villages. All proceeds go to community development projects in the area. *(☎ 098 503 567. Open daily 9am-5pm.)*

The best place to purchase **silver** is directly from the hill tribes, but if you can't make the trip, **Chompu Phuka** has a showroom with hill-tribe silverware and fabrics. Follow Suriyaphong Rd. west out of town toward Phayao for 1km; the showroom is on the right opposite PT Gas Station. There are no English signs, but look for the wagon wheels in the stone fence surrounding the parking lot. *(Open daily 8:30am-5:30pm.)*

▶ DAYTRIPS FROM NAN

Locals insist that no visit to Nan is complete without a trip into the area's rugged backcountry. They're right. Just a few kilometers away from town, the scenery is some of the most beautiful—and least touristed—in northern Thailand. However, because the area is quite rural, there is little public transportation. You'll have to rent a motorbike or hire a *songthaew*. Nan province is now almost entirely safe; though some mines remain buried in the most remote areas near the border with Laos, risks are minimal, especially on roads or trails. Getting lost is actually a greater danger, as English signs are sparse. Bring a detailed regional map, which you can find at Nan Guesthouse or the tourist office. In general, the roads are well-maintained and rarely busy. Combine that with the scenery, small towns, and lack of tourists, and Nan is a paradise for independent exploration.

For those who would prefer not to rent their own transportation, there is another terrific way to see the area. **Fhu Travel** (p. 342), in town, leads expeditions around the province. A **trek** with Mr. Fhu is the best way to visit the **Mlabri** (Phi Tong Lueng, "Spirit of the Yellow Leaves"), a tribe found only in Nan and Phrae provinces. Year-round **rafting** on the Nan River through **Mae Charim National Park** is also possible. *(☎ 054 710 636; www.fhutravel.com. 1-day trek to Mlabri territory 1400฿ each for 2 people, 800฿ each for 5 or more; 3-day trek 3200/1800฿, 1-day rafting trip 2300/1200฿.)*

▦ DOI PHUKHA NATIONAL PARK AND ENVIRONS

Using public transportation: take a bus from Nan to Pua (1hr., every hr. 5am-6pm, 40฿), then catch a songthaew to Bor Kleua (first songthaew departs between 8 and 10am, and others leave infrequently throughout the day; 50฿). Return transportation is difficult, as you'll have to wait for a passing songthaew to flag down. Motorbike rental available at the Yamaha dealership in city of Nan (see p. 341). If traveling by motorbike, leave Nan to the northeast, crossing the bridge north of the hospital. When you come to a T intersection, take a left, following signs for Rte. 1169 to Santisuk. After about 30km, you'll reach another T intersection. Turn left to remain on Rte. 1169. After another 10km, turn right for Rte. 1081 to Bor Kluea. To get to the village, wait until you see an intersection with a well-marked sign for Rte. 1256 and Doi Phukha National Park, and turn left, leaving Rte. 1081. To return to Nan from Pua by motorbike, take a left onto Rte. 1056, at the intersection near Pua. Do not follow the large marked signs to Nan unless you want to take the highway back (60km). Follow signs for either Bor Kluea or Santisuk. Rte. 1056 turns into Rte. 1081, then

Rte. 1169. In Santisuk (20km past the Silaphet waterfall), turn right onto Rte. 1169, and continue 30km back to Nan. Make a final right turn just before the bridge.

The best way to experience Nan's scenery is to explore Doi Phukha National Park, 85km from Nan. The park is home to the **Hmong** and **Mien** tribes, and contains a plethora of waterfalls and caves. Its most prized attraction is the extremely rare **Chomphu Phukha** tree (Bretschneidera sinensis), which blooms in February with foot-long clusters of red-veined, hibiscus-shaped flowers. Some choose to use public transportation to view the park, while the more adventerous rent motorbikes. Either way, the views are well worth the extra baht it takes to get around.

Though public transportation may be the easier way to see the park, it severely limits a traveler's flexibility and there is no assured return transportation. Still, the scenery from the bus as it winds through the park is breathtaking, and you can disembark at any point along the way. If you decide to get off, the best place is at the Chomphu tree, 30km from Pua. From there, it's a 2km walk downhill to the **park office** and **visitor's center,** with a scenic viewpoint, restrooms, campsites, and nature trail.

A much better way to explore Doi Phukha National Park is by motorbike. The **5-7hr. loop** is on well-paved back roads. Be sure to bring along a detailed regional map, along with sunblock and water. Also, make sure the motorbike you're renting has good brakes and alignment. Ask for a helmet with a drop-down visor. It's wise to fill up the gas tank in Nan, even though there are gas stations in Bor Kleua and Pua.

Each segment of the motorbike ride through the national park showcases a different aspect of Nan province's famed landscape. The gradual climb on **Route 1169** passes smiling farmers working on the hillsides. Narrow ridgelines, surrounded on all sides by views that stretch for kilometers, characterize the ride on **Route 1081,** which eventually weaves down to the tiny brookside village of Bor Kluea, with food and gas facilities. While there, be sure to check out the town's natural salt pits. **Route 1256** leads to **Pua** (47km), runs directly through Doi Phukha National Park, and goes over a couple of mountains. Along the way, you'll pass a large shrine (on your left 15km from Bor Kluea), the famous Chomphu tree, and a **camping area** (2km down the road from the Chomphu tree) with a viewpoint and nature trail. The park office, 3km past the camping area on the right, is next to the park's main entrance (admission 200฿). Pua is 25km farther along Rte. 1256.

PHRAE ☎ 054

Usually unnoticed by tourists on their way to Nan or Chiang Rai, Phrae (pronounced "*pleh*") is a small, peaceful town. Its popular attractions—Wat Phra Chaw Hae, a large temple structure, and mysterious rock formations billed as a "mini Grand Canyon"—lie on the outskirts of town. But Phrae itself is the real attraction here. Leisurely strolls through the busy night market and the historic old town make this secluded stop worthwhile, if uneventful.

TRANSPORTATION

Buses: Phrae is a gateway to Nan and Chiang Rai farther north, it has frequent and convenient transportation. The **bus station,** in the northeast corner of Phrae, east of Yantarkitkosol Rd., runs buses to: **Bangkok** (9hr., 13 per day 6:30pm-11:30am, 227-500฿); **Nan** (3hr., 10 per day 9:30am-1:30pm, 81-150฿); **Chiang Mai** (4hr., every hr. 6am-5:30pm and 12:30am, 92-176฿); **Lampang** (2hr., every hr., 53-101฿); **Chiang**

Rai (4hr., every hr. 7am-4pm, 114-205в); **Phitsanulok** (4hr., every hr. 6am-midnight, 83-150в); **Sukhothai** (3hr., every hr. 10:30am-2pm, 82-148в).

Trains: The nearest **train station** is in Den Chai, about 25km away on the Bangkok-Chiang Mai line. A **minibus** leaves from a stop on Yantarkitkosol Rd., 400m south of the intersection with Charoen Muang Rd. (45min., leaves when full 9am-6pm, 50в).

Local Transportation: Samlor (20-30в) and blue and crimson **songthaew** (10-20в) along Charoen Muang and Yantarkitkosol Rd.

ORIENTATION AND PRACTICAL INFORMATION

Phrae is 550km north of Bangkok and 200km southeast of Chiang Mai. There are two main roads in Phrae. The first is **Yantarkitkosol Road,** which runs north-south and leads to the bus station. The second is a road that is bisected by Yantarkitkosol Rd. The western section of the road has been named **Charoen Muang Road,** and leads to the old city; the eastern section, **Chor Hae Road,** runs to the hospital (1km) and the airport (2km). **Rob Muang Road** forms an oval around the circumference of the old city. Most daytime activity centers at the **day market,** just off Yantarkitkosol Rd. After dark, the crowds shift to the **night market** on Rob Muang Rd.

There is no official tourist office in Phrae, but the staff at the bus station's information booth can provide limited assistance and a detailed map of the city. **Bangkok Bank,** on Charoen Muang Rd., 100m past the intersection with Yantakaritkosol Rd., exchanges currency and has a **24hr. ATM** (open M-F 8:30am-3:30pm). The **police station** (☎054 511 089), at Rong Sor and Ratchadamnoen Rd., is open 24hr. There are **pharmacies, laundry services, and barbershops** along the stretch of Charoen Muang Rd. between Yantarkitkosol Rd. and the old city. To reach **Tewan Pharmacy** (☎054 511 131), go toward the old city on Charoen Muang Rd. and turn right on Rob Muang Rd., and it's 30m up on the right side. (Open daily 6-8am and 5-9pm.) You can find Internet access at **N'Joy** (☎089 953 1963), 50m past the **night market** on Charoen Muang Rd. (Open daily 10am-10pm. Internet 15в per hr.) The **post office,** with a **CAT Telecom** office inside, is located on Charon Muaeng Rd. before the central rotary in the old city. (Open M-F 8:30am-4:30pm, Sa-Su 9am-noon.) **Postal Code:** 54000.

ACCOMMODATIONS

As long as you're not averse to peeling paint or squat toilets, you'll find a number of cheap, centrally located hotels in Phrae. Because the town is not accustomed to a large number of foreign tourists, mid-range accommodations are limited. In general, the difference in room quality from a 100в-a-night hotel to a 250в hotel is well worth the upgrade.

▨ **Paradorn Hotel,** 177 Yantarkitkosol Rd. (☎054 511 177; www.phrae-paradorn.th.gs). Follow Yantarkitkosol Rd. from the bus station towards town for 50m. Lives up to its motto, "Absolutely Clean," with recently renovated rooms with TV, telephone, Western toilet, and hot shower. In terms of room quality for price, this is the best value in Phrae. The only downside is the 15min. walk to the old town. Restaurant open daily 6am-4pm. Singles with fan 300в, with A/C 480в; doubles 350/580в. ❸

Thepvong Place Hotel, 346/2 Charoen Muang Rd. (☎054 521 985), 100m from the Yantarkitkosol-Charoen Muang Rd. intersection, on the old city side; take a left down the 1st alley. The spacious, high-ceilinged rooms have cable TV, Western toilets, private balconies, and hot showers. With a great location near the old town, the Thepvong Place Hotel is an attractive option for those who aren't afraid of a few bugs. Rooms with fan 250в, with A/C 350в. ❸

Toongsri Phaibool Hotel (☎054 511 011), on Yantarkitkosol Rd., 30m north of the intersection with Chor Hae Rd. The aging yellow-painted rooms, arranged around a large open courtyard, aren't easy on the eyes, but are centrally located and inexpensive. All rooms have TV and private bath. Singles with fan and squat toilet 130฿, doubles 180฿, rooms with A/C and Western toilet 310฿. ❷

Tepviman Hotel, 226-228 Charoen Muang Rd. (☎054 511 003), in the center of town. One of the cheapest options in Phrae, with 37 hotel-style rooms that include baths and Western toilets. Spend the extra 20฿ for the rooms upstairs, as they're much nicer than those on the bottom floor. Manager Nuj speaks English and will happily provide information about the town. Singles and doubles with bath and fan 100-120฿, triples 170฿. ❶

⬡ FOOD

The **day market** on Muang Dang and Chor Hae Rd. is a gold mine for fresh produce and fish, the latter in various stages of life and afterlife. The **night market** on Rob Muang Rd., as you enter the old city from the town center, becomes increasingly crowded as the sun sets. The **food stalls** set out tables on the street, making this a great place to eat a cheap, delicious dinner.

▨ Ponjai (☎054 620 727), in the old city. Turn right on Weera Rd. just before the post office; it's the 2nd restaurant on your right. Ponjai's excellent *kanom jiin*-style food (pick your own noodles and sauce) is especially popular with locals and the university crowd. The sprawling open-air wooden terrace is ideal for relaxing. Try the *toto,* small servings of vegetables and pork fried with egg (30฿). Buffet-style noodles and sauce 25-30฿. Open daily 7am-4pm. ❶

Kamean Koei (☎054 523 399), on Rob Muang Rd., at the northeast corner of the small traffic circle. This traditional Thai eatery is located right in the thick of things and utilizes an industrial aesthetic to great effect. Try the spicy green curry with noodles (20฿) or papaya salad (20฿) as you watch the night market through the large streetside openings. Entrees 20-40฿. Open 10am-10pm. ❶

Khua Chaiwatthana (☎054 521 904), on Charoen Muang Rd., just south of the small traffic circle; look for the bright yellow Thai menu boards on the wall. Primarily Thai dishes (25-50฿) with a small menu of specialties (50-120฿; chicken with cashew nuts 50฿). English menu available at the same prices. Open daily 4-10pm. ❷

Tontarn (☎054 534 628), on Yantarkitkosol Rd., 5 doors down from 7-Eleven, opposite the Christian Hospital. A/C haven with a 20-page English menu of curries, noodle dishes, and soups catering to a local crowd. Red curry with boar's meat 70฿. Dishes 30-80฿. Open M-F 10am-10pm. ❷

⬡ SIGHTS

WAT PHRA THAT CHAW HAE. On top of a hill 9km outside of town, Phra That Chaw Hae looks out over the countryside from its marble terrace. Its 33m gilded pagoda and Phra Jao Than Jai Buddha image have established this *wat* as one of the most important pilgrimage sites in northern Thailand. (*Songthaew (40฿) leave roughly every hr. from a stop on the right, 500m down Chor Hae Rd., after Yantarkitkosol Rd. To return to Phrae, start walking back towards town; songthaew circle the neighborhood picking up passengers. Otherwise, charter a songthaew for 300฿.*)

PHAE MUANG PHI. About 18km away from town on Hwy. 101, Phae Muang Phi is a series of unusual rock formations caused by erosion, resembling a miniature version of the Grand Canyon in the United States. The mystery of its origin has superstitious locals convinced that phantoms haunt the area. The path that runs through the park takes 30min. to walk and gets quite hot at midday. *(Charter a songthaew (300฿ round-trip) to get here. They gather in front of the school on Yantarkitkosol Rd. Non-hired songthaew also make the trip from the school to Phae Muang Phi (45฿), but there is no easy return transportation. Open daily 7am-5pm.)*

WAT LUANG AND WAT PHRA NON. For those who don't want to make the trip out of the city, these two *wats*, situated in the northwestern blocks of the old city and a 10min. walk from the night market, provide in-town tourist attractions. **Wat Luang** is the oldest temple in Phrae, built in AD 829, the same year the city was established. It was constructed to enshrine the city's Buddha image, which was originally covered in gold. A small museum with antiques, Buddha images, and porcelain objects sits next to the *wat*. At only a century old, **Wat Phra Non,** on Pranomnuea Rd., is relatively modern. It houses an impressive reclining Buddha. *(Walking from the town center on Charoen Muang Rd., turn left on Srichum Alley, and continue past Wat Srichum. Museum entrance free.)*

WAT CHOM SAWAN. This *wat*, a 20min. walk north of the day market, features a fantastic Burmese/Shan-style temple built about 100 years ago. This *wat's* structural beauty is complemented by two holy artifacts: a 16-sheet ivory book with the teachings of Buddha written in Burmese and a bamboo basket covered in gold. *(To get to Wat Chom Sawan, continue north on Yantarkitkosol Rd. past the turnoff to the bus station and keep right when the road forks. The wat will be on your right.)*

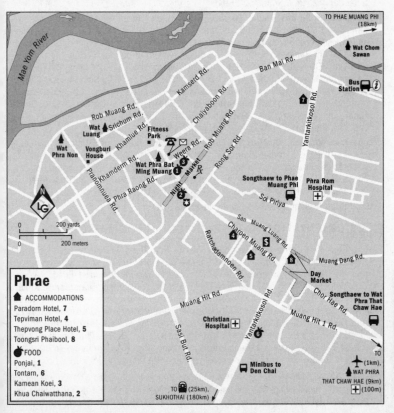

Phrae

🏠 ACCOMMODATIONS
Paradorn Hotel, **7**
Tepviman Hotel, **4**
Thepvong Place Hotel, **5**
Toongsri Phaibool, **8**

🍴 FOOD
Ponjai, **1**
Tontarn, **6**
Kamean Koei, **3**
Khua Chaiwatthana, **2**

NORTHERN THAILAND

PHITSANULOK ☎055

A pleasant, provincial river town, Phitsanulok is also a convenient base for exploring the lower north. As the proud home of Phra Buddha Chinnarat, one of Thailand's most revered Buddha images, Phitsanulok draws large crowds of Thai pilgrims. The town's characteristic houseboats, moored along the Nan river, add to the local color. Phitsanulok also has an excellent night bazaar, folk museum, and Buddha casting foundry. Little may remain of its one-time military importance as the capital of Thailand during the Ayutthaya period and as the headquarters of the Third Army during Communist uprisings in the nearby Nan hills, but Phitsanulok has plenty to keep visitors occupied.

▉ TRANSPORTATION

Flights: Phitsanulok Domestic Airport (☎055 258 029), on Sanambin Rd. **Thai Airways,** 209/26-28 Srithammatripidok Rd. (☎055 242 971). 50m to the right of TAT. Both open M-F 8am-5pm. Flights to **Bangkok** (4 per day, 1680฿).

Trains: Phitsanulok Train Station (☎055 258 005), on Akatossaroth Rd, next to the southern traffic circle. To **Bangkok** (Hua Lamphong Station; 6-8hr., 10 per day 3:51am-12:05am, 69-404฿), **Ayutthaya** (4-6hr., 4 per day, 54-258฿), and **Chiang Mai** (6-8hr., 5 per day 4:20am-1:34am, 52-269฿).

Buses: Bo Ko So Bus Station (☎055 302 716), on Phitsanulok-Lomsak Rd., east of town. Take a motorcycle taxi (60฿) or catch city bus #1, which shuttles between the train and bus stations. Schedules and prices change frequently; get an up-to-date schedule at the TAT. To: **Bangkok** (Northern Bus Station; 5-6hr.; 29 per day; 1st or 2nd cl. 238-299฿, VIP 406-650฿); **Chiang Mai** (6-7hr., 16 per day, 232-275฿); **Chiang Rai** (6-7hr., 24 per day, 275-346฿); **Khon Kaen** (6hr., 15 per day, 223฿); **Mae Sot** (5hr., 9 A/C vans per day 7am-4pm, 160฿); **Nakhon Ratchasima** (6-7hr., 10 per day, 270-393฿); **Phrae** (4hr., 14 per day, 66-119฿); **Sukhothai** (1hr., 17 per day 7am-6:15pm, 43-82฿); **Udon Thani** (7hr., 9 per day, 240-291฿) via **Loei** (4hr., 153฿). Multiple routes for major destinations. Duration of routes can vary significantly.

Local Transportation: City Bus Station, on Akatossaroth Rd., 1 block from the train station. 13 bus lines run daily 5am-9pm. Full schedule available at tourist office. Bus #1 to Bo Ko So Bus Station, Wat Yai, and Naresuan University. Bus #4 to airport. Regular buses 8-11฿, with A/C 11-14฿. Tourist office runs a tour **tram** to more than a dozen of Phitsanulok's major sights (6hr., daily 9am, 30฿); starts and ends at Wat Yai.

Car Rental: Avis, at Phitsanulok Youth Hostel (p. 351).

✦ ▉ ORIENTATION AND PRACTICAL INFORMATION

Phitsanulok lies along the east bank of the **Nan River,** 377km north of Bangkok. **Puttaboocha Road** runs alongside of the river and hosts an extensive night bazaar on its southern end. One block east is **Baromtrilokanart Road,** which encompasses the financial district. The main thoroughfare, **Akatossaroth Road,** lies two blocks east of the river and runs parallel to the railroad tracks. **Naresuan Road** leads west from the Phitsanulok Train Station on Akatossaroth Rd., cutting through the busiest part of town, as well as across Baromtrilokanart and Puttaboocha Rd., before crossing the river. The famous **Phra Buddha Chinnarat** is at Wat Yai at the northern end of Puttaboocha Rd. The **Bo Ko So Bus Station** is 2km east of the *wat* on the other side of the train tracks.

Tourist Offices: TAT (☎/fax 055 252 742), on Srithammatripidok Rd. Near Able Tours and Travel. Helpful English-speaking staff. Info, maps, and timetables for buses and train. Free Internet for tourists. Open daily 8:30am-4:30pm. **The Municipal Tourist**

Office (☎055 252 148), beside the river on Puttaboocha Rd, is located in a beautiful teak house that is worth seeing even if you don't intend to visit the office. Friendly staff but resources are not as comprehensive as at the TAT. Open M-F 8:30am-4:30pm.

Tours: Able Tours and Travel, 55/45 Srithammatripidok Rd. (☎055 243 851). Books regional tours along with domestic and international flights. Open M-F 8am-6pm, Sa 8am-4pm. MC/V.

Currency Exchange: Thai Farmers Bank, 144/1 Baromtrilokanart Rd. (☎055 241 497), at the clock tower. **24hr. ATM.** Cirrus/MC/Plus/V. Open M-F 8:30am-3:30pm. There are also several banks on Naresuan Rd.

Luggage Storage: At the train station. 10฿ per item per day. Open daily 7am-11pm.

Massage: The floating Thai Massage raft (☎055 243 389), down the stairs just south of the Naresuan Rd. bridge, offers well-priced massages on a spotlessly clean raft that bobs gently with the river. Massages 120฿ per hr., with A/C 150฿ per hr. Open daily 9:15am-9pm.

Shopping: Night bazaar, on Puttaboocha Rd., 2 blocks south of the Naresuan Rd. bridge. Large, well-organized, and touristy. **Topland Plaza,** at the rotary on the northern end of Akatossaroth Rd. Multi-level department store sells almost everything. Top-floor arcade. At the very least, a fun introduction to Thai consumer culture. Open M-F 9:30am-9pm, Sa-Su 10am-9pm.

Tourist Police: 31/15 Akatossaroth Rd. (☎055 245 357), 200m past back entrance to Wat Yai. Little English spoken. Open 24hr.

Medical Services: Buddha Chinnarat Hospital (☎055 219 844), on the southern extension of Akatossaroth Rd. The official street address is on Srithammatripidok Rd. 24hr. emergency room and **pharmacy.** 2 other hospitals, **Ruamphaet** and **Phitsanuvej,** both west on Srithammatripidok Rd., are nearby.

Telephones: Phitsanulok Telecommunications Center (☎055 243 116), on Puttaboocha Rd. near the Post Office. International phone and fax services. Open daily 7am-10pm. AmEx/MC/V.

Internet Access: The TAT offers free Internet access for tourists. For a faster connection, try any of the stores filled with teenagers playing computer games. Rates average 15฿ per hr. **Internet and Games** (☎055 258 207), across from the night bazaar on Puttaboocha Rd., is especially close to the guesthouses. (Open daily 9am-11pm. 15฿ per hr.)

Post Office: GPO (☎055 258 313), on Puttaboocha Rd., 500m north of Naresuan Rd. Poste Restante. Open M-F 8:30am-4:30pm, Sa-Su 9am-noon. **Postal Code:** 65000.

▚ ACCOMMODATIONS

Bon Bon Guest House, 77 Payalithai Rd. (☎055 219 058), beside the Lithai building, at the back of an alley. Little touches—doilies on the TV, floormats for the bathroom, paintings on the wall—make the large rooms feel like home. Cable TV, hot water, and private balconies. Rooms with fan 350฿, with A/C 450฿. ❸

Lithai, 73/1-5 Payalithai Rd. (☎055 219 626). Walk south from the train station and take the 2nd road to the right, and you'll see the sign 50m down on the left. High-quality hotel rooms surround a quiet, vine-draped inner courtyard. Some rooms have TV, hot water, and fridge. Full breakfast included at adjacent Steak Cottage with rooms 350฿ and up. Singles with fan and private bath 220฿, with A/C 350฿; doubles with A/C, private bath and hot water 460฿. ❷

Phitsanulok Youth Hostel (HI), 38 Sanambin Rd. (☎086 679 9425; www.tyha.org). Take bus #4 toward the airport. If walking, go about 2.5km south from the train station, cross the train tracks, turn right on Sanambin Rd., and look for the hostel signs on the left. As soon as you step off the main road, you'll feel like you're on a jungle safari. Brick paths overgrown with tree roots lead through overhanging vegetation to a converted old house. Those seeking a place with character won't be disappointed. Breakfast included. Dorms 120฿; singles with bath 200฿; doubles 300฿. ❶

NORTHERN THAILAND

London Hotel, 21-22 Soi 1 (☎055 225 145), off Puttaboocha Rd. From the train station, walk west on Naresuan Rd., and turn left on Baromtrilokanart Rd. You'll see the English sign as you pass Sairuthai Rd. Quirky decor for cheap. A stuffed elephant head watches over the main staircase, which leads up to a wood-shingled hallway with numerous rooms and 2 shared baths. Internet 20฿ per hr. Singles with fan and no window 100฿, doubles with window 150฿. ●

🗒 FOOD

Phitsanulok is a great place to eat. For lunch, locals head to the delicious, inexpensive restaurants in the city center, or sit at the umbrella-shaded terraces along the river and eat from the ubiquitous food stalls near Wat Yai.

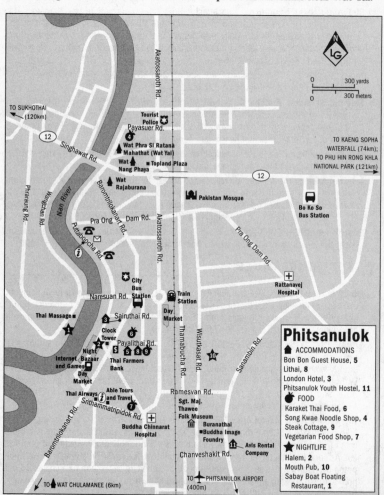

NORTHERN THAILAND

Phitsanulok

🏠 ACCOMMODATIONS
Bon Bon Guest House, **5**
Lithai, **8**
London Hotel, **3**
Phitsanulok Youth Hostel, **11**
🍴 FOOD
Karaket Thai Food, **6**
Song Kwae Noodle Shop, **4**
Steak Cottage, **9**
Vegetarian Food Shop, **7**
★ NIGHTLIFE
Halem, **2**
Mouth Pub, **10**
Sabay Boat Floating
 Restaurant, **1**

After dark, the **night market** on Puttaboocha Rd. becomes a popular destination for dinner and drinks.

Karaket Thai Food (☎055 258 193), on Payalithai Rd., across from the Lithai Building. One of several good Thai restaurants on this block. Although it is usually packed with a local crowd, Karaket eases the language barrier by setting out its pots of curries for customers to peer into before making their choices. Fresh and flavorful curries served with water, herbs, and cucumber slices. Curry with rice 20฿. Open daily 2-8pm. ❶

Song Kwae Noodle Shop (☎055 208 501), at the northern end of Puttaboocha Rd., past Wat Yai; non-English sign has an image of people sitting in a noodle bowl. A predominantly university-age crowd frequents this popular noodle shop, slurping down rice noodles as their feet hang over the edge of the relaxed roadside terrace. Pork, beef, or chicken noodle soup 25-60฿. Open daily 10am-4pm. ❶

Vegetarian Food Shop, 55/4 Srithammatripidok Rd. (☎055 246 416), beside the corner facing the hospital. A tiny underground outpost of vegetarian fare, with a small seating area along the side wall. Delicious, freshly squeezed orange juice 10฿. Veggie dish of the day with brown or white rice 15฿, 2 choices 20฿. Also sells rice and vegetarian food supplies. Open daily 6am-3pm. ❶

Steak Cottage (☎055 219 6269), in the Lithai Hotel (p. 351). Shares a kitchen with It's a Cake, which is usually open later in the day and focuses on delicious baked goods and coffee. This is the place to get your fix of Western food, including Western breakfast (70-90฿). Steak Cottage doesn't cater to vegetarians—the highlight here is the extensive steak list (80-150฿). Open daily 7am-2pm and 5-9pm. ❸

📷 SIGHTS

🖼**WAT PHRA SI RATANA MAHATHAT (WAT YAI).** This huge *wat* shelters Phitsanulok's jewel. Cast in 1357, the spectacular **Phra Buddha Chinnarat** ("Victorious King") is one of the world's most commonly reproduced Buddha images and one of Thai Buddhism's leading pilgrimage destinations. Wat Yai is also one of Thailand's most prominent *wats* in terms of the total donations that it receives each year. The Sukhothai-style image glimmers with a distinctive halo of flames that frames its head and torso. The architecture of the sanctuary itself is similarly striking, punctuated by mother-of-pearl inlay doors that Ayutthayan King Boromokat commissioned in 1756. A bustling marketplace complete with snacks, souvenir stands, and an ATM to get cash for merit donations surrounds the *wat*. The left wing of the *wat* (if you're facing Phra Buddha Chinnarat) has been turned into a small museum. *(At the northern end of Puttaboocha Rd. Wat open daily 7am-6pm. Museum open W-Su 9am-4pm. Suggested 20฿ entrance donation includes brochure. Sarongs provided free of charge to the bare-legged.)*

🖼**SERGEANT MAJOR THAWEE FOLK MUSEUM.** This museum is a remarkable project aiming to document and preserve rapidly vanishing Thai folk traditions. Spread throughout several traditional teak houses with fragrant gardens, the museum includes a traditional birthing room, an exhibit about the magical powers Thais ascribe to their tattoos, and a fascinating collection of such traditional animal traps as a snake guillotine and a porcupine snare. Visitors will leave armed with expertise about cattle castration techniques, hill-tribe costumes, and regional kite patterns. Has helpful English captions. *(26/43 Wisutkasat Rd. ☎055 212 749. Open Tu-Su 8am-4:30pm. 50฿, students 20฿; includes a souvenir postcard.)*

📷 NIGHTLIFE

Phitsanulok is not heavily touristed by Westerners, and so it's mercifully free of the hostess bars common in other parts of Thailand. Instead, students from the nearby universities contribute to a lively bar scene that is active most nights of the week. This crowd congregates at the row of open-air bars overlooking the Nan River along the far side of the night market. The downtown area is less busy after dark but has a few popular bars.

Halem (☎086 778 8884), toward the northern end of the night market. Uses red lighting to create a low-key mood, and is conveniently around the corner from spotless public bathrooms. Large Singha 75฿. Open daily 6pm-midnight.

Sabay Boat Floating Restaurant (☎055 251 970), across the river from Halem; go down the stairs, past Thai Massage and Wow! Food and Drink. This floating party attracts a slightly older clientele and features nightly karaoke and live music. Large beer 100฿. Open daily noon-11pm.

The Mouth Pub and Restaurant, (☎055 219 456), near the eastern end of Srithamma-tripidok Rd., attracts Westerners with indoor/outdoor seating and airy, tasteful interior design. Large Tiger beer 80฿. Open daily 11am-midnight.

🎵 ENTERTAINMENT

If it's the right time of year, you can partake in one of Phitsanulok's two major **festivals. Long-tailed-boat races** are the central attraction of a festival that takes place when the Nan River is at its fullest, generally in early October. The boats depart from the front of Wat Yai, and river processions accompany the races. On the waxing moon of the third lunar month, generally in January or February, the **Phra Nakhon Khiri Fair** gets under way. Wat Yai hosts a lavish six-day festival of homages, traditional entertainment, and dance and theater performances.

🔲 DAYTRIP FROM PHITSANULOK: PHU HIN RONG KHLA

Park headquarters located 125km northeast of Phitsanulok. To reach the park, take a bus to Nakhon Thai (2hr., every hr. 5am-6pm, 50-70฿) and then grab a songthaew 32km to Phu Hin Rong Khla (1hr., 3 per day, 80฿). Private transportation is necessary to see much of the park. Charter a songthaew for the day for 2000฿ from Phitsanulok, less from Nakhon Thai. Direct drive from 2hr. Phitsanulok. Take Rte. 12 from Phitsanulok, then take a left onto Rte. 2013 to Nakhon Thai. Turn right onto Rte. 2331, follow signs to Nakhon Thai or National Park about 70km out on Rte. 12. Contact the Forestry Department in Bangkok (☎02 579 7223) or Phu Hin Rong Khla Park (☎05 523 3527) for more info. Park headquarters open daily 8am-4pm. 200฿, students 100฿.

The area that is now Phu Hin Rong Khla gained notoriety in the late 1960s as the stronghold of the communist People's Liberation Army of Thailand (PLAT) and was the site of their clashes with the Thai army for almost 20 years. From 1967-1982, PLAT survived in the Phu Hin Rong Khla forests near the Laotian border. Recruits poured in after the crackdown on student demonstrators in Bangkok in 1976, but in 1982, the government struck a decisive blow to the movement by offering amnesty to all students who had joined after 1976. In 1984, the area was declared a national park.

Today, the park offers not only hiking trails, scenic views, and waterfalls, but also provides a close look into the scattered air-raid shelters and military barracks that survive from its embattled past. The most visited sight in the park is the **flagpole,** near the old Communist headquarters. A 3.2km nature walk leads to the flagpole, where the Thai flag now flies; here on the ridge of the mountain range, one can enjoy the panoramic view of the valley below. The start of the walk lies 2km from park headquarters along a marked and paved road. A map of the natural and historical attractions of Phu Hin Rong Khla is available at park headquarters.

Phu Hin Rong Khla's **park headquarters** offer some cheap accommodations. (Tent rental 100฿. Camping 30฿; bungalows 300-2500฿.) Those traveling with their own transportation will want to explore the many waterfalls that lie off Rte. 12. The best is the three-tiered, 40m drop of **Kaeng Sopha Waterfall,** 74km outside of Phitsanulok. The dry-season flow will leave you unsatisfied, but the large alley boulders entwined with trees warrant exploration. The turnoff to Kaeng Sopha Waterfall is 3km beyond the turn off to Nakhon Thai, and it's 2km from the main road to the waterfall. TAT has a regional map noting the relative positions of waterfalls along Rte. 12. All turnoffs are well-marked.

SOUTHERN THAILAND

As one of the most famous international beach destinations, southern Thailand is a full-blown vacation mecca. With some of the world's best dive sites, thousands of kilometers of white sand beach, rock climbing, high-profile nightlife, and a well-developed tourist infrastructure, it's not surprising that millions of tourists visit every year. The high volume of tourism does mean that nearly every island is hospitable to visitors and that English is an unofficial second language, but the convenience bred of such tremendous development has also begun to overwhelm both the environment and Thai culture. Farther south, mosques gradually replace *wats* as the ethnic mix shifts from Thai to Malay, and the number of tourists dwindles. Most travelers today enjoy a middle ground, balancing the extremes of the south.

CHUMPHON ☎077

For most travelers, Chumphon is simply a stop en route to the tropical trinity of Ko Tao, Ko Phangan, and Ko Samui, serving as a gateway to the south. With a tourist industry built to cater to those waiting for the next leg of a journey to or from the islands, Chumphon is a highly convenient and comfortable place to book onward tickets, check email, make overseas calls, and swap stories with other travelers. Those without immediate logistical or communication needs, however, might prefer to leave the rather charmless town and relax nearby on the undeveloped, pristine beach at Thung Wua Laen.

▐ TRANSPORTATION

Trains: Chumphon Train Station (☎077 511 103), at the west end of Krumluang Chumphon Rd. Luggage storage 10฿ per day. To: **Surat Thani** (3hr., 11 per day 9pm-6am, 100฿), **Bangkok** (7-10hr., 10 trains per day 7:30pm-2:30am, 480฿) via **Hua Hin** (3-4hr., 93฿) and **Phetchaburi** (4-5hr., 7 per day, 225฿).

Buses: The biggest Chumphon **bus station** (☎077 502 268) is located 12km to the east of Chumphon on Hwy. 4. A white *songthaew* with a red stripe goes from the intersection of Poramin Monka Rd. and Phinit Khadi Rd. to the bus station (50฿) and back from 8am-6pm. While buses going to all destinations stop at this main bus station, most destinations can be accessed from smaller bus stations located within the city of Chumphon. **2nd-cl. A/C Buses** to **Bangkok** (8-10hr., 8 per a day 8am-8pm, 360฿) via **Phetchaburi** (270฿) and **Hua Hin** (230฿) leave from a small bus station on Poramin Monka Rd. between its intersection with Thawi Sinkha Soi 2 and Rotfai Rd. VIP Buses to **Bangkok** (7hr.; 10:30am, 2:00, and 9:30pm; 350-550฿. **2nd cl. A/C buses** to **Phuket** (6-8hr.; 5:30, 8:00, 10:00, 11:50am; 370฿), **Hat Yai** (10hr.; 8:30, 9:30, 11:30am, 9:00pm; 350-450฿); all leave from near the market just off Pracha Uthit Rd. Unless you want to head to the bus station 12km. away from Chumphon and catch a bus at 2am, buy a ticket from one of the local travel agencies or hotels for a bus that will pick you up from your hotel and take you to **Krabi** (4hr.; 6:00am, 1:00pm; 470฿).

Minibuses: White minibuses to **Ranong** (2-3hr., every hr. 8am-6pm, 120฿) leave from Tha Thapoa Rd. across from New Infinty Travel, and will probably drop you off wherever you want in Ranong if you tell them in advance. Minibuses for **Surat Thani** (2-3hr., every hr. 8am-6pm, 170฿) leave from within a parking lot next to the night market; on the right side of Krumluang Chumphon Rd. when heading away from the train station.

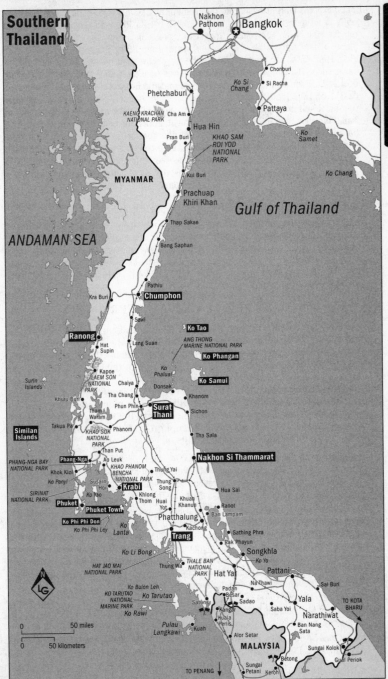

Boats: Express boat tickets for **Ko Tao** (Lomprayah Catamaran, 1½-2hr., 7am and 1pm, 550฿; Songserm Express Boat 3hr., 7am, 450฿), **Ko Phangan** (Lomprayah Catamaran, 3-3½hr.; 7am, 1pm; 750฿; Songserm Express 5hr.; 7am, 1pm; 600฿), and for **Ko Samui** (Lomprayah Catamaran 4½-5hr.; 7am, 1pm; 850฿; Songserm Express 6½hr.; 7am, 1pm; 750฿) can be purchased at their respective piers or at travel agencies for the same price. The **Lomprayah Catamaran** leaves from the **Thong Makham Pier** (☎077 558 212), 20km. south of Chumphon; the **Songserm Express** leaves from **Thayang Pier** (☎077 553 052), 10km. south of town. Both have taxi services that pick you up from your hotel and bring you to the pier for free. **Slow midnight boats** leave from the **Pak Nam Pier,** 6km from town (6hr., daily midnight, 200฿). The night boat does not provide transportation to the pier. Tourist agencies and guesthouses sell tickets and provide transportation (50฿), and can arrange a wake-up call for any of the times. Night boats are entirely exposed to the elements—check weather reports. In general, faster boats are also more likely to induce seasickness. To visit **Ko Maphraw (Coconut Island)** and some of the similar smaller and less developed islands contact Chumphon National Park (☎077 558 144), which sells package tours that vary by price and destination according to the number and interest of the participants.

Local Transportation: Motorcycle taxis (20-30฿) are all over town, especially near the train station, the markets, and the numerous bus stations. Almost every guesthouse and travel agency rents **motorbikes** (200฿ per day). Santawee New Guesthouse rents **bicycles** (100฿ per day with passport deposit). Fame Travel Agency rents **cars** (1200฿ per day). The Chumphon Cabana Resort (☎077 504 442) in Hat Thung Wua Laen rents **diving equipment.** Open daily 9am-8pm.

◢✦🔋 ORIENTATION AND PRACTICAL INFORMATION

Chumphon is 498km south of Bangkok. The town is small, but somewhat confusing to navigate. **Krumluang Chumphon Road,** home of the town's night market, runs east from the train station, forming the northern edge of town. **Poramin Monka Road** marks the southern limit; look for the hospital, post office, and official tourist offices here. *Farang*-oriented travel agencies and guest houses line **Tha Tapoa Road,** which runs north-south through the southwestern part of the city. Parallel to Tha Tapoa Rd. and one block east is hotel- and eatery-studded **Sala Daeng Road.** "V"-shaped **Pracha Uthit Road,** turns into **Phisit Phayaban Road** on the eastern side of Chumphon, and straddles the city center, the day market is on the west side along.

Tourist Office: Municipal Office (☎077 511 024, ext. 120), 100m. west of the post office. Left off Tha Thapoa Rd. onto Poramin Monka Rd., first left after the market onto Phinit Khadi Rd., right into the first parking lot. Questions can be answered more conveniently by better English speakers at one of the tourist agencies on Tha Tapoa Rd. and Sala Daeng Rd.

Tours: Commercial tourist agencies sell boat tickets and arrange tours on Tha Tapoa Rd. **New Infinity Travel,** 68/2 Tha Tapoa (☎077 570 176), near the Farang Bar. Employee Are speaks great English, and is incredibly helpful when booking tickets and planning out trips in any direction. She has pictures on her computer to help with directions. Open 8am-8pm. **Fame Tour & Service,** 188/20-21 Sala Daeng Road (☎077 571 077), provides ferry tickets, advance booking for trains and buses, luggage storage, and arranges for scuba diving on Ko Tao. Open daily 7am-midnight.

Currency Exchange: Bangkok Bank, 111/1-2 Sala Daeng Rd. (☎077 511 446). **24hr. ATM.** Open M-F 8:30am-4:30pm. Other 24hr. ATMs can be found on nearly every block of the city, especially in more touristy areas on Sala Daeng Rd. and Tha Thapoa Rd.

Police: (☎077 511 300), on Sala Daeng Rd., about 100m north of the intersection with Krumluang Rd. Little English spoken. Open 24hr.

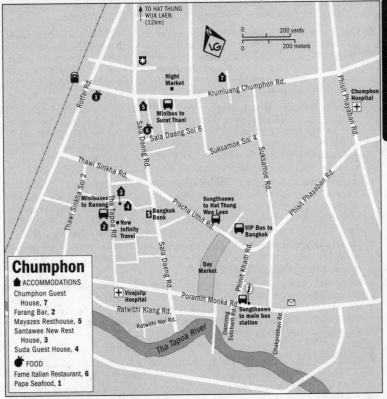

Chumphon

ACCOMMODATIONS
Chumphon Guest
    House, **7**
Farang Bar, **2**
Mayazes Resthouse, **5**
Santawee New Rest
    House, **3**
Suda Guest House, **4**

FOOD
Fame Italian Restaurant, **6**
Papa Seafood, **1**

Medical Services: Virajsilp Hospital (☎077 503 238), at the south end of Tha Tapoa Rd.; a 5min. walk from the bus station. Great service. Cash only. Open 24hr. Has **pharmacy. Chumphon Hospital** (☎503 672), on Phisit Phayaban Rd., at the corner of the intersection with Krumluang Rd., provides 24hr. emergency care.

Telephones: Most guesthouses and tourist offices have international phone service, though **TOT phone cards** can be purchased at most 7-Elevens for half the price (4฿ per min. to the US).

Internet Access: Farang Bar offers the cheapest Internet on their one computer, located behind the kitchen (30฿ per hr.). **New Infinity Travel** and **Fame Tour and Service** offer 1฿ per min. Internet and Wi-Fi.

Post Office: GPO, 192 Poramin Manka Rd. (☎077 511 041), southeast of town, past the tourist office, on the left. Poste Restante. Open M-F 8:30am-4:30pm, Sa 9am-noon. **Postal Code:** 86000.

ACCOMMODATIONS

Inexpensive sleeping options abound in Chumphon. Many of Chumphon's budget accommodations aim to be one-stop service centers for everything an island-hopping traveler might need or want: food, drinks, Internet, travel bookings, and massages. The positive side of this is convenience, while the downside is that some establishments may engage in high-pressure sells to convince travelers to use more of their services. Most hotels and guesthouses cluster on Tha Tapoa Rd., Sala Daeng Rd., or in the alleyways connecting them.

Suda Guest House, Bangkok Bank Tha Tapoa Rd. Soi 8 (☎077 504 366), just around the corner from New Infinity Travel, on a small alley of of Tha Thapoa Rd. The immaculate rooms are lovingly tended, but Suda herself really sets the place apart, with her warmth, excellent English, and wealth of useful info. Reserve in advance as rooms fill up even in low season. Spotless bathrooms have hot showers (non-guests 20฿). Singles 200-250฿, doubles 350-450฿. Add 80฿ for A/C. ❷

Santawee New Rest House, Bangkok Bank Tha Thapoa Rd. Soi 8 (☎077 502 147), right next to Suda Guest House. The incredibly energetic and friendly father and son duo that owns the place spends most of the day roasting coffee beans behind of the rest house. The rooms are new, airy, and freshly painted. Each comes with fan and shared squat toilet. Beware: the coffee roaster gets loud and smells intensely of roasted coffee by 9am. Singles 150฿, small doubles 200฿, and large doubles 250฿. ❷

Chumphon Guest House (☎077 502 900), on Krumluang Chumphon Soi 1, 600m from the train station. Nearby sounds of roosters and cows give Chumphon Guest House a surprisingly bucolic feel for a place so close to the train station. The owner speaks very good English. All beds come with mosquito nets. Breakfast 40-80฿. Small singles160฿, doubles 180฿, come with fan and shared bath; rooms with private bath 250฿. ❷

Mayazes Resthouse, 188/139 Sala Daeng Rd. (☎077 503 511), 100m north of Fame Tour and Service. Large, clean doubles with fan and shared bath 250฿, small singles without windows 200฿. ❷

Farang Bar (☎077 597 7381), right in the center of Tha Tapoa Rd. where all the VIP buses stop on the way back from the piers for dinner. Exudes backpacker mellowness. Cheap rooms, popular bar and vegetarian-friendly restaurant. Dishes 50-200฿. Beers 50฿. Open 6am-midnight. Shared stone and tile showers, rooms have bare floors and beat-up furniture. Rooms with fan 200฿. ❶

FOOD

For Chumphon's finest victuals, head to the markets. The **day market,** between Pracha Uthit and Poramin Manka Rd., offers *gluay lep meu* (fingernail bananas) and a variety of other fruits. (Open daily 5am-6pm.) The **night market,** on Krumluang Chumphon Rd. 300m east of the train station, offers *pad thai* (25฿) and other Thai staples. (Open nightly 6-11pm.) At another market along Tha Tapoa Rd., south of Farang Bar, excellent noodle and fried rice **stalls** gather outside a small pavillion (noodle dishes 20-35฿).

Papa Seafood, 2-2/1 Krumluang Chumphon Rd., across from the train station. The crowd of locals, peppered with foreigners waiting for their trains, comes to Papa's outdoor terrace to watch sports on the flat screen TV and snack on renowned seafood dishes (100-200฿). Beer 90-120฿. **Papa 2000,** next door, is the largest disco in town. Restaurant and terrace open daily 11am-3am. Disco open 6pm-2am. ❸

Fame Italian Restaurant, 188/20-21 Sala Daeng Rd. (☎077 571 077). Has a menu filled with pizzas (100-190฿), pastas (100-200฿), sandwiches (60-120฿), and Thai curries (60-120฿). Affiliated with Fame Tour & Service (see **Tours, p. 358**). Full bar gets lively at night. Beer 50-70฿. Open daily 4:30pm-midnight. ❷

DAYTRIPS FROM CHUMPHON

For extended excursions to caves and other sights in the vicinity, it's best to book a tour with a tourist agencies or guesthouses. The **Phato Rainforest Ecotourism Club** and **Runs 'n Roses** (☎086 172 1090; www.runsnroses.com) offer whitewater rafting adventures and ecotourism trips into the nearby Phato Rainforest.

A 3-day package starts at 1200฿ and includes hands-on educational studies of the rainforest watershed system. Bookings can be made through **Suda Guest House** (p. 360) or through most other travel agencies. Two popular destinations are the **Rab Ro Caves** and the **Ka Po Waterfalls,** 30km from Chumphon. Prices vary, but expect to pay at least 500฿.

HAT THUNG WUA LAEN

Bright yellow songthaew leave Chumphon's day market along Pracha Uthit Rd., across the street from the 7-Eleven, for Hat Thung Wua Laen (sometimes called Cabana Beach), 12km away. They leave every 30min. or whenever the car is full, and will stop near the south end of the beach (20min., 30฿) if you ask to go to Hat Thung Wua Laen. Return songthaew to Chumphon sometimes cruise Moo 8, the beachside road, but more often than not they bypass the beach and go straight from the nearby village to Hwy. 4. If you are in a rush to get back to Chumphon and haven't seen a yellow songthaew in a while, walk to the southern end of the beach and take a right shortly after you pass Tiger Bar on your left. Continue straight on the curving road for 3km back to Hwy. 4 and wait by the side of the road for the next songthaew. No taxis can be found on the beach; instead, you must order one from a hotel or guesthouse. Last return by songthaew 6pm.

Hat Thung Wua Laen (4km long) is the area's premier beach and a refreshing escape from Chumphon. It remains pristine thanks to rules that forbid further development and thus keep crowds of foreigners away. During the week, the beach is often deserted, save for fishing boats anchored several hundred meters out from the bay; on the weekend, it's popular with locals, who like to have picnics in the shade.

Along the beach, there are a number of good, affordable restaurants with picturesque thatched huts and bamboo tables. They all feature a similar simple English menu, cooking up spicy papaya salad (50-60฿) as well as various seafood curries (40-90฿). A self-described "seafood resort," **The View Restaurant ❷**, 13/2 Moo 8, has a Chinese-influenced menu that specializes in hot-and-sour soups and curries (45-150฿). **Funky's Beach Bar ❷**, 4/2 Moo 8, just and across the street from Seabeach Bungalows, is a fun outdoor beach bar. Enjoy the sounds of waves and funk music underneath the stars as you drink beers or mixed drinks (50-90฿) and play pool. (Open 10am-1am.)

Divers may want to visit two popular islands that are visible in the distance off the shores of Hat Thung Wua Laen. **Ko Ngam Yai** and **Ko Ngam Noi,** prized for their swallows' nests, coral reefs, and soaring cliffs, are seldom visited but well worth the trip. Chartering a boat is expensive (1500฿ or more for a day), and it's best to book with an organized tour. If you are interested, talk to the staff at Cabana Resort at the south end of Hat Thung Wua Laen.

RANONG   ☎077

It is a safe bet that the foreigners you'll see scattered around Ranong are here for a "visa run" to the nearby Myanmar border. Ranong serves this purpose well, and is a comfortable place to spend a day or two. Its large market is an exciting place to wander around looking for tasty Burmese curries, and the nearby natural hot springs are a scenic place to unwind. The bottom line is that although Ranong probably isn't interesting enough to merit a visit if you're not crossing the border, it has plenty of color to contribute to your visa run experience.

▐ TRANSPORTATION

Ranong Airport is about 20km south of town on Phetkasem Hwy. A taxi ride from town from the airport costs 200฿-500฿. **Air Asia** (www.airasia.com) flies from Ranong to **Bangkok** (1hr.; Tu, F, Su 3:30pm; 950฿). The **bus station** (☎077 811

548) is on Phetkasem Hwy., 1km south of the bridge just south of Kamlangsap Rd. **Buses** head to **Bangkok's Southern Bus Terminal** (7-8hr., every 2hr. 5am-8:30pm, 295฿) **Chumphon** (3hr., every hr. 6am-4pm, 100฿); **Krabi** (6hr.; 6, 7, 10am, 12:30pm; 150฿); **Phang Nga** (2-3hr.; 8, 9, 10am, 2pm; 135฿); **Surat Thani** (3hr., 10 per day 5am-3:30pm, 130฿); **Phuket** (3-4hr., 7:30am-5pm, 145-185฿). **Minibuses** to **Chumphon** (2hr., every hr. 6am-6pm, 100฿) depart from the eastern side of Ruangrat Rd., one block south of Dupkadee Rd. Within town, songthaew frequently run up and down Ruangrat Rd. from 6am to 6pm (10฿). Take the #2 *songthaew* (20฿) to get to the bus station. **Motorcycle taxis** will take you anywhere within the city for about 10฿ per km, from Ruangrat Rd. to the bus station for 30฿, and to the hot springs for 40฿. **Pon's Place** (see below) rents **bicycles** (100฿ per day) and **cars** (1500฿ per day) with a 10% discount longer than 10 days. Also books boats to **Ko Chang** (150฿); and **Ko Phayam** (200฿).

⊞ 🛈 ORIENTATION AND PRACTICAL INFORMATION

Ruangrat Road, which runs north-south, is the town's main street and the location of almost everything you'll need while here: market, hotels, restaurants, tour agencies, and ATMs. **Phetkasem Highway (Hwy. 4)** runs north-south on the eastern edge of the city. As Phetkasem Hwy. heads south from its central intersection with **Kamlagsap Road**, it passes by the road that leads to the hot springs, the bus station, and eventually the airport.

Tourist office: Travel agencies lining Ruangrat Rd. specialize in visa runs (4hr., 8:30am, 400-450฿), and trips to nearby Ko Chang and Ko Phayam. **Pon's Place** (see **Food**, p. 363) operates visa runs and tours, and arranges tickets and bookings. Open daily 7:30am-9pm.

Banks: Several on Ruangrat Rd. at Tha Meuang Rd., on the part of the road closest to Phetkasem Hwy. **Bangkok Bank** and **Krung Thai Bank** are right next to each other, have MC/V/AmEx **24hr. ATMs.** Both open M-F 8:30am-4:30pm. Additional 24hr. ATMs located 1 per block continuing north up Ruangrat Rd.

Police: (☎077 811 173), on Dupkadee Rd., just off Ruangrat Rd., near the road's northern end. Open 24hr.

Hospital: Ranong Hospital (☎077 812 630), on Kamlangsap Rd. 1 block west from Phetkasem Hwy., with 24hr. emergency care.

Pharmacy: 87/1 Ruangrat Rd., in the middle of town. Open daily 9am-9:30pm.

Internet: Kay Kai Internet, 293/6 Ruangrat Rd. (☎077 822 890), near the north end of Ruangrat Rd. 20฿ per hr. Open daily 8:30am-10pm. Additional Internet spots can be found about 1 per block up Ruangrat Rd., most with the same rates and hours.

Post Office: GPO on Chonraua Rd., about 1km down Dupkadee Rd. from Ruangrat Rd., at the intersection of Dupkadee Rd. and Chon Ra-U Rd. Open M-F 8:30am-4:30pm, Sa 9am-noon. **Postal Code:** 85000.

▌ ACCOMMODATIONS

The accommodations in Ranong, while modest in scope, are perfect for a quick night's rest before crossing the Myanmar border, or moving to other destinations within Thailand.

Sin Tavee Hotel, 81/1 Ruangrat Rd. (☎077 811 213), in the center of town, several blocks up Ruangrat Rd., past the new market on the left side of the street. Likely the best value in Ranong. Big beds, clean private baths with cold shower, TV, and friendly service are all part of the deal. While all the rooms are clean and decent, the corner singles are well worth the extra 40฿ for private balconies and superior air circulation.

Singles 200฿; corner singles with balcony 240฿, with A/C 320฿. Rooms with 2 twin beds and fan 280฿. ❷

Rattanasin Hotel, 226 Ruangrat Rd. (☎077 811 242), a bit farther up Ruangrat Rd., away from the market, across from J&T Restaurant. This newly refurbished hotel has bare, crisp, clean white rooms at very good prices. Singles 200฿; two twin beds in one room 300฿; with A/C 350฿/400฿. ❷

FOOD

From 8am to 10pm, there are a number of **food stalls** at the front of the **market** on Ruangrat Rd. that sell delicious chicken noodle soup (35฿), stir-fried dishes with rice (35฿), and Thai iced tea (10฿). In mango season, the **fruit market** right across the street from the main market serves excellent mango with sticky rice (*kow nee-o ma-moo-ang*) and coconut milk (25฿). The *farang*-oriented restaurants on Ruangrat Rd. are quite good.

Pon's Place (☎077 823 344), on Ruangrat Rd. 100m north of the Sin Tavee Hotel. Pon's arranges a number of tourist services (see **Practical Information,** p. 362), but also serves up good meals. The Thai curries served here pack more flavor, while at lower prices than those at other establishments. Dishes 35-70฿. Open daily 7:30am-9pm. ❷

J&T Restaurant, 267 Ruangrat Rd., at Luvung Rd., a few blocks up from the market, attracts a lunchtime wave of local schoolchildren hungry for inexpensive and tasty Thai-Chinese dishes like steamed minced fish curry (45฿) and local steamed egg with fresh shrimp paste (40฿). J&T's also specializes in ice cream sundaes (20-35฿). Dishes 25-60฿. Open daily 10am-11pm. ❷

PHANG-NGA TOWN ☎076

While most travelers choose to explore the breathtaking natural beauty of Phang-Nga Bay National Park via speedboat from nearby Phuket or Krabi, there are some advantages to staying in small Phang-Nga Town. The provincial capital of Phang-Nga (pronounced "PUNG-aah"), Phang-Nga Town is also a launch pad for numerous bay tours, many of which are less expensive than those offered in Phuket or Krabi. From enchanting Sa Nang Manora National Park to the ancient Buddhist temple caves at Suwankuha, Phang-Nga is a treat for travelers looking to get a little off the beaten path.

TRANSPORTATION

Phang-Nga's **bus station** (☎076 412 014) is on Phetkasem Highway, near the center of town, less than

ON THE MENU

OUTDOOR EATS

Visitors to Thailand intent on trying traditional fare without traditional intestinal issues often skip right past the outdoor food stalls (without a second thought).

In fact, upon closer inspection, most restaurants kitchens are remarkably similar to that of your typical food stall—just with a roof above it, if that. And while food stalls may not have a refrigerator, most vendors purchase their meat and fruits that morning, so the ingredients are typically fresh. Even if the food stalls' more authentic food won't sway you, the prices should. A noodle soup or pad thai costs somewhere between 30฿ and 50฿ on the street, you'll be hard-pressed to find the same dish at a restaurant for less than 60฿, and they can easily cost as much as 120฿.

Certain precautions should be followed when navigating street fare. Stay away from meat that looks like it has been out and uncovered for extended periods of time. Also be wary of any uncooked vegetables or fruits that are unpeeled; you should watch the vendor peel these items. Noodle soups and stir-fried dishes are safe bets as they are usually served hot and are prepared right in front of you.

1km away from most accommodations. **Buses** to **Bangkok** (11-13hr., 7 per day, 630-1039฿); **Hat Yai** (6hr.; every hr. 8am-3, 5:30, 7pm; 300-380฿); **Krabi** (1½hr., every 30min. 6am-8pm, 75-83฿) via **Trang** (3hr., 220฿); **Phuket** (1hr., every 30min. 6am-8pm, 80-90฿); **Surat Thani** (3½hr.; 7:30, 9:30, 11:30am, 1:30, 3:30, and 5pm; 90-170฿). Green **songthaew** run along the highway from the bus station to the pier (30฿), and to points around town (10-15฿). **Motorcycle taxis** also zip around town (20฿).

ORIENTATION AND PRACTICAL INFORMATION

The entire town is on or just off a 4km stretch of **Phetkasem Highway.** The bus station is located just off the highway, near the center of town. From here, Phetkasem Hwy. runs north to Phang-Nga Guest House (p. 364) and a few blocks beyond. To the south, the town clings to the highway for about 3km, with most of the government offices 2km south of the bus station.

Tours: The **travel agencies** near the bus station provide most tourist services and charge 400-500฿ less than the agencies operating out of Phuket and Krabi. ½-day tours approx. 3½ hours even if they tell you otherwise, 500฿; full-day tours approx. 6½ hours even if they tell you otherwise, 750฿; overnight tours to Phang-Nga Bay 1050฿, includes cost of a shared room in Panyee Bungalow and a hearty dinner and small breakfast; all of the options include Ao Phang-Nga Marine National Park's 200฿ admission. **Mr. Kean's tours** (☎076 430 613) in the bus station. Open 6am-7pm.

Bank: Bangkok Bank, 120 Phetkasem Hwy. (☎076 412 132), about 100m. north of the bus station, with a **24hr. ATM** Open daily 8am-8pm. Various other ATMs can be found all along Phetkasem Hwy., about 1 per each block.

Police: (☎076 412 075), on Soi Policestation, right off of Soi Thungchedi off of Phetkasem Hwy, 1km from the bus station, about 200m past Phang-Nga Inn.

Hospital: Phang-Nga General Hospital, 436 Phetkasem Hwy. (☎076 412 034), 2km from the bus station, in the same direction as the police station, after Phetkasem Hwy. forks and curves to the east. Emergency care open 24hr.; English spoken; cash only.

Internet Access: Internet and Game (☎076 413 240) immediately to the left as you exit the bus station, with Internet for 20฿ per hr. Open 9am-10pm.

Post Office: (☎076 412 171), on Phetkasem Hwy. in the same direction as the police station, about 100m past the hospital, with Poste Restante and international phone. Open M-F 8:30am-4:30pm, Sa-Su 9am-noon. **Postal Code: 82000.**

ACCOMMODATIONS

Phang-Nga is home to a wide range of accommodations. From the affordable with concrete floors, to the more expensive with gorgeous wooden interiors, there are plenty of places to get a good night's sleep.

Phang-Nga Guest House, 99/1 Phetkasem Hwy. (☎076 411 358), next to a 7-Eleven, 2 blocks to your right as you exit the bus station. Best budget lodgings in town. The owners of Phang-Nga are rightfully proud of their spotless rooms with blue tiled floors and comfortable mattresses. "American" breakfast 60฿. Singles with fan and TV 250฿, with A/C 400฿; doubles 300/600฿. ❷

Thaweesuk Hotel (☎076 411 686), 100m past Phang Nga Guest House in the same direction from the bus station, is the cheapest choice around. Rooms with large hard bed in a dusty concrete room with fan and tiny private bathroom 200-250฿. ❷

FOOD

Phang-Nga has several good dining options near the bus station. The **night market,** off Phetkasem Hwy., two blocks to your left as you leave the bus station, sells fruit, soup, curry, and *pad thai* from 6-11pm. A handful of **street vendors** set up shop near the bus station on Phetkasem Hwy., with standard banana pancake and fried dough fare. (Open daily dusk-midnight.)

Khrua Suan Thong, (☎040 560 057). Head left out of the bus station and take your second left on Rongrua Rd. Follow the road for 800m over a bridge. As the road winds to the right, the restaurant will be on your right. This popular local favorite has lamp-lit thatched huts situated next to the river. They specialize in fresh fish dishes and in southern curries (70-250฿). If you are feeling more adventurous, try the stir fried crocodile in red curry. Open daily 11am-11pm. ❷

Duang Restaurant, 122 Phetkasem Hwy. (☎076 412 216), next to the Bangkok Bank. Specializes in seafood, though it also serves excellent hot-and-sour soup. Dishes 50-150฿. Open daily 10am-10:30pm. ❷

Khun Thip Phang-Nga Satay (Mr. Satay) (☎076 411 322), located shortly before the Phang Nga Inn across the street from a DTAC phone store. Run by the same family for more than 30 years, this restaurant is home of the famous Malay-styled pork *satay*. 10 *satays* 45฿, 16 *satays* 72฿. Open daily 10am-6:30pm. ❷

SIGHTS

Most of Phang Nga Town's interesting sights lie a good distance outside of town, but the **Pung Chang Cave** off Phetkasem Hwy., past the post office, is worth a visit. A stream runs through the cave, which has entrances 1.3km apart on opposite ends of a towering tree-covered limestone mountain. This mountain is visible from town and is said to resemble an elephant. Pung Chang is especially notable for its well preserved ancient cave paintings. Although you can walk to the entrance of the cave, you can't get far inside without a raft. Sayan Tours and Mr. Kean (p. 364) operate half-day **rafting** trips through the cave for 500฿. (Open daily 8am-6pm. Motorcycle taxi to the cave from the bus station 50฿.)

WAT THAMTAPAN. The adventures at this sight are both riveting and appalling. As you enter the *wat* complex, head through the 50m dragon mouth. Once you exit the dragon mouth, continue straight on the dirt path leading to a beautiful cave with bridges that meander over the small river inside. Next, head back towards the rear of the dragon mouth bridge, take a right down the dirt path, and be prepared for some gruesome figures. This awesome but disturbing display is meant to be a portrayal of hell. The jarring images are not suitable for children. Upon exiting the hell portion of the *wat*, head right to the section portraying heaven, which is considerably less exciting. To the right of some monk dorms, past sofas, is a wooden ladder that leads up to a little pagoda with a view of the entire region. *(1.7km from the bus station. From the bus station, head towards the hospital and take a right on Soi Thamtapan about 200m before the hospital. ☎076 413 805. Open 6am-6pm.)*

WAT THAM SUWANNAKUHA. This cave complex is a pleasant Buddhist temple, known by locals as Wat Tham. It consists of several caves, the largest of which is 40m long and houses an impressive 15m reclining Buddha. The temple (and its resident monkeys) is best visited late in the afternoon when the tourist buses have returned to Phuket, leaving the temple relatively undisturbed. *(5-6 km. past Pung Chang Cave along Phetkasem Hwy. 8km outside of Phang-Nga, off Phang-Nga Koke Kloy Rd. To get there by motorcycle, continue down Phetkasem Hwy. until you see the sign for Wat*

Tham. Make a U-Turn and take a left into Phang-Nga Koke Kloy Rd. The cave is on your right 200m down the road. Roundtrip motorcycle taxi 200฿, roundtrip tuk tuk 400฿. Open 6am-6pm. 20฿.)

DAYTRIPS FROM PHANG-NGA TOWN

PHANG-NGA BAY NATIONAL PARK. This massive park stretches over 400 sq. km, 80% of which is water, and encompasses vast, low-lying mangrove forests punctuated by more than 120 towering, postcard-perfect limestone islands. Touring through the maze of waterways on a longtail boat is a rare opportunity to experience a piece of pristine Thai wilderness. Although the bay's status as a national park has aided in its conservation, responsible ecotourism is critical preventing damage to the islands. Most tourists make a beeline for the park's twin jewels: beautiful **Ko Khao Ping Gan** and its satellite, **Ko Tapu,** better known as "James Bond Island" (scenes from the Bond flick *The Man With The Golden Gun* were filmed here). While the view of the thin limestone rock that is Ko Tapu (literally, "Nail Island") slicing into the bay is quite striking, be prepared to wade through aggressive shell-vendors and tourists in order to stake out a prime photo-taking spot. If it gets too crowded on the beach facing Ko Tapu, take the trail that winds around Ko Khao Ping Gan for more spectacular panoramas. Another worthwhile destination is the **Tam Lod Grotto,** an open-ended, sea-level cave dripping with stalactites through which only small boats can maneuver. Ko Khien displays 3000-year-old drawings of boats and animals on the mountain's edge, presumed to have been painted by seamen who were looking for shelter from a monsoon.

While larger boats visit from Krabi and Phuket, the most common tours are from Phang-Nga are on longtail boats, which, while a bit shakier, are able to maneuver through the narrow caves and waterways unlike the larger speedboats. It is possible to charter longtail boats from the pier during the high season. Still, it's more relaxing to avoid the bartering and go with one of the reputable tour companies in Phang-Nga on a group tour. Phang Nga Town tour groups (p. 364) offer trips through the bay: ½-day 500฿, full-day 750฿, overnight trips 1050฿. The full-day trips include a stay at **Ko Panyi** and full-day kayaking trips (1500฿). The full day trip, also includes a couple more coves, swimming and lunch on the beach, and is probably the best deal of the four.

Whichever way you decide to visit the bay, be sure to dress to get wet. The "land" excursions may entail wading through knee-high water. Rainstorms on the bay, especially in the rainy season, can completely drench you in a matter of minutes. *(Park admission 200฿, which will likely be included in the cost of your tour.)*

KO PANYI AND THE MUSLIM FISHING VILLAGE. Though technically part of the Phang-Nga Bay National Park, Ko Panyi is certainly worth a visit by itself. About 250 years ago, Muslim fishermen from Indonesia settled on the island, constructing homes and businesses on stilts above the water. Almost three centuries later, the Muslim fishing village is still a vibrant community with over 200 households, though nowadays it seems to cater more to tourists than to fish. Most tourist boats pull up along the southern shore at the docks leading to expensive waterfront restaurants. Behind these restaurants is an arcade of vendors hawking dried seafood and your typical tourist trinkets. The prominent town mosque is the only real site to see in the village, but watching gorgeous sunsets and sunrises from Ko Panyi village make the trip worth it. For more than souvenir shopping, turn off the arcade and amble down one of the town's rickety, suspended streets to witness a fascinating community centered around the sea. Overnight stays are worthwhile, as the village assumes a different character after daytrippers return to the mainland. There is one hotel on the village. It is also possible to arrange a homestay with **Panyee Homestay,**

(☎076 450 636; 250-350฿)—speak with any of the tour agencies. If you plan to stay there overnight, bring bug spray along for ubiquitous mosquitoes.

SA NANG MANORA FOREST PARK. This park, a small, secluded patch of dense rainforest bisected by a brook, makes for an adventurous day of hiking. Well-marked trails criss-cross the brook and its accompanying waterfalls, often on precarious "bridges" that are actually just two logs nailed together. Beware: the park closes for rain. There are ten hiking trails with a handful of small waterfalls with swimmable pools. Points of interest along the main 2km path include limestone cliffs, Shell Cave (which serves as an impressive reminder of the area's oceanic past), giant trees, poisonous plants, and a finale known as Bat Cave. (9km from town, off a small, well-marked, winding road that branches to the right from Petchkasame Hwy. about 4km from town. Motorcycle taxis from the town center 150฿. The park headquarters at the entrance to the park offers free maps and will answer your questions, but does not conduct guided tours. There is no lodging or camping in the park. Open 8am-4pm. Free)

PHUKET ☎076

An internationally renowned tropical playground, Phuket Province begs comparison to Bali and other over-touristed, sun-drenched paradises. Thailand's biggest island in the Andaman Sea, and its wealthiest province, Phuket draws tourists looking for anything but a cultural or solitary experience. Most visitors arrive by plane and are swiftly shepherded into A/C taxis, which deposit them at five-star luxury resorts. As such, Phuket can be less than friendly for the budget traveler, but there are some good deals to be found, especially if you travel in the low season or if prime sleeping digs are not a priority. Likewise, there are still a couple of beautiful secluded beaches for those willing to get off the backpacker trail and settle for less comfortable bungalows. The majority of backpackers, however, come to relax with fellow *farang* on beaches like Hat Kamala and Hat Karon by day and cruise the discos in the infamous nightlife hub, Hat Patong, by night.

⊟ TRANSPORTATION

Thanks to Phuket's enormous size and lack of an extensive public transportation system, getting around is expensive. By far, the cheapest, most convenient way to explore the island is by motorbike. However, it is also the most dangerous and is the cause of regular casualties.

Flights: Phuket International Airport, 28km to the north of Phuket Town on Rte. 4026. **Bangkok Airways,** 158/2-3 Yao Warat Rd. (☎076 225 033; open daily 8am-5pm) and **Thai Airways,** 78/1 Ranong Rd. (☎076 360 444; open daily 8am-5pm), across from the local beach *songthaew* station, run domestic and international flights. To: **Bangkok** (1hr., approx. every hr. 7:25am-9:30pm, 1800฿); **Ko Samui** (50min.; daily 9:20am, 6:05pm; 1300฿); **Kuala Lumpur, Malaysia** (1hr., twice daily, 2500฿). **Singapore Airlines** flies to **Singapore** (3hr., daily 9am, 1900฿).

Buses: Phuket Bus Terminal (☎076 211 480), off Phang-Nga Rd., in eastern Phuket Town, behind a shopping plaza. TAT office has a good free bus schedule. A/C and non-A/C buses to: **Bangkok** (10-14hr., 21 per day 6am-7:30pm, 560-1120฿); **Hat Yai** (7hr., 5:30am-9:45pm, 307-613฿); **Khao Sok National Park** via **Takua Pa** (2-3hr., 8:50am-6:10pm, 60-90฿); **Krabi** (4hr., 5 per day 10:50am-3:50pm, 81-113฿); **Phang-Nga** (2½hr., 5 per day 10:10am-4:30pm, 44-66฿); **Surat Thani** (4½hr., 5 per day 7am-3:30pm, 220฿); **Trang** (5hr., 5:15am-8pm, 200-257฿). **Minibuses** to **Surat Thani** (4hr.,

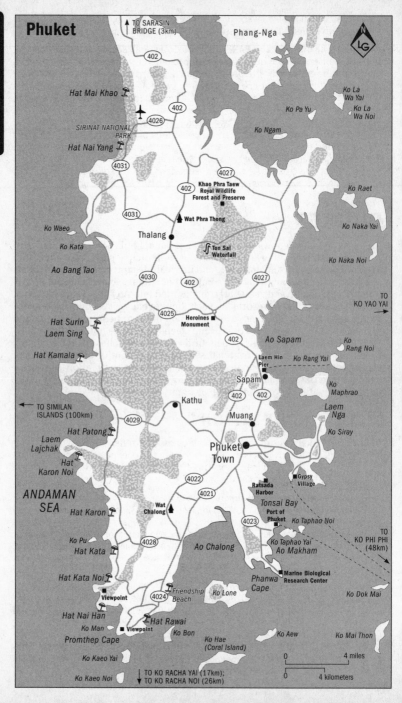

Phuket

every hr. 8am-4pm, 250฿) leave from Suthat Rd., just north of its intersection with Phang-Nga Rd., across the street from Montri Hotel.

Boats: Boats to **Ko Phi Phi Don** (8:30am, 1:30, 2:30pm; 500-600฿), depart from Ratsada Rd. on the eastern side of Phuket Town, about 3km from the city center. Tickets are cheapest in Phuket Town, where they are the same price as tickets purchased at the pier, but also include free transportation from your hotel to the pier.

Local Transportation: Local **bus and songthaew station,** on Ranong Rd., in Phuket Town, next to the market. Labeled **songthaew** leave every 30min. to: **Hat Kamala** (6am-6pm, 30฿); **Hat Karon** (7:30am-6pm, 25฿); **Hat Kata** (7:30am-6pm, 30฿); **Hat Patong** (7:30am-6pm, 25฿); **Hat Rawai** (6:35am-5:30pm, 30฿); **Hat Surin** (7am-5pm, 30฿). Return to Phuket Town between 6am and 4pm from each of the beaches, at the same price as the outgoing *songthaew* rides. **Tuk-tuks** and **non-metered taxis** that can be booked through a travel agent cruise between the beaches and the airport and are both about the same price. **Tuk-tuks** from Phuket Town to: **Hat Kamala** (360฿); **Hat Kata** (240฿); **Hat Nai Yang** (430฿); **Hat Patong** (210฿); **Hat Rawai** (230฿); **Hat Surin** (340฿). Note that these prices are the prices listed at TAT; the prices offered by the *tuk-tuk* drivers themselves will likely be double these prices. Trying to bargain them down will require serious persistence. **Metered taxis** (1st 2km 50฿; 8฿ per additional km) from the airport to any destination on the island. (**Phuket Town** 650฿.) To find a metered taxi, take a right out of the airport and pass through the hordes of shouting drivers, to the blue and yellow taxis. **Motorcycle taxis** are harder to find but are much cheaper, starting at around 40฿ from 1 beach on the island to another; they also will require some bargaining.

Rentals: Motorbikes (100-300฿ per day) and **jeeps** (1000-1400฿ per day) available all over the island. Like most everything else, vehicle rentals are cheapest in Phuket Town. Most vehicles are uninsured, and accident rates for *farang* are alarmingly high. Also note that these rentals do not include the cost of gasoline. Helmets, provided by most rental shops, are required for all motorcycle drivers in Phuket, a rule strictly enforced in the most touristed areas. Cops sometimes run stings to ensure that all *farang* drivers possess a valid International Driver's Permit (see **Essentials,** p. 33).

◪ ORIENTATION

Getting around Phuket is not particularly complicated, but given the island's size (570 sq. km), and its hilly terrain, traveling can take time. Phuket is connected to the mainland by **Highway 402,** the island's main north-south artery, and the **Sarasin Bridge** to the west of Hwy. 402. Bordered by the Andaman Sea, the west coast is lined with beaches. The northern beaches, especially **Hat Kamala, Hat Surin,** and **Laem Sing,** are quieter and prettier, while south of Kamala, party central **Hat Patong** has a sensory overload of tacky bars, cabaret shows, and gimmicky tourist stalls. Farther south are serene but ever-developing **Hat Karon** and **Hat Kata,** while a few smaller, more secluded, and for the most part less attractive beaches fringe the island's southern tip. Phuket's bleak and muddy eastern coast is filled with mangroves, prawn farms, and bobbing boats. On the island's southeast corner, **Phuket Town,** the island's capital, offers financial, postal, and telecommunications services in addition to a bevy of authentic budget restaurants.

🛈 PRACTICAL INFORMATION

Tourist Office: TAT, 191 Thalang Rd. (☎076 212 213), in Phuket Town, just west of the post office. Helpful, friendly, and organized English-speaking staff provides maps, bus schedules, and accommodations lists. Open daily 8:30am-4:30pm.

Tours: Tour operators are a dime a dozen in Hat Karon, Hat Kata, Hat Patong, and Phuket Town. Most arrange tours to Phang-Nga Bay and nearby islands (1200-1400฿), with canoeing 2200-2800฿ and can book bus or ferry tickets to just about anywhere you might want to go. Typically, the tour agencies in Phuket Town are cheaper than on the beaches, and **Mark Travel Service,** located in the On On Hotel (p. 371), is one of the cheapest in Phuket Town.

Currency Exchange: In Phuket Town, a slew of banks are on Phang-Nga Rd. across from the On On Hotel, and several more are 1 block south, on Ratsada Rd. **Bangkok Bank,** 22 Phang-Nga Rd., across from the On On Hotel, has a handful of **24hr. ATMs**. Open daily 8:30am-4:30pm. Additional 24hr. ATMs can be found about 1 every other block in Phuket Town. Currency exchange booths and ATMs abound on Hat Karon, Hat Kata, and Hat Patong.

Tourist Police: 100/31-32 Chalem Prakiat Rd. (☎076 355 015), in the far northwest part of town about 3km from the city center. English spoken. Smaller booths are on major beaches. Open 24hr.

Medical Services: Bangkok Phuket Hospital, 21 Hong Yok-U-Thit Rd. (☎076 254 4214), on the northwest side of Phuket Town just off of Yao Warat Rd. **Phuket International Hospital,** 44 Chalerm Prakiat Rd. (☎076 249 400), southwest of Bangkok Phuket Hospital, on the way to the airport. English spoken. Both open 24hr.

Telephones: CAT Telecom, 112/2 Phang-Nga Rd. (☎076 216 861), in the building under the radio tower. Cheapest international calls around, if you're willing to buy in bulk. A 300฿ phone card will get you 2฿ per min. calls to the US. Internet 100฿ for a 3-hr. card. Open daily 8am-8pm. Tourist agencies at the various beaches offer fairly expensive calls to the US (around 20฿ per min.), but you can always buy a 100฿ **TOT** card and use it on any international pay phone, which should get you 15 min. to the US.

Internet Access: Cyber cafes line the more southern area of Montri Rd. as well as Tilok Uthit 1 Rd., 1 block east, and charge 25฿ per hr. **Hi-Tel,** on Ong Sim Phai Rd., at Tilok Uthit 1 Rd., has particularly fast connections. Open daily 8am-midnight. Also available at. Several Internet shops on Phang-Nga Rd. and Thalang Rd., about 1 per block. **OA Internet,** 14 Talang Rd., offers Internet at 20฿ for 40min. and is open 8am-11:30pm. On Hat Karon, Hat Kata, and Hat Patong, there are tons of Internet shops, but don't expect to pay less than 1฿ per min.

Post Offices: GPO, 12/16 Montri Rd. (☎076 211 020), on the corner with Thalang Rd. Poste Restante. Open M-F 8:30am-4:30pm, Sa-Su 9am-noon. **Postal Code:** 83000.

PHUKET TOWN ☎076

With no idyllic beaches to speak of, Phuket Town lacks the immediate glamor of its neighbors. But, as the region's oldest town and its current center of finance and commerce, Phuket Town is a pleasant place to stay for late-night or early-morning transit or to stock up on supplies before heading out to the beaches. The Sino-Portuguese architecture (characterized by the use of arches) and the up-and-coming arts scene also lend a certain charm to the region. Moreover, Phuket Town has a solid tourist infrastructure with a good variety of budget hotels, restaurants, and extensive transportation links, make it a comfortable springboard for exploring the rest of the island.

ORIENTATION

Most of Phuket Town's tourist services and accommodations are concentrated within a small area. The island's intercity bus station is just north of the main road, **Phang-Nga Road,** which runs west from the station to On On Hotel (below) and houses many banks. Just east of the CAT Telecom (distinguished by its radio tower), Phang-Nga Rd. intersects **Phuket Road,** which runs south past **Nava-mindra Memorial Square** to the **Seiko Clock Tower,** a main landmark in the southern part of town next to the towering, Metropole Hotel. The local bus and *songth-aew* station is across from the day market on **Ranong Road,** on the west side of town. A newer part of town, near **Tilok Uthit 1 Road** (toward the bay from Metro-pole Hotel), contains a number of dining, shopping, and entertainment options, including landmarks, such as the **Ocean Shopping Mall** and **Robinson's Department Store,** each of which cater to *farang.*

ACCOMMODATIONS

Phuket Town has the widest selection of budget accommodations on the island.

Talang Guest House, 37 Thalang Rd. (☎076 214 225; www.talangguesthouse.com), located in a fairly historic neighborhood, is clean and well-maintained. The spacious rooms are tastefully decorated and include hot water showers and large, comfortable beds. The rooms with balconies cost a bit more, but the fresh air and views are worth it. Breakfast included. Single rooms with fan 300฿, for doubles 350฿; with A/C 400/450฿; with balcony is an extra 50฿. ❸

Thavorn Hotel, 74 Ratsada Rd. (☎076 211 3335), appears to have changed very little since it was built in 1963. Incorporating Sino-Portuguese designs into its 2 vast, 5-story buildings, there's something undeniably appealing about the Thavorn's expansive linoleum hallways and aging vinyl furniture. That said, its cracked wooden doors and aged tilework could definitely use some renovating. Rooms with double-bed and fan and private bath 180฿, with A/C 500฿. ❷

On On Hotel, 19 Phang-Nga Rd. (☎076 211 154), is the oldest hotel in town established in 1929. With wood plank floors and high ceilings it is a welcome contrast to Phuket's ubiquitous concrete monstrosities. Sparsely decorated rooms and low prices draw a devoted backpacker crowd. Singles with fan and clean shared bathroom 180฿, doubles with fan and bath 250฿; with A/C 460/560฿. ❷

Nana Chart Mansion 41/34 Montri Rd. (☎076 230 041), opposite Pearl Hotel, has modestly-sized rooms with crisp new sheets and clean Western toilets. Singles and doubles 250฿; with TV 300฿; with TV, A/C, and hot shower 350฿. ❷

Suk Sabai Hotel, 82/9 Thep Kasatri Rd. (☎076 212 287). West from the bus station on Phang-Nga Rd., make a right on to Thep Kasatri Rd., and turn right onto the small alley next to the Ford dealership; 50m forward on your left. Suk Sabai consists of clean, quiet, standard, concrete hotel rooms. Doubles with fan 240฿, with A/C 380฿. ❷

FOOD AND NIGHTLIFE

Phuket is famous for its culinary delights, including *tao sor* (Chinese crepes) and *kanom jin Phuket* (breakfast noodles in spicy curry). There are a number of delicious **food stalls** (most dishes 30-50฿, open daily 5am-10pm) in the **market** at the junction of Tilok Uthit 2 and Ong Sim Phai Rd. On the weekend, there is a **market** on Hong Yok U-Thit Rd., in the southeastern part of town about 2.5km from the city center, that offers even more food stalls and full blocks of **merchandise stalls** (Open 7am-6pm).

Bookhemian, 61 Thalang Rd. An arthouse, bookshop, gallery and cafe, this is where hip Thais hang out to enjoy high-quality coffee in a gallery-cafe setting. It also has an extensive independent film collection that can be watched in a screening room above the cafe. Espresso 45฿. Open daily 10am-10pm.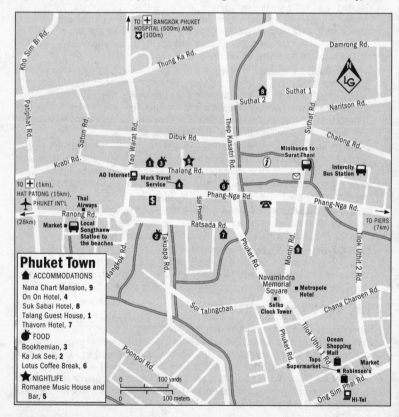

Lotus Coffee Break, 119 Phang-Nga Rd. Come here for a Western breakfast or sandwich. Tea 15฿. Thai dishes 35-70฿. Shakes 25-30฿. Open daily 7am-9:30pm. ❶

Ka Jok See, 26 Takuapa Rd., is a cozy, classy teak wood restaurant several shops south of Ratsada Rd., hidden by a screen of plants. At this expensive but excellent restaurant, the staff treats you like royalty. Try the *tom yum* (150฿). Chinese and Thai dishes 80-380฿. Open Tu-Su 6-11pm. ❹

Romanee Music House Bar, on a small alley off Thalang Rd. Live jazz and reggae bands play on M, Th, F, Su 10pm-midnight. The bands are great, and the beer is cheap (90฿). Don't be surprised, however, if you are the only foreigner enjoying the night here. Open M-F, Su 6pm-1am.

HAT PATONG

On Phuket's west coast, Patong is the island's nightlife and entertainment center, a tasteless mix of go-go bars, strip shows, Thai boxing, and gaudy souvenir stalls. With high-rise condos dotting the beach and streets that come alive at night amidst sex shows, prostitution, and general drunken debauchery, Hat

Phuket Town

🏠 ACCOMMODATIONS
Nana Chart Mansion, **9**
On On Hotel, **4**
Suk Sabai Hotel, **8**
Talang Guest House, **1**
Thavorn Hotel, **7**

🍴 FOOD
Bookhemian, **3**
Ka Jok See, **2**
Lotus Coffee Break, **6**

⭐ NIGHTLIFE
Romanee Music House and Bar, **5**

Patong is likely not what most people have in mind when they envision their beach holiday. It is overpriced, overcrowded, and oversexed. Regardless, Patong's intensity is undeniable and its neon-filled streets are worth a visit for the spectacle. Hat Patong is defined by two roads that run northwest, parallel to the 3km of beach. Closest to the water is **Thaweewong Road,** crowded with expensive seafood restaurants, outdoor bars, and souvenir stalls. One block east, **Song Roi Pee Road,** which is north of where **Ratuthit Road** intersects with **Bangla Road,** is home to more restaurants and Hat Patong's few budget hotels. Phuket's raciest bars and go-go shows cluster in alleyways off Bangla Rd., which is the main byway connecting Ratuthit Rd. and Thaweewong Rd.

HAT KARON AND HAT KATA

Popular with backpackers and package tourists alike, the adjacent beaches of Hat Karon and Hat Kata have the best balance of lively nightlife, plentiful dining options, sufficiently cheap accommodations, and beautiful sand. While the go-go bars that dominate Hat Patong overflow a little onto the northern end of Hat Karon, the further south you go, the fewer go-go bars you will see. Hat Karon and Hat Kata remain pleasant, comfortable getaways.

◆ ORIENTATION

Hat Karon and Hat Kata are actually three distinct beaches. To the north, luxury resorts dot the 3km of Hat Karon. There are some noteworthy exceptions; at the northern edge of the beach **Patak Road (East)** houses a number of budget accommodation and dining options. To the south, a hilly, rocky cape separates Hat Karon from Hat Kata. Here, more budget restaurants and hotels cluster around **Taina Road,** which winds inland from the beachside **Patak Road (West).** Hat Kata is split into Hat Kata and **Hat Kata Noi.** While Hat Kata is monopolized by the gargantuan Club Med fortress, the smaller and slightly rocky Hat Kata Noi, to the south, is the most solitary beach of the three. The tiny, tree-covered island of **Ko Pu** lies a few hundred meters out from shore between Hat Kata and Hat Karon, a manageable distance for experienced swimmers, though it should only be attempted when green flags are flying at the entrance to the beach.

◆ ACCOMMODATIONS

Budget accommodations branch off of the beach, along Patak Rd. (East) and Taina Rd.

P.M. Restaurant and Guesthouse, 528/19-20 Patak Rd. (☎089 647 4791), opposite the Karon Cafe on a small alley right off of the Patak Rd. The management of this newly renovated Guesthouse is friendly and laid-back, and the rooms are clean, with comfortable beds, new white sheets, A/C, and private baths with warm water. High-season rooms with double bed 900฿, low-season 400฿; additional mattress 100฿. ❸

Kata On Sea (☎076 330 594). On Taina Road, turn up the steep driveway next to the 7-Eleven, and walk up to the top of the hill. Accommodations are large, basic bungalows with fans, or recently renovated rooms with A/C, cable TV, and hot water. Motorbike rental 200฿ per day. 2-day advance reservations recommended in high season, when spots fill quickly. High-season basic bungalows with fan 500฿, low-season 400฿; deluxe rooms with A/C 1000/800฿. ❸

Bazoom Hostel (☎076 396 914; www.bazoom-hostel.com). Inland on Hat Karon, near the intersection of Luangpoh Chuang Rd. and Patak Rd. East This eclectically-painted dorm European-style is by far the cheapest around. Dorm beds 150฿. ❷

🞕 **FOOD.** Both Hat Karon and Hat Kata have a good selection of inexpensive restaurants, as well as some nicer, pricier ones. In between Hat Karon and Hat Kata, the restaurants line up along Taina Rd. closest to the beach. At the northern end of Hat Karon, there are several reasonably priced dining options located along Patak Rd. (East) heading inland. Head to the alleys on the left side as you make your way inland, especially the alley that houses Karon Cafe and P.M. Restaurant; you can find some outdoor soup (40฿) and rice dish (60฿) stalls if you're interested in delicious meals at the cheapest prices around. (Most open 8am-10pm.) **Kwong Shop Seafood ❸**, on Taina Rd., is also a good no-frills place to get a fast bite to eat. Chicken and beef dishes 80-100฿. Seafood dishes 100-200฿. Open daily 8am-midnight.

🞖 🎵 **ACTIVITIES AND ENTERTAINMENT**

For those with the cash, Hat Karon and Hat Kata are a good jump-off point for exploring some of the world's best snorkeling and diving around the Similan and Racha Islands. Head to PADI-certified **Siam Dive Asia**, 24 Karon Rd., north of Club Med, near Dino Mini Golf and across the street from Peach Hill Hotel. All of their trips include transportation from your hotel, tanks, weights, and most meals and drinks. (☎076 330 598; www.diveasia.com. Full-day trip 3900-4900฿, 4-day trip to the Similan Islands and Surin from 24,900฿. Open M-Sa 11am-8pm. AmEx/MC/V.) Hat Kata and Hat Karon's night scene offers loud music at nondescript bars lining the street. **Dino Park Mini-Golf** provides a form of more innocent fun. (Open daily 10am-midnight. 240฿, children 180฿.)

HAT SURIN, AO BANG TAO, AND HAT NAI YANG

The island's northwest shore was once famous for harboring the most beautiful and least-developed beaches on Phuket. Today, it has exploded with luxury resorts in the past decade. These resorts, however, faced a fatal blow in October 2005 when the Thai National Assembly placed all beaches in Thailand within the public domain, thus making it possible for lowly backpackers to sunbathe alongside the world's glitterati.

Located 10km from Patong, Hat Surin and the surrounding beaches provide a welcome respite, as a daytrip or a week-long holiday, for those with less lewd interests. But it is a challenge to find a roof over your head among Hat Surin's fair share of five-star accommodations. All accommodation rates drop considerably during the low season, and cheaper guesthouses are located closer to the highway. Although swimming is not recommended here due to strong winds and heavy surf, lounge chairs rented for 50-100฿ can make for a luxurious seaside experience.

Street vendors (daily 9am-10pm) set up shop in the parking lot behind Surin Beach. Take the lead of locals and order the superb grilled chicken (40฿) and *som tam* (papaya salad 30฿), and ask to be served at one of the many tables with umbrellas overlooking the sea. On the northern end of the beach, **Nok Seafood ❸** is an active beachfront restaurant with a friendly crowd. (☎08 444 594. Seafood 100-220฿. Open 5pm-2am.)

If you bring your own food, towel, and book, attractive **Ao Bang Tao** makes a decent daytrip, especially between May and July, before the heavy rains hit but after the crowds have fled. Located 1.5km north of Hat Surin, Ao Bang Tao is dominated by two resorts that monopolize access to the water. Squeezed between the two beaches on the road from Surin to Ao Bang Tao is **Bangtao Lagoon Bungalows ❺**, 72/3 Moo 3 T. With the ocean right at your fingertips, Bangtao's compact, comfortable huts with private bath and warm shower, as well as a blue patina and marble floors, makes this accommodation heaven on earth. The bungalows range from standard to deluxe. There is also an infinity pool and two somewhat expensive restaurants. (☎076 324 260; http://phuket-bangtaolagoon.com. Dishes 80-300฿. High-season bungalows 900-2700฿, low-season 550-1450฿; extra bed 200฿.)

Sirinat National Park, farther north at Hat Nai Yang, is a stunning, expansive park filled with coconut trees and coral reefs. Be careful at the beach, though: from May to September, Hat Nai Yang has Phuket's most dangerous riptides. The visitors office is near the entrance to the park. English spoken. (☎076 328 226. Open daily 8:30am-4:30pm.) It's possible to rent **tents** (2- to 3-person tent 225฿; 4- to 5-person tent 300฿; 7- to 8-person tent 600฿; camping 30฿; bungalows 600-1200฿.) Park entrance fee 200฿ per person.

HAT KAMALA AND LAEM SINGH

Escape to quiet Hat Kamala on the way to Hat Surin from Phuket Town (*songthaew* 30฿). Home to only two or three small luxury hotels, Hat Kmala itself is decent, less crowded, but also much less scenic than some of the nearby beaches. Though hit fairly hard by the 2004 tsunami, many of Kamala's resorts and restaurants have since been reconstructed, and you'd be hard pressed to notice any of the damage. Small **Kamala Police Station,** 96/52 Moo 3, is at the northern end of the beach. (☎076 385 31. Open 24hr.)

Most of Hat Kamala's accommodations lie on Moo 3, which runs along the beach from Highway 4025 at the northern and southern ends of the beach. Next to Benjamin Resort, **Pavilion Beach Restaurant** ❸ has commanding views of the ocean and is justifiably popular with backpackers. The stir-fried ginger chicken (70฿) is especially delicious. (☎08 4059 1712. Dishes 70-200฿. Open daily 10:30am-9:30pm.) The excellent **Gourmet Pizza Restaurant** ❸, where Moo 3 connects with Hwy. 4025 at the southern end of the beach, serves delicious, but expensive Thai and Western food. (Personal pizza 180-250฿. Thai dishes 100-150฿. Western dishes 200-380฿. Open daily 9am-11pm.)

Laem Singh is an especially picturesque and intimate beach located 1km to the north of Hat Kamala and 1.5km south of Hat Surin. To get to the beach, you must head up a mountain on Hwy. 4025 and get off at the signs for Laem Singh. Then, head down the path and steps to the small, 150m undeveloped beach nestled amid limestone cliffs. Beach chairs can be rented for 50-100฿ per day. There are two small restaurants a little ways back from the beach that play laid-back music and serve Thai (60-140฿) and Western dishes (120-220฿). Beware: waves can get especially ferocious here during monsoon season.

HAT RAWAI, AND AO CHALONG

Squeezed into the southeastern tip of Phuket, Hat Rawai caters mostly to locals. The beach's narrow strip of sand and muddy water render it unappealing for swimming; for salt-water basking, try its more attractive neighbor Hat Nai Han. However, underrated Hat Rawai looks out onto a lovely bay filled with picturesque red and yellow longtail boats flitting in front of beautiful islands in the distant green glassy waters. Amidst a number of identical open-air fresh seafood restaurants, **Esan Zab Seafood** ❸, the northernmost of them, is the most delcious, offering seafood dishes (80-180฿), papaya salad (60฿), and fresh pineapple (30฿). At night, these restaurants serve romantic candlelit dinners on the boardwalk underneath the stars. (Open 8am-10:30pm.) For those looking to spend the night at Hat Rawai, **Pornmae Bungalows** ❸, 58/1 Wiset Rd., located at the central part of the beach, has simple, bare rooms with fridges and private baths. (☎076 613 733. Singles and doubles 400฿.) Hat Rawai is also a great jump-off point for those looking to take a daytrip to one of the nearby islands, visible from the shore. Though prices can and should be bargained down, longtail boats for up to six people can be hired to go **Coral Island** (1200฿), **Racha Island** (3000฿), **Kai Island** (4500฿), and **Ban Island** (1000฿). Each longtail should also have snorkeling gear on board for those interested in seeing the fantastic marine life. Coral Island is the most popular for tourists.

Pleasant Ao Chalong, north of Hat Rawai on the island's southeastern side, is the largest bay on Phuket. Because of its size and shallow, muddy waters, the bay is primarily used for docking. Though it makes for mediocre swimming, Ao Chalong is a good place to stay if you want to learn more about the active Andaman Sea yachting culture. To meet sailors and laid-back visitors, go to **Friendship Beach ❺**, 27/1 Soi Mittrapap, on a secluded beach 1.5km north of Hat Rawai, toward the Ao Chalong pier on the southern side of the bay; across from a small market. Ao Chalong has immaculate bungalows with private and clean outdoor bath, and a pool, which is open to non-guests. The resort also boasts a **restaurant ❸**, beach bar, biweekly jam sessions, cable TV, and Internet at 1฿ per min. (☎076 381 281. Thai dishes 80-135฿. Delicious homemade Apple Pie 115฿. Live music F and Su 7-10pm. Bar open until midnight. Restaurant open 8am-10pm. High-season 2-person bungalows 3000฿, low-season 1600฿.)

SIMILAN ISLANDS   ☎076

While the southern Thailand backpacker superhighway swallows up other islands, Ko Similan, a national park consisting of nine small islands, remains the virgin beauty of the Andaman Sea. Relative inaccessibility and higher expenses have helped preserve Ko Similan both below and above water. Due to its outstanding 30m underwater visibility and magnificent coral gardens, the Similan Archipelago is one of the best deep-water dive sites in the world. Though it's primarily known for diving and snorkeling, Ko Similan also has spectacularly fine beaches, majestic rock formations, and fascinating wildlife. If time and budget are not an issue, Ko Similan is worth the trip. But plan ahead: it's only accessible Nov. 15-May 15. There are no services on the Similan Islands. For information on the islands, ask at the TAT in Phuket-Town (p. 370).

KO PHI PHI DON   ☎075

The secret is out. Beautiful Ko Phi Phi Don (generally known as Ko Phi Phi), once an untouristed island dotted with swaying palms and isolated spits of sand surrounded by shimmering turquoise waters, is now the second largest *farang* destination in Thailand. Today, backpackers, bikinis, bars, and buckets of booze fill the streets, and tourists seem to outnumber locals about five to one. Still, the commercialization of the island has not entirely destroyed its natural beauty; you just have to look through more people and construction to see it. The beaches are still clean and well maintained, and the ban on cars and motorbikes means teenagers on bicycles are the main road hazards. Nearby, the island preserve of Ko Phi Phi Ley, accessible only by boat from Ko Phi Phi, provides a more serene atmosphere, although it too has suffered, especially since its stint as the title role in the 2000 film *The Beach*. While Ko Phi Phi is no longer the tranquil getaway you might have imagined, if you're looking to have a good time it won't disappoint.

▐ TRANSPORTATION

Ferries depart regularly from Ko Phi Phi's **Thon Sai Pier** to **Ko Lanta** (1½hr; 1:30, 2, 3pm; 350฿; no low-season service), **Krabi** (1½hr.; 9am, 2pm; 400฿); **Railay** and **Ao Nang** (1½hr., 3:30pm, 390฿), and **Phuket** (1½hr.; 9am, 1:30, 2:30pm; 350฿). Tickets available at any of the travel agencies in Thon Sai Village. Boats to serene **Ko Phi Phi**

Ley depart from the pier. Tickets for tours of the island can be booked at any tour agency (½-day 450-600฿). You can also hire **longtail boats** (3 hr., max. 3 people, 1200฿) or **speedboats** (3 hr., 4000฿) to go to Ko Phi Phi Ley or more remote beaches.

ORIENTATION AND PRACTICAL INFORMATION

Ko Phi Phi is small and shaped like a lopsided dumbbell. The lack of street names makes the island quite disorienting at first, but the island's small size makes learning the lay of the land surprisingly easy. It is possible to walk the entire island, save the high cliffs, in 45min. The village too, is compact. The main port of call, **Ao Ton Sai**, is pretty but polluted. It is nestled in the narrow part of the island, just west of the main village where travelers come to eat, check email, and party. The main thoroughfare extends east-west, roughly following the coast. East of the pier, in the heart of the village, two streets extend off the main thoroughfare and house restaurants, tour agencies, dive centers, and tattoo and massage parlors. After 150m, these north-south streets converge into one street that leads, after a short walk, to **Ao Lo Dalam,** where you'll find most of the budget accommodations in the area perched around a steep path headed up to the viewpoint. The viewpoint in Ao Dalam, up the stairs past all of the budget accommodations, affords stellar views of the bays and surrounding islands. The narrow isthmus where **Ao Thon Sai pier** is situated connects the two main chunks of island, less popular **Ko Nok** to the west (left as you exit the pier) and the much larger **Ko Nai** to the east. Smaller, less-developed beaches ring the island's outer peninsulas, the most popular of which is **Hat Yao** (Long Beach), east of Ao Thon Sai on Ko Nai.

Tourist Office: TAT in Krabi (p. 382) serves Ko Phi Phi.

Tours: Most tour agencies on the island can arrange trips to Ko Phi Phi Ley and boat/train/bus combos to Bangkok, Malaysia, and other destinations. Likewise, they offer tickets for the same sunset snorkeling excursions around Ko Phi Phi Ley. 10-person snorkeling trips via longtail boat 450-500฿.

Currency Exchange: The Siam Commercial Bank, in Ao Thon Sai 100m to the right of the pier when getting off the boat. Exchanges cash and gives credit card advances. Open daily 9am-8pm. **24hr. ATMs** are abundant on the island, especially in the village. Long Beach is the exception, devoid of a single ATM.

Local Tourist Police: Booth (☎081 536 2427), off the main thoroughfare about 400m east of the village. English spoken. Open daily 8:30am-7:30pm.

Medical Services: Phi Phi Island's **Hospital** (☎075 600 719), in Ao Thon Sai, 150m to the left of the pier when getting off the boat. Basic medical services. English spoken. Open 24hr. The closest full-service hospitals are in Krabi and Phuket.

Telephones: Private travel agencies in Ao Thon Sai offer expensive connections starting at 20฿ per min. Buying a **TOT** international phone card at a 7-Eleven and using it on one of the international pay phones right outside will save you some money. Otherwise, unless it is an emergency, it's probably best to wait until you get back to the mainland.

Internet Access: It's hard to throw a coconut and not hit a computer with Internet in Thon Sai. But abundance doesn't make them cheap—the going rate is 2฿ per min. Further out on Long Beach, Internet is a whopping 3฿ per min.

Post Office: Take a right from the pier, then the first left past the Infinity Travel office. Very small office offering all of the standard mailing options. Open M-F 8:30am-4:30pm, Sa-Su 9am-noon. **Postal Code:** 81000.

ACCOMMODATIONS

Ko Phi Phi's bungalows are plentiful, but vary widely in price and quality, and guesthouses follow suit. Generally, the island is more expensive than its neighbors, but rooms are cheaper on the edges of the village and on the more isolated beaches. It pays to explore the outer rim of the island, where fewer mainstream backpackers venture. Don't trust the *touts* who meet your boat at the pier and tell you that there are no accommodations below 300-400฿ on the island; if you go with them, you're probably paying too much. Low-season discounts up to 50% are sometimes available, but be ready to haggle for them.

AO LO DALAM AND AO THON SAI. Most budget accommodations are near the northeast end of the isthmus, along the path that ultimately ascends a steep set of stairs to a viewpoint. On a hill to the right as you walk along the path to the northwest corner of the isthmus lies **The Rock Backpacker ❷.** Look for The Rock's large hull-shaped bar protruding from the hill. Not posh by anyone's standards, but the beds are the cheapest in town, especially the 16 dormitory bunk beds with shared bath. (☎075 612 402. High-season dorms 200฿, low-season 150฿.) **Tropical Garden Bungalows ❸,** also on the path past the viewpoint, close to Garden Home Bungalows, offers a singles with above average shared baths. Though the bungalows are pretty far from the beach, Tropical Garden has a small pool at the center of the complex. (☎01 968 1436. High-season single 500฿, large bungalows with fan and private bath 900฿; low-season 300/500฿). **Moonlight Guesthouse ❸** is located off the path that heads to the stairs and the viewpoint. Heading from the pier, take your first possible left shortly after The Rock Backpacker and continue straight for about 70m; it will be on your left. Moonhouse is one of the cheapest lodgings and is conveniently near both the village and Loh Dalum beach. May be loud at night thanks to the nearby beach bars. (☎075 675 1436. High-season singles with fan 600฿, low-season 300฿.)

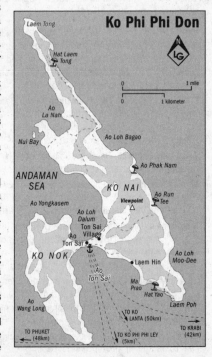

HAT HIN KOHN AND LAEM HIM. Just southeast of Ao Thon Sai and 150m from the pier, the main thoroughfare path continues west along the coast to several more upscale resort. The few cheap options exist along flat Hat Hin Kohn, a long stretch of sand. The beach is decent, but with the number of longtail boats moored at its shore, it is far from the island's best. **P.P. Rim Lay Travel and Bungalow ❸,** right next to the mosque, has spacious concrete bungalows with fans, and big beds, although the leaky faucets, dodgy sheets, and loud early morning prayers may not be for everyone. (☎01 728 6887. High-season rooms 800฿, low-season 400฿). A path to your left immediately after P. P. Rim Lay Travel and Bungalow leading inland past the mosque, brings you 150m later to **Gypsy 1 ❸,** which has decent, somewhat worn, bungalows at cheap prices. (☎075 601 044. High-season doubles with fan 800฿, low-season 300฿.)

◪ **HAT YAO AND MA PRAO.** Hat Yao, also known as Long Beach, is a 10min. longtail boat ride (150฿) from Ao Ton Sai pier and has Ko Phi Phi's best sand and swimming. During low tide, it is possible to walk along the beach from the pier, but use extreme caution, as algae-covered rocks can be extremely slippery. Alternatively, it is possible to walk here from Ao Thon Sai by walking through the Bayview Resort path and then up through another path once you have reached Ma Prao beach, but this 45min. walk from the village to Hat Yao or vice versa is tedious. Hat Yao does not have any ATMs. To get cash, you have to walk 20min. to the village. Likewise, if you are interested in experiencing the nightlife in the village, Hat Yao is not where you want to stay. Still, Long Beach does provide a couple of reasonably priced beachside bungalows on a stunning white sand beach. **Paradise Pearl Bungalow ❹,** the first resort on Long Beach after Ma Prao (the westernmost resort on this beach), has nearly 100 pleasantly decorated bungalows in varying price ranges. Paradise's restaurant occupies an ideal spot overlooking the beach and is deservedly popular. (☎075 618 050. High-season doubles with fan 700฿, with A/C 1800฿; low-season 300/900฿.)

◪ **KO NOK.** The westernmost beach on the island, Ko Nok is just past the hospital. It is a mediocre beach with lots of moored boats and Ao Ton Sai Pier clearly visible in the distance. There is one budget bungalow option here, **P.P. Sand Sea View Resort ❸,** which offers small, sparsely decorated bamboo bungalows near the beach, all with private baths and mosquito nets. (☎084 635 3855. High-season doubles with fan 800฿, with A/C 2300฿; low-season 400/1200฿.)

◪ ♫ FOOD AND ENTERTAINMENT

Ko Phi Phi, as a result of its expat population, offers an outstanding range of international cuisine. Homesick tourists munch on faux-Italian, -Mexican, and -Swedish fare in restaurants all over the island. A number of **open-air restaurants** geared towards locals serve up soups, *pad thai,* and excellent fish curries directly in front of the pier. (Dishes 50-120฿.) Plenty of **pancake stalls** on the streets of Thon Sai Village serve up a modified version of *roti* (50-60฿) for tourist consumption. **Phi Phi Bakery ❷,** on the main road parallel to the beach, about 100m east of the pier, offers delicious donuts (20฿), cakes (35฿), and wonderfully inauthentic chocolate chip cookies made with cornflakes (25฿), plus standard *farang*-friendly Thai dishes (80-120฿. Open daily 7am-9:30pm.) **Cosmic Restaurant ❸,** in Ao Ton Sai, serves delicious thin-crust pizza (150฿) and Thai curries (80-100฿. Open 10am-10:30pm.) **Garlic 1992 Restaurant ❷,** just past V Shop in the village, is proud of its relative old age (as compared to other Phi Phi restaurants) and loves its garlic. Everything is spicy, delicious, and a little less expensive than most nearby restaurants. Watch the board at the entrance for pizza-plus-beer specials. (Dishes 50-150฿. Open 7am-10:30pm.)

By night, Ao Thon Sai is an impressive hotbed of activity. There are a couple of mellow beach bars located on each of the beaches, and about a dozen louder and rowdier bars located all over the island. **Sunflower Beach Bar and Restaurant, Jordan's Irish Bar,** and **The Reggae Bar,** and **Cancun Bar** are all great options.

🎣 WATER SPORTS

Ko Phi Phi's waters are so clear that you almost don't need to bother with a mask to check out the marine life. **Bamboo Island** and **Mosquito Island** are famous **dive sites,** and there are many dive shops and tour agents in the area extremely eager to serve. Three-day PADI certification courses generally cost close to 12,500฿. **Visa Diving Center,** 50m to the east of the pier along the main drag, is one of the best. (☎075 601 157; www.visadiving.com.) In addition to diving, **snorkeling** is also popular and far cheaper (½-day 450-500฿, includes lunch and gear). Longtail boats provide for a more intimate, enjoyable tour than the larger motor boats. Nearly any privately hired longtail has snorkeling gear onboard, and most know places with good coral to explore (3 hr. trip 1200฿, max. of 3 people). If you'd rather chill out on the water, rent **kayaks** at Kayak Sunset, right next to Sunflower Bar and Restaurant, on Loh Dalum beach. (1st hr. 200฿, each additional hr. 100฿.)

🏝 DAYTRIP FROM KO PHI PHI DON: KO PHI PHI LEY

Getting to Ko Phi Phi Ley from Ko Phi Phi Don usually involves some sort of organized tour. Plenty of Ao Thon Sai agencies arrange package daytrips to the island (½-day trip 450-650฿ depending on boat or longtail trip; full-day 900-950฿),but individual longtail boat tours around the island cost slightly less (3hr., 3 people 1200฿).

Nearly every visitor to Ko Phi Phi ends up at Ko Phi Phi Ley at some point. And for good reason—the island's limestone cliffs shelter shallow, coral-filled coves teeming with sea life, and enclose stunningly gorgeous white-sand beaches. Ever since Leonardo DiCaprio filmed *The Beach* here, hordes of tourists from all over the Andaman region have flocked here to take in the sights. Although they haven't added to the experience, Ko Phi Phi Ley is still not to be missed.

Tours generally include stops at **Viking Cave, Pilah,** and **Maya Bay.** Viking Cave, on the northeastern side of the island, has paintings on its walls dating back about 400 years, but is more known for its long vertical shafts where swiftlets build their delicate saliva nests (a highly coveted Asian delicacy). Villagers have constructed intricate networks of bamboo scaffolding in order to collect the prized nests. It used to be possible to enter the cave and view the shafts, but after the shy swiftlets fled the scene, collectors put an end to that venture in favor of more lucrative nest collecting. Collecting nests is an extremely dangerous undertaking, and every year several collectors fall during the process, resulting in injury and sometimes death.

Pilah, on the eastern side of the island, is a sheltered cove with turquoise water perfect for swimming. There's a small patch of coral near the entrance, but because there are no permanent moorings, scarring from longtails has marred it. Regardless, the snorkeling here is still great. Other sites around Ko Phi Phi Ley do have permanent moorings, which make for better snorkeling experiences, and are more environmentally friendly.

Maya Bay, on the western side, was made famous by *The Beach* and is a spectacular white-sand beach that's surreal both in its natural beauty and in the number of tourists that can crowd onto its shore. If butting shoulders with fellow *farang* isn't your idea of a good time, try getting there early by hiring a longtail boat before 8am. Another interesting, but expensive, way to get a less touristy glimpse of Maya Bay is to camp on the beach. Many tour agencies offer a 20hr. camping package with food and gear included for 1600฿ per person.

KRABI   ☎ 075

The last bastions of serene beach beauty in southern Thailand are being invaded by droves of backpackers, and the town of Krabi is the staging ground for their assault. Tourists come here because the beaches of Ao Nang, Rai Ley, Ko Phi Phi, and Ko Lanta are within a short commute. Krabi itself is little more than a necessary transit point. It does, though, have a mellow vibe that's all its own, and the emergence of excellent budget accommodations more than justifies an overnight stay.

▐ TRANSPORTATION

Buses: The **bus station** (☎075 663 503) is 5km north of town in the village of Talat Kao at the intersection of Utarakit Rd. and Hwy. 4. To: **Bangkok** (12hr., 8 per day 7:30am-5:30pm, 461-944฿); **Hat Yai** (4hr., 15 per day 7am-5pm, 96-230฿); **Phuket** (3-4hr., about every 30min. 6:20am-5pm, 81-155฿); **Satun** (5hr.; 11am, 1pm; 187฿); **Surat Thani** (2hr., about every 2hr. 4:30am-4pm, 140฿); **Trang** (2½hr., about every hr. 6:50am-9:30pm, 90-117฿).

Minivans: Private travel agencies operate A/C minibus service to towns in Thailand and Malaysia. To: **Phuket** (3hr., 11am., 250-350฿); **Surat Thani** (2hr., every hr. 7:30am-4:30pm, 170฿); **Nakhon Si Thammarat** (3hr., every 30min. 7:45am-4pm, 180฿); **Hat Yai** (4hr.; 7, 11am, 5pm; 230฿). In low season, boats do not run to Ko Lanta; at this time, **minibuses from Krabi** are the primary mode of transit to **Ko Lanta** (3hr.; high season every hr. 7am-7pm, low season 3 or 4 per day by demand; 300-350฿). You can buy all minivan tickets at your hotel or at a nearby travel agency. Minivans pick up guests from all hotels in the Chao Fah area.

Ferries: Longtail boats leave from **Chao Fah Pier** (Kongka Pier) on Kongka Rd. for **Hat Rai Lay** (50min., 8am-6pm, 150฿) and **Ko Lanta** (1½hr.; 10:30am, 1:30pm; 350-400฿). You can only get tickets for a longtail boat to Rai Lay at the pier, and the boats will not leave until 8 people are on board. You will inevitably have to wait a while for more people to show up, or pay double if no one else comes. Check the ferry times from Ko Phi Phi to Krabi and head to the pier 30min. after the Ko Phi Phi boat arrival for a greater chance that 8 people will show up at that time. During the low season, service decreases and Ko Lanta ferry service shuts down altogether. From the new **Passenger Marine Port** (Klong Jilad Pier), 5km south of town, express boats go to **Ko Phi Phi** (1½hr.; 10am, 1:30 (only in high season), 3pm; 400฿). Most hotels in Krabi arrange for *songthaew* transport to the pier; they arrive 30 min.-hr. before your scheduled departure. Check tourist offices and travel agencies for current boat schedules and info.

Local Transportation: Red **songthaew** run up and down Utarakit Rd., especially near the TAT office and go to the bus station (20฿ from the center of town); white *songthaew* leave from Maharat Rd. in front of the 7-Eleven and circle the city before heading to **Ao Nang** (8am-6pm; every 30min. 50฿; 1½hr., 100฿) Catch a red *songthaew* heading in the direction of the bus station to get to the road that goes the 2km to **Wat Tham Sua** (frequent 8am-6pm, 20฿). **Motorcycle taxis** go from the new **passenger pier** (50฿), the **bus station** (50฿), and the **airport** (100฿) to the center of town.

Rentals: Travel agencies and guesthouses on Utarakit Rd. rent **motorbikes** for 200฿ per day. Some also rent **jeeps** (1000-1200฿ per day; depending on season).

▰ ▱ ORIENTATION AND PRACTICAL INFORMATION

Central Krabi is compact and easily navigable by foot. **Utarakit Road,** the main street, runs parallel to the **Krabi River** and is home to most services. To the north Utarakit Rd. heads to Wat Tham Sua and the bus station; the more southern part of the road, near **the pier,** has an abundance of guesthouses, Internet spots, and travel agencies. Parallel to Utarakit Rd. and one block over, **Maharat Road** has shops and eateries that are more geared to locals than to *farang*. Boats to Hat Rai Lay and Ko Lanta leave from **Chao Fah Pier** on **Kongka Road,** which branches off of Utarakit Rd. and runs along the river. **Chaofa Road,** running up the hill from the pier past Utarakit Rd., is home to more *farang*-oriented hotels and restaurants.

Tourist Offices: TAT (☎075 622 1634), in a white building on the side of Utarakit Rd. closest to the river, about 150m north of Chaofa Rd. Good free maps of all of the nearby islands. English spoken. Open daily 8:30am-4:30pm.

Tours: For boat tickets, it is most convenient to book out of your hotel. Most hotels provide transportation to the pier and allow you to leave belongings while you are gone. You can also directly book from **PP Family** (☎075 612 463), in the white building on Chao Fah Pier, which operates most ferry services from Krabi. However, beware that many of the salesmen in PP Family will often try to overcharge you by about 50฿. A little bargaining may be necessary. Open daily 7:30am-9pm.

Currency Exchange: Several banks line Utarakit Rd., including **Bangkok Bank,** 147 Utarakit Rd. Open M-F 8:30am-3:30pm.

Police: (☎045 611 222), 800m past the post office. Little English spoken.

Medical Services: Krabi Hospital (☎045 631 769), on Utarakit Rd., 2km north of town. Some English spoken. Cash only. Open 24hr.

Internet Access: All along Utarakit Rd., in cafes and guesthouses. The average rate is 1฿ per min. or 40฿ per hr., with a 10฿ minimum. **Eighty-nine Cafe,** across from Jam Bar on Chaofa Rd., has particularly fast connections, a flatscreen TV, and serves beer (45฿) and fruit shakes (50฿). It is open 8am-midnight, as are most of the Internet shops on Chaofa Rd. The Internet shops on Utarakit Rd. tend to close by 10pm.

Post Office: 190 Utarakit Rd. (☎045 611 497), on top of the hill, on the left. Poste Restante. Open M-F 8:30am-4:30pm, Sa 9am-noon. **Postal Code:** 81000.

ACCOMMODATIONS

Krabi has a good selection of budget choices, most of which lie near the pier along Utarakit Rd. and Chaofa Rd. Room prices can increase by as much as 100฿ during the high season.

Chan-Cha-Lay Guest House, 55 Utarakit Rd. (☎045 620 952), on the uphill slope. Some of the hippest digs in town, with clean, bright rooms and simple, clean shared outdoor showers. An airy blue palette successfully creates a pleasant seaside atmosphere. Everything from the bathrooms to the art on the walls is perfectly executed, making this guesthouse a real steal. Reservations recommended. Rooms with big beds and shared bath 200฿, with private bath 350฿, with A/C 600฿. ❷

K Guest House, 15-25 Chaofa Rd. (☎045 623 166), 1 block down from the intersection of Chaofa Rd. and Utarakit Rd. The more expensive wood-paneled upstairs rooms conjure up images of a tropical log cabin. Singles and doubles 200฿, upstairs rooms with fans, private bath, and balcony 300฿. ❷

Good Dream Hotel, 83 Utarakit Rd. (☎045 622 993), near the intersection of Utarakit Rd. and Chaofa Rd. Rooms are small, but offer all of the desired amenities at the right price. All of the rooms come with private bath, hot shower, and Wi-Fi. Small singles with fan 120฿; large doubles with fan 200฿, with A/C 450฿. Book ahead, as rooms fill up quickly even in low season. ❷

Siboya Guest House, 69 Utarakit Rd. (☎045 623 561). This guesthouse's small, cheap rooms are cozy, with funky, fresh decor. High-season double with shared bath 120฿, with fan 150฿. Low-season 100฿/120฿. ❷

City Hotel, 15/2-3 Sukhon Rd. (☎045 611 961; www.citykrabi.com), between Utarakit and Maharat Rd., in the heart of downtown on Soi Maharat 10, directly across from the local night market. Spacious, slightly dated, but well-furnished rooms, all come with cable TV and phone. Singles and doubles with fan 450฿, with A/C 650฿; newer rooms with hot water 950฿. ❸

🍴 FOOD

The **night market** (open nightly 3-9pm), opposite the City Hotel (p. 383), has a vast selection of edible fare, including multiple stalls selling a variety of excellent fruit (prices labeled by the kg). The amazing 📷**smaller night market** by the pier on Kongka Rd. has delicious food stalls serving freshly made Thai curries, chicken *satay*, soups (40-70฿), and *pad thai* (30฿). **Chaofah Panchano stall** is an especially good one, but the wait can sometimes be up to 40min. For a late-night meal, several open-air restaurant stalls set up shop along Maharat Rd., offering fried chicken and rice (40฿) and soups (30฿), and stay open until midnight.

Ruenmai Thai, on Maharat Rd., 2km north of town (motorcycle taxi one-way 30฿), on the corner just after the 7-Eleven; sign is in Thai. This huge outdoor restaurant has tables surrounded by jungle-like vegetation. Try the blissful coconut-cream prawn soup with *pak mieng*, or the edible ferns with fish, both 80฿. Open daily 10am-10pm. ❸

Ban Chaofa Restaurant, in the Ban Chaofa hotel, specializing in pizza and pasta dishes, and also serves a delicious vegetarian *pad thai* (50฿). Thai dishes 40-80฿. Italian dishes 130-170฿. Open daily 7am-10pm. ❷

Corner Restaurant, between Ban Chaofa and K Guest House (p. 382) on Chaofa Rd., has great daily curry specials for 70฿. Thai dishes 50-80฿, western dishes 80-160฿. Open daily 9am-11pm. The restaurant is closed in the low season. ❷

👁 SIGHTS

Krabi's most impressive sight is **Wat Tham Sua,** 8km north of town, on an access road off of Utarakit Rd. An operating monastery inhabited by hordes of monks and nuns, the *wat* is best known for its **Tiger Cave.** Legend has it that a large tiger once lived here, and its footsteps adorn the *wat*'s entrance. Apart from a fairly large Buddha statue, the cave itself isn't much to see. If you continue down the road to the rear of the monastery, you will arrive at the bottom of 1327 steps that provide a 45min.-1hr. strenuous walk up the mountain to a pair of Buddha's footprints.

ON THE MENU

GANG FLAVA

Farang often have difficulty distinguishing between curries (*gang*) thanks to their often-similar ingredients, explosive spiciness, and common coconut base. This list is meant to help you navigate the basics of this Thai favorite:

Red Curry (*gang pet*). Literally, "spicy curry," this delicious dish includes coconut milk, red curry paste, and fish sauce.

Green curry (*gang kee-o wahn*): Similar to red curry but a little sweeter; includes green curry paste.

Yellow curry (*gang ga-ree*): Includes coconut cream, tumeric, and pineapple. Potatoes are a common ingredient in its southern incarnation.

Massaman curry (*gang massaman*): A Thai-Muslim specialty. Cumin, cinnamon, and cardamom make it similar to Indian curry. Potatoes and beef are the usual ingredients, though other meats can be substituted.

Panang curry (*gang panang*): The Thai rendition of the Malaysian favorite is often made with less coconut milk, beef and is drier and spicier than other Thai curries.

Gang is generally accompanied by rice or *khanom jeen* (rice noodles), but often you have to order—and pay for—these separately. Many curries are served with or already include kaffir lime. *Gang* is eaten with a spoon and fork rather than chopsticks.

Enlightenment isn't easy: be prepared for a grueling climb. The platform at the top of the hike provides a fantastic view of Krabi and the surrounding area. A second set of steps in the rear of the monastery, about 20m from the steps leading to the climb, leads you on a 15min. walk to a fairly unimpressive cave and ancient tree with large roots, all within a preserved national forest filled with little shacks where the monks live. *Songthaew* from Utarakit Rd. (15min., 20฿) drop you off at an access road 2km from the *wat*. From there, hire a motorcycle taxi (they wait at the corner) for 20฿. A motorcycle taxi from the center of town will cost you 80฿ and will take 10min. to arrive. Donation requested at *wat*.

🖈 DAYTRIP FROM KRABI: KHLONG THOM

To get to the national park 50km from Krabi, take a motorbike from Krabi or a songthaew to Khlong Thom 50฿; motorcycle taxi to Khlong Thom 300฿. Songthaew run from Khlong Thom back to Krabi (every hr. 8am-6pm). Open 6am-6pm. Free.

The world-renowned beaches near Krabi are some of Thailand's most popular, so if you're planning on staying at **Ao Nang** or **Hat Rai Lay,** bypass Krabi, and head straight for the sand. If beaches aren't the only thing on your mind, try a daytrip to Krabi's nearby forest. The **Khao Nawe Choochee Lowland Forest** is one of the last remaining forests of its kind in Thailand. Among the 290-plus bird species that nest in the forest is *Pitta gurneyi*, a brightly colored, ground-dwelling bird of which only 150 remain. The **Thung Tieo Nature Trail** (2.7km), located in Khlong Thom, traverses some of Thailand's most lush and undisturbed slices of nature. **Park headquarters** is at the entrance to the park; they provide maps and can answer questions.

AO NANG   ☎ 075

Ao Nang's accessibility by car gives it a completely different atmosphere from either secluded Rai Lay or the nearby islands. With brightly colored shops, beachfront hotels, and a boardwalk perfect for an evening stroll, Ao Nang has a made-for-tourists feel.

🚍 TRANSPORTATION. White Krabi-bound **songthaew** crawl down Ao Nang Rd. **Motorcycle taxis** will take you to **Krabi** for 150-200฿. Regular **taxis** will make the trip for 400฿. **Songthaew** to **Ao Na Mao** (every 30min., 30฿), where you can take a 70฿ 8-person longtail boat to Rai Lay even during low season.

🖈🔢 ORIENTATION AND PRACTICAL INFORMATION. The main drag, **Ao Nang Road,** makes a U-shape, with the bottom of the U parallel to the beach, where you can find the most expensive ocean-front restaurants. Most of the restaurants and accommodations are east of the pier along the right side of the U. The left leg of the U has bigger, more expensive resorts. As you walk southeast on Ao Nang Rd. parallel to the beach, continue straight down the path to the right of the police station (rather than turning with the road to the left to all of the budget accommodations), and after 100m, find yourself at the nicest **swimming beach** in the area.

Sea Canoe Krabi (☎075 612 740), at the corner of the left leg of the U near the longtail boat ticket booth, offers half-day (500฿) and full-day (900฿) **canoe** rentals. Rent **mountain bikes** (100฿ per hr.) at **Thailand Travelling,** on the corner of the right leg of the U near the police station. They hand out free maps of the area. Full-day **snorkeling tours** of the nearby islands by speedboat cost 1400฿ per person with up to 22 seats, but only 500฿ per person by slower and noisier longtail boat that can hold up to four people. **Nosey Parker's Elephant**

Trekking and River Camp (☎075 612 048) offers 1hr. elephant treks (adults 750฿, children 450฿) and half-day tours, which include 2hr. of elephant and jungle trekking (adults 1650฿; children 850฿).

Along Ao Nang Rd., there are a number of moneychangers and **ATMs**, a **mini-market**, restaurants, and **tour offices**. There is a **police** at the corner on the right leg of the U. (☎075 695 163. Open daily 8am-midnight.)

⌐ ACCOMMODATIONS. Overnight stay options on Ao Nang vary, but most of the budget options are clustered on an alley along the right side of the right leg of the U where Sea World Guest House and P.K. Mansion are. All of these hotels and guesthouses offer the typical tourist services, including tour bookings, **motorcycle rentals,** and **Internet** (2฿ per min.). For something a little bit more rustic, **Anawin Bungalows ❸**, on Soi 6, on the left side, off the main drag 500m inland from the police station, has simple, immaculate, brightly painted cement bungalows. (High-season bungalows with fan and cold water 800฿, low-season 350฿; larger bungalows with A/C 1000/450฿.) There is an unnamed alley off of the main drag, just inland after the police station, that is about a 2min. walk from the beach. This lane is filled with budget guesthouses and hotels; they are especially affordable during low season. While the four guesthouses in this alley are very similar, the one with the best value is **Sea World Guest House ❸**, 247/10-11 Moo 2, which has sparklingly clean rooms with big windows and private balconies. (High-season, single with fan and private bath 400฿, bigger room with A/C 1000฿. Low-season prices are cut in half.

❐ FOOD. The best Thai food from the beachfront restaurants is available at **Ao Nang Cuisine ❷**, 245/4 Moo 2, in the middle of the strip near the central 7-Eleven. (☎045 637 253. Thai dishes 50-110฿. Western dishes 80-200฿. Open daily 9am-11pm.) **Last Cafe ❷** is at the southeastern end of Ao Nang Beach, past a ton of massage huts, 500m after the road becomes a dirt trail. (Muesli with fruit and yogurt 30฿. Omelettes 40฿. Thai noodle soup 50฿. Open high season daily 7am-7pm.) Italian restaurants line the beach road. To eat where the locals eat, head to the **food stalls** 800m inland on the western leg of the U. They will be on your left, serving up *pad thai*, fried rice, curries, and pancakes for 25-70฿.

KO LANTA YAI   ☎075

Ko Lanta Yai is an up-and-coming island on the *ko*-hopping backpacker trail. Because of its large size and its distance from Phuket, the island has not yet become overrun with tourists. There's a local flavor and a quiet charm here that is lacking in tourist hotspots like Ko Samui and nearby Ko Phi Phi. While the northern part of the island is fairly developed, quieter, more serene parts can be found to the south.

❰ TRANSPORTATION. During the high season, **boats** arrive from **Krabi** at **Ko Lanta Yai's Ban Sala Dan Pier** (1½hr.; 10:30am, 1:30pm; return 8am; 350-400฿) at the northern tip of the island. Also, in the high season, **express boats** leave from **Ko Phi Phi** for **Ko Lanta Yai** (1½hr.; 1:30, 2, 3pm; 350฿). In the low season, the only way to get there is by **minivan**, depart year-round from **Krabi** and connect via two **ferries** with **Ko Lanta Yai** (3hr.; every hr. 8am-3pm; 350฿ with 5-person minimum).

Outside of Ban Sala Dan, the island is extremely spread out. Most resorts offer free pickup from minivan and ferry drop-off points, as well as a free return, as long as you purchase your ticket through them. Because the **resort trucks** are the best mode of transportation, reservations are recommended one to two weeks in advance during the high season. Alternatively, hire a **motorcycle taxi** from the minivan drop-off in Ban Sala Dan to anywhere on the island for about 25฿ per km. **Motorbikes** can be rented from most tour agencies and resorts (200-250฿ per day). Many also rent **bicycles** for 100฿ per day; however, remember that the island is 28km long.

⬛🔃 ORIENTATION AND PRACTICAL INFORMATION. Ban Sala Dan is the island's largest town, with **tour operators, a police booth, post office, Internet** cafes, **banks,** a health center, cheap open-air restaurants, and other conveniences. There are two main roads on the island, one on the western side, and the other following the coast on the eastern side. There are a couple of smaller roads which traverse the island to connect these two main roads. During the low season, the island turns into a ghost town as many stores and hotels close, and many locals dependent on the tourism industry for their livelihoods move elsewhere for a couple of months to find work. However, the low-season quiet does not make for a boring scene; instead, the island becomes a wonderfully quiet getaway from the hubbub of many other tourist destinations. Around the corner from Ban Sala Dan is Ko Lanta Yai's biggest beach, **Hat Klong Dao,** a 2km beach sprinkled with quality resorts. Klong Dao has decent coral at its north end and the beach faces directly west, making for stellar sunsets.

🔃🔃 ACCOMMODATIONS AND FOOD. Even in low season, accommodations are expensive on Hat Klong Dao, so head south to find the cheaper options. In the middle of the island on the western coast, just below Phra-Ae beach, is **Lanta Emerald Bungalow ❷,** near Khlong Khoang village. The rooms are huge and clean with TV, fan, and private bath. It is located on a rocky beach, but its private pool, laid-back beachside bar (**Ting Tong Bar** with 60฿ beer), delicious restaurant (Thai dishes 60-100฿), and friendly staff more than make up for it. (☎075 667 037. Low season bungalows with fan 300฿, with A/C 500฿. Prices double Sept.-Oct. and triple Nov.-Dec.) On the southern tip of the island, overlooking the scenic Kanthiang Bay, the **Marine Park View Resort ❷** provides an excellent range of accommodations, from bungalows with TV and A/C to more rustic rooms, all with private bath. The beach here is fantastic, and the three-tiered **Marine Park Resort Restaurant ❷** overlooks the peaceful bay. (☎075 066 5063; www.lantamarine.com. Most dishes 60-180฿. High-season bungalows with fan 400-900฿, with A/C and bay view 1800฿; low-season 300/600฿.) Off of the main western road, on a smaller road that leads to the viewpoint in the center of the island, **Top View Restaurant ❸** is precariously perched atop a west-facing cliff. Though relatively expensive, especially for its small portions, it's more than worth the splurge for the absolutely jaw-dropping sunset views. (☎075 283 0135. Dishes 80-200฿.) Another popular restaurant among tourists and locals alike is **Lanta Seafood Restaurant ❷,** at the northern tip of the island in Ban Sala Dan. It has patio seating looking out on fishing boats in the ocean. The fish is certainly fresh, and the dishes (50-140฿) are reasonably priced. (☎075 684 106. Open year-round 11am-9:30pm.)

🔃 SIGHTS. There are eight other beaches on the island, including the beautiful **Khlong Nin** and **Kanthiang** beaches, both located on the southwest portion of the island and both known for their scenery. **Khlong Hin beach,** in the middle of Khlong Nin and Kanthiang, is renowned for its **snorkeling. Seaborn Ventures** (☎075 684 696) in Ban Sala Dan offers **kayak-snorkel** excursions for about 900฿ per person. You can also rent a longtail boat for up to four people for a day for 4000฿. Contact any hotel or travel agency for more information. The offshore islands also boast excellent diving and snorkeling. There are a few outstanding daytrips to the interior, most notably to the **viewpoint** at the center of the island and the **Tham Mai Ka caves,** 4km south of the viewpoint. (Open 8am-6pm. 200฿.)

You can also see **waterfalls** at the southern end of the island and go on **elephant treks** (400-500฿ per hr.) in four different locations scattered all over the northern and southern portion of the island.

TRANG ☎ 075

Though Trang province contains spectacular islands, beaches, and caves, which combined rival those of the more popular Krabi and Phuket, it has, for the most part, stayed off the tourist circuit. Its over 200km of coastline and more than 46 offshore islands have remained less developed than similar nearby islands like Ko Lanta and Ko Phi Phi. At the same time, the less developed tourist infrastructure means that you may need a little more patience and money to get where you want to go. Trang city is a pleasant and quiet jump-off point onto the sand nearby. It has deep historical roots, having served as an important trading point as early as the first century AD. Today, the city is wealthy from its rubber tree plantations, which were first established in 1899. Though the city of Trang does not offer many sights in and of itself, its compact center contains bustling day and night markets, indelibly charming *raan ko-pii* (coffee shops) that serve extra strong coffee, and well-established restaurants featuring delicious *mu yang* (Chinese-style roast pork). All in all, Trang can be a welcome relief from the southern Thailand tourist circuit.

◢ TRANSPORTATION

Flights: Trang Airport (☎075 218 224), at the end of Visetkul Rd., 5km south of the city. Some of the more expensive hotels may arrange free or discounted pickups if you book with them in advance. **Nok Air** to **Bangkok** (daily 11:50am, 1950฿). Motorbikes (100฿) and *tuk-tuks* (150฿) leave from Trang Airport for town. Flights can be booked at many of the travel agencies next to the train station, including **World Travel Service Limited**, 25/2 Pharam 6 Rd., on your left hand side when you are facing the train station. Open M-F 8:30am-5:00pm and Sa. 8:30am-noon.

Trains: Train station (☎075 218 012), at the west end of Phraram 6 Rd. Trang is not on the main Southern Line, so train service is limited, and buses and minivans are a better bet. Fares listed are 2nd-cl. to **Bangkok** (16hr.; 1:25, 5:20pm; 280฿) via **Chumphon** (6hr., 214฿) and **Surat Thani** (4hr., 189฿).

Buses: Bus terminal (☎075 210 455), on Huay Yod Rd., 1.5km. north of downtown. Check with tour agencies and TAT for buses that leave from other parts of city. To: **Bangkok** (10hr.; 9:00am, 5, 5:30pm, 651-900฿); **Hat Yai** (4hr., every hr. 8am-6pm, 80-175฿); **Krabi** (2hr., every hr. 6am-8pm, 60-135฿); **Phuket** (5hr., every hr. 7am-6pm, 127-220฿).

Minivans: Minivans to **Hat Pakmeng** leave from Taklang Rd., near the railroad tracks past the night market (50min.; high season every hr. 8am-5pm, low season every other hr.; 50-70฿). Minivans to **Kantang Pier** (every hr. 8am-4pm, 60-80฿) leave from Kantang Rd. 100m south of Phraram 6 Rd; to **Surat Thani** (3hr., every hr. 10am-5pm, 195฿) from the parking lot in front of the the train station; to **Nakhon Si Thammarat** (2hr., every 1-2hr. 9am-5pm, 150฿) from Visetkul Rd., 500m north of the city, just after the big movie theater; to **Ko Lanta** (2½hr., high season every hr. 9:30am-1:30pm, low season every other hr.; 250฿) right in front of KK Travel, across from the train station. Check with hotels or any travel agency in town for departure location of minivans to: **Hat Yai** (2hr., every 30min. 6am-6pm, 120-148฿); **Krabi** (2hr., every hr. 7am-6pm, 120-156฿); **Phang-Nga** (4hr., every other hr. 7am-6pm, 180-225฿); **Phuket** (5hr., every hr. 7am-6pm, 260฿); **Satun** (3hr.; 1:30, 3:30pm; 183฿).

Local Transportation: Pastel green *tuk-tuks* within the city run for 20-30฿ per person to just about anywhere in the city. **Motorcycle taxis** line every other street corner and are typically less expensive. Yamawa Hotel (see opposite page) and several of the tour agencies near the train station rent **motorbikes** for 150-200฿ per 24hr.

ORIENTATION AND PRACTICAL INFORMATION

Buses arrive at the bus station near the intersection of **Ploenpitak Road** and **Huay Yod Road,** a 20min. walk north of town or a 5min. ride by motorcycle taxi (30฿) or *tuk-tuk* (40฿). The train station sits at the west end of **Phraram 6 Road,** a large hotel-lined avenue with a landmark clock tower 200m east of the train station, at the intersection of Pharam 6 Rd. and Visetkul Rd. Most tourist services are also situated on Pharam 6 Rd. next to the train station. North of Phraram 6 Rd. and roughly parallel to it, **Ratchadamnoen Road** winds alongside the main day market, and becomes **Pattalung Road** to the northeast of town near the night

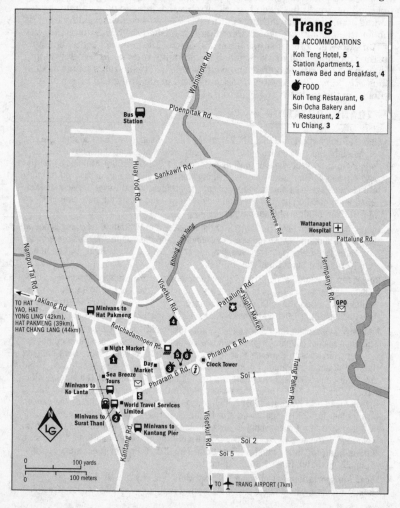

Trang

🏠 ACCOMMODATIONS
Koh Teng Hotel, **5**
Station Apartments, **1**
Yamawa Bed and Breakfast, **4**

🍎 FOOD
Koh Teng Restaurant, **6**
Sin Ocha Bakery and
  Restaurant, **2**
Yu Chiang, **3**

Wattinrote Rd.

Ploenpitak Rd.

Bus Station

Huay Yod Rd.

Sankawit Rd.

Kuankeeree Rd.

Wattanapat Hospital

Pattalung Rd.

Khlong Huay Yong

Visetkul Rd.

Jermpanya Rd.

Namput Tai Rd.

Taklang Rd.

TO HAT YAO, HAT YONG LING (42km), HAT PAKMENG (39km), HAT CHANG LANG (44km)

Minivans to Hat Pakmeng

Pattalung Rd.

Pattalung Night Market

GPO

Ratchadamnoen Rd.

Night Market

Day Market

Phraram 6 Rd.

Clock Tower

Soi 1

Sea Breeze Tours

Phraram 6 Rd.

Minivans to Ko Lanta

Trang Palien Rd.

World Travel Services Limited

Minivans to Surat Thani

Kantang Rd.

Minivans to Kantang Pier

Visetkul Rd.

Soi 2

Soi 5

0   100 yards
0   100 meters

N

LG

TO ✈ TRANG AIRPORT (7km)

market. **Kantang Road,** which runs roughly north-south one block east of the train station, intersects Pharam 6 Rd.; further north, intersects **Visetkul Road** where its name changes to **Huay Yod Road.**

Tourist Office: The **TAT** office in Nakhon Si Thammarat handles Trang queries. In town, the **Trang Tourist Association** offers the closest thing to non-biased tourist assistance (☎/fax 075 215 580). Next to the Trang Hotel on Phraram 6 Rd. Enthusiastic staff with passable English and free maps. Open daily 8:30am-5pm.

Tours: Travel agencies offering organized tours and transportation line Phraram 6 Rd. **Sea Breeze Tours,** 59/1 Sathanee Rd. (☎075 217 460), right on the right when you are facing the train station. Tissawan at the front desk speaks great English and is extremely helpful. Open 7:30am-10pm.

Currency Exchange: Bangkok Bank, 2 Phraram 6 Rd. (☎075 218 203), 1 block from the train station, on the right. **24hr. ATM.** Open M-F 8:30am-3:30pm.

Police: 6 Pattalung Rd. (☎075 211 311). Some English spoken. Open 24hr.

Medical Services: Wattanapat Hospital, 247 Pattalung Rd. (☎075 218 018), near the intersection with Ploenpitak Rd., about 800m northeast of the clock tower. Some English spoken. Open 24hr.

Internet Access: Connect, 142 Ratchadamnoen Rd., is almost always packed with kids playing loud war and dance computer games. 15฿ per hr. Open 24hr.

Post Offices: GPO (☎075 218 521), at the bend on Jermpanya Rd., a 20min. walk from the train station. Poste Restante. Open M-F 8:30am-3:30pm. **Tap Thiang Post Office** on Phraram 6 Rd. (☎075 218 021), 1 block from train station. Open M-F 8:30am-4:30pm, Sa-Su 9am-noon. **Postal Code:** 92000.

ACCOMMODATIONS

While the majority of hotels are geared towards business travelers, Trang has a few solid budget accommodations.

Koh Teng Hotel, 77-79 Phraram 6 Rd. (☎075 218 148), 4 blocks from the train station on the left, 1 block before the clock tower. Koh Teng pitches itself as a 5-star hotel for backpackers, and it's hard to argue. Large rooms are clean, comfortable, and a great value. Try to get a room facing outside for more fresh air. The rooms with satellite TV have a multitude of channels. On the 2nd-fl. corridor, where these rooms are located, the lighting is much better than it is in the large dark corridor of the 3rd fl. with the non-TV rooms. Singles and doubles 180฿, with satellite TV 220฿, with A/C 280฿. ❷

Yamawa Rooms for Rent, 94 Visetkul Rd. (☎075 216 617). Clean guesthouse is carefully decorated and far more personable than Trang's ubiquitous business hotels. Private baths, TVs, and massage parlor. Staff is very helpful and can assist in setting up tours or ferries. Also rents motorbikes (200฿ per 24hr.). Singles 200฿, doubles 350฿, rooms with big beds and A/C 450฿. ❷

Station Apartments (☎075 223 393). At 100m north of the train station, take a left out of the station and take your first right, it will be on your right in 20m. It's the closest budget option to the station. Enormous gray concrete rooms foster an institutional feel, and make Station Apartments best for a quick stay during a short train layover. Rooms with fan 280฿, with A/C 380฿. ❷

FOOD

Trang's cuisine has a distinct Chinese influence. Crispy, roasted, honey-dipped pork (*mu yang*), Chinese doughnuts (*paa tong ko*), and *dim sum* all make delicious breakfasts. The town is also famous for its strong fresh-brewed coffee, available at shops and restaurants everywhere. Trang has two **night markets,** both open nightly 5-9pm. The one east of the clock tower is especially impressive and worth a visit. There's also an expansive **day market,** just off Phraram 6 Rd., with fresh produce. English menus can be a bit hard to come by in town, but, as a rule, most restuarants and cafes have one buried away somewhere.

Sin Ocha Bakery and Restaurant (☎075 211 191), just south of the train station to the left when you are facing the station. Come here for an excellent hit of caffeine and yummy pastry. Be sure to ask for *"ko-pee"* or you might end up with Nescafé. Coffee 20฿. Pastries 10-25฿. Thai dishes 40-70฿. Open 7am-7pm. ❶

Yu Chiang, 112 Pharam 6, with a Thai script sign and a curry stall in front of it, halfway up Phraram 6 Rd. from the train station on the left. This hidden marvel serves equally delicious coffee and tea in a wooden room filled with antique circular marble tables. Coffee 15฿. Open M-Sa 6am-5pm. ❶

Koh Teng Restaurant, below the hotel of the same name, has tasty Chinese and Thai food for breakfast, lunch, and an early-bird dinner. The chicken curry (40฿), which is a cross between yellow curry and Masaman curry, is a house specialty. Dishes 40-70฿. Open daily 7:30am-5pm. ❶

🎵 ENTERTAINMENT

Trang's entertainment is quite unlike the usual Thai offerings. Makeshift **cockfighting** arenas set up below stilt houses and host fights every Thursday at 9am. (Direct *tuk-tuk* drivers to Sanam Wuah Chon near the bullfight field 30฿. Tickets from 200฿.) **Bullfights** are staged once or twice a year on Saturday mornings. Ask around at the travel agencies if you are interested. The Trang Chamber of Commerce organizes events like the **Cake Festival** (Aug.) and **Barbecue Festival** (Sept.), which celebrate Trang's famed dessert and pork.

🔍 DAYTRIPS FROM TRANG

The area surrounding Trang provides a bevy of attractions, from caves to natural oceanside Edens, most of them overlooked by travelers making a beeline from Surat Thani to Ko Phi Phi Don, Phuket, or Malaysia. Expect few travelers even in places like **Ko Mook** and **Hat Pakmeng**, and only a smattering of locals on isolated **Hat Yong Ling.** Though *Let's Go* doesn't list them here, **Ko Sukorn, Ko Lipe,** and **Ko Bulon** are also relatively *farang*-free, and if time and money aren't an issue, are incredible havens for relaxation and exploration.

Those interested in getting a taste of the beaches and islands without a prolonged visit should look into taking a one-day tour around the coast. Many tour agencies sell tickets for a full-day longtail boat ride that includes snorkeling as well as visits to Ko Mook, Ko Hai, Ko Kradan, and the Emerald Cave (855฿).

▨HAT YONG LING AND HAT YAO

Minibuses (80฿) to Hat Yong Ling leave every 1½hr. or when full from the Trang market. To get to nearby Hat Yao, take the same bus for the same price and ask to be dropped off 2km farther down the road at Hat Yao. In the low season, minibuses are much less frequent, and it may be necessary to rent a motorcycle (150-200฿ per 24hr.) or hire a taxi or minivan (500-700฿) from Trang or Pakmeng. To get to both of these beaches on your own, head east from Trang on Hwy. 403, following the signs to the beaches for 42km. To get to Hay Yong Ling, take a right at the sign for San Beach, 2km before Hat Yao. There is a clearly marked right turn for Hat Yao 1km before the Hat Yao pier. Sinchai Chaomai Resort is located on your right .5km after Hat Yao beach.

Hat Yong Ling and Hat Yao are separated by less than 2km, but the beaches are quite different. Hat Yong Ling has been made into a National Park, which requires a 200฿ admission fee for foreigners. Because of its national park status, there is no development around it, and because of its entrance fee, it is mostly empty. The park has retained its crystal clean waters surrounded by wild orchid-covered rocky mountains. Inquire at the office at the entrance of the park for possible treks through the forest and information on a bat cave. Or, simply walk along the beach to enjoy one of the best sand-and-sea combinations around. Spelunkers should bring flashlights. Along the mountain base, the waves have carved out coves where locals camp and grill seafood. Hat Yao, 2km south, is a little more popular, with a couple restaurants near the beach. Its waters are murkier than the Hat Yong Ling to the north and are not ideal for swimming. **Sinchai Chaomai Resort ❸,** on Hat Yao, .5km north of Hat Yao Pier, occupies a stunning location next to a towering limestone cliff. Simple bungalows are available overlooking the sea, and Sinchai can organize boat tours around the area and to nearby islands. (☎075 203 034. Small bungalows 300฿, bigger bungalows closer to the water 500฿.) **Hat Yong Ling's National Park Headquarters,** actually located on the southern end of Hat Chang Lang (below), also serves its distant neighbor Hat Chao Mai 20km to the north. (☎075 213 260. Open M-F 9am-5pm.) There is a ranger station in the center of Ban Yong Ling.

KO MOOK

Take a minivan to Hat Yao and ask to be dropped off at Khuan Tung Ngu, (1hr., 60-80฿) and hop on a boat to the island (1hr., 8am-noon, 100฿). In the low season, minibus service stops, boat service is sporadic at best, and it's usually necessary to hire your own transportation.

Easily accessible from Khuan Tung Ngu during the high season, Ko Mook with four resorts, is the most developed of the Trang Province islands. **Emerald Cave,** so named for its tinted waters, is a spectacular sight. Visitors must swim through an 80km tunnel to reach a beautiful cliff-surrounded lagoon. The lovelier and cheaper western side of the island boasts a great white-sand beach, called **Farang Beach.** Of the island's four resorts, **Had Farung Bungalows ❸** is the least expensive (bungalows 300฿, with bath 500฿). Had Farung is closed during low season. Similarly priced **Koh Muk Rubber Tree Bungalows ❺** is open year-round. (☎081 968 0332. High-season bungalows with fan 800฿, low season 500฿.)

KO KRADAN

In low season, there is no regular service between the mainland and Ko Kradan. Private longtail boat 1hr., 1200฿. In high season, you can buy a ticket from a travel agency for a minibus/ferry (daily, every hr. 10:30am-1:30pm, 350฿).

Beautifully pristine and under the protection of the Hat Jao Mai National Park is **Lost Paradise Resort ❹,** which offers comfortable bungalows with fan near the beach. (☎075 210 693. Open only in high season. 600-1000฿.)

ℹ REGIONAL UNREST. The coverage of Hat Yai, Satun, Ko Tarutao, Ko Bulon Leh, Sungai Kolok, and Songkhla could not be updated for the 2009 series due to continued, unrest in these areas that has kept travelers away and prevented us from updating our coverage. For more detailed information on sectarian violence and terrorist threats in the area, see **Southern Discomfort,** p. 63. Many national governments, including those of Australia, Canada, the US, and the UK, have issued warnings against traveling in the four southernmost provinces of Narathiwat, Pattani, Songkhla, and Yala. For an up-to-date assessment, visit your country's travel advisory website (see **Travel Advisories,** p. 21).

NAKHON SI THAMMARAT ☎ 075

Located off the backpacker circuit, Nakhon Si Thammarat is a bustling city whose long and weighted cultural history is evident in the town's markets and *wats*, including the largest temple in all of southern Thailand. Buddhists come here from all over the world to visit the massive Wat Phramahathat and stay for the several other religious points of interest in the area. Known also for its huge bazaars filled with clothing, fine jewelry, and basketry, Nakhon Si Thammarat is a perfect choice for those looking for both some cultural immersion and the chance to stock up on souvenirs.

⌨ TRANSPORTATION

Flights: Airport (☎075 346 976), 20km north of town on Hwy. 4103. **Thai Airways** (☎075 342 491) and **PB Air** (☎075 312 500), both at 1612 Ratchadamnoen Rd. Open daily 8am-7:30pm. While neither of these 2 airlines have direct flights from Nakhon Si Thammarat to Bangkok, they both can book tickets for you on **Nok Air,** which offers 2 direct flights a day to **Bangkok** (1hr.; daily 7:35am, 1:45pm; 2500฿).

Trains: Train station (☎075 356 364), on Yommarat Rd. where Pagnagon Rd. dead-ends, 1 block from downtown. Nakhon Si Thammarat is not directly on the Southern line, so service is limited. **2nd-cl. trains** to **Bangkok** (16hr.; 1, 3pm; 243-283฿), **Sungai Kolok** (9hr., 6am, 70฿), and **Phatthalung** (3hr.; 6, 9:30am, 2:20pm; 22฿). Ticket office open daily 8am-5pm.

Buses: Bus station (☎075 341 125), off Phaniant Rd., past the mosque and across the railroad tracks. To: **Bangkok** (12hr.; 7am, 4, 5, 5:10, 5:40, 6pm; 415-780฿); **Hat Yai** (3hr., every hr. 4:45am-4:15pm, 135-180฿); **Ko Samui** (5hr.; 11:30am; 232฿, includes ferry fare); **Phatthalung** (3hr., 7 per day 6am-3:30pm, 100฿); **Phuket** (8hr., 7 per day 5:20-11am, 210-245฿); **Ranong** (6hr., 7:30am, 310฿); **Surat Thani** (2hr., frequently 5am-5pm, 115-130฿); **Trang** (2hr.; 6, 9:10am, 2:50pm; 130฿).

Minivans: Leave from stands and travel agencies all over town, most within 1 block of Ratchadamnoen Rd., near downtown. Minivans to **Krabi** (3hr.; 8am, 4:30pm; 190฿) and **Phuket** (5hr., 8am-4pm, 270฿) leave from the parking lot right in front of city hall. Minivans to **Ko Samui** (1½hr., 7:30am-1pm, 229฿ including ferry fare) leave from the intersection of Ratchadamnoen and Ratnikom Rd. near the Thai Airlines office.; to **Surat Thani** (1½hr., 6am-5:30pm, 165฿) leave from near the intersection of Yommarat and Chumphol Rd. Minivans to **Trang** (2hr., 7am-5pm, 150฿) leave from Bo-Ang Rd. 50m west of its intersection with Phattanakarn-Khukhwang Rd. Inquire at TAT, tour agency, or your hotel for more information.

Local Transportation: An impressive and efficient **songthaew** fleet has rendered *tuk-tuks* obsolete in Nakhon Si Thammarat. Blue *songthaew* ply linear routes on virtually every major street in town (6am-8pm, 10-25฿). **Motorcycle taxis** (20-40฿)will do the same job for more baht and more adventure.

✦ 🛈 ORIENTATION AND PRACTICAL INFORMATION

Nakhon Si Thammarat is a large, 5km-long linear town. Most of the city's sights and services are on or within one block of **Ratchadamnoen Road,** the main street. Running parallel to Ratchadamnoen Rd. in the northern part of town are **Yommarat Road** to the west and **Si Prat Road** to the east. Yommarat Rd. holds the train station, while Si Prat Rd. is the site of banks, hotels, restaurants, and shops. Also between Ratchadamnoen Rd. and Yommarat Rd. is narrow **Jamroenwithi Road,** the location of the town's night market and the center of the bazaars that are open all day. **Pagnagon Road** is the city's largest east-west street, and runs from the train station past Ratchadamnoen Rd. in the heart of downtown to some good eateries, hotels, and a day market. A new portion of town lies east of the center near the intersection of **Bo-Ang Road** and **Phatthanakarn-Khukhwang Road** and contains a number of Western-style shopping centers and restaurant chains.

Tourist Office: TAT (☎346 515), behind Sanam Na Meuang Park next to tennis courts, a few blocks south of downtown, past the police station along Ratchadamnoen Rd. Helpful English-speaking staff dispense a full range of info. Open daily 8:30am-4:30pm. **Municipal Tourist Office,** more conveniently located inside the City Hall complex on Ratchadamnoen Rd., 4 blocks closer to downtown than TAT, has maps, bus schedules, and decent English. Open daily 8am-4pm.

Currency Exchange: Banks line Ratchadamnoen Rd. off the main road. **Krung Thai Bank,** 1452 Pagnagon Rd., 1 block from Ratchadamnoen Rd. heading away from the train station. **24hr. ATMs** outside. Open daily 8:30am-4:30pm.

Markets: The whole town seems like one big market. Good souvenir markets sell local jewelry, basketry, and pottery at good prices across Phatthanakarn-Khukhwang Rd., from Robinson's Department Store east of downtown, and right next to Wat Phramahatat. There are bazaars, some 3 stories high, selling cheap clothes, shoes, and electronics. Most of these are located in the various allies between Jamroenwithi Rd. and Ratchadamnoen Rd.

Police: (☎075 356 500), on Ratchadamnoen Rd., about 5 blocks south of downtown. Little English. Open 24hr.

Hospital: Christian Hospital (☎075 356 214), at the intersection of Si Prat and Bo-Ang Rd., is the traveler's best bet in terms of location and English skills. Open 24hr.

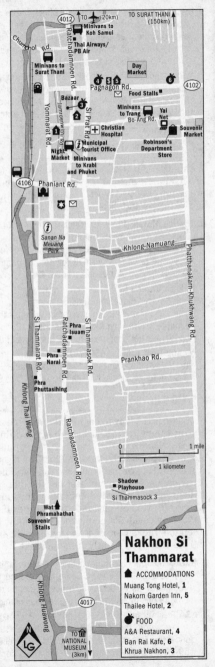

Nakhon Si Thammarat

🏠 ACCOMMODATIONS
Muang Tong Hotel, **1**
Nakorn Garden Inn, **5**
Thailee Hotel, **2**

🍎 FOOD
A&A Restaurant, **4**
Ban Rai Kafe, **6**
Khrua Nakhon, **3**

Internet Access: Several places offer 15-20฿ per hr. connections. The area near where Robinson-Ocean Rd. winds towards Bo-Ang Rd. behind Robinson's Department Store and also the area along Sri Prat near its intersection with Phaniant Rd. both have lots of Internet shops. **Yai Net,** 89/198 Robinson's Ocean Rd., near Robinson's Department Store is open daily 8am-midnight. 15฿ per hr.

Post Offices: GPO (☎075 356 1356), on Ratchadamnoen Rd., across the street from the police station about 5 blocks south of downtown. Poste Restante. Open M-F 8:30am-4:30pm, Sa-Su 9am-noon. Alternatively, a convenient downtown branch office at 1204/13 Pagnagon Rd., 3 blocks from Ratchadamnoen Rd., across from the Nakorn Garden Hotel. **Postal Code:** 80000.

ACCOMMODATIONS

Without the hordes of *farang* found in much of the rest of Thailand, Nakhon Si Thammarat has not developed the usual range of accommodations. There are really only two types of establishments here: nice, middle-class, air-conditioned hotels and dirt-cheap digs.

Thailee Hotel, 1128-30 Ratchadamnoen Rd. (☎075 356 948), at the corner with Boh-Ang Rd., 1 block before City Hall coming from the train station. Clean, spacious rooms in this hotel's 4-story building come fully furnished with soft beds, closet, and desk. The price is shockingly low for the quality of the rooms. Midnight curfew. Squat toilets. Singles and doubles 140฿. ❶

Nakorn Garden Inn, 1/4 Pagnagon Rd. (☎075 313 333; fax 342 926), just past Krung Thai Bank, 1 block from Ratchadamnoen Rd. heading away from the train station. This resort-style hotel has greenery and fountains that let you forget you're in a bustling city. Beautifully furnished rooms come with A/C, hot shower, mini-fridge, Wi-Fi, and satellite TV. Excellent attached restaurant. Singles and doubles 445฿. ❸

Muang Tong Hotel, 1459/7-9 Jamroenwithi Rd. (☎075 343 026), a 2min. walk from the train station right next to the night market. Rooms are clean with private bath and Western toilet. Singles with fan 250฿, doubles 300฿; with A/C 350/400฿. ❷

FOOD

Curbside is the way to eat in Nakhon Si Thammarat. There are two **day markets,** one on Yommarat Rd., just south of the train station, and one on Pagnagon Rd., past the Nakorn Garden Inn (p. 394) heading away from the train station, a few blocks east of Ratchadamnoen Rd. The **night market,** on Jamroenwithi Rd. near Pagnagon Rd., offering curries, rice, noodle soup, fried whole chickens, and other delicacies, is your best bet for dinner (20-30฿ per dish). Though these stalls don't get crowded until 6pm, they are open at noon and close around 10pm. All over the city, at least one per block in downtown, there are food stalls showcasing cans of condensed milk; these stalls serve *roti* and pots of green tea, the classic dessert or late-night snack for most locals. (Banana *roti* and tea 15฿. Open nightly 2pm-midnight.)

Khrua Nakhon, just off Ratchadamnoen Rd. in the heart of downtown. Turn into the small alley next to the 7-Eleven. Come here around lunchtime for a real taste of Nakhon Si Thammerat. Khrua serves delicious, authentic regional cuisine. Try the iced ginger drink (15฿) or one of several types of sea bass curries (50-60฿). Open daily 6am-3pm. ❷

A&A Restaurant (☎075 311 047), on Pagnagon Rd., just past Si Prat Rd. when heading away from the train station. A large, pleasant Western-style cafe with international foods, and international artwork, and A/C. Delicious ice cream (20-35฿) and Thai food (50-100฿). Fresh-brewed coffee 25฿. Open daily 7am-11pm. ❷

Ban Rai Kafe, on Pagnagon Rd., near its intersection with Phatthanakarn-Khukhwang Rd. Signs are in Thai, but look for the large, open-air bamboo hut-style restaurant on your left as you head away from the train station. Best known for its nightly music video sing-alongs in front of big screen TVs. Dishes 60-120฿. Beer 60฿. Sing-alongs start at 10pm. Open daily 5pm-1am. ❷

🔆 SIGHTS

WAT PHRAMAHATHAT WORAMAHA WIHAAN. The largest temple in southern Thailand, Wat Phramahathat covers an area of 40,800 sq. m and is said to be over 1000 years old. The temple is the home of the Lanka Wong sect of Buddhism in Thailand. In AD 1157, King Chantharaphanu sent a group of monks to study Buddhist teachings in Sri Lanka; in 1227, they returned to Thailand and set up shop at Wat Phramahathat. The province has been the home of the Lanka Wong ever since.

A number of important artifacts and historical sights are housed within the *wat*'s compound. The most significant is the **Phra Borom That Chedi,** a pagoda that houses relics of the Buddha and resembles a massive inverted concrete bell. It is estimated to have been built around AD 757, during the Si Wichai period. The pagoda has a base diameter of 23m and is 56m high, making it the second-tallest pagoda in all of Thailand. *(2km south of downtown on Ratchadamnoen Rd. Any songthaew heading south on Ratchadamnoen Rd. from the center of town will take 5-10min. and cost 10-20฿. Open daily 7am-4pm.)*

NATIONAL MUSEUM. The museum contains a number of interesting and historically significant artifacts. Most impressive, and a source of intense local pride, is the throne of King Rama V. While the throne's exact origin is unknown, its intricate carvings resemble the signature craftwork of Nakhon Si Thammarat artisans. The museum also contains several Sri Lakan, Hindu and Buddhist images and artifacts that are quite similar to those in Wat Pramahattat. In addition, there is a room devoted to local handcrafts. *(3km south of town, on Ratchadamnoen Rd. Southbound Ratchadamnoen Rd. songthaew (20-30฿) go past the museum entrance. Open W-Su 8:30am-4pm. 30฿.)*

OTHER SIGHTS. Nakhon Si Thammarat's **city walls** were built over 1000 years ago; the current ones occupy roughly the same location as the originals and date back to the 18th century. They run about 2239m north-south and 466m east-west.

Buddhism isn't the only religion in Nakhon Si Thammarat. The town **mosque,** two blocks toward the bus station from Ratchadamnoen Rd., with its large green cupolas, one of the most ornate in southern Thailand and is worth a quick look, even if it's just from the roadside. Nearby are several delicious Muslim food stalls. Nakhon Si was also the original settling point for Hindus journeying east from the Indian subcontinent, and their former presence is marked by the remnants of two temples facing each other across Ratchadamnoen Rd. On the west side (the same side as Wat Phramahathat), 1km south of the town center, lies **Phra Isuan,** a Brahmin temple dedicated to Shiva, the Hindu god of war. While the original chapel, constructed during the Ayutthaya period, has long since eroded away, a reconstructed replica rests on its former site. Across the street is **Phra Narai,** a Hindu temple from a similar time period dedicated to the god Narai.

SURAT THANI ☎ 077

Surat Thani's position as a gateway to and midpoint between Ko Samui, Ko Phangan, Ko Tao, Phuket, and Krabi makes it a necessary stopover for most travelers. A stroll along the colorful and bustling waterfront, home to a number of Chinese tea shops, is the best way to kill an hour or two. This transportation hub is also home to a superb night market that could keep you trying new Thai dishes for weeks, though after a day or two in Surat Thani, there won't be anything else to entertain you.

TRANSPORTATION

Flights: Airport (☎077 441 2301), 30km outside of town. **Thai Airways,** 3/27-8 Karoonrat Rd. (☎077 272 618), flies daily to **Bangkok** (1hr.; 11:30am, 7pm; 3800฿). To get to the Thai Airways office, 2km from the city center, head southwest down Talad Mai Rd., taking a left on Chonkasem Rd. Take your 2nd right onto Karoonrat Rd. and it will be 300m up on your right. **Thai Air Asia** (☎077 441 196) has an office in the airport; **Phantip Tour** (p. 398) is a reputable tour agency that handles flight bookings and also sends minivans to the airport 2hr. prior to departure. Phantip minivans that return from the airport to town 30-60min. after flight arrivals can be found outside the airport next to the taxi line (100฿).

Trains: Train station (☎077 311 213), in Phun Phin, 12km from Surat Thani. Orange Mercedes buses run frequently between the local bus station (Talaat Kaset 1) in town and the train station (25min., every 5min., 14฿); catch them anywhere on Talaat Mai

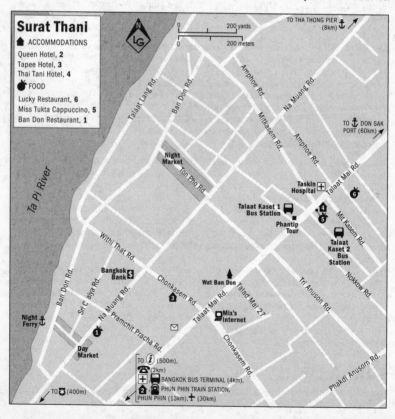

Surat Thani

ACCOMMODATIONS
Queen Hotel, **2**
Tapee Hotel, **3**
Thai Tani Hotel, **4**

FOOD
Lucky Restaurant, **6**
Miss Tukta Cappuccino, **5**
Ban Don Restaurant, **1**

Rd. or at the bus station. Coming to town from the train station, exit the station and turn right to reach an orange bus. The orange buses on the way to Surat Thani stop first at a bus station 4km from town before arriving at Talat Kaset 1 bus station in town. You can also get a taxi between Surat Thani and the train station for 140฿. **2nd-cl. trains** to: **Bangkok** (12hr., 10 per day 10:40am-11:20pm, 358-438฿) via **Chumphon** (3hr., 128฿); **Butterworth, Malaysia** (12hr., 1:00am, 992฿); **Hat Yai** (6hr.; midnight, 1, 2am; 236฿); **Sungai Kolok** (10½hr., midnight, 2am, 309฿); **Trang** (6hr.; 4, 6am; 139฿).

Buses: There are 3 bus stations. Tour and travel agencies will try to lure you to private buses, which often take about the same amount of time and may cost 50-100฿ more than public buses. On the other hand, these private buses do a better job of adhering to a schedule. As a general rule, try to avoid the private buses unless time is a priority.

Talaat Kaset 1: (☎077 212 182), on Talaat Mai Rd., behind Phantip Travel at Nokkon Rd. Offers mostly local and provincial travel. To: **Chumphon** (3½hr., every hr. 6:30am-5pm, 100฿) and **Surat Thani Province,** (25 min., every 5min. 5am-7pm, 14฿) with frequent orange buses to the train station.

Talaat Kaset 2: (☎077 272 341), behind Thai Tani Hotel (below). **Regular** and **A/C buses** to: **Hat Yai** (5½hr., every hr. 5am-3pm, 300-340฿); **Krabi** (3-4hr., every hr. 6:30am-5:10pm, 320-480฿); **Phang-Nga** (3hr., every hr. 6am-3pm, 90-220฿); **Phuket** (5-6hr., every hr. 5:30am-3pm, 195-220฿); and some other destinations.

Bangkok Bus Terminal: 4km outside of town toward the train station, with buses to **Bangkok** (9-11hr., 9-10 per day noon-9pm, 435-820฿).

Minivans: Run from Talaat Kaset 2 to **Nakhon Si Thammarat** (1½hr., every 30 min. 6am-6pm, 130฿); **Khao Sok National Park** (2hr., every hr. 5:30am-5:30pm, 150฿); **Chaiya** (1½hr., every 20 min. 6am-5pm, 80฿); **Penang, Malaysia** (6hr., every hr. 6am-5pm, 650฿); and some other destinations.

Boats: Ferries depart from several points in and outside of town. **Songserm Travel Center,** 6km outside of town, at Tha Thong Pier, operates daily express boats to **Ko Phangan** (4hr.; 10am, 2, 4:30, 5, 6pm; 280฿) and **Ko Samui** (3hr., every 2hr. 6:30am-7pm, 150฿). Ticket includes transportation to the pier. **Night ferry** from Surat Thani pier goes to **Ko Phangan** (7hr., 11pm, 400฿) and **Ko Samui** (6hr., 11pm, 360฿). **Phantip Tours** runs buses to **Don Sak Port,** about 75km from Surat Thani (1hr., every other hr. 6:30am-4:30pm, 120฿). Less dependable, cheaper minivans (every hr. 6:30am-4:30pm, 100฿) from Talaat Kaset 2 to **Don Sak Port.** From Don Sak Port, **Raja Car Ferry** sends ferries to **Ko Phangan** (2½hr., every other hr. 6am-6pm, 280฿) and **Ko Samui** (1hr., every 2hr. 5am-7pm, 150฿). Seatran, at Don Sak Port, operates ferries to **Ko Samui** (1½hr., every hr. 6am-7pm, 240฿).

Local Transportation: Motorcycle taxis (20฿), **tuk tuks** (30฿), and **songthaew** (20฿) roam the streets.

■ ▲ ORIENTATION AND PRACTICAL INFORMATION

Trains arrive at Phun Phin Train Station, 12km from Surat Thani. Phun Phin and Surat Thani are connected by the busy and noisy **Talaat Mai Road,** which enters Surat Thani from the southwest and passes the tourist and post offices on its way to the center of town. Local buses leave from two separate small markets, each just a block off Talaat Mai Rd., near the center of town. Night boats depart from the **night boat pier** on **Ban Don Road,** which runs along the banks of the **Ta Pi River;** other ferries leave from **Tha Thong** and **Don Sak Piers** located 6km and 75km outside of town, respectively. A significant number of budget accommodations, travel agencies, and conveniences are also in the Ban Don Rd. area, within easy walking distance of the night boat pier and bus stations. There are additional budget accommodations, Internet services, and restaurants located around the intersection of Chonkasem Rd. and Talaat Mai Rd.

Tourist Office: TAT, 5 Talaat Mai Rd. (☎077 288 8179). A 2.5km walk on Talaat Mai Rd. from the town center, or take a *songthaew* heading down the road. An oasis of accurate info with a helpful English-speaking staff. Open daily 8:30am-4:30pm.

Tours: Agencies abound near the pier and on Talaat Mai Rd., between the markets. A number of fraudulent agencies have sprung up in Surat Thani in recent years, so ask around and choose wisely. A common ploy is to tell you that the night ferry is not running with the intention of getting you to stay at their hotel for the night. The website www.backpackersthailand.com has some additional information and lists several of the known fraudulent tour agencies. **Phantip Tour** (☎077 272 230), a well-respected, full-service travel agency, located between the 2 bus stations on Talaat Mai Rd. Makes hotel, train, plane, bus, and boat bookings. Open daily 7am-5pm.

Currency Exchange: Surat Thani's exchange rates are better than those on the islands. Banks with **24hr. ATMs** line Na Muang Rd. Most banks open M-F 8:30am-3:30pm; a few operate extended hours. **Bangkok Bank,** 195-7 Na Muang Rd. (☎077 282 805), has a currency exchange booth in front. Open daily 8:30am-3pm.

Police: 188 Na Muang Rd. (☎077 272 095). Little English spoken. Open 24hr.

Hospitals: Surat Thani Hospital (☎077 284 700), just south of the bridge 1km past TAT on Talaat Mai Rd., on the way to Phun Phin. **Taksin Hospital** (☎077 273 239), on the northern side of town, 2 blocks north of Talaat Kaset 2 on the left side of Talaat Mai Rd. Staff at Taksin speak somewhat better English. Credit cards accepted. Open 24hr.

Telephones: CAT Telecom (☎077 283 050), on Donnok Rd., 2km from most hotels. Walk down Talaat Mai Rd. towards TAT from Chonkasem Rd. and turn left onto Donnok Rd., and it's 1.5km farther down on the left. A 300฿ phone card will get you 2฿ per min. phone calls to the US. Open daily 8am-10pm.

Internet Access: Internet places along Chonkasem Rd., just south of the intersection with Talad Mai Rd., all charge 20฿ per hr. and cater to local schoolchildren. The friendliest, which is also open the latest, is **Mix's Internet,** open 8am-midnight.

Post Offices: GPO (☎077 272 013), near the corner of Talaat Mai and Chonkasem Rd. Poste Restante. Open M-F 8:30am-4:30pm, Sa-Su 9am-noon. **Postal Code:** 84000.

ACCOMMODATIONS

Surat Thani has an odd assortment of budget accommodations, many of which fall within the genre of the aging Thai-Chinese hotel, uneven in the quality of their facilities and services. Most establishments are within a few blocks of the pier or around the markets.

Tapee Hotel, 100 Chonkasem Rd. (☎077 272 575), mid-block between Na Muang Rd. and Talaat Mai Rd. Large, immaculate rooms with TV, phone, and room service. A very professional staff and a quick walk from all intercity transit options. Singles and doubles with fan 440฿, with A/C 550฿. ❸

Queen Hotel, 12 Sisawat Rd. (☎077 311 831), on the street, directly opposite the train station in Phun Phin. Cross the street from the station, turn left, and then turn right at the fork in the road; the hotel is 50m down. The only hotel in Phun Phin. Convenient for early or late trains. Small rooms are clean enough. Tourist services available. Internet 2฿ per min. Singles 200฿, doubles 250-400฿. ❷

Thai Tani Hotel, 442/306-308 Talaat Mai Rd. (☎077 272 977), right next to Talaat Kaset 2. A curious mix of mid-range touches and low-budget gloom. While the rooms and bath have seen better days, it is surprisingly nice for stopover accommodations next to the bus station. Reception on 3rd fl. Singles with fan 240฿, with TV 280฿; doubles 260/300฿, with A/C 380฿. ❷

FOOD

The █night market, on Ton Pho Rd., between Na Muang and Ban Don Rd., is almost reason enough to spend the night in Surat Thani. From fried insects and duck eggs to enormous oysters and oil-drenched crepes, this is the place to sample Thai cuisine. During mango season, try *khao niaw mamuang*, sliced mango with coconut-sweetened sticky rice. Surat Thani is the trade hub of a coconut-growing region, so any dish involving coconut is likely to be especially memorable. There is also a less exciting **day market** on Na Muang Rd.

Ban Don Restaurant, 268/2 Na Muang Rd., just below the Ban Don Hotel. Very popular with locals, this restaurant focuses on a delicious selection of noodle and rice dishes (30-50฿). Chicken cooked with sweet basil and chili 40฿, iced coffee 10฿. English menu available. Open 7am-5pm. ❷

Tapee Hotel Restaurant, 100 Chonkasem Rd., on the ground floor of the Tapee Hotel (see above). Thai and Chinese dishes 35-80฿. Delicious duck and rice combo 40฿. Open daily 8:30am-10pm. ❷

Miss Tukta Cappuccino, 442/307 Talaat Mai Rd. (☎077 212 723), under a yellow sign that says "Internet." Internet 30฿ per hr. Cappucinos 35฿. Cheese and egg sandwiches 35฿. Open daily 9am-9pm. ❷

Lucky Restaurant, 452/84-85 Thathong, on the corner of Talaat Mai and Thong Rd. Those looking for Thai or Chinese food near the bus station can duck into this immaculately clean and densely staffed restaurant. Chicken noodle soup 50฿. Chicken with cashew nuts 80฿. Open daily 9am-10pm. ❸

DAYTRIPS FROM SURAT THANI

CHAIYA

Minivans leave from Talaat Kaset 2 station (1hr., every 20min. 6am-5pm, 80฿). Songthaew (20฿) run frequently between Chaiya and the wats. Wat Phra That is 1km from Chaiya town towards Hwy. 41, and the way is clearly marked. Wat Suan Mok, off of Hwy. 41, is located 50km north of Surat Thani and 5km southwest of Wat Phra That.

North of Surat Thani (56km is the town of Chaiya. This little town reached its peak as a powerful and important Srivijaya city-state between the 5th and 6th centuries AD, after many centuries as a regional trade center. While many significant Srivijaya artifacts unearthed here have been carted off to the National Museum in Bangkok, its impressive and important *wats* remain. The multi-layered history of **Wat Phra Borommathat,** known as Wat Phra That, spans more than 1200 years. The Buddha's relics are enshrined in the *chedi*. The centerpiece of this Mayahana *wat* is a spectacular *stupa* adorned with Indian-influenced bas-relief. Don't miss the adjacent statues of hermit sages striking yogic poses.

Next door, the small but interesting **Chaiya National Museum** houses artifacts dating from Chaiya's heyday. Highlights include shadow puppets and 2000-year-old bronze drums. A tranquil carp pond is at the center of the museum. (☎077 431 066. Open W-Su 9am-4pm. 30฿.)

Situated in a forest along Hwy. 41, **Wat Suan Mokkha Phalaram (Suan Mok),** the "Forest of the Untying of Sorrows," is more a working monastery than a tourist attraction. **Ajahn Buddhadasa Bhikkhu,** the monk who established the monastery, was a controversial figure during his lifetime, branded as a Communist during the 1970s for his Buddhist critiques of capitalism and materialism. Since his death, he has become one of Thailand's most highly revered monks. The Wat Suan Mok version of Buddhism is an unusually ecumenical one, as evidenced by the images of Christian, Muslim, and Hindu figures featured among the offbeat paintings that adorn the *wat*'s "Spiritual Theater." Meditation on death is also emphasized in the monastery's practice, and the meditation hall prominently features three human skeletons. The 120 acre forest behind the "Spiritual Theater" is perfect for a contemplative walk. A 5min. walk into the forest from the park entrance and up a small hill leads to the **Golden Hill Shrine,** the site of the monk's monthly gathering. It is a peaceful spot located right next to the burial site of Buddhadasa Bhikku, and is worth a short visit. Anyone can attend meditation retreats held by monks that start on the last day of each month and run to the 11th day of the following month. Just show up a few days before the end of the month. (☎077 431 597. *Food, accommodations, and expenses for the 12-day retreat 1500฿.*)

KHAO SOK NATIONAL PARK

From Surat Thani, catch a minivan from Talaat Kaset 2 to Khao Sok (2hr., every hr. 5:30am-5:30pm, 150฿). From Phuket, find a bus or minibus driving the Phuket-Surat Thani route (180฿) and confirm that it will go to Khao Sok—some buses take routes that bypass the park. The buses drop you off at the start of the Khao Sok road, which goes to the park entrance (3km). The road is full of bungalows. Surat Thani travel agencies also offer a number of minivan departures (180฿), but they're overpriced, and they may try to make you stay at their affiliated accommodation in Khao Sok. Park headquarters ☎077 395 1542. Admission 200฿, with student ID 100฿.

Nestled in the mountain ridge separating the eastern and western coasts of peninsular Thailand, splendid Khao Sok National Park is one of the most remarkable reserves of southern Thailand and definitely worth a visit. Almost halfway between Surat Thani and Phuket, this 160 million-year-old rainforest, a relic of the country's topological past (some date it as far back as 380 million years), covers roughly 650 sq. km of jungle-blanketed foothills and protruding limestone formations. Its unique geography and generous rainfall allow it to sustain a remarkable ecosystem. The park is also home to a plethora of wildlife, including gibbons, bears, elephants, *guars*, and *languars*. Tigers and panthers supposedly live here, but they are rarely spotted. Undoubtedly, the park's jewel is its native flora, which include dozens of species of orchids and ferns. Most spectacular is the Bua Phut, a lotus flower that can grow to 80cm.

The **park headquarters** near the entrance sells entrance tickets, dispenses trail maps, and arranges guided hikes to the waterfalls and caves in the park. The two major trails depart from behind the visitors center. A fairly easy 7km trek to **Ton Gloy Waterfall** leads through several picturesque falls and gorges. The trek there and back takes about 6hr. A somewhat steeper and trickier 4km hike to **Sip-et-Chan**, a majestic, 11-tiered waterfall, takes you through extremely dense rainforest and has six river crossings. This route takes about 4hr. round trip. Watch out for leeches. Both trails are well-maintained but have bridge crossings that can be tricky when wet. During the rainy season, if you plan to go more than 3km away from the headquarters, a national park guide is recommended. (4-5 hr. ½-day 500฿, full-day 800฿.) To cut costs, hang out by the headquarters and try to join up with a group, as the cost of the guide is fixed, and not affected by the number of hikers.

There are a considerable number of cheap lodging opportunities in Khao Sok. For those interested in a central location, the headquarters offers a **camping area ❶** (tent rentals 3-person 225฿, 6-person 600฿) and **bungalows ❺** (2-3 people, 800฿). Also, just inside the park at the **visitors center** is **Tree Tops River Huts ❷,** a set of tree houses and bamboo bungalows right on the river that puts you a mere stone's throw from the trailheads. (☎077 395 129. Free bus station pickup and dropoff if you reserve in advance. Rooms have private baths, and those that cost 500฿ and up have A/C and hot showers. Bare bamboo 2-person bungalows 200฿, concrete doubles with river views 500฿, lovely treehouses nestled in the forest 700฿.) Most accommodations in Khao Sok both have an attached restaurant and can help arrange treks.

KO SAMUI ☎077

Thailand's third-largest island has come a long way since the first backpackers arrived in the 1970s. Ko Samui ("Coconut Island"), now fully equipped with a slew of resorts and restaurants, an international airport, and some of the area's best hospitals, is one of Southeast Asia's most popular travel destinations. The shift in tourism away from the Andaman Coast in the wake of the 2004 tsunami has increased the flow of foreign visitors to Ko Samui's famed beaches. Despite its runaway popularity, Ko Samui still delivers on sunbathing and swimming options, and retains a number of colorful, somewhat secluded beach villages.

⌐ TRANSPORTATION

Some travelers arrive on Ko Samui by plane, but most come by boat, either from the transportation hub of Surat Thani or from neighboring islands.

Flights: Samui International Airport, between Hat Chaweng and Hat Bangrak. **Bangkok Airways** (☎077 425 0293; www.bangkokairways.com) flies to: **Bangkok** (1-1½hr., 16-25 flights per day 6am-9:20pm, 4600฿); **Phuket** (50min.; 9:35am, 6:20pm; 2450฿); **Singapore** (1½hr., 8:10pm, 6435฿). Most travel agencies on the island can book tickets.

Trains and buses: Most travel agents can book joint boat-and-train or boat-and-bus tickets to the mainland. Prices vary slightly from agent to agent. Packages to **Bangkok** (16hr., 700฿), **Ranong** (520฿), **Phuket** (550฿), **Hat Yai** (580฿), **Krabi** (480฿), and **Penang, Malaysia** (860฿).

Boats: There are piers located in 3 villages in Ko Samui: **Na Thon, Hat Bo Phut,** and **Hat Bangrak.** Both Lomprayah Catamaran and Seatran offer free pickup from anywhere on the island and delivery at their respective piers. Schedules and prices for all boats change frequently, so check for the most current info. The largest number of boats runs to and from Surat Thani, and departures are less frequent Feb.-Aug.

Na Thon: The main pie is dominated by **Songserm Travel Center** (☎077 420 157), which runs boats to: **Chumphon** (6hr., 11am, 1000฿); **Ko Tao** (2½hr.; 9, 11am; 450฿); **Surat Thani** via **Don Sak** (2hr., 1:30pm, 220฿), with 1hr. bus transfer; Ko Phangan's **Thong Sala** (45min.; 9, 11am; 220฿). **Seatran** also sends express boats from Na Thon to Don Sak Pier to **Surat Thani** (1½hr., every hr. 5am-6pm, 220฿) with 1hr. bus transfer. The **night boat** to the main pier in Surat Thani (7hr., once per week 5pm, 250฿). The **Raja Car Ferry** runs from a pier 10km south of Na Thon to **Surat Thani** (3hr., every hr. 5am-6pm, 260฿).

Hat Bangrak: Seatran sends boats to **Mae Hat** on Ko Tao (2½hr.; 8am, 1:30pm; 550฿) via **Hat Rin** on Ko Phangan (45min.; 8,10:30am, 1:30, 4pm; 200฿).

Hat Bo Phut: Lomprayah Catamaran sends boats to **Mae Hat** on Ko Tao (2½hr.; 8am, 12:30pm; 550฿) via **Hat Rin** on Ko Phangan (45min.; 8am, 12:30, 4pm; 200฿).

Local Transportation: Songthaew congregate near the piers and circle the island frequently. (6am-6pm. From Hat Chaweng to Hat Lamai 60฿, from Na Thon pier to Hat Chaweng 100, from Na Thon to other beaches 60-150฿). After 6pm, *songthaew* still roam the streets but are harder to find and charge double. Speedy **motorcycle taxis** provide a faster but more dangerous and expensive alternative to *songthaew.* (From Na Thon to Hat Bo Phut 260฿, to Hat Chaweng 200฿, to Hat Mae Nam 280฿). Many resorts on the island provide minivan transportation to and from the piers and the airport for a 50-100฿ fee.

BE TAXI SAVVY. Don't be fooled by the presence of yellow cars with "Taxi Meter" signs. These are surplus cabs from the Bangkok taxi fleet. Most of these cabs will not actually use their meters. The rare handful of taxis that do use the meter will charge a 90฿ surcharge. The A/C cabs that don't use the meter, while undoubtedly the most comfortable means of getting around, will try to charge double or triple what a *songthaew* will cost, anywhere from 200฿ to more than 2000฿ per ride.

Rentals: Rental stores are everywhere, but choose a reputable vendor; your hotel is usually a good choice. **Motorbikes** 150฿ per day (150cc automatic bikes 200฿). **Jeeps** 800฿ per day, with insurance 1000-2000฿. Passport deposit required. Samui's roads,

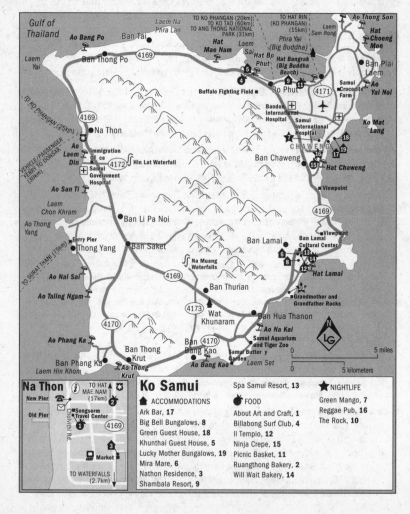

Ko Samui

🏠 ACCOMMODATIONS
Ark Bar, **17**
Big Bell Bungalows, **8**
Green Guest House, **18**
Khunthai Guest House, **5**
Lucky Mother Bungalows, **19**
Mira Mare, **6**
Nathon Residence, **3**
Shambala Resort, **9**
Spa Samui Resort, **13**

🍎 FOOD
About Art and Craft, **1**
Billabong Surf Club, **4**
Il Tempio, **12**
Ninja Crepe, **15**
Picnic Basket, **11**
Ruangthong Bakery, **2**
Will Wait Bakery, **14**

⭐ NIGHTLIFE
Green Mango, **7**
Reggae Pub, **16**
The Rock, **10**

which are sandy and filled with potholes, are overrun with drivers who are not used to such bad conditions. Exercise extreme caution when driving here. Also note that roadside petrol stands charge marked-up prices for gasoline of uncertain quality, so fill up at legitimate gas stations. There are numerous **bicycle** rental shops that charge 70-100฿ per 24hr. Besides a couple hills between Chaweng and Lamai, the island is actually surprisingly flat and bike-friendly.

🔲 🔁 ORIENTATION AND PRACTICAL INFORMATION

Ko Samui is encircled by one road, **Route 4169,** which makes navigating the deceptively large island simple but time-consuming. Island roads often flood at low points, even in the dry season. The main transportation hub and service center, **Na Thon,** lies on the west coast. From here, Rte. 4169 runs clockwise to **Ao Bang Po** and **Hat Mae Nam** on the northern coast before cutting down the east coast to **Hat Chaweng,** the island's most celebrated beach, and **Hat Lamai,** Hat Chaweng's smaller and more budget-oriented sibling. **Route 4171,** enveloping the island's northeastern peninsula, branches off Rte. 4169, just past Hat Mae Nam, and reconnects with it in Chaweng. It passes through **Hat Bo Phut** (Fisherman's Village), **Hat Bangrak** (Big Buddha Beach), and the smaller beaches of **Ao Thong Son, Ao Yai Noi,** and **Hat Choeng Mon.** In general, Na Thon, Hat Chaweng, and Hat Lamai are livelier and offer more services, while Hat Mae Nam, Hat Bo Phut, Hat Bangrak, and Hat Choeng Mon are more quiet and more relaxed.

Tourist Office: TAT (☎077 420 504), on Na Thon Rd. Located in a cluster of government buildings off a small road near the post office and Angthong Rd. Helpful, English speaking staff provides a wide range of maps and brochures on the island and environs. Open daily 8:30am-4:30pm.

Tours: Hundreds of establishments all over Na Thon, Hat Chaweng, and Hat Lamai sell identical boat/bus/train ticket combinations and arrange Ang Thong Marine Park tours (1100฿, with a 1hr. of kayaking 1400฿), fishing trips, and elephant treks. In Na Thon, agencies line Na Thon Rd., near the pier.

Immigration Office: (☎077 421 069), 2km south of Na Thon at the intersection of Rte. 4169 and Rte. 4172. Open M-F 8:30am-4:30pm.

Currency Exchange: Dozens of banks offering good rates for currency exchange and credit card advances, as well as **ATMs,** line the main roads of Na Thon, Hat Chaweng, and Hat Lamai. Bank exchange booths and ATMs also can be found along the main roads in Ban Plai Laem, Hat Bo Phut, Hat Mae Nam, Ban Thong Po, Ban Thong Krut, Ban Bang Kao, and Ban Hua Thanon. Most exchange booths open daily 11am-7pm.

Local Tourist Police: (☎077 421 281 or 421 360), on Rte. 4169, 200m south of the intersection with Cholvithi Rd. Fluent English. Open 24hr.

Medical Services: Samui International Hospital (☎077 230 781) on Rte. 4171 in the northern stretch of Hat Chaweng. **Bangkok Hospital** (☎077 429 500) in the southern stretch of Hat Chaweng on Rte. 4169. **Bandon International Hospital** (☎077 245 2369) just south of Hat Bo Phut. **Samui Government Hospital** (☎077 421 2302) to the south of Na Thon. All of these hospitals accept credit cards, have an English-speaking staff, and are open 24hr. Smaller nursing stations can be found in Na Thon, Hat Chaweng, and Hat Lamai.

Internet Access and Telephones: LoveNet, in a shack filled with locals located in Na Thon on the southern end of Angthong Rd., 1 block west of the fresh produce market. Internet 20฿ per hr. Open M-F noon-10pm, Sa-Su 9am-10pm. **CAT Telecom,** 2nd fl. of the post office, provides international phone, fax, and cheap Internet. Internet 300฿ for 10hr. Calls to the US 5฿ per min., but you have to buy a bulk 300฿ calling card. Open daily 8:30am-4:30pm. Travel agencies and Internet cafes around the island offer pricier international phone service and Internet access (usually 50-60฿ per hr.). A handful of restuarants and cafes on Hat Lamai and Hat Chaweng, including Starbucks, offer Wi-Fi at the same rates.

Post Offices: GPO (☎077 421 013), on Cholvithi Rd., 50m north of the main pier in Na Thon. Poste Restante. Open M-F 8:30am-4:30pm, Sa-Su 9am-noon. Licensed, private branches along Rte. 4169 offer more limited services. **Postal Code:** 84140.

⌂ ☐ ACCOMMODATIONS AND FOOD

Though Ko Samui caters more to wealthy tourists than it does to backpackers, you can expect to find at least one place with cheap beds on each of the island's beaches. Many budget travelers find Hat Lamai to be treasure trove of decent, affordable accommodations. Several websites have good information on accommodation, dining, and entertainment options in the different beach areas, especially **www.samuidirect.com** and **www.sawadee.com.** Reserve in advance during the high season (Dec.-May). Rates should be 30-50% lower in the low season (June-Nov.), so ask about discounts.

◉ SIGHTS

For the most part, Ko Samui's sights fall squarely into the category of tourist trap. The island has no shortage of overhyped animal-themed novelties with hefty admission prices. Most are located just off Rte. 4169 and are best reached by *songthaew* or motorbike. Some offer free pickup and return from anywhere on the island. Call in advance. Travel agencies also offer one-day tours of the island for around 1500฿. Relatively few foreigners stray from the beach to explore the island's interior. Those who do should be vigilant about safety, and **women traveling alone should exercise particular caution.**

WAT KHUNARAM. In this clash of Buddhist devotion and tourist gawking, Wat Khunaram houses the sunglasses-wearing, glass-encased mummified body of **Phra Khru Samathakittikhun,** a monk who died in 1973 but evaded decomposition through complex pre-death meditation. Before his death, he confidently predicted that his body would not decompose. He asked his disciples to build him an upright cask and to keep him in the Nirvana Room of the temple so that he could be a pillar of Buddhism for all to see. (*On Rte. 4169 in the island's southeast corner, about 4km inland from Hat Lamai. Open 6am-6pm. Free.*)

SAMUI BUTTERFLY GARDEN. One of Samui's most popular non-beach attractions, the Butterfly Garden maintains over 24 species of colorful southern Thai butterflies in addition to less spectacular (and less popular) species of insects, all amidst a lovely garden of bright and unusual flowers. (*Located near Laem Set, on the southeastern coast of the island. Off Rte. 4170, opposite Centara Villa Samui. ☎077 424 020. Open daily 8:30am-5:30pm. 170฿, children 100฿.*)

WATERFALLS. Ko Samui boasts several waterfalls scattered around the interior of the island. Two-tiered **Hin Lat Waterfall,** 3km south of Na Thon, is the most accessible, though not the most beautiful. The pool at the bottom is perfect for a swim. (*Located at the eastern end of Rte. 4172. A 50฿ motorcycle taxi from Na Thon.*) The **Na Muang II Waterfall,** 11km south of Na Thon, is more impressive but requires a 3km hike through a mountainous jungle path. (*Songthaew from Na Thon can drop you off at the foot of the path right off on Rte. 4169 on their way to Hat Lamai. From there, it is a 3km hike along a well-marked path to the Na Muang II Waterfall. Many travel agencies organize waterfall and trekking trips for 1200฿ per day.*)

GRANDMOTHER AND GRANDFATHER ROCKS (HIN TA AND HIN YAI). According to an old Samui legend, an elderly couple was en route to the mainland to procure a wife for their son when a fierce storm pummeled the ship and killed the two seafarers. Their bodies washed ashore, and their respective genitals somehow petrified in the shapes of "Grandfather Rock" and "Grandmother Rock," where tourists now gather to have their pictures taken with the natural rock formations in the shape of the couple's genitalia. The path leading to the Rocks is filled with vendors selling various brown, black, and green gooey coconut caramels, a delicious local specialty; a bag of the treats will run you 50฿. The vendors hand out warm samples to anyone interested. *(Amid the rocky outcropping at the southern end of Hat Lamai.)*

THE SAMUI AQUARIUM AND TIGER ZOO. Thailand's only privately owned aquarium features fish native to the Gulf of Thailand, as well as sharks and turtles, and an especially worthwhile collection of sea lions. The adjacent tiger farm houses several Bengal tigers. *(300m off Rte. 4170, south of Hat Lamai, about 150m northeast of the Butterfly Garden. ☎ 077 424 017. Open daily 9am-6pm. 350฿.)*

🎵 🎭 ENTERTAINMENT AND NIGHTLIFE

BOXING. Between the stadiums in Chaweng and Lamai, you can attend a **Thai boxing** match nearly every night of the week in Ko Samui. Watch for posters, flyers, and vehicles blaring announcements of upcoming matches. **Chaweng Boxing Stadium** and **Pelbuncha Boxing Stadium** in Chaweng, are located within a block of one another near the southern end of the beach on the small road between Rte. 4169 and Rte. 4170, right next to the lagoon. **Lamai Boxing Stadium** is located on the small east-west road that connects Lamai Rd. with Rte. 4169. When heading south down Lamai Rd., take a right on the road after Bauhaus Club, and head up the hill for 150m until you see the stadium on your left. A night of four or five fights typically starts at 9pm and lasts about 2hr. Admission can vary somewhat from night to night, but will usually cost 300-500฿.

BARS. With dozens of pubs and go-go bars, Hat Chaweng is Samui's nightlife capital. Most places are open until at least 2am. The mega-pub **Green Mango** is a massive complex of six bars that draws a young, European mainstream-clubbing crowd. The two-story complex often features live DJs. The mood picks up at around 11pm and doesn't fade until 3am. (Beer 100฿. Mixed drinks 120-200฿. Red Bull and vodka 140฿. Buckets 500฿. Open nightly 9pm-3am.) Outside of the main strip overlooking the picturesque nearby lagoon is the massive and popular **Reggae Pub,** which attracts an older, mellower crowd. Resembling a multi-story entertainment center rather than a pub, it comes complete with a tacky souvenir shop. The in-house band performs a nightly crowd-pleasing mix of vaguely reggae renditions of pop hits. Every Wednesday night, there is a Rasta Party, in which the band plays almost exclusively Bob Marley covers. To get there, follow the signs to the Chaweng Boxing Stadium across the lagoon and continue 50m past the stadium. (Beers 80-100฿. Mixed drinks 100-150฿. Open nightly 8pm-3am.)

Hat Lamai, just south of Hat Chaweng, unexpectedly has both the island's largest concentration of go-go bars and its best selection of backpacker-oriented nightlife. **The Rock,** just behind the Grandmother and Grandfather Rocks, has a great laid-back vibe and a beautiful view of the nearby large stone phallus standing in front of clear blue waters. Seemingly slapped together from tin, driftwood, and images of Bob Marley, Che Guevara, and marijuana leaves, the ultra-laidback Rock is a pleasant and relatively inexpensive place to while away an afternoon. (Large Singha beer 70฿. Open 9pm-2am.)

SOUTHERN THAILAND

DAYTRIP FROM KO SAMUI

ANG THONG MARINE PARK

The only way to visit the marine park is on a tour through one of Ko Samui's travel agencies. Daytrips that include breakfast, lunch, swimming, snorkeling, hiking, a visit to a crystal green lagoon, park admission, and transportation to and from the pier cost 1100-1300в. There are several different companies that lead tours to the national park. Samui Island Tour (☎077 421 506) is reputable and one of the cheaper tours available, with 1100в day trips, with kayaking 1400в. You can book your tickets at just about any tourist agency on the island although you might have to do a little bargaining. Grand Sea Discovery (☎077 427 001) runs tours that leave from Thong Sala on Ko Phangan. The trips from Ko Phangan have a nearly identical itinerary as those from Ko Samui, but are considerably more expensive (2100в with kayaking) because of Ko Phangan's additional distance from the marine park. Clean bare 2-person bungalows with ensuite bathroom on Ko Wua Talap 500в. Tent rental and camping for 2 people 150в, for 3 people 220в. Park office ☎077 286 025.

Ang Thong Marine National Park totals 102 sq. km and is a breathtaking collection of 42 limestone islands, 25km west of Ko Samui. Among the islands are **Ko Mae Ko** (Mother Island), popular for **Talay Nai** (Inner Sea), a saltwater lagoon that is connected to the sea by an underwater tunnel. **Ko Sam Sao** (Tripod Island) is famous for its huge rock archstone bridge that juts out into the sea, as well as for fantastic snorkeling. Lastly, **Ko Wua Talap** (Sleeping Cow Island), the largest of the islands, is home to the park office as well as two fantastic hikes. The **viewpoint**, over 500m above sea level, is one of the best sights in all of Thailand. The entire park is visible from its peak. The 450m path is quite steep, and the last 50m require steep bouldering. Closed-toe shoes are recommended. Round trip, the hike should take a little over an hour. There also is a gentler path to a cave with stalagtites and stalagmites that will take you a little less than an hour round trip and is definitely worthwhile. **Ko Lak** and similar limestone formations tower 400m above the water. Dolphins dance in the water around the longtail boats that motor near **Ko Thai Plao**. The water at **Hat Chan Charat** (Moonlight Beach) is as good for diving as that at Ko Tao. Arrange for a multi-day stay at the park bungalows by talking to your tour operator in advance.

NA THON

With no great beach to boast, Na Thon is Ko Samui's waiting room for visitors killing time until the next ferry. Unless you have an early ferry to catch or the last *songthaew* has skipped town, there's little reason to spend the night. If you must, **Nathon Residence ❹**, on Thaweerat Pakdee Rd. next to the Siam City Bank, is the best option in town. Freshly painted and tastefully decorated apartment-style rooms are well cared for by an attentive staff. (☎077 236 058. Rooms with double bed, A/C, and private marble counter-top baths with hot water 500-650в.) Na Thon does have a surprisingly good range of eating options. One of Ko Samui's most inventive and delicious eateries is **About Art & Craft ❷**, on Cholvithi Rd. by the pier, a gallery and charming organic vegetarian cafe run by a local artist couple. Try the rice soup with tofu and ginger (90в). A wide range of juices and teas is also available (60-100в), including soy lattes (70в). (Open daily 8am-5pm.) Popular **Ruangthong Bakery ❶**, on Thaweerat Pakdee Rd. at its intersection with Na Amphoe Rd., serves breads, pastries, and Thai dishes (40-100в). It's a great place to grab a quick meal, cup of coffee (30в), or snack before the ferry ride. (Open daily 7am-6pm.)

HAT BO PHUT

The charming Bo Phut ("Fisherman's Village"), with its delightfully quaint seaside strip, offers a pleasant combination of quiet atmosphere, seafood restaurants, and trendy shops. Friendly locals, traditional architecture, and lovely vistas of fishing boats in the blue bay make up for the small, steep beach that is not ideal for swimming. Bo Phut is spread around one narrow road, Bo Phut Rd., that branches off Rte. 4169 and runs along the coast before reconnecting with the main road farther west. Though the range of budget accommodations is not great, there are a couple worthwhile options, mostly near the eastern side of the beach. The best of them is **Khunthai Guest House ❹**, located on a small alley 50m east of Billabong Surf Club. (☎077 245 118. Rooms with fan, double bed, private bath, and a nice patio with a fine view of the ocean 500฿, with A/C 700฿.) If you want to stay on the main drag, the food is pretty expensive. To get some cheaper Thai food, head to the **food stalls** and soup and noodle shops located on Rte. 4169, a 5min. walk inland from Bo Phut Rd. Of the expensive restaurant options on the beach, the friendly **Billabong Surf Club ❹** is a good choice. It specializes in large cuts of juicy meat: burgers (190฿), steaks (290฿), and ribs (190฿). The view across the harbor is also excellent. At night, Billabong turns into a lively **sports bar,** one of the best of Ko Samui's many spots that show nightly soccer matches on TV. (Free Wi-Fi. Dishes 120-350฿. Open daily 10am-2pm.)

HAT BANGRAK (BIG BUDDHA BEACH)

Big Buddha Beach lies on the northern coast of Samui's northeastern peninsula, along Rte. 4171. Bungalows abound in this lively area, but the rocky, boat-filled beach is not the best for swimming. Regardless, the resorts here are decently priced, well-decorated, and relaxing. The expat couple that runs backpacker-gone-upscale **Shambala Resort ❹** creates one of the best guesthouse atmospheres on the island. The resort is located in the middle of the beach 300m to the west of the Seatran Discovery pier along Rte. 4171. Chill-out terraces and other relaxing spots are scattered throughout the lovely grounds and around the beachside bar, making this place feel like a tropical paradise. The most affordable bungalows with fan are spacious and well-decorated, and the attached restaurant serves some fantastic desserts, including banana in warm sweet coconut milk (60฿), in a delightful beach garden setting. (☎077 425 330. Night security provided. Bungalows with fan 600-700฿, with hot shower 800฿.) For food, try **Picnic Basket ❸**, 100m west of the Seatran pier along Rte. 4171. Scottish owner Jimmy cooks up hardcore traditional British breakfasts, meat pies (200฿), fish and chips (250฿), and build-your-own picnic items. (Fresh fruit, vegetables, meats, cheese, and fresh baked bread each 30-120฿. Sandwiches 100฿. Open daily 8am-6pm.)

LAEM THONGSON, AO THONGSAISON, HAT CHOENG MON, AO YAI NOI

The northeastern cape wraps around the island's most delightfully secluded coves and harbors some of its best views. Beaches lie down dirt roads off Rte. 4171 and are most easily accessed by motorbike. North of Ao Yai Noi, bordering Ao Thong Son, and 4km north of Hat Chaweng, Hat Choeng Mon is worth visiting for its serene, uncrowded beaches with pleasant swimming.

HAT CHAWENG

The biggest and brashest of Ko Samui's beaches, Hat Chaweng roars 5km along the eastern coast. A loud, happy mix of superb soft sand, clean waters, cheap booze, and music make it the sunbathing and party capital of Ko Samui. Although the Chaweng area teems with luxury hotels, upscale tourist shops, and aggressive taxi drivers, the quality beach makes it worth a visit. And if you don't want to swim, people-watching provides hours of entertainment. Hat Chaweng's main road, **Chaweng Road,** is parallel to the beach and connected to Rte. 4169 to the west via three access roads; most services are available along it.

☗ ACCOMMODATIONS. Affordable accommodations in Hat Chaweng are scarce and fill up quickly. **Green Guest House ❹** is on the northern stretch of the beach next to Al's Hut Bungalow. The popular clean concrete bungalows are situated in a quaint garden and are a stone's throw from the beach. (☎077 422 611. Doubles with fan and hot shower Dec.-Jan. 500฿, Jan.-Apr. 450฿, May-Nov. 400฿. With A/C 700฿/650฿/600฿.) **Lucky Mother Bungalows ❹** is right next door with fewer bungalows that are right on the beach. Wooden fan bungalows show their age with buggy rooms and stained floors. Cleaner, newer concrete bungalows have hot water. (☎077 230 931. Wooden bungalows 400฿; newer bungalows 600฿, with A/C 800฿.)

❏ FOOD. Budget food can likewise be tough to find on Chaweng. Western foods at near Western prices are most common, with Italian food and pub fare particularly rampant; Thai food tends to come in highly Westernized form. A longstanding budget favorite is the 24hr. **Ninja Crepe ❶,** at the southern end of Chaweng Rd., 150m north of the southernmost access Road to Rte. 4169. The food is good and cheap. It's the type of friendly, unpretentious eatery ubiquitous elsewhere in Thailand but fairly rare on Ko Samui. A huge variety of good curries (45-70฿), and other Thai standards are also served. For dessert, try the mango and sticky rice 60฿. If the staff thinks you're struggling with the spicy food, they'll give you a free banana to wash it down. (Beer served until 2am.) Otherwise, your best bets for budget food are the the mobile soup and noodle **stands** that are constantly moving up and down Chaweng Rd. during the daytime, serving the locals for 40-50฿ per bowl.

HAT LAMAI

☗ ACCOMMODATIONS. Hat Lamai's nightlife and pebble-filled beach are both second to Hat Chaweng's, but it has more budget lodging options, great cheap food, and fewer crowds. Hat Lamai's main road, Lamai Rd., runs parallel to the beach and connects at the north and south with Rte. 4169. Lamai Rd. offers some fantastic beachside accommodation deals right in the middle of the action-packed strip. **▨Big Bell Bungalow ❸** is located on the northern end of the beach 50m south of Pavillion Resort and across the street from the beach. This place would be a steal in most of Thailand, but it is an especially fantastic deal on Ko Samui, with tastefully decorated, immaculate wooden bungalows with clean soft bedding and ensuite clean bathrooms. (☎077 960 752. Basic bungalows 350฿, with TV 400฿, with A/C 500฿.) **Spa Samui Resort ❷,** on Rte. 4169 north of Lamai Rd., has everything an extremely health-conscious traveler could want: clean A/C rooms, a lauded **restaurant,** and an excellent health spa with tai chi, yoga, and massage service. Book in advance as rooms tend to fill fast even in low season. (☎077 230 855; www.spasamui.com. Yoga programs 3000฿. Daily morning meditation on the beach free. A/C bungalows 1000-1200฿.)

❏ FOOD. Most bungalows serve standard meals (60-120฿ curry dishes) until 10pm and let more expensive restaurants and pubs (about 100-250฿ per entree) along the main drag pick up the slack late at night. **Street food** abounds, more so than in other parts of Ko Samui. The best budget option on Hat Lamai and perhaps in all of Ko Samui is at the small ⊠ **night market** located right next to a cluster of go-go bars across the street from Il Tempio (see below). From 6pm-11pm, five stands clustered together serve all of your standard Thai street food: soups, kebabs, *pad thai*, curries, tempura, fried noodles and rice, pancakes, and fruit shakes, all for 30-60฿ per dish. The patrons of the market, locals and tourists alike, enjoy their meals at long open-air tables. Though small in size, the market offers up a sufficient variety to keep you satisfied for weeks. There also are roadside **day markets** along Rte. 4169 south of Hat Lamai and at Ban Hua Thanon that sells snacks and fresh fruit. **Il Tempio ❸,** in central Lamai, 100m south of Big Bell Bungalow, has good albeit pricey Italian food in a casual setting. (Open daily 11:30am-11pm. Pizzas and pastas 200-420฿.) **The Will Wait Bakery ❷,** in the center of Lamai Rd. 100m south of Bauhaus, serves a standard menu of Thai and Western favorites with a selection of freshly-baked breads. There also is an extesnive array of salads. (Dishes 70-280฿. Open daily 7am-11pm.)

KO PHANGAN ☎ 077

Ko Phangan can be a nonstop backpacker party locale or a secluded beach paradise, depending on where you are on the island. Highly developed Hat Rin, home to the legendary Full Moon Party, could give Bangkok's Khaosan Rd. a run for its money as the most popular backpacker spot on earth. On the other side of the island, not a single tattoo shop or Internet cafe mars the view from spectacular Bottle Beach, where even electricity can be hard to come by. Ko Phangan owes its uneven development in large part to the difficulty of traversing the island's rugged interior, so choose your beach wisely: whether it is wild and crowded or laid-back and secluded, you're not likely to venture far from it.

▛ TRANSPORTATION

Boats: From the pier at Hat Rin Nai, **Had Rin Queen Ferry** (☎077 375 113) goes to Ko Samui's **Hat Bangrak** (35min.; 9:30, 11:40am, 2:30, 5:30pm; 200฿). The **Raja Ferry:** goes to **Surat Thani** (3hr.; 7, 11am, 1, 5pm; 380฿). A **night Boat** goes to **Surat Thani** (6hr., 10pm, 400฿). The night ferry lands at the night ferry pier located just outside of downtown Surat Thani. Seatran, Raja, and Songserm ferries land at Don Sak port over 60km from Surat Thani. The same boats all take off from ports on the southwestern corner of the island in Thong Sala. The Songserm (☎077 377 704) and Raja (☎077 377 452-3) piers are located next to each other 1 block north of the Lomprayah, Seatran (☎077 238 679), and night ferry piers, which are all located right next to each other.

Lomprayah Catamaran: To **Ko Samui** (20min. 7am, 300฿; 11am, 4pm, 250฿) and **Ko Tao** (1hr., 8:30am, 350฿).

Songserm Express Boat: To: **Ko Samui** (45min.; 7am, 12:30pm; 220฿); **Ko Tao** (1hr., 12:30pm, 250฿); **Surat Thani** (3hr.; 7am, 12:30pm; 400฿).

Seatran Boat: To: **Ko Samui** (30min.; 11am, 4:30pm; 250฿); **Ko Tao** (1hr.; 8:30am, 2pm; 350฿); **Surat Thani** (3hr.; 6:30am, 1, 5pm; 430฿).

BUMP, BUMP, BUMP. Though paved, the last 5km of the road to Hat Rin is tremendously hilly, with enough traffic to result in a number of serious accidents each year. Before heading to any destination, inquire about the road conditions. The combination of inexperienced motorbike users and atrocious roads makes for an astronomical rate of accidents and injuries.

Local Transportation: Songthaew meet ferries at the piers in Thong Sala and run to the island's major beaches. Official rates to: **Ban Kai** (80฿); **Ban Tai** (60฿); **Chalok Lam**

(130฿); **Hat Rin** (100฿); **Hat Yao** (120฿); and **Thong Nai Paan** (150฿). Be aware that the official prices are minimums and actual prices can be higher in the rare instances when no other passengers are interested in going to the same destination. While **motorcycle taxis** are prevalent throughout the island (15-20฿ per km), **songthaew** serve as the primary means of transportation. In the center of **Hat Rin**, *songthaew* wait across from the police booth and go to **Thong Sala** (3 passenger minimum, 100฿ per person). **Longtail boats** make trips between the major beaches. They leave from **Hat Rin Nai** to: **Thong Sala** (1500฿); **Hat Thian** (600฿); **Hot Thong Reng** and **Than Sudet** (1500฿); **Thong Nai Pan** (1800฿); **Bottle Beach** (2000฿). A full-day round-trip longtail boat excursion to several beaches and back costs 3000฿. You will have to bargain somewhat aggressively with the drivers to get these aforementioned fares.

Ko Phangan

🏠 **ACCOMMODATIONS**

Bottle Beach 1, **5**
Bottle Beach 2, **7**
Bottle Beach 3 (Haad Kuad Resort), **6**
Chill House, **14**
Coral Bungalows, **9**
Paradise Bungalows, **15**
Pha-Ngan Bayshore Resort, **13**
Same Same Lodge & Restaurant, **16**
Sea Mew, **1**
Smile Bungalows, **4**
Star Huts, **8**

🍴 **FOOD**

Corner Kitchen, **2**
Nira House Bakery, **10**
Om Ganesh, **12**
Paprika, **11**
Swiss Bakery, **3**

Rentals: Motorbikes are available for rent around the pier, on the main street of Thong Sala, and from almost all guesthouses and travel agencies in Hat Rin (150฿ with passport deposit).

> **MOTORBIKE SCAM.** Beware that there is an unverified rumor that some independent motorcycle taxi rental shops are running a scam where they claim that you have scratched the bike and demand more money afterwards. Rent your motorbike from guesthouses, where such scams are rarer. Also, make sure and look over the bike for scratches and dents before you take it out for a spin.

ORIENTATION AND PRACTICAL INFORMATION

Ko Phangan is 100km northeast of Surat Thani and 15km north of Ko Samui. While a few boats depart and dock at the **Hat Rin pier**, most arrive at the island's main city and port of call, **Thong Sala**, where many conveniences are located, including ATMs, travel agencies, and the cheapest Internet on the island. From the Thong Sala pier, three paved roads cover most of the island. One runs 10km southeast along the coast to the party beach of **Hat Rin**. Hat Rin is split into **Hat Rin Nai** (Sunset Beach) to the west and **Hat Rin Nok** (Sunrise Beach) to the east. Midway along this paved road, a bumpy dirt road heads to the northeastern beaches of **Thong Nai Paan Yai** and **Thong Nai Paan Noi**. Other dirt trails branch off of this dirt road to more remote coves and beaches, like **Hat Thian** and **Than Sudet**. A second paved road from Thong Sala cuts 10km northward through the heart of the island to **Ao Chalok Lam**, a departure point for boats heading to lovely **Hat Khuat** (Bottle Beach). The third road runs a scenic course west along the coast to the less-developed bays of **Hat Yao, Hat Salat**, and **Ao Mae Hat**. Ko Phangan definitely rewards those who explore its far corners, but doing so is a transportation challenge that will require a little patience and money. Solo travelers who hop on a motorbike and venture out on their own should exercise caution in remote areas as roads can be really unsafe and confusing as you venture away from Thong Sala.

Tours: In Hat Rin, ▣**Backpackers' Information Centre** (☎077 375 535; www.backpackersthailand.com), next to D's Bookshop 1 block away from the Chicken Corner on Sunset Beach, is the best full-service tour agency on the island, and is likely one of the best in all of Thailand. Open daily 10am-10pm. Though it is affiliated with Songserm express boats, **Songserm Travel Center** (☎077 377 096), on the left side of the main road in Thong Sala which heads inland from the Songserm pier, can book tickets for any ferries or boats. Boat/bus packages to Bangkok (700฿), Krabi (600฿), Phuket (550฿), Had Yai (650฿), and Chumphon (700฿). Open daily 8:30am-10pm.

Currency Exchange: Several exchange booths line the street leading from the main pier in Thong Sala. **Siam Commercial Bank,** next to Songserm Travel Center, 30m from the Thong Sala pier on the left, has a **24hr. ATM.** Open M-F 8:30am-4:30pm. Currency exchange booth open daily 8:30am-6pm. In Hat Rin, banks and exchange booths with similar hours and 24hr. ATMs cluster right next to the pier. Bottle Beach has no banks, exchange booths, or ATMs.

Books: U Book Shop, next to the Siam Commercial Bank, has a decent selection of beach reads, and refreshing A/C. Open daily 8:30am-8:30pm. Similar shops selling and trading used paperback editions of backpacker classics abound in Hat Rin. **D's Book Shop,** next to Backpackers Information Centre, offers an especially good selection of books in many different languages. Open 8am-10pm.

Police: Main office (☎077 377 114), 2km north of Thong Sala on the road to Ao Chalak Lam. English spoken. Open 24hr. A small 24hr. **police booth** operates at Hat Rin right next to the *songthaew* drop-off and pick-up area at the end of the road that connects Hat Rin to Thong Sala. English spoken.

Medical Services: Koh Phangan Hospital (☎077 375 103), 3km north of Thong Sala, located on a road that leads northwest to Hat Yao. English spoken. Open 24hr. In Hat Rin, private 24hr. nursing stations provide basic medical services. **Hat Rin Medical Clinic** (☎077 239 5098) is located 30m from the pier right across from Om Ganesh. For serious medical attention, take a boat to Ko Samui; Ko Phangan Hospital can arrange emergency speedboat service there.

Internet Access: Internet on Ko Phangan is some of the most expensive in Thailand: 3฿ per min., in Hat Rin, 5฿ per min., in Bottle Beach, and the more reasonable 1฿ per min. in Thong Sala.

Post Office: GPO (☎077 377 118), in Thong Sala. From the end of the Songserm pier, take the 1st right at the large roundabout and follow the road along the shore; the post office is on the right 1km down the road. Poste Restante. Open M-F 8:30am-4:30pm, Sa 9am-noon. In Hat Rin, a private, licensed branch (☎077 375 204), on the road connecting Hat Rin Nok and Hat Rin Nai right next to Om Ganesh, 30m from the pier, offers somewhat more limited postal and courier services. Open daily 9am-midnight. **Postal Code:** 84280.

ACCOMMODATIONS AND FOOD

Most travelers to Ko Phangan head immediately to the southern coast and the beaches of Hat Rin. Those looking for more attractive and secluded beaches should head north to lovely Hat Khuat (Bottle Beach) or mellow Thong Nai Paan Noi. Accommodation prices and availability rise and fall with lunar tides. The island fills to maximum capacity two to four days before the Full Moon Party (see **Sex, Drugs, and Lunar Cycles,** p. 415). Whether you're looking to attend the party or to avoid it, be sure to research the dates in advance, as the party does not always coincide exactly with the full moon. Current schedules are available at www.fullmoon.phangan.info. If you plan to be there for the party, make reservations or arrive a few days early—otherwise, be prepared to commute to Ko Samui or to sleep on the beach.

SIGHTS

LONGTAIL BOAT TOURS. Lest you forget the extent to which Ko Phangan is a backpacker hot-spot, the most popular daytime activities on the island are two competing and widely advertised daily longtail boat tours: the **Munchies Boat Trip** (☎081 083 0968) and the **Reggae Magic Boat Trip** (☎077 859 137). The 5½hr. tours depart around noon to circle the island, stop at various beaches and waterfalls (Thong Nai Pan, Than Sudet Beach, Bottle Beach), and dabble in a bit of snorkeling on Hat Khom. Both promise lunch and snacks. Each tour is 700฿ per person. In Hat Rin, tickets for both are available at all of the tour agencies. If you have a group of five or more, it is most cost efficient to charter a longtail boat for the day (3,000฿) and go through with the exact same tour at your own pace. Longtail boats can be chartered at Sunset Beach and will require a significant amount of bargaining.

WATERFALLS. After parties and beaches, waterfalls are Ko Phangan's next biggest tourist attraction. The most famous stretches of river and small falls run through **Than Sadet Historical Park,** an easy 20min. walk from the beach. Kings Rama V, VII, and IX all walked along its bathtub-sized waterfalls and cascades, leaving their initials as seals of inspection. *(Longtail boats from Hat Rin (1-way 1500฿*

per boat) drop passengers off on the beach at Hot Thong Reng at the mouth of the river. From here, hike up the river for .5km to get to a small cascade of waterfalls perfect for swimming.)

WAT KOW THAM. A more contemplative alternative to the Hat Rin party scene, Wat Kow Tham, spreads through forested grounds on a hillside between Hat Rin and Thong Sala. Some of the many shrines scattered throughout the tranquil grounds offer good views of a relatively undeveloped stretch of the island's coast. Under the direction of Head Nun Mae Chee Ahmon Pahn and Australian-American couple Rosemary and Steve Weissman, the *wat* offers 10-day silent *vipassana* meditation retreats intended to teach compassion, loving kindness, and mindfulness. Beginners are welcome, provided they are serious about abiding by the *wat's* strict discipline: as a sign at the entrance reminds visitors, this is a monastery, not a guesthouse. Retreats begin between the 8th and 17th of each month, and participants must arrive in person to register. Check the website, www.watkowtham.org, for a schedule and more guidelines. The minimum age for participation is 20, and those under 26 must meet special participation requirements. The all-inclusive cost for participation in the retreat is 4000฿. Day visitors are welcome to participate in meditation and other retreat activities for free. (*To reach Wat Kow Tham, take a songthaew (80฿) running between Thong Sala and Hat Rin, and ask to be let off at the wat. From the drop-off, the wat is a 1km walk uphill along a clearly marked path.)*

◾ NIGHTLIFE

Even in the weeks preceding the full moon, all of Ko Phangan's nightlife is centered on Hat Rin Nok's beach, where open-air bars spread out cushions and low tables for drink-sipping loungers. Just about any phase of the moon—half moon, black moon, quarter moon, or "shiva moon"—is occasion for some smaller variation of the Full Moon Party. Almost every night on Hat Rin Nok brings out fire twirlers, fireworks, and trance beats. Big parties are also thrown on the beaches of Ban Thai and Ban Kai to celebrate the half moon and the black moon. Flyers on Hat Rin announce super-cheap drink specials, and occasionally direct people away from the beach to other venues for pool parties and the like. Sometimes, the venue will arrange free taxis from Sunrise Beach.

Almost every night on Sunrise Beach, dreadlocked people twirl whiskey bottles and fire sticks at **Drop-In Bar,** a Sunrise Beach institution located to the south of the small beach. (☎077 375 446; www.dropinclub.com. Singha 80฿, mixed drinks 100฿. Live entertainment 9pm-dawn.) With less fire, the expat-run **Outback Bar,** on the road between Hat Rin Nok and Nai, tends to draw a laddish crowd to its larger and football on the big-screen television. Outback has an extensive drink menu with just about every mixed drink around for 150฿ each. This bar serves delicious fried Western snacks and appetizers. (*Bruscetta* 60฿. Open daily 7am-2am.)

Hat Rin Nok's **Full Moon Party** is the stuff of legend. Each month, crowds of up to 12,000 gather on this strip of sand. DJs spin the latest imported mixes until well after dawn, and every inch of sand is packed with an international crowd dancing to the pulsating bass fueled by drink and more than a few club drugs. Half-naked people with fluorescent body paint glitter under the moonlight and blacklights, and fire jugglers light up the sand. It's beautiful, full of energy, and unlike anything you have seen before.

THONG SALA

Thong Sala may be a dull beachless town, but it's also a lifeline for the island, boasting the island's cheapest Internet connections the most tourist services, and the island's most aggressive barrage of *songthaew* drivers waiting at the pier. Staying here usually indicates an early ferry departure, an inability to find accommodation elsewhere, or a serious inertia problem, but some comfortable rooms do lie close to the pier. **Sea Mew ❷**, 71 Thong Sala Pier (☎077 377 795), on the waterfront road right between the Songserm pier and the night ferry pier, has a great staff. Unfortunately, the spirited atmosphere of its restaurant, the closest thing Thong Sala has to a backpacker hangout, doesn't extend to Sea Mew's somewhat bland, if clean, rooms. (Doubles with fan and private bath 400฿, with A/C 500฿.)

Thong Sala's main drag has several decent, but pricey, Western eateries. It is also the island's best bet for market eating: a modest **day market** offering 40฿ noodle soups and 50฿ curries is behind the 7-Eleven 150m inland from Songserm Travel Center. The equally small **night market** spreads along the first road to your left if you take a right exiting the Seatran pier. *Tom yum* (60฿) is a particularly good bet. The **Corner Kitchen ❷**, 1 Moo 1, three doors down from the post office, serves an extensive selection of run-of-the-mill, but delicious, Thai, European, and Chinese cuisine. (☎077 238 184. Dishes 60-120฿. Open daily 9:30am-9:30pm.) The popular Francophone outpost **Swiss Bakery ❷**, located in an alley just off the main road near Songserm Travel Center, is a lovely bakery tucked away in a quiet garden. (Open daily 7am-3pm.)

THONG NAI PAAN NOI

With sparkling water and a relaxed atmosphere, these twin beaches are a nice compromise between the solitude of Bottle Beach and the lunacy of Hat Rin. They offer ample reward for those willing to endure the hour-long **songthaew** ride from Thong Sala (150฿) or the **boat ride** from Hat Rin (1800฿). *Songthaew* stop first at Thong Nai Paan Noi, the more populated of the two, which has a small village, better swimming, but slightly more expensive accommodations.

Near the *songthaew* drop-off, popular **Star Huts ❷** is the largest operator on the beach and teems with long-term guests. Prices for the larger and nicer bungalows can rise by several hundred baht in the high season. (☎077 445 085. Double bungalows with fan 650฿, bungalows with A/C 1300-2000฿).

HAT RIN NOK (EAST)

Welcome to "Backpacker Land," where the word Reggae appears in the name of every other establishment, a kid calling home to ask for more money occupies every phone booth, and every phase of the moon occasions a beach party. Few places are as much of a self-contained backpacker universe as this village of travel agencies, clothing and book shops Internet cafes, and funky bars, each of which target the young, raging Full Moon Party crowd. With all that's going on in the village, the beach, which looks and smells polluted at times, seems like almost an afterthought—until the night of the Full Moon Party, that is, when the waterfront takes center stage.

▣ **TRANSPORTATION.** *Songthaew* from Thong Sala drop you off at the end of the main road, just inland from Hat Rin Nok. From here, it's a 5min. walk to Sunrise Beach or a 10min. walk to Hat Rin Nok's quieter twin, Hat Rin Nai, where the Hat Rin pier is located. The small village spreads between the two beaches, which are connected by several dusty roads that all offer similar bars, hotels, and tattoo parlors. These roads intersect **Haadrin Road,** the area's main artery, running parallel to Sunset Beach. Most basic services are in this area. If you ever get lost in this area, know that if you follow almost any of the roads to its end, you will end up at one of the two beaches.

SEX, DRUGS, AND LUNAR CYCLES. The Full Moon Party has attained legendary status in backpacker culture. As the story goes, on the tropical paradise of Ko Phangan, people gather under the full moon to leave all worries behind and party all night on a beach where the good vibes flow as freely as the drugs. The reality these days falls far short of this fantasy on several counts. While this beach party is still one of the best in the world, smart partiers will be careful and keep the following in mind:

1. **Research** in advance when exactly the party will be occurring, because it's not always held on the full moon. Many major Buddhist holidays fall on the full moon. The Thai Buddhist establishment took considerable offense at the manner in which the half-naked, drug-addled foreigners of Ko Phangan were celebrating sacred holidays. Conceding to their pressure, the party is now typically held a few days before or after the full moon. Check www.fullmoon.phangan.info for the latest schedules.

2. **Reserve in advance,** and arrive on Ko Phangan early. Accommodations on Hat Rin Nok and Nai fill up as many as 4 days in advance of the big party. If you don't have a week to burn on Ko Phangan, reservations are strongly recommended, although a significant number of places don't accept reservations around the time of the party. Fail to plan ahead and you may be stuck commuting from Ko Samui or sleeping on the beach.

3. **The Thai police are in the know.** You're not the only one who's heard about the ecstasy, acid, and opium here. Police regularly set up checkpoints on all roads leading to and from Hat Rin in the days leading up to the party, and you can expect a rigorous search of not only your person but also your vehicle. Contrary to popular belief, a few thousand baht cannot bribe you out of a drug offense in Thailand, and trust us: you don't want to end up in Thai prison.

4. **Thieves love to take advantage of the full moon** to rob you while you party. Protect your stuff. Do not keep your money or camera in your pocket. Likewise, avoid keeping valuable possessions in obvious hiding places in your bungalow, such as under your pillow or mattress. Most resorts and bungalows offer safety boxes; take advantage of these, especially if your bungalow or hotel room is located close to Sunset beach. Leave the expensive footwear behind: shoe theft on the beach is a major problem, much to the delight of nearby sandal vendors. Be wary of strangers who offer you a drink or drugs, as they may ultimately be trying to rob you.

ACCOMMODATIONS. Throughout the year, you can find a crowd of vacationing 20-something Europeans and Israelis here. If you are looking to join them in the hotels closeset to Sunset Beach, expect overpriced, flimsy bungalows. Venturing a few blocks inland or a 20min. walk south away from the action to Leela Beach will often get you a much better room value. **Same Same Lodge & Restaurant ❸** is perched above Hat Rin Nok on the Southern side of the beach right next to Soi Viking, off the dirt road that leads south to Leela Beach. It is your best bet if you are looking to sleep in the center of the action. Same Same anticipates a backpacker's every need with an attractive common area that includes a good restaurant, lively bar, pool table, and lounge area with a big-screen TV. Come full moon, Same Same gears up with an extensive 300฿ pre-party buffet with live music. (☎077 737 5200; www.same-same.com. No reservations accepted during the 5 days preceding Full Moon parties. Rooms with fan and private bath 500฿, with A/C 800฿.) **Pha-Ngan Bayshore Resort ❸**, at the northern end of Haadrin Rd., is a well-maintained set of bungalows reaching from the beach inland near to the *songthaew* dropoff. At night, it's quieter than other resorts. The splurge is worth it for those who have to be near the beach and want something better than the claptrap beach bungalow norm, but brace yourself for skyrocketing high-season and full-moon prices. (☎077 375 224. For the week preceding the full-moon, bungalow doubles with fan and private bath 900฿, normally 600฿; with A/C and hot water 400/1000฿; beachfront 4500฿/3500฿.) **Paradise Bungalows ❸** is at the opposite end of the beach from Pha-Ngan Bayshore, and reception is located in a mini-mart at the northern end of Haadrin Rd. The bungalows with fan are a great value for their location, just steps away from Sunrise Beach. However, some of the cheaper bungalows are suffering from serious neglect and may reek of perfumes intended to mask smells. Definitely take a look at the bungalow before you agree to it. (☎077 375 2445. Bungalows with fan 350฿, with A/C 800฿.)

🗐 **FOOD.** Hat Rin has the island's best selection of international food and provides ample vegetarian options and Western snack foods. Restaurants representing at least half a dozen nationalities line Haadrin Rd., which connects the southern ends of both Hat Rin beaches, and the small dirt alleys stemming from it. **Nira House Bakery ❷** is around the corner from Mr. K Chicken Corner, located inland in the direction of the 7-Eleven. With a cool, relaxing interior, Nira caters to an array of health-food types, those with a sweet tooth, and anyone craving real coffee. Excellent chocolate croissants cost 50฿, and hummus sandwiches on homemade bread run 90฿. (Kitchen open daily 8am-8pm. Bakery open 24hr.) **Om Ganesh ❸**, just uphill from the pier, serves tasty Indian and Tibetan food amidst protruding wall murals of the Himalayas and various Hindu deities. Chicken *tikka* (120฿) and mango *lassi* (40฿) are good choices. The 399฿ "vodka bucket" is probably not. (☎077 375 123. Dishes 60-180฿. Open 8am-11pm.) **Paprika ❸** is located towards Sunrise Beach, 250m from the pier. This casual Mediterranean spot serves the island's Israeli contingent with cheap and authentic falafel, hummus, and tabouli. There is a Hebrew book swap located inside. The falafel special includes a falafel and a fruit shake for 80฿. (Dishes 80-180฿. Open daily 9am-8pm.)

HAT RIN NAI (WEST) AND LEELA BEACH

Though a mere 100m west of Hat Rin Nok, the mellow atmosphere of Hat Rin Nai makes it feel like it's miles away from its party loving neighbor. The strip of muddy sand at Hat Rin Nai is hardly attractive, but the beach does have its perks: a good selection of bungalows, pretty sunsets, and a location that's close enough to take advantage of Hat Rin Nok's nightlife but far enough to retreat from it.

A number of basic accommodations, restaurants, and ticket agencies run along the ragged main road heading toward the Hat Rin Pier. Budget beachside bungalows lie at the northern end of the beach, a 15min. walk along the beach from the pier, past a rocky outcropping. **Coral Bungalows ❷**, popular with Full Moon partiers, is high quality, with a restaurant boasting an excellent sea view. In the nights preceding the full moon, the bungalows host a series of pool parties that last until dawn. Their more expensive bungalows, with inlaid pebble walls and vibrant colors, are a massive step-up in quality from their cheaper wooden counterparts, but their markedly un-scenic inland location is a huge flaw. (☎077 375 0234. Double bungalows with fan 500฿, with A/C 800฿.)

Located south down the peninsula from Hat Rin Nai is Leela Beach, a laid-back backpacker hub filled with some of the cheapest accommodations on the island, all of which is a short 20min. walk from Sunrise Beach. The rocky beach here is not the best for swimming, the rooms in some of the bungalows can be pretty dingy, and the area, which is nestled in the jungle, has more mosquitoes than the other beaches. Still, the the accommodations are some of the best deals on the island. **Chill House ❹**, located down Soi Viking, towards Leela Beach, is a great cheap option. Rooms are nestled in the mountains and have spectacular views of Sunrise Beach. The laid-back atmosphere at the sky bar with hammocks is a nice touch. Arrive early, before the full moon; these rooms fill up almost a week before the party. (☎086 012 2596. 2-person bungalows with fan and private bath 600฿. Discounts possible for smaller bungalows.)

BHAT KHUAT (BOTTLE BEACH)

Set against lush green hills, this gorgeous and quiet ▨beach—with perfect water for swimming—lures those who intend to stay for a few days into spending weeks or months, in part because it is so inconvenient to leave. Likely the most expensive Internet access (5฿ per min.) in all of Thailand can be found here; there is little mobile phone reception, and electricity in most bungalow rooms, only goes on at night.

▣ **TRANSPORTATION.** The most inexpensive way to get here is to take a **songthaew** from Thong Sala to **Ao Chalok Lam** (10km, 20-40min., 130฿). The bay is the departure point for boats to **Hat Khuat**. (To **Bottle Beach** 1:30, 4pm; return 2, 5pm; 100฿.) In the dry season, it may be possible to walk the 4km from Ao Chalok Lam to Bottle Beach. Inquire in Ao Chalak Lam. You can also charter a **longtail boat** from **Ao Chalak Lam** to Bottle Beach (400฿). Longtail boats also go from Hat Rin to Bottle Beach (2000฿).

▛ **ACCOMMODATIONS.** Once on Bottle Beach, your options are limited to five inexpensive bungalow operations, three of which are owned by the same family. **The Bottle Beach Bungalows** empire spreads across the majority of the beach. **Bottle Beach 1, Bottle Beach 2,** and **Bottle Beach 3** (Haad Khuad Resort) each offer an eclectic assortment of bungalows: beachside and inland, small and large, new and old. Quality varies considerably within each Bottle Beach outpost, so be sure to shop around. **Haad Khuad Resort ❸** offers the best value of the three. (☎076 445 127. Clean, comfortable 3-person bungalows 450฿, 4-person bungalows 850฿.) **Bottle Beach 2 Resort ❸** has the cheapest but also the dingiest and barest rooms. (☎076 445 156, double bungalows with fan 350฿.) All three have electricity in the rooms, but only at night. All three accept MC/V. Among the restaurants attached to the three outfits, Haad Khuad Resort has the best Thai food (dishes 60-180฿; red curry chicken 80฿), and Bottle Beach 2 Resort the liveliest backpacker scene. On the full moon, customers of Bottle Beach can buy a 400฿ round trip ticket to Hat Rin. Among the lodging accommodations, Bottle Beach 2 likely won't be filled around the full moon, while the other accommodations will be. **Smile Bungalows ❸**, at the northern end of the beach, has prices are similar to those at Bottle Beach. But, the bungalows here are far more attractive, with stone walls, soft mattresses, and lovely bathrooms. Electricity is also limited to nighttime here. (☎081 956 3133. Small bungalows with private bath and fan 350฿, large 550-600฿.) Its reggae-filled restaurant (dishes 80-250฿) is also quite popular.

KO TAO   ☎077

As one of Southeast Asia's most renowned dive sites, charming laid-back Ko Tao lures an international crowd of underwater enthusiasts ranging from scuba neophytes who seek cheap certification courses to veterans who relish its clear gulf waters and outstanding reefs. For non-divers, the island offers superb snorkeling and spectacular sun-baked coves, many of which are so secluded that they can only be reached by boat or a long hike. While there are many budget accommodations and more than enough bars to satisfy those on their way to or from the Full Moon Party, Ko Tao is also family-friendly. Many guesthouses, restaurants, and bars have a more upscale edge as a result. And despite having no airport, few luxury hotels, only a handful of well-paved roads, and a utilities crunch that causes power outages in most of the island, Ko Tao is still moving in the direction of larger crowds and higher prices.

⌐ TRANSPORTATION

Boats: Lomprayah Catamaran, Songserm Express Boat, Seatran Discovery, and a **night boat** send ferries to Chumphon, Ko Phangan, Ko Samui, Surat Thani, and Bangkok. Ferries leave daily from one of the 4 piers in Mae Hat. Boat service is subject to

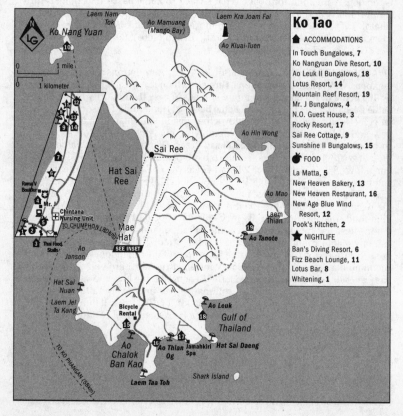

Ko Tao

🏠 ACCOMMODATIONS

In Touch Bungalows, **7**
Ko Nangyuan Dive Resort, **10**
Ao Leuk II Bungalows, **18**
Lotus Resort, **14**
Mountain Reef Resort, **19**
Mr. J Bungalows, **4**
N.O. Guest House, **3**
Rocky Resort, **17**
Sai Ree Cottage, **9**
Sunshine II Bungalows, **15**

🍎 FOOD

La Matta, **5**
New Heaven Bakery, **13**
New Heaven Restaurant, **16**
New Age Blue Wind
    Resort, **12**
Pook's Kitchen, **2**

★ NIGHTLIFE

Ban's Diving Resort, **6**
Fizz Beach Lounge, **11**
Lotus Bar, **8**
Whitening, **1**

Map labels: Laem Nam Tok, Ko Nang Yuan, Ao Mamuang (Mango Bay), Laem Kra Joam Fai, Ao Kluai-Tuen, Ao Hin Wong, Sai Ree, Hat Sai Ree, Ao Mao, Laem Thian, Rama V Boulevard, Mr. J, Chintana Nursing Unit, TO CHUMPHON (80km), Mae Hat, SEE INSET, Ao Tanote, Thai Food Stalls, Ao Janson, Hat Sai Nuan, Laem Jet Ta Kang, Bicycle Rental, Ao Leuk, Gulf of Thailand, Ao Chalok Ban Kao, Ao Thian Og, Jamahkiri Spa, Hat Sai Daeng, TO KO PHANGAN (55km), Laem Taa Toh, Shark Island frequent schedule changes, and the trip can be rough Nov.-Feb., when the sea is choppy. Bring your own Dramamine.

Lomprayah Catamaran: Company boats leave from the company's pier 2 blocks south of the Seatran Discovery pier. To: **Chumphon** (1½hr.; 10:45, 2:45pm; 550฿); **Ko Phangan** (1hr.; 9:30am, 3pm; 300฿); **Ko Samui** (2hr.; 9:30am, 3pm; 450฿).

Songserm Express: Boats leave from the company's pier 1 block south of Lomprayah Catamaran pier. To: **Chumphon** (3hr., 2:30pm, 450฿); **Ko Phangan** (1½hr., 10am, 250฿); **Ko Samui** (3hr., 10am, 350฿); **Surat Thani** (8½hr., 10am, 550฿).

Seatran Discovery: leave from the company pier on Mae Hat. To: **Chumphon** (2hr., 4pm, 550฿); **Ko Phangan** (1½hr., 9:30am); **Ko Samui** (2hr.; 9:30am, 3pm; 450฿).

Night boat: Leave from the main pier, 1 block south of the Seatran Discovery pier. To: **Chumphon** (5hr., 10pm, 300฿); **Surat Thani** (7hr., 10:30pm, 650฿).

Local Transportation: Pickup-truck taxis go Mae Hat to anywhere on Ko Tao that is accessible by the island's paved roads (4 or more people, 50฿-100฿ per person). **Taxis** between Mae Hat and Hat Sai Ree are 50฿ per person. Pricey **longtail boats** can be hired to reach otherwise inaccessible bays (at least 4 people, 200-500฿ per person).

Rentals: If you plan to explore the far reaches of Ko Tao's roads or to travel between Hat Sai Ree and Mae Hat, rent a **motorbike,** available everywhere (200฿ per 24hr., passport deposit required). A more stable option is an **ATV,** available at most motorcycle rental shops for 600฿ per day (passport deposit required). A more environment-and-wallet friendly option is to rent a high-quality **bicycle** available from a stall right next to 7-Eleven in Ao Chalok Ban Kao. (70฿ per day, 500฿ deposit. Open daily 8am-10pm.)

✈🛈 ORIENTATION AND PRACTICAL INFORMATION

Boats arrive at **Mae Hat** (Mother Beach), where a number of tourist-oriented services are concentrated, though there are few accommodations. A little more than 1km north of Mae Hat, **Hat Sai Ree** is Ko Tao's largest and most popular beach and the heart of the backpacker and scuba scene. If you head south from Mae Hat for 2.5km, you get to **Ao Chalok Ban Kao,** the main southern beach and the second most popular beach on the island.

Semi-paved roads branch off of the island's main north-south road to more beaches, including on the eastern coast **Ao Leuk, Ao Tanote** (a fantastic snorkeling destination), **Ao Hin Wong,** and on the island's southeastern corner **Ao Thian Og** and **Hat Sai Daeng.** Due to its hilly nature and the rarity of street lights, the island can be exhausting to explore by foot during the day and nearly impossible to navigate at night. Exploration possibilities include the 30min. walk from Mae Hat to Ao Chalok Ban Kao, the 30min. walk farther to secluded Ao Thian, the hour and 15min. walk from Mae Hat to Ao Leuk, and the 45min. walk farther to lovely and quiet Ao Tanote. Different colored jeeps with numbers on their windows serve as taxis and go to most destinations, though they are concentrated in Mae Hat. The free Ko Tao Info brochure is an excellent guide to the island, as is the free fold-out map produced and distributed by Jamahkiri Spa and Cafe del Sol. Both are available at hotels and tourist agencies all over the island.

Tourist Office: There is **no TAT office** on the island, but the TAT offices in Surat Thani, Ko Samui, and Chumphon can all answer your Ko Tao related questions. On the island, private agencies line the 2 east-west roads in Mae Hat as well as the main road in Hat Sai Ree, providing info and tickets. All offer similar services and prices. Local character **Mr. J** (☎077 456 0667) claims to provide any type of service, from scoring visa extensions to arranging emergency loans. *Let's Go reminds its readers that those who rely on Mr. J's "homemade condoms" do so at their own risk.* Find him at his shop on the hill just north of the pier, a 5min. walk down the semi-paved path off the Seatran Discovery Pier

Rd. This path is located to the left when exiting the pier, just before Cafe del Sol. Office open daily 8am-10pm.

Currency Exchange: Exchange booths and **ATMs** abound in Mae Hat and Hat Sai Ree, but are harder to find on the rest of the island. **Siam City Bank,** on the main pier road in Mae Hat 150m from the pier, offers Western Union service and a currency exchange booth. Open M-F 9am-4pm. Currency exchange booth open daily 9am-4:30pm.

Police: (☎456 077 631), a 10min. walk on the semi-paved path from Mae Hat to Hat Sai Ree, 250m past Mr. J's. English spoken. Open 24hr.

Medical Services: There is **no hospital on the island. Nursing stations** offering basic services are abundant around Ao Chalok, Hat Sai Ree, and Mae Hat; most open daily 8am-8pm. One such nursing unit is the **Chintana Nursing Unit,** located on the eastern edge of Mae Hat, on the main road, 100m from the Seatran Discovery Pier Rd., towards Hat Sai Ree. Open daily 8am-8pm. **Badalveda** (☎077 456 580) in Hat Sai Ree near Scuba Junction, has a hyperbaric chamber available 24hr. for the emergency needs of divers suffering from decompression illness. For serious illnesses, all of the nursing units can arrange transportation to a hospital in Ko Samui.

Telephones: Nearly all travel agencies and bungalows offer international phone service for around 20฿ per min.

Internet Access: High-speed Internet is widely available, though pricey. Mae Hat and Hat Sai Ree both have Internet for 2฿ per min., with a 20฿ minimum. On Ao Chalok Ban Kao and the more secluded beaches on the eastern coast, you can find Internet for 3฿ per min. with a 30฿ minimum. **PC Travel,** located in Mae Hat 100m. down the semi-paved northbound path starting next to Cafe del Sol, has good connections and likely offers the best deal in town at 100฿ per hr. A number of resorts, including the View Cliff Resort, and several bars, including the Safety Stop Bar and Whitening, offer free Wi-Fi.

Post Office: (☎077 456 869) on the Seatran Discovery Pier Rd. in Mae Hat, at the top of the hill near its intersection with the main north-south road. Poste Restante. Open M-F 8:30am-4:30pm, Sa-Su 9am-noon. **Postal Code:** 84280.

ACCOMMODATIONS AND FOOD

While dive agencies rent bungalows almost exclusively to their clients, there are plenty of budget places available if you're not scuba diving. The cheapest rooms, usually with fan and attached bath, run 300-500฿; the closer you are to the beach, the more you'll pay. Prices listed reflect high-season (Jan.-Aug.) rates; in the low season, some places knock off 100-150฿. Also, keep in mind that in the five days following Ko Phangan's Full Moon Party, especially in June, July, and January, there is a bottleneck on the island as partiers shack up to scuba dive. An available room on the island during these periods can be difficult to find, especially because most places will not accept reservations. Also, post-Full Moon Party (July, Aug., and Jan.), expect to have to forage a little or pay 800฿ and higher if you want a room on the beach.

ACTIVITIES

Scuba diving is popular year-round in Ko Tao, although late September through December often brings heavy rains and choppy waters. The island also has a unique tide; September to May is high-tide season and better for snorkeling, while May to September is low-tide season and better for basking on the beach. Ko Tao has more than 20 dive sites. **Chumphon Pinnacle** is a favorite for deep dives, while **Southwest Pinnacle** and **Shark Island** are known for gorgeous coral and leopard sharks. **Green Rock,** near Ko Tao, and **Sail Rock,** on the way to Ko Phangan, are famous for rock "swim-throughs." Closer to Ko Tao, **Hin Wong Pinnacle** and **Ko Nang Yuan** (p. 424) have coral suitable for snorkeling. **Japanese**

Garden, off of Nang Yuan, is a favorite spot for snorkelers and beginning divers. A **shipwreck** off the coast of Mae Hat is another popular dive destination.

For those just looking to **snorkel** on their own, snorkel-and-fin sets are available at any dive shop, travel agency, or corner store for about 100฿.

Scuba prices are largely standardized, so judge on friendliness and professionalism. Four types of classes are available. Beginners can choose from the four-day open-water certification course (9000฿) or the supervised one-day "discover scuba" dives (3000฿, additional dives 1000฿ each). Certified divers can hone their skills with the two-day advanced open-water course (8500฿) or tag along with any dive class on a one-day "fun dive" (1 dive 1000฿, 2-5 dives 900฿ each, 6-9 dives 800฿ each, 10 or more dives 700฿ each). Bring your own equipment for a 10-15% discount. Prices may or may not include accommodations in affiliated bungalows for the duration of the course; be sure to ask. Whether the price of the accommodation is fully included in the scuba package or not, the affiliated rooms will probably will be discounted such that it is a better deal, especially during high season, to stay there as opposed to a non-affiliated bungalow.

There are plenty of dive shops from which to choose, all sporting PADI certification. **Crystal Dive Resort** (☎077 456 106-7; www.crystaldive.com) is considered one of the most trusted dive shops on the island and has received a number of noteworthy PADI Member Awards. Its Ko Tao office is located on Mae Hat, along the beach, just north of the Seatran Discovery pier.

The following is a short list of some additional popular dive shop operations. Be sure to talk to the staff and patrons about teaching and equipment before committing. Larger shops have representative offices on Mae Hat.

Ban's Diving Resort (☎077 456 466; www.amazingkohtao.com).

Big Blue Diving Resort (☎077 456 415; www.bigbluediving.com).

Buddha View Dive Resort (☎077 456 0745; www.buddhaview-diving.com).

Easy Divers Koh Tao (☎077 456 010; www.kohtaoeasydivers.com).

Scuba Junction (☎077 456 164; www.scuba-junction.com).

Taa Toh Lagoon Dive Resort (☎077 456 503; www.taatohdivers.com).

MAE HAT

There are four piers on Mae Hat (from north to south): **Seatran Discovery pier, the main pier, Lompraya Boat pier,** and **Songserm Boat pier**. In Mae Hat, there are four roads, one extending east from each of the four piers. Both dead-end at the main road, which heads north to Hat Sai Ree and south to Ao Chalok Ban Kao. In addition, as you head east away from the Seatran Discovery pier, there is a semi-paved path just before Cafe del Sol that also leads north to Hat Sai Ree. Mae Hat is the food, fuel, and ferry center of Ko Tao. The beach is covered with boats, making it unsuitable for swimming. There is little reason to linger upon arrival; you'll find better beaches and vibes elsewhere on the island.

⌂ ACCOMMODATIONS. Budget guesthouses are are mostly found up two roads east of the main pier and the Seatran Discovery pier. **The N.O. Guest House ❸,** located up the hill on the main pier road, has decently large, comfortable rooms with ensuite bathrooms and is less than a 2min. walk from the pier. (☎077 456 648. Rooms with fan 400฿, with hot shower 500฿, with A/C 700฿; with both A/C and hot shower 800฿.) Jack-of-all-trades **Mr. J ❸** rents out several clean, well-maintained bungalows that are located just behind his main shop (see **Practical Information,** p. 419). The shop serves as reception. (Small rooms with shared bath 250฿. Rooms with double bed, private bath and newish bathroom fixtures 350-600฿; bigger rooms with A/C 1000-1200฿.) A number of similarly cheap bungalows are located past Mr. J's bungalows, on the rocky promontory at the northern edge of Hat Sai Ree. Though hardly beautiful, the area is closer to the beaches and dive shops of Hat Sai Ree and has lower prices than Sai Ree proper.

FOOD AND NIGHTLIFE. Ko Tao has less Thai food stalls than most other places in Thailand, but your best bet for finding a cheap bowl of noodles or some fresh **street vendor** fare is the main road near Mae Hat as you begin your journey south to Ao Chalok Ban. Mae Hat has the most restaurants on the island. Uphill from the Seatran Discovery pier on the right, diver hangout **Pook's Kitchen ❷** draws an affable crowd with tasty Thai standards and Western snacks. (☎087 888 1761. Delicious ginger and honey tea 25฿. Burger with fries 90฿. Open daily 8am-9pm.) One hundred meters uphill from the main pier, Italian-owned **La Matta ❷** is a reliable favorite for authentic Italian pizza and pasta (100-270฿), fresh salads (75-150฿), and wine (90฿ per glass). They also offer an all-you-can-eat pasta special for 200฿. (Open daily 11am-11pm.) A pair of Bangkok artists runs the most stylish nightspot in Mae Hat, **Whitening ❸**, on the southern end of town along the beach road between the Lomprayah and Songserm piers. It's a great place to sip a drink or snack on Thai-Indian fusion dishes (100-350฿) while watching the sunset. The scene here is mellow in the evening with a 6pm-7pm 95฿ mixed drink happy hour, but wilder late at night. Free Wi-Fi. (☎077 456 199. Open daily 11am-midnight. Kitchen closes 11pm.) **Safety Stop Bar,** right next to the pier and hard to miss, is an unpretentious diver hangout with 5pm-7pm happy hour drink specials (50-60฿ beers among others) that make it a good choice at sundown. Nightly sports on the TV and English-language newspapers keep the expat and tourist crowd happy. Free Wi-Fi. (Open 7am-2pm.)

HAT SAI REE

Backpackers and divers congregate in the bungalows along this 2km beach, which is Ko Tao's busiest bit of sand and rapidly becoming even busier. Despite its popularity, the beach retains some laid-back charm. Candlelight dinners with sunset views yield to easy-going nightlife. However, for higher-quality swimming and snorkeling, beaches on the southern and eastern coasts of the island have a clear advantage.

ACCOMMODATIONS. Those looking for a budget-friendly, sociable spot on Hat Sai Ree should look no further than **In Touch Bungalows ❸** at the southern end of the beach, near the rock bearing King Rama V's initials. The wood-paneled bungalows gathered in a shady courtyard have a brightly colored aesthetic. The highlight is the colorful restaurant with a pool table and bar, where both guests and the friendly staff while away their time. (☎077 456 514. Small bungalows with fan and private bath 300฿; bigger rooms 400-500฿, with hot shower 800฿. Restaurant open 7am-midnight. Bar open until the last person leaves.) A deservedly popular choice is the old-school **Sai Ree Cottage ❷**, just south of Scuba Junction (p. 421) next to Seashell Divers Resort. Their simple wooden bungalows get points for cleanliness, as does their social beachside **restaurant,** which boasts a menu of reasonably priced Thai dishes, milkshakes, and cocktails. However, they don't accept reservations and are often full. Your best time to try to get a room is between 9 and 11am when people are heading out for the morning boats. (Bungalows with fan and private bath 350฿, with A/C 1300-2500฿.) A modest step up in price yields a massive step up in quality at **Lotus Resort ❸**, which straddles the line between budget and mid-range. The fan bungalows here are large, airy, and well-kept, with comfortable beds and spacious balconies. Anyone is welcome to stay here, but those diving with Lotus are given priority and receive considerable discounts on lodging. The affiliated bar (see below) is not to be missed. (☎077 456 297. Bungalows with fan and private baths 400-800฿, with A/C 1200-2500฿.)

◘ **FOOD.** For culinary offerings on the island, Hat Sai Ree is second-best to Mae Hat. **Vendors** offering fresh sliced fruit (20-25฿) and various meats on sticks (10-40฿) can often be found in the area near New Heaven Bakery and the 7-Eleven. Around sunset, **food stands** also set up on the beach, barbecuing fresh fish and veggies to order (30-60฿). Most bungalows along the beach have beach-side restaurants strewn with cushions and low tables, ideal for quick between-dive meals and evening pre-party drinks. The best food on Hat Sai Ree is at **New Heaven Bakery ❸**, just north of Lotus Resort. This refreshing deli, cafe, and bakery serves fresh breads and pastries, stocks Western picnic essentials such as European cheeses and salamis, and offers excellent sandwiches, including vegetarian favorites like grilled vegetables or hummus with feta (both 80฿), either to eat in or to go. (Dishes 60-140฿. Open daily 7:30am-8pm.) A standout among the guesthouse restaurants is the one at the **New Age Blue Wind Resort ❸**. Ordering here is a self-serve process: you have to get yourself a menu and an order form. Thai curries and Western dishes are both good and vegetarian options abound. (☎077 456 116. Dishes 60-240฿. Delicious spicy Thai salad with chicken 70฿.Open daily 8am-9:30pm.)

◪ **NIGHTLIFE.** In the evening, divers put away their gear and sunbathers slather on aloe vera in preparation for nights passed drinking by the beach and watching pirated movies in nearby restaurants. Two beachside bars located right next to each other are particularly excellent around sunset. **Lotus Bar,** next to Lotus Resort, and **Fizz Beach Lounge** set out comfy cushions, torches, and candles on the sand in late afternoon and welcome sunset-watchers with great 4pm-7pm happy hour specials. Fizz is popular a little earlier as it has great big green bean bags that are perfect for reading around sunset. Crowds really start arriving at Lotus around 10-11pm during the middle of the fire juggling shows that last from 9-midnight. (Happy-hour spirits at Lotus Bar 50฿, regularly 100฿. Mixed drinks 120-160฿. Both Fizz and Lotus open nightly 4pm-2am.) The most popular guesthouse bar is the one at **Ban's Diving Resort,** in the center of the beach 200m south of Lotus Bar, where you can always find a lively crowd of hard-drinking divers. (4-7pm happy hour with 60฿ spirits, regularly 100฿. Look out for themed party nights held once or twice a week. Open 2pm-4am.)

AO LEUK AND AO TANOTE

The two major bays on the eastern side of Ko Tao are ideal for those seeking solitude and offer some of the best snorkeling on the island. Tiny Ao Leuk has a rocky, less-than-spectacular beach but is much more peaceful than the ever-packed Hat Sai Ree, and is home arguably to the best snorkeling of any of Ko Tao's beaches. Making this trip by motorbike is only recommended for experienced drivers because of its steep hills and sandy ditches. Alternately, taxis to both bays cost 100฿ per person from Mae Hat, but can occasionally be bargained down to as low as 50฿. Black Tip Diving and Water Sport, in the middle of the beach next to Diamond Resort, sends scheduled taxi jeeps back to Mae Hat every other hour from 8:30am-6:30pm for 100฿ per person.

The best choice for lodgings on the bay is **Ao Leuk II Bungalows ❹**, where the hill-side grounds are scattered with airy, wooden bungalows with porches. (☎077 456 779. 2-person bungalows with fan 550฿. Restaurant open daily 7am-10pm.) About 2km farther north from Ao Leuk, along a winding steep semi-paved road, is Ao Tan-ote, more populated and with a better beach than its neighbor. This picturesque little beach attracts an older crowd; as a result, many of the accommodations are more expensive than elsewhere on the island. For food, long-term vacationers recommend the restaurant at **Mountain Reef Resort ❷**, a popular spot on the southern end of the beach with good views. (Thai and Western dishes 50-150฿. Delicious homemade yogurt with honey 50฿.) Mountain Reef Resort has some of the cheapest rooms. (☎01 956 2916. 2-person doubles with fan and private bath 400฿. Larger, better maintained rooms with better views 800-1200฿.)

AO CHALOK BAN KAO

Chalok Ban Kao Bay is carved out of the island's south end, 2.5km from Mae Hat (30min. by foot, 50฿ taxi ride per person for 4 or more people). The bay is small but shelters a dense concentration of bungalows, dive shops, Internet cafes, and restaurants. Despite the density, Ao Chalok Ban Kao still is beautiful and relaxed. However, due to shallow waters, the bay is not very swimmable. The solution: head to gorgeous Ao Thian (see this page), a 20-30min. walk away. On the western side of the bay, **Sunshine II Bungalows ❸** (not to be confused with slightly more expensive Sunshine I Bungalows next door) is the closest thing to a budget accommodation on the beach, featuring plywood bungalows with private baths. (☎077 356 154. Small 2-person bungalows with fan 350฿, larger bungalows 400-500฿.)

All of the bungalows and resorts have similar attached restaurants looking out on the ocean, most open 8am-10pm and with standard Thai fare for 70-120฿. To find cheaper noodle and stir-fry **stalls** as well as an assortment of **bars**, head inland on the main road for 200m in the direction of Hat Sai Ree.

AO THIAN OG

An uphill walk southeast from Ao Chalok leads to a fork in the dirt road. The left path leads downhill to the small but stunning Thian Og Bay, also known as Rocky Bay or Shark Bay. Thian Og bay has an outstanding white-sand beach, perhaps the island's best, ideal for swimming and snorkeling (equipment rental available on the beach includes mask and fins, 100฿). **Rocky Resort ❸**, on the bay's rocky east end, has spectacular views, but some of the bungalows are quite worn and fairly ill-maintained. Rocky also has the only restaurant on the beach, with decent, relatively inexpensive fare. (☎077 456 035. Standard Thai dishes 80-130฿. Small 2-person bungalows on the water with fan and ensuite bathrooms 400฿, larger better-maintained rooms 600-1000฿.)

LAEM TAA TOH

This lovely cape juts into the gulf, separating Ao Chalok from Ao Thian. To get here, follow the dirt road from Ao Chalok, taking the right path leading uphill at the fork. You can also get here during low-tide by scrambling over the rocks and wading through the water on the eastern side of Ao Chalok. Besides spectacular views, the cape is home to the romantic and atmospheric ⬛**New Heaven Restaurant ❸**, which has delicious Thai dishes and desserts. New Heaven has a wide range of options—fruit juices include tamarind and dragon fruit, nightly seafood offerings often include barracuda and king prawn—but the real reason to come here is the unbelievably beautiful view of Ao Thian Og from atop a charming patio covered in pillows and short tables. (Excellent Thai dishes 70-200฿. Seafood 200-350฿. Coffees 60-100฿. Shakes and smoothies 80-120฿. Open daily 8am-10pm.)

▶ DAYTRIP FROM KO TAO: KO NANG YUAN

Ferries depart daily from the Mae Hat catamaran pier (10:30am, 3, 6pm; return 8:30am, 1, 4:30pm; round-trip 200฿), right next to the boat and ferry pier. Longtail boat drivers also camp out near the 7-Eleven in Mae Hat. You can rent a longtail boat roundtrip to Ko Nang

Yuan for 250฿ per person (at least 4 people). You can also book a 9am-4pm tour around the island through any travel agency; tour costs 550-650฿ and includes lunch and snorkeling as well as stops at Hat Leuk, Hat Hin Wong, Mango Bay, and Ko Nang Yuan.

About 1km off of Ko Tao's northwest coast, lovely Ko Nang Yuan is actually three separate islets connected by a three-pronged stretch of white sand. The beach not only makes a good photo opportunity, but its snorkeling is among Ko Tao's best. It is a great place to spot sea turtles, reef sharks, and other sea life, and the steep climb up one of the islets to the viewpoint is well worth it. The island is best visited as a daytrip from Ko Tao, although there is one accommodation option, the pricey but comfortable **Ko Nangyuan Dive Resort ❺**. Reservations are essential. (☎077 4560 8893. www.nangyuan.com. Lovely 2-person bungalows with fan 1500฿, with A/C 2100฿.) The resort's **restaurant ❹**, aware of its monopoly over edibles on the island, has steep prices. (Dishes 150-300฿.) The staff also can set up fun dives (1000฿ per dive). If you choose to avoid Ko Nangyuan Resort by packing your own food for the day, keep in mind that plastic bottles are not allowed on Ko Nang Yuan for environmental reasons.

APPENDIX

CLIMATE

The high and low tourist seasons roughly match up to the aptly-named rainy and dry seasons of Southeast Asia. Generally, rainfall peaks from May to September, falling off from November to April. There is no uniform seasonal pattern for Thailand, except that it is generally very hot year-round. Keep in mind that the rainy season's monsoons, while dramatic, are rarely severe enough to impede travel through the region.

AVG. TEMP. (LOW/ HIGH), PRECIP.	JANUARY			APRIL			JULY			OCTOBER		
	°C	°F	mm	°C	°F	mm	°C	°F	mm	°C	°F	mm
Bangkok	22/32	71/89	0.4	27/34	80/94	2.8	26/32	80/94	6.2	25/32	77/89	9.1
Chiang Mai	14/29	58/84	0.3	23/36	73/97	1.8	24/32	75/89	6.6	22/31	72/88	5.2
Phuket	23/31	73/88	1.4	25/33	77/91	6.4	25/31	77/87	10.4	24/30	76/86	12

To convert from degrees Fahrenheit to degrees Celsius, subtract 32 and multiply by 5/9. To convert from Celsius to Fahrenheit, multiply by 9/5 and add 32.

°CELSIUS	-5	0	5	10	15	20	25	30	35	40
°FAHRENHEIT	23	32	41	50	59	68	77	86	95	104

MEASUREMENTS

Thailand uses the metric system. The basic unit of length is the meter (m), which is divided into 100 centimeters (cm) or 1000 millimeters (mm). One thousand meters make up one kilometer (km). Fluids are measured in liters (L), each divided into 1000 milliliters (mL). A liter of pure water weighs one kilogram (kg), the unit of mass that is divided into 1000 grams (g). One metric ton is 1000kg. The only non-metric measurements used in Thailand are units of area; 1 *rai* is 1600 square meters, 1 *ngaan* is 400 square meters, and 1 *waa* for 4 square meters.

MEASUREMENT CONVERSIONS	
1 inch (in.) = 25.4mm	1 millimeter (mm) = 0.039 in.
1 foot (ft.) = 0.305m	1 meter (m) = 3.28 ft.
1 yard (yd.) = 0.914m	1 meter (m) = 1.094 yd.
1 mile (mi.) = 1.609km	1 kilometer (km) = 0.621 mi.
1 ounce (oz.) = 28.35g	1 gram (g) = 0.035 oz.
1 pound (lb.) = 0.454kg	1 kilogram (kg) = 2.205 lb.
1 fluid ounce (fl. oz.) = 29.57mL	1 milliliter (mL) = 0.034 fl. oz.
1 gallon (gal.) = 3.785L	1 liter (L) = 0.264 gal.

LANGUAGE

The Thai language, the nation's official language, is extremely different from English, which is spoken only in some sectors of the Thai population. Few tourists pick up more than basic rudiments during a short trip. Thai script is not based on an alphabet in the same way that English is, but is an abugida, relying on consonants with vowel notation. Some are used only to write Sanskrit words and some are only found at the ends of Thai words. Many of these consonants are the same sound except differing in tone, and are thus distinguished by an accompanying name. For the sake of brevity, *Let's Go: Thailand* provides only a guide aimed at providing the traveler with some speaking ability.

Since even spoken Thai is so difficult to learn and since few travelers make the effort, even the most basic attempts at Thai by *farang* will be greeted with excitement. This section will help you prepare for your trip and gives you a few key phrases to practice.

PRONUNCIATION

Thai (like Chinese, Lao, Burmese, and Vietnamese) is a tonal language, and word meanings are partially determined by intonation and pitch. The five tones in Thai are middle, low, high, falling, and rising. **Middle** tones (unmarked) are spoken in a level voice in the middle of a speaker's vocal range. **Low** (à) and **high** (á) tones are spoken in level pitch, and come from the bottom and top of a speaker's range respectively. **Falling** tones (â) begin high and end low, as in the English pronunciation of "Hey!" **Rising** tones (ǎ) begin low and end high, as in the English interrogative "What?"

Simple vowels are roughly pronounced as in English, except for the "a," "o," and "eu" sounds. Consonants are mostly similar in pronunciation to English, with notable exceptions listed below. Sometimes the "l" sound is substituted for "r" so that a word like *aroy* ("delicious") is pronounced "aloy." Occasionally, when there are two consonants next to each other in a word, Thai native speakers will drop the second consonant so that a word like *glai* ("far") is pronounced "gai." A more extensive guide to pronunciations counterintuitive to the English speaker is presented below.

PHONETIC UNIT	PRONUNCIATION	PHONETIC UNIT	PRONUNCIATION
a	as in "father"	t	hard t/d sound
o	as in "coat"	ph	as normal English "p," as in "panda"
eu	as in the French "bleu"	th	as normal English "t," as in "telephone"
ae	as in "cat"	r	rolled almost as an "l" (see above)
g	hard g, between g and k, as in "gat"	p	hard p/b sound

GRAMMAR

Grammatically, Thai is very simple. There are no indefinite or definite articles, and verbs do not inflect to express tense or number. Questions are formed by adding mai to the end of any verb; for example, to ask if someone is hungry *(hew)*, you would say *hew mai* ("Are you hungry?"). Answering a question is equally simple: to answer affirmatively, just repeat the verb. From the example above reply with, *hew* ("I am hungry"). To answer negatively, place *mâi* in front of the verb—from the example above, *mâi hew* ("I am not hungry").

PRONOUNS: Thai does have its own complexities, however, including its large number of pronouns. Some of these are gender specific, while others vary according to the relationship between the people conversing. The pronouns below are commonly used, and appropriate for informal use.

I	YOU	HE/SHE/IT	THEY	WE
pôm/di-chăn (m/f)	khun	khao	puak khao	Rao

POLITENESS: To be polite, men should add *krap* to the end of their sentences, and women should add *ka* to the end of theirs. These words have no specific meaning, but are used in place of words like please and other pleasantries.

PHRASEBOOK

MEETINGS/GREETINGS		DAYS OF THE WEEK	
Hello.	sà-wàt-dee	Monday	wan jan
How are you?	sà-bai dee mâi	Tuesday	wang ang-kahn
I am fine.	sà-bai dee	Wednesday	wan pút
What is your name?	kun chêu à-rai	Thursday	wan pá-réu-hàt
My name is...	pôm/di-chăn chêu...	Friday	wan sùk
Yes/No.	châi/mâi	Saturday	wan sŏw
Goodbye.	lah gòrn	Sunday	wan ah tít

NUMBERS			
1	nèung	9	gôw
2	sŏrng	10	sìp
3	sâhm	11	sìp-èt
4	sèe	20	yêe-sìp
5	hâh	50	hâh-sìp
6	hòk	100	nèung roy
7	jèt	500	hâh roy
8	bpàat	1000	nèung pan

EMERGENCY			
Help!	chôo-ay dôo-ay	insect repellent	yah gun má-laang
Call a doctor.	dahm mor nòy	mosquito	yung
accident	ù-bàt-dì-hèt	My...was stolen.	...korng tòok kà-moy
doctor	mor	passport	nâng-seu deun tahng
emergency	hèt chuk-chern	pharmacy	ráhn kâi yah
fever	kâi	police	dam-ròo-at
fire	fai	rain	fŏn
hospital	rohng pá-yaa-bahn	sore throat	jèp kor
ill	bpoo-ay	stomach ache	bpoo ut torng
immediately	tun tee	sunblock	kreem gan dàat

GLOSSARY

SIGHTS

Bot: prayer room, chapel
Wat: temple/monastery complex
Chedi: dome-shaped structure that houses relics
Wihaan: prayer chamber
Prang: temple spire

GETTING AROUND

Soi: side street branching off a main street

Samlor: three-wheeled vehicle
Klong: canal
Tuk-tuk: three-wheeled truck
Songthaew: four-wheeled pickup
Moo: component of Thai address

EVERYDAY LIFE

Wai: gesture of respect, see p. 65
Longan: tropical tree and fruit

LUNAR CALENDAR

The chart below should help you figure out the dates of local festivals, which are often based solely on the lunar calendar. Also, if you plan to attend a Full Moon Party, we've listed the optimum arrival date to ensure you get accommodations.

NEW MOON	OPTIMUM ARRIVAL DATE	FULL MOON
December 27, 2008	January 6, 2009	January 11, 2009
January 26, 2009	February 4, 2009	February 9, 2009
February 25, 2009	March 6, 2009	March 11, 2009
March 26, 2009	April 4, 2009	April 9, 2009
April 25, 2009	May 4, 2009	May 9, 2009
May 24, 2009	June 2, 2009	June 7, 2009
June 22, 2009	July 2, 2009	July 7, 2009
July 22, 2009	August 1, 2009	August 6, 2009
August 20, 2009	August 30, 2009	September 4, 2009
September 18, 2009	September 29, 2009	October 4, 2009
October 18, 2009	October 28, 2009	November 2, 2009
November 16, 2009	November 27, 2009	December 2, 2009
December 16, 2009	December 26, 2009	December 31, 2009

APPENDIX

INDEX

INDEX

INDEX

INDEX

ABOUT LET'S GO

NOT YOUR PARENTS' TRAVEL GUIDE

At Let's Go, we see every trip as the chance of a lifetime. If your dream is to grab a machete and forge through the jungles of Costa Rica, we can take you there. If you'd rather bask in the Riviera sun at a beachside cafe, we'll set you a table. We write for readers who know that there's more to travel than sharing double deckers with tourists and who believe that travel can change both themselves and the world—whether they plan to spend six days in Bangkok or six months in Europe. We'll show you just how far your money can go, and prove that the greatest limitation on your adventures is not your wallet but your imagination.

BEYOND THE TOURIST EXPERIENCE

To help you gain a deeper connection with the places you travel, our fearless researchers scour the globe to give you the heads-up on both world-renowned and off-the-beaten-track attractions, sights, and destinations. They dive into the local culture only to emerge with the freshest insights on everything from festivals to regional cuisine. We've also opened our pages to respected writers and scholars to hear their takes on the countries and regions we cover, and asked travelers who have worked, studied, or volunteered abroad to contribute first-person accounts of their experiences. In addition, each guide's Beyond Tourism chapter shares ideas about responsible travel, study abroad, and how to give back while on the road.

FORTY-NINE YEARS OF WISDOM

Let's Go got its start in 1960, when a group of creative and well-traveled students compiled their experience and advice into a 20-page mimeographed pamphlet, which they gave to travelers on charter flights to Europe. Almost five decades later, we've expanded to cover six continents and all kinds of travel—while retaining our founders' adventurous attitude. Laced with witty prose and total candor, our guides are still researched and written entirely by students on shoestring budgets, experienced travelers who know that train strikes, stolen luggage, food poisoning, and marriage proposals are all part of a day's work.

THE LET'S GO COMMUNITY

More than just a travel guide company, Let's Go is a community. Our small staff comes together because of our shared passion for travel and our desire to help other travelers see the world the way it was meant to be seen. We love it when our readers become part of the Let's Go community as well—when you travel, drop us a postcard (67 Mt. Auburn St., Cambridge, MA 02138, USA), send us an e-mail (feedback@letsgo.com), or sign up online (http://www.letsgo.com) to tell us about your adventures and discoveries.

For more information, visit us online: www.letsgo.com.

915.93
Let
12009

MAPS

MAP INDEX

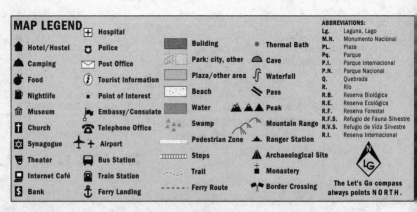

MAP LEGEND

✚ Hospital	
🏠 Hotel/Hostel	🚓 Police
⛺ Camping	✉ Post Office
🍎 Food	ⓘ Tourist Information
🍸 Nightlife	■ Point of Interest
🏛 Museum	Embassy/Consulate
✝ Church	☎ Telephone Office
✡ Synagogue	✈ Airport
🎭 Theater	🚌 Bus Station
💻 Internet Café	🚂 Train Station
$ Bank	⚓ Ferry Landing

▨ Building	⊙ Thermal Bath
▨ Park: city, other	⌒ Cave
▨ Plaza/other area	∬ Waterfall
Beach	≫ Pass
Water	▲▲▲ Peak
Swamp	Mountain Range
Pedestrian Zone	▲ Ranger Station
Steps	▲ Archaeological Site
Trail	⚕ Monastery
Ferry Route	Border Crossing

ABBREVIATIONS:
Lg.   Laguna, Lago
M.N.   Monumento Nacional
PL.   Plaza
Pq.   Parque
P.I.   Parque Internacional
P.N.   Parque Nacional
Q.   Quebrada
R.   Río
R.B.   Reserva Biológica
R.E.   Reserva Ecológica
R.F.   Reserva Forestal
R.F.S.   Refugio de Fauna Silvestre
R.V.S.   Refugio de Vida Silvestre
R.I.   Reserva Internacional

The Let's Go compass
always points NORTH.